The Manager in the International Economy, Seventh Edition

THE
MANAGER
IN THE
INTERNATIONAL
ECONOMY
SEVENTH EDITION

Raymond Vernon

Harvard University

Louis T. Wells, Jr.

Harvard University

Subramanian Rangan

INSEAD

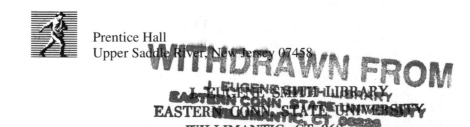

Prentice Hall
Upper Saddle River, New Jersey 07458

Library of Congress Cataloging-in-Publication Data

Vernon, Raymond,
    The manager in the international economy / Raymond Vernon, Louis
T. Wells, Subramanian Rangan.—7th ed.
      p.   cm.
    Includes bibliographical references and index.
    ISBN 0–13–232539–X
     1. International business enterprises—Management.
    2. International business enterprises—Case studies.
    3. International economic relations.   I. Wells, Louis T.
II. Rangan, Subramanian.   III. Title.
    HD62.4.V48 1996
    658.1′8—dc20

                                   95–4955
                                     CIP

Acquisitions Editor: David Shafer
Marketing Manager: Jo-Ann DeLuca
Project Management: J. Carey Publishing Service
Senior Project Manager: Alana Zdinak
Interior Design: J. Carey Publishing Service
Cover Design: Jayne Conte
Manufacturing Buyer: Vincent Scelta
Assistant Editor: Lisamarie Brassini
Editorial Assistant: Nancy Kaplan
Production Coordinator: David Cotugno
Cover Art: David Tillinghast Illustration
Text Illustrations: Burmar Technical Corporation

© 1996, 1991, 1986, 1981, 1976, 1972, 1968 by Prentice-Hall, Inc.
A Simon & Schuster Company
Upper Saddle River, New Jersey 07458

The copyright on each case is held by the President and Fellows of Harvard College and by other institutions and individuals, and they are published herein by express permission.

Case material of the Harvard Graduate School of Business Administration is made possible by the cooperation of business firms and other organizations which may wish to remain anonymous by having names, quantities, and other identifying details disguised while maintaining basic relationships. Cases are prepared as the basis for class discussion rather than to illustrate either effective or ineffective handling of an administrative situation.

Printed in the United States of America

10 9 8 7 6 5 4 3 2 1

ISBN 0-13-232539-X

Prentice-Hall International (UK) Limited, *London*
Prentice-Hall of Australia Pty. Limited, *Sydney*
Prentice-Hall Canada Inc., *Toronto*
Prentice-Hall Hispanoamericana, S.A., *Mexico*
Prentice-Hall of India Private Limited, *New Delhi*
Prentice-Hall of Japan, Inc., *Tokyo*
Simon & Schuster Asia Pte. Ltd., *Singapore*
Editora Prentice-Hall do Brasil, Ltda., *Rio de Janeiro*

Brief Contents

Contents

Preface

This is the seventh edition of a book that is intended to introduce the reader to the international economy from the perspective of a manager in international business.

The international economic environment, as the reader hardly needs to be told, has changed profoundly over the past two decades. Old institutions have been swept away; old assumptions have been altered. We were determined to try to capture some of the dimensions of that shift in the present edition.

Another factor of importance has shaped this edition. In the past decade or two, scholars all around the world have done exhaustive studies of operations of the multinational enterprise. In that period of intensive study, a stream of materials and concepts has emerged that illuminates the strategies, structures, practices, and effects of such enterprises. With the addition of a third author, Subramanian Rangan, we have tried to give these materials greatly added emphasis.

We have chosen the uninhibited course of presenting principles and concepts from the economic discipline (and other disciplines, for that matter) whenever we thought the ideas useful, while disregarding the contributions of the disciplines when we thought them irrelevant in this context. For instance, our use of trade theory and monetary theory in the explanation of international economic behavior is balanced quite differently from the presentation in standard textbooks.

Of course, many of the problems in the international economy can derive little help from the familiar precepts of the disciplines. As a rule, the problems encountered in the international economy are shrouded in uncertainty and risk. And commonly, the markets that managers encounter in the international economy are grossly inefficient.

Happily, economists in recent years have been giving greatly increased attention to the behavior of markets under such conditions. But it will be some time before their work produces much guidance for the manager. Besides, for many problems, such as those involving foreign exchange risk, there is a need to couple propositions from various disciplines, such as economics and political science, in ways that may not be satisfying to either. Accordingly, we have not hesitated to stray beyond the solid structure of the disciplines whenever we thought that something systematic might usefully be said bearing on the problems of enterprises in the international economy.

Most textbooks come very close to being stolen intellectual goods. Proper acknowledgments for the contributions that go into the making of a textbook, therefore, present a real problem for any author. The situation could hardly be otherwise. The job of a textbook is largely to present the current state of the art. Few scholars individually can do much more than add a few insights, a few clarifications, to a body of ideas already formulated by the culture that spawned them. Inevitably, that is the character of this book.

The present revision benefited from comments by Heidi Vernon-Wortzel, Robert Z. Lawrence, and F. M. Scherer.

Raymond Vernon
Louis T. Wells, Jr.
Subramanian Rangan

CHAPTER 1

The International Economy: A Manager's Perspective

Welcome to the seventh edition of *The Manager in the International Economy*. The goal of this text is to equip you, the reader-manager or reader-manager-to-be, with a solid understanding of the forces that influence and shape the economic environment in which you have to make your *international* business decisions, and in which you have to build and manage international economic relationships with foreign affiliates, parents, customers, suppliers, competitors, financiers, and host and home governments.

Consider just a few hypothetical illustrations of the challenges and opportunities that international business poses for corporate managers throughout the world:

- You are vice president of operations at Volvo of Sweden. The good news is that your 850 model is selling so briskly in the United States that you are barely able to keep up with demand. The bad news is that the U.S. dollar is continuing to weaken against the Swedish krona and, as a result, putting pressure on your U.S. margins. Should you raise the 850's sticker price and risk losing the momentum you presently enjoy? Should you take lower margins now and figure out another way to manage the exchange rate mismatch between your krona costs and dollar revenues? Can the strategy you devise to deal with this situation also incorporate a response to Mercedes' and BMW's decision to begin producing vehicles in the United States? How in your response do you plan to factor in the importance of scale?

- It is Monday morning in San Francisco. As you head to your job at Apple Computer, where you are chief of corporate strategy, you read the following newspaper headline: "U.S. to Continue China's MFN Trade Status." You are instinctively relieved since your company has substantial interests in China, but you ponder the headline as you drive in. What would be the strategic implications for your company if China were denied most-favored-nation (MFN) status? You also wonder whether China's application to join the World Trade Organization (WTO) will be ratified and then you ask yourself: How do the WTO and other international arrangements concerning trade and investment really affect my business and its future? Does today's news change the company's bargaining position vis-à-vis China's government?

- As a member of a special task force at USAir, a large passenger airline in the United States, you have been asked to brief the board of directors on the soundness of the carrier's proposed merger with British Airways. Although you believe the European Union market to be important, you know that economic forecasts for air traffic growth in Europe don't provide sufficient justification for the merger. On the other hand, you believe that the alliances that other U.S.-based carriers have with European-based ones—such as Delta's with Swissair, Northwest's with KLM, and United's with Lufthansa—make it important that USAir maintain and strengthen its links with British Airways. What risks and uncertainties are you using this alliance to hedge against? In what areas and to what degree do you anticipate learning as a result of this alliance? What arguments will you present to the board?

To be sure, these hypothetical illustrations pose hard, and even perplexing, questions. Clearcut answers will be difficult and rare. Indeed, the answer is likely to be: It depends. It depends on the particular competencies that the firm in question and its management possess; on management's perceptions of how lead rivals might react; and so on. Besides, the imponderables will often overwhelm the little information that is known for certain; at other times, random events, quite out of the control of the managers or the corporation, will determine the outcome. But there are also occasions when corporate managers are not well informed or exercise poor judgment because they lack an understanding of the economic, political, and institutional aspects of the international economy they operate in. It is here that this text will help. Although it is unlikely that the pages of a single text like this can capture the dynamism of the international economy in its entirety, you—the reader—should come away with

- A recognition and understanding of the primary actors in international business, namely, multinational enterprises; their origins, motivations, and modes of operating in the international economy.
- A thorough grasp of the core concepts and frameworks in international strategy and international management.
- An analytical understanding of the core precepts in international economics.
- An appreciation for the roles and motivations of the other set of key actors in international business, namely, host and home governments.
- A comfortable familiarity with the origins, domains, and functioning of international economic institutions and agreements—such as the General Agreement

on Tariffs and Trade (GATT), the World Trade Organization (WTO), the European Union (EU), the Organization for Economic Cooperation and Development (OECD), and the North American Free Trade Agreement (NAFTA)—that attempt to oversee and regulate the international economy.

* And most of all, a deep appreciation for the goals and roles of the corporate manager on the frontiers of international business.

Let us begin at the beginning. Let us consider briefly this question: What are the origins of international business, and how did the global economy come to take its present shape?

A Synoptic History of International Business

Looking at the clamor toward "internationalization" among businesses, we can easily be led to believe that the developments we are about to study are not only powerful but also *new*. On some aspects, such as Japan's prominence in outward foreign direct investment, both sentiments are justified, but by and large, the international economy has been a work in progress for some time.

The Early Period

Foreign commerce has been part of the human endeavor since very early times. Over 4,000 years ago, Egypt built a sea trade with cities in what we know today as the Middle East, and the Sumerians, who inhabited the region of present-day Iraq, traded with Asia Minor and Syria. What is more, as early as 2500 B.C., the Sumerians stationed their own agents to receive, store, and sell goods in foreign lands.[1]

Early *trade*, as the word itself connotes, was conducted largely in the form of barter, with goods being exchanged for goods. Progress in the form of coinage came around 700 B.C. when the king of Lydia, the western part of what is now Turkey, affixed his seal on *electrum*, an alloy of gold and silver, thereby attesting to its weight and quality. The innovation spread to other communities, and it is thought that by the 6th or 5th centuries B.C., primitive foreign exchange markets had begun to develop.[2]

Although international exchange, along with other aspects of civilization, suffered a setback during the period known as the Dark Ages (which began with the fall of Rome circa A.D. 400 and ended around the 11th century), trade picked up in the Middle Ages and flourished particularly after the fifteenth century when the European voyages of discovery began. These were the heady days of Portugal whose

[1]Mira Wilkins, *The Emergence of Multinational Enterprise* (Cambridge, Mass.: Harvard University Press, 1970), p. 3.

[2]Paul Einzig, *The History of Foreign Exchange* (London: Macmillan, 1970), chap. 2.

Vasco da Gama set sail on a historic expedition in 1497 and discovered the sea route to India by way of Africa's southern cape, a route still in use today.

As today, trade in early times allowed people to capitalize on regional differences in natural endowments, enabled them to consume variety, provided a method of enjoying the fruits of specialization, and created wealth. In fact, the creation of wealth was a central theme in the early theories of international trade that emerged during the seventeenth century. During this period, modern nation-states were being formed, and the rulers of these new nations sought to consolidate power and authority through the accumulation of gold and silver. They had to raise armies to fend off domestic challenge, and they had to build ships to compete for empire abroad. How to do this? By maximizing exports, minimizing imports, and bringing home the difference in precious metals. This powerful, but flawed, belief that trade surpluses, encashed in *specie*, created national wealth is termed *mercantilism*.

Mercantilism came under attack in 1756 from Scottish philosopher David Hume (1711–1776). He argued that the quantity and value of imports that a nation's exports can purchase is ultimately what is important to the people of the exporting nation, not the amount of gold or silver its rulers amassed. Furthermore, he argued, a rise in a nation's stocks of precious metals would cause domestic prices to rise, which, in turn, would lead to a drop in exports and an outflow of the very specie whose inflow was sought earlier.

A generation later, another famous Scotsman, Adam Smith (1723–1790), seconded Hume's attacks on mercantilism by arguing that international trade would bring an efficient allocation of resources. But it wasn't until an English economist named David Ricardo (1772–1823) came along in 1817 that the world was introduced to the theory of *comparative advantage*. For these contributions, Hume, Smith, and Ricardo are acknowledged as the founders of the body of knowledge we now call international economics. Of course, substantial advances in thinking have occurred since their day, and Chapter 6 will pick up on these and the later developments in our understanding of international economics.

Maturing of the Modern Corporation

Even while the rudiments of international trade theory were being developed and debated, a socioeconomic invention of critical importance was being made and slowly adopted in Britain and America. That invention was the modern business corporation.

Business historians identify the East India Company as perhaps the best known early example of a joint-stock private corporation. Initially, private investors in the company, which was chartered in 1600, pooled resources and bought shares in the individual ocean voyages that the company undertook. Later, investor participation grew more stable. Like the East India Company, other corporations in Britain were chartered and given official monopoly status to pursue "assigned missions," often entailing activities conducted on behalf of the Crown. In fact, many such corporations were used to colonize America before its independence. These were quasi-state enterprises, however, operating under the mantle of the king and deriving their power and right to immortality from the royal house itself.[3]

It was only after America won its independence that this mode of organizing economic activity really evolved under private, as opposed to quasi-state, ownership. Both in public and private spheres, from the building of turnpikes and railroads to banking and industry, private initiative flourished in America. Indeed, by 1801, just a few years after independence, the United States had more than 350 such enterprises. And half a century later, large industrial firms were making their mark, building their positions on the corporate form, on the advantages of large scale, and on the mastery of modern industrial technologies. Outside the United States, Britain, France, and Germany were prominent in spawning the leading firms in chemicals, pharmaceuticals, machinery, and electrical products, as well as in oil and the nonferrous metals.

These leaders, bearing such familiar names as Pechiney, Hoechst, Dupont, Standard Oil, and General Electric, seemed to have little stomach at the time for the rough-and-tumble competition in which they would be engaged a century later. Being leaders within their own national markets, they instinctively sought to avoid the bruising contact that international competition might produce.

Accordingly, until the outbreak of World War II, these national leaders were constantly forming and reforming international agreements among themselves aimed at suppressing international competition. Since only three or four leaders existed in world markets in any major product line, such agreements were feasible enough. Elaborate agreements in petroleum, pharmaceuticals, electric light bulbs, steel, and hundreds of other products were put in place, aimed at dividing markets, avoiding price-cutting, stabilizing production, and holding technological changes in check.

World War II ended the prominent role of such agreements in international trade. In any case the U.S. participants had always been uncertain partners in these arrangements, being concerned about the power and reach of the U.S. antitrust laws. From the outbreak of World War II until the 1960s, U.S. firms had no need for protection from European competitors and no desire to tie their own hands in international competition. By the 1960s, the eggs had been thoroughly scrambled, with U.S.-owned subsidiaries firmly established in the major markets of Europe and in many of the ex-colonies and other reserved areas of their European competitors.

Why was the modern corporation so critical in the evolution of international business? Because it provided both an excellent mechanism for raising huge amounts of capital and an effective organizational device for administering large ongoing enterprises. Indeed, the modern corporation was the institutional vehicle that made the Industrial Revolution and the growth of national enterprise possible. And, while we can find exceptions to the generalization, by and large, national scope was a prerequisite for international expansion.

Although the invention of the modern corporation was an indispensable element in the evolution and growth of international business, it is unlikely that the contours

[3]See Thomas K. McCraw, "The Evolution of the Corporation in the United States," in John R. Meyer and James M. Gustafson (eds.), *The U.S. Business Corporation* (Cambridge, Mass.: Ballinger, 1988).

of the international economy would look the way they do today were it not for the stream of technological innovations, particularly in telecommunication and transportation, that occurred during this period. Whereas in the mid-nineteenth century sailing-packets took about 21 days to cross the Atlantic, by the 1880s passenger-carrying steamships were making the voyage in 5 to 6 days. And whereas long-distance communication was earlier tied to transportation, the first transatlantic cable, which was laid in 1866, forever broke the tie. Later, with advances in electricity, mass production became possible. With radio and television, mass marketing appeared on the scene. Affordable air travel, telex, and long-distance direct-dial telephones totally revolutionized the manner in which commerce proceeded.

By the 1950s and 1960s, the United States and its corporations enjoyed an unprecedented lead in the world economy. To solidify and secure their foreign markets, from scale-intensive industries such as autos to research and development-intensive industries such as chemicals, computers, and scientific instruments, American companies branched out and set up foreign operations. Consumer-products companies such as Procter & Gamble were involved in similar expansion.

In a telling commentary about the period, *Business Week* declared in an April 1963 special report on multinational corporations that:

> To find a GM executive working out of a hotel in Johannesburg or . . . a Du Pont plastics expert conferring with a Japanese partner in Osaka is business-as-usual. . . . After all, American companies have spent the past decade running a helter-skelter race to get located overseas. . . . Shaped in the crucible of complex foreign competition, the largest of U.S. corporations—and smaller ones, too—have found themselves changing into a new form: the multinational corporation. . . . A multinational company's management sees its enterprise as a global entity. It sees its foreign and domestic interests interwoven into a web of carefully integrated parts. . . . What U.S. business is seeing, in the words of Chmn. Frederic G. Donner of General Motors, "is the emergence of the modern industrial corporation as an institution that is transcending national boundaries."

The Era of Globalization

Even though signs of internationalization were already visible during the 1960s, it was only during the 1970s and especially the 1980s that the trends we now associate with globalization emerged. Prime among them was a tremendous escalation in international competition. To appreciate the magnitude and speed with which things happened, consider the fact that during the oil shocks and stagflation-afflicted decade of the 1970s, world trade grew nearly 20 percent faster per annum than world output (4.0 percent compared to 3.4 percent per annum). The disparity intensified sharply during the 1980s and early 1990s, during which period international trade grew roughly 60 percent faster per annum than world output (4.9 percent compared to 3.0 percent).[4]

[4]World Bank, *World Development Report 1994* (New York: Oxford University Press, 1994), Tables 2 and 13.

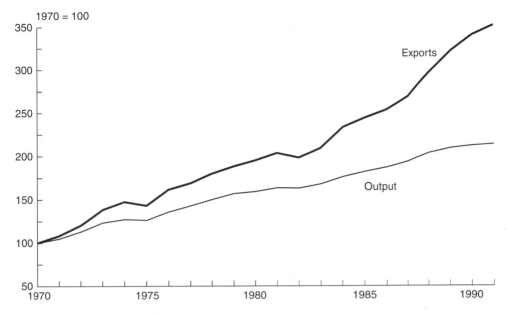

Figure 1-1   Growth in Volume of World Manufacturing Exports and Output, 1970–1991
Source: GATT, *International Trade: Statistics* (Geneva: GATT), various issues.

In terms of relative shares, two large countries, the United States and Japan, have been at opposite ends of these developments. For instance, in 1960 American companies manufactured nearly half the world's motor vehicles compared to about 2 percent produced by Japanese firms. But by the late 1970s Japanese firms had drawn even with their American counterparts.[5] The pattern is similar elsewhere, but nowhere more than in the area of foreign direct investment. In 1967 Japan accounted for slightly over 1 percent of the world stock of outward foreign direct investment; by 1990 its share had risen to nearly 20 percent. Over the same period, the U.S. share dropped from 50 percent to 26 percent.[6]

Another manifestation of globalization (and concurrent decline in American dominance) can be seen in rising intraindustry trade ratios. Intraindustry trade ratios indicate how much two-way trade takes place within industry groupings between two countries. So, for instance, if the United States exported only computers to Japan and imported only cameras from Japan, then its intraindustry trade ratio with Japan would be zero. But if, in addition to importing cameras, the United States also imported computers from Japan, then its intraindustry trade ratio with Japan would be positive.

[5]McCraw, 12–13.

[6]Figures for 1967 are from U.S. Department of Commerce, International Trade Administration, 1993, "Recent Trends in International Direct Investment: The Boom Years Fade," Appendix Table 1; figures for 1990 are from United Nations, *World Investment Report* (New York: United Nations, 1993), Annex Table 2, p. 248.

TABLE 1-1.   Intensity of Intraindustry Trade Between the United States and Selected Partner Countries, 1970, 1980, 1990[a]

Country	1970	1980	1990
Japan	32	31	48
Germany	44	48	64
France	52	59	69
United Kingdom	52	55	63
Italy	34	42	56

[a]Indices are calculated at the three-digit Standard International Trade Classification Level. Minimum value for indices is 0, and maximum value is 100. Low values indicate mainly one-way trade within product categories; high values indicate two-way trade within product categories.

Source: OECD, 1992, *Industrial Policy in OECD Countries, Annual Review, 1992*, pp. 206–209.

A rise in the ratio would indicate an increase over time in the ability of firms from different countries to compete internationally within industry groupings.

As Table 1-1 shows, not only were the intraindustry ratios of the five industrialized countries quite high back in 1970, but they rose substantially over the two decades of the 1970s and 1980s. As discussed above, this suggests that, increasingly, firms from developed countries have specialized within the same industries, differentiating their products as they did so.

Data shown in Tables 1-2A and B on share of national patents granted to nonresidents reinforce the impression of globalization and of a rise in the relative position of Japan. In the 1960s and early 1970s only a quarter of all U.S. patents went to entities based abroad, but by 1990 this ratio was up to nearly one-half. Especially noteworthy was the share of U.S. patents that went to entities based in Japan. Their share quadrupled (going from 5 to over 20 percent) during the 1970s and 1980s. Of course, the United States is not the only country that grants a large share of national patents to nonresidents. As Table 1-2B shows, by 1990 several countries were granting a very high proportion of national patents to nonresidents, with the notable exception of Japan.

TABLE 1-2A.   Share of U.S. Patents Granted to Nonresidents, 1963–1990

	1963–1977	1980	1985	1990
Patents to all nonresidents as a percent of total	27.7	39.6	44.8	47.6
Patents to entities based in Japan as a percent of total	5.0	11.5	17.8	21.6

TABLE 1-2B. Share of Patents Granted to Nonresidents in Selected Other Countries, 1990

Country	Patents to Nonresidents as a Percent of Total
Italy	98.7
Canada	92.2
Mexico	92.0
Brazil	86.5
United Kingdom	86.4
India	81.0
France	74.6
South Korea	67.1
Germany[a]	61.2
Japan	15.2

[a]Federal Republic of Germany before reunification.

Source: National Science Board, 1993, *Science and Engineering Indicators,* Appendix tables 6–12 and 6–21, p. 455 and p. 465.

Another facet of globalization is an increased level of integration of production across national borders. This trend is particularly visible in the manufacturing industry, where firms seeking global efficiencies have distributed and specialized either by product or stage their international production within individual countries.

A similar trend in outsourcing of components from affiliates located in low-cost regions is also clearly visible. In Table 1-3 consider the data which pertain to the non-electrical machinery industry. Whereas in 1966 foreign affiliates of American multinational enterprises in developing countries shipped only 3 percent of their output

TABLE 1-3. Exports to the United States by Affiliates of U.S.-based Multinationals Located in Developing Countries as a Percentage of the Total Sales of Those Affiliates, Selected Industries, 1966, 1977, 1988

Industry	1966	1977	1988
Machinery except electrical	3.0	5.9	30.7
Transportation equipment	na	3.8	29.4
Electric and electronic products	na	37.6	52.6

na = not available.

Sources: U.S. Department of Commerce, 1975, *U.S. Direct Investment Abroad: 1966;* 1981, *USDIA: 1977;* 1990, *USDIA: 1988.*

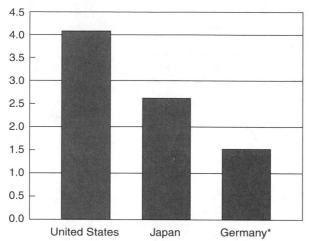

Figure 1-2   Ratio of Sales of Foreign Affiliates of Home-Based MNEs to Arm's Length Exports: United States, Japan, and Germany, 1989

[a]Data pertain to Federal Republic of Germany before reunification.

Sources: United Nations, *World Investment Report* (New York: United Nations, 1992), Tables II.1 and II.2, pp. 55–56.

*Data pertain to Federal Republic of Germany before reunification.

back to the United States, by 1988 the figure had jumped tenfold to 31 percent. Similarly, in the auto industry, by 1988 foreign affiliates were shipping back to the United States around 30 percent of their output, and in the electric and electronics products industries the figure was 53 percent.

The transshipment of intermediate products among affiliates of the same multinational enterprise—commonly known as intrafirm trade—is another phenomenon associated with globalization. By virtue of their early multinationalization, American firms have relied on such trade more frequently and for longer periods of time than firms from other countries. In the 1990s nearly 40 percent of nonaircraft U.S. manufacturing exports were made in this fashion.[7] In overall world trade, intrafirm shares are estimated to be around 25 percent.[8]

Even as the world's multinational enterprises helped integrate the world economy via trade, they pushed along even more forcefully in the area of foreign direct investment. In fact, for many observers, the word "globalization" has become synonymous with the widespread and growing presence of multinationals from various countries in various other countries. To see the phenomenon in numbers, consider that the world stock of foreign direct investment grew nearly tenfold between 1973 and 1993, going from $211 billion to over $2 trillion.[9]

As a result, even for multinational enterprises from traditionally export-oriented nations like Japan and Germany, foreign production and sales have become important channels through which foreign customers are gained and retained. In terms of value,

---

[7]Subramanian Rangan and Robert Z. Lawrence, "The Responses of U.S. Firms to Exchange Rate Fluctuations: Piercing the Corporate Veil," *Brookings Papers on Economic Activity*, Vol. 2 (1993), 341-379.

[8]United Nations, *World Investment Report* (New York: United Nations, 1992), p. 53.

[9]U.S. Department of Commerce, "Recent Trends in International Direct Investment," Appendix Table 1; and United Nations, *World Investment Report* (New York: United Nations, 1994), Table I.8, p. 19.

as Figure 1-2 shows, sales made by foreign affiliates of multinational enterprises based in the United States, Japan, and Germany far exceed exports as a means of reaching foreign customers.

In yet another manifestation of globalization, for many multinational enterprises today, the home market is no longer the largest source of revenues. This change may not be surprising for multinational enterprises like Electrolux, Asea Brown Boveri, or Nestlé whose home bases are small countries like Sweden and Switzerland. But as Table 1-4 shows, even for many of the largest U.S.-based corporations—such as Citicorp, Coca-Cola, and IBM—the share of total revenues generated abroad exceeds those generated at home.

As Frederic Donner, the then chairman of General Motors said to *Business Week* in 1963, "The great [companies] . . . of the free world . . . are no longer adequately described as Dutch, German, French, Italian, British or U.S. corporations . . . they are an international resource." If Mr. Donner's comments were a bit overstated when uttered in 1963, by the early 1990s, with the addition of Japanese firms to the list, they certainly reflected reality.

TABLE 1-4.   Sales Outside the United States, Selected U.S.-based Multinationals, 1993

Company	*Sales Outside the United States*	
	As a Percentage of Total Sales	In Billions of Dollars
Exxon	77	$75.6
Gillette	68	3.7
Bank of Boston	67	5.0
Coca-Cola	67	9.4
Citicorp	65	20.8
Colgate-Palmolive	65	4.6
Digital Equipment	64	9.2
Avon Products	61	2.5
IBM	59	37.0
Hewlett-Packard	54	11.0
Warner-Lambert	53	3.0
JP Morgan	52	6.3
Procter & Gamble	52	15.9
Du Pont	51	16.8
American International Group	50	10.1
Intel	50	4.3
Salomon	50	4.3
3M	19	6.9
Johnson & Johnson	49	6.9
Compaq Computer	49	3.5

Source: Brian Zajac, "Getting the Welcome Carpet," *Forbes,* July 18, 1994, pp. 276–279.

TABLE 1-5. Top 50 Multinational Enterprises Ranked by Size of Foreign Assets, 1992

Rank	Corporation	Country	Industry[a]	Foreign Assets	Total Assets	Foreign Sales	Total Sales	Foreign Employment	Total Employment
				(Billions of dollars)				(Thousands of employees)	
1	Royal Dutch/Shell[b]	United Kingdom/Netherlands	Petroleum refining	69.4	100.8	45.5	96.6	91.0	127.0
2	Exxon	United States	Petroleum refining	48.2	85.0	93.1	115.7	59.0	95.0
3	IBM	United States	Computers	45.7	86.7	39.9	64.5	143.9	301.5
4	General Motors	United States	Motor vehicles and parts	41.8	191.0	42.3	132.4	272.0	750.0
5	Hitachi[c]	Japan	Electronics	—	66.6	13.9	58.4	—	324.2
6	Matsushita Electric[c]	Japan	Electronics	28.7	74.4	29.9	60.8	94.8	252.1
7	Nestlé	Switzerland	Food	28.0	31.3	37.7	38.4	211.3	218.0
8	Ford	United States	Automobiles	28.0	180.5	33.2	100.1	167.0	325.3
9	Alcatel Alsthom[c]	France	Electronics	—	44.4	18.0	30.7	106.3	203.0
10	General Electric	United States	Electronics	24.2	192.9	8.4	57.1	58.0	231.0
11	Philips Electronics	Netherlands	Electronics	22.9	28.6	31.0	33.3	225.8	257.7
12	Mobil	United States	Petroleum refining	22.6	40.6	49.7	64.1	28.2	63.7
13	Asea Brown Boveri[d]	Switzerland	Electronics, electrical equipment	22.4	25.9	26.3	29.6	198.8	213.4
14	Elf Aquitaine[c]	France	Petroleum refining	—	45.1	13.2	36.2	—	87.9
15	Volkswagen[c]	Germany	Motor vehicles and parts	—	46.6	29.4	54.7	109.0	273.0
16	Toyota Motor Co.	Japan	Motor vehicles and parts	20.7	76.7	22.0	81.3	16.3	108.2
17	Siemens[c]	Germany	Electronics	—	44.6	27.0	50.3	160.0	413.0
18	Daimler–Benz[c]	Germany	Transport and communication	—	52.5	35.8	63.1	74.0	376.5
19	British Petroleum[c]	United Kingdom	Petroleum refining	—	31.5	34.0	58.6	71.7	97.7
20	Unilever[c]	United Kingdom/Netherlands	Food	19.4	24.2	35.0	43.7	247.9	283.2
21	Fiat	Italy	Motor vehicles and parts	19.2	58.0	20.3	40.1	82.6	285.5
22	Sony	Japan	Electronics	19.0	39.1	13.4	34.4	71.1	126.0
23	Hanson	United Kingdom	Building materials	17.5	36.6	8.2	15.7	54.0	75.0
24	ENI[c]	Italy	Petroleum refining	—	54.9	12.9	33.8	25.2	124.0
25	Du Pont	United States	Chemicals	16.0	38.9	17.5	37.8	36.9	128.7
26	B.A.T. Industries	United Kingdom	Tobacco	14.2	43.6	24.1	31.2	183.0	198.0

27	Philip Morris	United States	Food	13.8	50.0	20.0	59.1	70.0	161.0
28	Nissho Iwai[c]	Japan	Trading	—	40.7	35.0	91.6	2.1	7.3
29	Grand Metropolitan	United Kingdom	Food	13.0	16.7	11.2	79.8	—	102.4
30	Bayer	Germany	Chemicals	12.8	23.7	20.7	26.4	79.0	156.4
31	Chrysler[c]	United States	Motor vehicles and parts	—	40.7	4.3	36.9	35.1	113.0
32	Lyonnaise des Eaux[c]	France	Construction	—	24.3	7.4	16.4	83.9	161.1
33	Total[c]	France	Petroleum refining	—	20.9	14.9	25.9	28.5	51.1
34	Seagram	Canada	Beverages	11.3	11.8	5.9	6.1	9.3	15.8
35	Saint–Gobain[c]	France	Building materials	—	17.2	9.1	14.1	66.9	100.4
36	Dow Chemical	United States	Chemicals	10.8	25.4	9.4	18.9	28.2	61.4
37	Xerox[c]	United States	Scientific and photo. equipment	—	34.1	9.1	18.3	—	107.5
38	Toshiba[c]	Japan	Electronics	—	45.0	11.0	37.0	29.0	173.0
39	Ciba–Geigy	Switzerland	Chemicals	10.4	21.0	10.5	15.9	68.4	90.6
40	Procter & Gamble	United States	Soaps and cosmetics	10.2	24.9	15.9	30.4	59.4	103.5
41	BASF[c]	Germany	Chemicals	—	24.7	18.2	28.1	41.9	112.0
42	Chevron	United States	Petroleum refining	10.1	34.0	13.2	41.4	10.1	49.3
43	Michelin	France	Rubber and plastics	9.7	14.2	10.4	12.7	—	130.7
44	Petrofina[c]	Belgium	Petroleum industry	—	10.7	—	16.7	10.5	15.5
45	Honda[c]	Japan	Motor vehicles and parts	—	24.1	19.5	29.3	—	90.9
46	Sandoz	Switzerland	Pharmaceuticals	9.3	12.7	9.8	10.2	45.8	53.4
47	Bridgestone[c]	Japan	Rubber and plastics	—	14.8	7.5	14.0	54.0	85.8
48	Texaco	United States	Petroleum refining	9.2	26.0	17.2	36.8	13.1	38.0
49	Hoechst[c]	Germany	Chemicals	—	22.9	22.1	29.4	90.3	177.7
50	Electrolux[c]	Sweden	Electronics	—	11.5	12.4	14.2	104.9	121.1

[a]Industry classification for companies follows that in the Fortune Global 500 list in *Fortune*, 26 August 1991, except for Akzo, Daimler–Benz, GTE, ITT, and McDonald's. In the *Fortune* classification, companies are included in the industry or services that represents the greatest volume of their sales; Industry groups are based on categories established by the United States Office of Management and Budget. Several companies, however, are highly diversified. These companies include 3M, GE, Grand Metropolitan, Hanson, ITT, Sandoz and United Technologies.

[b]Foreign sales figures are outside Europe whereas foreign employment figures are outside the United Kingdom and the Netherlands.

[c]Data on foreign assets are not available; ranking according to foreign assets estimated on the basis of the ratio of foreign to total employment, foreign to total fixed assets and other similar ratios.

[d]Company's business include electric power generation, transmission and distribution, and rail transportation.

Source: United Nations, *World Investment Report*, 1994, Table I.2, p. 6.

TABLE 1-6.   Percentage Shares of World Manufacturing Exports Accounted for by the United States, and by U.S.-Based Multinational Enterprises and Their Majority-Owned Foreign Affiliates, 1966–1992, Selected Years

	1966	1977	1982	1992[a]
Share of world manufacturing exports accounted for by all U.S. companies	17.5	13.3	14.3	11.8
Share of world manufacturing exports accounted for by U.S.-based multinational enterprises and their majority-owned foreign affiliates	17.7	17.6	17.7	18.2

[a]Shares include nonmanufacturing exports.

Sources: Robert E. Lipsey and Irving B. Kravis, "The Competitiveness and Comparative Advantage of U.S. Multinationals, 1957–1983," NBER Working Paper No. 2051 (1986), p. 7, for figures prior to 1992; World Bank, *World Development Report 1994* (New York: Oxford University Press, 1994), Table 13, p. 187; U.S. Department of Commerce, *U.S. Direct Investment Abroad: 1992* (Washington, D.C.: U.S. GPO, 1994), Tables II.Q.1 and III.F.13.

In fact, the United Nations estimates that by 1992 multinational enterprises controlled about one-third of the world's private-sector assets.[10] The world's top 50 multinational enterprises ranked by foreign assets are shown in Table 1-5. As you look down this list of familiar names, notice that all 50 firms come from just 11 countries. If this list were expanded to include the top 100 companies, 96 would belong to these same 11 countries.

If we pause for a moment and reflect on the history of the developments traced so briefly in the preceding pages, we will notice that, gradually, the locus of decision making, organization, and action in *international business* has shifted from national to multinational enterprises straddling operations in multiple countries. More than ever before, it seems right to say: *Nations don't compete, firms do.*

Consider Table 1-6 which provides an illustration of the nation–firm distinction to which many observers are increasingly pointing. The first row in the table shows that when seen from the viewpoint of U.S. domestic labor and private citizens, the U.S. share in world exports has declined since the 1960s. But the second row shows that when seen from the viewpoint of U.S.-based multinationals and their international affiliates, this indicator of international competitiveness seems to have actually held course.

So, because the world's multinational enterprises have emerged as the primary actors in international business, they get pride of place in the schematic summary shown in Figure 1-3. The schematic and the table beneath it attempt to emphasize three points. First, to the extent that business affairs appear to be conducted in a "borderless" world today, multinational enterprises are the entities most responsible for the transformation. Second, although conventional export-import trade continues to be a vital part of the overall picture, international production and sales by multinational enterprises is increasingly becoming the dominant mode by which global business occurs in the 1990s. Third, even within trade, the intrafirm international transfers of multinational enterprises, not to mention their outsourcing and other trade-related operations, account for substantial portions of the total. This suggests that in finding, securing, and servicing world markets efficiently, multinational enterprises have discovered that both trade *and* foreign production are often required.

[10]United Nations, *World Investment Report,* 1993, p. 1.

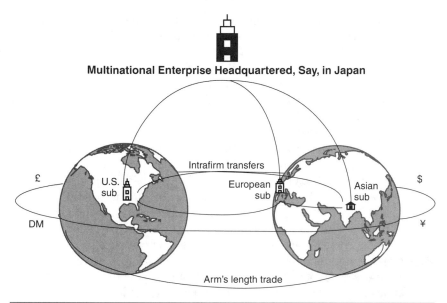

Multinational Enterprise Headquartered, Say, in Japan

Item	1991–1992 (U.S. $ in trillions)
Value of world exports of merchandise and services (1991)	4.4
Amount estimated to be intrafirm (1991)	1.1
Amount estimated to be arm's length (1991)	3.3
Value of sales made abroad by foreign affiliates of all multinational enterprises (1992)	5.5
Value of world foreign direct investment outflows (1992)	0.2
Value of world foreign direct investment stocks (1992)	1.9

Figure 1-3   International Business in the 1990s

Sources: GATT, *International Trade 91-92: Statistics* (Geneva: GATT, 1993), Table 1.1, p. 1; United Nations, *World Investment Report* (New York: United Nations, 1992), p. 53; UN, *WIR* (1993), p. 1; UN, *WIR* (1994), Table I.4, p. 12, and Table I.8, p. 19. Intrafirm exports are estimated by the United Nations (1992) to account for 25 percent of world totals.

National and Regional Patterns

Of course, the prominence given to the multinational enterprise should not leave the impression that nations no longer matter. Even in our so-called borderless world, nation-states are important actors not just because of the power of national governments to dictate terms at the border, but also because countries still provide a well-defined and relatively homogeneous unit for aggregating demand and supply, and often, therefore, for setting corporate strategy.

Generally speaking, purchasing power, economic growth rates, currency, customs, and tastes are more homogeneous among people within a nation than between people from different nations. Customs (like left- or right-hand drive), conventions (such as those that govern accounting practices), and environmental factors (such as the type of water or weather) might vary by nation. Being able to cater to as well as capitalize on these national differences are traits associated with successful multinationals.

Consider the concerns of a Matsushita executive who worked in the firm's microwave business in Europe. "British people like crispy fat on top of meat, so you need a stronger heating element in their ovens. Germans like their potatoes overcooked, but the British like them almost crunchy, so you have to design the cooking controls differently."[11]

Another reason why national units are important in business strategy is stressed by Michael Porter in his book *The Competitive Advantage of Nations.*[12] Some countries and regions may prove to be more important than others from a corporate strategy perspective because they offer the largest markets or have the potential to do so, or because they have a high concentration of suppliers and an attendant network of support industries (such as infrastructure and parts suppliers, shippers and distributors), or because the region is the crucible of innovation in a particular industry.

The central point is this: Geography can be an important dimension in international business, and it is therefore useful to view the world economy through a lens of nations. Which countries of the world harbor the movers and shakers? Well, several nations might qualify on one count or another, but let us begin with that summary indicator of economic importance, gross national product, or GNP. Table 1-7 presents GNP and population data for three clusters of countries and the world at large.

The Group of Seven (G7) nations—Canada, France, Germany, Italy, Japan, the United Kingdom, and the United States—lead the world in terms of GNP and economic size. Per capita GNP in the G7 was about five times as high as the world average; and as the GNP figures which have been adjusted for purchasing power indicate, the United States still led the pack in 1992. The so-called newly industrialized countries, or the NICs—Hong Kong, Singapore, South Korea, and Taiwan—stand out in terms of their recent sustained high rates of economic growth. Whereas world GNP grew at around 1.2 percent per annum between 1980 and 1992, the NICs had grown fast enough to nearly double their incomes over this interval.

Finally, Brazil, China, India, and Mexico merit attention largely for their potential. We will call this group of nations the Emerging Four, or the E4. The moderate but rising purchasing power within these countries coupled with their large populations promises vast markets for a spectrum of industries ranging from commercial aircraft to cars, consumer electronics, telecommunications, and financial services. Furthermore, because all four nations have a reasonable base of skills and technology, and all four are increasingly liberalizing their economies, they represent both a threat and an opportunity for firms in the advanced industrialized nations: a threat in the sense that some of tomorrow's world-class competitors will emerge from these countries, and an opportunity in the sense that foreign enterprises can locate their own facilities in these countries and partake in the dynamism and skill base that these countries have to offer.

---

[11]Brenton R. Schlender, "Matsushita Shows How to Go Global," *Fortune,* July 11, 1994, pp. 159–66.

[12]Michael E. Porter, *The Competitive Advantage of Nations* (London: The Macmillan Press, 1990).

TABLE 1-7.   Gross National Product and Population, Selected Countries, World, 1992

	GNP					Population
	Total	Per Capita		PPP Estimates Per Capita		
Country	Billions of Dollars	Dollars	% Change Per Annum 1980–1992	Dollars	United States = 100	Millions
The G7						
Canada	494	20,710	1.8	19,720	85	27
France	1,320	22,260	1.7	19,200	83	57
Germany[a]	1,789	28,859	2.4	20,610	89	62
Italy	1,223	20,460	2.2	17,730	77	58
Japan	3,671	28,190	3.6	20,160	87	125
United Kingdom	903	17,790	2.4	16,730	72	58
United States	5,920	23,240	1.7	23,120	100	255
The NICs						
Hong Kong	78	15,360	5.5	20,050	87	6
Singapore	46	15,730	5.3	16,720	72	3
South Korea	296	6,790	8.5	8,950	39	44
Taiwan[b]	207	9,936	12.8	na	na	21
The E4						
Brazil	360	2,770	0.4	5,250	23	154
China	506	470	7.6	1,910	9	1,162
India	215	310	3.1	1,210	5	884
Mexico	329	3,470	−0.2	7,490	32	85
World	23,061	4,280	1.2	—	—	5,438

[a]Data refer to Federal Republic of Germany before reunification; population is for 1989, and 1992 per capita GNP is based on these earlier population figures.

[b]GNP growth figure is for 1980–1991.

PPP = purchasing power parity; na = not available.

Sources: World Bank, *World Development Report 1994* (New York: Oxford University Press, 1994), Tables 1 and 3. For Taiwan, Economist Intelligence Unit, *Country Report,* 2nd Quarter 1994, and *Country Profile,* 1993; and Republic of China, *Taiwan Statistical Data Book,* 1992.

As Figure 1-4 shows, however, even though the E4 nations had over 40 percent of the world's population in 1992, they accounted for only 6 percent of world economic output. In contrast, the G7 nations accounted for only 12 percent of the world's population, but 66 percent of world economic output.

International exports and foreign direct investment activity are also disproportionately concentrated among a handful of nations. As Figure 1-5 shows, in both merchandise and commercial services exports, the 10 leading nations accounted for 64 percent of the world total in 1992. In foreign direct investment, the 10 leading nations accounted for 93 percent of all outward investment stocks and 73 percent of all inward investment stocks.

Given that almost the same handful of countries from North America, Western

Shares in World Population, 1992

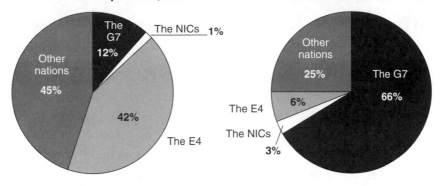

Shares in World GNP, 1992

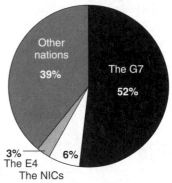

Shares in World Merchandise Exports, 1992

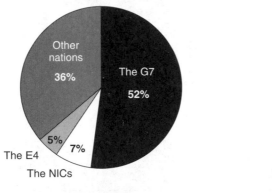

Shares in World Commercial Service Exports, 1991

Shares in World Outward FDI Stocks, 1990

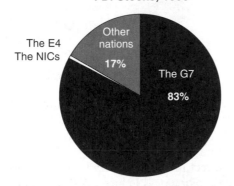

Shares in World Inward FDI Stocks, 1990

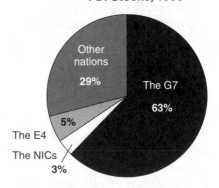

Figure 1-4 Shares in World Population, GNP, Exports, and Foreign Direct Investment, Selected Country Groups, 1990–1992. See Table 1-7 for countries that make up the G7, the NICs, and the E4.

Sources: Population and GNP data from World Bank, *World Development Report,* 1994, Tables 1 and 3. Taiwan GNP and population from Economist Intelligence Unit, *Country Report,* 1994. Trade data from World Bank, *World Development Report,* 1994, Table 13; GATT, *International Trade 91-92: Statistics,* Table 1.5. FDI data from United Nations, *World Investment Report,* 1993, Annex Table 2. FDI data for Hong Kong and Singapore pertain to 1989; and for Korea, Taiwan, China, and India to 1988.

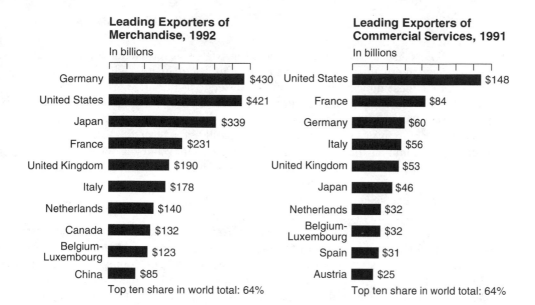

Leading Exporters of Merchandise, 1992

In billions

Germany	$430
United States	$421
Japan	$339
France	$231
United Kingdom	$190
Italy	$178
Netherlands	$140
Canada	$132
Belgium-Luxembourg	$123
China	$85

Top ten share in world total: 64%

Leading Exporters of Commercial Services, 1991

In billions

United States	$148
France	$84
Germany	$60
Italy	$56
United Kingdom	$53
Japan	$46
Netherlands	$32
Belgium-Luxembourg	$32
Spain	$31
Austria	$25

Top ten share in world total: 64%

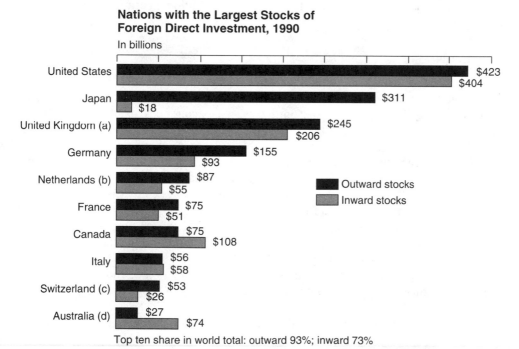

Nations with the Largest Stocks of Foreign Direct Investment, 1990

In billions

	Outward stocks	Inward stocks
United States	$423	$404
Japan	$311	$18
United Kingdom (a)	$245	$206
Germany	$155	$93
Netherlands (b)	$87	$55
France	$75	$51
Canada	$75	$108
Italy	$56	$58
Switzerland (c)	$53	$26
Australia (d)	$27	$74

Top ten share in world total: outward 93%; inward 73%

Figure 1-5 The Ten Leading Nations in Terms of Exports and Foreign Direct Investment Stocks, 1990–1992.

[a]Inward stock in 1988.

[b]1989.

[c]1989.

[d]1991.

Sources: Trade data from World Bank, *World Development Report,* 1994, Table 13; GATT, *International Trade 91-92: Statistics,* Table 1.5. FDI data from United Nations, *World Investment Report,* 1993, Annex Table 2.

Europe, and East Asia are prominent on these top 10 lists, it should not come as a surprise that their international economic transactions occur mainly with one another. For this reason, these three regions are often referred to as the Triad. The significance of this term is vividly apparent in Figure 1-6, which is based on the trade and investment patterns of 10 Triad nations.

The very high intra-European trade figure should be interpreted cautiously. The existence of a common market, the geographic proximity, and the relatively small size of their home markets, all tend to push European nations to integrate more like states or provinces within one nation.

To summarize: seen from a national or regional perspective, international business appears to be tightly concentrated in just a handful of nations and regions. From a manager's perspective, these regions—North America, Western Europe, and East Asia—jointly form the arena where the bulk of international production, consumption, and competition is taking place. Nevertheless, several developing countries including Brazil, China, Mexico, and India bear watching, and, in the 1990s managers on the frontiers of international business will have to factor in the threats and opportunities emerging from regions that lie outside the traditional perimeters of the Triad.

Industry Patterns

Some industries are more internationalized than others. A number of factors, including the nature of competition, transport costs, scale economies, availability of inputs, and the difficulty of successfully conducting arm's length trade (trade between unrelated parties) in research and development and other intangibles (such as brand names), influence the degree to which industries internationalize. Just look at Table 1-5 again. We can see that the world's top multinational enterprises are concentrated in a rather small set of industries, which include automobiles, petroleum, chemicals and pharmaceuticals, packaged foods, and machinery.

Figure 1-7 shows the sectoral breakdown of world exports and foreign direct investment (FDI) stocks. Two things are clear. Manufacturing dominates merchandise trade, and, within manufacturing, machinery and commercial aircraft account for almost two-fifths of the total of such trade. Motor vehicles, food, and chemicals—including pharmaceuticals—jointly account for another two-fifths within all manufacturing.

As is true of merchandise trade, manufacturing has also been the single largest sector with regard to foreign direct investment (FDI). Indeed, as late as 1980, manufacturing accounted for close to 45 percent of the world's total stock of FDI.[13] More recent data seem to indicate that commercial services FDI—primarily finance and trade-related activities—now accounts for half the total. This relatively recent shift is caused by two factors. First, with worldwide deregulation of certain service sectors,

---

[13]United Nations, *World Investment Report,* 1993, Table III.1, p. 62.

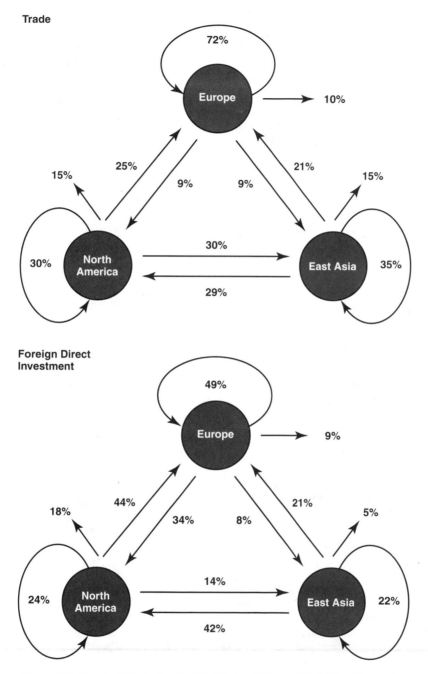

Trade

72%

Europe

10%

25%   9%   9%   21%

15%   15%

30%   North America   East Asia   35%

30%

29%

Foreign Direct Investment

49%

Europe

9%

44%   34%   8%   21%

18%   5%

24%   North America   East Asia   22%

14%

42%

Figure 1.6   Keeping It in the Family: Triad Nations' Shares of Trade (Exports plus Imports) and Outward Foreign Direct Investment Stocks by Partner and Host Region, 1990

Note: Europe refers to France, Germany, Italy, Netherlands, Sweden, and the United Kingdom; East Asia refers to Australia and Japan as sources and includes South-East Asia and the Pacific as hosts; and North America refers to Canada and the United States.

Source: United Nations, *World Investment Report* (New York: United Nations, 1993), Tables VII.3, and VII.5; pp. 168 and 170.

Sectoral Shares in World Exports, 1991

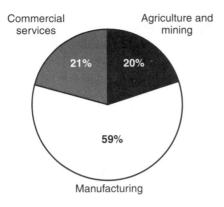

Sectoral Shares in Outward Foreign Direct Investment Stocks, 1990

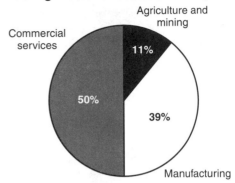

Industry Shares Within World Manufacturing Exports, 1991

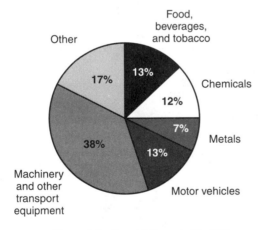

Industry Shares Within Manufacturing Outward Foreign Direct Investment Stocks, 1990

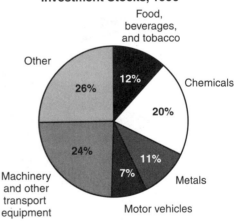

Figure 1-7   Sectoral Shares in World Exports and Foreign Direct Investment, 1990, 1991

Note: FDI shares are based on data for Australia, Canada, France, Federal Republic of Germany, Italy, Japan, Netherlands, United Kingdom, and United States only. These countries account jointly for 90 percent of worldwide outward FDI stocks.

Sources: GATT, *International Trade 91-92: Statistics,* Tables I.1 and III.1, pp. 1 and 30; and United Nations, *World Investment Report,* 1993, Tables III.1 and III.3, pp. 62 and 72.

particularly banking and insurance, FDI in services has grown rapidly. To this extent, the pie chart in Figure 1-7 reflects reality.

But a second factor related to reporting practices drives a wedge between reality and the pertinent pie chart in Figure 1-7. The problem is that FDI stock figures are reported at book value. As a result, the more recent service-related FDI is overrepresented and the less recent manufacturing-related FDI is underrepresented. Indeed, if appropriate adjustments were made so that the stock figures showed market rather than book values, it is quite likely that even in the 1990s the manufacturing sector would bulk substantially larger than the other sectors.

Putting Globalization in Perspective

Let us close our high-speed review of the international economy by putting matters in perspective. Important as international business has become, the bulk of our economic activity still takes place locally or nationally. Trade barriers, other government policies, and transportation costs make it almost impossible or uneconomic for international transactions to take place in large portions of our economy.

For example, haircuts, retail shopping, home construction, retail banking, transportation, radio and TV broadcasts, housing, and health care are just a few of the large number of goods and services that, even in the 1990s, we produce and consume mostly locally. As Table 1-8 shows, particularly within the world's most industrialized economies, these sectors are substantially larger than agriculture, mining, and manufacturing, which constitute the traditional "tradables" sector. Even within the United States, the world's largest trader of services, imports supplied only 4 percent of the market for services in 1993, whereas imports supplied nearly 25 percent of the market for merchandise during the same year.[14]

But at least two important trends are pushing patterns in another direction. First, international trade in services is picking up steam. Whereas in 1981 world exports of commercial services stood at $413 billion, by 1991 they had more than doubled to $890 billion—representing growth of 8 percent per annum.[15] Over the same period, the value of world merchandise exports rose from $2,011 billion to $3,506 billion—representing growth of 5.7 percent per annum.[16] Although better reporting and data collection practices may account for substantial portions of the large jump in services trade, without a doubt, real growth has taken place in this sector. The contents of Box 1-1 attest to this trend.

Second, and much more important, service corporations are multinationalizing rapidly. Whereas banks and insurance companies have long been global players, during the 1990s telecommunication firms, commercial airlines, accounting firms, advertising agencies, and even management consulting firms began globalizing rapidly by setting up foreign affiliates and entering into alliances.

These trends are being fueled both by shifts in the strategies of service corpora-

---

[14]President of the United States, *Economic Report of the President*, 1994, Table B-7, p. 278; and Table B-21, p. 292.

[15]General Agreement on Tariffs and Trade, *International Trade 91-92: Statistics* (Geneva: GATT, 1993), Table A5, p. 79.

[16]Ibid., Table A3, p. 73.

TABLE 1-8. Percentage Shares of Agriculture and Merchandise, and Construction and Services in the Gross Domestic Product of Selected Countries

| | | Agriculture and Merchandise | | | | Construction and Services | | | |
| | | | | | | | | Commerce, Transport, and Communications | Financial Services, Insurance, and Real Estate |
Country	Year	Total	Agriculture	Mining	Manufacturing	Total	Construction		
The G7									
Canada	1993	25.1	3.1	4.2	17.8	74.9	5.4	20.5	16.8
France	1992	25.3	3.1	4.4	17.8	74.7	5.7	17.8	13.9
Germany[a]	1990	35.2	1.8	3.3	30.0	64.8	4.8	15.0	—
Italy[b]	1990	33.2	4.4	—	28.8	66.8	6.9	28.3	13.3
Japan	1992	30.4	2.2	0.3	27.9	69.6	10.1	19.1	16.0
United Kingdom	1992	26.0	1.8	1.9	22.3	74.0	6.2	22.2	23.6
United States	1990	21.6	2.3	1.0	18.3	78.4	5.1	22.0	14.7
The NICs									
Hong Kong	1991	15.0	0.2	0.0	14.7	85.0	5.0	33.3	24.9
Singapore	1992	28.2	0.2	0.1	27.9	71.8	7.9	29.6	27.0
South Korea	1992	35.3	7.6	0.4	27.3	64.7	15.2	17.3	16.6
Taiwan	1992	38.2	3.7	0.3	34.2	61.8	4.3	22.6	18.1
The E4									
Brazil	1991	37.5	10.8	1.7	25.0	62.5	7.1	7.1	—
China[c]	1992	64.8	29.2	—	35.6	35.2	7.4	14.0	—
India	1991/92	53.1	30.8	2.0	20.3	46.9	4.6	18.0	10.7
Mexico	1991	33.7	7.5	3.4	22.8	66.3	5.0	32.9	10.7

[a]Data refer to Federal Republic of Germany before reunification.

[b]Finance, insurance, and real estate share is for 1992.

[c]Manufacturing share is for 1991.

Sources: Economist Intelligence Unit, *Country Report and Country Profile*, various issues; OECD, *OECD Economic Surveys: Germany*, 1993, Table B, p. 136; *OECD Economic Surveys: Italy*, 1992, Table O, p. 146; World Bank, *Trends in Developing Economies: 1992*, p. 119; United Nations, *Statistical Yearbook for Asia and the Pacific*, 1993, Table III, p. 129.

tions and by the waves of deregulation and privatization that are washing across many countries. According to the United Nations, by 1992 services accounted for 50 to 55 percent of the annual flows of foreign direct investment.[17] As a result, the distinction between tradables and nontradables, if it ever was valid, is becoming less and less important from the standpoint of managers in the international economy.

Even though companies like Deutsche Bank, Toys "Я" Us, and United Parcel Service are moving aggressively in directions that are likely to alter the sectoral patterns of trade and investment in the future, it is still manufacturing and resource-

[17]United Nations, *World Investment Report*, 1992, p. 105.

BOX 1-1. U.S. EXPORTS: MORE THAN PEANUTS

In 1992, American service firms exported to nonaffiliates abroad:

- Over two-thirds as much in passenger fares ($17.4 billion), such as seats on U.S.-flagged air carriers, as the United States exported civilian aircraft ($24.5 billion).
- More educational services ($6.1 billion) than the United States exported corn ($5.7 billion).
- More financial services ($5.4 billion) than the United States exported wheat ($4.6 billion).
- More equipment installation and repair services ($2.8 billion) than the United States exported agricultural machinery ($2.1 billion).
- More information services, including computer and data processing and database services ($2.6 billion), than the United States exported aluminum ($1.2 billion).
- More legal services ($1.4 billion) than the United States exported vegetable oils ($1.0 billion).
- More management consulting services ($0.78 billion) than the United States exported milled rice ($0.72 billion) or peanuts ($0.21 billion).

SOURCE: President of the United States, *Economic Report of the President* (Washington, D.C.: U.S. Government Printing Office, 1994), Box 6–1, p. 209.

---

intensive companies like General Motors, Matsushita, and Royal Dutch/Shell that dominate the international forest in the 1990s. The treatment of the issues considered in the balance of this text will reflect this fact.

Roadmap

The remainder of the book is divided into three parts. Part One, covering Chapters 2 to 5, locates us within the firm and addresses such questions as: Why do firms become multinational? What goals and strategies drive multinational firms? How do their managers identify opportunities, assess risks, and formulate responses? What organizational and network structures have these firms turned to in their efforts to compete effectively in world markets?

Part Two, covering Chapters 6 and 7, explores the interactions between the multinational enterprise and the nations in which it operates. It looks at how country factors, as well as national goals and policies, relate to and influence the competitiveness of multinational firms. Part Three, covering Chapters 8 to 11, discusses the key characteristics of the international economic system in which the manager operates. The chapters in Part Three touch on the role of exchange rates in the macroeconomy, the rules and operations of international financial markets, and the evolution and functions of international economic institutions and arrangements such as the GATT, WTO, EU, and NAFTA.

Suggested Reading

KOBRIN, STEPHEN J. "An Empirical Analysis of the Determinants of Global Integration." *Strategic Management Journal*, 12 (1991), 17–31.

KOGUT, BRUCE. "Country Capabilities and the Permeability of Borders." *Strategic Management Journal*, 12 (1991), 33–47.

UNITED NATIONS. *World Investment Report.* New York: United Nations, 1994.

U.S. CONGRESS, OFFICE OF TECHNOLOGY ASSESSMENT. *Multinationals and the U.S. Technology Base*, OTA-ITA-612. Washington, D.C.: U.S. Government Printing Office, 1994.

CHAPTER 2

Going Multinational: Firm Motives and Characteristics

For two decades the Lincoln Electric Company . . . maker of arc welders and welding supplies . . . [has managed to drive out many] small companies and a few large ones, including General Electric and Westinghouse. . . . As Lincoln saw it, the only true threat it faced . . . as it entered the 1980's was from ESAB of Sweden. As ESAB acquired European rivals, Lincoln, which had small operations in Britain, France and Canada, became increasingly concerned that the Swedish company would establish a fortress on its home ground and then invade the United States market. [In response, in a matter of just six years] 1986 to 1992, Lincoln expanded from 5 plants in 4 countries to 21 plants in 15 countries. *The New York Times,* September 5, 1994.[1]

Inside a factory complex . . . here [in Minas Gerais, Brazil], assembly lines are running three shifts a day, propelling Fiat Automoveis S.A. past Ford and General Motors to rank as Brazil's second-largest car maker [behind Volkswagen]. . . . "This will be the main plant for producing Fiat's new world car," [said] Pacifico Paoli, chief executive of the subsidiary. . . . Fiat of Brazil . . . is investing $1 billion in expanding the plant here. . . . Cheap land, relatively low-cost labor, and abundant steel and electrical expansion are cited as factors in Fiat's expansion. . . . Undoubtedly influenced by Fiat's track record, General Motors and Autolatina, a Ford-Volkswagen consortium, are reportedly leaning toward choosing Minas Gerais for factories they plan to build in Brazil next year. *The New York Times,* August 11, 1994.[2]

[A]t the behest of [Chairman] Welch and Vice-Chairman Paolo Fresco . . . GE is betting on the three developing giants—China, India, and Mexico—with Southeast Asia close behind. Total population: roughly 2.5 billion, some 10 times the U.S. In all four markets, political

---

[1] Barnaby J. Feder, "Recasting a Model Incentive Strategy," *The New York Times,* September 5, 1994 pp. 33 and 36.

[2] James Brooke, "Inland Region of Brazil Grows Like Few Others," *The New York Times,* August 11, 1994, pp. D1–D2.

and economic risks loom, but GE reckons that placing many small stakes of a few tens of millions of dollars each will cushion it. If the strategy "is wrong, it's a billion dollars, a couple of billion dollars," says Welch. . . . "If it's right, it's the future of the next century for this company." *Business Week,* November 8, 1993.[3]

Some kinds of enterprises are much more caught up than others in the opportunities and dangers that arise from developments that lie outside the home economy. Lincoln Electric, Fiat, and General Electric are just three examples of such entities, which we categorize as multinational enterprises.

As we saw in Chapter 1, in the course of the past few decades, most of the large enterprises of the world, whether engaged in manufacturing, mining, banking, or other services, now fall in this category. Such enterprises are characteristically made up of a parent firm located in one country and a cluster of affiliated firms located in a number of other countries. Enterprises of this sort commonly operate in such a way that the affiliated firms, though located in different countries, nevertheless share the following characteristics:

- They are linked by ties of common ownership.
- They draw on a common pool of resources, such as trade names and patents, information and systems, and money and credit.
- They respond to a common strategy, aimed at increasing the profit and reducing the risk of the enterprise as a whole.

About one-half of the industrial output of the countries outside the former communist world is produced by firms that have developed a multinational structure. These enterprises have some special problems that arise from their being multinational, but they also face the problems and opportunities of any importer or exporter, or any lender or borrower who deals across national boundaries. Accordingly, from the viewpoint of the manager who is interested in the international economy, our focus on the multinational enterprise does not narrow the range of problems that the book addresses.

Although multinational enterprises have come to account for a large part of the world's total output, they still consist of a very distinctive group of firms. Generally speaking, multinational enterprises are large in size. Practically all five hundred of the biggest enterprises in the world have substantial business interests in the form of operating units located outside their own country. Ford Motor Company, for instance, has 51 percent of its employees outside the United States; Philips of Netherlands, 88 percent of its employees outside the home country; British Petroleum, 73 percent; and Sony of Japan, 56 percent. In the past few years, the largest firms of Korea, Mexico, and other industrializing countries have begun to take on signs of a similar trend.

Firms that have developed a multinational structure tend to be engaged in cer-

---

[3]Tim Smart, Pete Engardio, and Geri Smith, "GE's Brave New World," *Business Week,* November 8, 1993, pp. 64–70.

tain kinds of business activities. By almost any measure, there are more multinational enterprises in manufacturing than in oil, mining, agriculture, or banking. Within the manufacturing sector, the multinational enterprise is especially strong in certain kinds of industries, especially in industries whose product markets are dominated by a relatively few large firms. These include motor vehicles, chemical products, petroleum refining, pharmaceuticals, electronic products, and prepared foods. However, some firms from developing countries such as Brazil and India have managed to create multinational networks in less complex manufacturing industries, including textiles, shoes, and bicycles (see Box 2-1).

Multinational firms have rapidly been acquiring dominant positions in the service industries as well. They have proved especially prominent in financial services, hotels, fast food, accounting, engineering and large-scale construction, and management consulting. Firms in certain developing countries have been particularly successful in establishing overseas activities that provide engineering and construction services.

Why have so many enterprises developed a multinational network in the past few decades? Why did they not, instead, conduct their international business through arm's length exports or through licensing arrangements with independent firms, or some combination of such mechanisms? After all, managing a multinational network entails special difficulties and generates special costs. Managers must set up costly systems of communication and coordination, expose their enterprises to the hazards of investing in foreign currencies, and risk the possibility of being discriminated against as foreign investors by the governments of other countries. Yet the fact that multinational enterprises have expanded so rapidly suggests that managers see some reasons for developing a multinational structure.

Numerous scholars have tried to make some generalizations regarding the forces that have pushed firms to create a multinational network. The generalizations below represent our rendition of the collective wisdom of others, including Stephen Hymer, John Dunning, Peter Buckley, and Mark Casson. In brief:

- Firms that have acquired some firm-specific capability sometimes find that they must operate through a foreign subsidiary in order fully to exploit that capability. Think about GE's venture in China, India, and Mexico.
- Firms that wish to take advantage of a lower cost structure in a foreign country sometimes find that they must establish a subsidiary in that country in order to take advantage of those lower costs. Consider a U.S. semiconductor company's assembly operations in Malaysia.
- Firms that wish to protect and strengthen the position of the network they have created sometimes conclude that additional subsidiaries will increase the competitive position and prospective profits of the multinational network as a whole, even if the added subsidiaries do not generate a profit on a stand-alone basis. Recall the explosive foreign expansion by Lincoln Electric cited at the beginning of this chapter.

BOX 2-1. INDIAN MULTINATIONALS: ON THE WINGS OF HOPE

Indian companies, long buffered from foreign competition, are now beginning to appreciate the threats that accompany the opportunities brought by their government's
economic liberalization programs. The drawing down of previously high import tariffs
and the entry of foreign multinationals are forcing many Indian firms to streamline operations, consolidate capacity in "global-sized plants," and go multinational.

In the words of one Indian executive, "Competition is getting more and more
rough. . . . How . . . do you counter the threat of other multinationals, unless you are
one yourself?" Many Indian firms are taking these words to heart. The Birla group, a
large producer of rayon fiber and industrial products such as insulators and carbon
black, has initiated 20 international joint ventures in four countries. Many of its products reach markets in developed countries, and foreign sales already account for half
the company's total sales.

Another Indian firm, Asian Paints, went multinational in 1977 by starting production in Fiji. The director of the company explains, "The decision to take such a
step, despite the presence of established foreign paints manufacturers such as British
Paints and Jensen and Nicholson, stemmed from the fact that there was a large Indian
expatriate community in Fiji which had shown a great interest in Asian Paints. Exports
from India were ruled out because of the high freight costs." The company now plans
to expand in Australia and New Zealand.

Similarly, Ranbaxy Laboratories, India's second largest pharmaceutical company, is targeting the international generic drugs market. The company has set itself a
sales goal of $1 billion for the year 2003–2004, which it hopes to achieve by exporting
off-patent generic drugs from India and by forming foreign joint ventures to make
new generation drugs in India. The company operates plants in Malaysia, Thailand,
Hong Kong, China, and the Netherlands.

In the bicycle industry, Hero of India controls 50 percent of its domestic market. Now it is "gearing up for a plunge into the global market." The company has applied for brand registration in 45 countries. Its sister company, Hero Motors, already
assembles mopeds in Egypt, Bangladesh, Iran, and Brazil.

In the textile industry, India's Arvind Mills is thought to be a "world leader in
the making." The company supplies denim to makers of the Lee, Wrangler, and Levi
Strauss brands of apparel. Although Arvind produced considerably less than U.S.-
based Swift's 115 million meters in 1992, its planned expansion in Sri Lanka and
Mauritius is expected to take capacity to 140 million meters by the mid- to late 1990s.

SOURCE: Based on Dakesh Parikh, "Indian Multinationals: On the Wings of Hope," *India
Today*, September 15, 1994, pp. 86–90.

- Firms that wish to reduce the political and competitive risks to the network as a whole sometimes conclude that a foreign subsidiary will contribute to that objective, even if the subsidiary will not generate a profit on a stand-alone basis. Think about the move by Japanese car manufacturers to begin production in the United States in the 1980s.

In the paragraphs that follow, let us explore more closely these four motivations that lead firms to create multinational networks.

Exploiting Firm-Specific Capabilities

Practically every large firm develops some capability that distinguishes it from others. It may be a valuable technological skill such as that possessed by Sharp, a leading manufacturer of color flat-panel displays, or a trade name such as that of Kodak. The existence of that capability is usually what the firm relies on to overcome its initial handicap as a foreigner operating in foreign markets. Exploiting that asset, whether by increasing the earnings it generates or by reducing the risks that it may lose its earning power, is usually the first major objective of the firm's strategy. Of the various firm-specific capabilities that we are likely to encounter, those based on a unique technological skill or on a strong trade name are likely to head the list.

Technological Innovations

Since the beginning of modern industry over one hundred years ago, a good deal of the research and development undertaken by industrial firms has resulted in new products. The emphasis on new products has been especially typical of the efforts of firms in the United States, whose expenditures on research and development are responsible for almost half of the research and development expenditures in the industrialized world.[4] Some of the products resulting from research and development, such as instant cameras, simply perform a familiar job for the consumer better than the existing products. Others, such as computer-controlled machine tools, help the producer perform certain tasks more efficiently. But many products, such as penicillin and commercial aircraft, were not in serious competition with any existing products at the time of their introduction and could be regarded as satisfying wants that were never previously addressed.

The location of a firm's headquarters has strongly influenced the firm's propensity to innovate and the direction in which it was likely to innovate. Any country in which industrial innovation occurs on a substantial scale is bound to contain a body

---

[4]National Science Board, *Science and Engineering Indicators* (Washington, D.C.: U.S. GPO, 1993), Figure 6-15, p. 169.

of trained engineers and interested managers. But that is not quite enough. Managers and engineers need an incentive to innovate: the hope of gain or the fear of loss must be strong enough to justify the effort. In some national environments, firms engaged in the sale of some products or services feel little incentive to innovate because of existing agreements with potential competitors; in many European countries, for instance, retail services operate under tight local agreements. On the other hand, many governments offer special incentives to enterprises to innovate in high-tech products and services, offering, for example, to share the financial risks of such activities.

Where the capacity and incentive to innovate are strong enough, innovators have tended to concentrate on those products that seem most widely demanded in the national environment in which the innovators operate. In a country where, say, skilled labor is exceedingly scarce and expensive while capital is abundant and cheap, business managers and engineers have concentrated on labor-saving devices (such as washing machines and food processors). In a country where raw materials and space are scarce, the innovations that capture the interest of business managers and engineers have tended to be material and space saving (such as fuel-efficient cars and small TVs). Moreover, countries with high per capita incomes offer opportunities for the sale of new products or services that have not been seen before, whereas countries with low per capita incomes offer unique opportunities for the adaptation of existing products to lower priced versions, or for the adaptation of production processes to small volumes and low labor costs.

Yet other variables have influenced the propensity for industrial innovation in any economy and the direction those efforts take. Countries in which the military buys large quantities of hardware from their producers generate one kind of market, and countries in which the government buys large quantities of medicines, quite another. In big countries, the presence of a large internal market induces innovations that are associated with economies of scale; in small countries, that kind of innovation may be less likely. And so on.

Once a firm establishes a technological lead in some product, it must face the problem of finding the best way to exploit the lead. Sales to foreign markets can sometimes be achieved well enough through exports. A producer of a new line of earth-moving equipment located in the United States or Japan, for instance, may not feel especially handicapped when selling its product in Australia. Besides, at the early stage of a product's development, managers are not acutely concerned with questions of production cost. Their focus at that stage is on other factors because:

- The lines separating the development stage, the pilot-plant stage, and the first commercial production stage for a new product are often not clean-cut. In these early stages, the manager is likely to be most concerned with maintaining effective communication among the key development engineers, production specialists, controllers, salespeople, and prospective first users of the product. (Think, for instance, of the development of a new parallel-processing computer.) If the product proves successful, the manager is likely to produce the first units of the new product at the site where the development occurred. More than any other factor, this explains the U.S. automobile industry's early location in Detroit and the chemical industry's early location in New Jersey.

- Even if managers could take their choice of locations, they would have great difficulty determining the least-cost points of production and distribution. Products that are in their infancy often come in a variety of experimental shapes, sizes, and materials. Moreover, new products often cater to markets whose ultimate size and geographical bounds cannot be readily determined.

- At these early stages, the character of the demand and of the competition is such that the manager will not likely feel great pressure to minimize production and distribution costs. In new products such as battery-powered electric cars and laser-aiming devices, the number of competing producers is small, at least at first. And the sensitivity of customers to small differences in price is not very high.

As a result, the initial international strategy of innovative firms is quite simple: Manufacture at home and supply foreign markets from that single production site. In time, however, the manager is forced to worry about costs. The reasons for the increased worry are various:

- As the product matures, it begins to assume characteristics that permit easier comparison from one producer to the next. Think of how much the personal computer industry has developed since its birth in the early 1980s.

- As the product matures, the original producer's special knowledge and special skills, whatever they may be, are shared with others at home and abroad. The threat of price competition becomes more tangible.

- As the demand for the product grows, the later users are generally found placing much more weight on questions of price than the first users. In economic terms, the price elasticity of demand is higher for the later users than for the original users. Moreover, differences in price between brands are generally of greater importance to these later users.

- As the product matures, importing countries may begin to ask whether there are ways of encouraging local production to take the place of imports. Import restrictions sometimes develop at this stage. Some are overt restrictions, such as tariffs and import-licensing requirements. Others are more subtle restrictions, stemming out of "buy-at-home" policies on the part of government agencies or regulations that require some minimum domestic content.

At this stage, one possibility the exporter might consider is to license the innovation to an independent producer in the market in which local production seems indicated. A prime question for the firm, then, is whether an efficient market exists in which it can sell or license its technology and patents at a favorable price. Such a license may provide for a flow of unpatented technical information to the licensee; it may grant patent rights to the licensee covering specified countries; it may authorize the licensee to use the licensor's trade name in given markets; and it may make provision to supply some exotic line of machinery or industrial supplies. In return, the licensee will be obliged to make various payments to the licensor, typically on the order of 3 or 4 percent of its gross sales. The licensee may also be obliged to take on various commitments to the licensor, such as confining its sales to certain markets or buying its intermediate products from the licensor.

However, the market for such licenses or other contractual agreements often proves quite imperfect, for several reasons.

- For one thing, the buyer cannot tell if the technology being offered is worth the price until after the purchase has been completed and the technology has been applied. Accordingly, the buyer has a poor basis for determining a price.
- In addition, it is often very difficult to communicate subtle and complex systems and technologies successfully from one firm to the next, especially if the recipient is an independent firm operating in another culture. Accordingly, heavy costs may be involved in effectively transmitting the necessary information.
- It is also difficult as a rule for licensors to be sure that licensees are maintaining adequate quality control in their production. This is a particularly worrisome point for the licensor when the licensee is using the licensor's trade name. Moreover, the licensor may find it difficult and expensive to police other provisions of the licensing agreement, such as the licensee's adherence to the territorial limitations set out in the agreement.
- Finally, if the facilities required for exploiting the innovation are highly inflexible and cannot easily be adapted to other products or services, prospective licensees may be quite hesitant to invest, fearing the risk associated with the foreign firm's bargaining power in the future. Imagine a local firm in Ireland contemplating whether or not to construct and operate a half-a-billion dollar semiconductor fabrication plant in exchange for a limited license to manufacture chips designed by an Intel or NEC.

In any event, the maturing of technologically advanced products tends to press enterprises toward the establishment of overseas production units, whether through independent licensees or through subsidiaries. Where that choice exists, the subsidiary, as we will see further in Chapter 4, commonly proves to be the more attractive choice for many firms.

Strong Trade Names

The fact that firms cannot always sell or license their assets for use in foreign markets is also illustrated by the problems of exploiting a strong trade name. In the modern world of easy international movement and communication, trade names can sometimes gain strength in a foreign market without much conscious effort on the part of the firm that owns the name. Casual unplanned exports sometimes establish a position for a foreign brand. International tourists, business travelers, movies, magazines, and television can also be the carriers. The enormous popularity of Levis jeans in countries like Russia and India, which were previously closed to such foreign products, provides an illustration of these forces at work.

As a rule, the strength of the foreign trade name is associated with the fact or the illusion of superior performance. Whether fact or illusion, the expectation of superior performance is often strengthened and fortified by copious promotional expenditures, as is often the case for name-brand toiletries, pharmaceuticals, food preparations, and other products. Colgate toothpaste, Gillette blades, Pantene shampoo, Cadbury chocolates, Nescafe instant coffee, Lipton tea, Marlboro cigarettes, and Ray-Ban sunglasses are just a few examples of products that enjoy worldwide brand recognition.

Sometimes, too, the strength of a brand name is associated not with superior performance but with predictable performance. The international traveler may seek out a familiar hotel name mainly because he or she wants to know what to expect on arrival in an unfamiliar country. In some cases, the existence of a strong trade name rests on some technological capability. For instance, delivering a packaged food product such as chocolates in a standardized condition and on a reliable basis can be a technically exacting job that only a limited number of firms has mastered.

In any event, whether based on illusion or substance, some trade names command a premium in foreign markets. With regard to some products, such as packaged foods, soft drinks, and drugs, where trade names play a critical role, enterprises often discover that they cannot exploit their advantage by way of exports, and so they commonly establish plants, hotels, or other facilities in their foreign markets. Yet, once they are established in such markets, these firms generally have to confront national competitors who are operating on roughly the same cost basis. Indeed, the foreigners are sometimes handicapped by additional factors, such as the costs of communication and the discriminatory policies of host governments. In such cases, the special strength of the trade name is usually indispensable for the foreign firm to maintain a competitive position.

Although foreign trade names have been known to endure in such markets for long periods of time, their ability to command a price premium in a given type of product against the competing offers of national producers often erodes in time. As long as the product or service itself remains unchanged, national producers learn either to match the performance of the foreign product or to overcome the illusion of a difference that was never there. When that happens, multinational enterprises find themselves obliged to share their foreign markets with national producers.

In sum, both kinds of innovative firms—those that have come up with new products and those that have built strong brand names—face similar problems as their innovations age. Figure 2-1 presents an idealized version of typical competitive developments in markets originally dominated by such foreign-owned multinational enterprises. In the earliest stage, the multinational enterprise relies on its trade name or

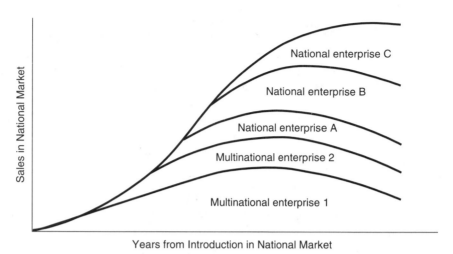

Figure 2-1   Schema of Changing Industry Structure in a National Market

its technology, or both, to introduce a new product or service. Its monopoly is usually short-lived, for its presence in the market is joined by rival multinationals. At some later point, the technology becomes sufficiently diffused and the product or service becomes sufficiently standardized to permit national firms to produce and market it in competition with the leaders.

Lowering the Cost Structure

A focus on costs is a second major motivation for firms to become multinational. In the simplest situation, as Figure 2-2 depicts, a firm that has been servicing a foreign market through exports may discover that the volume of its foreign sales has grown sufficiently large that on a delivered cost basis it will prove cheaper to service the foreign market through foreign production.

Figure 2-2 incorporates various arbitrary assumptions, such as the assumption that the marginal cost of production is rising in the home facility throughout the range of production under consideration, but these assumptions can be changed without altering the general approach.

In the 1990s, in sheer quantity terms, most of the output of multinational enterprises has been in products whose sale depends on costs and prices rather than on a strong technological lead or a strong trade name. Although innovation may have been a factor in the initial decisions to become multinational, firms in industries such as automobiles, heavy chemicals, certain ball bearings, and many other standardized products can no longer rely on firm-specific advantages arising solely from technology or trade names. In these circumstances, firms tend to focus on ways of minimizing costs, and often, a multinational *network* is the response.

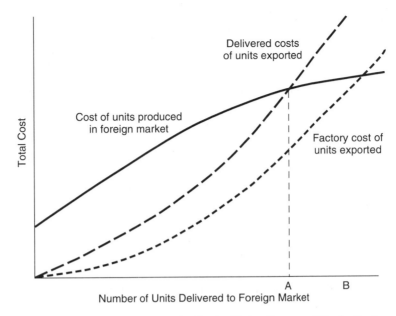

Figure 2-2   Costs of Product Delivered to Foreign Market: Exports and Foreign Production Compared

For most industries, the lowest costs are likely to be associated with some combination of plants in different countries, balancing the gains from low production costs in those countries with the added expenses of management coordination, import duties, and transportation. The result can be a network of coordinated plants around the world, with some plants specializing in manufacturing certain components and models of a product and others doing assembly, repair, or other operations. In a very few industries, the lowest costs may come from one plant that supplies the world; jumbo aircraft and some types of semiconductors, for instance, fall in that category.

One pattern, sometimes dubbed the "hub and spokes" model, places most production capacity at a single location, loosely tied to a network of affiliates abroad. The hub may dominate when economies of scale are so large that no one national market is big enough for efficient production. Other patterns of multinational networks, however, do not display a dominant central facility but instead rely on a network of plants of roughly equal importance to the network.

Protecting Returns to the Network

A major principle in the management of multinational enterprises is that foreign subsidiaries exist to serve the system as a whole, and that returns therefore are not measured by the standards of a stand-alone enterprise. Illustrations of the distinction are easy to find.

Shut-out Pricing

One illustration involves the pricing strategies that multinational enterprises commonly adopt in response to the appearance of a newcomer in one of its markets. Typically, the enterprise introduces a drastic, albeit temporary, reduction in the going price. If the established firm operates in a number of markets, it can exercise this option with special effectiveness.

Picture a well-defined market in which the leaders of an industry have settled down into an acceptable equilibrium. Each leader has a stable share of the market and no great uncertainties about the price. Since entry into the market is not easy, profit rates are likely to be fairly high. Now a newcomer appears in the market and may be in a position to cut prices in a bid for a share of the market. Confronting the newcomer, the leaders may respond in various ways, but one of two possibilities is likely:

- The leaders may disregard the newcomer's bid and permit it to capture some share of the market, relying on the expectation that the newcomer's goal in share-of-market terms is limited and that equilibrium will reassert itself once the goal has been achieved. In this case, the minimum cost to the leaders of the newcomer's appearance is the quantity of sales lost multiplied by profit per unit.

- An alternative strategy for the leaders is to reduce the price to a shut-out price, thereby retaining the previous volume of sales but accepting for the necessary period a lower profit margin on those sales. In that case, the cost to the leaders is the quantity of shut-out sales multiplied by the decline in profit per unit. Such a strategy, it is apparent, is particularly effective for multinational leaders if the newcomer has made its challenge in only a limited number of national markets, as is likely. Where transshipment between markets involves some significant costs, multinationals can reduce their profits only in the markets being challenged and continue to operate at their usual profit margin in other countries.

Subsidiaries as Information and Experience Gatherers

Another purpose that a foreign subsidiary commonly serves for its multinational network is to acquire information or experience that can be used not only by itself but also by other units in the network. Multinationals headquartered in Europe and Japan often acquire subsidiaries in the United States with the ostensible purpose of absorbing a new technology or gaining experience in distributing in the U.S. market. Multinationals headquartered in the United States sometimes regard their Mexican subsidiaries as training grounds for the penetration of markets further south.

Take the case of the 50–50 joint venture by General Electric and the appliance maker Mabe of Mexico. Through this venture, GE gets access to Mexico's low-cost labor and growing appliance market. Mabe "piggybacks" on GE's worldwide purchasing power and its modern technology. "They learn some things from us, and we learn from them," says J. J. Dupuis, the joint venture's president. Indeed, when Japanese competitor Sanyo began to use Tijuana as a base to produce the over one million mini-refrigerators it sells in the United States, GE was able to counter quickly by turning to Mabe. The GE-Mabe venture now accounts for nearly 30 percent of U.S. imports of these small appliances. Furthermore, in an "unusual reversal of roles," Mabe taught GE how to make gas ranges, a product the American firm had never manufactured before. Thanks to the successful partnership, the venture has a 33 percent market share in gas stoves sold in the United States.[5]

The power of an effective information-gathering network in international business is evident not only in the occasional big decisions to establish a new foreign source or invade a new foreign market but also in the day-to-day operations of some foreign business activities. Numerous studies have demonstrated the advantages of internalizing certain kinds of information flows. Two observations regarding the communication of information can be made:

- Failure rates in effective communication between two widely separated parties are extremely high. The party at the source may be unaware of the information needs of the user; the user may be unaware of the capabilities of the source; the user may be inattentive to the messages actually sent; the message may be garbled or diverted, without the parties being aware.
- Failures are less likely when both parties perceive themselves as members of a common group responding to a set of common goals.

The growth of multinational banking networks over the past two decades illustrates the importance of an effective communication network within a single organization. Most of what multinational banks do for their customers in the international field can technically be done by a global network composed of national banks operating as independent correspondents. But multinational banks have managed to capture a high proportion of the international business that was once handled by national banks, an achievement that rests in part on their ability to internalize the communication function.

Another illustration of the strategic role played by the internal communication network is provided by the historical role of the Japanese trading company. These trading companies are traditionally involved in two distinct activities: in importing standardized bulk commodities and raw materials, such as coal and iron ore, and in exporting the manufactured products of relatively small Japanese manufacturers, especially products that sell in world markets largely on a price basis. In both connections, the trading companies collect information about sources and markets, schedule shipments, and finance transactions, relying for their competitive strength mainly on their communication network. Each unit of the trading company, distributed over

---

[5]Geri Smith, "This Venture Is Cooking with Gas," *Business Week,* November 8, 1993, p. 70.

many foreign locations, must be gauged for its contribution to the network as a whole. (See Box 2-2.)

Subsidiaries in Vertical Chains

Perhaps the most common situation in which the performance of the foreign subsidiary is judged by its contribution to the multinational enterprise as a whole is one in which the subsidiary forms part of a vertical chain that creates, produces, or distributes a product or service. The motivations for creating such chains are complex. Some are aimed at minimizing cost, whereas others are targeted at reducing risk.

The risk-reducing objectives are dealt with in the section that follows. The cost-reducing aspects of vertical integration take various forms.

- Reducing the cost of transmitting information and maintaining coordination, already noted above.
- Reducing transaction costs, such as the cost to the producing firm over the prices and specifications of raw materials and intermediate products. Such costs, as Japanese multinationals have often demonstrated, can be held to a minimum by developing long-term relationships with nominally independent firms. Yet membership in a common multinational network can serve that purpose as well.
- Adapting a downstream processing facility, such as an oil refinery or a smelter in another country, to the chemical and physical peculiarities of the crude oil or ore that the facility receives. This strategy is common to the petroleum and mining industries.

Reducing Risk to the Network

Very often, the function of the foreign subsidiary of a multinational enterprise is to contain or reduce the risk to which the enterprise as a whole is exposed. These risks take various forms, some of them stemming from random events, some from the threats of governmental action, and others from the aggressive moves of explicit rivals in an oligopoly.

Multiple Markets and Multiple Sources

An enterprise that serves several different markets is less vulnerable to the random variation of demand that affects any single national market. If the market is shrinking for any reason in one nation, it may possibly be increasing in another. Thus, for example, construction firms, often faced with cyclical business, can seek a certain de-

BOX 2-2.   THE SOGO SHOSHA: JAPAN'S EARLY MULTINATIONAL NETWORKS

Because Japan was a relative latecomer to economic development and international trade, its industrial and commercial revolutions had to occur simultaneously. In order to meet established competitors from Europe and the United States, Japan knew it needed large scale. It also needed access to raw materials, new technology, information, and financing. The lack of resources and expertise, combined with a sense of urgency, defined the circumstances in which an ingenious Japanese institution known as the *sogo shosha*, or "trading house," emerged. This unique institution would become "a window to the world for a nation long isolated."

Starting out as large-scale traders, the sogo shosha evolved to become a provider and coordinator of an entire range of services. To give an example of the breadth of its expertise, take the steel industry. A sogo shosha may make arrangements with some far away coal and iron mines for large volumes of the materials to be transported to Japan, lease ships to the shipping lines, provide insurance, arrange for delivery to the steel producer's factory, provide financing, and even manage inventories in the process.

But perhaps the sogo shosha's most valuable service is the one it provides as worldwide information network *par excellence*. It is estimated that on a typical business day, the largest sogo shosha in Japan transmits and receives more than 50,000 telexes. Most of these come from its managers around the world who are constantly searching for potentially useful information. Their acute ability to gather and direct the appropriate information in a timely fashion to someone within the network, perhaps in another part of the world, translates into a powerful competitive weapon in the sogo shosha's arsenal.

In order for this network to function effectively, the sogo shosha has had to develop a strong ability to integrate internally. After all, the "mere fact that two subunits belong to the same overall organization is no guarantee that they can work together effectively." Research reveals that formal organization has little to do with the mentality of sogo shosha managers who think system- rather than subunit-wide. Instead, informal interaction and social systems within the firm appear to be the underlying factors making integration possible. Creative human resource policies and shared culture are also believed to contribute to the special network abilities of the sogo shosha.

SOURCE: Based on Michael Y. Yoshino and Thomas B. Lifson, *The Invisible Link* (Cambridge, Mass.: MIT Press, 1986).

gree of stability by operating in several markets. Furthermore, in industries threatened by interventions of national governments, an act of nationalization in one market can be offset by an expansion elsewhere.

Reducing Risk Through Vertical Integration

The producers of standardized products that are manufactured under conditions of high fixed costs have an especially compelling need to stabilize the demand for their product; small variations in such demand create especially large changes in profits. One method of reducing uncertainties regarding demand is to establish close relationships with customers. In some cases, contractual arrangements are adequate; in others, for reasons similar to those that lead to foreign investment of other kinds, security can be obtained only by owning the customers. The existence of captive customers may not eliminate all the sources of variation in demand, but at least it protects sellers from the uncertainties that the producer feels when customers can switch between suppliers. When Venezuela's state-owned oil company, PDVSA, acquired refining and distribution facilities in the United States and Europe, that consideration was uppermost.

In such cases, however, a move by any firm toward vertical integration increases the uncertainties of all the other firms in the market. Buyers of the product that do not wish to be absorbed by their suppliers are confronted with a growing need to capture their own sources of supply. For as vertical integration proceeds, the users that remain independent find themselves more and more obliged to buy their materials from vertically integrated firms with which they are in direct competition. Under those conditions, the vertically integrated producer may decide to supply its captive downstream users in more generous quantities and on better terms than its independent customers, thereby endangering the independent's existence. A realization of that risk has led to the pattern of expansion portrayed in Figure 2-3.

The process of vertical integration often leads to the multinationalization of op-

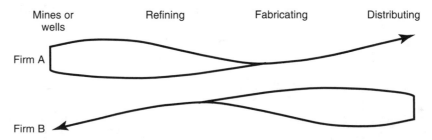

Figure 2-3   Typical Paths of Expansion in Industries Producing Standardized Products with High Fixed Costs

erations. As enterprises move upstream or downstream to complete their vertical structure, they commonly reach beyond the national economy in which the integrating process began. Either they need new sources of supply that are not to be had in their part of the world, or they need markets that do not readily exist at home. In either case, national enterprises often become multinational enterprises as they pursue the integration strategy.

Follow-the-Leader as Risk Reduction

In an industry made up of a small number of firms that see each other as competitors, another risk-reducing strategy that often leads to the multinationalization of the dominant enterprises is the follow-the-leader pattern. This phenomenon is often seen in industries that are oligopolistic in structure. Although the strategy may appear in any industry in which a few large leaders dominate, it is especially visible in industries in which the leaders are selling nearly identical products.

Picture the limiting case, that is, the case in which an industry consists of only two firms, both producing the same standardized product and both located in the same country (Coke and Pepsi or Mercedes and BMW come readily to mind). Other firms are barred from entry because of the problem of sheer scale in the industry, and overt agreements between the two firms are illegal.

Now firm L (the leader) learns about a new site in another country from which production and distribution would be less costly, or which offers an attractive new market. Should it set up in the new location?

The answer, of course, depends in part on its anticipation of the way in which firm F (the follower) is likely to respond.

- One possibility firm L may consider is that firm F will not react at all and will passively accept firm L's improvement of its profit margins. That hypothetical possibility would seem unlikely. The existence of major differences in profit margins would place firm F at the mercy of firm L, exposing firm F to the possibility that firm L might try to increase its share of the market at some later date. Moreover, the cash flow of firm L would exceed that of firm F, adding to firm L's aggressive strength. So firm L cannot ordinarily count on inaction from firm F.

- Firm L must consider another possibility: Firm F may follow firm L to the new location; there will be a period of uncertainty, during which each assesses the aggressive intentions of the other in the light of the new cost structures; and the new equilibrium established at the end of the period of uncertainty will generate a price level and profit margin no more favorable than the one that existed before the move. In that case, firm L will hesitate to move. (According to some analysts, this situation is one reason why the U.S. steel industry delayed so long its introduction of oxygen topping in steel production and why U.S. tire companies delayed so long their introduction of radial tires.)

- A third possibility is that firm F will follow firm L to the new location, with favorable results for both. This can occur if both firms retain their old price structure; it would be better still if both—acting as a profit-maximizing monopolist would act—adjust their prices to a new level that would increase their total sales and total profits. (The reader who is not familiar with the concept of optimum pricing in a monopoly situation should pause here to digest the point that it sometimes pays a monopolist to reduce the price of its product because the price reduction may increase both total demand and total profits.) This outcome, seen through the eyes of firm L, would be a happy one.

In the real world of multinational enterprise, of course, industries are rarely made up of just two firms, and barriers to entry are rarely so high as to eliminate the existing firms' worry that newcomers may enter. Indeed, in oil, aluminum, copper, steel, basic chemicals, telecommunications, and banking, the number of large enterprises in world markets has been increasing, not decreasing, in the decades since World War II.

Managers, therefore, are generally obliged to worry about the possibility of newcomer firms. If such newcomers appear, however, the existing firms may resort to imitative behavior to protect their positions. The existing firms, for instance, may locate an added productive facility where the newcomer has located. If the new location imparts special strengths to the new firm, imitation by the established firms will have the effect of matching the new firm's strengths. That matching will limit the new firm's ability to upset the existing equilibrium in the market.

The facts about production costs or other characteristics relating to some new location are never all that clear. Neither the new investing firm nor the established firms can avoid the possibility that estimates may be prone to major error; the new firm may have a bonanza or a disaster on its hands. Nevertheless, although both possibilities exist, a follow-the-leader policy may be the best available response. For if the new location proves more advantageous than the best prior estimate might have suggested, the desirability of imitation is even stronger. If, on the other hand, the new firm's move proves to be ill-considered and to afford no advantage over existing facilities, the error may still not prove very costly. For if the oligopoly is small enough in number and imitative enough in behavior, the cost of the error may be absorbed by a general increase in the price.

Figures 2-4A and B illustrate in more detail some typical sequences and indicates more precisely why imitative behavior commends itself as a strategy. In both cases shown, the failure of firms to follow the leader entails high risks, whereas the cost of following the leader is limited. But as Box 2-3 suggests, in some cases a firm feels sufficiently secure or sufficiently chastened by experience that it will hold back from following the leader.

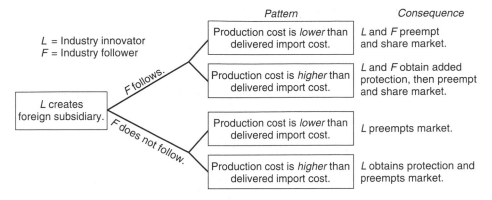

Figure 2-4A   Foreign Subsidiary Created to Produce and Sell in Its Local Market

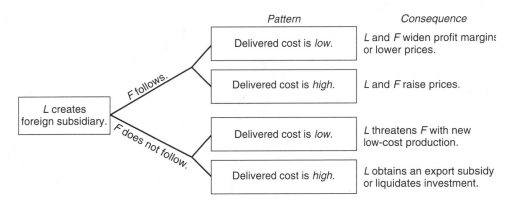

Figure 2-4B   Foreign Subsidiary Created to Produce Supplies for Its Affiliates

In the end, this kind of strategy may break down. Too many firms may enter the industry, and imitation as a hedge against risk may prove impossible. In that case, a strategy based on the existence of barriers to entry must come to an end.

The various sequences described in earlier pages have pushed many enterprises toward the creation of a multinational network of affiliates. The existence of such a structure, however, does not necessarily bring a global perspective to the network. The home market may continue to dominate the network's strategic thinking, and the parent firm may continue to be the principal source for the generation of new information and new strategies. In the case of U.S. firms in particular, the continued dominance of the U.S. market and the traditional home focus of U.S. business managers have favored such a pattern.

In the 1980s, however, significant shifts in perspective could be seen in a number of firms. With a global network in place, these firms began to regard their foreign

BOX 2-3.   EXXON DOESN'T FOLLOW

While follow-the-leader behavior is typical in oligopolistic and sharply rivalrous industries, sometimes firms in such industries do things differently. Exxon's deliberate and almost hesitant response to invitations by countries like China, Algeria, Angola, and parts of the former Soviet Union, all of "which had long been coveted for exploration but were off-limits," provides a case in point.

In the 1990s, while rivals Shell, Mobil, Chevron, and Amoco have embraced many of these opportunities, Exxon has preferred to wait "and see how volatile politics, particularly in areas like Russia, play out before committing the billions of dollars it will take to develop the most promising fields." Partly as a result of this strategy, rival Shell has passed Exxon in size and is "growing faster and risking more capital in exploration." Chevron and Amoco are also moving aggressively to the new frontier areas because their U.S. reserves are declining. Analysts are concerned that Exxon's relatively flat spending on exploration and development of new fields will mean that the firm may not be able to replace reserves quickly enough. For its part, Exxon says it is under less pressure to explore in these untested frontiers because it has a large number of existing, but untapped, reserves.

Exxon's reluctance to follow is also visible in another area—liquefied gas—which rivals like Mobil have been developing for decades. This is surprising given that the liquefied gas business is "highly profitable and fast-growing." Experts note that the decade of the 1990s may come to be known as "an era of gas, rather than oil." Frank Knuettel, an analyst at Prudential Securities, comments: "Exxon is not taking any big risks. Shell is surpassing Exxon in many ways. . . . They [Exxon] are missing out on growth. . . . They are doing well on the rate of return, but at the expense of some future projects."

SOURCE: Based on Agis Salpukas, "Exxon's Go-Slow Strategy," *The New York Times*, September 19, 1994, pp. D1 and D8.

affiliates as sources of new information, including new technologies, and new opportunities. Moreover, some firms began to look on every locational decision, such as a decision to create a new unit for production, distribution, or research, as one for which any country could be considered on its merits.

This change in perspective was due to many factors, including improved channels of communication, the realization by large firms that new products and new competitors could come from any corner of the globe, and the growing importance of costs as a factor in competitive survival. One visible effect of the change in perspectives is that multinational firms the world over are considering anew their corporate strategies for competing in global markets. Let us pick up on this important topic in the next chapter.

Suggested Reading

BUCKLEY, PETER J., and MARK CASSON. *The Future of the Multinational Enterprise.* London: Holmes and Meier, 1976.

CASSON, MARK. *The Firm and the Market.* Cambridge, Mass.: MIT Press, 1987.

CAVES, RICHARD E. *Multinational Enterprise and Economic Analysis.* New York: Cambridge University Press, 1982.

DUNNING, JOHN H. *International Production and the Multinational Enterprise.* London: Allen and Unwin, 1981.

DUNNING, JOHN H. (ed.). The United Nations Library on Transnational Corporations. Vol. 1, *The Theory of Transnational Corporations.* London: Routledge, 1993.

HENNART, JEAN-FRANCOIS. *A Theory of Multinational Enterprise.* Ann Arbor: University of Michigan Press, 1982.

LIFSON, THOMAS, and MICHAEL Y. YOSHINO. *The Invisible Link: Japan's Sogo Shosha and the Organization of Trade.* Cambridge, Mass.: MIT Press, 1986.

CHAPTER 3

Managing the Multinational: Goals and Strategies

[In the 1990s] . . . competition comes in relentless waves from all directions. And CEOs . . . must examine the place of their corporation in a world where national boundaries are blurring and the global market is becoming integrated at a dizzying pace.

Not all the questions the CEOs ask themselves are easy or pleasant: What new products will be offered and at what price from Thailand and Korea, as well as from Japan and more traditional sources of competition? How can we get our prices down to challenge both new and old competitors and still make adequate returns for our shareholders? How can we compete against giant transnationals that enjoy huge economies of scale and offer world-wide responsiveness to local markets? Is our organizational structure adequate in this emerging transnational world? To keep pace, should we pursue joint ventures? Strategic alliances? International mergers? Wendt, 1993: 5.[1]

These concerns raised by Henry Wendt, former chairman of SmithKline Beecham, throw into stark relief the challenges that confront managers in large multinational enterprises in the 1990s. The forces of globalization, it appears, are demanding that managers simultaneously achieve multiple, and sometimes conflicting, objectives.

How should we address these challenges? Let us take up this question in two parts. In this chapter let us consider the evolution and current thinking on the goals and strategies of multinational enterprises, and in the next chapter, let us follow up with a discussion on the organizational and management structures needed to achieve the goals and carry out the strategies outlined here.

---

[1]Henry Wendt, *Global Embrace* (New York: HarperCollins, 1993), p. 5.

Let us begin by considering how multinationals have changed over the past few decades. As we saw in the two previous chapters, most multinationals in existence today began as national firms that competed in one or another oligopolistic industry. Although they were found in a wide range of industries—from food to chemicals to automobiles—the firms that went multinational all shared one attribute: They possessed some "firm-specific advantage"—an intangible asset such as a brand name, sophisticated technology, or scale—that they were trying to exploit through internalization.

At most early multinationals, products and processes typically originated in the home office and were adopted abroad with minor adjustments to suit local needs. Control and decision making rested in the home office, and top management positions at the subsidiary were staffed by home country nationals. Howard Perlmutter, in a pioneer study of multinational strategies, classified these multinationals as *ethnocentric* because they had a sharp home focus and managed their foreign subsidiaries from the home base.[2]

Eventually, however, bending to the threats of competitors and the demands of host governments, multinationals broadened the functions of many of their foreign subsidiaries. In manufacturing in particular, some foreign assembly plants eventually moved into actual manufacturing, drawing on components and materials in the country where they were located.

As manufacturing was undertaken locally or regionally, and products and processes were developed with the local market in mind, some multinationals based in North America and Europe found themselves creating "miniature replicas" of the home operation. "Miniature replicas" referred to foreign affiliates that performed locally most, if not all, business functions. Typically, such affiliates operated on a stand-alone basis. Consequently, these subsidiaries were granted relatively more autonomy over their operations and strategies, and began to be managed by nationals of the host as opposed to the home country. Perlmutter's word for these multinationals was *polycentric.*

Even as this trend was taking shape, new cost-competitive international competitors from Asia, especially from Japan, thrust sharply into the markets of U.S. and European multinationals. Christopher Bartlett writes:

> [T]he typical Japanese company [entering the international market] . . . had new efficient, scale-intensive plants, built to serve its rapidly expanding domestic market, and it was expanding into a global environment of declining tariffs. Together these factors gave it the incentive to develop a competitive advantage at the upstream end of the value-added chain. Its competitive strategy emphasized *cost advantages* and quality assurance, and required tight central control of product development, procurement, and manufacturing (emphasis added).[3]

---

[2]Howard V. Perlmutter, "The Tortuous Evolution of the Multinational Corporation," *Columbia Journal of World Business,* January–February (1969), pp. 9–18.

[3]Christopher A. Bartlett, "Building and Managing the Transnational: The New Organizational Challenge," in Michael E. Porter (ed.), *Competition in Global Industries.* Boston: Harvard Business School Press, 1986, p. 373.

Consequently, the organizational structures that these cost-competitive firms developed were built typically along product rather than geographical lines. In many respects, these were *geocentric* multinationals in the Perlmutter classification.

So successful were these firms that, in just 10 years, between 1975 and 1985, they changed the rules of the game in industry after industry. In autos, where once General Motors and Ford dominated, Toyota, Nissan, and Honda had moved in. In consumer electronics, where GE and RCA once led, Sony and Matsushita had made major inroads. In heavy equipment, Komatsu had successfully challenged Caterpillar. As a result, American and European firms, such as ITT and Philips, were discovering at the hands of rivals, such as NEC and Matsushita, that being responsive to the demands of host governments and to differences in national markets wasn't sufficient; cost structures and pricing had to be extremely competitive too.

The sharply different approaches with which U.S., European, and Asian firms had entered international markets prompted Michael Porter and others during the mid-1980s to propose that industries varied along a spectrum from *multidomestic* to *global* in their competitive scope.

Consumer banking, fast food, toiletries, and other industries where competition was country-centered, were labeled multidomestic. In these industries, consumer tastes and preferences often varied substantially from country to country. Consequently, products configured to satisfy preferences in one country had a low likelihood of succeeding in others. Moreover, scale economies were not particularly significant in multidomestic industries. In such circumstances, these writers deemed, polycentric firms would do just fine because to be competitive in local or multidomestic industries, decisions on products, prices, and distribution channels had to be made at the local level. And even though costs were not unimportant, responsiveness to local tastes was the primary focus in such businesses. Accordingly, organizational structures based on geography rather than on products were deemed more suitable to the achievement of these goals.

On the other hand, automobiles, semiconductors, TV sets, and other industries where linkages and commonalties between national markets were high were labeled global. Such industries demanded regional or global scale for two reasons. First, the volumes needed to minimize unit manufacturing costs were large. Second, the cost of developing new products and services was rising rapidly, while the life of those products and services was becoming shorter. In global industries, production had to be centralized or, alternatively, each activity or operation had to be carried out where it made the most economic sense.

Of course, by the end of the 1980s and the start of the 1990s, several pressures were at work nudging global players to reformulate their strategies. One set of pressures came from governments of host countries which, including industrialized host countries in Europe and America, showed signs of becoming more protectionist. In these countries, rising levels of import penetration often brought from domestic labor and business demands for local content rules, voluntary export restraints, and, increasingly, dumping penalties (see Box 3-1).

Another set of pressures came from exchange rates, which, as Figure 3-1

BOX 3-1.   SUBDUING GLOBAL PLAYERS: HOW WEAK DOMESTIC FIRMS PLAY THE POLITICAL CARD

Successful penetration of the home market by foreign rivals has often elicited a political response from less competitive domestic firms. As illustrated by a 1994 case from Europe's television industry, charges of dumping by firms and the levying of dumping penalties by their governments appear to be becoming the tactic of choice in this game.

In the case in point, Philips of the Netherlands and Thomson of France, two major consumer electronics firms, complained to the European Union (EU) in September 1994 that "five Asian countries had achieved a sharp rise in their EU market share by pricing their televisions below the levels charged in their home markets." Of course, the charges were not being directed at "countries"; they were being directed at specific rivals: Hitachi, Funai, and Sanyo, all of Japan, and Goldstar and Samsung of Korea.

Critics of these tactics contend that price comparisons in such instances are made in "opaque and arbitrary" ways that allow officials wide latitude to find that dumping has occurred and that domestic producers have been injured. Indeed, at the time this book went to press, the *Financial Times* anticipated that the EU would levy provisional antidumping duties on color TVs originating from the five countries named. The 20 to 30 percent duties were expected to provoke a substantial rise in the prices paid by European consumers of color TVs.

Indicative of the popularity of such tactics, the EU modified its rules in 1994 to make it easier for dumping duties to be imposed. Previously, a qualified majority vote was necessary for the imposition of dumping penalties. But, on France's insistence, the rules were changed so that a simple majority vote would suffice. The change is expected to "make it easier to protect European industries against low-priced imports, particularly from Asia."

SOURCE: Based on Emma Tucker and Guy de Jonquieres, "EU Plans Dumping Duties on Asia TVs," *Financial Times*, September 16, 1994.

---

shows, changed quite dramatically during the 1980s. In the past, when a very few large firms—typically sharing a common home-base—dominated world markets in one or another product line, a strengthening of the home currency just meant that they risked having to charge a higher price for their products in foreign markets than they might otherwise have chosen; but that, usually, was the extent of the damage. Their superiority in technology or size or both protected them from loss of share in their biggest and, usually, most important market—the home market. That no longer is the case.

As Table 3-1 shows, in most industries today, lead rivals come from countries that are in different currency zones. Besides competing vigorously in various third

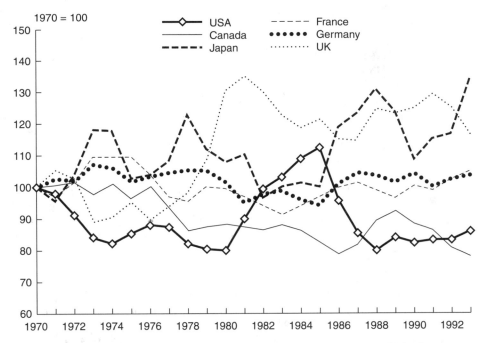

Figure 3-1   Movements in Exchange Rates Adjusted for Changes in National Price Levels, Selected Countries, 1970–1993

country markets, lead rivals have inter-penetrated one another's home markets. As a result, swings in real exchange rates, such as those experienced during the 1980s, can have an enormous impact on the competitiveness and profitability of centralized global firms. This is causing many global players to establish operations in a number of different currency zones.

Moreover, producers in some global industries are discovering that despite some convergence in national tastes and needs, important differences persist. According to *The Economist,* in response to cultural differences, the global player McDonalds, which "issues its employees worldwide with an operating manual as thick as a phone book, which lays down the law from how to greet customers to how to clean the lavatories," now serves "Teriyaki burgers in Tokyo and wine in Lyons."[4] In short, global players are having to become more attuned to national differences and, now, increasingly to the formation of regional trading blocs.

On the other side, multidomestic or locally-responsive players—whose foreign expansion was based on the "miniature replica" strategy—are having to increase the level of integration in their worldwide operations in an effort to become cost-efficient. These firms are also attempting to make more intensive the internal transfer and sharing of knowledge. Consider the widely cited example of Procter & Gamble's

---

[4]*The Economist,* July 30, 1994, "The discreet charm of the multicultural multinational," pp. 57–58.

TABLE 3-1.   Lead Multinationals in Selected Industries, 1994

Industry	Country of Headquarters		
	United States	Japan	Europe
Food	*Philip Morris*	—	*Unilver*
	CPC		*Nestle*
Petroleum refining	*Exxon*	—	*Royal Dutch/Shell*
	Mobil		*British Petroleum*
Chemicals	*Du Pont*	*Sumitomo*	*Hoechst*
	Dow		*BASF*
Pharmaceuticals	*Bristol-Myers Squibb*	—	*Sandoz*
	Merck		*Roche*
Earth-moving equipment	*Caterpillar*	*Komatsu*	*Mannesmann*
	Deere	*Hitachi*	
Computers	*IBM*	*Toshiba*	*Olivetti*
	DEC	*Fujitsu*	
Semiconductors	*Intel*	*Toshiba*	—
	AMD	*Hitachi*	
Industrial machinery	*General Electric*	*Hitachi*	*Siemens*
		Mitsubishi	*Asea Brown Boveri*
Consumer electronics	*Emerson*	*Sony*	*Philips*
		Matsushita	*Thomson*
Telecommunications	*AT&T*	*NEC*	*Alcatel*
	Motorola		*Ericsson*
Automobiles	*General Motors*	*Toyota*	*Volkswagen*
	Ford	*Honda*	*Fiat*
Commercial aircraft	*Boeing*	—	*Airbus*
	McDonnell Douglas		
Medical equipment	*General Electric*	*Toshiba*	*Siemens*
	Johnson & Johnson		
Scientific and photographic equipment	*Eastman Kodak*	*Fuji Photo Film*	—
	Xerox	*Cannon*	
Rubber and plastic products	*Goodyear*	*Bridgestone*	*Michelin*
Commercial banking	*Citicorp*	*Sumitomo*	*Union Bank of Switzerland*
Reinsurance	*General Re*	—	*Munich Re*
			Swiss Re

Sources: Companies chosen from "Fortune's Global 500: Ranked Within Industries," *Fortune,* July 25, 1994, pp. 164–182; "The World's Largest Service Corporations," *Fortune,* August 22, 1994, pp. 180–208; and from David B. Yoffie (ed.), *Beyond Free Trade* (Boston: Harvard Business School Press, 1993).

Liquid Tide. When the product was introduced in the mid-1980s, it was heralded as having a truly international heritage because the new ingredients that helped suspend dirt in wash water came from P&G's headquarter city, Cincinnati; the cleaning agents came from P&G technicians in Japan; and the chemicals that fought mineral salts found in hard water came from P&G scientists in Brussels.

Although such intrafirm international transfers of knowledge do occur to varying degrees, many observers believe that relative to the potential, American and European multinationals are just beginning to exploit this opportunity systematically. A recent study by Reading University's John Cantwell found that "only 9% of the patents granted to American multinationals in the 1980s were for work done by [their] overseas operations; for European firms the ratio was 30%."[5]

The Strategic Challenges

Based on the preceding discussion, we can identify four broad challenges that managers in multinational enterprises must continually work on if they are to become and stay competitive in the 1990s. Figure 3-2 summarizes these strategic challenges:

- Taking account of the competition.
- Upgrading productivity and efficiency.
- Being responsive to local stakeholders.
- Leveraging the multinational network to achieve operational flexibility and systemwide exploitation of local learning.

Taking Account of the Competition

In international business, neither monopoly nor perfect competition is an applicable model. Oligopoly—competition among the few—is the dominant reality, and most large companies are readily able to identify the enemy. Indeed, there is perhaps no more important motivation for the actions of large corporations than the plans and actions of their rivals.

Look again at Table 3-1, which shows a list of leading competitors in various industries. What the table does not capture is the intensity and extent to which these rivalries are personalized. Some rivalries, such as the ones between Pepsi and Coke, Caterpillar and Komatsu, Boeing and Airbus, or Kodak and Fuji, are well known. But even if not as well known, the situation is often similar in most other industries where competition is international.

From the standpoint of corporate strategy, this element of interaction and tight rivalry has three implications. First, in deciding what markets to penetrate, what technologies to pursue, where to procure raw materials, whether to enter into alliances, and so on, the choices that managers face are not totally open. Rather, they are shaped, and even delimited, by the actions and strategies of rivals.

Second, along certain key dimensions such as geography, product breadth, and technology, firms may have to be relatively clear about their strategic intentions vis-

[5]*The Economist,* July 30, 1994, "The discreet charm of the multicultural multinational," pp. 57–58.

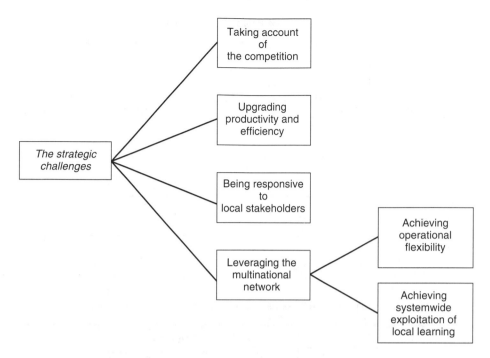

Figure 3-2   The Strategic Challenges Facing Managers in the International Economy

à-vis rivals. On some issues, firms may decide to cooperate with rivals. Take the case of IBM and Apple Computer. Although the two corporations compete vigorously against one another in the personal computer market, they nevertheless have chosen to work jointly to produce a new microprocessor that would match Intel's Pentium chip.

If firms choose to cooperate, they need to settle on which markets they will go after and which markets they will cede to rivals; which products to offer and which products to pass over; and when and how to enter into alliances. If, instead, firms choose to compete, they may need to decide whether to dominate, match, follow, or undermine the competition. In order not to put the system as a whole at risk, sometimes firms decide to withdraw from a particular arena or product.

Accordingly, as Figure 3-3 shows, strategic posture or intent vis-à-vis rivals can be mapped along such dimensions as core competencies, geography, business segment, product line, or value-added function. Successful strategies in international business are often built around the identification and targeting of particular rivals. At Komatsu, the slogan "Maru C," or encircle Caterpillar, was a powerful way for top management to focus companywide efforts. Similarly, at Hewlett-Packard, the "Beat Epson" motto energized employees at the company's printer business to track and, eventually, trump the Japanese rival.

The third and final implication of oligopolistic rivalry comes from the word

A: Mapping Strategic Posture Vis-à-vis Rivals by Geography

	Compete					Cooperate
Region	Lead and Dominate	Match Head-to-head	Follow and Imitate	Selectively Undermine	Call It Quits and Withdraw	**Cooperate**
North America						
Europe						
Asia						
Latin America						

B: Mapping Strategic Posture Vis-à-vis Rivals by Business and Value-added Function

Business	**Value-added Function**	Compete					Cooperate
		Lead and Dominate	Match Head-to-head	Follow and Imitate	Selectively Undermine	Call It Quits and Withdraw	**Cooperate**
	R & D						
Business A	Input Sourcing						
Business B	Manufacturing and Assembly						
Business C	Marketing and Sales						
Business D	Distribution and Logistics						
Business E							

Figure 3-3   Mapping Strategic Posture Vis-à-vis Rivals Along Strategic Dimensions

"strategy" itself. As borrowed from the military lexicon, strategy refers to the task of preparing "to meet the enemy in combat under advantageous conditions,"[6] and this is what we have been discussing. But given that "the enemy" has the same objective in mind, *interaction* among rivals in the form of moves and countermoves plays a critical role in shaping corporate strategy. Managers, therefore, must continually anticipate the strategic intent of their rivals along the dimensions we outlined above, compare these intentions with their own, and identify the course of action best suited to the circumstances.

After all, as C. K. Prahalad and Yves Doz have argued:

> if we believe that competitors influence the patterns of competition as much as the underlying characteristics of a business and that often they [meaning rivals] change those characteristics through competitive innovation, then we need to pay special attention to . . . *key competitors' strategic intentions in determining the patterns of global competition.*[7]

Upgrading Productivity and Efficiency

A challenge that managers confront every day is that of raising their firms' productivity and cutting unit costs. Although the markets in which multinationals compete are far from perfectly competitive, price still matters in most businesses in which they compete.

Scale has been one of the key advantages drawn on by multinational enterprises to drive costs down. For example, in the construction equipment industry, owing partly to a rise in design costs and partly to changes in production processes, minimum efficient scales for hydraulic excavators rose between 1980 and 1990, from 2,000 to nearly 10,000 units per year. During this period, Komatsu was able to increase production and achieve scale economies because it had an advantage in tapping a surge in demand in its protected home market. One observer estimates that these economies gave Komatsu a 10 to 40 percent advantage, depending on the product, over arch-rival Caterpillar's costs in Japan.[8]

Another consideration on the cost side is factor costs. Low costs of wages have long been a consideration in firms' decisions to source from Asia and Latin America. The decision to locate facilities abroad is not limited to assembly (as in semiconductors) or manufacturing (as in home appliances). Increasingly, even research, engineering, and development are becoming suited for shifts to lower cost–same value locations. Motorola, for instance, is developing one of its most sophisticated new products in India's computer capital, Bangalore.

But costs alone should not dominate the manager's attention; the revenue side

---

[6]Webster's Ninth New Collegiate Dictionary, 1983.

[7]C. K. Prahalad, and Yves L. Doz, *The Multinational Mission* (New York: Free Press, 1987), p. 39.

[8]Michael G. Rukstad, "Construction Equipment: From Dominance to Duopoly," in David B. Yoffie (ed.), *Beyond Free Trade* (Boston: Harvard Business School Press, 1993), p. 321.

matters too. Kodak, for example, is routinely able to set prices above those of rival Fuji because in most world markets (with the exception of Japan), its brand is differentiated and its market share is much larger. Sony and IBM provide other examples of companies that have established their brands successfully. As a result, these firms enjoy high prices and margins.

Being Responsive to Local Stakeholders

A multinational enterprise operating abroad faces three local stakeholders: employees, customers, and governments. Each has the potential to become either a source of strength or a stumbling block.

Take the case of Lincoln Electric, one of America's most successful welding equipment manufacturers. What set the company apart and made it the leader in its industry in the United States was its productivity-based bonus pay. Workers at Lincoln are compensated on the basis of factors such as output and quality, and since 1934 the company has paid its employees almost as much in merit bonuses as in salaries.

In the late 1980s, Lincoln saw its position threatened by Sweden's ESAB, which was consolidating its position in Europe. Feeling threatened, Lincoln expanded rapidly, going to 11 new countries in a matter of just six years between 1986 and 1992. Struggling to digest the expansion in the midst of a worldwide recession, Lincoln "determined to cram the labor system so successful at home down the throats of its new foreign employees."[9]

The plan backfired badly. The company discovered too late that in Brazil once bonuses have been paid for two years, the law may require them to be regarded as base pay to which the worker may be entitled indefinitely. In Europe workers valued vacation more than extra money, and unions resisted the plan that made "workers feel like independent entrepreneurs." And, in France, when workers finally took to the system, "the subsidiary had no profits to distribute as bonuses, infuriating employees."

Customers, too, may be seen as stakeholders. In most industries, the concept of the "global consumer" is still a glint in the eyes of large producers. Differences in national tastes, distribution channels, advertising media, weather, and so on are factors that ought to receive attention at firms operating in many countries (see Box 3-2). For instance, vending machines are a key retail distribution channel in Japan, and Coke has a dense network of them in the country. This led Nestle to join forces with Coca-Cola to sell its Nestle iced tea and coffee in Japan.

Finally, host governments have long been important local stakeholders in the eyes of multinational enterprises. Perhaps no facet of the operation of multinational enterprises distinguishes them more from their purely domestic counterparts than

---

[9]Barnaby J. Feder, "Recasting a Model Incentive Strategy," *The New York Times,* September 5, 1994, p. 33.

BOX 3-2.   CHINESE TO GET A TASTE OF CHEESE-LESS CHEETOS

At last, Cheetos, the snack, has come to China, the country. The catch? They don't taste like Cheetos.

The maker of Cheetos, Pepsico, announced a $1 million joint venture to produce the little crispy-tasting cheese puffs in Guangdong province. . . . It marks the first time a major brand will be produced in China for Chinese tastes, Pepsico said.

But these Cheetos don't taste like cheese, which is hardly a mainstay of the Chinese diet. . . .

In focus groups for more than 1,000 people in Guangzhou, Shanghai and Beijing, the cheese-ish taste of American Cheetos did not, as they say, test well. Pepsico had to try more than 600 flavors, ranging from Roasted Cuttlefish to Sweet Carmel, before settling on Savory American Cream ("a buttered popcorn flavor," . . .) and Zesty Japanese Steak ("a teriyaki-type taste"). . . .

The introduction of Cheetos will be backed by television and print advertising and promotions based on Chester Cheetah, the brand's feline band symbol, riding a Harley-Davidson motorcycle. The packages will carry the Cheeto logo in English along with Chinese characters "qi duo" (pronounced CHEE dwaugh).

"Luckily," Mr. Goh [general manager of Pepsico Foods International] said, "the translation is 'new surprise,' instead of some phrase that might offend people."

SOURCE: Glenn Collins, "Chinese to Get a Taste of Cheese-Less Cheetos," *The New York Times*, September 2, 1994, Business Section.

---

their exposure to host governments. This subject is explored in some detail in Chapter 7, but let us preview the main issues here.

Many factors affect how governments approach their relations with multinational enterprises. In resource-rich countries, the prime objective of governments when dealing with multinationals is to maximize the rents that their local resources command in world markets. In other instances, governments usually concentrate on upgrading the national economy and the skills of their citizens. In decades past, a common strategy was to restrict imports and to subsidize local producers, often including the subsidiaries of multinational enterprises. Companies such as Fiat have grown and prospered "by negotiating with host governments for protection from more efficient global competitors in exchange for establishing local joint ventures and licensing agreements."[10]

In the 1980s and the 1990s, import restrictions were less common than before, but government provision of subsidies and tax exemptions persisted and even in-

---

[10]Bartlett, 1986, p. 371.

creased. When locating subsidiaries in low-cost production sites, managers of multi-national enterprises have been particularly alert to such opportunities.

If upgrading economically is the focus in developing countries, fear of down-grading economically looms large in the view of governments in developed countries. As home-based multinationals reorganize their global production networks, often shifting large chunks of production outside the country in the process, these govern-ments confront the daunting problem of easing the transition of displaced workers. As a result, unemployment and the competitiveness of domestic firms have become major concerns of national and local governments. In many instances, state and local governments have set up "economic development agencies" whose primary task is to attract multinational firms to the region via the offering of sizable incentive packages. In other instances, developed country governments have put in place or increased ex-isting requirements concerning the local content of products sold on their soil by for-eign multinationals.

Multinationals, however, do enjoy a capacity for flexibility in their relations with governments not available to other firms. For instance, U. S.-based Kaiser mines bauxite in Jamaica but transports it all the way across the Atlantic to Ghana, where it has a "world-class" aluminum smelting facility. The company uses Jamaican bauxite, even though Ghana itself also has bauxite and even though "each conversion step (bauxite to alumina, alumina to aluminum) cuts the weight to be shipped by half, and local processing facilities can demonstrably be made economic."[11] Why? The an-swer, of course, is that, by locating its processing facilities in a country other than the one in which it mines ore, Kaiser mitigates the risk of nationalization in both coun-tries.

Leveraging the Multinational Network

As Bruce Kogut has noted, multinational enterprises enjoy an important advantage over their purely domestic counterparts: namely, "differences in national markets cre-ate profit opportunities" and improve competitiveness. Moreover, as Kogut writes:

> the benefits of coordinating the flows within a *multinational network* . . . [come not only from] exploiting differentials in factor, product, and capital markets, but also . . . [from] the transfer of learning and innovations throughout the firm, as well as [from] the enhanced leverage to respond to competitors' and [as we just saw above] governments' threats.[12]

As many writers have acknowledged, although the opportunity is now amply apparent, the challenge lies in execution. Explicitly recognizing flexibility and trans-fer of learning as strategic goals, and adhering to them even as work on the other

[11]Louis T. Wells, Jr., "Minerals: Eroding Oligopolies," in *Beyond Free Trade,* pp. 335–336.
[12]Bruce Kogut, "A Note on Global Strategies," *Strategic Management Journal,* 10 (1989), pp. 383–389.

challenges is undertaken, can be extremely difficult. For instance, economic efficiency might dictate that all production be consolidated in one worldwide plant. But operational flexibility might call for two plants in two distinct currency areas.

Some firms have squared the circle by creating a network of product-focused core plants in strategic regions around the world. These firms accommodate operational flexibility by ensuring that a reasonable proportion of intermediate inputs are common to all major products. When exchange rates change, at least the common intermediate components can be sourced from the exchange-rate-favored location.

Other strategies for enhancing flexibility might include "a shift from ownership to rental of resources; from fixed to variable costs. . . . Incrementalism and opportunism may be given greater emphasis in . . . comparison to pre-emptive resource commitments and long-term planning."[13]

The Bartlett-Ghoshal "Transnational"

In an effort to help managers respond to the changing dynamics of international business, numerous management scholars have pondered over corporate international strategy and written a considerable amount on the subject in the 1980s and 1990s. Among such contributions is a study by Christopher Bartlett and Sumantra Ghoshal which seeks to capture the essence of what senior international executives are struggling with.

The central element of Bartlett and Ghoshal's study is a model that the authors call the transnational.

> The transnational company . . . seeks efficiency not for its own sake, but as a means to achieve global *competitiveness*. It acknowledges the importance of local responsiveness, but as a tool for achieving *flexibility* in international operations. Innovations are regarded as an outcome of a larger process of organizational *learning* that encompasses every member of the company.[14]

To clarify, the authors distinguish the transnational model from three traditional models, which they label *multinational, global,* and *international* (see Table 3-2). In their nomenclature, *multinational* firms are those that primarily pursue country-oriented, locally responsive strategies. Decentralization is the watchword at such firms. Companies such as Philips, ITT, and Fiat are identified with this category. By contrast, at *global* firms, the watchword is centralization. The strategy that these firms pursue is

[13]Sumantra Ghoshal, "Global Strategy: An Organizing Framework," *Strategic Management Journal,* 8 (1987), pp. 425–440.

[14]Christopher A. Bartlett, and Sumantra Ghoshal, *Managing Across Borders: The Transnational Solution* (Boston: Harvard Business School Press, [1989] 1991), p. 59.

TABLE 3-2.   The Organizational Characteristics of Bartlett and Ghoshal's Multinational, Global, International, and Transnational Firms

Organizational Characteristics	Multinational	Global	International	Transnational
Configuration of assets and capabilities	Decentralized and nationally self-sufficient	Centralized and globally scaled	Sources of core competencies centralized, others decentralized	Dispersed, interdependent, and specialized
Role of overseas operations	Sensing and exploiting local opportunities	Implementing parent company strategies	Adapting and leveraging parent company competencies	Differentiated contributions by national units to integrated worldwide operations
Development and diffusion of knowledge	Knowledge developed and retained within each unit	Knowledge developed and retained at the center	Knowledge developed at the center and transferred to overseas units	Knowledge developed jointly and shared worldwide

Source: Christopher A. Bartlett, and Sumantra Ghoshal, *Managing Across Borders: The Transnational Solution* (Boston: Harvard Business School Press, [1989] 1991), p. 65.

built on global-scale and cost advantages. Matsushita, NEC, and Toyota are identified with this category.

International firms, the third model, are classic product-cycle firms whose core ideas and innovations occur first at home and then snake their way outward to foreign affiliates that later adapt the products and technologies to suit local needs and tastes. Here the watchwords are top-down and sequential. Companies like General Electric in consumer electronics, Procter & Gamble, and Ericsson are identified with this category.

Set apart from these three types is the Bartlett-Ghoshal *transnational.* At its core, the transnational eschews dichotomous structures—product-based or geography-based, centralized or decentralized, independent or dependent—and, instead, pushes for solutions that are tailored to suit the situation. It advocates the replacement of systemwide symmetry by differentiated structures, a notion which is illustrated in Figure 3-4.

As Figure 3-4 shows, some businesses at Unilever, such as chemicals, might be appropriate candidates, relatively speaking, for centralized, worldwide management. The presence of large economies of scale, a high value-to-weight ratio, and worldwide consensus on designated use and form might all be factors that account for why the chemicals business is placed on the top left-hand corner of the first integration-responsiveness grid in Figure 3-4. On the other hand, a business such as packaged foods might require a high degree of adaptation to local tastes and distribution channels, and its output might be most economically delivered to the local market via local manufacture. This is why the packaged foods business is placed on the bottom right-hand corner of the integration-responsiveness grid.

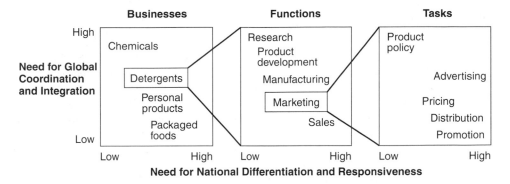

Figure 3-4   Integration and Differentiation Needs at Unilever

Source: Christopher A. Bartlett, and Sumantra Ghoshal, *Managing Across Borders: The Transnational Solution* (Boston: Harvard Business School Press, [1989] 1991), p. 97.

As the second box in the figure shows, however, just because a business occupies a particular position on the integration-responsiveness grid does not mean that all the functions performed within the business ought to performed at the same level. The detergents business, for instance, occupies a spot in the middle of the first box. But research on detergents might be performed in just one worldwide center, whereas marketing and sales of detergents might be undertaken at the local and national level. Likewise, not all tasks within the marketing of detergents will be suitable candidates for execution at the local or national level. Unilever detergents might be promoted in one country in a fashion highly independent of how it is promoted in other countries, but pricing policies across nations will have to be slightly more integrated.

The transnational also is based on the assumption that the relative importance of foreign affiliates and their host environments is rising. Accordingly, in the words of the model's authors:

> The transnational centralizes some resources at home, some abroad, and distributes yet others among its many national operations. The result is a complex configuration of assets and capabilities that are distributed, yet specialized. Furthermore, the company integrates the dispersed resources through strong interdependencies. . . . The British subsidiary may depend on France for one range of products, while the French depend on the British for others. Some of these interdependencies are automatic outcomes of the . . . configuration of assets and resources. Frequently, however, they are specifically designed to build self-enforcing cooperation among interdependent units.[15]

Of course, the challenge in ambitious conceptions such as these lies in organizing and managing. And it is to these issues that we turn in the next chapter.

---

[15]Christopher A. Bartlett, and Sumantra Ghoshal, *Managing Across Borders: The Transnational Solution* (Boston: Harvard Business School Press, [1989] 1991), p. 60.

Suggested Reading

BARTLETT, CHRISTOPHER A., and SUMANTRA GHOSHAL. *Managing Across Borders: The Transnational Solution.* Boston: Harvard Business School Press, 1989.

EDEN, LORRAINE. "Who Does What after NAFTA? Location Strategies of U.S. Multinationals." In Lorraine Eden (ed.), *Multinationals in North America.* Calgary: University of Calgary Press, 1994, 193–245.

KIM, W. CHAN and RENÉE A. MAUBORGNE, "Making Global Strategies Work," *Sloan Management Review,* 34 (1993), 11–27.

KOGUT, BRUCE. "A Note on Global Strategies." *Strategic Management Journal,* 10 (1989), 383–389.

PORTER, MICHAEL E. (ed.) *Competition in Global Industries.* Boston: Harvard Business School Press, 1986.

PRAHALAD, C. K., and YVES L. DOZ. *The Multinational Mission.* New York: Free Press, 1987.

YOFFIE, DAVID B. (ed.). *Beyond Free Trade.* Boston: Harvard Business School Press, 1993.

CHAPTER 4

Managing the Multinational: Organizations and Networks

From Henry Ford's earliest days . . . , [the] Ford Motor Co. was an international enterprise. Five years after its founding in 1903, it set up its first overseas sales branch, in France. By 1911, it was making cars in Britain. But more than 80 years and dozens of overseas operations later, Ford is still trying to figure out what it means to be a global company. Ford, which announced a massive reorganization in April [1994] isn't alone. *Business Week,* May 23, 1994.[1]

Many of tomorrow's most intriguing opportunities—interactive television, on-board navigational systems for cars and trucks, cell therapy, remote at-home medical diagnostics . . . — will require the integration of skills and capabilities residing in a wide variety of companies. Competition for the future often takes place between coalitions as well as between individual firms. . . . Sometimes they involve the creation of a new joint venture company, as . . . when [U.S.-based] Warner-Lambert formed joint ventures with [Britain-based] Wellcome and Glaxo Holdings [now Glaxo-Wellcome] to develop and market over-the-counter versions of its partners' popular prescription drugs. And some[times] coalitions simply involve close, collaborative development work such as Apple's cooperation with Sharp for the production of the Newton [hand-held computer]. Hamel and Prahalad, 1994: 187.[2]

---

[1]John A. Byrne, Kathleen Kerwin, Amy Cortese, and Paula Dwyer, "Borderless Management: Companies Strive to Become Truly Stateless," *Business Week,* May 23, 1994, pp. 24–26.

[2]Gary Hamel, and C. K. Prahalad, *Competing for the Future* (Boston: Harvard Business School Press, 1994).

This chapter focuses on how multinationals organize themselves internally and how they manage their networks across national and firm boundaries. The issues in this realm are among the most vexing that corporate managers face. Indeed, some writers on international management believe that "limited organizational capability is the most critical constraint" that multinational enterprises confront as they attempt to respond to the challenges brought about by global competition.[3]

Recall from Chapter 3 that these challenges cover a wide range: taking account of the competition; striving for higher productivity and efficiency; being responsive to local stakeholders; and leveraging the network to achieve operational flexibility and systemwide exploitation of local learning. As we have noted, firms are realizing that if they want to be players in future rounds of competition, they must work simultaneously on a number of different fronts.

Take the case of Ford's 1994 announcement that its organization would now be oriented around global product divisions. According to the company, the primary aim of the shift was to reap firmwide efficiencies. As Gunnar Hedlund notes, however, "centrally guided global strategies for given products . . . [which look] at the world as one market . . . may lead to neglect of opportunities to exploit . . . differences between nations."[4] Recognizing this risk, Ford intends to establish close contact between its North American and European operations.

But it is widely believed that, at least in the foreseeable future, the most dynamic car markets will be those in Asia and Latin America. Accordingly, the executives at Ford acknowledge that even as they concentrate on their transition to a new internal organization, they must also manage diligently their external links with Mazda of Japan, in which Ford has a 25 percent equity stake, and with Volkswagen of Germany, with which Ford had until 1995 a joint venture in Brazil (Box 4-1).

In a quite different industry, IBM finds that, in order to be competitive, it too must divide its attention between designing an effective internal organization and managing its external links with companies such as Apple, Motorola, Siemens, and Toshiba. In its industry, the high rate of change in technology (rather than local responsiveness) appears to be the primary driver of alliances.

While we can point to numerous examples of companies that are using multiple modes to expand abroad, to share or reduce risks, to penetrate nationally protected markets, and to gain efficiencies, the fundamental questions these illustrations raise are: How should multinational enterprises organize themselves for maximum effectiveness? What role will networks external to the multinational enterprise play in the process of adaptation?

Let us begin to answer these questions by looking at the evolution of the organizational characteristics of multinationals; the strains and new demands created by the

---

[3]See, for instance, Christopher A. Bartlett and Sumantra Ghoshal, "Managing Across Borders: New Strategic Requirements," *Sloan Management Review (SMR)* (Summer 1987), pp. 7–17; and "Managing Across Borders: New Organizational Responses," *SMR,* (Fall 1987), pp. 43–53.

[4]Gunnar Hedlund, "The Hypermodern MNC—A Heterarchy?," *Human Resource Management,* 25, no. 1, (Spring 1986), p. 19.

BOX 4-1. GLOBAL MANAGEMENT, FORD STYLE

In 1994–1995, American car maker Ford launched a major initiative to globalize the development and management of its automotive products. Under the leadership of chairman Alex Trotman, the company established five vehicle program centers: one run jointly out of Germany and Britain to manage small cars, and four others—located in the United States—to manage large cars and trucks. Ford's aim in revamping, according to the company, is to "to break down national barriers" inside the company and to "make more efficient use of its engineering and product development money against rapidly globalizing rivals."

Under the plan, Ford expects the individual centers not only to design and develop the new generations of vehicles for which they have worldwide mandates, but also to take responsibility for their worldwide production, marketing, and profitability. The product-based centers will be overseen by worldwide functional heads—one each for product development, manufacturing, and marketing. These three officers will operate out of the company's U.S. headquarters.

One risk that Ford's new plan is said to run is the amplification of mistakes. As an executive from Ford told *Business Week*, "If you misjudge the market, you are wrong in 15 countries rather than only in one." Indeed, Ford acknowledges that if it is to successfully pull off its plan, the group designing small cars in Europe will need to work closely with the Americans, and eventually, as Ford expands there, the Asians. Likewise, the groups designing worldwide products in the United States will need input from their counterparts in other regions.

The result, one observer claims, is that "the interdependency ratio within Ford has gone from 1 to 30." In this regard, one immediate obstacle Ford faces is that its European and North American computer systems aren't wholly compatible with one another. Nevertheless, it is anticipated that eventually "engineers and executives will talk to each other daily across the Atlantic through video conferences and computer nets."

Finally, although Ford aims to have the innards of its global cars be the same across continents, the company will permit country modifications in styling and specification in order to cater to regional differences. The hoped-for net gain: efficiencies to the tune of $3 billion, most of which are anticipated from the use of fewer suppliers, worldwide procurement, other pooling of resources, and the elimination of unneeded redundancy.

SOURCE: Based on "The World Car: Enter the McFord," *The Economist*, July 23, 1994, p. 69; and John A. Byrne, Kathleen Kerwin, Amy Cortese, and Paula Dwyer, "Borderless Management: Companies Strive to Become Truly Stateless," *Business Week*, May 23, 1994, pp. 24–26.

forces of globalization; and the responses and proposals to address these new demands offered by corporate managers and business scholars. Our review starts with
the structures inside the multinational enterprise proper and then moves to the links
that are external to the enterprise itself.

First Principles

Organizations are created to pool the efforts of individuals. Those efforts will be devoted to collecting and sharing information, skills, or capital, putting these resources
to work, monitoring performance, and making midcourse changes in goals and actions. Good internal communication networks and well-designed channels of decision
making are minimal prerequisites for the effective coordination of such firmwide efforts.

In the multinational enterprise, four types of building blocks are almost invari-
ably involved in creating an organization to serve these purposes.

- *Activities* which fall within a particular function (such as advertising, pricing,
  and distribution in the marketing function).
- *Functions,* which generally include production, finance, marketing, personnel,
  research, and government relations.
- *Business units* within the firm, which are generally grouped according to some
  key product or market characteristic, so that the items in any such group are
  more like each other with respect to the key characteristic than like those in any
  other group.
- *Countries or regions,* which are generally grouped on the same principle of
  maximum homogeneity within a class.

The challenge for the manager is to use these building blocks to design an organization that is best suited for achieving of the firm's strategic goals. The problem of
developing an appropriate organization is rendered all the more difficult by several
considerations:

- The strategy associated with any given line of business is likely to change as the
  business itself changes and as the market evolves. The direction of these
  changes may be reasonably predictable, but they still leave the manager with
  the problem of adapting the organization to its current strategic needs while at
  the same time allowing for future changes in these needs.
- The organization appropriate to one line of business within an enterprise may
  be quite different from the organization appropriate to another line within the
  same enterprise. The firm that produces both aircraft engines and electric refrig-

erators is likely to find that the organizational requirements for the two lines
will be quite different.

- Finally, even within a business line and at a given moment in time, the organizational needs may differ by country. The best organization arrangements may
well be different for affiliates in Japan and, say, Thailand.

Considerations such as these sometimes lead to the creation of organizations
that appear very complex to the outsider. In practice, however, functioning organizations evolve over time by adjusting to visible strain. As this strain develops, informal,
out-of-channel contacts are generally used at first to deal with the new problem.
When the formal adjustment is finally made, it is greatly influenced by the structure
that preceded it and by the personalities that have to be accommodated within it.

Despite all the qualifications, as the well-known Stopford and Wells study of
1972 showed, there have been some visible regularities in the organizational change
of multinational enterprises.[5] That study, based on an examination of the foreign expansion patterns of more than 150 U.S.-based multinational enterprises, proposed
what is widely called a "stages" model. Let us review the evolutionary patterns suggested by the model and then consider subsequent developments.

Evolutionary Patterns of Organization

Let us begin with Figures 4-1A and B. These figures describe some of the features of
two typical organizations before they have embarked on a program of overseas investment. At this stage, the organizations can be regarded as relatively "small" by the
standards of multinational enterprises, confined to a few product lines or a few markets and wrestling with a comparatively limited number of strategic decisions. In organizations of this sort, the president typically makes the strategic decisions based on
the contributions of the vice presidents. Contact with foreign markets is achieved
mainly through exports. An export manager, if one exists, is considered an adjunct to
marketing. Naturally, the export manager's principal communication takes place with
the marketing vice president and others in the marketing group.

As the enterprise grows, the diversity of its problems increases, especially when
growth occurs by adding to the number of product lines. Each product may well require a different kind of integration between marketing and production as well as different ties with research. At the same time, if the products are increasing, the chances
are that the exports of the enterprise will be growing too, perhaps even faster than domestic sales. Out of the growing choice of products, several will have reached a stage
of rapid growth in overseas demand. At first, the increased traffic may be handled by
an export manager using the pattern suggested in Figure 4-1. Eventually, however,

[5]John M. Stopford and Louis T. Wells, Jr., *Managing the Multinational Enterprise* (New York: Basic Books,
1972).

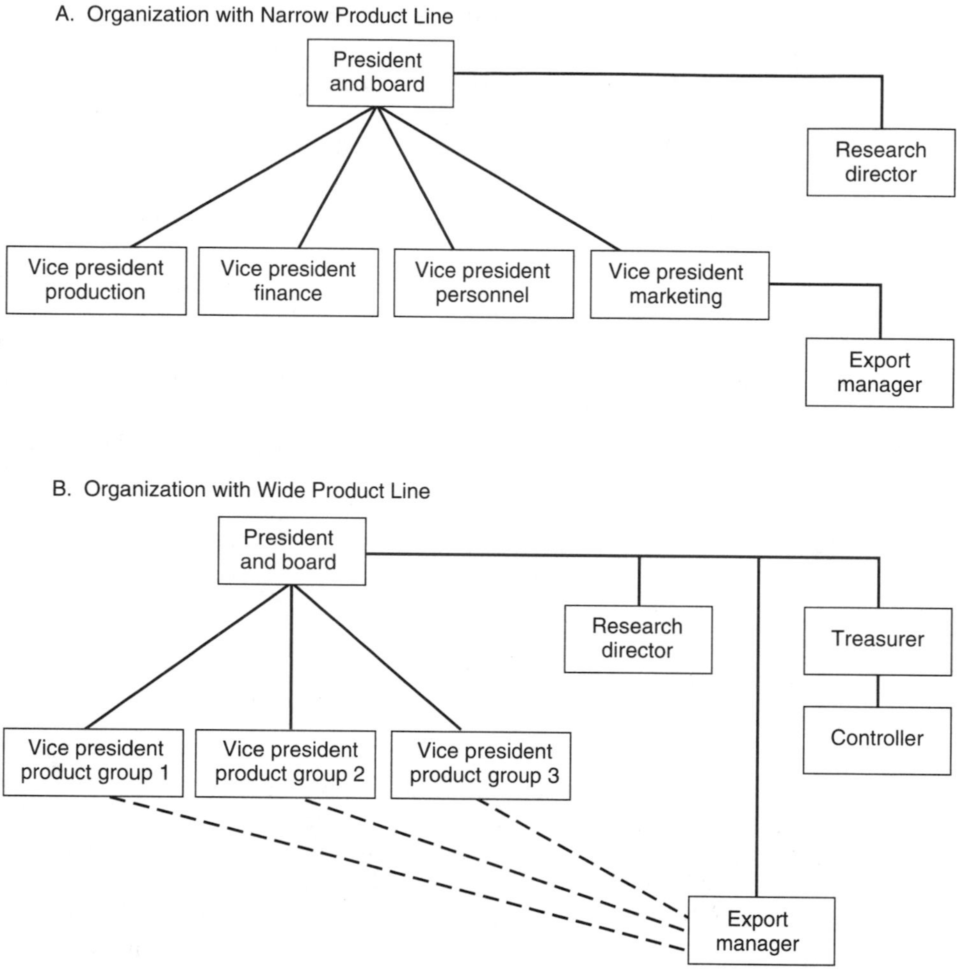

A. Organization with Narrow Product Line

B. Organization with Wide Product Line

Figure 4-1   Typical Organization of Multinational Enterprise Before Establishment of First Overseas Manufacturing Subsidiary

many firms create an international division, and the resulting organization is likely to be along the lines of the one depicted in Figure 4-2.

One key assumption about the communication patterns that lie behind the organization shown in Figure 4-2 is fairly evident. Those concerned with production and marketing for areas outside the home market, it is assumed, will have more to communicate with one another than with their counterparts in the product groups. This key assumption is widely made in the first stages of overseas expansion, especially by U.S.-based firms and other firms with large home markets.

Typically, however, the production and marketing specialists in the interna-

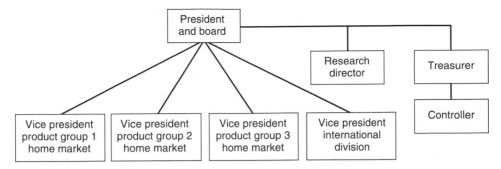

Figure 4-2 Typical Organization of Multinational Enterprises at Early Stage of Overseas Expansion

tional division increasingly find themselves obliged to consult with their counterparts in the various home product divisions. Information must be exchanged; plans must be coordinated. Accordingly, various sources of strain begin to break the international division apart: (1) the strain of a heavy flow of communications with other divisions, involving attenuated links between sender and receiver; (2) the strain of sheer size of the international division, creating a problem of declining efficiency in communications within the division; and (3) the strain associated with rapid growth, and the attendant claim on corporate resources, creating jealousies within the enterprise. By that time, too, the volume of overseas business is seen as sufficiently large to justify locating international specialists within each of the main product divisions.

The results were seen in the short life and high rate of mortality for international divisions in large U.S.-based multinational enterprises and in the strains that have been visible in the structures of European-based enterprises and Japanese trading companies. Once the international division is gone, the organization shown in Figure 4-2 is no longer representative and is superseded by that portrayed in Figure 4-3. As

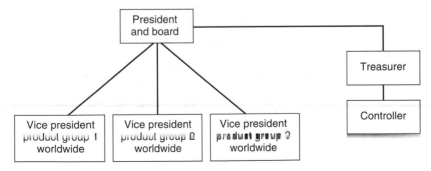

Figure 4-3 Typical Organization of Multinational Enterprise with Wide Product Line after Establishment of Overseas Manufacturing Subsidiaries

the international division disappears, the product group divisions are concurrently assigned worldwide responsibility for production and marketing. In theory, such divisions are freed to pursue a global strategy according to which they are prepared to locate activities at optimal points anywhere in the world. At this stage, too, the product divisions may be delegated responsibilities for some or all of their related research activities, this delegation reflects the fact that the communications of the researchers need no longer be directed to two different constituents—the international division and the appropriate home product division.

A special point has to be made with regard to enterprises that expand overseas on the basis of comparatively narrow product lines. Enterprises with narrow product lines, such as IBM or Volkswagen, have tended to organize their operations on a highly integrated basis in any region of the world and to link the separate production and marketing facilities of the region into fairly tight interdependent patterns. Within their regional markets, the pricing practices, trademark practices, quality-control standards, and production patterns of the enterprises are closely related. A plant in one country may be assigned to a specialized task, such as the manufacture of a limited range of components for assembly and sale in a number of contiguous countries.

Enterprises of this sort have been relatively slow to adopt a product-division organization. For instance, these firms have shown a preference at home for an organization based on functional divisions. Once such firms establish an international division to handle their overseas business, they tend to find this division adequate for a relatively long period of time. Eventually, however, enterprises of this sort based in the United States have been found to break up their non-U.S. interests into regional divisions and to produce the new structure depicted in Figure 4-4.

Finally, operating largely by trial and error, some firms conclude that the most desirable pattern is one that allows for a "grid" or matrix structure. In these organizations, subsidiary managers operate with dual reporting relationships—one to the worldwide product divisions and the other to the area division under whose jurisdiction the subsidiary falls.

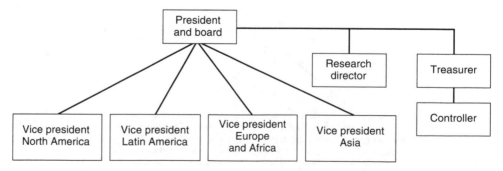

Figure 4-4   Typical Organization of Multinational Enterprise with Narrow Product Line at Advanced Stage of Overseas Expansion

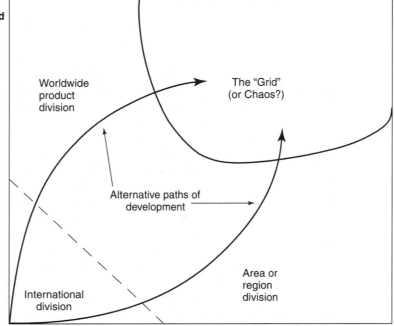

Figure 4-5   Typical Organizational "Stages" in the Evolution of U.S.-Based Multinationals

Source: Adapted from Christopher A. Bartlett and Sumantra Ghoshal, *Managing Across Borders: The Transnational Solution* (Boston: Harvard Business School Press, 1989).

Thus, starting with the export manager and international division, firms that sell abroad a wide range of products typically opt for worldwide product divisions, whereas those with narrower product lines but high and widely spread foreign sales organize along region or area divisions. Firms that are high on both dimensions often resort to matrix structures. These findings led Stopford and Wells to a central conclusion: A firm's *strategy* (of product or geographic diversification) largely determines its organizational *structure*. Their "stages" model is commonly summarized as shown in Figure 4-5.

New Strains and Demands

Whatever the choice of organizational structure, whether in the directions suggested by Figure 4-2, 4-3, or 4-4, the process of coordination and communication has repeatedly uncovered several shortcomings in the structure.

Dilution of International Expertise

One shortcoming to which U.S.-based firms have seemed particularly vulnerable has arisen out of the premature movement of enterprises from the international division stage (shown in Figure 4-2) to the worldwide product divisions stage (shown in Figure 4-3). Studies suggest that, contrary to expectations, a reorganization of that kind sometimes reduces both the interest and effectiveness of a firm in foreign markets.

As long as firms have an international division, they can count on pressure for overseas expansion coming from that division. With the dissolution of the division and the dispersal of its specialists to various product divisions, the focus on foreign markets sometimes declines and the skills nurtured in the division are weakened. The managers put in charge of the new worldwide product divisions often have neither the expertise nor the interest to exploit opportunities abroad. This lack of interest can be attributed to the fact that for most U. S.-based multinationals the home market is the largest single market of the enterprise. The home market, therefore, commonly serves as the training ground for high-level managers, and thus the source of their expertise. For such managers, economic opportunities in foreign markets have appeared marginal in comparison to the prospects for further expansion in the United States.

In response, some firms retain the international division longer than was once thought appropriate, abandoning it only when international activities are so well established that their importance to product divisions becomes self-evident. Other firms, recognizing that the international division represents only a transitory stage, try to find other ways of ensuring that product divisions are sufficiently responsive to foreign opportunities, including rotations to the field, special training, and special pecuniary incentives. Without such special measures, experience suggests that the neglect of foreign markets can be a substantial risk.

The Product-Region Dilemma

The choice of a product-based organization, such as that in Figure 4-3, or a region-based structure, such as that in Figure 4-4, or even the matrix system leaves many questions of organization unanswered.

When the product-based structure is chosen, one common problem is how to coordinate the firm's activities within some given geographical territory. This problem arises, for instance, when a host government insists on viewing the firm's activities within its territory as a single unit for a regulatory purpose, such as taxation. To deal with that kind of situation, enterprises sometimes create umbrella committees or umbrella companies that act to pull together the diverse interests of the enterprise in a given territory whenever such action is needed. Another difficult task in a product-based organization may be to coordinate advertising or to provide services for products of more than one division.

Furthermore diversified firms sometimes find that the choice of structure suitable for some product lines is not appropriate for other parts of the business. The strategy for one product line, for example, might well call for close integration of activities within regions. The need is for a region-based structure similar to that shown in Figure 4-4. For other parts of the business, however, the strategy may depend on rapid communication of innovations from headquarters to subsidiaries around the world, and thus call for a structure similar to that of Figure 4-3.

Similarly, when a region-based structure is chosen, the enterprise may find it difficult to manage the transfer of new technology across regions. Temporary or permanent coordinating teams are often created to deal with such issues. In the matrix organization, where the different viewpoints of the two supervisors suggest different courses of action, it remains for the supervisors themselves to find ways of reconciling their differences.

Many managers find matrix organizations uncomfortable because authority and accountability are divided. Such division of authority tends to create high overhead costs: to resolve differences, communications must be frequent and intense. In practice, power in such organizations often begins to tilt in one direction or the other; the influence of the product managers or that of the area managers comes to dominate. Reestablishing an equilibrium then requires a major effort. Influenced by such experiences, in the mid-1990s several multinationals including Digital Equipment, Dow Chemical, and Citibank abandoned their matrix organizational structures.[6]

Different Requirements for Different Business Functions

A business is made up of different functional areas: finance, marketing, production, and so on. There is, of course, no reason to believe that all business functions should be handled in the same way within a given firm. The finance function, for instance, has typically been a candidate for close coordination across different regions and different products because money and credit come close to being fungible resources of the firm. Hence, those concerned with the finance function tend to communicate frequently, regardless of their product and area association. As a result, many multinationals have centralized the finance function; it falls under neither product nor regional managers, but reports directly to headquarters. The personnel function, on the other hand, has usually been decentralized to the various national markets because wages, working conditions, and labor practices tend to vary by country.

The production function has been organized differently for different kinds of enterprises. In spite of the multinationals' claims that they are pursuing a global strategy, most of them have organized their production on a regional basis. In spite of improved communications facilities, the problems of coordinating production facilities in widely dispersed plants remain enormous, while the benefits of global systems seem elusive.

[6]"The Discreet Charm of the Multicultural Multinational," *The Economist,* July 30, 1994, pp. 57–58.

A region such as North America, Europe, or East Asia generally includes countries that in the aggregate can satisfy a firm's needs for scale, skills, specialized suppliers, and low wages. Thus, many firms can meet their requirements without trying to coordinate production facilities across different regions. A U.S. automobile firm, for example, is likely to obtain many of its labor-intensive parts from Mexico for its U.S. plants; its European affiliates and European competitors, on the other hand, will probably obtain many of their labor-intensive parts from Ireland, Portugal, or Spain. In other industries where scale economies and transportation costs loom high, production may even take place on a purely national basis. Regardless of geographic scope, the management of the production function usually is organized on a basis quite different from that which governs the finance function.

Different Subsidiaries with Different Roles

Organizations designed to provide for two-way flows of goods and intangibles among their units are bound to differ from those based on the hierarchical principle of a dominant headquarters unit that provides the critical tangible and intangible inputs. Even within a particular line of business, a firm may find that it wants to assign different kinds of roles to particular subsidiaries. No one stereotypical structure is likely to satisfy all needs without some adjustment.

For instance, when U.S. firms first ventured abroad, most of them assumed that new products, new technologies, and new marketing ideas would originate in the U.S. parent. The subsidiaries would be responsible only for learning from headquarters, perhaps adapting innovations somewhat to local needs and marketing their products in the markets where they were located. The relationship between headquarters and subsidiary was a fairly straightforward one.

On the other hand, the subsidiaries of European and Japanese enterprises, particularly those in the United States, sometimes have had a more complicated assignment. One of the prime objectives of some of these subsidiaries has been to transfer back to headquarters ideas that could be gleaned from what was the world's most advanced market. In fact, Canadian, European, and Asian firms have often established U.S. subsidiaries to serve as a source of information and training for the enterprise as a whole. These subsidiaries, therefore, maintain a special relationship to their headquarters unit.

In the past two decades, many U.S.-based multinationals have had to reconsider the role of some of their overseas subsidiaries. As we observed in Chapter 3, the sources of information and expertise in today's world are widely dispersed. The dramatic changes in income levels and market size in Europe and Japan, and the increasing importance of manufacturing bases in low-wage countries, have made the simple model of an earlier era obsolete for many enterprises. New ideas may arise in Japan or Europe; a subsidiary located there may therefore be charged with research, monitoring of developments of other firms in those markets, and so on. Similarly, the output of, say, a Malaysian plant may well be the input of an affiliated manufacturing plant in the United States or elsewhere, rather than a product for sale primarily in Malaysia. But the organizational changes required to deal with these developments are just being conceptualized.

New Paradigms for Internal Networks

The new demands placed on multinational enterprises since the onset of heightened competition in the 1980s have forced managers across the globe to search for new organizational paradigms. Working with and studying the large corporations struggling to rise to these challenges, several management scholars have come up with ambitious proposals for ways in which multinational enterprises can better organize themselves. Of such proposals, two—Hedlund's *heterarchy,* and Bartlett and Ghoshal's *transnational*—have captured the attention of both managers and academics. Let us consider these proposals in turn.

Hedlund's "Heterarchy"

To understand Hedlund's heterarchy,[7] we need to learn some new nomenclature. The nomenclature has to do with two archetypal and polar modes of governing economic activities, namely, markets and hierarchies. When economic activities are conducted at arm's length between unrelated parties (suppliers and their customers, for instance), *and* when explicit contracts or prices are the primary mechanism by which the activities are coordinated, then these activities are said to be governed by markets or market mechanisms. In pure markets, neither transacting party has authority over the other, and it is expected that each party will do what is in its own best interest in each individual transaction.

On the other hand, when economic activities are conducted between parties related to one another, either by ties of common ownership (such as those that exist between a multinational enterprise parent and its foreign affiliates) or by implicit contracts (such as those commonly assumed to exist between employers and employees), and when vertical authority (rather than price) is the primary method by which activities are coordinated, these activities are said to be conducted within a hierarchy. In the case of the multinational enterprise, as we noted earlier, it is generally assumed that the parent has the authority to direct and control the actions of its subsidiaries.

If markets represent horizontal, two-way relations between independent entities and if hierarchies represent vertical, top-down relations between, say, the multinational enterprise parent and its foreign affiliates, then Hedlund conceives the heterarchical multinational as lying somewhere in between, incorporating attractive features from the two polar modes of governance. In his words:

---

[7]Based on Hedlund, 1986.

The heterarchical MNC differs from the standard geocentric one both in terms of strategy and in terms of [the direction of the relationship between strategy and] structure. *Strategically,* the main dividing line is between exploiting competitive advantages derived from a home country base on the one hand, and actively seeking advantages originating in the global spread of the firm. . . . [W]hen it comes to the *structure* of the enterprise and the process of managing it . . . the idea of structure determining strategy [rather than the other way around] . . . is a fundamental one for the heterarchical MNC. Rather than identifying properties of the industry in which it competes and then adapting its structure to the demands thus established, the [heterarchical] MNC . . . first defines its structural properties and then looks for strategic options following from these properties.[8]

That is, in Hedlund's heterarchy, managers do not view the multinational enterprise as a traditional hierarchy where ideas, technology, and other resources originate just from the top (from the parent and its home base) and move down to the affiliates. Rather, managers conceive of and design the new multinational enterprise in such a manner that core resources and ideas may originate from any affiliate or branch, located in any country, in the system. New ideas from, say, the affiliate in Mexico or Taiwan, can be internalized and diffused within the network of the enterprise wherever its home base may be.

Furthermore, if managers can design and effectively coordinate such a system, argues Hedlund, then this organizational ability can itself, as we observed in Chapter 3, become a source of competitive strength based on which firms can launch new products, enter new markets, and pursue new strategies. So, rather than working from products and markets and then setting on appropriate organizational structures (as the firms in Stopford and Wells's study did), heterarchical multinationals retain the option of going the other way too.

Hedlund enumerates several other features of the heterarchical multinational enterprise:

- The heterarchical multinational enterprise has multiple centers, each with competence in one or another business, product, or function. Resources are diffused within the network of affiliates, and it is implicitly assumed that ideas can come from any country.
- Subsidiary managers play strategic roles not just within their own units but within the enterprise as a whole. The notion of "headquarters" is diluted.
- Thinking and decision making are not restricted to the center; every part of the enterprise can participate. In this manner, the feedback loop between action and thought is tightened.
- Integration is achieved primarily through normative control and only secondarily through coercive or bureaucratic means. Socialization and "corporate culture" become more important.

[8]Hedlund, p. 20.

- In contrast to a matrix, a heterarchy recognizes that organizations may be built along more than two dimensions. Thus, R&D may be organized one way, production a second, and marketing a third.
- Finally, managers have flexibility in the selection of governance modes. A subsidiary may purchase components from or sell its production externally. Similarly, coalitions with other firms and actors may be frequent in the heterarchical multinational enterprise.

The heterarchical multinational enterprise is an idealized conception whose emergence, as Hedlund himself acknowledges, has yet to occur on a wide scale. Nevertheless, like the transnational model that we will take up next, it represents an early contribution to the process of conceptualizing the characteristics of new organizations designed to meet the changing economic realities and the tough new demands of globalization.

Bartlett and Ghoshal's "Transnational"

In terms of intellectual heritage, Bartlett and Ghoshal's transnational both preceded Hedlund's heterarchy and appeared subsequently in a more refined form. Recall from Chapter 3 that within the transnational, organizational design is guided by the characteristics of the particular business, function, or activity under consideration, not by a need to do things "one way." Formal structures within affiliates in one region may be quite different from those in another. Moreover, the transnational emphasizes interdependence rather than dependence or independence.

To flesh out the organizational characteristics of the various models in their classificatory system, Bartlett and Ghoshal describe four separate structures, each paralleling one of their archetypes.

Within firms categorized as multinational, the formal structure is like a *decentralized federation.* Under this system, "the dominant management mentality [views] the company's strategy as developing positions in key markets worldwide and managing offshore operations as a portfolio of independent businesses."[9] Early European multinationals are often identified with this model. To the extent that these enterprises could be regarded as hierarchies, their control and coordination systems are built around informal links between headquarters and subsidiaries, and were supplemented by simple financial systems that permitted accounting consolidation. We can see that in terms of relative emphasis, this structure is similar to Stopford and Wells's region-based divisions and to Perlmutter's polycentric firm.

Within firms categorized as international, the formal structure is described as a

---

[9]Christopher A. Bartlett, and Sumantra Ghoshal, *Managing Across Borders: The Transnational Solution* (Boston: Harvard Business School Press, [1989] 1991), p. 49.

coordinated federation. Under this system, top management controls and guides the actions of foreign subsidiaries, whose primary task is to adapt to local needs the products and strategies that emanate from the home office. Partly due to their historical leadership in technology and partly due to the large size of the home market, the managerial culture of many U.S.-based multinational enterprises fits this mold. Formal management and tight top-down links between parents and affiliates are hallmarks of these organizations. In terms of relative emphasis, this structure is similar to Stopford and Wells's international division and to Perlmutter's ethnocentric firm.

Within firms categorized as global, the formal structure is like a *centralized hub.* Under this system, headquarters tightly controls the worldwide operations of the enterprise. Foreign subsidiaries engage primarily in sales and service, and, compared with their counterparts in multinational or international organizations, they have relatively less freedom (and, ostensibly, less need) to create new products and strategies or even adapt ones emanating from headquarters. The management style of Japanese corporations in the 1970s and 1980s is frequently associated with this model of organization. In terms of relative emphasis, this structure is similar to Stopford and Wells's worldwide product divisions and to Perlmutter's geocentric firm.

Finally, within transnational firms, formal structures take a variety of quite differentiated and complex forms. As the schematic in Figure 4-6 suggests, under this model, resources and centers of decision making are dispersed among the various affiliates. In addition to the parent, foreign affiliates within the firm might also be worldwide centers of expertise along one or another dimension. Shared learning and transfer of knowledge are effected by developing a high degree of interdependence and integration among the affiliates and between the affiliates and the parent. In fact, to promote systemwide integration, informal systems are encouraged and emphasized. Given these characteristics, at transnationals, the organizational structure is labeled an *integrated network.*

Managers who want to adopt the transnational way of thinking, according to Bartlett and Ghoshal, must master three extremely ambitious tasks:

- First, they must develop an organizational sensitivity that is oriented not around one or two, but multiple, dimensions. For instance, managers whose firms are traditionally focused on product or efficiency must also develop their organizations along the dimensions of geography (local responsiveness) and functions. Once developed, this balance in perspectives must be legitimized and sustained by top management. According to the model's authors, this investment will, enhance the firm's ability to face the changes and new challenges thrown up by the dynamic global economic environment.
- Second, rather than relying on one "way of doing things," firms must use a heterogeneous mix of modes to govern the flows and activities that occur within their organizations. Flows of products (such as intermediate and final goods) may be coordinated through *formal* processes and systems; flows of scarce re-

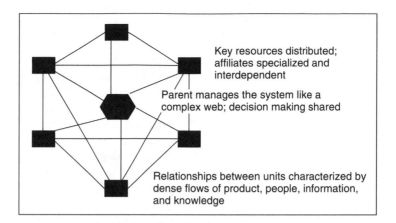

Figure 4-6   Bartlett and Ghoshal's Transnational

Source: Adapted from Christopher A. Bartlett, and Sumantra Ghoshal, *Managing Across Borders: The Transnational Solution* (Boston: Harvard Business School Press, 1989).

sources (such as money, technology, and key personnel) may occur under the *centralized* supervision of senior management; and flows of information and ideas may be facilitated through less formal *social* processes that integrate managers culturally.

• Finally, because the transnational engenders enormous complexity, and because it has a high potential to raise the level of conflict inside firms, top management must employ sophisticated means to unify their employees under a common corporate vision. "To develop such commitment, each individual must understand and share the company's purpose and values, must identify with the broader goals and objectives and must accept and internalize its key strategies."[10]

Other Links in the Network

Having reviewed the new paradigms for organizing operations wholly internal to multinational enterprises, let us now consider why and how these entities enter into alliances and joint ventures, and licensing relationships.

---

[10]Ibid., p. 70.

Alliances and Joint Ventures

Alliances and joint ventures (addressed here as one phenomenon) have been increasingly popular in recent years, often among multinational enterprises with home bases in different countries. Some long-standing international alliances, however, go back half a century or more in the raw materials industries, notably in aluminum and oil. By contrast, the striking increase in alliances in recent decades is found mainly in high-tech industries. In the computer industry, for instance, one study counted only four such international alliances in 1975 but identified 35 such alliances 10 years later. Other studies have found that international alliances today are common not only in computers, but also in biotechnology, semiconductors, telecommunications, software, and aviation.

Firms have entered into alliances for a number of different purposes:

Spreading risk. Among the reasons for alliances among the oil or mineral producers was the desire to spread the financial risk created by physical and political uncertainties in large-scale projects. In high-tech projects entailing high front-end costs, technological risks pose a similar problem for firms and lead to a similar response.

Multinational alliances often reflect the advantages that managers associate with multiple locations. Accordingly, firms have frequently tried to increase the number of locations by pooling their resources with those of other firms with similar objectives. By creating such partnerships, multinational enterprises can spread a given amount of investment across a larger number of locations and thereby reduce risk. As a result, in the aluminum industry, considerable number of bauxite mines of the world located outside the United States were joint ventures among competing multinational aluminum firms, often of different nationalities. The same pattern was once quite common in large oil fields and large copper mines throughout the world before a wave of nationalizations in the 1970s changed many of these facilities from privately owned firms to state-owned enterprises.

Reducing competition. Oil and mineral producers entered into alliances in the past primarily to reduce competition. Some observers fear that reduced competition may also become one of the consequences of some of today's high-tech alliances. A few governments are already expressing concern, for instance, over the possibility of increasing concentration in the manufacture of commercial aircraft and telephone switching equipment.

Bringing complementary capabilities together. When firms with unique capabilities are reluctant to offer them in an open market, other firms that can use such capabilities to their advantage are faced with a choice of either developing the capabilities internally or developing a mutually advantageous alliance with the reluctant firm, including possibly an exchange or a guarantee to provide a market.

All parties may see the internal development of the complementary capabilities as entailing higher costs than satisfying the alliance terms. Thus, automobile firms that are strong in mechanical engineering have felt inadequate in developing the electronics associated with new antilock braking systems, fuel systems, and emission systems. So some firms have decided to enter into alliances with electronics firms to provide such needs rather than to develop their own internal capabilities.

European car makers have also sought alliances with one another to share product lines and distribution systems, as well as to pool research and development. At various times producers of luxury or sports cars have, for example, built alliances with manufacturers of lower priced family cars in order to economize on distribution. Similarly, in the aircraft industry, alliances have brought together mainframe manufacturers with parts manufacturers in another country, especially when the arrangements can improve market access for the aircraft to that country.

The same firm may build up alliances with different purposes. AT&T, for example, has entered collaborative arrangements to gain access to the European market for telecommunications equipment. At the same time, it has established links for access to technology for personal computers. AT&T's arrangements have included agreements with Philips of the Netherlands and Olivetti of Italy.

Alliances that share research and development costs or that seek to meld complementary technical skills may well have a temporary life. The research project that led to the arrangement may be completed, and the partners see no more need for cooperation; or the firms may internalize the skills they need in order to proceed without the partner. As a result, many alliances don't last; yet, that is not necessarily an indicator that they failed. They may well have accomplished their original objectives.

Many of the alliances that last go through substantial changes. Xerox, for example, joined with Fuji Photo Film of Japan in 1962 to market copiers in Japan. At the outset, the arrangements that created the joint-venture company, Fuji Xerox, were little more than the common national partner strategies chosen by many firms to enter the Japanese market. By 1971, however, Fuji Photo Film had effectively dropped out of the alliance. By 1993, the relationship between Xerox and Fuji Xerox had turned into a very complex arrangement under which Fuji Xerox not only handled local marketing in Japan but also was involved in product development and manufacturing for Xerox's global business.

The very frequent collapse of alliances suggests that many were not well thought out from the beginning or that they were not well managed. As with so many other management decisions, there has been a certain element of fashion in alliances, especially during the 1980s. A number of arrangements, it appears, were formed hastily, without much attention to the goals and the management task. Even those with well-thought-out goals have sometimes proved difficult to manage. Powerful partners have often struggled for control; working out mechanisms for joint decisions has been a challenge, especially since multinationals from different countries often have different views of decision making. But adjusting to changing goals has probably proved the most difficult task facing managers of international alliances.

Some alliances have grown to include a number of firms; those are often labeled alliance networks. One of the best known is Mips Computer Systems, a microprocessor design firm that brought in more than 40 partners, including Japanese, U.S., and German multinationals. Some members of the network developed and produced semiconductors; others supplied inputs; and still others were customers. Not surprisingly, such moves often lead rival firms to build their own networks of alliances. As a result, competition sometimes begins to be among networks rather than simply among multinational enterprises.

To summarize, from the viewpoints of participants, three features of the alliance are attractive: (1) The parties involved usually see themselves as retaining greater control over their contributions than they would have in an arm's length sale or licensing arrangement; (2) they avoid the unambiguous domination by one partner of the other, such as happens in a merger or consolidation or in a one-way licensing arrangement; and (3) they usually remain able to terminate the arrangement as the costs and benefits change. At the same time, an alliance may be continually modified and extended as the reasons for its existence change.

Licensing

As we noted in Chapter 2, the licensing agreement or technical assistance agreement is often between a multinational enterprise parent and a company located in a host country. The company located in the host country may be a foreign affiliate of the licensor, or it may be an independent entity. Here we focus on licensing arrangements with independent entities.

In licensing arrangements, the licensor provides a combination of management services, technical information, or patent rights and receives payment in money (called a royalty). Although such agreements generally entail only a limited amount of control by the foreign licensor, some licensing agreements tie the local enterprise hand and foot. They may require it to buy its intermediate products from the foreign licensor, adhere to quality standards set by the licensor, and confine its marketing efforts to areas defined in the license. Indeed, practically all licenses include some of these limitations.

When is it advisable to use licensing arrangements? When should managers turn to joint ventures and alliances, and when to wholly owned foreign affiliates? The next section takes up this question of choice of links and elaborates on the licensing mode in that context.

A Choice of Links

How does a corporate planner charged with the job of selecting the appropriate mode of foreign participation go about making that choice in a given situation? At a minimum, the corporate planner exploring these possibilities is obliged to answer two questions:

- Do the benefits that the firm would derive from any of these arrangements exceed the associated costs?
- If the answer is yes, which arrangement provides the largest net benefits?

The formal methods of calculating the net benefits to the firm from any given arrangement are well developed and can be found in any standard text that deals with capital budgeting. Underlying such methods is a comparison of a stream of future costs with a stream of future benefits. Each benefit will be suitably discounted to its present value; each may be adjusted for the risk or uncertainty associated with the projection. If some modes are less restrictive than others in terms of future action, the value of such flexibility may be factored in. Similarly, if substantial differences are perceived between the various modes in the rate at and degree to which learning and knowledge transfer will be facilitated, then this consideration may also be factored into the decision. Indeed, the internalization hypothesis of Chapter 2 is predicated on the assumption that business managers make some such calculations and that multinational enterprises come into existence as a result.

In practice, however, the conscientious analyst will recognize that the problems of developing credible estimates of some costs and benefits in such circumstances are usually formidable. Moreover, these hard-to-quantify elements may sometimes prove to be the dominant ones in the decision. Table 4-1 lists the costs and benefits that ordinarily have to be weighed in such arrangements, including not only those that are conventionally included in cost-benefit calculations but also the hard-to-quantify factors that may weigh heavily in the decision.

A glance at Table 4-1 indicates that, when measured in terms of costs and benefits, none of the arrangements emerges uniformly as the most desirable. Judgments on the relative merits of the different arrangements depend on two kinds of questions:

- Where one arrangement outranks another in some element of cost or benefit, what is the size of the difference?
- Where an arrangement is ranked high in one element and low in another, is there some common measure that can be applied to the elements so that the manager can reach a single net judgment?

Some of the factors that lead to the rankings in the table are self-evident. Take, for instance, the question of capital commitment and management commitment on

TABLE 4-1. Costs and Benefits of Operating Abroad Through Licensing Arrangements, Joint Ventures and Other Alliances, and Wholly Owned Affiliates

	Licensing Arrangement	Joint Venture and Other Alliances	Wholly Owned Affiliates
Costs			
1. Cost of capital commitment	1	2	3
2. Cost of management commitment	1	2	3
3. Restraint on strategic and operational flexibility of rest of multinational firm	3	2	1
4. Cost of enforcing terms of arrangement	3	?	1
Benefits			
1. Amount of payment to parent	?	?	?
2. Stability of payment to parent	3	?	?
3. Political security for parent	3	2	1
4. Contribution to parent's store of knowledge	1	2	3
5. Contribution to value of parent's trademark and trade name	1	2	3
6. Future availability of local outlet to parent	1	2	3

the part of the foreign parent. When a license is all that ties the local enterprise to the foreigner, the foreigner ordinarily supplies very little capital or management. Similarly, joint-venture alliances generally draw less capital and management from the foreign parent than does a wholly owned subsidiary. The order of ranking for capital commitment and management commitment, therefore, is usually straightforward.

In terms of flexibility, however, the licensing agreement generally imposes a heavier cost on the foreign licensor than do most ownership arrangements. Whereas a foreign owner may be able to reshuffle its arrangements with a subsidiary as circumstances require, the rights and obligations of an independent licensor and licensee presumably cannot be changed without an arm's length renegotiation. In the licensing case, for instance, the foreign licensor may be irrevocably tied during the life of the license to using the licensee as its instrumentality for serving some given market. In arrangements in which the parent is linked to the local venture by ownership ties, the capacity to redefine the function of the local venture from time to time is likely to be greater.

Another cost of considerable importance is that of enforcing the terms of the arrangement. In the case of licensing, there is often a risk that the licensee will breach some of the provisions of the agreement, such as provisions that impose geographical limitations on sales, that require quality control, or that require the licensee to purchase intermediate products from the licensor.

Table 4-1 gauges not only costs but also benefits. A priori, nothing can be said as to the relative amounts of payment to parents associated with the various alternatives; a licensing agreement that called for payments of, say, 3 or 4 percent of gross sales may yield just as much revenue to the licensor as an equity commitment. The return would presumably be less on a joint venture than on a wholly owned subsidiary, at least in absolute amounts, but it could be more or less than the income from a licensing agreement.

The question of risk and stability of payment, however, is more determinate. The stability associated with the anticipated income flows is ordinarily higher for the licensing arrangement because such arrangements generally provide for payments that are fixed in amount or are a function of production volume, rather than for payments that are a function of profits. Thus, in the licensing arrangement, the multinational bears less of the risk associated with low or uneven profits; on the other hand, it stands to make less if the project turns out to be especially profitable.

The other rankings almost speak for themselves, although none is altogether beyond question. The table assumes (despite some occasional evidence to the contrary) that licensing arrangements involve less political risk than ownership arrangements. It assumes, too, that the existence of a wholly owned subsidiary allows the foreign firm to capture certain other advantages that are not so surely available through other types of links. If the link is with a wholly owned subsidiary, the knowledge that foreign firms pick up about the local market, the spread of their trade names in the country, or the access they gain to local distribution systems will usually be greater than if the arrangement entails a lesser degree of control.

Although the cost-benefit calculations suggested by Table 4-1 are difficult to make, the job is rendered a little easier by the fact that they vary predictably according to certain explicit conditions. These conditions have been carefully studied in connection with the choice between joint-venture alliances and wholly owned subsidiaries.

- Some countries regard local ownership as an important national objective. Western European governments, though nervous about the possibility of foreign ownership in some industries, are less concerned about the question than are some other governments. India, for example, at least until the early 1990s, strongly preferred licensing to ownership and joint ventures to wholly owned subsidiaries. Accordingly, in some countries, managers may not have the full range of choices suggested by Table 4-1; or, if they do, they may have to weigh the differences in political risk associated with the various alternatives against the differences in the other costs and benefits listed in the table.
- Local partners in some countries are in a position to provide local capital and management more readily than are local partners in others. A foreign parent that is in a joint venture with a local partner located in Europe, Japan, or the United States may very well be receiving a genuine contribution of capital, management, or information; in Haiti or Ecuador, however, tangible contributions from local partners are less likely.

Although some of the factors that determine the manager's choice may be imposed by the circumstances in the country where the operations occur, the manager's choice is likely to be determined even more strongly by the kinds of resources that are already available to the firm and the kind of strategy that the firm is pursuing. A few key propositions that have emerged from the studies so far offer some guides to an optimum strategy from the manager's point of view:

- Firms that have had long overseas experience generally prefer wholly owned subsidiaries to joint ventures and any kind of subsidiary to a license. It may not be the experience itself that causes this tilt, however. Instead, firms with overseas experience may also have readier access to the information, skills, and capital needed to launch a foreign subsidiary. Although local partners in a joint venture may provide information, skills, and capital, the implicit cost to the parent of acquiring these resources from a local partner may be relatively high. In the terms of Table 4-1, the rankings assigned to capital commitment and management commitment might still be right; but the absolute size of the differences might be smaller for the more experienced firms, thereby tipping the preference of the firm toward a wholly owned subsidiary.

- Where an effective strategy demands that the firm should be able to exercise a high degree of control over its foreign affiliate, the presence of others participating in the direction of the affiliate will be counted as a negative factor, especially if the interests of the others threaten at times to be adverse to those of the parent. Although a licensee or a local partner is likely to share many common interests with the foreign parent, there are also issues over which their interests may conflict. Accordingly, where control is important, a wholly owned subsidiary will be preferred.

Principles such as these suggest that, from the viewpoint of the multinational enterprise, the optimum ownership arrangement may vary from one foreign affiliate to the next. Moreover, from the viewpoint of the multinational enterprise, the optimum ownership arrangement for an affiliate with a given function in a given country may vary over time. When foreign affiliates are set up in protected markets, separated from world competition by high import and high export barriers, a subsidiary's operations may be relatively isolated, bearing very few links to a global strategy. In such cases, joint ventures (or licenses) may not be confining. But as the barriers come down, the utility of the original joint-venture choice is often questioned. The introduction of the North American Free Trade Agreement (NAFTA), for instance, has provoked a scramble among U.S.-based multinationals as they have reconsidered whether the various licenses and joint ventures they set up in Mexico in years past make sense in light of liberalized trade and investment that NAFTA promises to bring.

In any event, in view of these large uncertainties it is hardly surprising that most firms do not appear to rely on formal calculations of anticipated costs and benefits when they choose among their alternatives, preferring instead to use other decision rules as a basis for their choice see (Box 4-2).

BOX 4-2. OOPS! I THOUGHT ALL DOWNSTREAM ACTIVITIES WERE CANDIDATES FOR "DIFFERENTIATED LINKS"

Memorandum

To: Messrs. Vernon, Wells, and Rangan
From: Amanda T. Nicolaidis, C. E. O., Healthcare Products, Inc.
Subject: Your advice on organization

Thanks so much for the guidance you provided in our seminar on "Managing the Multinational Enterprise." I wonder, however, if we will ever really have the last word.

Let me give you a problem to think about, one that has arisen inside my own company. (To protect the innocent, I have altered the names and places.)

One of our hottest items is an antidepressant drug, Omnibel, which has patent and trade name protection in most major markets of the world. Nevertheless, its therapeutic properties are not unlike those of other antidepressants, with which it is in direct competition. Following your sage advice on differentiated structures, we have placed marketing and pricing strategies in foreign countries in the hands of our packaging subsidiaries located in each of these countries. And we reward the marketing departments in each country in part on the basis of their gross sales in that country.

Our subsidiary in the prosperous nation of Argilia was approached by the ministry of public health of that country to make an offer for the sale of Omnibel, to be used in the extensive network of hospitals and clinics that the government maintains. Up to that time, practically all of its sales of Omnibel had been in relatively small quantities to the private distribution network in the country. In her eagerness to get the business, fearing strong competition from other antidepressants, our marketing manager in Argilia offered a price well below any that had previously been offered in world markets.

Unbeknown to her, however, the various national ministries of public health in the region regularly exchanged information on the prices at which they purchased their drugs. Suddenly we were confronted with demands from four other countries to renegotiate our prices for Omnibel and to make an adjustment for previous sales of the product to the public health ministries in those countries.

How do you suggest we organize ourselves to deal with this kind of problem?

Suggested Reading

BARTLETT, CHRISTOPHER A., and SUMANTRA GHOSHAL. *Managing Across Borders: The Transnational Solution.* Boston: Harvard Business School Press, 1989.

CONTRACTOR, FAROK, and PETER LORANGE (eds.). *Cooperative Strategies in International Business.* Lexington, Mass.: Lexington Books, 1988.

EGELHOFF, WILLIAM G. *Organizing the Multinational Enterprise: An Information-Processing Perspective.* Cambridge, Mass.: Ballinger, 1988.

GHOSHAL, SUMANTRA, and NITIN NOHRIA. "Internal Differentiation Within Multinational Corporations." *Strategic Management Journal,* 10 (1989), 323–337.

GOMES-CASSERES, BENJAMIN. "Group Versus Group: How Alliance Networks Compete." *Harvard Business Review,* July–August (1994), 62–74.

GOMES-CASSERES, BENJAMIN. *Collective Competition: International Alliances in High Technology.* Cambridge, Mass.: Harvard University Press.

HEDLUND, GUNNAR. "The Hypermodern MNC—A Heterarchy?" *Human Resource Management,* 25, no. 1, (Spring 1986), 9–25.

YOSHINO, MICHAEL Y. and U. SRINIVASA RANGAN. *Strategic Alliances.* Boston: Harvard Business School Press, 1995.

CHAPTER 5

National Units in Multinational Networks

As we saw in Chapter 2, a multinational enterprise is composed of a number of corporations or branches situated in different countries, bound together by a common parent, a common overall strategy, and a common use of resources. At the same time, the managers of a multinational enterprise constantly find themselves obliged to treat their business as if it were made up of national units, however artificial the breakup may be. Thus, the multinational enterprise is engaged in constant efforts to reconcile its identity as an integral enterprise with its identity as a series of national units.

National Boundaries and Multinational Operations

In response to the requirements of a common strategy, the units of a multinational enterprise are engaged in a variety of transfers among themselves. Figure 5-1 portrays in a schematic way some of the transfers among such units, which characteristically come about as follows:

- A given unit of the enterprise may specialize in the production of some intermediate material, component, or final product on behalf of the enterprise as a whole. Transfers are dubbed "sales" and ordinarily bear a transfer price, even when both sides of the transaction fall under the general direction and control of a single global product manager and lie within the ambit of the same profit center in the enterprise.

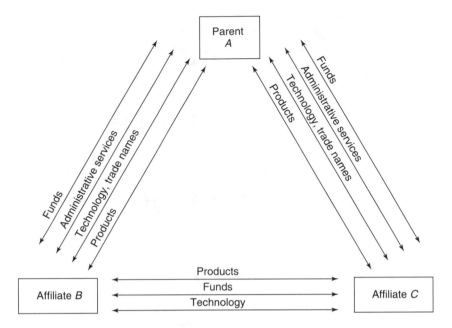

Figure 5-1   Typical Interaffiliate Transfers in a Multinational Enterprise

- Another unit may specialize in research and development for the benefit of the multinational enterprise as a whole. At some point, transfers of patent rights and know-how must take place between affiliates. These transfers are often regarded as sales, and the payments generally appear as "royalties" or administrative charges.
- The cash generated in some units of the enterprise can sometimes be used more efficiently in other units. Accordingly, cash transfers are arranged. If the desired cash flows do not take place in the form of interest, dividends, royalties, charges, or payment for goods, they are generally arranged as loans and advances or as purchases of equity among the affiliates.

For a multinational enterprise that is composed of a parent and wholly owned subsidiaries, it may not be immediately apparent why any of these internal transfers should be explicitly identified and priced. The transfers, after all, are taking place within the bounds of one integral business unit and under the direction of the same management. There are at least four reasons why such explicit identification and labeling are required. (1) There is a need to develop a separate figure to show income for each affiliate, to serve as the basis for taxation in each national jurisdiction. (2) There is a need to measure the performance of various parts of the enterprise for internal control purposes, such as evaluating and motivating managers, and generating yardsticks to guide managers in routine decisions or in decisions about added investment. (3) There may be a need to establish a profit figure in a foreign subsidiary because a portion of the ownership of the subsidiary is held by some outside interest, such as a local partner. (4) There may be a need to report the operations of parts of the enterprise for purposes other than taxation, including those concerned with credit, import licensing, price control, or disclosure to the public.

Because several objectives exist, an inescapable problem arises: From the viewpoint of the firm, no one set of prices is optimal for all these purposes. The transfer prices that bring taxes down to the minimum level permitted by law are not necessarily those that best measure the performance of each affiliate. The figures that are useful for measuring performance for internal control purposes are not usually appropriate for reporting the firm's operations to stockholders or to public authorities.

The problem is not generally one of deception or avoidance, as is so often supposed. Although deception or avoidance may sometimes occur, the main problem is that there is no such thing as a wholly objective description of the operations of a firm and no such thing as a description optimal for all purposes. For example, if a unit in a multinational enterprise produces components for others in the same network, and if the unit has surplus capacity, a transfer price that reflects only marginal costs might be appropriate for sending the right price signals to other units in the enterprise and for maximizing the network's profits. But a tax authority in the country of the supplying unit is likely to view that price as wholly inappropriate, insisting that the price charged by the supplying unit should reflect full cost.

Although taxation is only one of the factors that will influence the way a multinational enterprise distributes its income among its subsidiaries, it is so important that it deserves special attention.

Issues in Taxation

Minimizing Taxes

Managers of multinational enterprises share with most of the human race a common reaction to the problem of taxation: Where choices exist in the law, they tend to elect the course that reduces their tax obligations. Multinational enterprises, however, confront some opportunities and some risks in this regard that do not normally apply to national enterprises:

- Affiliates that perform certain specialized functions, such as the distribution of products and licensing of patents, may be just as readily placed in one country as another without greatly affecting their efficiency. In such cases, countries with low tax levies or none at all, such as Bermuda and Luxembourg, have a special attraction.

- When a multinational enterprise sells a big-ticket item, such as a mainframe computer or a steel mill, several different units of the enterprise may be involved in the development, production, and installation of the product sold, and it is often not clear which unit of a multinational enterprise should be credited with the sale. Identifying the seller is even more difficult when a multinational service company, such as an advertising agency, a management consulting firm, or a bank sells its intangible service to a multinational client for its global use.

- When one affiliate provides capital to another, the multinational enterprise is often free to choose whether the capital should be advanced in the form of debt or of equity. Debt entails subsequent payments in the form of interest; equity, in the form of dividends. The choice generally affects the paying affiliate's taxable income and sometimes the receiving affiliate's taxable income as well.

- In the transfer of most products and services between affiliates, no "true" measure of value exists, because there are no arm's length prices to provide guidance. In such cases, the manager is not greatly inhibited in choosing a transfer price, and the choice can be influenced by its effects on the firm's tax bill.

- Finally, even where a price exists that is unequivocally arm's length in nature, local authorities may not be willing to accept it, on the grounds that the market is a monopoly or otherwise imperfect.

Moreover, multinational enterprises are exposed to the risk that the profits of their foreign subsidiaries may be subjected to double taxation—once in the foreign country where the profits arise, and again at home when the profits are remitted to the parent. To deal with that possibility:

Some countries, including Germany and the United States, impose taxes on the income earned abroad by their enterprises but offer relief from double taxation by allowing credits for income taxes that have already been paid to other governments on such foreign income.

Some countries, such as Sweden, tax the foreign income of their firms and do not provide relief from double taxation in all cases. Instead, they rely on bilateral tax treaties to establish relief on a country-by-country basis. Since treaties may establish different approaches, the taxpayer's obligation to its home government with regard to income earned abroad may vary according to the source of that income. In the absence of a treaty, the home tax will be applied on all income remaining after the host country has imposed its tax.

Another approach, found in Dutch law, relies on a proportionality principle. The parent's tax liability at home is based on its worldwide consolidated income. But that income is divided into two parts: income originating abroad and entitled to exemption, and other income. The parent's tax liability is then reduced in proportion to the share of worldwide income that is entitled to exemption. In other words, if one-third of the parent's total worldwide income is entitled to exemption, then the domestic tax liability of the parent corporation is reduced by one-third.

Still other countries deal with the double-taxation problem simply by exempting their corporations from income taxation on income earned abroad.

U.S. Tax Law

Two features of U.S. tax law deserve special mention: the handling of the double-taxation problem; and the handling of problems in transfer pricing.

Double taxation.   As we have already noted, U.S. tax law is built on two general principles:

- That the U.S. taxpayer's global income, not its U.S. income alone, is subject to U.S. taxation.
- That, in order to avoid double taxation, the U.S. government credits the taxpayer for income taxes already paid to foreign governments on income earned abroad.

However, where the income is earned abroad, as in the case of the profits earned by a subsidiary, the U.S. parent has no obligation to pay taxes to the U.S. government on that income until the subsidiary has actually declared a dividend to the parent. That critical point has the effect of distinguishing the profits generated by a branch sharply from the profits generated by a subsidiary. For under U.S. law, a branch is simply a part of the parent enterprise and has no separate juridical personality. Accordingly, the parent "receives" the branch's income as soon as it is earned.

For the manager, this distinction presents both problems and opportunities. For instance, a parent company may anticipate that there will be losses in a new overseas operation for the first few years. If the overseas operation is a subsidiary, then there is usually no way for the parent to use that loss as an offset against its own profits in the United States. If, however, the overseas operation is nothing more than a branch of the parent establishment and therefore a part of the parent, then the loss will offset income earned elsewhere inside the parent company and will reduce the aggregate tax liability of the parent to the U.S. government.

Contrariwise, where profits are anticipated, the U.S. parent usually finds it advantageous, from the point of view of taxes, to incorporate overseas establishments as separate entities under the laws of the countries in which they operate. These subsidiaries, of course, are obliged to pay taxes to their host governments (for that matter, so are the branches of U.S. parents, as a rule). But because the subsidiary is a separate legal entity from the parent, the parent can defer paying U.S. taxes on that income, assuming any are due, until it has received the income in the form of dividends.

This approach has some interesting consequences. One of these arises when a foreign government grants a "tax holiday" to a selected enterprise. When such an exemption is granted to the subsidiary of a U.S. parent, the exemption has the effect, in many cases, of reducing the size of the foreign tax credit that its U.S. parent will eventually be entitled to take in the United States. Therefore, U.S. investors who repatriate the earnings of their foreign subsidiaries acquired during a tax holiday may gain little or nothing from the holiday. Other countries have different rules. Japan, for example, will in many cases grant its enterprises tax credits for taxes that other governments have forgiven under the terms of a tax holiday.

Many complexities and technicalities surround the calculation of the U.S. tax credit. Ultimately, the calculation must be left to the tax experts. But certain concepts are sufficiently important to merit special attention from the general manager.

- A U.S. taxpayer that has subsidiaries in more than one foreign country must usually pool its income from its various foreign subsidiaries, together with the tax credits applicable to such income, as if they came from a single foreign source. Yet, for certain kinds of businesses such pooling is not allowed, particularly in various stages of the petroleum industry. One result of pooling is that surplus tax credits arising in one foreign country are applied to reduce the U.S. tax liability on income from another foreign country.
- U.S. tax authorities reserve the right to recalculate the profit earned by a foreign subsidiary according to the rules of U.S. tax accounting. If the recalculated profit of the subsidiary is less than that on which the foreign subsidiary paid its foreign income tax, the U.S. tax credit is appropriately reduced. Particularly important for many U.S.-based multinational firms has been the U.S. tax authorities' practice of allocating a portion of the parent's research and development expenses to foreign subsidiaries. The result has been to lower the foreign subsidiaries' income and hence the allowable tax credits in the United States based on such income.
- Foreign taxes that qualify as income taxes are designated by U.S. tax authorities on a case-by-case basis in accordance with certain criteria. But ambiguous cases often arise. For instance, when a U.S. firm operating under a management contract receives payment in kind, such as crude oil or copper ore, the implicit tax in such payments may not be eligible as an income tax.

The U.S. government has taken various steps to place limits on the ability of U.S. firms to avoid the payment of U.S. taxes on profitable overseas operations. Some of the most important have been the limits placed on the use of foreign subsidiaries as tax havens.

As was pointed out earlier, a U.S. parent company normally does not incur a U.S. tax liability on income from a foreign subsidiary until after the subsidiary has declared dividends. One way by which the parent can avoid receiving dividends in the United States is to create and interpose a foreign holding company, preferably situated in a country whose income tax rates are very low, such as Panama or the Grand

Caymans. Intermediaries such as these can receive royalties, interest, and dividends from foreign subsidiaries, and can channel such funds to other foreign subsidiaries in need of financing. In 1962, however, the U.S. government drastically reduced the attractiveness of such foreign holding companies by making the income of such companies immediately subject to U.S. taxation.

U.S. tax law has also been used in ways that sometimes encourage the use of foreign subsidiaries, notably when such subsidiaries would be helpful in promoting U.S. exports. Under U.S. law, a U.S. taxpayer may create a corporation in a foreign country to perform specified economic functions with respect to exporting from the United States, such as advertising, invoicing, and collections. If the corporation so created meets various criteria, a specified fraction of its income is exempt from U.S. tax, even when remitted to the U.S. parent. (This tax feature is widely used by other countries as well.)

Transfer price guidance.   Like practically all other national tax systems in the world, U.S. tax law is built on the assumption that, with enough analysis and good-will, the U.S. taxpayer can allocate every sale unerringly to the appropriate unit of a multinational enterprise, and can determine the "true" transfer price for every product and service transferred between the taxpayer and an affiliated unit. On the problem of allocating sales among the units of the multinational enterprise, U.S. authorities offer little explicit guidance to the taxpayer. On the fixing of transfer prices, however, the taxpayer is offered numerous rules, guidelines, and procedures, all aimed at reducing the ambiguities created by the basic premise of the law.

The authorities, for instance, recognize various estimates of the "true" price as legitimate (see Table 5-1):

- A price in a comparable transaction undertaken at arm's length (comparable uncontrolled price, or CUP).
- The resale-minus method, applicable for cases in which the taxpayer transfers a product to a foreign subsidiary, which then sells to an uncontrolled buyer, thus establishing a resale price.
- The cost-plus method, based on production cost estimates plus a reasonable markup.
- The "fourth method," that is, anything reasonable that the tax authorities have previously reviewed and accepted.

Following Thomas Schelling's dictum that, where all else fails, a 50–50 split will seem reasonable, the authorities are even prepared to accept a 50–50 split of profits in some circumstances as a reasonable way to determine the transfer price.

In 1986, the U.S. Congress addressed the especially knotty problem of determining transfer prices for intangibles, having in mind particularly the license fees and royalty payments that U.S. taxpayers were making and receiving in transactions with

TABLE 5-1.   Alternative Methods Used in Transfer Pricing Cases (percentages of total cases)

Report	CUP	Resale-minus Method	Cost-plus Method	"Fourth Method"
1972 Conference Board Report	28	13	23	36
1973 Treasury Report	20	11	27	40
1981 General Accounting Office Report	15	14	26	47
1984 Internal Revenue Service survey	41	7	7	45
1987 Internal Revenue Service survey	32	8	24	36

CUP = Comparable uncontrolled price method

Source: U.S. Department of the Treasury. *A Study of Intercompany Pricing.* Washington, DC: U.S. Department of the Treasury, 1988.

their foreign affiliates. Thereupon, a new statutory standard was created, namely, that the transfer price in such cases should be "commensurate with" the income generated by those intangibles. Then, in 1994, to give some meaning to that amorphous yardstick, the tax authorities once again proposed a series of approaches. These largely repeated the standards proposed for products, beginning with the usual CUP, and were supplemented by elaborate efforts to indicate how the CUP might be approximated. However, it was plain that, in the end, the "fourth method" would be applied extensively. The estimate of one industry source, reported in the *New York Times,* was that the new approach "was liable to produce chaos," as tax disputes increased and revenue disappeared.

Despite the giant uncertainties that the multinational enterprise confronts in apportioning its profits among the various national taxing jurisdictions, there is little likelihood that the U.S. government or other governments will provide much relief on this front. If any one government were to attempt unilaterally to use global profits as a point of departure, for instance, multinational enterprises would be exposed to the risk of double taxation. And if several governments were to move simultaneously in that direction, the move would require an intergovernmental apparatus for determining global profits and allocating them fairly among the taxing jurisdictions involved, an apparatus that shows no signs of coming into existence. Accordingly, multinational enterprises and their governments are doomed to a continuing struggle over the allocation of their profits.

Measuring Performance

It would be a staggering coincidence if the figures that had been generated for tax purposes inside the multinational enterprise served equally well to measure performance for other purposes, such as satisfying the disclosure requirements of the accounting profession or measuring the performance of managers. For these purposes, changes in exchange rates create a particularly important challenge.

Foreign-Exchange Exposures

Any business manager, whether or not in a multinational network, may be found from time to time paying or receiving funds in a "foreign" currency, that is, a currency different from the one in which the manager's unit ordinarily conducts its business. In that case, the commitment is likely to generate special problems.

- A firm in Leeds, England, for instance, may borrow U.S. dollars, use these dollars to buy sterling, and pay its local bills with the sterling proceeds. Problems arise because the value of the pound sterling may vary from month to month or even day to day in relation to the U.S. dollar. Accordingly, the borrower in Leeds may find that the repayment of its dollar debt 60 days later requires more sterling than it received at the outset. If no prior provision is made for the contingency, the firm in Leeds will find that it has suffered a loss in sterling.
- By the same token, an exporter of machinery from Pittsburgh who accepts a 60-day note from a Paris buyer denominated in francs may find that the dollar value of the note has changed when the time for payment arrives. (For an indication of what firms may do to forestall such losses, see Chapter 6.)

Losses or gains from foreign-exchange variations affect the units of a multinational enterprise just as they do any national enterprise. At times, however, in measuring the performance of a manager of a unit of a multinational enterprise, it may be necessary to consider whether the policies that generate gains or losses of this sort should be counted as part of the manager's responsibilities.

- The interests of the enterprise may, for instance, suggest that a subsidiary in a weak currency area that has borrowed from the parent should denominate its debt obligation in the parent's currency; yet this might be quite contrary to the interests of the local manager.
- At times, too, the managers of two different affiliates of the same multinational enterprise may have sharply conflicting interests—one wanting a prospective payment to be denominated in one currency, and the other in another currency.
- Furthermore, there may be savings to the enterprise in the form of lower hedging costs if obligations in a particular currency in one subsidiary can be offset by expected receipts in the currency in another subsidiary.

Such decisions, therefore, are usually handled by delegation to some higher center. When they are, the problem of measuring the performance of individual managers takes on an added difficulty.

Another issue created by variations in the value of currencies is of special importance to the multinational enterprise: As values change, how should the enterprise as a whole and its constituent parts located in various currency areas record their assets and liabilities? There are two aspects to this issue—the conversion problem and the translation problem.

The *conversion problem* is simply an extension of the issue already discussed. Any firm at all, whether in Leeds, Pittsburgh, or Paris, will find itself adjusting the value of assets or liabilities already on its books whenever those assets or liabilities are not denominated in its own currency. Accordingly, if our Pittsburgh exporter were obliged to produce a balance sheet at a time when it was carrying accounts receivable denominated in francs, the dollar value of the franc account would have to be calculated on an up-to-date basis.

The *translation problem*, however, involves wholly different issues, which have embroiled the accounting profession in the United States in acrimonious debate with the managers of multinational enterprises. The problem arises from the fact that each unit of a multinational enterprise ordinarily does its business in the currency of the country in which it is located. Local currency is received from local sales, and local currency is used to pay local taxes, meet local payrolls, and buy local supplies. Accordingly, the assets and liabilities as well as the income and outgo of the subsidiaries are commonly denominated in a currency that differs from that of the parent. When the parent is faced with the need to consolidate the statements of the various units into a single statement for the multinational system as a whole, the existence of many different currencies can create considerable difficulties.

Picture a specific situation. The country is Italy in the year 1994. The value of the lira in relation to the dollar has been falling steadily, while internal prices in terms of the lira have been going up continuously. There is every expectation that more of the same is in the offing. A parent company located in the United States is assessing the implications of the change in the value of the lira upon its investment and is wondering what adjustments ought to be made upon its books to reflect the changes.

Suppose, then, that the manager of the parent company, being innocent of accounting-translation practices, simply requests his or her staff to undertake two groups of projections for the years ahead: (1) a projection of the balance sheet and profit-and-loss statement for the Italian subsidiary, denominated in lire; and (2) a projection of the net flow of earnings to the parent across the lira–dollar exchange, taking fully into account the probability of a continued decline in the value of the lira.

The staff, of course, could make all sorts of assumptions about price trends, projecting item by item the prices of goods and services that the company would have to buy, and item by item the prices of goods it would have for sale. By estimating cash needs and cash flow, it could come to some kind of estimate of cash throw-off. And on given assumptions about the change in the exchange rate and the parent's policies toward the subsidiary, it could estimate the schedule of dollar yield to the parent.

Since the price relationships among different goods and services do not remain forever fixed, and since the depreciating price of foreign exchange cannot be a perfect negative image of every domestic price within an inflating economy, there is nothing foreordained about the outcome of such a calculation. It may show that the prospective inflation-with-devaluation spells trouble for the subsidiary because of a squeeze between raw material prices and sales prices and because of the need for an increase in working capital; or it may show that the inflation-with-devaluation will provide a bonanza for the subsidiary, even after due allowance is made for increased working-capital needs.

The staff, let us assume, has made its projections and has concluded that, by and large, inflation-with-devaluation will leave largely unimpaired the subsidiary's capacity to generate a net flow of dollars to the parent. Lira prices may change inside Italy, and the dollar–lira relation may change as well. But, all told, the effect of two different kinds of price changes will simply be to leave the dollar cash flow roughly where it is.

That outcome is no less plausible than any other. Table 5-2 lists the changes that occur inside the Italian subsidiary as inflation, punctuated by devaluations, takes its course. As we run down the list of effects, we realize that the net effect of inflation-with-devaluation upon the subsidiary's generation of local currency depends on the circumstances of the subsidiary. On balance, the effect may increase cash flows or diminish them. Accordingly, it is unclear whether the net flow of funds to the parent across the exchanges, that is, the flow of funds converted to the currency desired by the parent, will rise or fall. Even with periodic devaluations, the flow may well increase. This is especially likely to be the case if exports account for a large fraction of the subsidiary's sales.

Accounting Requirements

Logic is one thing and accounting requirements are another. U.S. requirements are promulgated by a private body, the Financial Accounting Standards Board (FASB), whose regulatory mandate is based on the power of accountants to grant or withhold certification. That body's requirements contain two elements:

TABLE 5-2.   Typical Effects of Inflation and Devaluation on the Italian Subsidiary

Item	Cause	Effect in Lire
Sources of funds		
Gross revenues from local sales	Inflation	Increase
Gross revenues from export sales	Devaluation	Increase
Windfall profit from non-lira assets	Devaluation	Increase
Uses of funds		
Expenditures on local materials and labor	Inflation	Increase
Expenditures on imported materials and labor	Devaluation	Increase
Taxes	Inflation or devaluation	Indeterminate
Additions to working capital	Inflation	Increase
Additions to fixed capital	Inflation or devaluation	Increase
Windfall loss from non-lira liabilities	Devaluation	Increase

- The rules specify just what exchange rates are to be used for each item in the subsidiary's balance sheet when translating the subsidiary's accounts into a consolidated systemwide report.
- If resulting dollar amounts on the asset side of the balance sheet are no longer equal to those on the liability side, as is usually the case, rules specify how such "gains" or "losses" are to be reflected in the consolidated statement of the U.S. parent.

The relevant FASB rule, so-called FASB-52, spells out two methods of translating the statements of the Italian subsidiary. The appropriate method depends on the "functional currency" of the subsidiary. The functional currency is usually the currency in which the entity normally generates and expends cash. Most frequently, the functional currency is the local currency of the country in which the subsidiary operates—the lira in the case of our Italian subsidiary. In the cases in which the foreign entity is regarded as a direct extension of the company's U.S. operations, however, the functional currency is the U.S. dollar; this would be the case for a branch that handles U.S. exports, for example. Moreover, if the subsidiary is located in a highly inflationary country such as Brazil, the translations also must be handled as if the functional currency were the U.S. dollar. Once the functional currency is determined, it is not to be changed except under special circumstances. The choice of translation method is made as follows:

- If the functional currency is the local currency, translation is made using the current-rate method.
- If the functional currency is the U.S. dollar, translation is made using the monetary-nonmonetary method.

TABLE 5-3. Translation Rates Applied to the Italian Subsidiary's Balance Sheets After Devaluation

Item	Lire per Dollar	
	Current-rate Method	Monetary-nonmonetary Method
Assets		
Cash	1,500	1,500
Accounts receivable	1,500	1,500
Inventories	1,500	Historical rates[a]
Fixed assets	1,500	Historical rates
Liabilities		
Accounts payable	1,500	1,500
Unremitted declared dividends	1,500	1,500
Long-term debt	1,500	1,500
Net worth	Historical rates	Historical rates

[a]That is, 1,000 or less.

Assume in the case of our Italian subsidiary that on December 31, just a split second before the close of business, the value of the lira had changed from L1000 = $1 to L1500 = $1. Table 5-3 lists the main items of the balance sheet, together with two sets of translations, one according to the current-rate method and the other according to the monetary-nonmonetary method.

As noted earlier, the effect of all these manipulations of lira amounts is to produce an inconsistency in the accounts of the subsidiary as they are calculated in dollars in preparation for consolidation with the accounts of the parent. This requires a balancing adjustment somewhere in the consolidated accounts. Under the current-rate method, the balancing item that results from the translation process is accumulated as a separate component of equity directly on the balance sheet. It is not reflected in an income statement until the subsidiary is sold or liquidated. Under the monetary-nonmonetary method, the balancing adjustment must be passed through the consolidated profit-and-loss statement for the current year, as it is recorded in the net worth of the firm.

Whether a positive or a negative adjustment is generated by either of these methods depends on the relative size of the items on the two sides of the balance sheet that must be evaluated by the current exchange rate. Call these items the adjustable items. The translation adjustments are as follows:

	IF ASSET ADJUSTABLES EXCEED LIABILITY ADJUSTABLES	**IF LIABILITY ADJUSTABLES EXCEED ASSET ADJUSTABLES**
If foreign currency has depreciated	Negative	Positive
If foreign currency has appreciated	Positive	Negative

Regardless of the method used to handle translation gains and losses, gains or losses from actual foreign-exchange transactions undertaken by the subsidiary are included in its current income accounts and, on translation, in the consolidated income statement of the parent. (However, gains or losses resulting from certain transactions undertaken to hedge net investments in foreign subsidiaries go directly to stockholders' equity in the consolidated balance sheet.)

A careful examination of the translation methods shown in Table 5-3 reveals one reason why the rules call for the monetary-nonmonetary method of translation when the subsidiary is operating in an inflationary environment. The alternative method would require the application of the current exchange rate to fixed assets. Since the value of fixed assets is not adjusted for inflation, a rapid devaluation would quickly erode the translated value of any fixed assets.

If the currency of a subsidiary is threatened with devaluation, the firm can take any one of several courses of action to avoid a translation loss, regardless of the translation method to be used.

- It can eliminate the risk by assuring that the asset adjustables of the subsidiary do not exceed its liability adjustables. The subsidiary, for instance, can declare dividends to the parent, thereby depleting its cash position. (You will find it useful to reconstruct the effect of various policies on the balance sheet; then, by referring back to Table 5-3, note how these maneuvers affect the translation adjustment under the two methods.)
- It can look on the threatened translation loss as requiring a hedge and can respond in the same way as a U.S. exporter who is worried about the fact that he will be paid in lire on some future date. (As noted earlier, Chapter 6 deals with such hedging techniques.)

These cautionary measures have a cost, however. Whether the cost is worth the benefit is for the manager to determine according to the circumstances of the firm. The assumption that the answer is yes, so common in many enterprises, is far from self-evident.

Note that the translation adjustments discussed in the past few pages are required of the firm only for purposes of securing the certification of public accountants. They therefore affect the firm's public statement to its stockholders. But they have no bearing on the firm's report for income tax purposes. Nor need the firm use them in its appraisal of the performance of its foreign managers or in the making of investment or operating decisions.

Appraising Managers' Performance

Enterprises that take their own certified records seriously as a basis for management control sometimes develop quite misleading impressions of how subsidiaries located in such countries are performing. In some years, prices inside the country may rise considerably while the country's exchange rate remains relatively unchanged. During these years, even though local prices and local profit margins may be rising in terms of the local currency, the translation of the results into the home currency of the parent takes place at unchanging rates. These are the bonanza years, if there are any bonanza years at all; in these years, the subsidiary's paper performance, translated into the home currency, is at its best. Then comes the devaluation. Abruptly, the less favorable rate is applied to sales and profits, and the erstwhile bonanza is suddenly seen as a disaster. Yet throughout the cycle, the local subsidiary's performance, if measured in terms that might have been applied to a production unit at home, may be quite unchanged and exemplary. Small wonder that managers of foreign subsidiaries are sometimes bewildered by the roller-coaster quality of home-office appraisals.

To prevent that result in internal evaluations, some enterprises (1) use arbitrary rates of translation for sales and profits of subsidiaries; and (2) reserve from profits, both in local currency accounts and in dollar accounts, such sums as they anticipate will have to be added to working-capital requirements as a result of the inflation. These measures are intended to distribute the impact of the inflation–devaluation process over the full period of overvaluation and undervaluation of the local currency.

Determining the Subsidiary's Contribution

There is a more basic problem, however, and it calls for a quite different type of adjustment in appraising the performance of a foreign subsidiary. In the end, every subsidiary should be judged by its contribution to the multinational enterprise as a whole, and not just by the record of the subsidiary itself. Yet, both in the internal calculations of multinational enterprises and in the external evaluations of their performance, a common tendency is to overlook the systemwide costs and benefits of the operations of any subsidiary. Fortunately, when staff work inside the multinational enterprise is based on an incomplete approach of this kind, senior managers in the enterprise, drawing on their experience, sometimes sense that the staff's seemingly refined calculations are providing the wrong answers. Top-level decisions are likely to reflect at least an intuitive appreciation of the wider effects of investment decisions.

The "ideal" solution for estimating the yield on any added investment anywhere in the multinational enterprise, therefore, involves the multinational enterprise as a whole. It requires a calculation of the incremental return to the whole multinational enterprise system, regardless of where the investment may take place. Oil companies calculating the yield on an investment in new producing wells, for instance, sometimes include a provision for the capital that will have to be invested in seemingly unprofitable downstream refining and distributing facilities to bring the oil to market. But such treatment is exceptional.

The difficulties of carrying out such an approach systematically are considerable. Many of these difficulties arise because the resources used and the benefits provided by the subsidiary are not easily priced. Table 5-4 provides a list of some difficult items.

The items listed in Table 5-4, do not, of course, wholly defy quantification. For instance, the parent's management commitment in the establishment of a foreign subsidiary could be charged on the basis of the opportunity cost to the parent that was involved in the diversion of the parent's energies. In theory, at least, if the top management of Dow Chemical were diverted from planning the expansion of a plant in Peoria because it was completely absorbed in planning the expansion of a plant in Brussels, the cost of expanding the plant in Brussels should include the profits that were foregone in Peoria. On the same principle, a parent's guarantee of funds could be carried as a running cost to the subsidiary equivalent to the increased burden, if any, that the rest of the system would have to bear by virtue of the guarantee.

Pricing of the benefits, however, presents rather more formidable difficulties. Reducing the cash flow of rivals in a foreign market is a benefit that is hard to evaluate. If the existence of a subsidiary provides assurances to affiliates that a predictable source of supply or a predictable market exists, then the affiliates are capable of planning for production on a basis that involves lower risks. The caustic soda plant operated by the chemical enterprise can plan its output against a more predictable de-

TABLE 5-4.   Resources Used and Benefits Generated by a Subsidiary
That Are Difficult to Price

Resources Used
1. Parent's management commitment in the establishment of the subsidiary and in its subsequent operation
2. Subsidiary's use of parent's guarantee in raising funds
3. Subsidiary's use of accumulated information and procedures of the enterprise
4. Subsidiary's use of trademark and trade name of the enterprise

Benefits Generated
1. Subsidiary's availability to parent and affiliates as a source of supply or as an outlet
2. Subsidiary's competitive impact on profits of rivals
3. Subsidiary's contribution to parent and affiliates of information regarding local economy or similar economies
4. Subsidiary's contribution to parent and affiliates in extending use of trademark and trade name

mand. The oil enterprise can plan its refining activities with less worry about threats to supplies. Accordingly, a subsidiary's presence may either reduce the risk to affiliates or reduce their costs, or both. But none of the factors involved is easily expressed in money terms.

The manager in the international economy will be tempted to disregard these factors in a return-on-investment calculation simply because they are so difficult to quantify. That is a temptation that should be resisted; otherwise, the investment decision may well be made on false premises.

Suggested Reading

EDEN, LORRAINE. *Taxing Multinationals: Transfer Pricing and Corporate Income Taxation in North America.* Toronto: Toronto University Press, 1995.

HUFBAUER, G. C., *U.S. Taxation of International Income.* Washington, DC: Institute for International Economics, 1992.

JARILLO, J. CARLOS, and JON I. MARTINEZ. "Different Roles for Subsidiaries: The Case of Multinational Corporations in Spain." *Strategic Management Journal*, 11 (1990), 501–512.

KOGUT, BRUCE, and NALIN KULATILAKA. "Operating Flexibility, Global Manufacturing, and the Option Value of a Multinational Network." *Management Science*, 40, no. 1 (1993), 123–139.

MARTINEZ, J. I., and J. C. JARILLO. "The Evolution of Research on Coordination Mechanisms in Multinational Corporations." *Journal of International Business Studies*, 20 (Fall 1989), 489–514.

U.S. CONGRESS, OFFICE OF TECHNOLOGY ASSESSMENT. *Multinationals and the U.S. Technology Base.* Washington, DC: U.S. Government Printing Office, September 1994.

PLASSCHAERT, SYLVAIN (ed.). *Transnational Corporations: Transfer Pricing and Taxation.* Vol. 14, U.N. Library. New York: Routledge, 1994.

CHAPTER 6

Comparing National Economies

Managers in multinational enterprises are constantly engaged in analyzing national economies, appraising their relative strengths and weaknesses. In making those analyses, the manager usually has two large questions in mind:

- When I face a competitor with a home base in another country, does the difference matter? Does a U.S.-based firm, for instance, have some distinctive advantages over a Japan-based firm?
- When I consider establishing a production facility in a given foreign country, what should I expect in the way of costs and opportunities? What are the signs, for instance, that such a facility might produce at lower cost than one presently in my enterprise network?

In either context, some basic ideas regarding the sources of the strengths and weaknesses of different national economies can create a framework for the manager's analysis.

A Variety of Approaches

Among economists, comparing the strengths and weaknesses of different countries is an old question, at least as old as Adam Smith. As is usual for two-handed economists, however, members of the profession have approached the subject on the basis of some widely different starting assumptions.

For several centuries, ever since David Ricardo made his mark on the profession, economists framed their thinking around the following query: Given the endowments of the country in natural resources, labor, and capital, what are its relative strengths and weaknesses? That query set the stage for *the doctrine of comparative advantage*, which in the nineteenth century explained to the satisfaction of all why Portugal specialized in the production of wine and Britain in the production of cloth.

More recently, however, many economists have pursued a very different question in their efforts to understand the relative strengths and weaknesses of countries. Their basic query has been: What effects do public policies have on the competitive performance of firms in a given national economy? Under that general heading, one finds numerous contributions associated with such names as Anne Krueger, Paul Krugman, Michael Porter, and Laura Tyson.

Because both approaches contribute a little to an understanding of the competitive performance of different national economies, this chapter pursues each in turn.

Comparative Advantage

The beliefs and convictions of national leaders, John Maynard Keynes reminds us, can usually be traced to the influence of professors long departed. So it is with the doctrine of comparative advantage. A centerpiece in every course on the theory of international trade, the doctrine still influences policymakers throughout the world. Indeed, some observers go so far as to attribute the liberal trade policies of Mexico and Argentina in the mid-1990s to the Ec-101 courses that so many of their leaders took at Yale, Chicago, Harvard, Berkeley, and Penn 20 years earlier.

Our reasons for dwelling on the comparative advantage doctrine here are twofold: first, because the doctrine may provide glimpses of the real world to managers; and second, because it may help managers understand some of the underlying convictions of the public policymakers they face.

The theory of comparative advantage provides the bedrock for estimating the relative advantages in a given country for the production of a specified product or service that is tradable on world markets. Although the starting assumptions of the theory are narrow and unreal in various respects, the final implications of the theory for trade in goods cannot be disregarded.

One way to develop an understanding of the theory is to trace through a simple example.

Picture the United States and Mexico, each with its supply of land, labor, and capital. Imagine that each is producing only two products, cotton and cars. The United States is more fortunate than Mexico, being blessed with natural resources and an industrial history that allows it to produce both cotton and cars far more efficiently than Mexico. When a production unit (some given mixture of capital, labor, and land) is put to work in the United States, therefore, it generally produces both more cotton and more cars than a production unit would produce in Mexico.

At this point, we may be tempted to conclude that it makes no sense for an enterprise to produce anything in Mexico. The physical superiority of the United States in the two products is likely to suggest that producers in the United States would be wise to do all their producing at home. But a moment's reflection will indicate that this is a fallacy. There is a well-known corporate lawyer on Wall Street whose legal skills and legal fees are among the highest in the profession. At the same time, he is a superb house painter, capable of doing interiors far more swiftly and efficiently than any available painter in the business. Like the United States, therefore, he excels at two lines—in his case, at the law and at house painting. Yet he has long since learned that it makes no sense for him to paint his own house. Instead he hires painters, even though they are slower and less efficient than he. In effect, although he is an outstanding painter and an outstanding lawyer, he "exports" his legal services, relying on the high price it can command, and he "imports" his painting needs.

This exchange seems to make sense; intuitively, one can accept it as wise. Now, let us return to the United States-Mexico cotton–cars case to trace out the arithmetic that supports the same kind of conclusion in that case.

In Table 6-1, the assumption is that the United States and Mexico have not yet discovered each other's existence. Each, in isolation, is producing and consuming its own cotton and cars. Assume that each country has the same number of production units to begin with and, as before, that the United States is capable of producing more cotton per production unit and more cars per production unit than Mexico. Let each country have 10,000 production units. One production unit yields, say, 10 bales of cotton in the United States and 8 in Mexico. And one production unit yields, say, 6 cars in the United States and 2 in Mexico. Table 6-1 summarizes various production possibilities that the United States and Mexico have available.

The reader will observe that one pair of the cotton–cars figures for each country carries an asterisk (*). This is the pair of production possibilities that it is assumed each country has in fact chosen. For their own reasons, the people of the United States have chosen to produce and consume 25,000 bales of cotton and 45,000 cars, while the Mexicans have elected a combination of 40,000 bales of cotton and 10,000 cars.

Now let us suppose that the United States, playing the role of rich lawyer who cannot afford to spend his time on house painting, decides to concentrate all its production units in the activity it does best and to trade off its surplus for the things it

TABLE 6-1.   Production Possibilities of the United States and Mexico[a]

Use of Production Units	United States		Mexico	
	Cotton (000 bales)	Cars (000)	Cotton (000 bales)	Cars (000)
10,000 in cotton, 0 in cars	100	0	80	0
7,500 in cotton, 2,500 in cars	75	15	60	5
5,000 in cotton, 5,000 in cars	50	30	40	10
2,500 in cotton, 7,500 in cars	25	45	20	15
0 in cotton, 10,000 in cars	0	60	0	20

[a]Each country contains 10,000 production units.

needs. What does the United States do best? Table 6-1 suggests the answer. The table not only shows that the United States produces both cars and cotton more efficiently than Mexico, but it also shows that the advantage in cars (6:2) is larger than its cotton advantage (10:8). To state the same proposition the other way around, Mexico's cotton disadvantage is less than its cars disadvantage. Comparatively speaking, the United States' advantage is greater in cars than in cotton, while Mexico's disadvantage is less in cotton than in cars.

Then let the United States specialize fully in cars and Mexico fully in cotton. If that were to happen, the two countries would have both more cotton and more cars to divide up between them. In isolation, as Table 6-1 shows, their combined production is only 65,000 bales of cotton and 55,000 cars. But with each specializing in what it does best, their combined production will be 80,000 bales of cotton and 60,000 cars. Then one can conceive of a pattern of production and trade like that envisaged in Table 6-2.

Observe the final consumption patterns as a result of specialization and trade. Mexico is now consuming 50,000 bales of cotton and 12,000 cars instead of the 40,000 bales and 10,000 cars it consumed when in isolation. The United States, meanwhile, is also doing better in all products: under the regime of specialization and trade, it is consuming 30,000 bales of cotton and 48,000 cars, as against only 25,000 bales and 45,000 cars in isolation.

All that has been illustrated so far is the possibility that, under certain conditions, international trade may turn out to benefit both parties. Although this is a modest conclusion, it is also a powerful one, of which all countries are acutely conscious. Neither the most efficient country nor the least efficient feels altogether free to abandon the search for that hypothetical advantage. Accordingly, the impulse to open up the economy to foreign trade is never wholly lacking among government policymakers.

When policymakers succumb to that impulse, as has typically been the case in the 1990s, comparative advantage will play a major role in determining what products can efficiently be produced in the country that has been opened up. To see why, let us introduce prices and exchange rates into the discussion.

As a first step, let us assume that the production units in both countries are

TABLE 6-2.   The United States and Mexico in Specialization and Trade

	United States			Mexico		
	Produces	Trades (Imports + Exports−)	Consumes	Produces	Trades (Imports + Exports−)	Consumes
Cotton (000 bales)	0	+30	30	80	−30	50
Cars (000)	60	−12	48	0	+12	12

being paid in a single currency, say, U.S. dollars. Obviously, it makes no sense to assume that the production units of both countries will command the same price. Intuition urges that the U.S. production unit, being more productive, will be paid more for its work. A U.S. production unit produces 10 bales of cotton to the Mexican figure of 8; hence, it might be valued at 125 percent of the Mexican unit by this measure. And a U.S. production unit produces 6 cars to the Mexican output of 2; this suggests a value of 300 percent for the U.S. unit in comparison to the Mexican.

Suppose, then, we strike a value of 250 percent for the U.S. unit, that is, a figure somewhere between the indicated limits. If Mexican production units are paid the equivalent of $1.00, then U.S. units might be paid $2.50. At those levels of payment, the prices of cotton and cars prevailing in the two countries, just before they begin to trade, are those shown in the upper half of Table 6-3.

The upper half of the table portrays a situation in which two-way trade is occurring. Because the U.S. production units are being paid more than Mexican units, Mexico is able to offer an attractive cotton price to U.S. buyers. But despite the higher payment to U.S. production units, U.S. sellers are still able to offer an attractive car price to Mexico. The willingness of Mexico's production units to accept a price that reflects their relative inefficiency is what keeps Mexico's cotton price competitive. So two-way trade is possible. And the pattern suggested in Table 6-2, or something very much like it, is not foreclosed.

This simple model suggests a number of things about the real world:

- As long as a country contains a fixed amount of production units, it cannot hope to excel in all products. Here we have a glimpse of the problems of countries such as Venezuela and Zambia. In these cases, the efficiency with which they

TABLE 6-3.   Payments and Prices in the United States and Mexico in Equilibrium and Disequilibrium

	United States	Mexico
In Equilibrium		
Payment per production unit	$2.50	$1.00
Cotton—bales per unit	10	8
cost per bale	$0.250	$0.125
Cars—number per unit	6	2
cost per car	$0.417	$0.500
In Disequilibrium		
Payment per production unit	$2.50	$2.50
Cotton—bales per unit	10	8
cost per bale	$0.250	$0.312
Cars—number per unit	6	2
cost per car	$0.417	$1.250

produce oil and copper, respectively, exceeds the efficiency with which they produce manufactured goods, at least under current circumstances. As a result, they are pushed back to specializing in their leading export and are handicapped in their efforts to diversify their respective economies.

- As long as a country contains a fixed amount of production units, it cannot decree higher rewards for those units, such as by arbitrarily raising the price for labor, without moving into disequilibrium. If such demands were made and granted in the case of Mexico, as the lower half of Table 6-3 indicates, the price of both cotton and cars would be higher in Mexico than in the United States: that is, Mexico would have priced itself out of the market.

Even though the doctrine of comparative advantage builds on premises that are crude and oversimple, it provides hints of the behavior of the real world that are often quite consistent with reality. In general, the factors of production of any nation tend to be compensated at a rate, relative to other countries, that roughly reflects their efficiency relative to those other countries. The relation is not perfect, nor need it be. But in general, when a country's performance is grossly out of line, some kind of disequilibrium sets in.

In Chapter 8 we shall be exploring how disequilibria of this sort affect a national economy and what their consequences are likely to be. Here, it is sufficient to note that if the country attempts to overcompensate its production factors in terms of their international efficiency, the country's prices are likely to rise, and this in turn will increase its imports and reduce its exports. Strain on the balance of payments can be expected to follow, eventually demanding some form of readjustment that brings payment to the production factors back toward a tolerable level.

Governments and Competitiveness

The doctrine of comparative advantage leaves any business manager with a sense of incompleteness, a story half-told. That sense has been shared by many scholars, especially those in contact with the real world of international business rivalry. Scholars have made numerous efforts to break out beyond the confining assumptions of comparative advantage doctrine. Two themes in particular have been common to those efforts:

- In determining the competitive profile of any country, scale plays a major role: in the size of the individual plant, in the size of its relevant market, and in the size of the surrounding industrial agglomeration. Can the scale factor be taken systematically into account in the calculations of managers?
- The resources of any country cannot be taken as given, as if endowed by the accidents of nature and the vagaries of history. Such cases do exist, of course, witness Saudi Arabia. For most countries, however, public policies have played a

critical role, as in the case of Singapore and Japan. Can anything systematic be said about such policies?

Scale and Strategic Trade Policy

When the effects of scale are introduced, the competitive position of different nations has to be seen in a new light. Having in mind the possibilities of increasing returns to scale, managers are obliged to ask whether the circumstances of each country, including the size of the market and the policies of its government, are compatible with capturing the advantages of scale. In that context, the government's trade and subsidy policies take center stage.

Consider, for example, the problems of a small country producing manufactured goods. Before world trade opens up, the country's manufacturers produce a large number of products to satisfy the needs of the local market. Faced with a small market for such products, local firms produce at relatively high costs. If the firms could expand their volume, costs would fall and opportunities to sell abroad would develop. However, in the real world, most firms are initially hesitant to make the commitments needed to move into foreign markets. The initial costs of entering foreign markets, when coupled with the ignorance and uncertainty of the local producers, usually represent a significant barrier to action.

Governments such as Korea, therefore, have usually responded with two policies: They have protected the domestic market from the importation of foreign goods, hoping to capture some of the advantages of scale for their local firms; and they have subsidized those firms in various direct and indirect ways in order to increase their exports. As a result, factor costs alone have not been sufficient to explain the success of some industries in these countries.

The trade patterns of countries are influenced, however, not only by economies of scale internal to the firm but also by scale factors that transcend the individual firm, including economies that go with the increased size of the industry to which the plant belongs or even to a complex of interdependent industries.

As a cluster of industrial plants grows, it lays the basis for large, low-cost common services, such as a large power plant or a firm specializing in the software of the dominant industry. The cluster also lays the basis for common risk-reducing facilities that no single plant, taken by itself, could easily afford. All producers confront unavoidable contingencies, such as the shutdown of the plant of a major supplier, the failure of an electric power supply, the breakdown of a carrier delivering essential materials, the failure of a piece of critical machinery, or the loss of key repair personnel.

Finally, the existence of the cluster may encourage competition among its constituent firms, adding to the efficiency of their performance.

Until very recently, theorists have preferred to ignore or belittle the influence of scale economies in the production of goods and services. One reason has been that it has been difficult for theorists to accommodate the idea of scale economies within the existing structure of theory. However, by making a few highly heroic assumptions about how business managers behave in the presence of entry barriers, theorists can now incorporate the existence of scale economies in trade models. The assumptions themselves—known to economists as the Cournot-Nash conditions—may appear highly improbable in the eyes of experienced business managers. But the models that emerge, which go under the rubric of *strategic trade theory*, do manage to produce results that seem intuitively reasonable.

Starting from the observation that many modern industries are characterized by increasing returns to scale, strategic trade theory adds the assumption that those same industries tend to be oligopolistic, and thus able to earn higher than average returns. The first countries to develop those industries are likely, according to the theory, to strengthen their lead positions by virtue of having been first. Furthermore, the returns to the country from those industries will be greater than the returns from other industries, where economies of scale are less significant and where competition drives down profits.

In the absence of government intervention, according to the theory, it is difficult to predict in which countries such new industries will first appear. The manufacture of VCR equipment, high-definition TV, or other such products could begin in any of several industrialized countries, especially if they contain large high-income markets. By timely support to its own firms, however, governments might well play a role in helping those firms take the lead. Once a country has seized such a lead, potential producers in other countries will recognize that the leader has an insuperable cost advantage, created by learning-by-doing and by economies of scale in production and marketing.

Strategic trade theory, therefore, simply reaffirms what most managers have long taken for granted: that when governments institute policies that support home industries in their early growth, those industries may develop an early lead that others will find it extremely difficult to overcome. Moreover, because the lead is based partly on learning-by-doing, it will provide a basis not only for successful export campaigns from the home base but also for successful penetration of foreign markets through the establishment of production units in those markets.

Others have been more cautious in interpreting the policy implications of the new theory. They have wondered whether governments are really capable of choosing winners, or whether they are simply likely to respond to political pressures. They have speculated, too, that rival governments may tend to support the same industries with subsidies and protection, negating the advantages to be gained by the first country. Despite these demurrers, theorists have begun to accept the idea that scale economies and learning curves can measurably affect the competitive advantage of a given country.

Porter's Diamond

Uninhibited by the constraints imposed by formal trade theory, Michael Porter has gathered up the various ideas of different scholars who have attempted to break out of the comparative advantage mold, and has refined and extended them in a framework he has labeled the "national diamond." Seeking to identify the national characteristics that affect the international competitiveness of firms based in any given country, he identifies those characteristics under four headings (hence, his "diamond"):

Factors of production
Conditions of demand
Links with supporting industries
Conditions and practices in national competition

Under Porter's four headings, we consider some of the factors that various scholars have emphasized.

Factors of production.   Factors such as land, labor, and capital have to be analyzed in much finer detail than comparative advantage theory would require, primarily because substitutability of one kind of land for another or one kind of labor for another is often so difficult. Where labor is concerned, for instance, variations such as manual dexterity, response to factory discipline, and other such characteristics may prove critical for the manager in any cross-national comparison.

On the other hand, some substitutability among the factors does occur in the long run, often creating new national capabilities that may enhance the competitiveness of a country. As numerous scholars have long observed, Germany's historical lack of natural resources, for example, accounts in considerable part for its educational emphasis on chemistry and its consequent supply of skilled chemists. And Japan's endemic lack of space has encouraged a skill in the miniaturization of products as well as an indigenous planning capability, such as "just-in-time" inventorying, which economizes on the use of space.

Influences such as these endow enterprises operating in a given national environment with unique skills that enhance their competitiveness in international trade. Some of these skills can be carried over into the producing subsidiaries of their multinational enterprises that operate in other countries.

Conditions of demand.   Various studies have demonstrated that managers are more conscious of demand conditions close to home than of demand conditions in distant markets. Where such conditions happen to be the forerunner of conditions that will appear later in other markets, the firms that have already built up their experience in satisfying such demands at home enjoy a competitive advantage. Explanations of the competitive strength of U.S. manufacturing firms in the decades following World War II, for instance, usually emphasize that U.S. firms were ahead of firms in other countries in satisfying a large high-income market and in producing under conditions of high labor costs. Explanations of the competitiveness of Japanese firms in the 1960s and 1970s usually assign some weight to their experience in responding to the demands of cramped households in Japanese cities. And explanations of the influx of the subsidiaries of Japanese and European firms into the United States in the 1980s and 1990s usually assign some weight to the fact that the home markets of these firms have grown sufficiently in size and income that they are no longer fearful of the challenge involved in tackling the huge U.S. market.

Links with supporting industries.   The advantages of agglomeration in industrial societies, discussed earlier, have long been a subject of study among locational economists. Clusters of interrelated services are epitomized around the world by Silicon Valley in the United States, by the Grenoble high-tech cluster in France, and by Tokyo's cluster of computer chip producers, not to mention the gunsmith villages of Pakistan's northwest frontier, the textile factories of Mauritius, and the mushroom cellars of Kennett Square in Pennsylvania. These agglomerations, where they exist, can offer major competitive advantages to national industries.

The same agglomerations, however, may inhibit the firms that depend on them from setting up producing subsidiaries in other countries. To set up a production facility in a foreign country away from the agglomeration is to increase uncertainty and raise costs. Accordingly, firms that feel compelled to set up a foreign facility often try to persuade others in the home-based agglomeration to follow them to the new foreign location (see Box 6-1).

Conditions and practices in national competition.   The conditions of rivalry that firms encounter in their own national markets exert a major influence on the behavior of those firms in international markets, affecting both their export practices and the practices of their foreign subsidiaries. For instance, firms that are vertically integrated at home in response to the conditions of the home market are likely to prefer a vertically integrated structure for their operating subsidiaries in foreign markets. And firms that engage in vigorous competition in home markets are likely to compete vigorously in foreign markets.

Managers should guard against too readily assuming that firms which do not experience a high measure of competition at home are unlikely to compete vigorously abroad. To be sure, cases consistent with that generalization are common, witness the moribund U.S. steel industry for several decades after World War II. But contrary cases also are common. For instance, Korea's entry in some international markets, including automobiles and shipbuilding in the 1970s, was spearheaded by firms that enjoyed heavy protection from imports and little domestic competition at home. Similar cases are encountered in the history of Brazilian and Mexican firms that eventually entered international markets.

Indeed, as we saw in Chapter 2, the practice of shut-out pricing in foreign markets is made more feasible when the producer enjoys monopoly rents at home. Where such rents exist, producers find it easier to cover their overhead in their home sales while pricing their exports simply to cover their marginal costs. That practice, therefore, is endemic among firms in industries with high fixed costs.

Is the diamond forever?   In the past few decades, there has been a visible convergence among the world's industrialized countries in capital and labor costs, in

---

BOX 6-1. JAPANESE MAGNETS

In coming to the United States, Japanese carmakers quickly discovered that American parts suppliers could not adapt to just-in-time quality and delivery requirements. Even obtaining basic inputs like high-quality steel or glass proved difficult. Unfamiliar with the just-in-time system and deeming Japanese quality demands unreasonable, many U.S. parts suppliers simply chose not to sell to the transplants.

The shortage of qualified parts suppliers left Japanese auto assemblers little choice but to build a new parts industry in the United States. Today, Japanese companies own wholly or in part more than 270 automotive parts suppliers in this country. Having conducted a detailed survey of 73 of these Japanese-owned and joint-venture parts suppliers, we estimate that they employ more than 30,000 American workers and represent an investment of $5.5 billion.

Most of these organizations supply glass, brake systems, seats, and other components directly to the production plants. Nippondenso, Japan's leading automobile parts supplier, makes air conditioners, heaters, clutches, filters, fuel pumps, and other components for transplant automakers at plants in Michigan, Tennessee, South Carolina, and California.

A second group of companies makes replacement parts for Japanese imports. Japan's two leading battery companies, Storage Battery and Yuasa Battery, recently launched a Memphis-based joint venture that produces 6,000 car batteries a day. A third group provides manufacturing equipment to transplant assemblers. For instance, 16 Japanese machine tool companies, including Yamazaki Mazak, now operate in the United States, along with two conveyor-belt makers and two makers of automotive painting machines.

According to our survey, two-thirds of the transplant supplier companies came to the United States on direct request from a major Japanese automaker.

SOURCE: From Martin Kenney and Richard Florida, "How Japanese Industry Is Rebuilding the Rust Belt," *Technology Review*, February–March 1991, 28.

---

consumer tastes, and in available technologies. The emergence of the single market in Europe and the growth of Japan have produced a convergence in the size of the markets of those areas. As a result, the differences in environments arising in different areas have tended to shrink. National specializations in innovation such as the traditional U.S. concentration in labor-saving machinery and high-income products, the German concentration in chemical substitutes for natural raw materials, and the Japanese concentration in miniaturized and quality-sensitive products have become less distinctive. So the export patterns of the countries relying on innovations also have grown less distinctive; personal computers, synthetic materials, automotive parts, camcorders, software, and banking services have crossed borders in both directions.

The same has been true of foreign direct investment flows; the outward flows of subsidiaries from each of the major industrialized areas have been concentrated largely in the same manufacturing and service industries as the inward flows to those areas.

At the level of the individual product or service, the process of convergence that is suggested by these data may be equally apparent. For any specific product falling in one of these industries, the trade pattern portrayed in Figure 6-1 is likely to persist, beginning with exports from the innovating country, moving swiftly to production in other areas with high marketing potential, and moving eventually to production in countries that promise the lowest costs of production.

Customs Unions and Other Preferential Blocs

When appraising the competitive conditions provided by any national economy, the manager should take into account the increasing importance of preferential trading blocs—that is, blocs created by groups of countries that agree to extend preferential treatment to the importation of goods and services originating in the territory of another member of the group. Of these arrangements, two are especially common:

- Customs unions: blocs whose members abolish trade barriers in trade between them while maintaining a common set of trade barriers, especially including tariffs, against the products of nonmembers.
- Free-trade areas: blocs in which each member maintains its own national restrictions against the products of nonmembers, while abolishing trade barriers between members for products originating in the area.

In their efforts to exploit the advantages of large internal markets, governments all over the world have shown a considerable interest in creating customs unions or free-trade areas with their neighbors, hoping thereby to increase the efficiency and trading opportunities of their industries. That increased interest has led to the creation of a rash of such schemes, described in Chapter 11.

The contribution of economists to the debate has been to demonstrate that some schemes may produce conditions that add to the efficiency of industries in the participating countries, but some may have the opposite effect. The manager must decide in individual cases which of these two possibilities is the more likely.

A preferential trade arrangement, according to conventional analysis, can either (1) divert existing trade from a country not participating in the arrangement to a country that is a participant, or (2) create more trade among its members without diversion. Table 6-4 presents the first of these two possibilities in a simple model. There we assume that two countries, A and B, have formed a customs union. By its terms, A and B

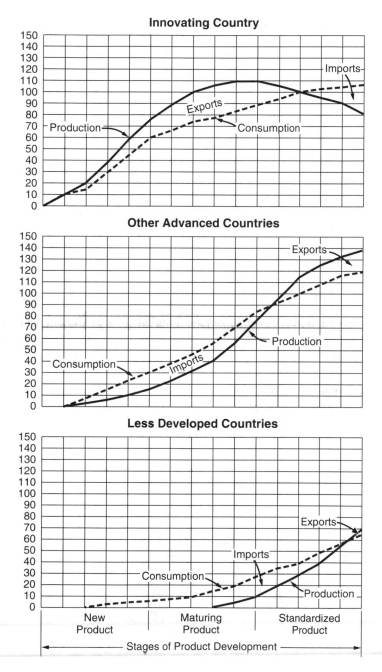

Figure 6-1 International Trade and Production in the Product Cycle

abolish all tariffs in trade between them, but they maintain a common tariff in their trade with country C. The table suggests what happens to trade in products X and Y.

According to the assumptions of Table 6-4, an outside source, represented by country C, is the most efficient supplier of products X and Y.

Before union, country C managed to export product X to country A; C's cost of production 8, plus the duty levied by A, 5, had permitted C's producers of X to under-sell A's producers in A's markets. C had been unable, however, to sell its relatively cheap X in B's market because B's duty of 3 was sufficient to make C's price non-competitive against B's producers. With product Y, the situation is similar. C is the most efficient producer, but this time C is unable to overcome A's tariff wall while being able to surmount that of B.

Now union takes place. Countries A and B strike an average of their previous tariff rates of 5 and 3, respectively, in product X to produce a common tariff of 4; but that rate is now applicable only to imports from Country C. The same process produces a tariff rate of 4 for product Y. Now C is barred from A and B. In product X, Country B's producers drive country C out of A's market; and in product Y, country A's producers drive C out of B's market. Trade diversion has occurred; the most efficient world producer has been driven out of the markets of the countries in a customs union in favor of more costly suppliers inside the union.

A different outcome, however, is offered in Table 6-5. Here, a customs union creates international trade instead of merely diverting it. In this model, the production costs and import duties before union are so great that C has been unable to export to A or B; tariffs of A and B are so high as to bar C's product and to protect higher cost local producers. When the customs union between A and B goes into effect, it opens up the possibility in product X that country B may export to A, and in product Y that country A may export to B.

TABLE 6-4. Trade Diversion Attending a Customs Union of Countries A and B (Figures in dollars per unit of product)

Country	Product X				Product Y		
	Production Cost	Import Duty	Market Price		Production Cost	Import Duty	Market Price
				Before Union			
A	14	5	13		10	3	10
B	10	3	10		14	5	13
C	8	0	8		8	0	8
				After Union			
A	14	4[a]	10		10	4[a]	10
B	10	4[a]	10		14	4[a]	10
C	8	0	8		8	0	8

[a]Applicable only to imports from Country C.

TABLE 6-5.   Trade Creation Attending a Customs Union of Countries
A and B (Figures in dollars per unit of product)

Country	Product X				Product Y		
	Production Cost	Import Duty	Market Price		Production Cost	Import Duty	Market Price
				Before Union			
A	12	5	12		10	3	10
B	10	3	10		12	5	12
C	8	0	8		8	0	8
				After Union			
A	12	4[a]	10		10	4[a]	10
B	10	4[a]	10		12	4[a]	10
C	8	0	8		8	0	8

[a]Applicable only to imports from Country C.

If this were all there were to the effects of preferential areas, these arrangements could be summarized as efforts at the achievement of the second best. Where trade does not exist, a preferential bloc opens up the possibility that it may be created. But where trade already exists, a preferential bloc may divert the trade from the most efficient sources to second-best producers.

The effects of customs unions and other preferential arrangements, however, are much more profound than the simple trade-diversion, trade-creation possibilities suggested by reference to the tables themselves. Observe that in both Tables 6-4 and 6-5, after the customs union is in effect, the price of product X can be expected to fall in country A and the price of product Y can be expected to fall in country B. The price declines will presumably stimulate the consumption of X and Y in A and B, thus increasing the output of those products. This combination of consequences may have more economic effects than the static trade-diversion and trade-creation analyses would suggest.

Even wider implications are opened up if one introduces the possibility of economies of scale, whether they are economies of the individual plant or the economies of industrial agglomerations. This possibility largely explains why customs unions and other preferential arrangements are so attractive to the less developed areas. One small country, perhaps, cannot provide a sufficient market to sustain a steel mill of effective size, but several small countries, all pledged to buy from one another initially on a preferential basis, may collectively provide the market necessary to support a steel mill of reasonable efficiency. On similar lines, one small country may not be able to provide enough market to justify the cluster of interrelated facilities that are needed directly or indirectly to sustain a modern automobile-producing complex, but several such countries can jointly provide the necessary market.

Shifting Capabilities

The history of national strategies suggests that, over the years, countries frequently modify or abandon their existing strategies in favor of another that reflects their changing position in world markets. Managers, therefore, will commonly find that they must reconsider their estimates of the strengths and weaknesses of any given country as conditions and policies change within the country.

The most striking illustration of these changes in recent decades has occurred in developing countries that have moved out of the import-substituting stage in their industrial development to an export-led strategy. That shift has been visible in some of the fast-growing economies of South-East Asia such as Korea and Thailand, and in much of Latin America. With it, subsidiaries that multinational enterprises originally established to overcome the import barriers of the country have been retooled and reoriented to serve as export platforms for the multinational network. Volkswagen's subsidiary in Brazil, for instance, has evolved from a supplier of the local Brazilian market to a global supplier of some Volkswagen models.

These shifts have not been confined to developing countries. Both Japan and the United States have observed that the functions of many of their parent enterprises have been changing substantially, as their relative capacity to provide skilled manufacturing labor has given way to a relative capacity to produce high-grade service skills. Once the principal exporters in any multinational network, parent firms in such networks have gradually become more specialized in the provision of services and capital, as well as in the coordination of their global supply and marketing networks. Managing such a shift sucessfully has presented a compelling challenge for multinational enterprises.

Suggested Reading

DUNNING, JOHN H. "The Competitive Advantage of Countries and the Activities of Transnational Corporations." *Transnational Corporations*, 1, no. 1 (February 1992), 136–168.

KOGUT, BRUCE. "Country Capabilities and the Permeability of Borders." *Strategic Management Journal*, 12 (1991), 33–47.

KRUGMAN, PAUL R. (ed.). *Strategic Trade Policy and the New International Economics*. Cambridge, MA: MIT Press, 1987.

PORTER, MICHAEL E. *The Competitive Advantage of Nations*. New York: Free press, 1990.

RUGMAN, ALAN M., and ALAIN VEIBEKE. "Foreign Subsidiaries and Multinational Strategic Management: An Extension and Correction of Porter's Single Diamond Framework." *Management International Review*, special issue 1993/2, pp. 71–84.

U.S. CONGRESS, OFFICE OF TECHNOLOGY ASSESSMENT. *Competing Economies: America, Europe, and the Pacific Rim*. Washington, DC: U.S. Government Printing Office, October 1991.

CHAPTER 7

Exploring National Policies

Facing global competition, managers of multinational enterprises must always be alert to opportunities in foreign countries for superior technology, cheaper inputs of labor, capital and materials, and promising markets. At the same time, they also have to answer to national governments and national interest groups, which continually judge multinationals by their contributions to national interests.

Therein lies a dilemma—or several different dilemmas. Different countries often pull the multinational enterprise in conflicting directions. And stockholders exert pressures to move the enterprise in yet another direction.

Can we identify the country pressures that are likely to arise and the forms they are likely to take? In this chapter, first we explore that terrain, starting with the economic goals of national governments and national interest groups. Then we deal briefly with political and social goals.

The Economic Goals

- Volkswagen faces a sharp decline in the world market's demand for its little Beetles. So its managing board decides to cut back drastically on production in its German plants. German unions bitterly protest the company's action. The company responds by reversing its decision and cutting back its Brazilian production instead.

- Hoover is seeking to cut its production costs for big-ticket consumer durables in its European markets, as competition in that market stiffens. In its efforts to cut costs, it plans to close its vacuum-cleaner plant in France and to move the 600 jobs to Scotland, where lower labor costs, more favorable tax concessions, and added scale economies seem to answer its needs.
- Honda expands its small-truck factory in Marysville, Ohio. The Office of Technology Assessment of the U.S. Congress wonders whether the expansion will reduce the profits and vitality of U.S.-owned competitors such as Chrysler and Ford.
- Kazakhstan invites the world's oil companies to submit proposals for the exploration and development of its gas and oil fields. The Nigerian government fears that the Kazakhstan opportunity will reduce its chances for securing similar commitments from the leading international oil companies.
- Sony acquires Columbia Pictures. The U.S. Department of Commerce wonders whether the acquisition in the long run might weaken the dominance of the U.S. entertainment industry in world markets.

In the pages that follow, we want to sort out conflicts such as these, real and potential, examining the measures that governments have taken affecting multinational enterprises and the responses of their managers. To survey that complex field, we separate international business in goods from that in services. Within each of these major fields, we distinguish the measures of governments affecting the multinational activities of their "home" enterprises from the measures taken toward foreign-owned enterprises in their respective jurisdictions. Finally, we try to take account of the differences among various countries that are in different conditions of economic and political development.

In outline, therefore, the pages that follow touch on each of the categories portrayed below, highlighting major tendencies.

	Manufacturing	Services
Developed countries		
As home country		
As host country		
"Emerging" and "developing" countries		
As home country		
As host country		
Eastern Europe, former Soviet		
Union (FSU), People's		
Republic of China (PRC)		

The Manufacturing Industries

The Setting

As we saw in Chapter 1, the global networks represented by multinational enterprises in the manufacturing industries have grown substantially in recent decades, along with international trade and international investment.

In the 1990s most governments in the world seem to have accepted the proposition that, where the international movement of goods is concerned, open markets are by and large advantageous and that any governmental restrictions on the international movement of goods should bear the burden of justification. That general attitude is reflected in the fact that in 1993 representatives of over 120 countries agreed on the provisions of a new World Trade Organization and that over 170 countries accepted the Articles of Agreement of the International Monetary Fund.

The same general situation exists with respect to governments' attitudes toward the continued expansion of the international manufacturing operations of multinational enterprises. In the 1990s, governments have tended to look on the expansion of multinational enterprises as more or less consistent with their national interests. Indeed, practically all countries have been providing some special support to firms to expand their multinational operations, both inbound and outbound. Once again, therefore, proposals to impose restrictions on the operations of multinational enterprises usually have to bear the burden of providing some special justification.

This does not mean, however, that the managers of multinational enterprises have had a clear field for pursuing the objectives of their respective enterprises, without regard for the desires of governments. Far from it. Despite a general desire to promote trade and investment, most governments have deliberately sought, by many different means, to push the development of multinational enterprises in one direction or another that differed from the firm's preferred strategy.

Most of the measures that governments take to influence the development of multinational enterprises can be summarized under the following wide-ranging headings:

Government licensing policies
Subsidy policies
Trade policies
Patent policies
Antitrust policies
Capital-market policies

We now review these policy instruments, highlighting differences in the treatment of home enterprises from that of foreign enterprises, and noting differences among different country categories where these merit special attention.

Government Licensing Policies

Foreign firms that wish to create a business establishment in a particular country need various authorizations from the government agencies of that country before setting up shop. For a few countries—most of them being advanced industrialized countries—this is a perfunctory requirement, involving little more than the creation of a corporation or the registration of a business entity. But most governments in the world retain the right to screen proposals by any foreign firm to open up a business facility in their jurisdiction. For most countries, therefore, the licensing of a manufacturing business is a substantial undertaking.

Most governments, however, claim to adhere to the rule that a foreign-owned firm lawfully established in its jurisdiction receives the same treatment as any firm owned by its nationals. Numerous international agreements, some of which are summarized in Chapter 11, tend to reinforce that general position.

Despite the widespread screening of proposals for investment by foreign enterprise, the risk that a foreign-owned manufacturing enterprise will be refused a license to do business in a foreign country is lower today than it has been in decades.

- Among the advanced industrialized countries that once were identified with restrictive policies in the licensing of foreign-owned enterprises, notably Japan and France, substantial liberalization has taken place.

- Many countries in the developing world that maintained highly restrictive licensing policies against foreigners a decade earlier, including Mexico, Argentina, India, and Taiwan, have dramatically reduced their requirements. Some countries have even created "one-stop" licensing agencies, hoping to expedite the process by which foreign applicants accumulate the necessary authorizations to do business.

- Eastern European countries have been opening up their borders to foreign-owned enterprises, in an ambitious effort to reshape their economies and to demonstrate that they are serious candidates for eventual entry into the European Union. Even the countries that were formerly fragments of the Soviet Union (today designated as the FSU) have allowed several thousand foreign-owned enterprises to surmount the many formal barriers to entry created by their disorganized and complex licensing systems.

- Ironically, in the mid-1990s the United States appeared to be one of the few countries of any importance contemplating new restrictions on foreign-owned enterprises.

Yet, despite the decline in licensing restrictions in most countries of the world and despite the growing strength of the nondiscrimination norm, the regulatory jungle that foreigners face can still be threatening. *The Economist* states in its September 24, 1994 issue: "It took America's W. R. Grace some 15 years to progress from negotiations [with the PRC] about building a plant to starting production." The problems surrounding licensing stem from various causes.

- Where extensive licensing requirements still exist, as they do in Eastern Europe, the FSU, the PRC, and many developing countries, the standards that any applicant faces, whether foreign or domestic, are vague and variable. In the summer of 1994, for example, Russia was changing its investment rules "like a drunken sailor" (a *New York Times* description) and was arbitrarily allowing some regions to add rules of their own.

- Even when the licensing requirements for investors are clear, the foreign applicant is likely to find that the nondiscrimination principle itself is not strong enough or clear enough to ensure entry. For instance, a foreign applicant who is introducing a high-tech manufacturing process that is not yet employed by domestic rivals cannot rely on the "national treatment" principle to determine the safety requirements that are to be imposed.

- With licensing authorities exercising high levels of discretion in most developing countries, in China, the FSU, and Eastern Europe, as well as in a few advanced industrialized countries, accusations of corruption and favoritism are commonplace. Such possibilities are increased by the fact that tax and tariff exemptions are tailor-made to selected applicants.

- Whether or not corruption plays a part, licensing authorities who exercise substantial discretion generally seek some concessions from foreign applicants. Typical demands include:
  - Taking on a local partner in a joint venture, at terms that seem advantageous for the local partner.
  - Establishing the proposed facility in a backward region of the country.
  - Transferring technology.
  - Accepting a designated local supplier or distributor.
  - Achieving export goals and accepting import limits.

- Licensing systems of government units below the national level, such as provinces and cities, are not always subject to the provisions of international treaties or to the commands of national governments. This problem is particularly acute for national systems in transition such as those of the FSU and it sometimes affects federal systems as well, such as those of the United States, Germany, and Canada.

- Governments engaged in large-scale privatization programs, such as those in Eastern Europe or the FSU, can be expected to place a lid on the size of foreigners' acquisitions in some industries. One reason is political, a response to public concern over foreign ownership. Another reason is economic, a sense that the foreign buyer is in a position for the time being to acquire national assets at bargain-basement prices.

- Enterprises that face a breach of treaty provisions guaranteeing their right to establish a business in a foreign country can press their claims only if they can persuade their home governments to support their case. Whether the government of a home country decides to champion an individual case depends on larger political issues, such as the state of the home country's political relations with the foreign country.

Subsidy Policies

Luring new enterprises.   Although governments commonly impose special restrictions on foreign-owned enterprises, they also offer subsidies in various forms aimed at attracting foreign-owned enterprises to their jurisdictions. Exemptions from taxation, discussed below, can often be the economic equivalent of a subsidy. In addition, governments provide structures on concessionary terms, roads and other infrastructure without charge, and training programs for less skilled labor, such as welders and secretaries. Measures such as these are taken not only by national governments but also by lower governmental units such as states and cities.

As a rule, governments that are wooing enterprises to set up a new unit in their jurisdiction offer just as good terms to foreigners as to a domestic competitor similarly situated. Indeed, a typical complaint in many countries runs the other way: that foreigners are being favored over domestic firms in the grant of subsidies or other incentives. In a few countries, including the PRC, governments sometimes do grant more generous incentives to foreigners than to their domestic rivals, hoping thereby to capture better technological, managerial, or marketing resources.

In advanced industrialized countries such as the United States and Europe, the fact that foreign-owned firms are so often the beneficiaries of subsidies from states and provinces stems from more subtle causes. As a rule, foreign-owned enterprises are freer to establish a large facility at a new location than are their domestic rivals. The automobile industry in the United States is a case in point; U.S.-owned firms such as Ford and General Motors are anchored in the Midwest by numerous ties, including union contracts, whereas foreign-owned firms such as Nissan and Daimler-Benz feel free to settle in the South and Southeast (see Figure 7-1).

Support for research.   Among the various channels by which governments dispense subsidies to enterprises, support for industrial research in various forms ranks high on the list.

In the U.S. case, Congress has struggled hard to include provisions in various laws that would channel official research support away from firms controlled by foreign interests, without too obviously violating the many treaty commitments that guarantee "national treatment" for such firms. Extending beyond military procurement, the discrimination has carried over into programs that provide official support for industries that produce "dual use" items and even some industries that are principally civilian in character. A considerable part of the funds for such purposes is funneled through the Department of Defense in ostensible support of military hardware

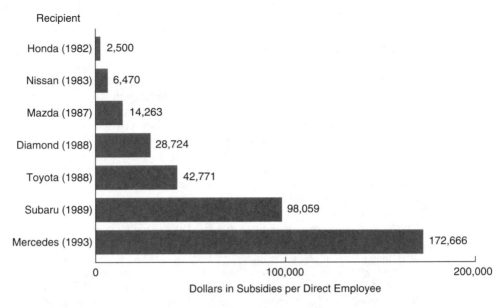

Figure 7-1

Recipient

Honda (1982)   2,500

Nissan (1983)   6,470

Mazda (1987)   14,263

Diamond (1988)   28,724

Toyota (1988)   42,771

Subaru (1989)   98,059

Mercedes (1993)   172,666

0   100,000   200,000

Dollars in Subsidies per Direct Employee

Figure 7-1   Subsidies per Direct Employee Provided to Foreign-Owned Automobile Manufacturers
in the United States

Source: Adapted in part from Office of Technical Assessment, U.S. Congress, *Multinationals and the
National Interest,* (Washington, D.C.: U.S. Government Printing Office, 1993), p. 68; *The Wall
Street Journal*, September 30, 1993, p. A12; and Daimler-Benz press release, September 30, 1993.

and software. Accordingly, discrimination against foreign-owned firms is built into
the system, even though they are producing in the United States.

In Europe, such support comes partly from national governments and partly
from the European Union. Like the U.S. programs, the support of national governments in Europe is commonly provided under the heading of national security.
France, in particular, has actively supported programs in such fields as aeronautics
and nuclear energy in the name of national defense. The extensive programs of the
European Union, briefly described in Chapter 11, are more frankly commercial,
aimed at keeping European enterprises competitive in world markets.

The Japanese case, as usual, is more obscure. Although recorded expenditures
by the government in direct support of industrial research are relatively low, government agencies have frequently taken the initiative in organizing research efforts by
various sectors of Japanese industry. The widespread assumption is that some of the
risks of large research efforts in industry are borne by the government by various indirect means (Box 7-1).

In other parts of the world, governmental support for industrial research, to the
extent that it exists, largely takes the form of helping local firms keep pace with technological developments in other countries. Brazil and Korea are especially noted for
such efforts.

BOX 7-1.   JAPAN'S VLSI PROJECT

The classic case of a government-supported project to capture an innovational lead over competitors is Japan's VLSI (Very Large Scale Integration) program, which is credited with catapulting Japanese industry into a world leadership position in the manufacture of computer chips. In the 1970s, Japan's telecommunication and computer industries were heavily dependant on U.S. chip production, especially for the critical DRAM (Dynamic Random Access Memory) chips. NTT, Japan's (then) state-owned telephone company, guaranteed a market for the chip output of Japan's three leading electronics firms for use in telecommunications. These joined together to produce a 64K DRAM, a goal reached in 1977.

Meanwhile, Japan's Ministry of International Trade and Industry (MITI) financed another program, designed to stimulate chipmaking for computer applications. MITI provided interest-free loans to finance 40 percent of a $200 million project stretching over four years. The same three firms, joined by two others and by specialists from MITI's own laboratories, launched a research program aimed at improving Japan's capabilities in memory devices and logic. The program is widely credited with having given Japan world leadership during the 1980s in various process technologies, notably in the fields of electron beam lithogaphy, as well as silicon crystal growth and processing.

One of the open questions with regard to governmental support for industrial research in the future is the eventual fate of the many state research institutes that once formed an essential part of the industrial structure of the FSU. In the Soviet Union, it was standard practice for the research of any major industry, whether civilian or military, to be centralized in institutes that were not directly linked to production units. Although some of these institutes appeared to be dissolving during the 1990s as national governments cut back drastically on nonessential expenditures, many are likely to continue to receive substantial support from their respective governments.

Governmental programs in support of industrial research pose obvious problems in the competition among multinational enterprises. Needless to say, those enterprises that have access to generous government grants have an obvious advantage over rivals that do not receive governmental support. Such support is particularly attractive to multinational enterprises because the granting governments cannot realistically confine the enterprises in their subsequent use of the acquired technology, even when such subsequent use takes place in foreign countries.

Nevertheless, various governments, including the United States, Japan, and the European Union, continue to dispense research funds directly to firms operating within their national jurisdictions. In the dispensation of such funds, governments seem to be moving toward policies that accept the concept of discrimination between "home" multinationals and other multinationals. True, governments seem disposed to reduce or eliminate such discrimination for the units of multinationals that are based in countries prepared to do the same—a policy of "conditional" national treatment. But that approach has not yet been formally acknowledged as the dominant principle in this area of government policy.

Trade Policies

The level of restrictions.   With multinational enterprises accounting for more than half the world's trade in goods, it is apparent that the trade policies adopted by governments can have a considerable effect on the operations of those enterprises. For instance, governments sometimes reduce the general level of their import restrictions in an effort to make their economies attractive to multinational enterprises as a base for processing and exporting products to world markets. And governments frequently grant foreign-owned enterprises exemptions from national import duties, covering both capital goods imports and materials required for the manufacturing process.

Although a reduction of trade barriers probably encourages the spread of multinational enterprises in most cases, an increase in trade barriers can also be the trigger that leads to such an expansion. When Nissan or Toyota or any other large automobile producer is doing a thriving export business in a large foreign country, for instance, merely a threat of trade restrictions from the government of the importing country can galvanize the firm to set up a producing subsidiary in that country.

Protecting vulnerable industries.   The spectacular decline in trade barriers during the past few decades has stimulated some governments to look for new ways of protecting some vulnerable industries from import competition. That stimulus led in the 1980s to a marked increase in the number of cases in which governments accused foreign exporters of "dumping" their goods in the complaining government's markets or of receiving subsidies for their exports from foreign countries. ("Dumping" is usually defined as the exporter's setting its export prices below those it maintains in home markets or in third countries, or pricing below cost.)

A number of countries, including the United States, the European Union, and Canada, have been particularly responsive to the complaints of their home producers in investigating cases of alleged dumping and subsidies. (See Box 7-2.) The United States alone instituted over 800 such investigations during the 1980s. By the end of the decade, a number of developing countries were emulating the U.S. example with cases of their own.

Not all such instances involve multinational enterprises, but such enterprises do pose a special problem in their application to dumping and subsidy cases. For when the exporter and the importer are units of the same enterprise, as often happens, the price they set for transfers of goods between them can be highly arbitrary. Such prices, public authorities usually assume, are fixed at a level that best serves the inter-

BOX 7-2.   PROTECTING DOMESTIC INDUSTRY: HARLEY DAVIDSON

During the 1970s, Harley Davidson Motor Company, maker of big powerful motorcy-
cles, found itself facing growing competition in its U.S. market. With its own formidable reputation for quality having slipped badly, Harley was facing increasing competition from Honda, with an assembly plant in Ohio, as well as from several Japanese
exporters. Although their products were mainly lightweight vehicles as distinguished
from Harley's heavyweight and superheavyweight bikes, Harley was rapidly losing
out even in its specialized segment of the market. In 1978, Harley Davidson petitioned
the U.S. Treasury Department to impose an antidumping duty on imports of motor-
bikes from Japan. Harley Davidson secured a finding that Japanese exporters were indeed dumping their smaller, lighter bikes in the U.S. market. But because the Harley-
Davidson machines were heavier, more expensive bikes that were demanded
principally by policemen, speed demons, and devotees, Harley Davidson was not
granted the protection that an antidumping duty might have offered against the offending Japanese exports.

  In the closing years of the 1970s, as Japanese producers began to elbow Harley
Davidson out of its specialty niche in heavyweight bikes, the company turned once
again to the government for protection. This time, however, Harley Davidson petitioned the U.S. International Trade Commission for protection under a little-used provision of U.S. trade law, Section 201, the so-called escape clause. At the same time,
the company took vigorous measures to overcome its performance gap, evident from a
comparison with Honda's Ohio assembly line. Honda's Ohio plant, for instance: had a
5 percent reject rate as compared with Harley's 50 to 60 percent; a labor productivity
rate at least 25 or 30 percent higher than that of Harley; and far lower inventories and
"work in progress" relative to output.

  To secure protection from imports under Section 201, a U.S. producer had to
demonstrate that there had been a substantial increase in competing imports, that the
U.S. producer was suffering serious injury or serious threat of injury, and that the increase in imports was the substantive cause of the injury. Under that section, the International Trade Commission recommended and the president granted protection for
Harley Davidson. In 1983, duties on big bikes, regardless of source, were raised from
4.4 percent to 49.4 percent, to be followed by graduated declines in such duties over a
five-year period; by the end of the period, the duty level would have returned to 4.4
percent. The idea was to offer Harley Davidson breathing space to cut its costs and
improve its product.

  Instructed by the Japanese example, Harley Davidson introduced major reforms
in its motor designs, its production processes, and its marketing techniques. By 1986,
to the astonishment of experienced observers, Harley Davidson was sufficiently transformed to refinance its operations through a public offering of its stock. By 1992, despite the end of its period of extraordinary protection, the company had managed to
build up its share of a shrinking big bike market in the United States from less than
one quarter to over 60 percent. By that time, too, it was beginning to look abroad for
added sales.

ests of the enterprise as a whole, taking into account the effects of any selected price on corporate taxes, on the tariffs to be paid on the shipment being valued, and on other factors affecting the multinational network's consolidated profits.

As a result of such investigations, governments frequently impose an antidumping duty or a countervailing duty on the importation of goods from a foreign unit of a multinational enterprise to a related unit in the national jurisdiction. Where dumping is alleged, the duty is fixed in theory in an amount equal to the difference between the government's estimate of the import's "fair" value and the price at which the goods were actually transferred. Where subsidization is alleged, the duty is fixed in theory to offset the subsidy. The means of estimating these figures, being determined unilaterally by the agencies of the importing country, are often utterly indefensible.

- In dumping cases, arbitrary yardsticks fixed by law or regulation often substitute for hard data or reasonable estimates.
- In subsidy cases, governments often base their findings that subsidies exist on tenuous grounds, such as the existence of regional development schemes in the exporting country.
- For products emanating from countries without a well-developed market system, governments in importing countries sometimes artificially "construct" a price, simply by looking at other market economies in a similar state of development to the exporting country and guessing at what the price would have been if a market had existed in the exporting country.

Another problem that multinational enterprises sometimes face involves the perception of governments that such firms can readily avoid an antidumping duty by switching the sources of imports or making minor modifications in product designs. If, for example, Source A is saddled with the dumping charge, Source B from the same multinational network may be able to provide the export without being subject to the same dumping duty. And if assembled baby prams are subject to a duty, unassembled kits may be able to avoid the duty.

In the history of the administration of antidumping duties, governments such as the United States and the European Union have become increasingly aggressive in dealing with what they perceive to be the avoidance tactics of multinational enterprises. For example, administrators in importing countries have been authorized and directed to impose such duties promptly where they conclude that sources have been shifted or products have been modified in order to escape imposition of the duties. The European Union, for instance, imposes antidumping duties on a product assembled inside the Union whenever 60 percent or more of the components in the product are already subject to antidumping duties.

Free-trade areas.   Another issue in trade policy that directly affects the operations of multinational enterprises involves the standards used in determining the "regional content" of a product in free-trade areas. Such areas, epitomized by the North

American Free Trade Area and described in Chapter 11, have proliferated in the past decade. Free-trade areas, the reader will remember, are created by agreement among a group of countries stipulating that products originating in the area will be free to cross the frontiers of member countries without payment of duties. Since each of the member countries in free-trade areas retains the right to set its own import duties in trade with third countries, the member countries have a joint interest in confining the free-trade right to products originating inside the area.

For multinational enterprises, the determination of "regional content" poses both special opportunities and special problems. Some of the products seeking the free-trade privilege are bound to contain some materials or components originating in third countries, especially if they are the products of multinational enterprises.

What criterion should be established by which such products are to be deemed products originating in the free-trade area? Most free-trade areas operate according to the standard that any product which changes its tariff classification by virtue of processing inside the area is to be regarded as being of domestic origin. So an imported set of bicycle gears that is eventually assembled into a bicycle inside the area loses its foreignness in the process.

But not in the case of NAFTA. In that agreement, as described in Chapter 11, over 200 pages of provisions elaborate the standards to be used in measuring regional content for different types of products. The object of these provisions is to deny free-trade rights to a large range of products that contain materials and components from outside sources. In that elaboration, the standards vary from one product category to the next, with automobiles and textiles being assigned a particularly distinctive set of standards. In the case of automobiles, special provisions even credit the value added by the Mexican subsidiaries of U.S-owned firms in a more generous way than the value added by the Mexican subsidiaries of Japan-owned firms.

Where multinational enterprises are involved, however, governments confront the same problems in the application of these standards as they encounter in the application of antidumping duties. Transfer prices between affiliates in the same multinational network will not be taken at face value. Ironically, governments operate with a different bias in the two situations. Where antidumping duties are concerned, importing countries want to find the highest possible cost for the product in the exporting country. When calculating the content added by other countries in the free-trade area, however, the bias of governments of the importing country is to put the lowest possible value on such content.

Patent Policies

Recall from Chapter 2 that multinational enterprises are highly concentrated in industries in which barriers to entry are substantial. These industries are usually dominated by large enterprises that possess some very distinctive capabilities. Commonly, those capabilities are seen in a strong patent position or a strong trade name. Singer Sewing

Machine, one of the earliest of the multinational enterprises, built its phenomenal growth one hundred years ago on both its patents and its trade name. The pattern persists today in pharmaceuticals, electronic products, and many other industries.

Yet the patents that different national governments issue vary greatly in the rights they confer.

- One difference in national patents is found in the life of the patents issued. Although a 1993 agreement under the GATT guarantees a minimum life of 20 years from the date of filing, the life of the patent itself varies from one country to the next. One survey of national patent laws in 1990, covering 32 countries at various levels of development (but not including the United States), shows that the lives of patent grants at that time ranged from 5 to 18 years, with fewer than half the countries at the 18-year level.

- A second difference is in the areas of invention that different governments include as patentable. For instance, some governments refuse to grant patents to cover a process, such as the use of electricity in the making of aluminum, or refuse to grant patents on some products, such as pharmaceuticals or food preparations. The pharmaceutical exclusion, for instance, appeared in 13 of the 32 countries in the survey.

- A third difference is the scope of the monopoly granted to the patentholder. All 32 countries made provision for compulsory licensing of patents where the patentholder fails to "use" the invention in the national jurisdiction; some also provided for cancellation of the patent grant as a remedy for nonuse.

- Other differences of importance also exist, both in the terms and conditions of the grant and in the means of enforcement. It remains to be seen, for instance, whether a patent grant by China or Russia will provide effective rights to the patentholder.

Multinational enterprises are interested not only in the terms and conditions of patent grants in the countries in which they operate but also in the treatment of foreigners in the application of the patent laws. Practically all countries insist that their patent laws are framed and administered without distinguishing between domestic and foreign applicants. Complaints to the contrary have been numerous, however. Foreigners point out that the provisions requiring "use" of the patent have a differential effect on them, inasmuch as they may wish to exploit their patent through exports to the protected area rather than through production within it. Foreigners claim, too, that their applications go to the bottom of the "pending" pile in overworked patent offices. Weak judicial systems, they state, may not be able to provide effective remedies for the violation of patents, especially if the patentholder is a foreigner.

The differences in patent policies among countries have been reduced somewhat by a number of international agreements. Of these agreements, the International Convention for the Protection of Industrial Property, usually dubbed the Paris Convention, is of longest duration. That agreement constrains governments in their application of remedies for the "abuses" by patentholders by discouraging the cancellation of patents and limiting the terms of compulsory licenses. These restraints were enlarged by a 1993 agreement, to be administered by a new World Trade Organization, which includes:

- An undertaking to grant a 50-year copyright protection to "authors" of computer programs, databases, movies, and the like.
- Undertakings to limit compulsory licensing of patents, and to guarantee at least 20 years of protection from the date of application for a patent.
- Commitments to provide more effective protection of trade names, trade secrets, and industrial designs.

It is difficult to know how important patent considerations may be in shaping the strategies of a multinational enterprise. From time to time, cases emerge that involve patentholders defending major stakes in foreign countries. Numerous countries, including China and Brazil for example, appear to be able to attract a considerable number of multinational enterprises over a wide range of industries, even though foreign patentholders have good reason to question the quality of the protection their patents will receive. Moreover, careful studies fail to reveal any relationship between the strength of the patent grant in a country and that country's capacity to attract foreign-owned enterprises. Even after correcting for the obvious factors that might otherwise obscure such a relationship, such as the size and structure of the national economy, the nature of its trade barriers, and the level of political risk, researchers have been unable to detect any evidence to suggest that the patent grant has been influencing the strategies of multinational enterprises. But the testimony of managers suggests that the studies may be misleading.

Antitrust Measures

The background.   From the viewpoint of multinational enterprises, only a few countries apply antitrust measures of any significance. One is the United States, another the European Union, and two recent surprising additions, Mexico and Korea. The pervasive emphasis in many countries on maintaining open markets, however, suggests that the importance of antitrust policies will grow. That expectation is supported by a number of other considerations.

- The proliferation of international alliances among potential competitors in the past decade has sometimes raised questions about the business practices likely to emerge among these competitors in cases in which they succeed in dominating the market.
- Despite the increase in the number and geographical spread of large industrial

firms in recent decades, the barriers to entry in some product lines appear to have grown, especially in some high-tech products. In the automobile and commercial aircraft industries, for example, the number of effective competitors in world markets has declined rather than increased.

- With the sharp increase in the number and coverage of free-trade areas in the past decade, governments are being obliged to confront the question of whether they should replace trade policy with competition policy in dealing with questions of competition and monopoly within such areas. The European Union already applies its common antitrust policy in lieu of restrictive trade measures when problems such as shut-out pricing and predatory dumping arise inside its single market.

U.S. policies.   Time was, 40 years ago, when multinational enterprises with an interest in the U.S. market had to pay the closest attention to U.S. antitrust law in shaping their strategies. At that time, the United States was the only country with an antitrust policy of any practical importance. In addition, international cartels, such as the restrictive prewar agreements among Dupont, Imperial Chemicals, and I. G. Farben dividing up world markets in chemicals, and between the world's principal oil companies fixing world prices, were being vigorously investigated and prosecuted. Moreover, some joint ventures between a U.S. firm and an international rival—arrangements that had some elements in common with those found in various alliances today—were being held in violation of U.S. law.

Today, the fervor that was evident in earlier antitrust prosecutions by the U.S. government is much reduced, especially where such cases involve firms operating in foreign jurisdictions. The number of participants engaged in most international product markets is typically greater than it was 40 years ago, thus limiting the power of restrictive business agreements. On the other hand, where increased concentration occurs in any product line or where collaborating firms learn to divide markets between them, national remedies will prove less adequate for dealing with the problems of restoring competition.

In the absence of international agreements, how are national authorities likely to apply their national laws? Will U.S. statutes, for instance, be applied in ways that discriminate against foreign-owned enterprises? Apart from a period in which I. G. Farben and other German firms were viewed as agents of the Nazi government, there is little in the enforcement history of such statutes to suggest such a possibility. Some recent trends, however, need to be taken into account in assessing future possibilities. For instance, in 1993 when Congress enlarged the existing exemption from U.S. antitrust laws for cooperative research ventures, it limited the exemption in various ways: first, to ventures with their "principal facilities" in the United States; and second, only to those foreign-owned enterprises whose governments extended similar treatment to U.S.-owned firms. Once again, U.S. policy seemed to be moving toward the concept of "conditional" national treatment.

The European Union.   Despite much initial skepticism, the antitrust policies of the European Union have turned out to have real substance. Read literally, they have at least as much sweep as the U.S. Sherman and Clayton antitrust acts, although the terms are less general and the procedures for enforcement different.

- Firms are required, for instance, to clear with the Commission any arrangements that may serve to divide up markets inside the European Union, such as territorial dealership agreements. Whereas conditional exemptions have been granted to various categories of agreements, such as joint R&D undertakings, numerous specific agreements have been rejected or subjected to specific restraints. (See Box 7-3).
- Where firms engage in restrictive business agreements or other predatory practices that affect crossborder trade inside the Union, the remedy lies in antitrust proceedings conducted by the Commission. Using these powers, the Union has forced the revision or abandonment of numerous schemes by enterprises to divide up national markets inside the Union and has imposed heavy fines on offending firms.
- Where large firms in different member countries propose a crossborder merger, the proposal requires the Commission's prior approval to determine whether the resulting entity will dominate any EU market. Although the Commission has rarely blocked such mergers, its review of such proposals is far from perfunctory.

Ample opportunities exist, therefore, for discrimination against foreign-owned enterprises in the enforcement of the Rome treaty's antitrust provisions. Like the U.S. Clayton Act, for instance, one provision of the treaty prohibits firms from abusing a "dominant position" in the common market. Two of the landmark cases on the "dominance" issue, however, have involved U.S.-based Continental Can and Gillette, stirring doubts in the minds of some observers regarding the nondiscriminatory application of the provision (Box 7-4).

Capital-Market Policies

The background.   In the early 1990s, the world's daily transactions in foreign currencies amounted to about $1 trillion, a total that is about 75 times the world's daily international transactions in goods and services. Overwhelmingly, therefore, foreign exchange transactions were arising out of activities associated with the capital accounts. Governments see this vast volume of transactions as containing highly volatile elements, including speculative operations in floating currencies and bets by speculators against governments that are attempting to maintain a given exchange rate. The total amount of foreign currencies that governments collectively hold comes to only a fraction of the daily transactions on foreign exchange markets. It is therefore

BOX 7-3.   TREATY OF ROME, ARTICLES 85 AND 86

ARTICLE 85

1. The following shall be deemed to be incompatible with the Common Market and shall hereby be prohibited: any agreement between enterprises, any decisions by associations of enterprises and any concerted practices which are likely to affect trade between the Member States and which have as their object or result the prevention, restriction or distortion of competition within the Common Market, in particular those consisting in:

(a) the direct or indirect fixing of purchase or selling prices or of any other trading conditions;

(b) the limitation or control of production, markets, technical development or investment;

(c) market-sharing or the sharing of sources of supply;

(d) the application to parties to transactions of unequal terms in respect of equivalent supplies, thereby placing them at a competitive disadvantage; or

(e) the subjecting of the conclusion of a contract to the acceptance by a party of additional supplies which, either by their nature or according to commercial usage, have no connection with the subject of such contract.

2. Any agreements or decisions prohibited pursuant to this Article shall be null and void.

3. Nevertheless, the provisions of paragraph 1 may be declared inapplicable in the case of:

—any agreements or classes of agreements between enterprises,

—any decisions or classes of decisions by associations of enterprises, and

—any concerted practices or classes of concerted practices which contribute to the improvement of the production or distribution of goods or to the promotion of technical or economic progress while reserving to users an equitable share in the profit resulting therefrom, and which:

(a) neither impose on the enterprises concerned any restrictions not indispensable to the attainment of the above objectives;

(b) nor enable such enterprises to eliminate competition in respect of a substantial proportion of the goods concerned.

ARTICLE 86

To the extent to which trade between any Member States may be affected thereby, action by one or more enterprises to take improper advantage of a dominant position within the Common Market or within a substantial part of it shall be deemed to be incompatible with the Common Market and shall hereby be prohibited.

Such improper practices may, in particular, consist in:

(continued)

BOX 7-3.   TREATY OF ROME, ARTICLES 85 AND 86 (CONTINUED)

ARTICLE 86

(a) the direct or indirect imposition of any inequitable purchase or selling prices or of any other inequitable trading conditions;

(b) the limitation of production, markets or technical development to the prejudice of consumers;

(c) the application to parties to transactions of unequal terms in respect of equivalent supplies, thereby placing them at a competitive disadvantage; or

(d) the subjecting of the conclusion of a contract to the acceptance, by a party, of additional supplies which, either by their nature or according to commercial usage, have no connection with the subject of such contract.

apparent why many governments see capital transactions as a potential threat to the stability of their national currencies and why many feel the need to maintain some control over such transactions.

In the course of exercising those controls, governments are likely to distinguish multinational enterprises from national enterprises in a number of different contexts.

BOX 7-4.   THE GILLETTE CASE IN THE EUROPEAN UNION

In November 1992, the European Commission ordered Gillette, a U.S-based company in the wet-shave business, to divest itself of its interests in Wilkinson Sword, a British-based company in the same business. Gillette's interest in Wilkinson Sword arose indirectly through its interest in Eemland Holdings N.V., a company in the Netherlands; Eemland, in turn, was the parent of Wilkinson. Gillette was a substantial creditor of Eemland as well as holding 22 percent of its stock.

The Commission noted that Gillette commanded over half of the shaving products market of Europe, and concluded that it held a "dominant" position in that market. Its involvement in Wilkinson was therefore seen as an "abuse" of that dominant position and hence a violation of Article 86 of the Rome treaty. Gillette was directed not only to sell its equity stake in Eemland but also to transfer to Eemland some Wilkinson Sword plants it held in Europe outside of the Community, including Turkey. Eemland meanwhile was directed to repay the loans it had received from Gillette, thus completely severing the connection between the companies.

SOURCE: *The New York Times*, November 12, 1992, p. C2.

- As we noted earlier, where the capital movement is part of a project by a foreign-owned firm to set up a branch or subsidiary, many governments wish to be in a position either to impose conditions that increase the economic benefits, or to weigh the security implications of the project, or to screen the project for other purposes.
- Where the capital movement is an outflow rather than an inflow, as in the case of a project by a domestic firm to set up a branch or subsidiary in a foreign country, some governments want to be in a position to review the project for its employment implications and balance-of-payment implications.
- Where the capital movement would substantially affect the money-generating capacity of the national banking system, some governments want to modify the transaction for its monetary effects, distinguishing in the process between foreign-owned firms and domestic firms.

As was observed earlier, the 1980s and 1990s represented a period in which governmental controls were lightened throughout the world, bringing capital markets in different countries in greater contact with one another. Nonetheless, the distinctions between foreigners and domestic participants continued to play a significant role.

Foreign-exchange controls.   Any international transaction, whether for the purchase or sale of goods and services or the movement of an investment across a national border, usually entails the conversion of money from one currency to another. Although none of the 22 member countries of the IMF classified as "industrial nations" restricts the use of foreign exchange for the purchase of goods and services, 92 of the 156 "developing nations" do maintain such restrictions. Where capital-account transactions are involved, 8 of the 22 "industrial nations" and 130 of the 156 "developing nations" impose restrictions. In the granting of licenses under most of these systems, governments commonly distinguish between applicant firms that are foreign-owned and those they regard as nationals.

Where multinational enterprises encounter restrictions in current-account transactions, they are usually of the following kind:

- Limits on the remission of profits to foreign parents and on the payment of interest or license fees to parents.
- Limits on payments for imported goods and services, and requirements for the surrender of foreign exchange acquired from exports of goods and services.

Restrictions on the capital-account transactions of foreign-owned enterprises, always much more common than restrictions on current-account transactions, have taken on added importance in some countries in recent years. Although those restrictions have not always been part of the foreign-exchange licensing system in a formal sense, they have served to produce similar restraints. Two special types of transactions have figured prominently in the exercise of these controls.

One has been the use of "swaps" by foreign multinationals in acquiring investments in countries with heavy foreign indebtedness, such as Mexico and Brazil (see Box 7-5). In such transactions,

- Foreigners acquire the debt of a foreign government at discount prices in a public market.
- They then tender this debt to the government for redemption in the national currency, usually sharing the discount with the debtor government.
- They are permitted to use that currency to buy an equity interest in local enterprises.

The second type of transaction that has helped to extend controls over capital-account transactions has been the ambitious programs of many countries, including some in the FSU and Latin America, for the sale of their state-owned enterprises. Such privatization programs have been extremely widespread in the 1990s, involving scores of countries and hundreds of billions of dollars in assets.

Governments have usually maintained close control over purchases by foreign

---

BOX 7-5. BRASMOTOR'S DEBT-EQUITY SWAP

Brasmotor is a large Brazilian company, a leader in the country's domestic appliance industry. It holds a dominant position, for instance in washers, refrigerators, and air conditioners. In 1987, wishing to raise additional capital in local currency in order to finance a new washing machine factory, Brasmotor explored the use of a debt-equity swap. The amount of local capital needed came to the equivalent of $50 million.

Operating within the provisions of Brazilian regulations at the time and subject to the government's approval, Brasmotor sold 4.5 million nonvoting preferred shares of its stock to five foreign banks, located in Canada, England, and Spain. In payment, the banks proffered for conversion $50 million of the external debt of Brazil, then selling in secondary markets at $31 million—that is, at a discount of 38 percent. By the time the deal was approved by the Brazilian government some months later, the discount had widened to 62.5 percent.

On approval, Brasmotor tendered the $50 million of external debt to Brazil's Central Bank, which thereupon credited Brasmotor with the equivalent amount in Brazil's local currency, calculated at the exchange rate then prevailing. On the basis of expert estimates of the value of the stock at the time the deal was approved, it appeared that the banks were giving up assets worth $18.8 million to secure assets worth $25.6 million. The Brazilian government began to wonder at that point whether its regulations governing swaps needed supplementing and, if so, what provisions should be introduced.

buyers in such operations, with various concerns in mind. In some cases, they have been fearful that foreigners might be in a position to acquire national assets at bargain-basement prices, with long-term injury to the domestic economy. In other instances, they have feared that opposition parties might make political capital out of large foreign acquisitions in sensitive areas of the national economy.

The Service Industries

Many of the issues discussed in this chapter with regard to the product industries also apply to the services industries. But the special characteristics of the service industries often lead governments to apply some distinctive measures. As a rule, those special characteristics stem from a number of factors common to services:

- *Protecting the buyer.* In many cases the buyer of services is substantially more vulnerable than the buyer of goods. Is the seller of the service actually qualified to perform? Does the accountant or the engineer or the architect have the requisite training and experience? Does the bank have the requisite assets and lending capabilities? To cope with such problems, practically all countries designate a list of licensed professions and licensed service industries, using criteria for licensing that are usually hostile to foreigners.
- *Entrenched protection.* Of course, once such professions and industries are designated, they constitute an interest group devoted to protecting and strengthening their franchises, to the further detriment of foreign applicants. Indeed, in many countries, governments have delegated the control of new entrants to organizations staffed and controlled by the designated professions and industries.
- *Natural monopolies.* Another problem is that the seller of some services commonly holds a monopoly position. Although new technologies are rapidly changing their situation, telephone companies and electric-generating plants have faced little or no competition in the national markets in which they hold a franchise. Accordingly, such industries are typically subject to special supervision from regulatory authorities, raising questions about the nondiscriminatory treatment of foreign-owned enterprises.

Because of the variety of situations presented by different service industries, it is difficult to generalize about the governmental measures of greatest interest to multinational enterprises. When governments invite multinational enterprises in service industries to establish themselves in the country, it is usually because they hope to obtain the added technological boost and capital that such enterprises can sometimes provide. Nevertheless, foreign-owned enterprises in such industries frequently encounter measures that impede their operations in the country, including impediments to the movement of foreign specialists into the country and other such limitations on their activities.

Finally, those service industries whose products are most transparent and most competitive, such as hotels and retail chains, generally encounter the fewest special difficulties. The success of McDonalds and other such food purveyors in penetrating Moscow and Beijing, therefore, is not accidental, but even such industries may face unique hurdles at times. In Japan, for instance, numerous local regulations and various national laws are designed to protect small neighborhood retail shops against effective competition. So the path of the multinational enterprise in the service industries promises to remain somewhat rocky.

Beyond Economics

The constraints that governments impose on multinational enterprises do not always stem from the country's economic interests or its interest groups. Some of the most draconian restraints arise from other considerations: a desire to protect the national culture; to bolster national security; and to deal with environmental issues.

Cultural Constraints

Various governments impose restrictions on foreign-owned enterprises in radio, television, newspaper publishing, and motion picture exhibition for a variety of motives. Sometimes the object is to protect a local industry, and sometimes to preserve a local culture. With the proliferation in the means of communication across international borders, from e-mail to satellites, many of these measures seem increasingly futile. Yet they manifest themselves in various ways, from the control of television broadcasting to the imposition of quotas on films displayed in public theaters.

Security Constraints

Most countries have developed regulations purportedly related to the national defense, ranging from restrictions on the export of goods and services to restrictions on foreign ownership in designated industries. As in the case of the measures protecting the culture industries, the power of these restraints seems to be declining. In particular:

- The prototypes of high-tech weaponry continue to increase in cost so rapidly that only the United States and a few European transnational consortia seem capable of financing such weaponry. Therefore, in this area only a few countries maintain controls of any practical consequence, but they are obviously of considerable importance to multinational enterprises.
- The technology of low-tech weapons of destruction, such as weapons of chemi-

cal and biological warfare, is already widely disseminated. (The technology of nuclear weapon production seems headed in the same direction, as technologies mastered in the FSU leak outward into other countries.) In this area, the national controls on exports maintained by countries that might be the source of such technologies probably have only transitory and limited effects.

- Modern instruments of war, such as tanks and aircraft, are produced from components, subcomponents, and specialized materials, assembled in different locations, usually containing substantial foreign elements. In this area, effective controls are difficult and costly, especially because many of the elements in the final products also are produced for civilian use.

- Finally, the United States, various European governments, Russia, and China, among others, find themselves promoting the export of military hardware. The U.S. record in the 1990s in this respect is particularly striking. The rationalization for such exports is that it contributes to maintaining the national production capability of the exporting country and it holds down the costs of the defense establishment. It also reduces the effectiveness of security control systems.

Most governments, including the United States and European countries, recognize the prospect of a decline in the effectiveness of security export controls. So far, the response of governments has been limited to measures that seem unlikely to do more than buy a little time, such as the Nuclear Nonproliferation Treaty and various national systems of export control directed at "outlaw" nations such as Libya and Iran. This is a field in which managers of multinational enterprises may confront major international initiatives in the immediate future, as the increasing threats become more palpable.

Environmental Constraints

Many governments maintain active programs aimed at controlling the environment, and multinational enterprises must take these programs into account in the development of firm strategies. Various international agreements already limit the manufacture and use of products threatening to the environment. And managers must count on individual countries imposing added limitations from time to time.

As a rule, however, measures for the control of the environment make no distinctions between domestic enterprises and multinational enterprises. If multinational enterprises seem to be disproportionately affected by environmental controls, that is due largely to the fact that firms engaged in such pollution-generating activities as raw materials exploitation, chemicals production, and automobile production tend to have a multinational structure. Still, some programs of environmental control will likely present especially strong challenges to enterprises organized along multinational lines.

Numerous proposals have been advanced urging governments to compel their multinational enterprises to apply home environmental standards to the activities of their subsidiaries and affiliates abroad. A few governments, Germany, for example, have been zealous in the promotion of environmental controls, reflecting a strong grass-roots sentiment for such controls. Most governments, however, including those with strong environmental programs at home, have been slow to compel their multinational enterprises to adhere to those standards in other countries. One reason has been a desire not to handicap their enterprises in international competition. Another has been a desire to avoid restraints affecting other countries that those countries have not adopted on their own initiatives.

In some cases, the proposal is that such subsidiaries should live up to home standards in the *products* they manufacture abroad, such as including antipolluting exhaust systems on automobiles manufactured in foreign countries and avoiding the production of pesticides that are banned in the home country. In these instances, home countries have taken a few hesitant steps in the indicated direction, such as setting up systems of notification to importing countries when exports include items banned in the home country. However, they have rarely gone so far as to impose restrictions on subsidiaries located in other jurisdictions.

The reluctance of home countries to intervene in the production activities of subsidiaries in other jurisdictions has been reinforced by the seeming indifference of many developing countries in the use of pollution-reducing products. Automobile owners in some countries have routinely stripped pollution controls from their vehicles. Even in countries where such devices are required, some governments have made no effort to enforce their requirements.

Environmental groups have also sought to discourage the installation of *processes* in foreign countries that fail to meet home standards. Their objective has been to prevent the development of international pollution havens, sanctuaries in which pollution-generating industries can pursue undesirable practices banned in their home environments. Apart from the programs of the EU, however, governments have done scarcely anything in that direction.

Nevertheless, pollution control is a field in which multinational enterprises are likely to encounter considerable governmental activity in the years ahead. Although few governments will be eager unilaterally to take the lead in this area, grass-roots pressures, as well as the example of some governments such as Germany and Japan, will overcome such constraints from time to time. Intergovernmental agreements of a regional kind, such as agreements under the aegis of NAFTA and the EU, could prove common. Managers must be constantly aware of the implications of such agreements for the strategy of the enterprise.

Exporting National Norms

The case of environmental controls exemplifies a large class of problems to which the managers of multinational enterprises must be particularly sensitive. Operating in various countries with differing norms, multinational enterprises cannot escape the

---

BOX 7-6.   PIZZA HUT'S POLICIES

An editorial in the *New York Times* (July 22, 1994) reports that Pizza Hut, which is a subsidiary of Pepsico, provides far less generous health coverage to its employees in the United States than to those in Germany and Japan, where it is subject to governmental mandates.

   In the United States, employees get no coverage for the first six months of their employment, according to the editorial, and thereafter receive company contributions only for additional coverage, not for the basic plan. A bill produced by a Senate committee would have required companies like Pizza Hut to pay 12 percent of a worker's wages for insurance premiums, far less than the existing requirements of Germany and Japan. Pizza Hut's business in these countries, according to the *New York Times*, is booming.

---

pressures created by those differences. With continued improvements in international communication, interested parties in different countries are likely to use those differences with increasing effect (see Box 7-6).

   Apart from the environment, the area of policy in which such differences are likely to play a considerable role is that of labor relations. In setting their norms in different countries, the protection of child and female labor, the promotion of safety in the workplace, and the creation of fringe benefits are among the subjects that multinationals will find themselves increasingly obliged to consider. In some instances, in setting their standards, such enterprises will find themselves between a rock and a hard place: obliged either to violate the norms of the host country or to disregard the pressures from abroad.

Suggested Reading

BOLTLUCK, RICHARD, and ROBERT E. LITAN (eds.). *Down in the Dumps: Administration of the Unfair Trade Laws.* Washington, DC: Brookings Institution, 1991.

DOZ, YVES L. "Government Policies and Global Industries." In Micheal E. Porter (ed.), *Competition in Global Industries.* Boston: Harvard Business School Press, 1986, 225–266.

GRINDLEY, PETER, DAVID C. MOWERY, and BRIAN SILVERMAN. "SEMATECH and Collaborative Research: Lessons in the Design of High-Technology Consortia." *Journal of Policy Analysis and Management,* 13, no. 4 (1994), 723–758.

MORAN, THEODORE H. "Introduction: Governments and Transnational Corporations." In T. H. Moran (ed.), *Governments and Transnational Corporations.* London: Routledge and the United Nations, 1993, 1–36.

CHAPTER 8

The National Economy in an International Setting

This chapter introduces the third and final section of this text. To put the chapter in context, recall what each of the three sections covers:

Part One, covering Chapters 2 to 5, views the international economy through the eyes of the firm manager, identifying opportunities, assessing risks, and formulating responses.

Part Two, covering Chapters 6 and 7, explores the interactions between the multinational enterprise and the nations in which it does business.

Part Three, beginning with this chapter, explores the central characteristics of the international economic system in which the manager is obliged to operate.

To develop an understanding of the international economic system, however, we must begin inside the national economy. For example, for managers to understand the changes in value of a national currency in international markets, they must begin with economic conditions at home. For that purpose, some fundamental concepts of macroeconomic analysis prove to be of great value, providing a richer understanding of what the manager is actually observing.

Matching Payments to Output

The Isolated Economy

Let us begin by reviewing a few simple ideas of how an economy works when it is totally isolated from the world, without links to an international economy. Each year, our isolated economy produces a variety of goods and services. For present purposes, we can say that the goods and services so produced are of three different kinds:

> **Consumer goods and services** (C): fuel, clothing, recreation, and other products and services acquired by the country's households for their consumption.
>
> **Investment goods and services** (I): machines, plants, engineering, and other goods and services acquired by the country's enterprises for production.
>
> **Government goods and services** (G): construction supplies and services, teaching supplies and services, and other goods and services used for the operations of governments, or acquired by governments to be dispensed other than through sale.

In the production of these goods and services during the year, those who have contributed are paid for that contribution. All told, these payments are exactly equal to the value of the goods and services they produce. What form do these payments take? The answer is

> **Payments to labor, net of taxes** (W).
>
> **Payments to capital (profit, rent, interest), net of taxes** (P).
>
> **Payments to governments, taxes** (T).

So . . .

$$C + I + G = W + P + T$$

In economic parlance, either sum represents gross national product (GNP). (There are a few awkward definitional problems and oversimplifications in the identity just stated, but problems of this sort are not significant here.)

The preceding relationship looks more obvious at first than it may appear on reflection. Remember that all we have been talking about so far is final goods and services—that is, products elaborated to the stage at which they are ready for consumption or investment. But how do the figures capture all the goods and services that pass as intermediates between business firms: the steel that goes to make refrigerators, the fuel that goes to make electricity, and so on?

The answer is that, insofar as the output of one industry gets used up to generate another's output, the aggregate value of output of the second industry reflects that fact. In short, the final value of a camcorder destined for a home in a Chicago suburb or of a lathe destined for a machine shop in San Francisco includes the value of all the design work, steel, copper, plastic, and distribution effort that went into the final product. Each industry's output, therefore, incorporates all the payments for all the inputs that have preceded it. In the end, as one traces back every input, its price is eventually accounted for by a payment to labor or capital or government, and the value of all the final output is an accumulation of all such payments. Accordingly, intermediate goods and services do not have to be taken into account explicitly in achieving the basic statistical identities set out above: the final value of all output is equal to all the payments to labor, capital, and government in the making of that output.

One might suppose that an economy of this isolated variety could operate with completely stable prices forever. The income placed in the hands of buyers of goods and services—that is, of consumers, of buyers of investment goods, or of government—is exactly equal to the goods and services that are being produced. To be sure, the mix may not be quite right; there may be too much of one good and too little of another to suit the marketplace. If small shifts in price could be counted on to restore equilibrium, however, the price level in general might well be stable.

Of course, there are numerous reasons why such stability is unlikely.

- *Saving and dissaving.* Consumers might hoard part of their income, putting it under the mattress; if they do that, the income withheld will not go into the market to bid for the available goods and services. Or consumers might go on a spending binge, drawing on the sums they had previously hoarded. If they do that, they will be demanding goods and services that were not produced in the period under consideration.
- *Varying the money supply.* Governments or banks may take steps that change the supply of money. Governments commonly possess the power to run the printing press. Banks often have the power to increase their loans to the public, giving them money in the form of a checking account.

If increases in money exceed increases in output, sellers may be able to draw on their inventories to fill the demand. If inventories are not available, however, bidders in the country will compete for the limited available goods, driving up prices. If changes in output exceed changes in money, producers may be obliged to inventory the surplus; otherwise, they will have to lower their prices to clear the market. Eventually, in the periods that follow, the output and the money flow may come back into equilibrium. For a time, however, even the closed economy may be unstable.

The Open Economy

So far, we have assumed a closed economy that produces all its own consumer goods and investment goods. It pays all its wages, profits, and taxes to entities inside the country; and all investment decisions and savings decisions affecting the country are made from within.

Now we open up the borders. Suddenly, a number of new alternatives present themselves. Goods and services produced inside the country can be exported; goods and services produced outside can be imported. Entities inside the country can receive income from without; entities outside the country can receive income from within. Obviously, the old identities between national production and national payments may not hold any longer. Can any shreds of the old identity be restored?

The answer is yes. Equilibrium is a bit more complex to achieve, but it is not wholly out of reach.

Begin with a country whose situation involves only one or two of the complexities suggested.

- With the borders open, national firms will be producing not only for national households (C), enterprises (I), and governments (G), but also for the export markets (E). The proceeds deriving from such production will provide not only national wages (W), profits (P), and taxes (T), but also the wherewithal for purchasing imports (M). So:

$$C + I + G + X = W + P + T + M$$

or

$$C + I + G + (X - M) = W + P + T = \text{GNP}$$

All these relationships are accounting identities; if the numbers have been compiled correctly, the equalities are inescapable. By opening the economy, however, we have added to the sources that might disturb the equilibrium between goods and services available and money available. The supply of goods and services can now be affected by imports and exports. And the supply of money can now be affected by the in-movement and out-movement of funds.

The next few pages demonstrate that when an open economy gets out of equilibrium in the sense that payments and output become unequal, a series of forces is launched in the economy that may nudge the economy back toward balance. Some of these forces can be traced through the country's income and others through the country's price structure.

Income-Equilibrating Effects

Let us suppose that the measure that produced the imbalance between the supply of money on the one hand and the output of goods and services on the other was the government's decision to print $100 and to make a gift of that sum to the country's farmers. In the closed economy, the infusion of new money could lead to more production, higher prices, or both. In the open economy, the possibilities are more complex.

To trace out the consequences, we have to make a few simple assumptions about the behavior of the mythical country of our example. Assume that whenever a national of that country receives an added dollar of income, the national spends 60 cents on local goods and 20 cents on imported goods, and fails to spend the other 20 cents. Then, if the increase in money supply is $100, Table 8-1 suggests what would happen.

The first line of Table 8-1 shows how the recipients of the original $100 dispose of their new income: $20 is paid out to foreigners through payments for imports, another $20 will drop out of circulation through saving, and only $60 will be respent in the domestic economy. In the next line of Table 8-1, the distribution course of the $60 is followed, line by line, until the original $100 has all "leaked away."

As a result of the process, nothing in the country would be the same. According to the totals shown in the table, the excess $100 would have generated a total of $250 of added domestic sales and added money income before its effects were dissipated. Of every $100 of injected money, $50 would leak out to foreigners to pay for increased imports, whereas $50 would be neutralized by remaining unspent.

The government's decision to inject $100, therefore, will drain its foreign exchange by $50, according to this simple model, before the effects of the injection are dissipated. If nothing further happened to the economy, its income flows and its goods flows would be back in equilibrium. (At this point, you may wish to try your hand at the converse possibility. Assume that the government withdraws $100 from circulation through a special tax; then trace the results for income, imports, and savings.)

Now, let us change our assumptions in one critical respect. Assume this time that the injection of added money into the economy comes from outside the country. A foreigner writes a check on her home bank in her home currency equivalent in value to $100. She sends the check for deposit to a bank that is located in another country. The bank, we assume, turns over its check denominated in the foreigner's currency to its central bank, receiving a credit for $100 in return. The bank then credits the foreigner with $100. The foreigner proceeds to spend the money in the local economy to purchase local labor and local goods.

For the moment, the country has made a solid gain in foreign exchange reserves. But can the country hold on to all its gain? The answer, according to the

TABLE 8-1. Result of Injecting $100 of Excess Funds into the Local Economy—Model 1

	Increase in Income	Increase in Imports	Increase in Saving	Balance for Respending
Injection	$100.00	$20.00	$20.00	$ 60.00
1st respending	60.00	12.00	12.00	36.00
2nd respending	36.00	7.20	7.20	21.60
3rd respending	21.60	4.32	4.32	12.96
•	•	•	•	•
•	•	•	•	•
•	•	•	•	•
TOTAL	$250.00	$50.00	$50.00	$150.00

model portrayed in Table 8-1, is no. Once the $100 begins to be used inside the country, its effects, according to the model, ought to be exactly like those of the government-generated money; before these effects are dissipated, they will have generated $50 of added imports to be offset against the original $100 gain in resources.

Although the exercise in Table 8-1 is simple in concept, its lessons are very real. When excess funds are turned loose in an economy, a series of forces gets to work to diffuse their unsettling effect. In the illustrations used so far, it was assumed that the excess funds came into the country by way of international capital movements or by way of the government's use of the printing press. However, one could picture their coming into a country from other directions: by way of foreign aid or export surpluses, or even by way of individuals' dishoarding currency previously stuffed into the country's mattresses.

However the funds may be generated, the channels by which they are withdrawn are imports and savings. Just how much of each depends on the economy's characteristics. In a country in which the marginal propensity to import was high, the release of new funds into the economy obviously would place comparatively heavy pressures on imports. On the other hand, if the marginal rate of imports was low and that of savings was high, new funds could be injected into the system with only moderate concern about increasing the country's imports.

These close ties among money injections, imports, and savings clarify a great many aspects of monetary policy. They explain why countries in balance-of-payment difficulties are urged to reduce their money supply and to increase their savings. They also explain why countries that are receiving large infusions of foreign capital, although grateful for the apparent contribution to their balance of payments, still worry about the consequent effect on their internal money incomes. These effects may subsequently lead to new strains on their supplies of foreign exchange.

Price-Equilibrating Effects

Like all simple models, Table 8-1 assumed that everything else in the world would stand still. In the real world, however, many things will change. One likely change will be the country's exchange rate, that is, the price at which the country's currency is exchanged for the currencies of other countries. Let us put that possibility aside for the present, however, to be addressed below.

There is another likely change that we can address here. In a closed economy, it will be recalled, an infusion of new money could lead to price increases. In a country with open borders, the possibility of such an infusion from abroad constitutes an added hazard. The waves of capital moving among countries today constitute a powerful force for varying the national money supply, and, as Table 8-1 indicates, the money income of the country would be pushed upward by the spending and respending of the $100 excess that its economy was trying to absorb.

In all these reactions to the injection of new money, of course, an economy that is already making full use of its productive resources at the time the new money is injected will react differently from one that is capable of increasing its output. By definition, the fully engaged economy is incapable of increasing its real income; so all the reactions described above have to be read as reactions in money terms alone. Table 8-1 tells us, therefore, that in money terms, a multiplier of 2.5 converts a $100 injection of new money into a nominal increase in income of $250, but it does not tell us what the increase may be in real terms. (For that purpose, economists often use other multipliers, sometimes entitled Keynesian multipliers.)

In any event, if the domestic economy's production capacity is already pressed to the limit and cannot yield another pound of rice or another yard of textiles, the money churning around in the country can raise the country's prices without increasing its real income. Accordingly, if new money is injected into the economy, the first effect might be a sharp rise in prices. If that occurred, Table 8-1 might prove to be a poor predictor of how the country would bring itself back into balance. Inflation could lead the country's nationals to behave quite differently from the initial assumptions incorporated in Table 8-1. Influenced by the increased prices at home, they might feel disposed to import more. Let us reflect these changed assumptions in Table 8-2. Here, with each respending, the import propensity of the economy is assumed to have risen a little, from 20 to 25 percent, and so on, until a ceiling of 40 percent is reached. At the same time, savings are assumed to have fallen by an amount equal to the increased spending on imports.

As Table 8-2 indicates, the balance-of-payment drain is greater in the new model, $67.40 against $50.00. Equilibrium is restored in the sense that the injection of new money eventually fritters itself away through imports and saving. But the restoration of equilibrium is accompanied by more imports, and hence more demands for foreign exchange to pay for these imports. If a country's supply of foreign exchange is limited, the increased import demand will increase the risk of imperiling the country's balance-of-payment position.

At this point in the exposition, let us look back at the structure of the ideas that have been crammed into the last few pages. Throughout, we have assumed that the

TABLE 8-2. Result of Injecting $100 of Excess Funds into the Local Economy—Model 2

	Increase in Income	Increase in Imports	Increase in Saving	Balance for Respending
Injection	$100.00	$20.00	$20.00	$ 60.00
1st respending	60.00	15.00	9.00	36.00
2nd respending	36.00	10.80	3.60	21.60
3rd respending	21.60	8.64	0	12.96
•	•	•	•	•
•	•	•	•	•
•	•	•	•	•
TOTAL	$250.00	$67.40	$32.60	$150.00

exchange rate of a country will remain unchanged. With that caveat in mind, the basic structure is relatively simple:

- When the money supply of a country increases, adjustments begin to take place. When measured in money terms, incomes and savings increase. And as prices change, so do imports and exports.
- Eventually, increased nominal savings and increased net imports drain away the increase in the money supply. Just how much each of these factors plays a role depends on the economy's structure. If there is a very high propensity to save (hence, a low propensity to consume), the balance-of-payment strain generated by the adjustment need not be great; if there is a low propensity to import, the adjustment is smaller still.
- The price adjustments that accompany the change in money supply may lead to an increase in imports (or a decline in exports). Just how these work out depends on the sensitivity of the country's price structure to increases in nominal costs. If these reactions are strong, the price increases could change the country's trade balance substantially. The changed trade balance in turn would eventually reduce income and dampen prices, thus moving the economy back toward equilibrium.

One Disturbance or a Series

All these generalizations, however, call for a loud word of caution. Throughout our discussion, we have traced the effects of a single disturbance in the economy. But what if the government persisted, year after year, in printing $100 for distribution to farmers? The models reflected in Tables 8-1 and 8-2 tell us that, year after year, we would see elevated income, imports, and savings, at least in nominal money terms. That pattern, however, does not lead to equilibrium; the country would in the end have to find some way of paying foreigners for the elevated imports.

Besides, expectations and responses in the country are bound to change as a result of the government's behavior.

- If the government's deficit spending raises the prices of things that farmers buy, for instance, farmers are likely to demand that the government raise its subsidy from $100 to, say, $150, thereby increasing the import balances to be financed in the future.
- On the other hand, if farmers spend their first $100 windfall on increasing the productivity of their land, the country might be able to count on increased national production and, hence, less imports to meet the increased demand generated by the government's deficit spending.

The models we have explored in the past few pages, therefore, only set the stage for debates over the most appropriate policies to be pursued. Any policy that blithely disregards the macroeconomic relationships outlined there is fraught with peril and is likely to generate responses that the policymakers never intended. On the other hand, framing the appropriate policies requires critical judgments about national responses that the models themselves cannot readily provide. (See Box 8-1.)

The Banking System's Key Role

In modern economies, the national banking system plays a crucial role in all these processes. Managers who are concerned about the cost and availability of credit would do well to understand that role.

We can begin to build that understanding by picturing the items that would appear on the consolidated balance sheet of the commercial banks in a modern nation.

BOX 8-1.   TRADE BALANCES AND SAVINGS

Politicians often blame a country's negative balance of trade on the trade restrictions of other countries. Economists, however, assert that a country's foreign trade balance is equal to the amount of its savings; they want to know, therefore, whether savings can be increased. How do they justify their position?

The savings of a country's households is roughly approximated by the difference between wages and consumption

$$S_c = W - (C_d + C_m - C_x)$$

The savings of industry is approximated by the difference between profits and investment

$$S_i = P - (I_d + I_m - I_x)$$

The savings of government is approximated by the difference between taxes and government services

$$S_g = T - (G_d + G_m - G_x)$$

Add the three equations together and you can see why economists conclude that a change in the country's savings, other things being constant, means a change in its trade balance.

These are shown in Table 8-3. The figures in the table, of course, are quite arbitrary, but they will prove useful in showing how the system works.

As a rule, modern banking systems operate on the principle of fractional reserves. For every $100 that a bank takes on deposit from a customer, the bank is obliged to maintain some fraction on deposit with the nation's central bank, say, $20. Let us suppose that a 20 percent reserve requirement exists for the demand deposits of every bank. Suppose that the commercial banking system is in the situation as portrayed in Table 8-3, a situation in which the system has just enough reserves deposited at the central bank to meet the 20 percent requirement. Any increase in the bank loans of the country, however, automatically increases its deposits as well; so the banking system is blocked from making any further loans. When a national banking system has reached that standstill state, the behavior of foreigners may provide a critical ingredient, allowing it to escape from the ceiling.

Suppose for a moment that a French firm has decided that it needs an increase of $50 in its dollar working balances in the United States. One way for the French firm to secure those balances is to sell francs and buy U.S. dollars. These dollars can come from various sources, including other firms that happen to be unloading some of their U.S. dollar holdings at the time. If the supply of dollars being offered at the time is scarce, however, the French firm's demand for dollars may have the effect of pushing up the price of dollars in relation to the price of francs. If the U.S. monetary authorities are unwilling to see that happen, they may decide to offer more dollars on the foreign exchange market. When that happens, the logjam that the U.S. commercial banks confront is broken. Why?

When the French firm sells its francs for dollars, the U.S. government, operating through the Federal Reserve Bank, provides the dollars for the purchase. To do so, it must draw on its supply of dollars; that is, it must draw on an account it maintains in a commercial bank. When that happens, however, the effect is to increase by the same amount the net deposits that the country's commercial banking is maintaining with the Fed, a result fraught with strong implications.

Table 8-4 portrays the altered situation. The big change for U.S. banks is the development of surplus reserves in the central bank. Although the $50 transaction that was responsible for this change may have seemed small at first, its potential effects on the national money supply are actually multiplied. Operating on a 20 percent fractional reserve, the banking system increases its reserves by $50, which elevates its

TABLE 8-3.   Consolidated Balance Sheet of Nation's Commercial Banks

Assets		Liabilities and Capital	
Reserves deposited with central bank	$20	Customers' demand deposits	$100
Short-term loans and advances	60	Customers' time deposits	10
Long-term loans	20	Capital and reserves	10
Other assets	20		
Total assets	$120	Total liabilities and capital	$120

TABLE 8-4. Consolidated Balance Sheet of Nation's Commercial
Banks after Dollar Purchase by French Firm

Assets		Liabilities and Capital	
Reserves deposited with central bank	$70	French firm's demand deposits	$50
Short-term loans and advances	60	Other customers' demand deposits	100
Long-term loans	20	Other customers' time deposits	10
Other assets	20	Capital and reserves	10
Total assets	$170	Total liabilities and capital	$170

ceiling on demand deposits by $200. Since every new loan in the system creates a new deposit in the system, the increase in reserves means that the banking system is free to make $200 more of new loans. (With the starting conditions portrayed in Table 8-3, you may want to trace through another transaction, arising from a decision by the French firm to reduce its dollar working capital by $50.)

The Exchange Rate as Policy Tool

As the models in Tables 8-3 and 8-4 suggest, almost any significant economic measure taken by government is bound to have repercussions on the international position of the national economy. One policy tool in particular has a direct and immediate impact on managers in the international economy, namely, the exchange rate.

Abandoning a Fixed Rate

A government that decides to maintain a fixed rate of exchange for its national currency with the currency of another country is committing itself to buy or sell that foreign currency as necessary, at a price that reflects the chosen rate of exchange. To carry out that undertaking, the country must have access to a supply of the foreign currency sufficient for the purpose.

As long as the demand for foreign currencies comes only from sources that are buying foreign goods and services, governments can estimate the demand for foreign currencies with some degree of predictability. As was noted earlier, however, daily transactions in foreign exchange markets today total on the order of $1 trillion, about 75 times the value of goods and services sold daily in international markets. So the demand for major currencies is coming from many sources other than buyers of foreign goods and services. And most of these other sources have far more volatile demands.

One such source is the speculator who is betting that the government will soon abandon its commitment to hold its currency at a given rate (see Boxes 8-2 and 8-3).

Where fixed rates exist, such speculations can build up to a self-fulfilling prophecy. At little risk to themselves, speculators can sell so much local currency and accordingly demand so much foreign exchange as to force the government to abandon the fixed exchange rate at which it provides that exchange.

Stimulating Exports

Consider a country whose products and services have been losing position in world markets. At current exchange rates, its exports are priced too high for easy sale. At the same time, at current rates, the goods and services offered to its residents by foreign sellers seem cheap. The government is distressed by that situation for many reasons, including its depressing effects on the country's industries that produce exports and compete with imports.

As long as the government is committed to a fixed rate, the government must

---

BOX 8-2.   GERMAN MONETARY UNION AND THE CONVERSION OF OSTMARKS TO DEUTSCHE MARKS

Following the demolition of the Berlin Wall, a massive exodus began from east to west Germany. By February 1990, the number of migrants reached 2,000 to 3,000 per day, crippling the economy of the east and placing a massive strain on the facilities of the west. Alarmed by this situation, the governments of the two regions hastened the arrangements for German reunification.

As the first step toward the reunification, the German monetary union took place on July 2, 1990 when the west German deutsche mark became the single currency for a unified Germany. East German ostmarks were converted to deutsche marks at a prearranged set of conversion rates. The central bank of east Germany turned over its functions to the Bundesbank, the central bank of west Germany, and restrictions on the capital movements between the two Germanys were also removed.

Although the ostmark at the time was worth only one-fifth to one-tenth as much as the deutsche mark in real terms, large quantities of ostmarks were converted to deutsche marks at parity. In addition, the state-owned enterprises of east Germany restated the wages of their workers in deutsche marks on a basis that failed to reflect the vast differences in productivity between their workers and those in west Germany.

In the years immediately following reunification, the German government made transfers to east Germany of about $120 billion annually. By 1993 east Germany had lost 3 1/2 million jobs, and industrial production for Germany as a whole had dropped by 15 percent. The government deficit had risen to over 7 percent of GDP, the German current account had swung from surplus to deficit; and long-term interest rates had increased measurably.

BOX 8-3.   GEORGE SOROS AND STERLING

In August 1992, the Exchange Rate Mechanism (ERM) governing the relations of the principal members of the European Union (then the European Community) was under stress. Helmut Schlesinger, president of Germany's central bank, the Bundesbank, had repeatedly announced his intention of keeping Germany's interest rates high regardless of the growing unemployment in the country. Gratuitously, too, he made it clear that he thought present exchange rate values fixed under the ERM could not be held. Given the independence of the Bundesbank and the German postwar tradition of suppressing any hint of inflation, regardless of other consequences, Schlesinger's words were being taken very seriously in the currency markets.

The United Kingdom, it was widely known, was far more preoccupied with the dampening effect of interest rates on economic growth and less concerned about the threat of inflation. But the pound sterling was linked to the deutsche mark by the ERM agreement, committing both countries to maintain a relationship in the exchange rate market that kept the value of the two currencies inside a 2.25 percent band. With German interest rates high and the commitment to maintain such rates firm, capital flowed out of the United Kingdom to Germany, pushing the value of sterling to the bottom of the range permitted under the ERM.

In September 1992, George Soros, chairman of the Quantum Fund, committed the Fund to massive short sales of sterling, betting that he and other speculators could force the two central banks to abandon their efforts to hold sterling inside the 2.25 percent band. It was a lopsided bet, with limited risk and high potential gain. Besides, both governments had an incentive to abandon their stabilization efforts at an early stage, because in each instance such efforts were weakening their ability to achieve their major objective. In the case of Germany, the central bank's efforts were increasing the supply of deutsche marks and adding to inflation, while in the case of the United Kingdom the efforts of the central bank were reducing the supply of sterling and inhibiting economic growth. According to newspaper reports, Soros's profits on the operation could be reckoned in billions of dollars.

try to fill the gap by providing increasing amounts of foreign currency. But what if it abandons its role as balance wheel? The outcome would be a devaluation, a decline in the value of the local currency relative to other currencies.

To see what the devaluation may mean for imports and exports, consider what would happen if Italy were to devalue the lira sharply in relation to the U.S. dollar. Suppose that the lira was valued at L.1000 to the U.S. dollar just before the devaluation and at L.1500 to the dollar just after. Italy, we suppose, is anxious to promote the export of shoes and discourage the import of executive aircraft. Table 8-5 sets up hypothetical unit prices for shoes and aircraft before and after devaluation.

As a result of the devaluation, Italy's shoe producers are likely to see various reasons for increasing their shoe production. If they leave the dollar price unchanged, as Table 8-5 assumes, then the price they receive in lire will have gone up considerably. And if they reduce the dollar price a little, thereby deviating from the assumptions of Table 8-5, their sales will presumably increase. In either case, the incentive to increase shoe production for exports will grow.

On the import side, analogous price effects take place. The dollar price of executive aircraft continues to be just what it was before the decline in the value of the lira, $3 million. But the Italian price is sharply increased, thereby discouraging importation of the aircraft.

It follows that, if the Italian economy is capable of providing more shoes for export or more executive aircraft for domestic use, or both, then Italy's trade balance may be improved and the government's objectives met.

Despite the power of the foreign exchange tool, governments have numerous reasons for limiting recourse to its use.

- Devaluations may help increase the country's exports by increasing profits to exporters in the home currency and by reducing the price of exports to foreigners in the foreign currency. Experience, however, indicates that the effects of a devaluation on exports take time, often as much as three or four years, as exporters gear up to their new opportunities. Besides, devaluations increase the price of imports in the home currency. Eventually, therefore—indeed, sometimes very quickly—a devaluation may strengthen inflationary tendencies in the country and thereby imperil the favorable effects sought by the devaluation.

- Devaluations create a loss in the short run for foreigners who own assets in the devalued currency. So foreigners who fear further weakness in the currency may refuse to invest following the devaluation, and local savers may transfer their savings into other currencies.

- Devaluations may create a black mark for the government in power, suggesting that they have lost their control over national economic policy. Take note of France's attraction to the *franc fort* at various stages in its history.

TABLE 8-5.   Hypothetical Price of Shoes and Executive Aircraft Before and After a Lira Devaluation

	Before Devaluation L1000 = $1		After Devaluation L1500 = $1	
	Shoes	Aircraft	Shoes	Aircraft
In lire	L100,000	L3 billion	L150,000	L4.5 billion
In dollars	$100	$3 million	$100	$3 million

The Interest Rate as Policy Tool

In addition to the exchange rate, another tool of policymakers likely to have substantial international repercussions is the interest rate, especially the interest rate applicable to short-term government instruments such as 90-day Treasury paper. Policymakers are sometimes motivated primarily by domestic considerations, such as inflation and unemployment, in their efforts to change such rates. At other times, it is the international position of the country that provides the trigger for policy changes.

Domestic Triggers

Governments have various ways of exerting a direct influence on interest rates, especially short-term rates. Three routes in particular are widely used:

- The central bank engages in open-market operations; that is, it buys or sells government short-term debt in the open market, thereby influencing the national interest rate (as well as the balance sheet of the nation's commercial banks, as the banks sell or buy the government paper).
- The central bank changes the rediscount rate applicable in transactions with the nation's commercial banks, thereby altering the interest costs of the banks (with predictable effects on their balance sheet, as they alter the amounts of their rediscounted paper).
- The central bank alters the fractional reserve requirements imposed on the nation's commercial banks (again, with predictable effects on their balance sheet, as they seek to meet the new requirements).

With these policy tools in hand, the government appraises the performance of its national economy. Suppose in this case that it finds the level of unemployment in the country unacceptably high and is determined to do something about it. One possibility is to try to reduce interest rates in the expectation that a reduction will help to reduce unemployment. Why?

- The answer to that question flows from what we learned when studying Tables 8-1 and 8-3. The decline in interest rates, it is hoped, will encourage the public to borrow more from banks in order to spend more on goods and services: to replace a truck in the business, to buy a second car, or to take a vacation.
- The increases have the same direct effects as any injection of new money, portrayed earlier in Table 8-1. That is to say, the injection increases national income, national imports, and national savings—at least, in the first instance. But with unemployment high, it is assumed, some part of that increased demand will be satisfied by an increase in national production.

If unemployment is the Scylla for national policymakers, inflation is the Charybdis; both are to be avoided, and both invite the use of the interest rate. (Suppose that the government fears inflation more than unemployment and therefore proposes to raise the interest rate rather than to lower it. Trace out the effects of that decision, following Tables 8-1 and 8-3.)

External Triggers

The national interest rate comes into play as a policy tool, as well, in order to deal with problems arising out of transactions with the rest of the world.

Consider Canada's position when the United States raises its short-term interest rate. The U.S. motive, we shall assume, is to dampen inflationary pressures in the U.S. economy. Suppose that Canada has the same concerns. As a result of the U.S. action

- Canadian savers switch their savings out of Canadian government paper into U.S. government paper . . .
- To make the switch, however, they must sell their Canadian dollars and buy U.S. dollars . . .
- Their sales lower the price of Canadian dollars in relation to U.S. dollars . . .
- The prices of Canada's imports from the United States go up as in Table 8-5, creating inflationary pressures in Canada . . .

Canada's response is obvious: If inflation is its principal concern and remains so after the U.S. move, it can counter the U.S. move by raising Canadian interest rates.

Now consider the opposite possibility. The United States lowers its interest rate in order to stimulate its economy. But Canada has the same concern. The consequences for Canada are now easy to trace. If stimulating the Canadian economy remains the Canadian government's principal concern after the U.S. move, the pressure will be on Canada to follow the U.S. lead and to lower its interest rate as well.

The moral of the story? No country is a monetary island. Not even the United States, Germany, or Japan.

Keeping Track of the Pressures

Most governments periodically publish a record that reports the transactions between their residents and the outside world. The record is generally referred to as the country's balance-of-payment accounts. For the major countries, most key figures in the accounts are available quarterly and a few key figures can even be obtained monthly.

To understand better how the figures are usually arranged and what they purport to measure, it is useful to pretend that every transaction between a resident of the country concerned and the rest of the world was recorded in the first instance by the conventions of double-entry bookkeeping. In standard double-entry bookkeeping, every transaction is recorded as if it consisted of an exchange of something for something else, that is, as both a debit and a credit.

In the case of merchandise imports, for instance, goods are ordinarily acquired for money or for debt; according to bookkeeping convention, the imported goods are recorded as a debit and the payment for those goods as a credit. In the case of merchandise exports, the exports are recorded as a credit and the receipts as a debit. Debits consist principally of (1) imports of goods and services, (2) increases in assets, or (3) reductions in liabilities. Credits consist principally of (1) exports of goods and services, (2) increases in liabilities, or (3) reductions in assets. The principal categories of debits and credits are shown in Table 8-6.

You may have already recognized a certain similarity between the credits and debits of balance-of-payment accounting and the double-entry accounts of business firms. The parallel is summarized in Table 8-7.

In practice, of course, no government actually knows enough about each foreign transaction to be able to record the transaction according to the entries required in double-entry bookkeeping. Instead, each category of debit and credit is laboriously estimated from separate sources, such as customs house records and special question-

TABLE 8-6.   Principal Balance-of-Payment Accounts

Debits	Credits
Current Items	
D.1 Imports of goods and services, and foreign tourism of residents	C.1 Exports of goods and services and tourism of foreigners
D.2 Interest, dividends, rents, and royalties to foreign entities	C.2 Interest, dividends, rents, and royalties from foreign entities
D.3 Gifts to foreign entities	C.3 Gifts from foreign entities
Capital Items	
D.4 Increase in private short-term claims on foreign entities (such as private holdings of foreign bank deposits and foreign short-term paper)	C.4 Decrease in private short-term claims on foreign entities
D.5 Increase in long-term claims on foreign entities (such as foreign stocks, bonds, and real estate)	C.5 Decrease in long-term claims on foreign entities.
D.6 Decrease in foreigners' short-term claims on domestic entities	C.6 Increase in foreigners' short-term claims on domestic entities
D.7 Decrease in foreigners' long-term claims on domestic entities	C.7 Increase in foreigners' long-term claims on domestic entities
Reserve Items	
D.8 Increase in official short-term claims on foreign entites (such as public holdings of foreign bank deposits and short-term paper)	C.8 Decrease in official short-term claims on foreign entites
D.9 Increase in gold stock	C.9 Decrease in gold stock

TABLE 8-7. Corporate Accounts and Balance of Payment Accounts Compared

Corporate Accounts		Balance-of-Payment Accounts		
Debits	Credits	Debits	Credits	Relation to Table 8-6
Profit and Loss Items		Current Items		
	Sales		Exports	C.1
	Other income		Other current account income	C.2 and C.3
Cost of goods sold		Imports		D.1
Other costs except depreciation		Other current account expenditures		D.2 to D.3
Taxes and dividends	Net retained earnings before depreciation		Current account balance	C.1 to C.3 minus D.1 to D.3
Balance Sheet Items		Capital and Reserve Items		
	Increase in current liabilities		Increase in foreigners' short-term claims	C.6 minus D.6
	Increase in long-term liabilities and equity		Increase in foreigners' long-term claims	C.7 minus D.7
Increase in current assets except cash		Increase in private short-term foreign assets		D.4 minus C.4
Increase in fixed assets		Increase in long-term foreign assets		D.5 minus C.5
Increase in cash		Increase in official holdings of foreign exchange (including gold)		D.8 and D.9 minus C.8 and C.9

naire returns. In theory, the debits and credits should balance. In fact, they never do. So an artificial balancing item, "net errors and omissions," is introduced to bring about balance. The balancing item is just that—a measure of the difference between debits and credits. So its size says little or nothing about the size of the debits and the size of the credits that have been omitted. If clandestine transactions are important, or if the reporting system is weak for other reasons, the omissions can be very large.

A little practice in the recording of typical transactions helps to clinch the relationships between the items. Even without such exercises, however, a couple of points will be apparent almost at once.

- Just as in the case of a corporate statement, no item of the balance-of-payments accounts taken by itself indicates very much about the strengths or weaknesses of a nation's foreign-exchange position. What is needed is the whole record.
- An analysis of the future supply of the government's foreign currencies has certain striking parallels to that of the corporation's cash-flow analysis. In both instances, it is necessary to rearrange the items listed in Table 8-7 into a conventional "sources and uses of funds" analysis. The national economy counts the following items as its sources of foreign exchange: exports, earnings from investments abroad, and increases in foreigners' short-term and long-term claims. An economy's uses of foreign exchange appear in various categories, including imports, payment to foreigners of interest and dividends, increases in its short-term and long-term assets abroad, and official holdings of foreign exchange. (Of course, any of these items can decrease as well as increase, in which case they shift their classification from "source" to "use" or from "use" to "source.")

When an effort is made to project the likely sources and uses of foreign exchange by a national economy, however, it begins to be evident that the project involves dimensions that have no obvious analog in a projection of corporate fund flows. As we saw earlier, exports and imports of a national economy are an intimate function of the internal demand of an economy. If the domestic demand for goods is very strong, the economy can suck up potential exports and pull in excessive imports. Although some developments inside a business entity can be thought of as a parallel phenomenon, the parallel begins to be a little strained when pushed very far.

In efforts to detect future trends in national liquidity, analysts are constantly reviewing the behavior of the balance-of-payments accounts, looking for added light. In the process, certain measures have tended to be given special weight. One is the *merchandise balance*, or *trade balance*, often calculated as the difference between exports and imports (C.1 minus D.1). Another is the current account balance (the sum of C.1 to C.3 minus the sum of D.1 to D.3).

Of the various payment account balances, the simplest from some points of view is the change in the gold stock and foreign currencies held by the government. Since no country that wishes to intervene in the foreign-exchange market dares to run out of convertible foreign currencies, all analysts watch with exquisite attention the changes in supplies of such currencies (D.8 and C.8). The sum of these changes plus changes in gold holdings (D.9 and C.9) in a given period is sometimes called the *payments balance* of the country for that period.

The accounts reported by government have changed in the past, and they will change again in the future. The important point to remember is that no single account or limited group of accounts can tell the whole story. The data are a reflection of a series of underlying processes. The processes have to be understood if any useful projections are to be made. A careful perusal of the balance-of-payment data can make some contribution to that understanding.

Suggested Reading

CAVES, RICHARD E., JEFFREY A. FRANKEL, and RICHARD W. JONES. *World Trade and Payments*. 6th ed. New York: Harper Collins, 1993.

KENEN, PETER B. *The International Economy*. 3rd ed. New York: Cambridge University Press, 1994.

CHAPTER 9

International
Money Markets

Linking the capital markets of the national economies are a number of institutions that are of prime importance to the manager who operates across borders. These institutions, which include international banks and securities markets, serve two interrelated functions:

- They help to move capital across borders by providing facilities for matching lenders with borrowers and matching buyers with sellers of foreign exchange and securities.
- They provide facilities for hedging against short-term and long-term foreign exchange risk, using so-called derivative instruments of various kinds, including foreign-exchange futures, foreign-exchange options, and currency swaps.

These institutions owe their vastly increased importance in recent years to the growth in business transactions across borders, including the growth of international trade in goods and services and the growth of cross-border investment. Many of the changes of the 1980s and 1990s, however, have been due to developments in the regulatory and competitive environment in which financial institutions have operated.

A Changed Environment

The Regulatory Structure

Throughout the world, governments have been relaxing their regulations affecting financial flows, encouraging increased competition among financial intermediaries.

These charges have been particularly important in the United States, the European Union, and Japan.

The United States.   Changes in the regulatory environment of the United States have been especially important in altering the role of banks. The principal U.S. banks operating in international markets grew up under the Glass-Steagall Act, a statute that requires the separation of commercial banking from investment banking. Accordingly, in the United States the business of accepting deposits and making loans has been largely separated from the business of trading in securities. Traditionally, too, state regulations in the United States have supplemented federal provisions in complex ways that limit the banks' rights to expand both geographically and by function.

In the 1980s, however, commercial banks in the United States were facing increasing competition from nonbanking enterprises. They were competing for deposits, for example, with money market funds. And they were competing for loans not only with credit card companies such as American Express, but also with a growing commercial paper market where leading corporations could raise money by selling their short-term notes directly to investors. To illustrate how rapidly such competition was growing, the amount of commercial paper outstanding in the United States quadrupled during the 1980s, reaching a level that was more than half the total of U.S. bank loans outstanding to commerce and industry.

Threatened by such developments, U.S. banks increased their efforts to have federal and state laws and regulations relaxed so that they could expand their activities in the United States beyond the commercial banking business into other fields of finance, especially underwriting and trading in securities. Some were already engaged in the securities business outside the United States through subsidiaries in London and elsewhere. By the end of the 1980s, a few large U.S. banks had secured permission from the Federal Reserve Board to deal in specified types of securities under carefully circumscribed conditions. Even more important, however, were the changes that the banks themselves were initiating in the mix of their activities. For as they encountered competition in their traditional commercial banking business, they moved into other operations, including notably the buying and selling of derivative securities. The implications of that change for U.S. managers are discussed below.

Japan.   In Japan during the 1980s, the leading commercial banks also experienced a loosening of the regulatory restraints that the government had imposed on their activities. But Japanese banks began the process of liberalization from a very different starting position.

Traditionally, Japan's financial markets have been under far closer governmental control than those of the United States, with the powers of control centralized in a single agency, the Ministry of Finance. Until the 1980s, the Ministry of Finance carefully limited the types of securities eligible for public sale and approved the substance and timing of each public offering. The ministry also confined each financial enterprise to a specified segment of the market, limited the number of firms operating in any such segment, and in numerous ways restricted the freedom of the firms operating in their respective segments.

Only a dozen or so banks, the so-called *city banks*, have traditionally been authorized to act as commercial bankers for Japan's large industrial firms. During this era of tight control that lasted into the 1980s, the city banks were allowed only to receive large deposits and make loans for the short term at officially prescribed interest rates. Meanwhile, three so-called *long-term banks* were granted a virtual monopoly on medium-term lending for industry and infrastructure. And four *securities dealers* were allowed to dominate the country's securities business. As for *foreign banks*, these were limited in both number and function, being largely confined to financing foreign trade.

By the 1990s, however, practically all these controls had been nibbled away. As Japan was drawn into the international money market network, Japanese banks and other firms were allowed far greater freedom to participate in capital markets abroad. Finally, in 1994, Japanese banks were permitted to participate as brokers and dealers in Japanese securities markets, ending the traditional monopoly of the securities dealers. At the same time, foreign banks and other foreign firms have gained increasing access to Japanese financial markets. True, the reactions of foreign firms to these liberalizing measures have been slow in showing themselves. For instance, foreign bank activity in Japan was not much greater in the beginning of the 1990s than it had been 10 years earlier. But the trend seemed reasonably assured.

Europe.   As for banks headquartered in Europe, these were enjoying a new era of liberalization brought on by the dismantling of capital market restrictions within the European Union. Moreover, as one of the measures for building a single market within the Union, a "single passport" had been created for banks inside the Union. In brief, the Union's member states were required to lift practically all barriers that had previously impeded banks and other financial institutions headquartered in a member country from doing business in the other member countries. All member states were required to meet some very general requirements laid down by the Union for the regulation of banks headquartered in their respective territories. A bank whose home country had satisfied such requirements was entitled to the "single passport," thus permitting it to do business in all the member states of the Union. Some host government requirements were still retained, such as the banks' adherence to national monetary policies and to various residual measures aimed at protecting customers. In other major respects, however, such as the right to couple commercial banking with investment banking, the regulations of the home country provided the determining set of controls.

The Union's single passport for banks also opened up the possibility that financial institutions outside the Union might gain access to the European market on the same terms as their rivals headquartered in Europe. The Union, however, conditioned such access on a reciprocity requirement—that is, a requirement that the home country of the foreign institution should offer substantially similar access to the Union's banks. By 1993, banks headquartered in the United States and Japan appeared to have met the necessary tests, despite the fact that neither of these countries was offering exactly the same rights to foreign banks as was the Union.

Transborder Investments

Responding to the giant increases in money flows across international borders during the 1970s and to the loosening of national regulations, large banks throughout the world substantially expanded their networks in foreign countries. By the end of 1993, the cross-border claims of banks, denominated in various currencies, exceeded $6,400 billion. (For comparison, the total domestic bank credit of the principal industrialized countries at that time was only about three times that total.)

At the same time, transactions in stocks and bonds across international borders have grown at a phenomenal rate. Table 9-1 provides data showing the greatly increased role of cross-border transactions in stocks and bonds experienced by the G7 (the United States, the United Kingdom, Canada, France, Germany, Italy, and Japan).

Accompanying the growth in cross-border transactions has been an expansion in the relative position of foreign securities in the portfolios of institutional investors such as pension funds, insurance companies, and mutual funds, as shown in Table 9-2.

As transborder investments have grown, the role of organized exchanges in cross-border investment has grown as well, especially those located in developing countries. Listings on securities exchanges in some developing countries grew spectacularly between 1985 and 1992, notably in Mexico, Korea, Malaysia, and Thailand. At times, the linkage between transborder investments and exchange listings has been quite direct. For instance, securities sold to foreigners that are issued by companies in developing countries benefit considerably from a stock exchange listing, because the listing is thought to offer some minimum promise of liquidity and some minimum guarantee of transparency in the affairs of the company. Concurrently, a sharp rise

TABLE 9-1.   Purchases and Sales of Securities between Residents and Nonresidents, Seven Countries, 1975–1993, Selected Years (as percentage of GDP)

Country	1975	1980	1985	1990	1993
United States	4.2	9.3	36.4	92.1	134.9
Japan	1.8	7.7	62.5	121.0	78.7
Germany	5.1	7.5	33.9	54.9	169.6
France	3.3	6.7	29.1	58.7	196.0
Italy	0.9	1.1	4.0	26.6	274.6
United Kingdom	n.a.	n.a.	366.0	689.0	1,015.8
Canada	3.3	9.6	26.7	64.2	152.7

Source: Bank for International Settlements, *64th Annual Report*, Basel, 1994.

TABLE 9-2. Selected Institutional Investors' Holdings of Foreign Securities, 1980–1993, Selected Years (as percentage of their total holdings, year end)

	1980	1985	1990	1993
Japanese private insurance companies	8.1	23.2	29.9	22.3
Netherlands insurance companies	6.9	22.9	20.2	26.0
United Kingdom pension funds	10.8	17.3	23.2	23.8[a]
U.S. mutual funds			4.0[b]	8.0
U.S. private pension funds			4.1	7.1

[a]1992.
[b]1991.

Source: Bank for International Settlements, *64th Annual Report*, Basel, 1994.

has occurred in equity placements in international markets by enterprises from developing countries; in 1992 such placements amounted to $9.4 billion, nearly eight times as much as two years earlier.

Exchange Rate Instability

Paradoxically, the extraordinary growth in transborder transactions has occurred during a period when exchange rates have been more unstable than they had been in many decades. In Chapter 10, we review the changes that produced that instability. Here, it is sufficient to observe once again, as we did in Chapter 3, that since the 1970s the relative values of the world's principal currencies have changed dramatically. These developments have greatly increased the desire of managers to find some means of avoiding the accompanying uncertainties.

Key Currencies

Managers try to avoid the risks of foreign exchange variations in many different ways. One such way is for the manager to insist that purchases and sales as well as loans and borrowings, even though undertaken with foreigners, should be denominated in the currency of the manager's country. If the manager is British, she may insist that her transaction be denominated in sterling; if American, in dollars. In that way, she can avoid the risk of a change in the nominal value of the receipts or the payments that she anticipates from her transactions, at least to the extent that the change might be the result of a devaluation.

To be sure, this strategy does not wholly insure against losses of a certain kind. If the value of sterling declines in relation to deutsche marks, for instance, a British seller or lender may wish that the transaction had been conducted in deutsche marks.

More important to the manager is the fact that by conducting her international transactions in her home currency, the main money inflows and outflows of her business
are denominated in the same medium.

One difficulty with a solution of this kind is that it cannot apply to both parties
in an international transaction; either one or the other, but not both, can trade in his or
her home currency. A further difficulty is that the manager who insists on doing her
buying and selling, borrowing and lending, in only one currency ordinarily handicaps
her negotiating position to some extent. If the manager is selling goods or services,
her insistence on designating the currency may have the effect of discouraging the
prospective buyer because it would force the buyer to borrow a currency that the
buyer has some trouble in getting. The same problem exists in international borrowing; if a firm is a borrower of funds, its designation of the currency may cut off many
prospective lenders.

That is one of several reasons why certain currencies have been accepted from
time to time as near-universal media of international payment—as "key" currencies,
in the parlance of international finance. The pound sterling played that role until
World War II, and the U.S. dollar performed that role in the decades following.

In 1971, however, the U.S. government ended its long-time commitment to convert U.S. dollars held by foreign governments into gold. That step meant that the
value of the U.S. dollar, no longer linked to a fixed price for gold, had lost the principal anchor that stabilized its value in foreign-exchange markets. Gradually over the
succeeding two decades, the U.S. dollar lost a little of its dominant position as a key
international currency. Nevertheless, the U.S. dollar continued to occupy the position
of the world's principal key currency, followed at a distance by the yen and the
deutsche mark. The dollar, for instance, was involved in over one-third of the
turnover in foreign-exchange markets, more than double that of the deutsche mark
and triple that of the yen. The dollar, too, remained the principal currency in which
banks' cross-border claims were denominated, exceeding the deutsche mark and the
yen by a factor of three. As Table 9-3 indicates, the dollar continued to figure prominently in the foreign-exchange reserves of governments.

TABLE 9-3. Share of Specified Foreign
Currencies in Official Holdings, End of 1982,
1986, 1991 (in percent)

Currency	1982	1986	1991
U.S. dollar	70.5	67.1	56.2
Deutsche mark	12.3	14.6	17.3
Yen	1.7	7.9	9.9
Other	12.5	10.4	16.6
Total	100.0	100.0	100.0

Source: International Monetary Fund, *Annual Report*,
1992.

In all likelihood, however, the primacy of the dollar will continue to weaken further over time. Countries in Asia are making more substantial use of the yen than countries in the rest of the world; the increase in the relative importance of Asia opens up the possibility of further relative declines in the dollar's dominance. That dominance, however, rests on some enduring factors, including the vast size and ready availability of the U.S. capital markets, the seeming stability of the U.S. political system, and the innovative strength of the U.S. banks in forging new instruments. Therefore, any decline in the relative importance of the U.S. dollar is likely to be slow.

The Market for Hedges

Managers in the international economy, it is evident, cannot easily escape exposure to the risk of exchange rate variations. With increasing frequency, therefore, managers have turned to the possibility of hedging their exchange rate risks.

Short-Term Hedges

Those who wish to hedge against adverse fluctuations in foreign currencies for relatively short periods, such as three months, have a number of alternative courses available. Take the manager in the United States who wishes to preserve the dollar value of an expected stream of earnings from a U. K. subsidiary. The earnings are expected to be available for remission in 90 days. The market for sterling appears to be under strain, however, and the manager would like to protect the value of the expected stream with a hedge. To create such a hedge, the manager can take any of three routes.

Using the forward exchange market.   One way would be to sell the anticipated sterling proceeds in the forward exchange market, receiving a specified price in dollars for delivery of the sterling on the target day 90 days hence. In this case, the cost of the insurance would be the 90-day forward discount—that is, the difference between the specified forward price and the current spot price.

Using loans and deposits.   A second way consists of

- borrowing sterling for 90 days,
- converting the funds at once into U.S. dollars,
- purchasing with the dollars a 90-day certificate of deposit denominated in dollars, and
- 90 days later, paying off the sterling loan with the expected sterling remittances.

In this case, the cost of the insurance would be the difference between the interest paid on the borrowed pounds and the interest earned on the deposited dollars. In theory, that difference ought to be close to the cost associated with the alternative, that is, the forward discount for sterling.

Using option contracts.   A third choice would entail the manager's purchase of a contract that gives her the option to sell her anticipated pounds for dollars at a specified rate during a 90-day period. "American" options allow for the manager's exercise of her right at any time during the period, and "European" options, only at the close of the period. Unlike the forward exchange contract, the manager would not be obliged to make an actual sale of the pounds unless she decided it was in her interest to do so. The exercise price in the option contract will ordinarily be less favorable to the manager than will the exercise price in the futures contract. Nevertheless, the option contract may be especially attractive if the manager is uncertain whether the prospective flow of sterling funds will actually materialize or if she is eager to retain the alternative of selling her sterling on the spot market when the funds become available.

Long-Term Hedges

Corporate treasurers, however, sometimes have a need for much longer hedges, well beyond the period covered in the forward exchange or option markets. To illustrate:

> A U.S.-based multinational enterprise that has successfully penetrated the Japanese market with its line of consumer products finds a need for added long-term capital. On investigation, it learns that an issue of 10-year bonds in the Eurobond market, denominated in yen, would provide the most favorable terms. The hitch, however, is that the firm will expose itself for 10 years to the risks associated with changes in the dollar-yen exchange rate, which will make uncertain the dollar costs of its periodic interest payments and of its final payment to redeem the bonds. The existing markets that provide foreign-exchange hedges, being typically limited to three-month hedges available in limited amounts, appear unable to provide the necessary hedge at reasonable terms. What to do?

In their efforts to find new sources of business, multinational banks have gradually moved into the writing of long-term contracts that provide such a hedge. In the first stages of providing such a service, during the early 1980s, the banks had typically confined themselves to an intermediary role. At that early stage, the banks tried to bring parties together whose hedging needs could offset one another. These were "swap transactions" in which each of the two parties assumed the foreign-exchange obligations of the other, with the intermediating bank providing a guarantee of performance. So the U.S. firm whose hedging needs were to ensure that its yen commitments remained stable in dollar terms would be matched with a Japanese firm whose needs were to ensure that its dollar commitments remained stable in yen terms.

Such swaps, however, proved difficult to arrange, because they required a matching of needs that involved the same currencies in similar magnitudes and with similar maturities. Soon, therefore, banks began to offer hedging contracts directly to parties that requested it, tailor-made to their needs. Like any future contract or future option, these contracts are classified as "derivative securities." The challenge for the bank that enters into such a business is to develop a portfolio of commitments that tend to offset one another, leaving no more net exposure to the bank than it wishes to assume. The portfolio itself may include various types of positions taken by the bank, such as deposits and securities denominated in foreign currencies, foreign-exchange futures, and options.

These developments in the demand for the services of multinational banks have profoundly affected the mix of their activities. An extreme example of that shift is provided by the record of Bankers Trust, which reports that its profits from "trading, positioning, and client risk management" increased from 21 percent of its total business income in 1985 to 71 percent in 1992.

Table 9-4 presents data for the world's principal international banks that reflect these shifts. The data confirm two basic trends: the slowing up in the growth of traditional international bank loans, and the sustained growth in over-the-counter currency swaps of the kind described above. With much higher profitability in swaps than in lending, the figures indicate a marked shift in the structure of international banking.

Hedging on Organized Exchanges

The facilities offered by organized exchanges to facilitate international money movements continued their long-term growth during the 1980s and the first half of the 1990s. Although the largest growth in the trading of hedging instruments lay in the over-the-counter markets maintained by the international banks, organized exchanges for foreign-exchange futures and future options thrive in a number of different coun-

TABLE 9-4.   Indicators of the Activities of International Banks, 1973–1991 (in billions of U.S. dollars)

	International Bank Loans	Over-the-Counter Currency Swaps
Annual averages		
1973–1977	$289	n.a.
1978–1982	395	n.a.
1983–1987	1,358	$100[a]
1988	2,545	316
1989	2,920	434
1990	3,535	578
1991	3,615	807

[a]Estimate for 1986.

Sources: The bank loan series is calculated from data presented in Group of Ten, *International Capital Movements and Foreign Exchange Markets*, Washington, DC, April 1993, p. 69, based on data from the Bank for International Settlements; and the currency swap data are from *International Capital Markets, Part II*, I. M. F., Washington DC, 1993, p. 24.

tries, including notably the United States, the United Kingdom, France, Germany, the Netherlands, and Singapore. In the United States, for instance, such markets are provided by the Chicago Mercantile Exchange in its International Money Market, the Mid-America Commodity Exchange, and the Philadelphia Stock Exchange. The currencies represented in these markets include the deutsche mark, the pound sterling, the yen, the French franc, the Swiss franc, the Australian dollar, and the Canadian dollar, as well as the ECU. The futures and options are usually traded in units valued at about $100,000 for specified durations, usually no more than a year.

These markets as a rule have neither the flexibility nor the scale to satisfy the hedging needs of multinational enterprises with large long-term stakes abroad, needs that have commonly been handled by banks operating over the counter. But the exchanges have proved sufficient to handle the needs of shorter duration and smaller size, while providing a convenient public facility for speculators in foreign exchange.

Suggested Reading

EDWARDS, FRANKLIN R., and HUGH T. PATRICK (eds.). *Regulating International Financial Markets*. Boston: Kluwer Academic, 1992.

GROUP OF THIRTY. *International Capital Markets*. Washington, DC, 1993.

LESSARD, DONALD R., and JOHN B. LIGHT-STONE. "Volatile Exchange Rates Can Put Operations at Risk." *Harvard Business Review* (July–August 1986), 107–114.

SUNDARAM, ANANT K., and J. STEWART BLACK. *The International Business Environment: Text and Cases*. Englewood Cliffs, NJ: Prentice Hall, 1994.

CHAPTER 10

The International Rules of the Game: Money

As we saw in earlier chapters, multinational enterprises are obliged to deal in many different currencies if they are to remain competitive. Dealing in different currencies, managers constantly face two challenges: moving money efficiently from one currency to another, without encountering high costs and official roadblocks; and protecting the enterprise from changes in the value of the currencies in which they have an interest. As they go about these tasks, managers constantly encounter international institutions and agreements among governments affecting the movement of money across borders. Some of these, as we shall see, provide opportunities for the manager, while others may throw up obstacles.

The Background

Throughout modern history, governments have wrestled with the fact that, where the international movement of money is concerned, no country is an island. The forces that stimulate the holders of one currency to buy or sell that currency for another are bound to make waves for the second currency. Today, with something like one trillion dollars being traded daily in the foreign-exchange markets, those waves can be very threatening.

Yet, governments have been very slow to enter into agreements that might limit their freedom in setting national monetary policy and exchange rate policy. More than 60 years ago, at the London Economic Conference in 1933, some countries talked of such a possibility. But the U.S. government, absorbed in its efforts to deal with widespread bank failures and unprecedented levels of unemployment at home, summarily killed off any international movement in that direction.

A few years later, in 1936, after extended negotiation, the United States, Britain, and France each issued a statement, very cautiously worded, announcing that it intended to take into account the interests of the others in its measures relating to the exchange rate of its currency. In the years that followed, however, this declaration simply meant that the United States would stand still, passively maintaining a fixed price in gold for the U.S. dollar, and leaving it for the others to find a way of stabilizing their currencies in relation to the dollar.

World War II introduced a new era, one in which the United States made huge contributions to the stability of other economies, reflected in the creation of the International Monetary Fund (IMF), the International Bank for Reconstruction and Development (the World Bank), and the European Recovery Program (the Marshall Plan), as well as some large government-to-government loans to the United Kingdom and France. The articles of the IMF, it is true, committed its members to maintain a fixed rate of exchange linked to the U.S. dollar and to seek the agreement of the IMF when instituting any major change in that rate. As far as the United States was concerned, however, any change in the gold content of the U.S. dollar seemed inconceivable at the time. When, a few years after the founding of the IMF, the United Kingdom and Canada changed their exchange rates, they simply disregarded the requirement to seek the IMF's agreement.

In practice, then, neither the U.S. government nor any other industrialized country was prepared at the time to limit its right to set monetary policies and exchange rates. Under pressure from the U.S. government, some cooperation developed among the European countries as part of the Marshall Plan. But only the developing countries, recipients of loans and grants from international institutions and other governments, could be made to submit to monetary discipline over extended periods.

It was not until the 1960s that the leading industrialized governments began to show signs of cooperation in the management of international money movements. By that time, the U.S. dollar was in trouble, with declining gold reserves and runaway deficit financing. At about the same time, the French franc was undergoing disastrous periods of weakness. With these two governments under pressure in a system of fixed exchange rates, some cooperation became a possibility.

One result of the stresses of that period was that nations agreed to the creation of a new international instrument within the structure of the International Monetary Fund, so-called Special Drawing Rights (SDRs). These were essentially new credits extended by the IMF to each of its members, denominated in a new basket of currencies that could be converted into existing national currencies. The creation of such credits in effect increased the volume of money in the world and opened up the possibility that the IMF might play a much greater role in the management of international liquidity. That potential, though it still exists today, has never been realized. The course of international money continues to be determined by the measures of individual countries.

In 1971 the U.S. government formally ended its practice of providing gold at a fixed \$35 price to the central banks of other countries. Thereafter, the price of the dollar would be determined by whatever the foreign-exchange market could generate, thus ending an era of stable exchange rates fixed to the dollar and introducing a new source of instability in international economic relations.

Since the end of the era of fixed exchange rates, anxiety has proved the mother of cooperation. From time to time in the decades since, leading governments have come together in a series of cooperative efforts to stabilize exchange rates. In this period, various institutions have played a key role. The IMF has continued to ride herd over its debtor countries, practically all of which are in the category of developing economies. The heads of state of the G7 (the United States, Canada, Japan, the United Kingdom, France, Germany, and Italy) have met in annual meetings, seeking to define general directions for cooperative economic measures among them. Occasionally, those meetings have produced coordinated movements in national monetary policies. Meanwhile, the G3 (the United States, Germany, and Japan) have engaged in more frequent and more intimate efforts to intervene in currency markets, operating through their central banks and finance ministries. During these years, too, the European Community (later the European Union) has created, modified, and reconstituted a series of arrangements, intended to stabilize the exchange rates of its member states. In the mid-1990s, it stood committed to the most ambitious effort of all, the creation of a monetary union and a common currency.

Supplementing such activities, the monetary authorities from various countries have made use of other institutions to deal with some of the fallout created by the growing volume of international money movements. From the viewpoint of the business manager, a few of these centers of activity have sometimes been important. One such center has been the 25-member Organization for Economic Cooperation and Development (OECD), sometimes dubbed the rich men's club, which has sponsored a series of agreements aimed at limiting the competition among governments in providing subsidized loans for the financing of their exports. Another has been the Bank for International Settlements (BIS), the traditional host for regular meetings of the central bankers of 33 countries, including all the leading countries in international finance, which has sponsored the so-called Basel accords among its members. The agreements, named after the city in which the BIS is located, seek to ensure that the international banks of the leading countries are adequately capitalized and supervised by the national authorities charged with bank oversight.

Not surprisingly, this hodgepodge of institutions and accords has not produced the tranquility and stability that most governments and most managers would prefer. As we saw in Figure 3-3 in Chapter 3, portraying the exchange rate movements of a number of major currencies since 1970, acute instability prevails in currency markets. And governments continue to demand substantial autonomy in the management of their monetary policies. Nevertheless, the role of international institutions in affecting international money markets is not trivial. The survey that follows provides a snapshot of the leading governmental institutions and programs that the manager will encounter in that role.

The International Monetary Fund

The influence of the IMF has stemmed from various sources:

- From the commitments of the member countries under the IMF's Articles of Agreement, limiting their use of financial restrictions.
- From the Fund's capacity to lend foreign exchange to countries in balance-of-payment difficulties.
- From the leadership role the Fund has assumed in evaluating whether and when countries in such difficulties are entitled to support from other potential lenders such as national governments and private sources.

Commitments and Loans

By 1994, as noted in Chapter 7, 93 of the IMF's 179 members had accepted a commitment not to impose any restrictions on the use of their currencies in the settlement of current-account transactions or to engage in discriminatory currency arrangements or multiple currency practices. Practically all of those that had not yet accepted such commitments were developing countries, most of them with relatively small volumes of international trade and investment. These commitments, therefore, covered a very large portion of the world's current-account transactions. Nonetheless, national controls over capital transactions were still endemic.

The IMF's direct lending role to countries in balance-of-payment difficulties, however, has been comparatively modest. The resources on which the IMF depends in making such loans come principally from its member governments. On joining the Fund, each government must make deposits to the Fund in an amount equal to a quota that the government has negotiated on entry. Three-quarters of the quota may be supplied in the government's own currency, and the rest in specified hard currencies. Another source of liquidity for the IMF consists of special borrowings that the IMF arranges from one or another of its more affluent member countries. Saudi Arabia and Japan, for instance, have loaned the IMF large sums, which have been especially earmarked for the poorest countries of the Fund.

All told, by drawing on quotas and loans, the IMF in the mid-1990s commanded liquid resources of about $100 billion, about half of which was uncommitted. The credits that the IMF in turn was extending to its members at the time came to about $45 billion. Added credits were being doled out at the rate of about $9 billion per year, a modest sum in a world of huge foreign-exchange flows.

A country desiring to avail itself of IMF credits has to demonstrate its eligibility for such credits. In principle, the IMF's support must be in order to meet a "temporary" disequilibrium in its balance of payments. In that case, the country may "buy" the required currencies from the IMF pool. Members actually buy such currencies by paying with their own, and eventually they have to repay the currencies originally bought. So perhaps it is more accurate to think of their purchases from the IMF's supply of foreign exchange as if they were borrowings rather than purchases.

The IMF's sale of currencies to member countries by now follows some well-developed patterns. For example, if Argentina needs sterling to meet a temporary crisis, the IMF has supplies of sterling available for sale to Argentina, to be paid for by Argentina in pesos. Under IMF policy, Argentina will be required "as a general rule" to return the sterling and retrieve its pesos within a three- to five-year period. Meanwhile, Argentina has acquired added elbowroom in trying to move back to a position of external equilibrium.

Argentina's right to buy the needed sterling from the IMF, however, is not always automatic. It depends on the state of Argentina's financial position with the IMF and on the circumstances that have created the foreign-exchange need. One of the questions that any analyst will want to be able to answer is how the country concerned stands in its capacity to buy currencies from the IMF. Each month, the IMF publishes that information in its regular **International Financial Statistics** series. What the manager will discover from such a source is that a member country's right of access to the IMF's pool of currencies is graduated: the more a country has already borrowed, the greater are the difficulties and conditions that attach to further borrowing. As the country approaches the limit of its capacity to borrow from the IMF, it may be required, for example:

- To accept restraints on the expansion of credit in its economy.
- To increase the level of its taxes.
- To lower its spending in the public sector, including its subsidies to businesses and consumers.
- To eliminate losses among its state-owned enterprises.
- To lower its exchange rate.

Requirements such as these represent the "conditionality" feature of the Fund's lending, a feature that dominates its relations with countries that are deep in debt.

The Leadership Role

Despite the limited amounts of the Fund's direct lending, it has come to occupy a leadership or coordinating role in the handling of the foreign-exchange crises of developing countries. When a member country encounters trouble in its foreign-exchange position, the Fund's decisions often determine what other governments and private banks will do in helping the troubled country out of its difficulties.

That role of the Fund has been especially important in the financial support that the world has been providing to eastern Europe and the countries created out of the break-up of the Soviet Union. The IMF "conditionality" approach developed over many decades in influencing the behavior of developing countries; but these were countries that were already familiar with such concepts as the private ownership of the means of production, competition, and market prices.

In eastern Europe, and even more obviously in the FSU, these concepts have been unfamiliar and even threatening to much of the population, and some of the related institutions for realizing them are still feeble or nonexistent. To be sure, governments have been in the process of selling off the equity interests in the state-owned enterprises that heretofore dominated their national economies. But many of these enterprises are monopolies that have never previously been involved in markets, and many could not remain in production without large cash advances to meet their payrolls. The burning question, therefore, has been whether the IMF's "conditionality" approach has any relevance for the problems of those areas.

By the mid-1990s, the IMF was beginning to recognize the limitations of its past experience in the environment of the FSU. All signs pointed to a long period in the construction of institutions and the restructuring of industries, necessary for a transition to a market economy.

The European Union

The European Union represents a common market that has no parallel in the world economy. Launched in 1959 by six countries, the Union has expanded in number to 15 countries, with the likelihood of even further extension in the decade ahead. The Union is well on the way to creating the largest economy in the world, one in which goods, services, money, and people can move freely without encountering any national frontiers. A critical part of that process has been the elimination of some of the barriers inside the common market to the movement of money and to the cross-border spread of financial institutions. Some of the details of the Union's structure and underlying agreements are reserved for Chapter 11, where we review the international rules of the game in the movement of goods and services. Here, we review the developments in the Union that have directly affected the flows of money among its member states.

As with goods and services, the member countries of the EU have led the rest of the world in their undertakings to remove existing barriers to the movement of money inside their common market. From the time of the Union's founding, its members had been committed to the elimination of restrictions on the movement of money in the financing of transactions on current account. Until the EU treaty was amended in 1993, however, the commitments in the treaty on the elimination of controls over capital movements had been quite equivocal, and no timetable (such as existed in the case of trade in goods) was imposed for eliminating the existing restrictions. Still, the Union developed a series of directives that required the lifting of restrictions over a wide range of capital transactions. By the time the 1993 Treaty of European Union (the so-called Maastricht agreement) went into force, controls over capital movements had almost disappeared inside the common market.

The adoption of the 1993 amendments, however, went a great deal further. With those amendments, the EU members (the United Kingdom excepted) stood committed to measures that would create a monetary union and would eventually merge all their currencies into one currency, the ECU. The union as contemplated would require the creation of a European System of Central Banks (ESCB), with a single monetary policy and a European Central Bank to implement that policy. These commitments, however, were conditional, being coupled with the requirement that countries joining the new system should have satisfied certain specified criteria, including:

- A prior period of exchange rate stability.
- A record of relatively good price stability.
- A record of relatively low interest rates on public debt.
- A cap on total public debt and on current fiscal deficits.

At the time the Maastricht Treaty was ratified in 1993, only Luxembourg was in a position to satisfy all these requirements. In the mid-1990s, there was widespread skepticism in Europe as to whether the timetable provided for in the treaty, envisaging completion of the process as early as 1997 and in any event by 1999, could be realized.

The prospects for an eventual monetary union in Europe have also been clouded by the failure of various efforts in the past to achieve that difficult objective. Throughout the late 1960s and 1970s, various schemes were tried and found wanting. The schemes generally entailed an undertaking by countries with leading European currencies, including the deutsche mark, the guilder, and the franc, to link those currencies firmly to one another while allowing them to float together in their relation to non-European currencies such as the U.S. dollar or the Japanese yen.

On the basis of analysis presented in Chapter 8, the reader should be able to reconstruct the conditions that are needed to make any such system work. Two conditions are clearly indispensable:

- The countries concerned must be willing to coordinate their internal economic policies, especially their monetary policies and employment policies, sufficiently so that their economies move more or less in step with one another.
- The countries concerned must be willing to lend one another the necessary currencies on such terms as would allow the central banks to maintain the agreed rates in the foreign-exchange market.

Throughout the 1970s, a succession of such schemes came unraveled, as one or another of these conditions was breached. At various points, for instance, Germany was unwilling to allow its economy to inflate at a rate that would match the inflation in France and Britain. At other times, Britain was unwilling to intervene in the foreign-exchange market to support its falling exchange rate.

In 1979 the most ambitious of these various efforts was launched—the European Monetary System (EMS). Its principal features were as follows:

- **The parity grid (ERM)**. In a network of bilateral commitments, member countries agreed to link their currencies together at specified rates, with a narrow band of variation permitted.
- **The European Currency Unit (ECU)**. A new unit was created, the ECU, consisting of a weighted basket of the currencies concerned. The ECU served (and indeed continues to serve) two key functions. It is the unit that EMS members use in borrowing from and lending to a central fund. And it provides an anchor point to which the value of each national currency is linked.
- **Short-term lending**. Members can borrow currency from one another very liberally as long as the borrowing is on a very short-term basis. Longer term loans denominated in ECUs are made from a European Monetary Cooperation Fund, created by contributions from each member.

In the second half of 1992, during enormous turmoil and heavy speculation in the foreign-exchange markets, the United Kingdom and Italy found it impossible to hold their currencies inside the bands prescribed by the EMS. In retrospect, a new period of instability had been introduced by the collapse of the Berlin Wall and the decision of the two Germanys to reunify. (To trace the sequence, the reader may find it helpful to go back to the processes described in Chapter 8.) Reunification created the prospect of a Germany preoccupied with offsetting its own internal inflationary forces and unwilling to shape its internal policies in order to help other countries in the system maintain the stability of their currencies.

In September 1992, after a massive hammering from speculators (described in Chapter 8), the United Kingdom gave up trying to hold the pound sterling inside the limits prescribed by the ERM, and announced its withdrawal from the ERM system. Concurrently, Italy suspended its stabilization efforts for the lira. Thereafter, various countries announced changes in the par values of their currencies, devaluing them in relation to the deutsche mark.

In July 1993, therefore, the rules of the ERM were changed. The permissible bands around which member currencies could vary were widened from 4.5 percent to 15 percent, thus dramatically raising the risks for speculators who wanted to bet on a devaluation of any currency in the system. But the United Kingdom still refused to rejoin the system.

The North American Free Trade Agreement

Far less significant than the treaties of the European Union have been the provisions of NAFTA, the agreement consummated in 1993 among Mexico, the United States, and Canada for the establishment of a free-trade area among them. NAFTA, unlike the European Union, does not purport to pool the sovereign powers of its members in an economic union. In contrast to the European Union, this agreement deals with money primarily in two limited contexts:

- In providing guarantees of certain rights to investors and investments originating in another member country.
- In providing specific rights to banks and other financial institutions headquartered in any member country to engage in cross-border trade and to establish subsidiaries and branches in another member country.

The existence of NAFTA, however, has made it easier for the United States to retain and even enlarge a practice that has commonly existed between pairs of countries, namely, to enter into a temporary swap of currencies between the central banks, thus providing a temporary supply of foreign currencies to the country with the weakening national currency. With NAFTA in the background, the United States and Canada several times in 1993 and 1994 extended short-term loans to the Mexican central bank, thus providing that bank with the means for stabilizing the peso.

The rights guaranteed to investors and their investments in NAFTA are based on a traditional set of provisions developed over a century or two in numerous bilateral agreements, so-called treaties of investment summarized below. Drawing on those provisions, NAFTA guarantees to investors from other member countries:

- National treatment—that is, treatment indistinguishable from that available to nationals, except for some extensive enumerated exceptions.
- Most-favored-nation treatment—that is, treatment indistinguishable from the treatment accorded the most-favored foreign nation.
- Fair treatment in the event of nationalization.
- Mechanisms and ground rules for the settlement of disputes.

The provisions of NAFTA that open up members' markets to an exchange of financial services are essentially adapted from the provisions of the General Agreement on Trade in Services (GATS), an agreement administered by the new World Trade Organization, summarized in Chapter 11. Although the members of the World Trade Organization were unable to complete their negotiations on financial services in time for inclusion in the agreement consummating the Uruguay Round in 1993, the basic provisions of that agreement guided the NAFTA members in liberalizing financial services among the three member countries. In effect, financial institutions in member countries acquired

- The same rights as those accorded to national investors when setting up business establishments in the markets of other members.
- The right to "export" their services across the borders of other members.

Time will tell whether these provisions will greatly increase cross-border investment flows in the free-trade area. But early indications in the mid-1990s pointed to the likelihood of considerable growth.

Treaties of Investment

Long before capital movements were being addressed in multilateral agreements and international institutions, governments were already attempting to secure some minimum rights for the investments of their nationals in foreign countries. Those efforts contributed to the development in the nineteenth and twentieth centuries of numerous bilateral agreements of variable scope under a variety of titles, such as Treaties of Friendship, Commerce, and Navigation, and Treaties of Investment. In the decades immediately following the creation of the IMF and the IBRD, these bilateral agreements fell into disuse. Following the lead of Germany in the 1970s, however, a number of industrialized countries revived their bilateral agreements programs with the aim of securing rights for their investors in developing countries. By the mid-1990s, such bilateral agreements could be counted in the hundreds.

These agreements, nominally reciprocal in form, typically leave host countries free to screen incoming foreign investments, but grant certain rights to the foreign-owned enterprises that are legally established in the country. Such rights, as noted earlier, purport

- To guarantee national treatment for foreign investors, subject to specific exceptions.
- To grant most-favored-nation treatment to foreign investors.
- To provide for fair treatment on expropriation or nationalization.
- To provide for the settlement of disputes, sometimes providing explicitly for resort to the International Center for the Settlement of Investment Disputes (ICSID), an appendage of the World Bank.

Experience tells us, however, that such agreements are of only limited value to the foreign investor.

- In most countries, governments enjoy wide latitude in making selections among individual enterprises, whether owned by nationals or by foreigners, when extending privileges and imposing obligations. Thus, "national treatment" may prove no guarantee against discriminatory treatment.
- In many countries, the control and regulation of the sale of services in the national market are in the hands of private organizations, such as securities exchanges and trade associations. So it is difficult for foreign sellers of such services to obtain a remedy against discrimination.

- The time and cost associated with the use of governmental dispute-settling institutions are sufficiently high as to render their use impracticable in most cases.

All told, therefore, the rights of foreigners in capital markets continue to be subject to significant uncertainties, putting managers of multinational networks on guard.

Agreement on Export Credits

Various narrower agreements among countries affecting the movement of money across borders are of some interest to managers. Among these, an agreement among the principal industrialized countries of the world regarding export credits has been substantially affecting the financing of big-ticket items in international trade. An agreement sponsored by the OECD, dubbed the Arrangement on Guidelines for Officially Supported Export Credits, limits the credit terms that signatory government agencies can provide in the promotion of exports.

Governments have long made a practice of promoting their exports through subsidized loans, especially for agricultural products, military supplies, and major items such as ships, planes, industrial plants, and electric-generating plants. In the 1980s, for instance, about one-third of the exports of OECD member countries were receiving some kind of public financing. As a rule, such support was being channeled through national agencies set up especially for the purpose, such as the U.S. Export-Import Bank, the Japan Export-Import Bank, and the U. K. Export Credit Guarantee Department.

The Arrangement seeks to limit the subsidies on exports through a number of provisions:

- At least 15 percent of the contract supported by the export credits must be covered by cash payments.
- The payment terms, with a few exceptions, may not exceed eight and one half years.
- Minimum rates of interest are prescribed, adjusted every six months. If a country's commercial lending rate falls below such minima, the official lending agency of the country may match the commercial rate.
- Except that governments may grant more favorable terms if those terms apply to 35 percent or more of the value of the sale (in which case the transaction is regarded as representing a noncommercial case of foreign aid).

By the 1990s the Arrangement appeared to be operating quite effectively in the range of transactions to which it applied, that is, in the subsidization of exports that were not predominantly financed by grants of foreign aid. Some countries—notably France and Japan—were continuing generous flows of grant aid to developing countries, tied to the acquisition of capital equipment from the donor country. It was not clear how the objective of encouraging the growth of developing countries would be reconciled with the objective of maintaining equal opportunities for exporters.

Capital Adequacy Agreements

Worth mentioning also are the Basel accords, sponsored by the Bank for International Settlements, which have brought all the major countries with substantial international banking facilities together in a common effort.

These agreements attempt to clarify the range of responsibilities of national banking authorities when dealing with the units of international banks, including the function of lender-of-last-resort. Contrary to the general tendency of most governments to guard their sovereign rights jealously in most matters, the general principle in this instance is that the country in which the parent bank is located is to assume the ultimate responsibilities for the financial support of the whole of the international network. The BCCI scandal of the early 1990s served to demonstrate that the adoption of the principle had not yet solved all the problems of the supervision of international banking facilities.

The accords also define minimum capital standards for banks engaged in international banking. In setting such standards, the agreement has been crafted to take into account the differences in accounting practices, capital markets, and regulatory schemes that are encountered in the major countries. Thus, a simple summary of its provisions is out of the question. Nonetheless, at least two unique features should be mentioned now.

- The capital requirements of banks falling under the agreement are adjusted to take account of the nature of their assets. Assets with high issuer risk generate a requirement for more capital than those with lower issuer risk.
- Off-balance-sheet obligations of the banks, such as guarantees of the debt of other enterprises, figure in the calculation of the banks' required minimum capital.

The impact of the agreement on international banking has been indisputable, obliging many banks to raise fresh capital in order to meet the agreement's standards.

Suggested Reading

KENEN, PETER B. *The International Economy.* 3rd ed. New York: Cambridge University Press, 1994.

O'BRIEN, RICHARD R. *Global Financial Inte-* *gration.* New York: Council on Foreign Relations, 1992.

OECD. *The Export Credit Financing System in OECD Member Countries.* 3rd ed. Paris: OECD, 1984.

CHAPTER 11

The International Rules of the Game: Goods and Services

Since the end of World War II, half a century ago, the 200-some sovereign states of the world have been building up networks of international agreements relating to the movement of goods and services across their borders. These agreements frequently play a substantial role in shaping and limiting the trade practices of these countries, described in Chapter 7. In some cases, as in the World Trade Organization (WTO) and the International Monetary Fund (IMF), more than 100 countries are signatories. In other cases, as in the treaty establishing the North American Free Trade Agreement (NAFTA), only two or three countries are involved.

The result is an intricate maze of international agreements that offer both opportunities to the alert manager and threats to the unwary one. But the systems that these agreements create, though quite complex, do have some general contours. To explore those contours, this chapter deals with various categories of agreements, moving in each instance from those with global scope to those of more limited geographical application.

Trade in Merchandise

The rules of the game in merchandise trade have taken on particular importance because most countries have gone further in dismantling their restrictions on such trade in the 1990s than at any time in recent history. Only a few decades ago, most governments in the world were imposing severe restrictions on their imports. Duties of 30 or

40 percent were not uncommon, and import licenses of various kinds were frequently required. Through the agreements and negotiations consummated under the General Agreement on Tariffs and Trade (GATT), and through various regional arrangements such as those of the European Union (EU), and NAFTA, countries are being thrown into direct competition in their merchandise trade as never before. For the manager in the international economy, it is critical to know whether these relationships are durable in the long run or simply represent a flash in the pan, and whether they offer new opportunities or new threats.

The GATT and WTO

Where merchandise trade is concerned, the GATT provides the take-off point for any description of the existing global system. The GATT was created in 1948 as a stop-gap "provisional" agreement among 23 countries, pending the time when a much broader International Trade Organization (ITO) would come into existence. The U.S. government, having led the international campaign for the negotiation and initialing of a draft ITO agreement, never submitted the agreement to the Congress for ratification. The power of opposition from groups in the United States plus the distractions of the Korean War led to the U.S. government's decision to abandon the ITO.

Because of the circumstances of its birth, the GATT suffered from some basic weaknesses that would plague it for most of its later existence. Among other things, the U.S. government's participation in the GATT for a long time was based solely on presidential powers, with the Congress refusing to take official cognizance of its existence; it was not until 1979 that Congress became directly involved in the ratification of GATT agreements.

Despite GATT's unpropitious beginnings, by the 1990s it would become the world's peak trade organization, with a membership of over 120 countries. In 1993 the member states agreed to strengthen the international structure supporting the liberalization of trade by creating a WTO (Figure 11-1). That organization is to oversee not only the agreements relating to trade in merchandise but also those relating to trade in services. Moreover, the organization is to have much stronger powers than the pre-1993 GATT to entertain complaints and adjudicate disputes among the member states.

With considerable particularity, the agreements heretofore administered by the GATT (and in extended form, to be administered by the WTO) lay down rules regarding merchandise trade aimed at four goals:

- A reduction in import restrictions, including a gradual reduction in existing tariffs through periodic negotiations and the ultimate elimination of import licensing restraints.
- The employment of the principle of most-favored-nation treatment by each member country in applying its trade restrictions to the commerce of each of the other member countries, a principle that prevents trade discrimination.

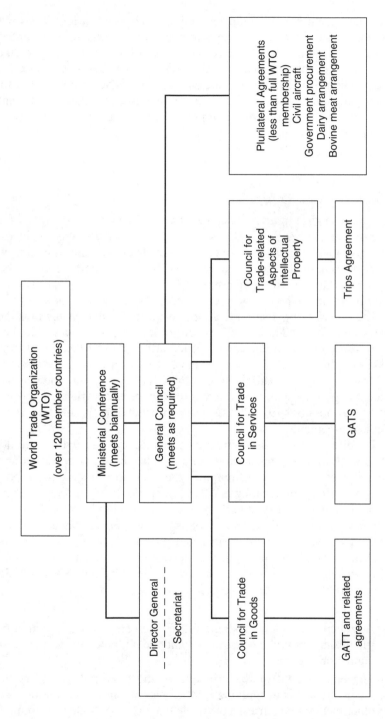

Figure 11-1 World Trade Organization

- The settlement of trade disputes.
- The grant of waivers from any commitment on the basis of an international consensus.

Since the GATT's founding, its member countries have reduced their tariffs through a series of giant bargaining sessions. There were eight such sessions between 1947 and 1993. In each of them, a complex bargaining process was applied that eventually culminated in a schedule of commitments undertaken by each member on the duties it would apply to each category of its merchandise imports. In accordance with the most-favored-nation principle, whenever a member agreed to reduce a tariff rate on any product, the reduction in that product was made available to all members of the GATT. The cumulative effect of these negotiations was to reduce the world's tariff levels to a small fraction—perhaps one-eighth or one-tenth—of what they had been at the end of World War II.

These achievements contributed to a vast growth in the volume and relative importance of international trade. As Figure 11-2 shows, the relative importance of international trade in merchandise grew substantially in all major areas, with the notable exception of Japan.

Nevertheless, as described in Chapter 7, member states have concurrently main-

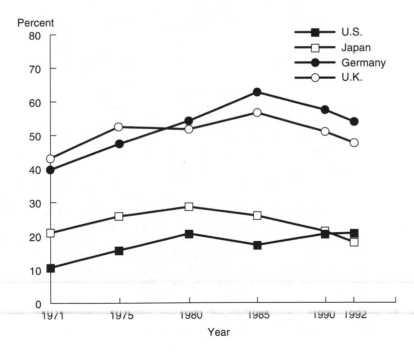

Figure 11-2   Foreign Trade as Percentage of GDP

Source: International Monetary Fund, *International Financial Statistics Yearbook, 1993.*

tained and even extended a number of different practices that significantly inhibit the growth of international trade. In the giant agreement concluded by GATT members in 1993, the so-called Uruguay Round agreement, one objective was substantially to curb a number of these practices inhibiting trade.

- **VERs**. So-called voluntary export agreements had proliferated over the years, as importing countries took up the practice of threatening potential exporters with official import restrictions on specified products unless the exporters agreed to hold the volume or the price of their exports in check. By threatening exporters, the importing country could avoid both applying import restrictions and discriminating overtly against the exporting countries it had targeted. The United States, Japan, and the European Union have made extensive use of such threats, notably in steel and automobiles. The 1993 agreement provides for a phasing out of almost all such agreements over a four-year period and for a virtual ban on future agreements.
- **"Safeguard" provisions**. From the first, the GATT had included a clause authorizing its members, under specified circumstances, to impose temporary restrictions on imports that threatened serious injury to a domestic industry. That right has occasionally been applied by the United States and other countries as

---

BOX 11-1. THE MONTREAL PROTOCOL ON CFCS

In September 1987 in Montreal and June 1990 in London, the United States, the countries of the European Union, Japan, and several scores of other countries entered into agreements to phase out the production of CFCs (chlorofluorocarbons) and a number of other substances that were believed to be contributing to the depletion of the ozone layer in Antarctica. The agreement provided for periodic assessments and reviews of the situation as well as for continuous research on the issue. In laying down the timetable for the phaseout process, distinctions were made between producers in industrialized countries and those in developing countries.

  Dupont took the lead in the United States, and Imperial Chemicals Industries took the lead in the United Kingdom in pressing for the termination of production. Both were substantial producers of the substances restricted under the protocol. Having determined that CFCs constituted a threat, these companies were prepared to terminate production. At the same time, however, it was apparent that an international agreement would be required if producers in other countries were to be restrained from filling the gap in the market created by their withdrawal.

SOURCE: Based on Richard Benedick, *Ozone Diplomacy* (Cambridge, MA: Harvard University Press, 1991).

an "escape clause." In the 1993 agreements, the provision has been redefined in much more specific terms. For instance, restrictions are to be limited to a maximum period of eight years, and rules are to be developed that would discourage repeated applications of the provision to the same industry (see Box 11-1).

- **MFA quotas.** An extensive set of import restrictions has been in effect under the GATT-sponsored Multi-Fiber Arrangement (MFA), which legitimates the importing countries' use of country-by-country quotas on a wide range of textile products. Under the 1993 agreements, industrialized countries are expected to phase out these restrictions over a 10-year period, at least for products from countries that in turn are relaxing their restrictions on high-quality textiles and clothing. Tariffs, however, are expected to replace the quantitative restrictions that are in force under MFA agreements.

- **Antidumping duties.** From the first, GATT rules authorized governments to impose special duties to offset dumping by foreign sellers. As noted in Chapter 7, such duties have been increasingly applied by major importers, including the United States and the European Union. Purporting to operate in conformity with GATT rules, governments introduced their own definitions of what constituted dumping and made it easier for their domestic producers to secure the imposition of such duties. The 1993 agreements circumscribe the use of antidumping duties, with stricter definitions of dumping and with more timely and effective provisions for exporters to secure remedies against the arbitrary imposition of such duties by governments.

- **Subsidies.** All governments provide subsidies to some industries under some conditions, a practice that gives rise at times to importing countries applying countervailing duties against the exports of those countries. The 1993 agreement distinguishes three types of subsidies:
  - Those that are prohibited outright and hence are subject to countervailing duties, such as direct payments for exports.
  - Those that might create unfair trade effects and are therefore "actionable" (that is, subject to countervailing duties), such as the financing by governments of the losses of state-owned enterprises.
  - Those that are "nonactionable," and hence not subject to countervailing duties, such as general support for depressed regions or disaster-relief assistance.

- **TRIMs.** Many governments, especially those in developing countries, impose trade-related investment measures (TRIMs) on enterprises producing goods in their jurisdiction. These measures require the firms involved, as a condition of doing business in the country, to generate some specified minimum domestic content in the products they produce or sell in the country; to achieve some specified balance between their exports and their imports; or to attain some other specified objective. Where such measures are applied, they usually are targeted at foreign-owned subsidiaries. Under the 1993 agreements, some of these measures are to be phased out, with a five-year transitional period provided for developing countries and a two-year period for developed countries.

- **Government procurement**. Practically all governments, when purchasing goods or services, practice systematic discrimination in favor of domestic producers. In a so-called plurilateral agreement, a subset of member countries of the GATT, including the United States, Japan, and the EU, are to broaden very substantially the range of goods and services for which foreign suppliers will be invited to bid on a nondiscriminatory basis.

- **Agriculture**. The GATT's rules with respect to trade in agricultural products have always been highly permissive, allowing for the widespread use of import restrictions, price support programs, and export subsidies. A standstill agreement has been framed covering such restrictions, along with an undertaking to reduce the restrictive impact of existing measures over a period of years. Nontariff import barriers such as quotas are to be converted to tariff equivalents, which then are to be reduced by more than one-third. Moreover, under domestic price support programs, governments are to lower their target support prices by about 20 percent. Subsidies paid to farmers for domestic production or exports are to be cut back substantially.

- **Technical standards**. With the decline in border restrictions on international trade, the world trading community has begun to realize the importance of numerous other restrictive devices, some very long in place, that inhibit the international movement of goods. For example, governments commonly impose technical requirements on goods offered in their national markets, such as safety standards for food, toys, automobiles, and electrical equipment, in forms that are sometimes intended to shut out foreign products. Some steps were taken in the 1993 GATT agreements to constrain such practices, but it remains to be seen whether these general measures can be made operational. In any event, the GATT measures acknowledge the right of governments to set national standards that are higher than any internationally agreed standards, if they are intended to protect any form of life or the environment, or to prevent deceptive practices. (See Box 11-1.)

- **Intransigence**. About 150 disputes have been referred to the GATT during its existence. Many have been effectively settled. Under the disputes procedures of the GATT in effect until 1993, however, governments accused of having violated GATT provisions have had numerous ways of stalling the GATT's consideration of the complaint and of preventing a definitive outcome of the complaints process. So various major disputes have dragged on over many years without resolution. A new disputes procedure has been agreed on, which provides automatic deadlines and timetables for the disputes process, from the filing of a complaint to the ultimate application of a remedy. Under the new procedure, the findings of a complaints panel, the disposition of any appeals, and the determination of a remedy all are to be completed pursuant to a timetable that covers about 10 months. The losing party must bring itself into compliance within 15 months thereafter. It remains to be seen how this ambitious undertaking will operate in practice.

The European Union

Inside the overarching global structure provided by the GATT, with its bedrock principle of nondiscrimination in merchandise trade, lie dozens of agreements among smaller groups of countries all over the world that in effect carve out exceptions from the general principle of nondiscrimination. The agreements may provide for the creation of a customs union or free-trade area among their signatories, in which case they are entitled, under Article XXIV of the GATT, to an exemption from the basic GATT rule on nondiscrimination. Or the agreements may have been the subject of a waiver from GATT rules, especially when undertaken among developing countries.

Of the various customs union and free-trade agreements found around the world, the most important arrangement by far is that of the European Union. Its importance is reflected in the fact that most of the GATT's deliberations under Article XXIV have involved one aspect or another of the EU agreements. In 1995 the EU's membership included 15 countries in western Europe, with the prospect that Hungary, Poland, the Czech Republic, and Slovakia would be members within another decade (see Figure 11-3).

The EU is a structure without precedent in the history of international economic relations. Far more than in an intergovernmental agreement, its members surrender their powers over international trade matters to a common set of EU institutions, as portrayed in Figure 11-4.

Four elements in the EU's arrangements exercise a particularly important role in the world's merchandise trade: its common internal market; its common agricultural policy (CAP); its numerous preferential arrangements with selected nonmember countries; and its common external tariff (CXT).

The common internal market.   Where merchandise trade between member countries is concerned, member countries have surrendered their sovereign powers to the Union and in principle have dismantled all trade barriers at their national frontiers. Except in some well-defined cases, goods inside any member country of the Union can circulate freely throughout the Union without regard to national frontiers. More specifically:

- Member states may impose neither tariffs nor quantitative restrictions nor other devices that have an equivalent effect on trade between members.
- Financial aid provided by member states to enterprises in their jurisdiction, including state-owned enterprises, is subject to review by the Commission. Such reviews are not perfunctory and have led to some landmark cases in which the EU has forbidden governments to provide state aid to major enterprises.
- Since 1993, the protection of the environment has been placed on a par with the achievement of a single market as objectives of the Union. In that connection, member states that wish to maintain environmental controls that exceed those required by the Union may do so with the Union's approval.

Figure 11-3   Membership in the European Union, by Accession Dates

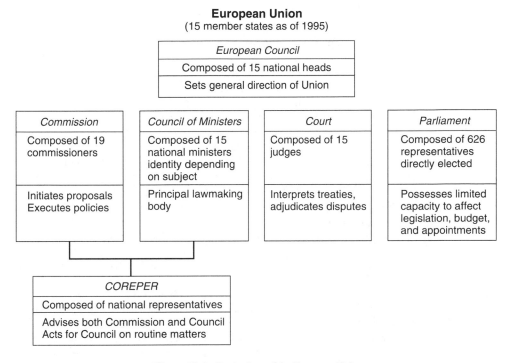

European Union
(15 member states as of 1995)

European Council
Composed of 15 national heads
Sets general direction of Union

Commission	Council of Ministers	Court	Parliament
Composed of 19 commissioners	Composed of 15 national ministers identity depending on subject	Composed of 15 judges	Composed of 626 representatives directly elected
Initiates proposals Executes policies	Principal lawmaking body	Interprets treaties, adjudicates disputes	Possesses limited capacity to affect legislation, budget, and appointments

COREPER
Composed of national representatives
Advises both Commission and Council Acts for Council on routine matters

Figure 11-4   Institutions of the European Union

- Nonetheless, where member countries apply regulations on products for reasons of health, safety, or environmental control, they are enjoined from applying such provisions in a manner that would constitute a disguised import restriction. In implementing that objective, the Union has introduced a highly innovative program that could prove to be a major precedent for future global trade relations. Under the Union's program, a principle known as mutual recognition has been introduced. It includes the following elements:
  - For any product category in which countries impose controls aimed at health, safety, or environmental objectives, the Union adopts general standards that are deemed necessary to satisfy those objectives.
  - The means of achieving those standards, however, are left to individual member states.
  - Each member is free to issue certificates for any export affirming that the export fulfills the home state's requirements.
  - Each member must recognize that the regulatory measures in effect in any other member state that satisfy the Union's standards are equivalent to its own. (See Box 11-2.)
- Where quantitative restrictions exist applicable to the goods of nonmember countries, as in the case of the Multi-Fiber Arrangement, the restrictions are ne-

BOX 11-2.   THE CASSIS DE DIJON CASE

In 1979 the European Court of Justice received a complaint from a small German importing firm, Rewe Zentral AG, claiming that the German authorities were preventing it from selling a French liqueur, *Cassis de Dijon,* in the German market. The liqueur is ordinarily used with white wine to create kir, a product little known at the time outside of France. As it frequently has done, the court used the case to pronounce a general principle of fundamental importance to the Community.

The German authorities were not prohibiting the actual importation of the liqueur but rather its sale on German territory. The alcoholic content of Cassis ran between 15 and 20 percent. Its sale as a liqueur therefore would violate a German law that forbade the marketing of liqueurs unless their alcoholic content exceeded 25 percent. And its sale as a wine would violate a German regulation that placed a ceiling on the alcoholic content of wines. Rewe Zentral AG decided to challenge the German regulation on the grounds that it was inconsistent with the obligations embodied in the Rome treaty, which in Article 30 prohibited "measures having equivalent effect to quantitative restrictions."

The German government argued that its prohibition of the sale of Cassis did not constitute a breach of treaty obligations since it was meant for two purposes: to protect public health; and to protect consumers against unfair commercial practices. Such measures, according to the German government, came under the exemption for measures instituted on grounds of "public morality," "public order," and "public safety," contained in Article 36 of the treaty.

As regards the protection of public health, the German government stated that one purpose in fixing minimum alcohol contents for liqueurs was to avoid the proliferation of alcoholic beverages on the national market, in particular those with a low alcohol content, since, in its view, such products could more easily induce a dependence on alcohol. A second purpose was to protect consumers against unfair commercial practices on the part of producers and distributors of alcoholic beverages, including destructive competition based on the concealed reduction of alcoholic content in rival products.

The court rejected these arguments. It acknowledged the principle of Article 36, permitting restrictions in some circumstances necessary for large public purposes. It even went further and indicated that the range of acceptable purposes enumerated in the treaty should be enlarged and refined. But it refused to accept the German arguments, observing that the alleged public purposes of Germany's prohibition could be achieved simply by disclosing the national origin and the alcoholic content of the product.

"In practice," said the court, "the principal effect of requirements of this nature is to promote alcoholic beverages having a high alcohol content by excluding from the national market products of other member states which do not answer that description."

(continued)

BOX 11-2.   THE CASSIS DE DIJON CASE (CONTINUED)

The German prohibition, therefore, was found to be "disproportionate" to the problem it claimed to address and not sufficiently justified to override the principle of free circulation of goods sought by the treaty.

The court concluded: "There is therefore no valid reason why, provided that they have been lawfully produced and marketed in one of the member states, alcoholic beverages should not be introduced into any other member state." With that pronouncement, the court succeeded in laying the foundation for the mutual recognition principle.

---

gotiated by the executive arm of the Union, the European Commission, and are applied on a Union-wide basis, thereby minimizing the existence of country-by-country quotas inside the Union.

The common agricultural policy (CAP).   As with nonagricultural products, the Union's programs are Union-wide in scope and are managed by the institutions of the Union. The Union, however, applies a special set of arrangements for agricultural products, arrangements that may require substantial alteration under the new GATT agreements. With the GATT itself having previously adopted special provisions for trade in agricultural products that were highly tolerant of protectionist practices, the Union was free to take the same approach. The 1993 agreements in the GATT, curtailing the use of protectionist devices for agricultural goods, promise to alter the EU's practices in this area. The modifications would take some time to be put in place.

The system that the EU is in the process of modifying has included the following features:

- An agreed target price has been fixed for the major commodities, a figure that would theoretically generate a "fair return" to relatively efficient producers in the Union.
- A variable levy has been imposed on imports of such commodities, calculated to ensure that the imports purchased by Union importers at world prices do not undermine the achievement of the Union's internal target price. (Tariff equivalents may eventually take the place of such levies.)
- An internal price support mechanism, usually implemented through the Union's purchases in the open market, has aimed further to support the achievement of the target price.
- Exports have been subsidized sufficiently to allow them to be sold at world prices.

These programs have generated mountains of grain and butter from time to time inside the Union, have absorbed most of the Union's annual budget, and have been a major source of friction between the Union and the world's principal exporters of grains, meat, and dairy products.

Under the GATT agreements of 1993, the fixed tariffs are to take the place of variable levies, export subsidies are to be substantially curtailed, and the agricultural support system is to be shifted to direct payments to farmers.

Preferential arrangements.   The various preferential arrangements of the Union with nonmember countries have been variable in their terms and extensive in scope, covering over 100 such countries. These have included:

- A European Economic Area agreement (EEA), which has included free-trade arrangements with five countries in Europe—Austria, Norway, Sweden, Iceland, and Finland. With Austria, Sweden, and Finland becoming full-fledged members of the EU, membership in the EEA agreement now has only limited application. Under the agreement, the EU maintains a free-trade area with the affected countries, covering nonagricultural products and services. The arrangement is unusual for free-trade areas, however, in subjecting its non-EU member participants to the full panoply of EU measures relating to the creation of a single European market, including notably
  - the provisions against restrictive business practices,
  - the provisions limiting state aids, and
  - the provisions for controlling the application of regulations relating to safety, health, and the environment.
- Bilateral agreements with each of several dozen countries in North Africa, the Middle East, and eastern Europe, extending various preferential rights to such countries for access to the Union's markets, typically without demanding reciprocal preferential privileges from such countries. For nonmember countries within Europe, including Hungary, Poland, the Czech Republic, and Slovakia, these agreements include a recognition that the ultimate long-term objective is membership in the Union.
- A five-year renewable agreement with over 60 former colonies of the Union's members, the Africa-Caribbean-Pacific Agreement (ACP), under which the Union provides
  - Duty-free access to the Union's markets in most products.
  - A package of development aid and technical assistance programs.
  - A stabilization fund against declines in export earnings for specified agricultural products and minerals.
- A General System of Preferences (GSP), providing some reductions in duties on selected products to developing countries other than the ACP members.

Relations with other countries.   The common external tariff (CXT) of the Union, therefore, has its principal application mainly in trade with countries that are not partners in any preferential arrangement, notably the United States, Japan, and the Latin American countries. Although every member of the Union is also a member of the GATT, the rules and procedures of the GATT have no standing in disputes among Union members regarding trade inside the Union. (Indeed, at the time this book went to print, Germany was arguing before the Court of Justice that the provisions of the Treaty of Rome dominated those of treaties with nonmember countries wherever inconsistencies existed.) Although the Union itself is not a member of the GATT, it alone is authorized to conduct negotiations with other members of the GATT.

Other Preferential Arrangements

Apart from the European Union's preferential arrangements with nonmember countries, a considerable number of other preferential arrangements exist in various parts of the world that affect the terms on which merchandise moves across national borders. Free-trade agreements between pairs of countries and among larger country groups have been proliferating throughout the world. A few are of sufficient importance to affect the basic strategies of enterprises.

The North American Free Trade Agreement (NAFTA).   NAFTA is commonly regarded as the nucleus of a preferential arrangement that may one day equal the European Union in scope and significance. Such a possibility is given credence by the fact that many countries, including most countries in the Western Hemisphere, have expressed an interest in joining. But NAFTA in its present form must be distinguished sharply from the European Union.

- NAFTA is an intergovernmental agreement, administered in effect through intergovernmental committees composed of officials from the various signatory governments; but these intergovernmental committees are obliged to act strictly within the limits of the treaty's detailed provisions. By contrast with the EU, therefore, NAFTA lacks any strong institutional support for its application and enforcement, such as a rule-making capability, an executive arm, and a court.
- NAFTA's members, unlike those of the EU, have surrendered none of their powers to negotiate with third countries.
- Because NAFTA is a free trade agreement rather than a customs union, each member country continues to levy its own tariff rates against the products of nonmember countries.
- NAFTA therefore contains extensive "rules of origin"—that is, provisions that lay down standards for identifying products that are to be denied duty-free treat-

---

BOX 11-3.   CALCULATING DOMESTIC CONTENT IN FREE-TRADE AGREEMENTS: THE HONDA CASE

In determining whether a product is of domestic origin inside a free-trade area, two criteria are customarily applied:

1.   Components and materials in the product are counted as domestic even if they contain materials of foreign origin, provided that the foreign components are sufficiently transformed by further processing inside the free-trade area as to alter their tariff classification.
2.   The aggregate value of the domestic inputs, so calculated, exceeds 50 percent of the value of the final product.

Under the U.S.-Canada Free Trade Agreement, in effect before the adoption of NAFTA, U.S. authorities ruled that Honda automobiles produced in Canada from parts generated in Canada, the United States, and foreign countries did not qualify as products eligible for duty-free treatment when brought in from Canada to the United States. In reaching that conclusion, U.S. authorities refused to include the cost of workers' health benefits and the cost of borrowed capital as part of the U.S. value added in the manufacture of Honda engines in the company's Ohio plant.

NAFTA provisions reduced the discretion of national authorities to make such arbitrary unilateral decisions by specifying the items to be included in domestic value-added calculations. At the same time, however, NAFTA provided, in the case of automobiles, that

1.   The customary 50 percent standard should eventually be fixed at 62.5 percent.
2.   In making the calculation of area content for any product, each input to the product should be tracked back to its ultimate origin, including the components and materials brought in through other member countries from third countries.

---

ment inside the free-trade area by virtue of including some ingredients from foreign countries (see Box 11-3).

Indeed, one of the distinguishing characteristics of NAFTA is the elaborateness and particularity with which these rules of origin are formulated. The rules are designed to maintain as much protection as possible in some industries inside the free-trade area. Reflecting that objective, the applicable rules of origin are presented product by product, covering over 200 pages in the treaty's text, with automotive products and textile products getting especially detailed treatment. (See Box 11-4.)

Apart from its free-trade area agreements, the United States, like the EU, favors

---

BOX 11-4.   A TYPICAL "RULE OF ORIGIN" FROM NAFTA

"Men's or boys' shirts of cotton or man-made fibers shall be considered to originate [in NAFTA] if they are both cut and assembled in the territory of one or more of the Parties and if the fabric of the outer shell, exclusive of collars and cuffs, is wholly of one or more of the following: . . . .

Fabrics of subheading 5208.42 or 5208.49, not of square construction, containing more than 85 warp ends and filling picks per square centimeter, of average yarn number exceeding 85 metric . . . "

---

some developing countries with special trading privileges. In the U.S. case, the areas especially benefited are in the Caribbean Basin. In addition, like the EU, the United States also maintains a General System of Preferences for the benefit of developing countries, although its terms and coverage bear no relation to those of the Union.

Asia-Pacific Economic Cooperation Forum (APEC).   The possibility of building on APEC, heretofore a forum for discussion and consultation, to create a preferential trading area in the Pacific Basin, has been a gleam in the eye of the U.S. government. The Forum includes 18 participating countries bordering the Pacific from Asia, Australia, North America, and South America. The object of creating a preferential trade arrangement in the area from the U.S. viewpoint is manifold: to head off the creation of preferential regimes in the region from which the United States would be excluded; and to anchor the U.S. economy more firmly to the high-growth economies on the Asia mainland.

There are few signs, however, that any broad preferential arrangement will materialize in the early future. The possibility of creating a free-trade area by the year 2020 has received official endorsement. However, some countries in South-East Asia, including Malaysia, resist the idea of maintaining formal preferential ties with Japan or with the United States. Besides, how to integrate China into a world trading system, whether through regional agreements or the WTO or both, was still an unresolved issue in the mid-1990s. Nevertheless, it appears likely that APEC will continue to exist, to be used by the countries in the Pacific Basin as a means of promoting economic ties and monitoring one another's behavior in the region.

Other arrangements   Preferential arrangements for trade in goods have been especially common among developing countries. Some are so limited and conditional that they can hardly be dubbed free-trade areas; instead of laying down some broad rules that cover a wide range of industries, they simply create narrow preferential commitments in a limited range of items. Some, however, are extensive enough in product coverage to approach status as a free-trade area. Worth noting are:

- The Andean Pact, which includes a set of preferential trading arrangements among Peru, Bolivia, Ecuador, Colombia, and Venezuela.
- MERCOSUR, an agreement among Brazil, Argentina, Uruguay, and Paraguay, intergovernmental in form, that provides for the adoption of a common external tariff among its members, along with the elimination of trade barriers inside the common market.
- The Association of Southeast Asian Nations (ASEAN) consisting of Singapore, Indonesia, Malaysia, Brunei, and the Philippines, which has declared its intention to create a free-trade area among its members.
- A network of bilateral free trade agreements involving Mexico, Central America, Colombia, Venezuela, and various other countries in Latin America, in flux.
- The Economic Community of West African States (ECOWAS), the Gulf Cooperation Council (GCC), and the Australia-New Zealand Closer Economic Relations Trade Agreement (ANZCERTA), all involving varying degrees of trade preferences.

Where trade in merchandise is concerned, the global structure generated by these overlapping agreements offers numerous opportunities to those managers determined to master its complexities. Although factor costs such as wages and land rents may matter in the selection of production sites, the complex mosaic of global trade arrangements may matter just as much in determining the merits of alternative sites. The strong interest of U.S.-based firms in Mexican locations and of German-based firms in eastern European locations is explained in part by the potential advantages to the firm created by these preferential agreements.

Trade in Services

The regimes that exist for international trade in services are strikingly different from those in trade. The reasons for those differences are evident, having been touched on in Chapter 7.

Delivering the Service

Although sellers of tangible products must ensure that their goods will physically cross borders if they are to be a part of international trade, sellers of services can provide their wares in a variety of ways. Engineering or accounting advice can be provided by telephone, fax, or letter; where surgery is involved, the surgeon or the patient may to pay a visit across an international frontier; and where banking services are involved, a foreign firm providing the service is likely to require a permanent establishment in the country. So the delivery of services commonly involves such delicate areas of policy as

- The granting of visas.
- The granting of rights to practice a profession.
- The granting of rights of establishment.

As noted in Chapter 7, governments are ordinarily not prepared to grant unlimited rights to foreigners in such areas. As a result, the delivery of services across international borders is typically hampered by restrictions that have no direct counterpart in the delivery of goods.

The General Agreement on Trade in Services (GATS)

In an effort to fill the void that has existed in the rules of the game for trade in services, the 1993 negotiation sponsored by GATT produced a General Agreement on Trade in Services (GATS). That agreement, operating under the umbrella of the WTO, is subject to its general provisions, including notably the dispute-settlement provisions. The general rules of the GATS for the international sale of services differ from those provided in the GATT for goods, the differences reflecting the unique characteristics of trade in services.

In effect, governments retain the right to protect their nationals from international competition. For the time being, they are free to provide subsidies, to discriminate in government procurement, and to tolerate restrictive business practices on behalf of their nationals. Nevertheless they must meet two requirements:

- To reduce their protective barriers (in GATS parlance, their limitations on market access) through negotiations with other GATS members.
- To grant national treatment and most-favored-nation treatment to all GATS members for those categories of services that they have designated for liberalization in the course of these negotiations, except to the extent that they have specified otherwise in the negotiations.

In these service negotiations, as in the negotiations historically conducted over the tariff rates applicable to merchandise, members are free to choose the services in which they propose to liberalize, as long as they satisfy the requirement of broad reciprocity. Moreover, each of the main channels for the delivery of services mentioned earlier—through cross-border communication, through the establishment of a commercial presence, or through the physical movement of the provider or the consumer of the service—can in theory be addressed separately. (See Box 11-5.)

Country A's principal "concession" in the liberalization of services, for instance, might be the opening up of its banking business to foreign banks, while Country B's principal concession might be the opening up of its cellular telephone business to foreign providers.

The first round of negotiations under GATS, completed in 1993, produced thin results; nonetheless, the results that were achieved were of considerable importance as precedents. For instance, although basic telecommunication services such as voice telephone services were set aside for future negotiation, there was agreement that "value-added" services offered by foreigners such as proprietary computerized data banks should have open access to the basic facilities. In 1995, a group of GATT members (notably excluding the United States) reached a thin agreement on the liberalization of financial services. Ongoing negotiations offered some promise that trade liberalization in banking, maritime services, advertising, and the "culture" industries might eventually be forthcoming.

Specialized International Regimes

Meanwhile, in some service areas, governments have developed specialized global institutions operating under rules fashioned especially for each service.

In the case of air transport, the fundamental principle accepted by 160 governments is that each is the undisputed sovereign of its own air space and that nothing happens in that space without its explicit permission. Guided by that overriding principle, the firms involved have been allowed to form an International Air Transport Association (IATA), while the governments involved have formed an International Civil Aviation Organization (ICAO). Between them, these institutions provide rules

---

BOX 11-5. FORMAT FOR COUNTRY OFFERS IN THE GATS NEGOTIATIONS OVER SERVICES

Mode of Supply	Limitations on Market Access	Limitations on National Treatment
Cross-border communication		
Commercial presence		
Consumer crossing border		
Producer crossing border		

of the game for the allocation of routes, the setting of prices, the sharing of proceeds from joint tickets, environmental protection, customs procedures, and safety regulations. Until the 1980s, with most national air industries subject to very close regulation, the international agreements tended to stifle international competition. Subsequently, as national regulations on competition were relaxed in many countries, including the United States, competition on international routes was allowed to grow.

Similar regimes exist in the fields of maritime transport, telecommunications, and banking, each highly specialized to its own area of service. As the WTO expands its agreements in some of these fields, complex questions of jurisdiction among competing international agencies are certain to arise. Already, for instance, such conflicts have arisen between the WTO and the World Intellectual Property Organization over which entity is to determine the international rules with regard to patents, trademarks, and copyrights.

The European Union

When in 1987 the European Union adopted the goal of creating a single European market by 1992, it was evident that the Union was still far from that objective in the case of services. The Union's drive to remove the obstacles to the sale of services in the common market was facilitated by the fact that the Rome treaty already provided in principle for the free movement of workers and capital among the member states, thereby narrowing the range of restrictive devices that could have impeded the movement of services. The principal remaining impediments, therefore, were national regulations ostensibly imposed by public authority to protect consumers, such as bank depositors, home buyers, and medical patients, and to protect the environment.

Obviously, for many services, governments and their publics would still insist on regulations of some sort. As with the health and safety regulations that affect international trade in goods, the challenge for the EU has been to find a way of permitting states to maintain the desired level of regulation without creating disguised barriers to trade. In response, the Union applied the "mutual recognition" principle to services, which it had already developed in order to deal with the health, safety, and environment regulations affecting trade in goods.

As it had done with goods, the Union in a series of enactments identified the general standards that each member government would be required to fulfill in the sale of each specified service, leaving the precise means largely to the home country of the seller. In most cases, a service that satisfies these minimum standards could be offered freely across frontiers inside the common market. As Box 11-6 indicates, however, the Union authorizes importing countries to impose additional requirements in some cases, including banking and medicine, provided they are not disguised barriers to trade.

In the early 1990s, it was still too early to tell whether the Union's extraordinary approach through the mutual recognition principle would greatly increase the cross-border flow of services inside the Union, and much too early to tell whether the

---

BOX 11-6.   THE UNION'S SECOND BANKING DIRECTIVE

Adopted in 1989, the Second Banking Directive is designed to create for "credit institutions" in the Union a single banking license that will permit banks to do business throughout the Union.

The directive was only adopted, however, after capital controls inside the Union had been ordered abolished and after common principles had been adopted governing capital adequacy standards and the conditions of solvency for banks in the Union.

1. The license applies only to "credit institutions," not, for instance, to firms that simply deal in securities.

2. Nevertheless, what a credit institution is free to do under that license is to be determined by the laws and regulations of their home state in the Union that define the powers of credit institutions.

3. However, host countries in the Union do retain some residual powers over banks from other Union countries. Vaguely defined, these residual powers include measures taken to conform to national monetary policies and to protect bank customers.

4. The European Commission may challenge a foreign bank that wishes to set up an establishment in a member country if the foreign bank comes from a third country that "is not granting Community credit institutions effective market access comparable to that granted by the Community." What is meant by "comparable" market access is not specified.

---

approach might be effectively applied beyond the Union itself. A first step toward such an extension, however, was already being launched in the EEA, covering the EU and the EFTA countries. Under that agreement, the EFTA countries are included in the liberalizing measures for services made possible by the mutual recognition approach.

The North American Free Trade Agreement

Like the EU, NAFTA also makes provisions for the liberalization of services among its members; but lacking a supranational rule-making capability, an executive, and a court, NAFTA uses an approach to the liberalization of services that is very different from the approach of the EU. In contrast, NAFTA patterns itself after a network of bilateral intergovernmental agreements, sometimes called treaties of investment, whose origins go back to the nineteenth century. As in such agreements, NAFTA lays down a general rule that nationals of a signatory country, when doing business in another signatory country, are entitled either to national treatment or to most-favored-nation treatment, whichever is superior. Each signatory then lists a string of exceptions, areas in which it proposes to reserve freedom of action.

In the case of NAFTA, some substantial liberalization is provided for in services, especially on the part of Mexico. Yet the exceptions stipulated by each of the three signatory countries are extensive and significant.

The United States, for instance, has listed reservations with respect to national treatment or with respect to the right to establish a local presence in the fields of financial services, telecommunications, pipelines, legal services, air transport, trucking and busing, water transport, cable television, social services, and newspaper publishing. In some cases, the reservations are intended primarily to ensure that the United States eventually secures reciprocity in the particular field from its partners. In other cases, the reservation stakes out an area in which the United States intends to retain freedom of action indefinitely.

Suggested Reading

ANDERSON, KYM, and RICHARD BLACKHURST (eds.). *Regional Integration and the Global Trading System.* New York: Harvester/Wheatsheaf, 1993.

FATEMI, KHOSROW (ed.). *North American Free Trade Agreement.* New York: St Martin's Press, 1993.

HARROP, JEFFREY. *The Political Economy of Integration in the European Community.* 2nd ed. Brookfield, VT: Edward Elgar, 1992.

KENEN, PETER B. *The International Economy.* 3rd ed. New York: Prentice Hall, 1994.

LOW, PATRICK. *Trading Free: The GATT and U.S. Trade Policy.* New York: Twentieth Century Fund, 1993.

PRESTON, LEE E., and DUANE WINDSOR. *The Rules of the Game in the Global Economy.* Boston: Kluwer Academic Publishers, 1992.

Balance-of-Payments Exercises

Make the appropriate entries into the U.S. balance of payments for each transaction. (When doing the exercises, use the system of accounts immediately following.)

1. Opel (Germany) sells $50,000 of cars to General Motors (f.o.b.). General Motors ships by German freighter (cost $2,000) but buys U.S. insurance (cost $500). All payments are made by drawing checks on General Motors' Morgan Guaranty account in New York.

2. A U.S. firm exports $600,000 worth of machinery to a German manufacturer by U.S. ship (cost $20,000), insured by a U.S. company (cost $4,000). Payment is made by drawing checks against the German manufacturer's account in Morgan Guaranty in New York.

3. Repeat the first two problems assuming that payment is made through accounts in German banks.

4. Gentle Sigh Investments, a New York investment trust, buys 100,000 shares of VW stock at DM400 per share, paying for half from its New York bank, the other half from its Berlin bank. (Assume for simplicity that 2.0 deutsche marks equals $1.)

5. VW pays DM8 dividends per share, through its Berlin bank. Gentle Sigh owns 100,000 shares.

6. A U.S. company exports to its Brazilian subsidiary machinery worth $500,000 and accepts $500,000 in stock as payment.

7. The U.S. government grants $1,000,000 of wheat to India under PL 480, accepting in payment blocked local currency equivalent to $1,000,000.

8. Karl Goldfinger of King of Prussia, Pennsylvania, sends $500 to his grandfather in Frankfurt. The check is drawn on the First National Bank of Philadelphia.

9. The Brunei central bank converts $50 million, which it had been holding as part of its reserves, into German marks and buys gold on the private market with another $10 million.

10. The U.S. and German governments enter into an agreement under which, on request, the U.S. government will automatically make available up to $100 million to the German government and the German government will automatically make available up to DM200 million to the United States. Term of loan is three months.

11. The U.S. government requests and receives a loan of DM200 million under the agreement described in 10.

12. The German government purchases $20 million in special three-year U.S. Treasury notes at 8½ percent, bearing the option on the part of the Germans to tender on three-day notice. The notes are denominated in DM and are paid for by drawing down the German account in the Federal Reserve Bank of New York.

System of Accounts in the United States Balance of Payments

Exports of Goods and Services

1. Merchandise, adjusted, excluding military
2. Transportation
3. Travel
4. Miscellaneous services:
   (a) Private
   (b) Government, excluding military
5. Military transactions
6. Income on investments (received by U.S. resident from overseas):
   (a) Direct investments
   (b) Other private
   (c) Government

Imports of Goods and Services

7. Merchandise, adjusted, excluding military
8. Transportation
9. Travel
10. Miscellaneous services:
    (a) Private
    (b) Government, excluding military
11. Military transactions

12. Income on investments (paid by U.S. resident):
    (a) Private
    (b) Government

Unilateral Transfers, Net

13. Private remittances
14. Government:
    (a) Military grants of goods and services
    (b) Other grants
    (c) Pensions and other transfers

U.S. Capital, Net

15. Private, net:
    (a) Direct investments, net
    (b) New issues of foreign securities
    (c) Redemptions
    (d) Transactions in outstanding foreign securities
    (e) Other long-term, net
    (f) Short-term, net
16. Government, net:
    (a) Long-term capital
    (b) Repayments
    (c) Foreign currency holdings and short-term claims, net

Foreign Capital, Net [Increase in U.S. Liabilities (+)]

17. Direct investments in the United States
18. Other long-term investments
19. Other capital excluding liquid funds:
    (a) U.S. private short-term liabilities
    (b) U.S. government liabilities
20. Increase in foreign holdings of liquid dollar assets

Reserves and Balancing Item

21. Gold and convertible currencies, net authorities
22. Unrecorded transactions, errors, and omissions

Definitions of Accounts

Account Number

Current Account

1 and 7 *Merchandise, adjusted, excluding military:* Includes all movable goods that are sold, given away, or otherwise transferred from U.S. to foreign ownership, or vice versa. The following exceptions exist, however:

    (a) Gold movements, except for net domestic consumption or production, are recorded in a separate capital account (21).

    (b) Purchases in foreign countries by U.S. tourists and purchases in the United States by foreign tourists are incorporated in the "travel" account. Personal expenditures by members of the armed forces in foreign countries are classified as "miscellaneous services."

    (c) Expenditures abroad by U.S. diplomatic missions and in the United States by foreign missions plus purchases of office supplies by U.S. government nonmilitary agencies operating abroad are included in the "miscellaneous services" account.

    (d) Electric power is treated as a miscellaneous service.

    (e) Bunker fuel, ship stores, and other port expenditures are accounted for in the transportation accounts. However, bunker fuel supplied overseas by foreign countries under contracts with military agencies of the United States is included in the "merchandise" account.

    (f) Household and personal effects of emigrants and immigrants are excluded from the balance of payments.

    The value of exports and imports should reflect the actual price paid to the seller, adjusted to include all charges to the point where the goods are placed alongside the vessel on which they are shipped (f.a.s.).

2 and 8 *Transportation:* Includes all international transactions arising from the transportation of goods and passengers by ocean and inland waterway shipping, air, rail, road, and pipeline transportation. Included are expenses of transportation companies consisting of purchases outside their own country of goods and services. Capital movements in the transportation industry are not included. The nationality of the recipient of payment is determined by the nationality of the company making or receiving payment and not by the flag of the ship on which the goods are carried.

3 and 9 *Travel:* Includes expenditures by travelers for lodging, food, amusements, gifts, and other personal purchases. Expenditures for transportation within foreign countries or between two foreign countries are in general included as a travel payment. Expenditures for transportation to and from the United States are included in the transportation account. Expenditures of government employees abroad are included in "Miscellaneous services, government."

4a and 10a   *Miscellaneous services, private:* Includes all private service transactions not already discussed. It excludes all transactions to which the U.S. government was a party, but does include transactions of foreign governments with private U.S. individuals or corporations, and the foreign transactions of state and local administrations. Important items are communications, reinsurance, motion picture rentals, engineers' and contractors' services, home office charges, rentals, royalties, and foreign representational expenses in the United States.

4b and 10b   *Miscellaneous services, government:* Includes all service transactions of the nonmilitary agency of the government and its personnel abroad; with the exception of freight and shipping and the service of capital. Post office department payments to foreign steamship companies for the carriage of mail and freight and fair payments for the overland transportation of government goods and personnel in foreign countries are included. Also included are:
   (a) Government purchases of lands and buildings not of an income-producing nature.
   (b) Cost of construction materials and labor for (a).
   (c) Expenditures of U.S. government personnel abroad.
   (d) Payments for participation in international organizations with the exception of relief, aid, and capital contributions such as subscriptions to the IBRD and IMF.

5 and 11   *Military transactions:* Includes transactions where the reporting federal agency is military. The account includes payments by U.S. military personnel for goods and services obtained from the foreign economy.

6a, 6b and 12a   *Income on investments, direct; other private:* Includes receipts of income on direct investments and on securities. Direct investment implies a degree of management control and is generally limited to those cases in which at least 25 percent of the equity is held by a single U.S. resident or group of business-related residents. If some control is evident, however, equity ownership may be as low as 10 percent. Private investment income includes dividends and interest on bonds, bank loans, real estate mortgages, deposits, short-term claims, etc.

6c and 12b   *Income on investments, government:* Includes government receipts on various long- and short-term loans and credits.

13   *Unilateral transfers, private remittances:* Includes noncommercial remittances of individuals and institutions including gift parcels, relief payments, missionary support, etc.

14   *Unilateral transfers, government:* Includes transfers from foreign-aid programs, military aid, pension and annuity payments, claim payments, settlements, recoveries and refunds, etc.

Capital Account

Capital items include all international claims payable in money, including equity securities; net equity in a foreign branch or other form of business enterprise not incorporated in the country of operation, in estates, trusts, annuity contracts; and real property held for the major purpose of producing income. Monetary gold is also considered a capital item.

Long-term capital includes items of indeterminate maturity or with a stated *original* maturity of more than one year from the date of issuance.

Short-term capital includes claims or liabilities with a maturity of one year or less.

15. *U.S. capital: private, net:* Transactions to which the U.S. government is not a party:
    (a) *Direct investments, net:* See definition of direct investment in account 6.
    (b) *New issues of foreign securities.*
    (c) *Redemptions.*
    (d) *Transactions in outstanding foreign securities.*
    (e) *Other long-term, net:* Contains primarily bank and corporate loans.
    (f) *Short-term, net:* Includes private holdings of short-term bank deposits, commercial paper, etc.

16. *U.S. capital: government, net:*
    (a) *Long-term capital:* Includes U.S. government loans and credits with an original maturity of more than one year.
    (b) *Repayments.*
    (c) *Foreign currency holdings and short-term claims, net:* Includes claims with restricted use, such as inconvertible currency holdings arising from PL 480 sales, counterpart funds, loan repayments in inconvertible currencies, etc.

17. *Foreign capital: direct investments in the United States:* See definition of direct investment in 6.

18. *Foreign capital: other long-term investments:* Includes transactions in U.S. equities, bonds, mortgages, etc.

19. *Foreign capital: other capital excluding liquid funds:*
    (a) *U.S. private short-term liabilities:* Includes commercial liabilities, primarily from advanced payments on orders, progress payments, postponed payments.
    (b) *U.S. government liabilities:* Includes advances on foreign military purchases, non-interest-bearing special government non-marketable securities given to international organizations, and dollar funds held by foreign governments under tied-aid operations.

20. *Foreign capital: Increase in foreign holdings of liquid dollar assets:* Includes demand and time deposits, deposit certificates, and all marketable U.S. government securities.

Reserves and Balancing Item

21. *Gold and convertible currencies, net, authorities:* Includes U.S. government holdings of gold and freely convertible foreign currencies.

22. *Unrecorded transactions, errors, and omissions:* The balancing item due to errors and omissions in the data-gathering process. As this account is the net of debits and credits, it gives no idea of the total size of the omitted items.

Note on transactions with the International Monetary Fund. The IMF is treated for most transactions as a foreigner. There are some important exceptions to the principle, however. The original capital contribution of IMF members includes a part payment in gold or its equivalent. To the extent that this gold contribution is unencumbered by offsetting obligations, such as borrowings by the country from the IMF, it is almost automatically available to the member. Accordingly, the U.S. gold tranche with the IMF is counted as a part of the U.S. reserves. Hence, an increase in the gold tranche position is recorded as an increase in U.S. gold holdings. If the IMF makes a dollar loan to the United Kingdom, there is an increase in the U.S. liabilities to the United Kingdom and a corresponding increase in the U.S. gold tranche position, cancelling any effect on the reported deficit or surplus.

If the United States draws on the IMF, U.S. holdings of foreign currencies increase and the gold tranche position decreases, again washing out the transaction. If the drawing is for more than the gold tranche position, a net liability is recorded.

Lotus Development Corporation: Entering International Markets

Events were moving rapidly at Lotus Development Corporation, the fastest growing microcomputer software company in the United States. Lotus was in its twelfth month of accelerating growth in December 1983 when Jim Manzi, vice president of marketing, decided it was time to do something about international sales. "We've been getting bombarded with requests," he reported. "Overseas distributors have been calling to carry our product. We get customer support calls from France. There's been a flood of telexes from all over Europe. All these signs have been telling us that we need to get serious about international markets. That's why we hired Chuck Digate as our director of international operations two months ago. When we offered him the position, we suggested that he live in the U.S. for two years and then move overseas. His reply was 'You've got that exactly backwards.' So we told him, 'Everything is up for grabs. The job is yours to make.'"

Digate's experience was in the hardware side of the microcomputer industry. After earning his MBA at Michigan, he held a number of positions at Texas Instruments (TI), including financial control management and consumer products marketing. He spent a year and a half managing market research for all TI consumer products, managed 1000 salespeople in the company's home computer demonstration network, and in late 1982 was sent to the south of France as director of European operations for TI's home computer division. By the middle of 1983 the spectacular

This case was prepared by Research Assistant John J. Coleman, under the supervision of Associate Professor David B. Yoffie, as the basis for class discussion rather than to illustrate either effective or ineffective handling of an administrative situation.

boom in home computers was waning; Digate thought it might be time to take on a new challenge in computer software. Starting with Lotus in December 1983, he immediately began working on an international business plan. Manzi would have to approve Digate's proposal before Lotus's international operations could begin in earnest.

Background of Lotus Development

Lotus was founded in April 1982 by Mitch Kapor, a former psychology student who believed that "I was going to make my greatest contribution to the field of human services by leaving it." Kapor wrote the popular VisiPlot and VisiTrend programs, graphics and statistics companion items for the best-selling electronic spreadsheet, VisiCalc. When International Business Machines Corp. (IBM) announced it would enter the microcomputer marketplace with an advanced, powerful computer based on the 16-bit Intel 8088 microprocessor, Kapor saw an opportunity to create a more functional and easier-to-use spreadsheet and productivity tool. VisiCorp, the marketers of VisiCalc, rejected Kapor's plan, so Kapor decided to set up his own company to do the job. Kapor received $1.2 million by selling the rights to VisiPlot and VisiTrend and another $1 million in venture capital. In October 1982, Lotus announced 1-2-3, a software program for the IBM PC providing spreadsheet, database, and graphing capabilities. The program was conceived and developed by Kapor and Jonathan Sachs, Lotus's vice president of research and development. Sachs, an accomplished programmer who had a hand in three earlier spreadsheet projects, wrote much of the actual program code. Lotus booked $1 million in dealer orders for 1-2-3 at a major trade show in November. By this time Lotus had also amassed an additional $3.7 million in venture capital.

1-2-3 was shipped on time in January 1983, accompanied by a huge advertising and promotion campaign (**Exhibit 1**). The three-month campaign cost over $1 million, far beyond the reach of most microcomputer software companies. In addition, Lotus embarked on a major training program for computer store personnel and produced vast quantities of point-of-sales promotional literature. By March, 1-2-3 was the top-selling business program on the Softsel "Hot List" (a popular industry barometer published by a major software distributor), displacing VisiCalc from its long reign at the top. One industry observer remarked that "1-2-3 has single-handedly changed the face and direction of the personal computer software industry."

During the year, 1-2-3 was being adapted for other computers such as the Wang Professional Computer and Digital Equipment's Rainbow, which were also based on the same microprocessor as the IBM PC but not strictly compatible with it. Lotus explicitly stated it would not adapt its software (or write new software) for 8-bit machines, most notably the Apple II. The company was also working on a follow-up product to 1-2-3 that would add integrated word processing and telecommunications capabilities (referred to internally as Lotus II). Lotus went public in October.

The Personal Computer Industry, December 1983

Hardware

The rise of the personal computer software industry paralleled the rise of smaller computers made possible by the development of integrated circuits and microprocessors and their rapid reduction in cost. By the end of the 1970s the markets for small home and business computers had grown substantially and the 8-bit Apple II series and TRS-80 computers from Tandy/Radio Shack were the leading business microcomputers. Computers based on more powerful 16-bit microprocessors, specifically the IBM PC, hit the market in 1981. These machines typically processed data at least twice as fast as their 8-bit counterparts and could run much larger and more sophisticated programs; software on the IBM PC could access up to 640K bytes (characters) of memory.

IBM was fast becoming the "industry standard" in the business-oriented personal computer industry (**Exhibit 2**). *Business Week* (3 October 1983) estimated that 75% of all personal computers in use in 1985 would be IBM PCs or PC-compatibles. Strong growth was expected in microcomputer hardware. A leading research firm expected the average number of microcomputers installed in *Fortune* 1300 companies to increase from 120 at year-end 1983 to 500 by December 1987. Another well-known firm estimated U.S. revenues for office personal computers would jump from $6 billion in 1983 to $20.7 billion in 1987 ($28.9 billion in 1989).

Software

Software was a billion dollar industry by 1983; back in 1979 it was hardly on the map. A Dallas-based market research firm estimated that the U.S. personal computer software market would total $1.4 billion in 1983 and would grow to $8.1 billion by 1989. Basic productivity programs—word processors, spreadsheets, databases, and especially integrated programs that combined these functions—were expected to grow most rapidly. The lion's share of the market was oriented toward business programs (**Exhibit 3**).

The software market was no longer viewed as a cottage industry. As one industry observer put it, "The days of putting your program in a Baggie, stapling it, and selling it by mail are ending." Entering a new product on the market in late 1983 required an estimated marketing investment of $50–100,000. (By contrast, VisiCorp launched VisiCalc on a $500 budget in 1978.) Software distributors played an increasingly important role as the link between the thousands of software companies seeking space on retail shelves and the software retailers who invested $10,000 simply to stock an inventory of 75 to 100 titles. Distributors bought software at a 55% to 60% discount and then resold and shipped it to retailers at a 40% to 50% discount. Softsel, the largest distributor, screened 400 products a month and agreed to distribute perhaps 10 to 12. One industry observer warned that "The pipeline is only so big, and it's full." Indeed, many analysts in late 1983 perceived an oncoming software shake-out. A common estimate was that 60% of the industry volume in sales would be dominated by about a dozen companies, while the other 40% would be taken by smaller companies offering specialty programs.

Competitors

Virtually all of the major vendors in 1983 got to the top on the basis of one product and rarely competed with one another (**Exhibit 5**). But this situation was expected to change. Lotus's four primary competitors—VisiCorp, Microsoft, Micropro, and Ashton-Tate—were working on one fashion or another of integrated software products to challenge the market strength of 1-2-3.

VisiCorp marketed VisiCalc, developed in 1978 for the Apple II and considered a primary factor in that machine's success. Approximately 600,000 copies of Visi-Calc had been sold worldwide for all machines by September 1983, but VisiCorp was struggling. Monthly sales of the relatively unchanged VisiCalc had decreased 75% from the beginning of the year, and sharp internal management disputes threatened to erupt into legal battles. VisiCorp was placing its hopes most strongly on VisiOn, an "operating environment" that provided users "windows" through which to look at more than one program simultaneously and transfer data between them.

Microsoft, one of the oldest and most influential companies in the microcomputer software industry, was beginning to move strongly into the applications area, where it planned to release a line of independent products which would be highly compatible with each other. Microsoft had opened a European sales and marketing office in April 1982. Its products (operating system and languages) were translated into French and German, and the company made wide use of locals in its hiring. There were approximately 50 to 60 Microsoft employees in Europe. In August 1982 Microsoft began shipping its Multiplan spreadsheet program in the U.S. Multiplan, which ran on a wide variety of 8-bit and 16-bit machines, did well in its first year but did not offer database or graphing functions. Microsoft was planning to introduce its applications line into Europe; Multiplan was sold by the company's European distributors and subsidiaries in 1983.

Micropro became a major player in the software industry on the basis of its extremely successful, multi-machine word processor known as WordStar. The company was in the process of releasing a line of software programs that were to be compatible with WordStar but would be stand-alone products. Micropro had an installed base of 600,000 users and registered 15,000 WordStar sales per month. The firm had operations in 27 countries, more than any of its competitors, and had a particularly strong European presence. Over 20% of Micropro's revenue came from overseas.

Ashton-Tate's dBaseII was the dominant microcomputer database program in the business world. The company was expected to go public, and was working on a highly integrated, multifunction product designed to compete with any new Lotus products on the high end. Ashton-Tate moved into Europe at the beginning of 1983, and translated programs were projected for year's end. Ashton-Tate worked through distributors (as many as 10 in a single country), did no product development or manufacturing in Europe, and used a high proportion of Americans in its operation. The company was considering OEM arrangements, offshore subsidiaries, and direct corporate selling.

Inside Lotus Development

By December 1983, 150,000 copies of 1-2-3 had been sold, and revenues and earnings were increasing rapidly (**Exhibits 4a** and **4b**). 1-2-3 was still number 1 on the Softsel list. Part of the reason for this success was that Lotus was the first software company to use a dealer introduction kit for its product. The 1-2-3 kit was glossy, extensive, and high quality. Lotus included a disk-based tutorial with 1-2-3 to teach buyers how to use the product. The tutorial was also sent to dealers who were encouraged to make copies for potential customers in their stores. Advertising and promotion totaled over $3.5 million for 1983, an amount far exceeding that spent by Lotus's competitors on any single product.

Manzi stressed that Lotus did not think of its markets in segments but, rather, considered 1-2-3's audience to be all business people and professionals whose jobs required the manipulation of quantitative data:

> Obviously a number of groups—middle manager types doing financial analysis, consultants, accountants, economists—find the program useful. But, in reality, we haven't tried to identify these specific groups. We've advertised to the wide range of people who need to manipulate quantitative data and tie it into graphs and databases. Our message is uniform: 1-2-3 is fast, powerful, flexible, and integrated. People who can use the product buy it. So far we haven't had to worry about what specific types of people buy the product. All we've noticed is that people from large corporations have different problems than do independent professionals, and we try to reflect that in our service and support.

In general, Lotus downplayed price and stressed support and training. At $495 retail, 1-2-3 was more expensive than the VisiCalc ($250) and Multiplan ($275) spreadsheets, but was $200 less expensive than Context MBA, the first integrated program for the PC. Particularly with larger, *Fortune* 2000 corporations—the one "segment" Lotus saw with distinct needs—Lotus helped train users and "train the trainers" in the corporation, and provided extensive assistance in using Lotus's command language to tune the package for specific applications.

Lotus distributed 1-2-3 through four primary outlets. First, and most important, were retail computer stores, accounting for at least 80% of Lotus's sales. Larger stores (e.g., the ComputerLand chain) could purchase directly from Lotus; independent and smaller stores purchased 1-2-3 from Lotus's distributor, Softsel. The second outlet was "national accounts," direct selling from Lotus to large corporations. This channel provided less than 10% of Lotus's sales. The third distribution channel was through value-added-resellers (VARs). VARs added value to 1-2-3 by packaging it with an additional product or providing special end-user support for specific or advanced applications. For example, one VAR provided the capability to load its proprietary database from an external mainframe computer onto individual personal computer workstations for use with 1-2-3. The VAR channel accounted for less than 10% of Lotus sales. The final outlet was third party sales. Major companies such as Digital Equipment and Hewlett Packard participated in this channel. These companies packaged, printed, and promoted special versions of 1-2-3 adapted for their machines. They were responsible for supporting the product, which they sold through their direct sales channels. Lotus retained the right to sell retail versions of 1-2-3 for these machines.

Another outlet for 1-2-3 existed, but it was not Lotus-approved. This consisted of sales through mail-order outlets, often available at from 25% to 50% off the retail price of 1-2-3. Lotus distributed no product to these so-called "grey market" dealers; they got their product mostly from authorized dealers looking for a quick infusion of cash. Lotus's policy was to discontinue relations with any dealer found selling to the grey market. Lotus did not, however, make any distinctions in customer service based on where the product was purchased. All registered owners of the product had equal access to support and service.

Lotus set up several regional retail sales offices to service dealers. Each dealer was sent a complete support kit containing sample product, advertising materials, point-of-sale items, and information to minimize ordering and stocking problems. Lotus sales representatives offered information, advice, demonstrations, and assistance. Training specialists conducted all-day training sessions with store personnel to familiarize them with 1-2-3's features and operation. Lotus also provided personnel and materials for dealer-sponsored promotions and customer seminars. The telephone support staff handled technical questions and product ordering on dedicated phone lines. These basic principles for aiding dealers were adapted for customers as well. Manzi pointed out that "Management has stressed that the company's image and success depend directly on customer satisfaction with product support and product performance."

Human Resources

In December 1983 Lotus had 292 employees, 257 more than at the beginning of the year. Many employees were overqualified, but the company tried to provide these people opportunities to move up while the company was growing rapidly. In an industry so young it wasn't easy to demand highly technically trained applicants, so one found teachers in customer support and consumer products people in marketing. Janet Axelrod, Lotus's first employee and its vice president of human resources, believed the company was making a number of mistakes in the general area of hiring:

We get ripped off by headhunters and do a lot of expensive hiring by gut feeling. Keeping up with, even defining, departmental and personnel needs is a gigantic problem. We have to say "screw conventional wisdom" because almost all of it is bull for a company growing as fast as we are. Right now, there's no head count control at all. This just can't go on. Add new operations overseas? That's just nuts! My first reaction is: "Are you out of your mind?!"

Lotus, which was non-unionized, consciously tried to establish itself as a "progressive" employer. The company deliberately maintained itself in the top quartile of pay in the industry and had a generous and extensive benefits package. Axelrod defined the Lotus philosophy as: fairness and justice are most important; employees at all levels have a right to speak their minds; every job has value; all people have a right to expect respect; the company is nothing without its employees; and diversity is best. "These values are important to me and the company," she observed, "and I have to insist that they'll be transferred overseas. But I'm not sure any of us knows the various cultures enough to do it."

Finance

In 1983 Lotus had no formal financial objectives, nor was any system in place to analyze potential new markets. Lotus had no real budget procedure but rather used more of a "wish list mentality," and there was no cost control system in place. A general concern in finance was developing an infrastructure for a control system while coping with very rapid growth. Digate knew there was a long way to go in that regard: "Perhaps the ultimate irony is that we're still doing our general ledger on a [Tandy/Radio Shack] TRS-80."

Research and Development

Mitch Kapor was convinced that future success for Lotus meant undertaking research and development with an eye toward ongoing technological changes. If the company was going to enter a major new market (e.g., word processing), Kapor wanted to avoid entering "just this side of a major new technology." But Lotus also emphasized product development for the short term. The driving forces, according to Manzi, were to "keep the spreadsheet market, because that pays the salaries, leverage the spreadsheet market with add-ons, and keep poking around with the existing product."

Manufacturing

Once a software program was developed, written, and debugged, it was ready to be manufactured. Manufacturing involved two different processes—disk duplication and assembly of the diskettes, literature, binders, and so on. The various printing jobs (manuals, reference books, etc.) were done outside Lotus. Of Lotus's production costs, 80% was for materials, another 15% was overhead, and the last 5% was labor.

Entering International Markets

Lotus officials assumed from the start that business productivity software had a natural global market. Before Digate was hired, Lotus had thought about international issues but the situation was still "essentially a gigantic mess" according to Manzi. Lotus's first attempt at an international plan was a "weird psycholinguistics doctoral thesis. It was bizarre," Manzi laughed, "and needless to say it never went anywhere." Until Digate came aboard, no single person was really in charge of international business on a full-time basis.

Softsel had been Lotus's exclusive worldwide distributor since 1-2-3 hit the market, but Manzi thought the arrangement was unsatisfactory. Softsel did not provide end-user support and dealer support—services Lotus had stressed in the U.S. Manzi wanted to resist the temptation to just take the U.S. version of 1-2-3 and "dump the product overseas." His first task, he said, was to "renegotiate everything." Manzi cancelled Softsel's exclusive worldwide distribution rights and raised 1-2-3's price to Softsel by 20%. He didn't feel Lotus had to worry about access to distribution channels and saw no good reason to ignore or kill a French distributor, for example, simply to maintain the relationship with Softsel.

In the interim between changing the Softsel arrangement and hiring Digate, Lotus hired a small European consulting firm to do a study of the European market. The consulting firm put Lotus in touch with Reflex Ltd., which Lotus subsequently hired in September 1983 as its U.K. distributor. Reflex was responsible for a "minirollout" and some dealer training to take place in fall 1983. One person from headquarters was sent to Reflex to handle customer support. Lotus's first overseas subsidiary was also opened in September in Windsor, England. 1-2-3 had sold well in the U.K. even before these direct moves; Manzi estimated that by year's end $1 million of product had been sold there.

Manzi was looking to Digate for the answers to a series of important questions. What strategy should Lotus adopt towards overseas markets? Should Lotus move slowly or quickly? Where should Digate be stationed? How should international operations be organized? Several of these issues had caused debate at headquarters. The individual in charge of the Cambridge-based business development group argued strongly that international business development be under his purview. He felt that Digate should be reporting to him, not to Manzi. At the very least, he wanted international software development to be separate from any new international group. Similarly, the CFO had some international finance experience and wanted responsibility for Lotus's international finance. Manzi also sensed a bias among top managers in the company that senior managers should be based at headquarters. Manzi, on the other hand, wanted to see a completely separate international unit that would be self-sustaining. He wanted to leave Digate as much open field as possible. "Chuck inherited a big mess," Manzi said, "including loose promises and commitments made by people without the power to make them. I've made it clear to Chuck that he should not worry about Lotus politics or financial constraints affecting the international strategy."

One market Digate considered entering was Japan, but Japan posed enormous problems, including dominance of 8-bit machines, lack of a standard operating system, complex characters and symbols, and weak microcomputer penetration into corporations. The other major market was Europe. The market there was highly segmented by country, language, leading microcomputers, and business practices. Still, the market was growing; it stood at about half the size of the U.S. market and many analysts expected its rate of growth to match or outpace the U.S. rate within the next few years (**Exhibit 6**). The level of development of the European market was considered by Digate to be 2 to 3 years behind the U.S.

U.S. firms dominated the European personal computer market, holding three-fourths of the installed base of microcomputers in Western Europe. Part of the American advantage could be laid to the cash built from operating in the huge American domestic market. The IBM PC was introduced to the European market in 1983 and, although doing well, it had not achieved dominant market share (**Exhibit 7**). Digate estimated that IBM held perhaps 20% of the 16-bit market. But industry expectations were that IBM might be helped in Europe by the hardware shakeout going on in the U.S. and the failure of some West German companies. Analysts speculated that European businesses would begin to look for stable vendors, and IBM was considered nothing if not stable.

Different microcomputer firms dominated different countries. Triumph-Adler and Siemens did well in West Germany. Micral was expected to increase its share in France. Olivetti had a leading position in Italy. In Great Britain, the Victor Sirius, repackaged and distributed by a local firm, Applied Computer Techniques (ACT), had an estimated 90% of the sales of 16-bit machines for the twelve months from April 1982 to March 1983 (approximately 10,000 units). ACT also released a 16-bit hit of its own, known as the Apricot. Neither of these machines was IBM-compatible.

The segmented nature of the European market was even more apparent in software. Software companies had to deal with 13 countries and languages, contrasting business styles, different laws, regulations, and business practices which could make certain types of software (e.g., accounting or banking) extremely difficult to market throughout Europe. Applications programs were considered the most difficult to transfer, with systems and utilities programs somewhat easier. One sign that the European market was difficult was that European companies were seriously trying to gain a foothold in the American market, primarily because the market was huge and, compared to Europe, relatively homogeneous.

No major European software firms had emerged in Lotus's 16-bit market. This was partly due to a lack of venture capital in Europe. Although there was some government support of fledgling software companies in Britain, and most European countries were concerned about their inferiority in large computer systems, Digate was not concerned about government protectionism because "there just isn't that much to protect." Tariffs on imported software were applied only to the value of the medium (diskettes and documentation, etc.) and not the value of the software itself. In Britain an estimated 70% of the software sold was imported.

Digate believed that European buyers were driven by the same needs as U.S. buyers. "The *Fortune* 500 type companies are the trendsetters. And not only European companies: there are a large number of American multinational corporations in Europe, and our product is used at many of them in the U.S. These large European and multinational companies could be our gateway to the small and medium size businesses where the bulk of personal computer sales will be for the next three to four years." Despite the basic similarities between European and American buyers, one way buyers differed across Europe was the centralization of purchasing. "In the U.K. buying is dispersed like in the U.S. Outside the U.K. there is more centralized control by data processing managers, which makes for slower purchasing. Germany is particularly conservative in this regard."

Operating in Europe presented many challenges. Top managerial talent was hard to come by because of the relative immaturity of the industry. The European Community posted a 6% tariff on imported software, while manufacturing in Europe required an investment of $2.5 to 3 million. Grey marketing—the undercutting of European dealers by U.S. distributors—posed yet another serious problem. And unauthorized copying of program disks (which had led Lotus to go to court in the U.S.), was known to be a real problem in parts of Europe. "Chuck tells me that the closer you get to the equator the more serious the problem becomes," Manzi joked. On the positive side, trouble with counterfeiting was relatively minor, and mail order outlets were insignificant in Europe. Pricing didn't seem to be much of an issue; American software companies generally charged the U.S. price plus or minus 10% in dollars. Demand appeared to be price inelastic.

Translation of 1-2-3 promised to be a major task. "First, we have to port for non-IBM hardware (i.e., write a series of drivers to support keyboards, screens, and other non-IBM system components). Then we have to translate the language, and I suspect that each translation will take from 9 to 12 months," Digate reported. 1-2-3 was not written with language translations in mind. "If we had only thought about going international 6 months earlier," Manzi noted, "we could have saved ourselves a lot of trouble." Text which would have to be translated was embedded in the computer code, rather than being separated into specific modules. Lotus would have to "start from scratch," and that meant reading through the thousands upon thousands of lines of computer code. Beyond that was the problem of the translation itself. 1-2-3's user interface was highly dependent on full-screen layout, but it was highly unlikely that this interface could remain unchanged across national borders. Some things that could be expressed by one word in English might require two, three, or four words in another language. Even if a single word could be found, it might be too long. Differences in local currency, characters, and punctuation on dates, times or decimals were not easily accommodated. In a sense, Digate observed, you were forced to create somewhat different products for the different markets. Even a small change such as requiring 2 screens rather than 1 to show a list of options could let a "bug" creep into a program. Furthermore, all the help screens in 1-2-3 (there were over 200) and the tutorial would need to be rewritten, requiring changes in screen layouts and fine attention to idiomatic language. And of course the extensive 1-2-3 documentation also required translation.

Digate sifted through these various issues while working up his international business proposal. Manzi received Digate's preliminary plan for entering international markets, reprinted in the Appendix, two weeks after Digate joined the firm. Digate was clearly convinced that Lotus should act quickly. He stayed in Cambridge for only two weeks before moving to England to talk with dealers, headhunters, the distributor, and others knowledgeable about the European market. Manzi, in Cambridge, studied Digate's sketch of where Lotus should be headed internationally. Did this path hold the most promise for Lotus?

Sample Copy from First Advertising Campaign

Meet 1-2-3 - the remarkable new software package that puts more raw power at your finger tips than anything yet created for IBM PC. 1-2-3 actually combines information management, spreadsheet, and graphing in one program that can perform all three functions interchangeably and instantly at the touch of a key. That's power.

To explain: since 1-2-3's information management, spreadsheet and graphing functions reside in memory simultaneously, you can go from retrieval to spreadsheet calculation to graphing instantly, just by pressing a few keys. So now you can experiment and recalculate and look at data in an endless variety of ways. As fast as your mind can think up new possibilities. There's no lag between you and the computer. And that's a new kind of power – power that's greater than the sum of its programs.

The spreadsheet function.

If 1-2-3 were just a spreadsheet, you'd want it because it has the largest workspace on the market (2048 rows by 256 columns). To give you a quick idea of 1-2-3's spreadsheet capabilities: VisiCalc's spreadsheet for the IBM PC offers 15 arithmetic, logical and relational operators, 28 functions and 32 spreadsheet-related commands. 1-2-3 has 15 operators, 41 functions and 66 commands. And if you include data base and graphing commands, it actually has 110!

In addition, 1-2-3 is up to 50 times as fast as established spreadsheets. With all the features you've ever seen on spreadsheets. 1-2-3 also gives you the capability to develop customized applications (with 26 macro keys) and lets you perform repetitive tasks automatically with one keystroke. If 1-2-3 were just a spreadsheet, it would be a very powerful tool. But it's much, much more.

The information management function.

Add to 1-2-3's spreadsheet a selective information management function, and the power curve rises at an awesome rate. Particularly since 1-2-3's information management capability reads files from other programs such as WordStar, VisiCalc and dBase II. So you can accumulate information on a limitless variety of topics and extract all

or pieces of it for instant spreadsheet analysis. Unheard of before. Specific 1-2-3 information management features include sorting with primary and secondary keys. Retrieval using up to 32 criteria. 1-2-3 performs statistical functions such as mean, count, standard deviation and variance. It can produce histograms on part or all of the data base. 1-2-3 also allows for the maintenance of multiple data bases and multiple criteria.

The graphing function.

1-2-3 enables you to create graphs of up to six variables using information already on the spreadsheet. And have it on screen in less than two seconds! Once you've made a graph, three keystrokes will display it in a different form. If data on the spreadsheet changes, you can display a revised graph with one keystroke. This instant relationship of one format to another opens up a whole new application area. For the first time graphics can be used as a "what if" thinking tool!

For a full demonstration of 1-2-3's remarkable power, visit your nearby 1-2-3 dealer. For the name and address, call 1-800-343-5414 (in Mass. call 617-492-7171).

Lotus Development Corporation, 55 Wheeler Street, Cambridge, MA 02138.

Spreadsheet, graphing, information management all-in-one

EXHIBIT 1   Lotus Development Corporation *Sample Copy from First Advertising Campaign*

EXHIBIT 2   Lotus Development Corporation
Microcomputers Installed in U.S. Corporations

Percent of sites with	1979	1980	1981	1982	1983[a]
Apple	16.8	24.7	42.0	39.0	23.6
DEC	—	—	—	1.7	5.7
IBM	—	—	—	13.1	35.4
Tandy	42.5	27.7	26.1	17.5	9.3
Others	40.7	47.6	31.9	28.7	26.0

[a]Estimate.

Source: *Datamation*, November 1983.

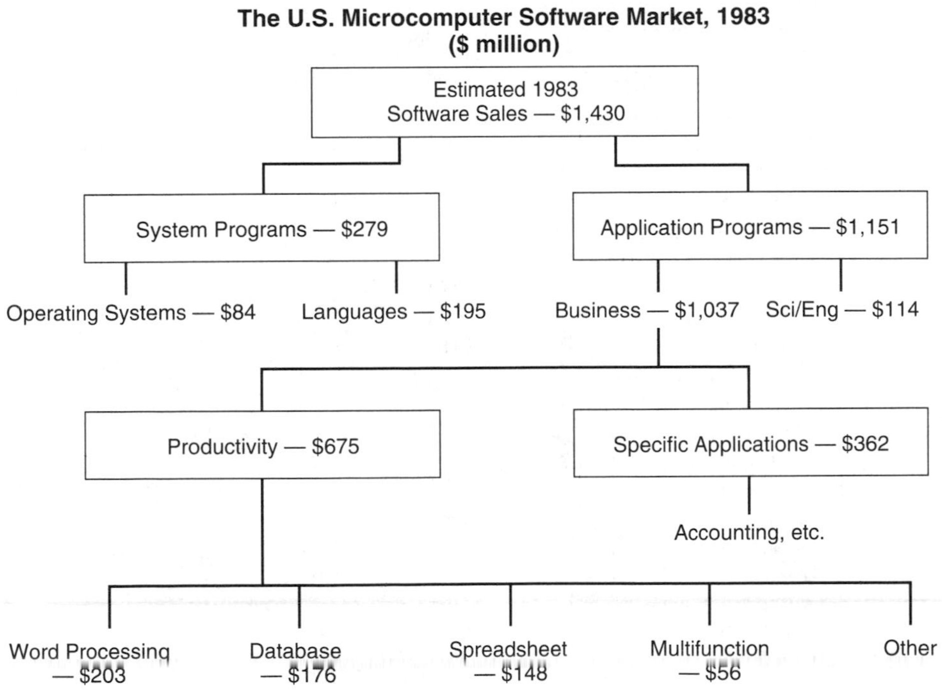

**The U.S. Microcomputer Software Market, 1983
($ million)**

Estimated 1983
Software Sales — $1,430

System Programs — $279   Application Programs — $1,151

Operating Systems — $84   Languages — $195   Business — $1,037   Sci/Eng — $114

Productivity — $675   Specific Applications — $362

Accounting, etc.

Word Processing   Database   Spreadsheet   Multifunction   Other
   — $203   — $176   — $148   — $56

EXHIBIT 3   Lotus Development Corporation *The U.S. Microcomputer Software Market, 1983* ($ million)
Source: *New York Times*, October 16, 1983.

EXHIBIT 4A   Lotus Development Corporation
Consolidated Statement of Operations, 1983

	Q1	Q2	Q3	Q4
Net Revenues	$ 4,787	$ 7,851	$16,465	$23,904
Costs and Expenses:				
Cost of Sales	812	920	1,933	3,133
Research and Development	289	311	495	1,105
Sales and Marketing	1,824	2,352	3,083	4,827
General and Administrative	815	1,077	1,682	2,349
Total Operating Expenses	3,740	4,660	7,193	11,414
Income from Operations	1,047	3,191	9,272	12,490
Interest Income	44	50	112	738
Other Income	1	3	167	317
Interest before Provision for Income Taxes and Extraordinary Item	1,092	3,244	9,551	13,545
Provision for Income Taxes	529	1,571	4,843	6,772
Income before Extraordinary Item	563	1,673	4,708	6,773
Extraordinary Item[a]	529	71	—	—
Net Income	$ 1,092	$ 1,744	$ 4,708	$ 6,773
Net Income per Share				
Income before Extraordinary Item	$0.04	$0.12	$0.35	$ 0.43
Extraordinary Item	0.04	0.01	—	—
Net Income per Share	$0.08	$0.13	$0.35	$ 0.43
Weighted Average Common Shares and Common Share Equivalents Outstanding	13,316	13,462	13,576	15,875
KEY FINANCIAL RATIOS (% of Net Revenues)				
Cost of Sales	17.0%	11.7%	11.7%	13.1%
Research and Development	6.0	4.0	3.0	4.6
Sales and Marketing	38.1	30.0	18.7	20.2
General and Administrative	17.0	13.7	10.2	9.8
Income from Operations	21.9	40.6	56.3	52.3
Net Income	22.8	22.2	28.6	28.3

[a]Utilization of a net operating loss carryforward.

EXHIBIT 4B   Lotus Development Corporation
Consolidated Balance Sheet, 1983 ($000)

	Q1	Q2	Q3	Q4
ASSETS				
Total Current Assets	5,112	8,585	17,544	72,631
Inc: Short-Term				
Investments	$ 910	$ 3,332	$ 5,136	$56,181
Accounts Receivable	4,008	4,553	10,775	14,234
Inventory	107	553	978	1,846
Total Assets	$ 6,042	$10,210	$20,612	$78,343
LIABILITIES				
Total Current Liabilities	1,168	3,541	9,141	19,183
Inc: Accounts Payable	$ 777	$ 1,625	$ 1,946	$ 5,091
Accrued Income Taxes	—	1,442	6,208	12,796
Total Liabilities	1,338	3,760	9,429	19,503
STOCKHOLDERS' EQUITY				
Inc: Common Stock	139	141	141	166
Paid-in Capital	4,686	4,715	4,715	45,547
Retained Earnings	(54)	1,691	6,399	13,172
Total Stockholders' Equity	4,704	6,450	11,183	58,840
Total Liabilities and Stockholders' Equity	$ 6,042	$10,210	$20,612	$78,343

EXHIBIT 5   Lotus Development Corporation
Estimated Sales for 1982 and 1983

Firm	1982	1983
Microsoft	$33 million	$70 million
VisiCorp	36	53
Micropro International	28	51
Digital Research	22	46
Lotus Development	1	40
Ashton-Tate	8	35
Peachtree Software	9	21

Source: *New York Times,* October 16, 1983. © 1983 by
THE NEW YORK TIMES COMPANY. Reprinted by permission.

EXHIBIT 6   Lotus Development Corporation
*Business Microcomputer Sales
in Western Europe* (000 units)

	1982	1986[a]
United Kingdom	80	180
West Germany	64	190
France	52	160
Italy	28	110

[a]Estimate.

Source: *Mini-Micro Systems,* April 1983.

EXHIBIT 7   Lotus Development
Corporation *Top Ten Microcomputer
Brands in Western Europe, 1983*[a]

Manufacturer	Market Share %
Apple	19.2%
Commodore	18.7
IBM*	9.8
Olivetti*	7.0
Victor*	6.5
Hewlett-Packard*	4.6
Intertec*	3.0
Tandy	2.8
Digital*	2.4
Bull*	2.1

[a]Estimate.
* = 16-bit microprocessor
Source: *Mini-Micro Systems,* May 1984.

APPENDIX
LOTUS DEVELOPMENT CORPORATION
MEMORANDUM

TO: Jim Manzi
FROM: Chuck Digate
SUBJECT: Business Plan Attached

The summary business plan (below) for our European operations encompasses 1984 and a cursory look at 1985 in order to get a perspective of where we are going. The section on operations issues should be used as a basis for discussion with the management committee and myself upon my next visit to Cambridge. With respect to detailed marketing, sales, and finance plans, I haven't included them because they are still in process.

U.K. Business Plan

Organization. The attached chart shows the proposed organization and staffing plan. The U.K. Managing Director will also have responsibility for the site and for the Human Resources function for all Lotus employee residents in the U.K. Initial areas of organizational focus will be in Product Support and Corporate Accounts Sales. A Finance and Accounting function will also be developed immediately to enable revenue generation in the U.K. company.

Key milestones. The organizational goals for the year are to be staffed with sufficiently trained personnel to enable direct sales to large accounts in late 2Q, to terminate Reflex's exclusive dealer distributorship in 3Q and to launch Lotus II by September using U.K. personnel for all marketing and sales and product support needs. We will spend $700,000 in the Lotus Ltd. launch campaign and expect to have 32 employees (20 exempt) by 4Q.

Germany/France Business Plan

Organization. Small marketing, sales and support staffs will be developed in these countries to support the Lotus name and our distributors.

Key milestones. Selection and training of distributors will be completed by mid-2Q followed by the launch of 1-2-3 in English supported by a local language self-tutorial manual (being prepared in English).

General start-up procedures.   Generally speaking, our distributors will adapt and translate promotional materials which will then be edited and approved by our in-house local marketing staff. In some cases, our advertising agencies will be commissioned to do this work. Initial training of distributors will be handled by U.K. personnel and then followed through by local staff and/or central European marketing staff as they come on board. Local software copyright laws and warranty issues will be incorporated in each country's product packaging *prior to shipment*. These processes will be managed by the manager of European marketing, who will be located in the U.K.

Minor Country Business Plan

Organization.   The European Marketing Manager will assist in selecting distributors for these countries and in hiring appropriate Lotus staff—generally training and support personnel for 1984. A Northern European Marketing Manager based in Scandinavia will report to the European Marketing Manager while the rest of Europe will be handled by a small staff in the U.K. Over time, business entities with full Lotus personnel will be established in three or four countries.

Key milestones.   Scandinavia will be started up first, due to reasonably widespread knowledge of English and 1-2-3 will be launched in English. The rest of Europe will not be supported by Lotus or its distributors until local language versions of Lotus II are available. The exception to this rule is the sale of English 1-2-3 to hardware manufacturers for their resale in volume to corporate accounts. The manufacturers will be trained by Lotus personnel from the U.K. and the U.S.

Operation Issues

Non-U.K. versions of 1-2-3.   A small team of temporary employees will be used to assemble product to be shipped outside the U.K. to hardware manufacturers who are selling into non-Lotus supported countries. This team will also prepare 1-2-3 products for shipment to Lotus distributors in Germany, France, and Scandinavia.

Lotus II.   All local language versions of Lotus II will be manufactured in Europe from day one in order to maximize control over the language, legal, and packaging problems. Initially, this process will be on a contract basis to U.K. vendors. Ultimately Lotus will bring this process in-house in a location that optimizes both Lotus' tax liabilities and operational control.

Transfer pricing for 1-2-3.   Transfer prices to the U.K. for both finished goods and bulk-packed product need to be established, taking into account the Lotus

U.K. investments in marketing and development and the support Lotus will provide to other European countries for products that are packaged in the U.K. and shipped to Europe.

Corporate structure in 1984. Branch offices will be established in all countries where Lotus has staff except for France and Germany, where subsidiaries should be established by 2Q84. These subs will begin generating local revenue when Lotus 1-2-3 is available in local packaging.

Rest of world in 1984. To the extent that American versions of either 1-2-3 or Lotus II are useful in other countries, product will be shipped directly from the U.S. Should versions be required that are available in Europe, product will be shipped from Europe. No subsidiaries will be established outside of Europe in 1984 with the possible exception of Australia. All Lotus staff will belong to Lotus U.S. branch offices.

Proposed 1984/1985 International Operations Organization

EXHIBIT A   Lotus Development Corporation *Proposed 1984/1985 International Operations Organization*

Poland 1989

No . . . absolutely not. Communism does not fit the Poles. They are too individu-
alistic, too nationalistic. Poland's future economy should be based on private
enterprise. Poland will be a capitalistic state.

—Joseph Stalin, 1944

On September 12, 1989, the Solidarity-led government of Tadeusz Mazowiecki took
office in Poland. As the first popularly elected government in the Soviet bloc, Solidarity was in a unique position. From its improbable beginnings in the shipyards of
Gdansk, the former trade union had become a significant political force. It had won
virtually unanimous support from the Polish people, as well as the goodwill of most
of the Western world. Its leaders came to power determined to build a new Poland.
They promised to dismantle the existing system of socialist control and to construct
in its place a liberal democracy and a market economy.

The Poland that Solidarity had inherited from its predecessors in 1989, however, was standing on the brink of economic disaster. Inflation was raging, the cost of
living was rising rapidly, and basic foodstuffs had all but disappeared from the
shelves. The government's external debt stood at $42 billion; servicing this debt
alone would require over 90% of foreign exchange earnings.

Solidarity's leaders believed that the people were behind them. But they also
knew that they had to move quickly to provide tangible evidence of the benefits of
economic liberalization. If Solidarity did not deliver on its promises, it risked pushing
the country even further into economic and political chaos.

Professor Debora Spar prepared this case as the basis for class discussion rather than to illustrate either effective
    or ineffective handling of an administrative situation.

Poland Under Communism

Since 1795, a fully sovereign Polish state has existed during only 21 years, from 1918 to 1939; for the rest of this time, the Poles have been at the mercy of their more powerful neighbors—partitioned, protected, and ruled by a series of adjacent empires. Following its brief flirtation with autonomy after the First World War, Poland was an early victim of the Second World War and lay for six years at the center of Nazi aggression. When the war ended, Poland was reorganized once again and quietly consigned by the great powers to become a member of the Soviet bloc, nominally independent but politically and economically under the sway of the Soviet Union.

Political system. From 1947 until 1989, Poland was effectively ruled by the Polish United Workers party (PZPR), an indigenous Communist organization that had been boosted into office at the behest of the Soviet Union. A Peasant party (ZSL) and a Democratic party (SD) also existed, but they consistently played the role of subordinate members in the PZPR's "coalition." Officially, the People's Republic of Poland was a parliamentary democracy, complete with guaranteed civil liberties and universal suffrage. In practice, all power in the country lay in the hands of the PZPR. Following closely upon the Leninist principle of "dual power," all offices of the government were "shadowed" by replicas within the party. Thus, the country's Council of Ministers and Council of State were under the control of the party's Political Bureau; the president and prime minister were actually subordinate to the party first secretary; and all local officials took their orders from local party secretaries. Administrative positions within the government were staffed by the nomenklatura, professional bureaucrats who rose to power through party ranks. In many cases, members of the nomenklatura held dual appointments in both the government and the party. Meanwhile, the principle of "democratic centralism," (also borrowed from the Soviet model) required every party member to obey the orders of his superior; as a result, all power in the country flowed directly from the top.[1]

As was the case in the other countries of the Soviet bloc, the communist party reinforced its control through an extensive system of internal security. In addition to the regular army, there existed an internal security corps, a heavily armed state police force, and several volunteer reserve forces. Together with the Security Service, which was closely linked to the Soviet KGB, these units kept all of Polish society under surveillance and deterred any would-be opposition. Poland's foreign policy, meanwhile, echoed that of the Soviet Union. Moscow retained the prerogative to intervene whenever the Polish government seemed to stray too far from the path of socialist unity.

Within these constraints, though, Poland had still managed to create its own brand of communism. Censorship was not as efficient as it was elsewhere in the Soviet bloc, and the secret police never became quite as powerful as they did in Rumania or East Germany. A degree of public expression was generally permitted by the

---

[1]Norman Davies, *Heart of Europe: A Short History of Poland* (Oxford: Clarendon Press, 1984), p. 36.

regime, and "national unity" was upheld more vigorously than was Marxism-Leninism.

Most important, the power of the Communist party in Poland had consistently been under quiet attack from a number of other organized groups—the trade unions, the intellectuals, and the Catholic Church. While none of these groups had been able to acquire any real power, they were able to chip away at the dominant authority of the party, pushing it to adopt a series of political and economic reforms. Likewise, the Parliament (or Sejm) did not always act merely to rubber-stamp the decisions made by the party. Although nearly all of the delegates were party members, they did occasionally block the leadership's decisions and act as a sounding board for political opposition.[2] The political system was thus somewhat more fluid than it was elsewhere in the Soviet bloc. Poland was still a harsh, one-party state, and it was still undeniably under the sway of Moscow, but the communists' hold on power had been contested actively throughout the tenure of their rule.

The church.   One of the most durable sources of opposition was the Catholic Church, for centuries a central element of Polish society and Polish politics. Although the power of the Church was officially denied by the Communist regime, 96% of the population was Catholic, and most people put their faith in Catholicism far before their commitment to Marxism-Leninism.

Under the Communists, church and state co-existed in an uneasy compromise. The government generally ignored the Church and its officials, but did little to stop religious activities. The Church, meanwhile, collected the people's grievances against the state but was usually careful not to translate these concerns into political action. In return for its quiescence, the Church was permitted to maintain free contact with the Vatican and to keep its own seminaries, social clubs, and even its own university.

Whenever the political situation heated up, however, the Church quickly became a convening point for the opposition. Throughout the 1970s, religious demonstrations were used as political protests: Polish citizens would place flowers, or attend ceremonies, or light candles at religious monuments, not just to demonstrate their support for the Church but also to flaunt their disapproval of the state and its policies. Sometimes members of the Catholic hierarchy were directly involved with opposition politics. Ignoring the orders of their own superiors, some priests became not only the confidantes of Polish dissidents but also the organizers and mobilizers of the opposition. By the late 1970s, several young priests had begun using their pulpits to preach sermons of reform and to urge their congregations to resist the government's policies and support instead the growing power of the trade unions.

Labor   Long before the Communist regime came to power, the working class was widely considered to be the backbone of the Polish economy and a key element of Polish society. As early as 1918, laborers were organizing workers' councils and

---

[2]George Kolankiewicz and Paul G. Lewis, *Poland: Politics, Economics and Society* (London: Pinter Publishers, 1988), p. 84.

insisting that they be given a role in determining wages, working conditions, and the limits of managerial prerogative. When these councils emerged again after World War II, they seemed so directly in line with the ideals of socialist organization that they were officially sanctioned by the Communist regime.[3]

Over the next 30 years, the workers' councils—like the Catholic Church—carved out an awkward compromise with the government. On one side, there was a "participatory ethos" in the country, a sense that workers had the right to manage their own enterprises and participate in economic decisions. This was an attitude that the government supported and in fact often emphasized and expanded. This idea of self-management peaked in 1956, when the Communist regime held up the workers' councils as the linchpin of its policy of economic decentralization. The state expectation was that councils would give workers a greater sense of ownership and thus a stronger incentive to improve production. Accordingly, the councils were empowered to shape their enterprises' policies, to negotiate wages, and to participate in choosing the manager.[4]

The price of all this power, however, was the consolidation of the workers' councils under the party's control. In 1958, the rights of all individual workers' councils were pooled into a national Conference of Workers Self-Management (KSR). Because the KSR also included representatives from the Communist party and from the state-sanctioned trade unions, it effectively transformed the workers' councils from instruments of the workers to tools of the state. By the mid-1970s, the workers' councils had effectively disappeared.

Still, the ideas of self-management and workers' rights persisted. Throughout the 1960s and 1970s, the strikes that periodically swept Poland started in the factories and were led by the industrial workers. Each time, the strikes were sparked by an increase in food prices; but the demands of the workers centered on the return of true self-management and economic decentralization.

The "Economics of Chaos": The Polish Economy, 1946–1979

Whereas Poland's culture made it resistant to the wholesale adoption of Soviet political ideology, the country was more willing to accept Soviet models of economic organization. Indeed, from its very inception, the PZPR was committed to the principles of collective ownership, central planning, and government control over virtually all aspects of the national economy.

The development of a command economy in Poland meant, in practice, that the central government set production targets, allocated resources, administered wages,

---

[3]George Kolankiewicz, "Employee Self-Management and Socialist Trade Unionism," in Jean Woodall, ed., *Policy and Politics in Contemporary Poland: Reform, Failure and Crisis* (Pinter Publishers, 1982), p. 130.

[4]Martin Myant, *Poland: A Crisis for Socialism* (London: Wishart and Lawrence, 1982), p. 71.

and fixed prices for most goods and services. Priority was given to heavy industries and in particular to the basic industries such as coal, iron, steel, and weapons manufacture. All industries were controlled by state ministries and produced goods in accordance with centrally derived planning targets. Agriculture was collectivized and large "Polish Agricultural Enterprises" established. Government agencies, known as Foreign Trade Organizations, handled all external trade. Banks and other financial institutions were owned and administered by the state.

This basic pattern of central control remained in place throughout the era of Communist rule. Over time, however, a recurrent series of economic crises forced the leadership to tinker with the specific mechanisms of the system, trying always to make the economy more competitive without undermining the socialist foundations upon which it was built.

Industrialization: 1946–1959.   During the early years of Communist rule, the overwhelming priority was to rebuild Poland's industrial base, which had been devastated by six years of warfare. The PZPR launched a series of extraordinarily ambitious plans, following closely the Stalinist model of forced industrialization. The focus of these plans lay in the construction of massive industrial complexes. The expectation was that once basic industries such as steel had been developed, they would serve as springboards for future economic growth. Workers would be asked to sacrifice consumption in the short run in order to attain a real increase in future living standards.

The initial results were positive. By 1949 industrial production had surpassed its prewar level, and 3.5 million people were employed outside of agriculture. From the regime's perspective, industrialization had not only begun to restore economic prosperity but had also laid the basis for a new and vibrant working class.

After 1949, however, momentum seemed to shift. It became clear that the industrialization drive was falling short of its ambitious goals.[5] While an industrial base had indeed been created, it was concentrated in a few specific industries, and had yet to produce widespread economic benefits. Consequently, workers began to chafe at what they regarded as "production for the sake of production."

Meanwhile, the party's attempt to collectivize agriculture was collapsing under the weight of protracted resistance by the peasantry. There were at this time over three million peasant households, most of them wed for generations to their land, and most producing at just above a subsistence level. When the party introduced its policy of "voluntary collectivization" in 1949, many peasants simply refused to join the new state farms. They argued that larger farms would demand investment—in tractors, roads, and machinery—that the state obviously could not yet afford. When pushed, many peasants left their land, and took jobs in nearby towns. After hours, and unofficially, however, they continued to farm their personal plots.

[5]Myant, p. 30.

Eventually, this combination of urban and rural discontent led to widespread strikes. In 1956, there were armed clashes between workers and the security police. In the wake of the turmoil, a popular leader—Wladislaw Gomulka—was reinstated as prime minister,[6] and took office pledging to liberalize the economy, decollectivize the agricultural sector, and "follow consistently the path of democratization."[7] Gomulka condemned the earlier plans' emphasis on large-scale investment and promised to address the workers' concerns through a reorganization of industry and the creation of new workers' councils.[8] How these changes would be enacted, though, was never made clear.

Efforts at reform: 1960–1979.   Under Gomulka, a new mode of economic thinking emerged within the PZPR. Seeing the severe imbalance in the economy, party officials realized that it was largely the result of overcentralized planning. Because plant managers were rewarded only for their ability to fulfill the central plan, they had little incentive to innovate or become more productive. The only way around this obstacle, the leadership saw, was to increase the autonomy of plant managers and individual enterprises. Accordingly, Gomulka abolished many of the central industrial boards and replaced them with smaller "industrial associations."[9] Workers' councils were re-established to give workers a say in the management of their enterprises. Most cooperative farms were disbanded and greater investment in the agricultural sector was promised. The government also considered a reform of the price system but rejected it out of fear that an increase in food prices would incite popular unrest.

Throughout the 1960s, government leaders continued to experiment at the margins of the economic system. Yet always, they ran into contradictions. They wanted to liberalize the economy, but not to abandon their control over the direction of investment or to permit any decrease in nominal wages or employment. If they allowed prices or wages to float, they risked a revolt by the workers.

By 1970 it was clear that the reforms had not worked. Although the economy had been relatively stable throughout the 1960s, it had not shown any substantial improvement; indeed, it was still largely characterized by a low growth in real wages and consumption, as well as by a slowdown in productivity.[10] Social conditions, moreover, had actually deteriorated in some respects. Newly married couples had to

---

[6]Gomulka had been a prominent member of the Polish Workers' Party until 1948, when he was ousted from
    power by Stalin, and eventually imprisoned.

[7]Myant, p. 45.

[8]Keith John Lepak, *Prelude to Solidarity* (New York: Columbia University Press, 1988), p. 37.

[9]Zbigniew Landau and Jerzy Tomaszewski, *The Polish Economy in the Twentieth Century,* translated by Wojciech Roszkowski (London: Croom Helm, 1985), p. 250.

[10]Lepak, p. 37.

wait an average of seven years before receiving an apartment of their own, and periodic shortages of meat were occurring.

In a last attempt to bolster the economy, Gomulka decided in December of 1970 to make a real change in the system of price controls and labor incentives. Almost immediately, the price of basic foodstuffs soared, and workers rioted in the streets of Gdansk, Gdijnia and Szczecin. Gomulka was ousted from power and replaced by Edward Gierek, a former miner.

Like his predecessor, Gierek took power determined to reform Poland's economic system, and in particular to improve the level and quality of consumer goods. His strategy was similarly straightforward: to invest massively and simultaneously in both heavy industry and the consumer sector. Rather than tinkering with the methods of administration, he went directly after the economic targets themselves. In a return to the classic Stalinist program, investment in heavy industry increased dramatically. Simultaneously, the consumer economy was boosted by a surge of imported Western goods. In order to finance this ambitious program, Gierek turned to a new and untested source: Western banks.

As expected, this double-pronged strategy of investment proved impressive in the short run. Real incomes rose by 40% from 1971 to 1976,[11] and industrial production increased by over 70%.[12] Production in the consumer sector rose by 79% in the five-year period from 1971 to 1975.[13] Full employment was maintained throughout the period, the provision of social services was expanded, and food prices remained frozen.

Once again, however, success proved unsustainable. By 1975 Poland was suffering a severe bout of inflation, created by the combination of rising incomes and an insufficient supply of consumer goods. People were spending an increasing portion of their day waiting in line to purchase basic foodstuffs. There was also a growing housing shortage and a general decline in the provision of social services. Most ominously of all, Poland's external debt was rapidly mounting.

In the summer of 1976, Gierek and his advisors tried to bring the economy back into balance by allowing the price of meat and other agricultural products to rise by an average of 69%.[14] Almost immediately thereafter, the country was swept by a wave of strikes and protests. The leadership quickly rescinded the price increases and began to search for new ways to rein in the economy and forestall widespread shortages. Publicly, party officials blamed the country's problems on a spate of bad weather and a global recession. Privately, as one journalist observed, they began to search for new solutions with "an urgency that seemed to verge on desperation."[15]

---

[11]Jerry F. Hough, *The Polish Crisis: American Policy Options* (Washington, D.C.: The Brookings Institution, 1982), p. 12.

[12]Adam Bromke, *Poland: The Last Decade* (Oakville, Ontario: Mosaic Press, 1981), p. 68.

[13]Bromke, p. 68.

[14]Hough, p. 14.

[15]Flora Lewis, *The New York Times,* September 19, 1976. Cited in Hough, p. 14.

The Rise of Solidarity

In 1976, workers in the Ursus tractor factory near Warsaw and in the nearby town of Radom took to the streets in protest. When Communist authorities arrested the people involved, a number of prominent intellectuals rallied to their defense, and formed the Committee for Defense of the Workers (KOR). Within nine months, all but five of the workers were quietly freed, but KOR remained active, and other opposition groups began to form around it. Suddenly, it seemed that something in the Polish political system had cracked. As one Polish scholar described it, 1976 saw "the emergence of a fundamentally new political situation in the country. Opposition, which in the past had been largely passive and scattered has now become active—it has taken an organized, vocal and increasingly political form."[16] The government actively persecuted the leaders of the opposition, but to little avail. On the contrary, dissident activity continued to spread. In March of 1977 the Movement for the Defense of Human and Civil Rights was organized; it was followed several months later by a student group—the Committee for Student Solidarity—pledged to "initiate the forming of an authentic independent student organization."[17] Independent newspapers sprouted, and a "flying university" emerged in Warsaw, offering courses that were not permitted at the state-run universities.

All of this activity culminated in the summer of 1980, when, in response to the growing demands of Western creditors, the government took its first tentative steps toward price reform by raising the prices of just a few cuts of meat. Almost immediately, local strikes once more broke out, with workers demanding a compensatory wage increase.[18] Surprisingly, the party advised managers to negotiate and took no measures against the strike leaders.

Encouraged by this unprecedented relaxation, workers struck all across the country throughout the summer of 1980. At the Gdansk shipyards, rather than negotiate with their own management, the workers demanded that the government negotiate jointly with a newly formed union of over 100 enterprises. After several weeks of threats, the government relented, accepting a long list of concessions that included the right of workers to strike, the right of free trade unions, and a relaxation of censorship.[19] In the aftermath of the negotiations, delegates of strike committees from across Poland formed a Coordinating Committee known as Solidarnosc (Solidarity) and elected as their chairman the charismatic leader of the Gdansk strike, an unemployed electrician named Lech Walesa.

---

[16]Adam Bromke, "The Opposition in Poland," *Problems of Communism,* vol. 27 (September–October 1978), p. 37.

[17]Cited in Peter Raina, *Independent Social Movements in Poland* (London: London School of Economics and Political Science, 1981), pp. 327–28.

[18]Hough, p. 20.

[19]Davies, p. 18.

The Regime Responds: 1980–1981

For the next year and a half, Solidarity functioned as a legal organization in Poland, the first independent trade union in the Soviet bloc. It established regional branches, negotiated with the Communist party, and won the support of the overwhelming majority of the Polish people.[20] Soon the Solidarity flag became a symbol famous throughout the western world.

Meanwhile, the Communist party was disintegrating from within. Its Marxist-Leninist ideology, which had never sat comfortably in Poland, was becoming more and more ambiguous as the party leaders responded to economic crisis with quasi-capitalist solutions. Even within the top ranks of the PZPR there was conflict. The leaders could not agree on a common response to Solidarity, on an appropriate economic program, or even on the tenets of their own ideology. By the summer of 1981, even the party's first secretary had publicly acknowledged the "ideological bankruptcy" of the PZPR. The only thing keeping the party together, it seemed, was a common fear of a Soviet invasion.

The economy was also deteriorating. In 1980, the nation's GNP had fallen by 6%; in 1981, it plummeted another 10%. By this point, nearly half of the country's industrial capacity had fallen idle. Loss of output translated into a 18% drop in exports in 1981. Poland's hard currency debt to the West had reached $25.9 billion by the end of 1981. By nearly all indicators, the Polish economy was on the verge of collapse.

In December of 1981, just as a Soviet invasion seemed imminent, the Communist regime moved to destroy Solidarity and restore its own control. Catching the opposition by surprise, the party launched a successful midnight coup that forced Solidarity back underground and imposed a regime of martial law under the direction of General Wojciech Jaruzelski. The spontaneous protests that broke out across the country were swiftly broken by heavily armed units of the security police. Tens of thousands of citizens were arrested and forced to signs of "pledges of loyalty" to the regime. All of the major industrial enterprises were put under military command, and their work forces subjected to army discipline. Virtually all of the Solidarity leadership was imprisoned, and the union itself was declared abolished. Basic civil rights were suspended and full censorship reinstated. This new regime of martial law would rule Poland until 1989.

Stalemate: 1982–1989

During the period of martial law, the political situation in Poland was relatively quiet. Although the opposition was very much alive during this time, it went underground. The strikes and protests that had marked earlier eras became less frequent and more subdued.

[20]Davies, p. 19.

The imposition of martial law allowed Jaruzelski's government to gain some control over the economy and, paradoxically, to start down the road to economic reform. In 1982, prices of all consumer goods were allowed to increase by 300% to 400%, bringing them considerably closer to their real market value. The power of the industrial ministries was reduced, and individual enterprises were given correspondingly greater authority to set their own production targets.[21] In an attempt to boost the country's hard currency receipts from exported coal, the regime invested heavily in the mining sector.

As a result of these efforts, Poland's economy improved somewhat by the mid-1980s. Industrial output grew by 6.7% in 1983 and 5.3% in 1984.[22] Agricultural production increased, and GNP experienced a modest upturn. Compared with the crisis period of 1979–1981, the 1980s were a time of stabilization. By most other measures, however, the country was still politically and economically in stalemate.

When the Wall Came Down: The Changes of 1989

When Mikhail Gorbachev's two-pronged program of *perestroika* and *glastnost* opened the way to reform in the Soviet bloc, Poland was one of the first of the Eastern European states to undertake serious political transformation and economic liberalization. The first steps occurred in the autumn of 1988, when government officials began to acknowledge that they needed help in boosting the economy and in regaining the support of the population. Quietly, party officials and local observers were starting to suggest that Solidarity, which was legally still banned, could potentially be of great use to the regime. "Without it," asserted one economist, "the regime—and the country—will go down the drain."[23]

It appears that the about-face concerning Solidarity had little to do with a political change of heart by the party officials; rather it was one more attempt to appease popular discontent and to do something that would make the economy work. Thus, after months of tentative approaches and retractions, the government held a "Round Table" discussion with leaders of Solidarity in the spring of 1989. From the government's perspective, the purpose of the discussions was to create a "social contract" that would enable Solidarity to join the government in a "consulting" capacity. From Solidarity's perspective, the talks offered the hope of allowing the union to gain legal status in Poland and play some role in determining the country's economic policy. To many Polish workers, however, the talks still represented nothing more than an "agreement between elites, the elite of power and the elite of opposition."[24]

[21]Kazimierz Poznanski, "Economic Adjustment and Political Forces: Poland since 1970," in Ellen Comisso and Laura D'Andrea Tyson, eds., *Power, Purpose, and Collective Choice: Economic Strategy in Socialist States* (Ithaca: Cornell University Press, 1986), p. 306.

[22]Poznanski, p. 307.

[23]"Solidarity's second coming." *The Economist,* October 8, 1988, p. 54.

[24]"Only if . . . ," *The Economist,* January 21, 1989, p. 52.

In any case, though, the results of the talks were dramatic. The government agreed to hold genuine elections in summer of 1989, opening seats in the Senate (Poland's upper house) to all candidates, and reserving one-third of the seats in the Sejm (the more powerful lower house) to be contested by Solidarity and the other outside parties. When the elections occurred in June, Solidarity won 99 out of 100 seats in the Senate and all of the 161 seats in the Sejm that it had been allowed to contest.[25] Together with the other two parties (the Peasant party and the Democratic party), and with the agreement of the Communist party, Solidarity formed a coalition government that took office in September 1989 with Tadeusz Mazowiecki at its head.

As the first non-Communist government in the Soviet bloc, Solidarity was hailed by the Western world and revered by the Poles as a tangible symbol of national pride and hope. Upon taking office, the leaders of Solidarity pledged to "return Poland to Europe." The Solidarity-led government declared its commitment to the creation of multiparty democracy, to free trade, and to a free-market economy.

Simultaneously, however, Solidarity was also forced to contend with an economy that had now deteriorated even further. During 1988, the Jaruzelski regime had unleashed a vicious cycle of wage and price controls. Trying to liberalize the economy, the government had let prices rise; trying to mollify the population, however, it had guaranteed a compensatory increase in wages.[26] The result was an inflation rate of 60% for 1988, with an upward spiral into hyperinflation. The spiral was exacerbated, moreover, by the legalization of the country's foreign exchange markets, which led to a dramatic flight from the Polish zloty. By August of 1989, the monthly inflation rate had hit 40%; by October, it stood at 54%.[27]

At the same time, the country was experiencing a balance of payments crisis, with a current account deficit of $2 billion (about 3.5% of GDP) projected for 1989. Total accrued debt service (interest plus amortization) had amounted to $6.7 billion in 1988, or nearly 10% of GDP. Although Poland had actually paid only one-fifth of this amount, even that had accounted for 2.3% of GDP and 16% of foreign exchange earnings.[28]

Structural problems: industry.   In addition to the immediate problems of inflation and debt, Solidarity's leaders had to deal with the consequences of four decades of socialist control and central planning. In the industrial sector, this meant that most industrial capacity was still in the hands of the state. Despite years of piecemeal reforms, factories and industrial complexes remained closely tied to the central ministries and set their production levels in accordance with centrally derived targets. Since managers had typically been rewarded only for their performance in meeting the plan, there were few incentives for innovation or efficiency. Likewise, since all

[25]*Poland: Economic Management for a New Era* (Washington, D.C.: World Bank, 1990), p. 1.

[26]David Lipton and Jeffrey Sachs, "Creating a Market Economy in Eastern Europe: The Case of Poland," *Brookings Papers on Economic Activity,* vol. 1, 1990, p. 109.

[27]World Bank study, p. 20.

[28]Ibid., p. 9.

investment funds came from the state, managers had little reason to limit their capital investment and no familiarity with the discipline of the market. In addition, the entire industrial sector was still skewed towards heavy industry; most enterprises were large complexes, vertically integrated throughout their chain of production.

Even so, Poland's industrial sector was still marked by a strong emphasis on self-management and by the wide range of discretionary power that was legally held by the workers' councils. Since 1981, laws had been on the books that empowered democratically elected employee councils to fire managers, to veto managerial appointments made by ministries, and to have some input into their enterprises' investment and wage decisions.[29] Although the precise role of these councils was still ambiguous in 1989, it was clear that they could be a major force in the industrial sector.

Agriculture. Although agriculture had never been fully collectivized, the plots that remained in private hands were small and suffered from a lack of key inputs such as fertilizer and animal feed that were distributed primarily to the "socialized sector" farms.[30] Prices for nearly all agricultural products were regulated by the state; marketing and processing were handled by state-sponsored monopolies. Increasingly, however, private farmers (who accounted for 75% of total agricultural output) were ignoring official channels and selling their produce for much higher prices on the black market.

As of 1989, private and state farms together produced 15% of the gross national product and accounted for 27% of the labor force. Poland was a leading European producer of rye and potatoes and a major exporter of pork products.[31] Although agricultural productivity was low by European standards, Poland was more than self-sufficient in food, and agriculture was generally regarded as one of the few bright spots in the Polish economy. There was a strong tradition of private farming, a wide range of products (meats, fruits, vegetables, grains) that were potentially competitive on world markets, and a peasantry that, for the moment at least, was committed to economic liberalization and to Solidarity.

The price system. Undergirding the entire Polish economy was an extensive system of price and wage controls. Despite all of the earlier attempts to tinker with the pricing mechanism and make it more realistic, the system itself remained, and prices for the majority of commodities were determined by central planners. The intent of the system was to direct government investment as efficiently as possible and to ensure that all citizens could afford to purchase basic necessities such as food and clothing. The unfortunate result, however, was that prices in the Polish economy bore little relation to the interaction of supply and demand. The market for both consumer

---

[29]Janusz M. Dabrowski, Michal Federowicz and Anthony Levitas, "Polish State Enterprises and the Properties of Performance: Stabilization, Marketization, Privatization," *Politics and Society,* pp. 406–407.

[30]World Bank study, p. 15.

[31]Central Intelligence Agency, *World Factbook 1991,* p. 254.

and industrial goods appeared to suffer from excess demand even while goods were abundantly available on the country's extensive black market.

For years, distortions caused by the system of price controls had contributed to growth of an extensive black market. Nearly everything, from food to spare parts to foreign exchange, was available on these markets, which were officially illegal but rarely shut down. The size and sophistication of these markets had always reflected the fundamental problems that plagued the official pricing system. By the same token, however, they had also served to give the Poles some experience with market capitalism and to create a small but powerful group of black-market entrepreneurs.

Banking.   Here, as elsewhere in the economy, the state controlled all assets and made all investment decisions. At the core of the system was the National Bank of Poland (NBP), which served as the government's bank, issued the currency, administered all foreign exchange reserves, and designed the nation's monetary policy. The state also owned a handful of smaller banks, which performed regional, or more specialized, tasks. All foreign exchange facilities were under the control of the state, as were all credit facilities. Historically, the NBP provided investment credit to industrial enterprises at the discretion of and with the guarantee of the government. As of 1989, the entire banking system suffered from a lack of capital and an extremely high concentration of credit. There was little familiarity with standard Western accounting practices, with asset valuation, or with audits.

Foreign trade.   For decades, Poland's trading position had been determined primarily by its role as a member of CMEA (Council for Mutual Economic Assistance), the Soviet-run trading bloc. Poland's task in the CMEA was largely to provide raw materials, heavy machinery, and some consumer goods to the Soviet Union and other bloc countries. In exchange, it received Soviet-subsidized oil and gas. All transactions within CMEA were conducted in "transferable rubles," a nonconvertible currency whose transaction value was set periodically by the member countries. The upshot of this system was that Poland's export economy was skewed toward the specialized production of heavy machinery and a handful of consumer goods which, although popular in Eastern Europe, were not likely to be competitive on Western markets. In addition, the sheer weight of CMEA had made Poland dependent upon it; Poland had historically sent over 50% of its exports to the bloc, and received virtually all of its energy imports from the Soviet Union. As a result, it was extremely vulnerable in 1989 to the economic disintegration that was occurring throughout the Soviet bloc, and in particular to a dramatic decrease in Soviet import purchases and energy exports.

Facing an imminent loss of CMEA trade, the Polish government had already begun to focus its sights on the West, and in particular on the European Community. Yet, the Polish economy was simply not geared for extensive trade with the West. As of 1989, foreign exchange was still not readily available, and the chronic overvaluation of the zloty served as an implicit subsidy to those importers who were able to obtain foreign currencies at the official rate. In addition, years of state control meant that Poland had few private exporters and little experience in world markets. And those product sectors in which the Poles were most efficient—tractors, coal, copper, agriculture—were also those for which world demand in 1989 was sluggish.

Preliminary Reforms

Just before Solidarity came to power, the Communist government had taken some tentative steps towards structural economic reform. For the first time, it officially placed private enterprise on an equal footing with the state sector and removed nearly all restrictions on private business. It passed a law that allowed individuals to buy and sell shares in companies, and a law on foreign investment that permitted the establishment of wholly owned foreign subsidiaries. It began to restructure the nation's banking system, establishing nine independent commercial banks, and transforming the National Bank of Poland into a conventional central bank. Finally, a law was passed at the end of 1988 which allowed for the unrestricted purchase and sale of foreign exchange.[32]

Bold as these reforms may have been, they had done little to improve the economic situation that had developed by the end of 1989 or to address the basic contradictions of Poland's economy.

Balcerowicz's Choice

By the time they entered office in 1989, Solidarity's leaders realized that they would have to undertake drastic measures not just to transform the economy, but also to prevent it from collapsing. From the start, they declared their commitment to two broad objectives: first, stabilization of the economic situation, and then structural adjustment and systemic reform. The job of formulating and then implementing a strategy was given to Leszek Balcerowicz, a former economics professor who had just been named the country's new finance minister.

Balcerowicz was a determined and dedicated man, described as a "genius" by his colleagues and respected even by his opponents.[33] Along with a small group of young academics, he began working to come up with a workable plan.

One of the great unknowns, however, was just how much power Balcerowicz had to launch his plan. Although Solidarity was officially at the helm of the Polish government, the majority of seats in the Sejm were still held by Communist party members, as were some of the key ministries, such as defense and interior. All of the nomenklatura were still firmly entrenched in their old positions. Theoretically, they

---

[32]World Bank study, p. 13.

[33]"The man behind the plan," *The Economist*, December 23, 1989, p. 58.

still had the ability to block or at least ignore any policy that Balcerowicz might make.

Outside the government too, there were bound to be problems. Already, workers at many state enterprises were beginning to protest that Solidarity had betrayed them. Any economic reform that entailed a rise in unemployment or a fall in workers' living standards was likely to be interpreted as a betrayal of Solidarity's trade union roots.

The challenge for Balcerowicz was thus largely one of timing and sequence. He, along with the rest of the incoming leadership, realized that the government could not transform the country's entire economic structure until the economy itself was relatively stable, and especially until inflation was under control. By the same token, he knew that the very process of transformation would create a certain amount of chaos in the economy, as enterprises were restructured and liquidated, and as workers were laid off. He needed to move quickly, but he also needed to ensure that the transformation worked and that it did not cause more chaos than it cured.

"Leaping to the market."   One of the earliest options that Balcerowicz received for consideration was a plan devised by a young Harvard economist named Jeffrey Sachs who had helped the Bolivian government to reduce its hyperinflation in 1986. Sachs's plan was based on the notion that reform would succeed only if it was quick and all-encompassing. He advised Balcerowicz to "leap to the market," breaking apart all of the remnants of the prior economic system as quickly as possible. "If you are going to chop off a cat's tail," he argued, "do it in one stroke, not bit by bit."[34]

Sachs's plan emphasized the interconnectedness of reform. As he described it:

> The transition process is a seamless web. Structural reforms cannot work without a working price system; a working price system cannot be put in place without ending excess demand and creating a convertible currency; and a credit squeeze and tight macroeconomic policy cannot be sustained unless prices are realistic, so that there is a rational basis for deciding which firms should be allowed to close. At the same time, for real structural adjustment to take place under the pressures of tight demand, the macroeconomic shock must be accompanied by other measures, including selling off state assets, freeing up the private sector, establishing procedures for bankruptcy, preparing a social safety net, and undertaking tax reform. Clearly, the reform process must be comprehensive.[35]

Sachs advised Balcerowicz to undertake a three-stage program of comprehensive adjustment.[36] In the first stage, the government needed to combat inflation (or "chronic excess demand") through a radical program of fiscal and monetary austerity as well as a devaluation of the zloty. The second stage, which could be implemented

---

[34]Lipton and Sachs, p. 100. The authors here are quoting a former Bolivian Planning Minister, referring to his own country's stabilization process.

[35]Lipton and Sachs, p. 99.

[36]The following section draws heavily on Lipton and Sachs, pp. 100–101.

simultaneously with the first, was the creation of a true market economy. According to Sachs, the Polish government needed at this stage to deregulate all prices, demonopolize the entire state sector, and remove all barriers to trade, both internally and internationally. The third stage would be the privatization of all state assets. During this stage, which would occur over a period of several years, all elements of the "socialist sector"—industrial complexes, state farms, financial institutions, natural resources, transportation networks—would be transferred to private owners and run on a competitive basis.

Sachs's plan stuck a responsive chord with Balcerowicz and other members of the Solidarity leadership. They saw it as a way to address the problems of Poland's economy straight on, and to minimize the length of the adjustment period. Building on Sachs's ideas, Balcerowicz and his advisers crafted a tentative economic stabilization program that would simultaneously (1) remove all price controls; (2) limit wage increases; (3) allow layoffs and bankruptcies; (4) reduce subsidies for all basic goods and services such as coal, bread, and housing; and (5) devalue the zloty and make it completely convertible.

In suggesting this plan, Balcerowicz claimed that it would "open new perspectives of proper living, free development and fruitful and satisfying work."[37] More prosaically, he argued that "if we try to put it off, the ailing Polish economy would get even worse."[38]

The gradual approach. Even as this plan was being formulated, however, many observers were registering doubts. Critics inside and outside government argued that Poland was ill-equipped to make the rapid leap that Sachs was advising. The reform plan, they argued, would impose a tremendous economic and political toll on the nation—a toll that Solidarity was not capable of sustaining. How, for instance, could a nation with no official unemployment (and thus no unemployment insurance or job placement programs) cope with the sudden layoffs of hundreds of thousands, and perhaps millions, of people? How would an economy already on the brink of collapse respond to such a drastic program of shock therapy? How could a society run by bureaucrats and planners instantly create the mechanisms of a free market? How would workers and farmers react when they saw their champion, Solidarity, implementing programs that not only caused a precipitous decline in their standard of living, but also removed the socialist benefits of job security and income equality to which they had become accustomed?

Overall, the critics urged that Poland needed to adopt a more gradual program of reform. They argued that before the country could leap to capitalism, it had to develop the institutions of a capitalist economy: a stock market, a private sector, more sophisticated distribution channels, a comprehensible legal framework. Without these institutions, they warned, the shock therapy would be all shock and no therapy; the people would suffer, but would receive no reward for their pains.

[37]*New York Times,* December 18, 1989, p. A1.

[38]*New York Times,* December 31, 1989, p. A9.

In addition, some critics were worried about the social aspects of the Balcerow-icz plan. For decades, Poland had had a system of relative income equality. There were, of course, many sectors of the population that did better than others, but the discrepancies had not been that conspicuous. A leap to capitalism would mean creating huge inequities. Many people would be out of work. Many would see their standard of living plummet. But some, the first entrepreneurs, would be able to get very rich very quickly. What could make matters even worse is that the people most likely to make this money were the old communists, for they had the foreign connections and access to the best resources. In economic terms, creating a capitalist class was necessary, but in social terms, it could be devastating.

Even under the most optimistic forecasts, moreover, the effects of the Balcerowicz plan would be drastic. Price increases of 25% to 50% a month were to be expected as state subsidies were removed. Real incomes were projected to drop by 20% in 1990 and industrial output to decline by 5%. At a minimum, 400,000 workers could be left jobless as a result of enterprise cutbacks and bankruptcies.

Balcerowicz himself acknowledged that Poland would be launching its reform program in "extremely unfavorable conditions." He argued, though, that shock therapy was the only way to transform the country and make capitalism work. His critics, however, continued to stress the fragility of Poland's economy, and the anxiety of its people. As one economist explained, "It's a program of economic transition by shock therapy, but considering the weakened condition of the nation, I'm worried about how well it will be able to handle shock therapy."[39] Added another, "The economic plan's biggest weakness is that it doesn't have anything concrete for the man in the street. Since the Solidarity government came to power in August, they have been saying you have to plan for austerity, you have to expect to suffer, and now this. I'm worried about an explosion of malcontent."[40]

One of the most powerful comments came from the Hungarian-American economist Janos Kornai, a leading expert on socialist economics:

> One has a strange feeling of deja vu when people who are noncommunists or even anticommunists get into power and think that they can manage the state sector in the right way. They think that because they are not communists, they will be able to run their central bank, their Ministry of Finance, and their state-owned enterprises efficiently. They are sure to fail.[41]

As the December 31 deadline approached, Balcerowicz began to worry that the critics might be right, and that the adoption of a radical plan might be too much for the country to bear. He worried too, that economic hardship could force the Poles to turn away from Solidarity, and to embrace another, more dangerous, type of party. He really had no idea how the Sachs proposal would work, or how it could be implemented politically. He began to wonder if perhaps there was another way.

---

[39]Quoted in *New York Times,* December 26, 1989, p. D1.

[40]Ibid., p. D8.

[41]Comment on paper by Sachs and Lipton, in *Brookings Papers on Economic Activity,* vol. 1, 141–142.

Eastern Europe

EXHIBIT 1

Poland

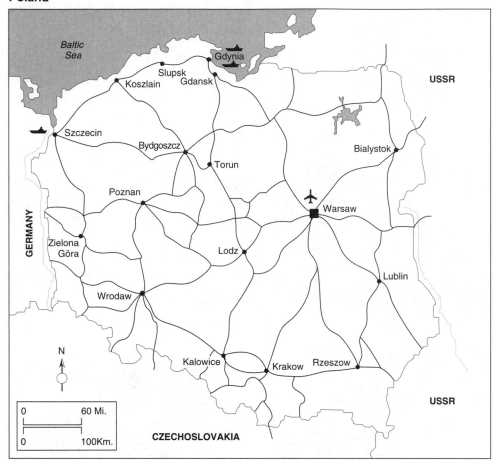

EXHIBIT 1   (*Continued*)

EXHIBIT 2 National Income Accounts 1980–1988 (billions of constant zlotys)

	1980	1981	1982	1983	1984	1985[a] I	1985[a] II	1986	1987	1988
			1982 Zlotys					1984 Zlotys		
Gross domestic product	6,268	5,643	5,374	5,763	5,993	6,211	9,018	9,398	9,582	9,975
Government consumption	471	450	461	475	511	550	850	850	859	860
Private consumption	4,201	4,049	3,543	3,734	3,893	3,994	5,603	5,955	6,106	6,283
Investments	1,714	1,330	1,287	1,357	1,443	1,532	2,341	2,446	2,449	2,658
Fixed investments	1,606	1,300	1,122	1,221	1,341	1,399	1,872	1,957	2,037	2,161
Changes in stocks	108	33	165	136	102	133	469	490	412	497
Exports	1,241	1,015	1,078	1,177	1,316	1,320	1,520	1,584	1,663	1,820
Imports	1,384	1,111	962	1,018	1,114	1,190	1,441	1,518	1,588	1,731
Domestic savings	1,608	1,147	1,378	1,421	1,527	1,637	2,517	2,655	2,743	2,832
Growth Rates (%)										
Gross domestic product		-10	-5	6	6	4		4	2	4
Government consumption		-5	2	3	8	8		0	1	0
Private consumption		-4	-13	5	4	3		5	3	3
Investments		-22	-3	5	6	6		5	0	9
Fixed investments		-19	-14	9	10	4		5	4	6
Changes in stock		-70	400	-18	-25	30		5	-16	21
Exports		-18	6	9	12	0		4	5	9
Imports		-20	-13	6	9	7		5	5	9
Domestic savings		-29	20	4	7	7		6	3	3

[a]In 1985 the Polish statistical authorities changed the formula used to calculate constant zlotys. The two columns of figures listed under 1985 represent the old and the new method of calculation.

Source: World Bank, p. 94.

EXHIBIT 3   Poland—GDP by Source in Current Values (billions of zlotys)

	1970	1975	1980	1985	1988
Material sectors	839.5	1,479.8	2,158.4	8,910.9	24,994.6
Industry	454.7	868.6	1,177.4	4,334.1	12,031.1
Construction	79.3	161.9	196.1	1,056.2	3,542.6
Agriculture	131.1	207.1	323.6	1,401.9	3,207.1
Transport and communications	67.7	117.0	184.2	635.1	1,461.9
Trade	75.6	77.0	207.0	1,190.5	4,110.6
Nonmaterial services	96.3	182.3	302.0	1,456.3	4,634.1
Satisfying population's needs	63.8	113.4	192.3	1,006.9	—
Housing	11.6	16.6	31.8	260.5	—
Education	21.1	41.0	68.0	298.0	—
Culture and art	4.0	5.8	9.5	37.4	
Health and social welfare	13.5	26.6	46.4	207.2	—
Satisfying society's needs	32.5	68.9	109.7	449.4	
Total, value-added unadjusted	935.8	1,662.1	2,460.4	10,367.2	29,628.7

Source: World Bank, p. 92.

EXHIBIT 4   Basic Indicators, 1960–1986 (1960 = 100)

	1970	1975	1978	1980	1982	1985	1986
National income produced (at constant prices)	180.2	287.2	331.7	304.7	253.4	293.2	307.6
Consumption of goods and services	162.1	243.0	284.3	299.9	245.0	278.0	291.9
Investment in national economy	204.5	458.7	487.9	394.1	268.8	347.2	364.9
Cost of living index	120.3	135.5	161.8	188.3	471.9	768.9	909.9
Real monthly wages in state sector	119.5	169.0	176.8	187.8	144.2	152.2	156.3

Sources: *Rocznik Statystyczny*, 1986; *Rocznik Statystyczny*, 1987 (author's own calculations).

EXHIBIT 5   Polish Industrial Production, 1970–1986

Product	1970	1978	1980	1982	1985	1986
Electricity (TW/h)	64.5	116	122	118	138	140
Coal (000 tons)	173	234	230	227	249	259
Copper (electrolyte) (000 tons)	72.2	33.2	357	348	387	388
Refined oil (000 tons)	7,471	16,970	16,126	13,405	14,067	14,300
Rolled steel (000 tons)	8,136	13,565	13,551	10,477	11,845	12,300
Washing machines, automatic (000s)	NA	273	360	232	303	277
Refrigerators and freezers (000s)	444	890	694	509	579	572
Color TVs (000s)	NA	60.6	147	144	158	173

Source: *Rocznik Statystyczny*, 1986; and *Rzeczpospolita*, 3 February 1987.

EXHIBIT 6 Employment by Sector, 1970–1987 (percent of total)

	1970	1980	1984	1987
Socialized industry	27	27	26	25
Construction	7	8	7	8
Agriculture	34	30	29	28
Trade	7	8	8	9
Education	4	4	5	5
Other	21	23	25	25
Total employment (thousands)	15,175	17,325	16,998	17,245
Total population (thousands)	32,658	35,735	37,203	37,700

Source: GUS, *Statistical Yearbook*, 1988; World Bank, p. 89.

EXHIBIT 7 Output, Inflation, and Real Wages in Poland, 1970–89 (average annual percentage change)

Year	Industrial Output	Consumer Prices	Average Wages	Real Wages
1970–78	7.9	3.8	10.3	6.3
1979–81	−6.8	13.1	16.3	2.8
1982	−5.5	100.1	56.0	−28.7
1983	6.0	22.0	27.7	19.0
1984	5.6	15.1	13.6	−1.3
1985	3.4	15.1	19.9	4.2
1986	4.9	17.7	21.1	2.9
1987	1.7	25.2	21.4	−3.1
1988	4.7	60.0	83.9	15.0
1989	−1.0[a]	257.1[b]	298.6	11.6

[a]Estimate

[b]Changes are calculated from annual averages. With the acceleration of inflation in 1989, the rate of price increase was much higher on the basis of an end-of-year comparison. Consumer prices rose 636% between December 1988 and December 1989.

Source: Sachs and Lipton, p. 105.

EXHIBIT 8 State Revenues and Expenditures, 1980–1989 (billions of zlotys at current prices)

	1980	1981	1982	1983	1984	1985	1986	1987	1988	1989E
Total revenue	1,214	1,149	2,405	2,708	3,403	4,224	5,171	6,169	10,544	29,098
Total expenditures	1,243	1,463	2,568	2,850	3,595	4,196	5,315	6,389	10,610	35,365
Purchases of goods and services	93	106	221	260	317	434	491	611	967	—
Payments of wages and salaries	87	114	184	224	279	329	411	510	891	—
Social insurance payments to Pension Fund in respect to government employees	16	26	44	82	107	126	158	194	296	—
Social insurance and welfare benefits paid to the population	31	43	203	212	230	231	247	—	—	—
Subsidies	720	849	1,146	1,140	1,487	1,672	2,108	2,688	4,394	—
Of which: To the population	300	363	573	576	649	807	1,183	1,691	2,967	8,057
To enterprises and economic units	420	486	574	564	738	865	925	977	1,427	—
Transfers to other units[a]	79	104	251	262	331	366	542	683	1,248	—
National defense and public security	91	103	233	259	337	384	505	617	987	2,795
Investment and modernization	105	100	268	382	452	540	760	943	1,580	2,197
Other[b]	20	18	18	30	56	116	95	143	248	—

[a]Consists mainly of transfers to extrabudgetary funds and other organizations to finance expenditures for various cultural, educational, and social purposes.
[b]Includes interest payments on foreign credits extended by the government.

Source: World Bank, pp. 103–104.

EXHIBIT 9   Poland's Fiscal Deficit, 1982–1989 (trillions of zlotys)

	1982	1984	1986	1987	1988	1989 Projected
Revenues	2.4	3.4	4.8	6.2	10.5	29.1
Expenditures	2.6	3.6	4.3	6.4	10.6	35.4
Unpaid interest on external debt	.1	.2	.3	.8	.9	9.0
Surplus/deficit	(.3)	(.4)	.2	(1.0)	(1.0)	(15.3)
Deficit as % of GDP	5.4	4.6	1.5	5.8	3.4	9.0

Sources: **Exhibit 8**; World Bank.

EXHIBIT 10   Poland's External Debt, 1981–1988 (US$ billions)

	1981	1982	1983	1984	1985	1986	1987	1988
Convertible currency	$25.9	$26.5	$26.4	$26.9	$29.7	$33.5	$39.2	$39.1
Short-term	1.1	1.3	1.3	1.3	1.4	1.4	1.5	1.4
Medium- and long-term	24.3	23.6	22.4	21.5	23.9	28.8	32.6	30.6
Nonconvertible currency[a]	2.6	2.9	2.7	2.8	3.4	4.2	2.9	3.0
Short-term	1.0	0.5	0.2	0.6	-	0.1	-	-
Medium- and long-term								
Total debt, including arrears	28.5	29.4	29.1	29.7	33.1	37.7	42.1	42.1

[a]The external debt in nonconvertible currencies was converted from transferable rubles (TR) into US$ using cross rates derived from the commercial rates of the zloty vis-à-vis the TR and US$: prior to 1982 the period average exchange rate was used but since 1982 end-of-period rates have been used.

Source: World Bank, p. 101.

EXHIBIT 11 Poland—Balance of Payments, 1980–1988 (US$ millions)

	1980	1981	1982	1983	1984	1985	1986	1987	1988
Current Account									
Exports (fob)	$14,170	$10,464	$10,457	$11,000	$11,800	$10,912	$11,538	$11,602	$13,211
Imports (fob)	15,806	12,564	10,654	10,582	10,962	10,436	10,914	10,803	12,064
Trade balance	–1,636	–2,100	–197	418	838	476	624	799	1,147
Total services	–2,320	–2,788	–2,653	–2,356	–2,967	–2,219	–2,538	–2,790	–2,883
Of which:									
Travel, net	16	–101	–65	–111	–123	–61	–45	–8	–16
Freight and insurance, net	64	288	332	271	89	85	88	–26	–23
Interest, net	–2,357	–3,060	–2,963	–2,592	–3,021	–2,383	–2,663	–2,915	–2,955
Other current items, net	–43	85	43	76	88	140	82	159	111
Transfers, net	656	655	323	380	467	768	946	1,413	1,434
Current account balance	–3,300	–4,233	–2,527	–1,558	–1,662	–975	–968	–578	–302
Capital Account									
Medium- and long-term capital	2,659	898	–2,371	–982	–107	84	–1,652	NA	NA
Revolving credits, net	0	0	196	338	240	–2	139	106	30
Short-term capital, and errors and omissions	239	–172	478	295	191	540	–421	NA	NA
Changes in Reserves	402	–35	–369	–119	–340	236	173	–797	–561
Change in Arrears		3,542	4,593	2,026	1,678	117	2,729	NA	NA

Source: World Bank, p. 95.

EXHIBIT 12   Exchange Rates,
1950–1989 (zloty per US$)

1950	4.0
1955	4.0
1960	4.0
1965	4.0
1970	4.0
1975	3.32
1980	46.05
1981	55.84
1982	86.45
1983	98.37
1984	126.24
1985	147.88
1986	197.62
1987	315.54
1988	502.55
1989	6,500.00

Source: International Monetary Fund,
International Financial Statistics.

EXHIBIT 13   Selected Indicators, 1989

	Real Wage (Index, January 1989=1.00)	Monthly Change in Real Wage (%)	Monthly Rate of Inflation (%)	Official Exchange Rate (zlotys per dollar)
1989				
January	1.00	−40.1	11.0	506
February	1.18	18.2	7.9	526
March	1.46	24.0	8.1	566
April	1.29	−12.0	9.8	631
May	1.15	−10.9	7.2	746
June	1.24	8.1	6.1	849
July	1.19	−4.1	9.5	836
August	1.73	45.2	39.5	988
September	1.30	−24.5	34.4	1,340
October	1.06	−18.2	54.8	1,970
November	1.08	1.9	22.4	3,077
December	1.36	25.6	17.7	5,235

Source: Sachs, p. 110.

EXHIBIT 14   Density of Housing Occupation

	Average Number of Rooms per Unit	Average Number of Persons per Room	Average Living Space per Person (M^2)
1960	2.46	1.66	NA
1970	2.87	1.37	12.9
1978	3.15	1.16	14.7
1984	3.31	1.07	15.8
1986	3.27	1.03	16.6

Source: *Kierunki*, January 1986; *Rocznik Statystyczny*, 1987, p. 439, Table 6.

EXHIBIT 15   The Sources of Social Antagonism in Poland (percentage mentioning factor)

Pay, earnings	75.6
Property, material possessions	60.5
Power, official position	42.2
Political opinions	41.8
Membership of PZPR	32.6
Division between manual and white-collar work	29.4
Urban/rural residence	27.3
Difference between older and younger generation	23.2
Education	18.4
Faith and religious practice	17.5
Social origin	15.5

Source: *Polityka*, 11 July 1987.

Gerber Products Company: Investing in the New Poland

Tangible structural changes in the Polish economy will not emerge without more vigorous investment processes. They will certainly not be stimulated artificially and arbitrarily by the Government, which, even if it wished to, has no means to achieve that. There is a recession and the industry is weak. What is available is virtually only foreign aid, foreign credit, and foreign direct investment.

—Dariusz Ledworowski, Polish Minister
of International Economic Cooperation

If adults from different countries had as much in common as babies do, there would be fewer problems in the world.

—Gerber official at an Alima press conference

In December of 1991, Fred Schomer and Steve Clark were caught in a delicate position. For months, Schomer, the chief financial officer of Gerber Products Company, and Clark, the company's general counsel, had been shuttling between Michigan and Warsaw, putting together a deal that would allow Gerber to acquire Alima S.A., one of Poland's largest and most successful food processing plants. On all sides, the deal had seemed to make sense. Gerber would modernize the aging plant, boost its sagging export trade, and give the Polish government $11 million of the hard currency it so desperately needed. In exchange, the world's largest baby food producer would

Research Associate Allegra Young prepared this case under the supervision of Professor Debora Spar as the basis for class discussion rather than to illustrate either effective or ineffective handling of an administrative situation.

gain a low-cost base for its European operations and an early advantage in the growing markets of Central and Eastern Europe.

Until this point, the negotiations had progressed smoothly. After winning a competitive bidding process sponsored by Poland's Ministry of Privatization, the Gerber officials had signed a Purchase and Sale agreement on October 1. Under the terms of this agreement, Gerber had formally committed itself to the Alima deal and agreed to work with the government in resolving a series of complicated issues such as property ownership and taxation. Everyone involved in the negotiations had acknowledged that these issues were critical to the deal's success, but because the discussions were going so well both sides were confident that they could resolve all issues by the end of the year.

But then on October 27 politics had intervened. After months of internal squabbling Lech Walesa's Solidarity government had bowed to popular pressures and convened the country's first fully democratic elections since World War II. The results were chaotic. Twenty-nine parties, including such novices as the Beer Lover's party, the Give Us a Chance party, and the Alliance of Women Against the Hardships of Life party, won seats in the Sejm, none with more than 13% of the vote. Solidarity splintered into a number of rival factions, the communists emerged as the second strongest party in the nation, and for weeks the newly elected representatives could not even form a coalition capable of selecting a Cabinet. Most ominously of all perhaps, the elections had revealed a wellspring of discontent with Poland's economic reform. After two years spent on an ambitious "leap to the market," many Poles had grown disenchanted with capitalism and wanted their new government to embrace policies of looser money, more social insurance, and fewer foreign investors.

And thus Fred Schomer and Steve Clark found themselves reconsidering their options. They knew that, at a minimum, the new government was going to want to renegotiate the Purchase and Sale agreement and take a tougher stance on the issues of ownership and taxation. Most likely, the government would also tinker with existing policies on profit repatriation, currency devaluation, privatization, and worker compensation—all if which could have a serious impact on Gerber's bottom line. Likewise, it was clear that the new government would be unable to deliver many of the promises that its predecessor had made in the October 1 agreement.

In principle, Schomer, Clark, and the rest of the Gerber team were still committed to Poland and the Alima plant. The facilities were in good shape, the enterprise was well-managed, and the entire operation fit nicely with Gerber's plans for global expansion. But before they spent $25 million for an overseas acquisition, the Gerber officials needed to reevaluate the merits of investing in such an uncertain situation.

The Gerber Products Company

Founded in 1928, the Gerber Products Company specialized in the care of the world's smallest consumers: babies. Daniel Gerber, Sr. founded the company in 1928 in the small town of Fremont, Michigan. At the core of Gerber's line were the 165 varieties of jarred baby food that the company distributed worldwide. In addition, Gerber manufactured basic baby apparel under its own product name and children's wear under the Buster Brown label.

The location of Gerber's main plant in the small farming town of Fremont, Michigan (1991 pop. 3,800) was a critical element of the company's operations. Most of the fruits and vegetables used in the factory were grown within 100 miles of Fremont, including 7.3 million pounds of peas, 60 million pounds of apples, 8.4 million pounds of peaches, and tons of pears, carrots, squash, green beans, blueberries, cherries, plums and wheat.[1] A nearby glass manufacturer provided glass for the approximately 600 million jars that the plant used each year.

Gerber employed 1,200 people at the Fremont site, which also served as its corporate headquarters. The offices of Gerber reflected the culture of the corporation: babies' pictures adorned the walls and desks of the employees, many of whom were also shareholders. Nameplates were created from children's blocks and automated toy soldiers guarded the entrance to the chairman's office. At one point in the company's 63-year history, corporate officers had considered a corporate office move to Chicago, but Fremont's loyalty to Gerber persuaded them to stay. As Robert Johnston, the company vice chairman explained, "It is a dedicated group of people. They used to blow the whistle when they needed people to come in to help process peas. People would give up whatever they were doing and come in to help out. That's pretty hard to walk away from."[2]

Since Gerber introduced processed baby food, the company had dominated the United States market, with a 1991 market share of 72%. The company's commitment to providing a child with nutritional food was central to its philosophy and paramount to its appeal. The company's managers prided themselves on the fact that doctors had been known to use Gerber's 1–800 number as an emergency resource for their patients, and focused on producing whatever was necessary to maintain the medical community's endorsement. The entire company was devoted to its founder's original determination to "do everything we can to deserve and maintain the confidence mothers have in our products."[3] Or as one current executive vowed, "If the pediatrician says we need to make artichokes to provide a baby with a balanced diet, we'll make artichokes."

Gerber's commitment to quality paid off handsomely on its bottom line. Despite flattening birth rates in the United States, the company had managed an 11% increase in sales in FY 1991, propelling its superbrand to total sales of over $1.2 billion. Of the 4% of U.S. houses that had babies, Gerber reached a full 92% of them. Gerber's other U.S. competitors, Heinz and Beech-nut, shared about equal amounts of the rest of the market.[4]

With a dominant position in the American market, therefore, Gerber's challenge

---

[1]"Gerber: Attention to Heritage and Values Has Defined and Helped Develop One of Michigan's Largest Multinational Corporations," *North Force Magazine,* Vol. 4, No. 2 (January 1991), p. 17.

[2]*North Force Magazine,* p. 17.

[3]Daniel Gerber, cited in *Gerber Annual Report,* 1992, p. 1.

[4]Margaret Littman, "Processor of the Year," *Prepared Foods,* September 1992, p. 30.

was to find some means of expansion or diversification. For awhile the company had experimented with ventures in day care centers and toys, but when these operations failed to provide any significant growth for the company, Gerber's management had decided to divest from all but the most basic lines of infant clothing, refocusing instead on the production of baby food. This streamlined strategy doubled Gerber's return on equity, taking it from 14.5% during the 1980s to around 29% since 1990.[5] Still the company wanted to grow.

The most obvious place for growth was the global market. In 1991, 90% of Gerber's sales were still occurring in the United States, a country with only 3% of the world's babies.[6] The company also did very well in Puerto Rico, Central America, and especially Mexico, where a joint venture with Pepsi controlled 100% of the local market. Elsewhere, though, Gerber's presence was limited. In Canada, Heinz effectively controlled the domestic market. And in Western Europe, Australia, the Middle East, and Africa, Gerber had already licensed their technology to local firms and thus were precluded from expanding their own sales operations. In the Far East, Gerber had had some success in penetrating the Korean and Taiwanese markets, but its success was limited by these countries' traditional reliance on cereal-based foods. In Japan, meanwhile, the company had encountered cultural barriers. Apparently many women felt that their mothers-in-law and husbands would look down at the use of commercially prepared baby food. Gerber executives were thinking of ways to market their product across this cultural divide, but prospects for the Japanese markets were still not overwhelming.

Against this backdrop, Al Piergallini, Gerber's chairman and CEO, had decided in 1990 to make Central and Eastern Europe a target for Gerber's international expansion. With the fall of communism, the markets of Central and Eastern Europe were positioned to grow rapidly, and consumers were eager for the Western-style goods that had been forbidden to them for so long. Despite a poor local economy Gerber was already doing well in the region, having exported around $3 million of baby food to Poland since 1988. Exports, though, were not the best means of servicing the Polish markets, since they left Gerber at the mercy of foreign exchange rates. If the company could instead establish a local plant, it would be able to minimize the vicissitudes of exchange rate swings and also develop an anchor for exports to neighboring countries such as Hungary and Czechoslovakia. More importantly, a Polish plant would also help Gerber improve its sales in France. Since the French licensee's license had just expired, Gerber had recently entered more aggressively into the French market where per capita consumption of baby food was higher than in the United States. Gerber officials knew that they could be competitive in France in terms of quality. While many of their competitors' products tasted better because they included sugar and other seasonings, Gerber's more natural formulas had already won the endorsement of a majority of French pediatricians.[7] Gerber also needed, though,

---

[5]Marcia Berss, "Limited Horizons," *Forbes,* October 12, 1992, p. 66.

[6]Berss, p. 66.

[7]Interview with Gerber executive, December 7, 1992.

to make its food competitive on price, and a plant in Central Europe would do this. It would allow Gerber to move closer to the European market, gain valuable economies of scale, and avoid the duties that fell heaviest on goods imported from the United States.[8]

In order to gain this potentially lucrative opportunity, however, Gerber had to move fast. Already the CEO of Heinz had announced that his company was considering using Central Europe as a base of operations and was researching cites in Ukraine, Hungary, and Poland. Clearly, Gerber's competitors had also noticed the potential of Central Europe and they were beginning to act.

Then, in May of 1991, the investment firm of Wasserstein Perella called Gerber with an interesting prospect. John Simpson, a director in Wasserstein Perella's Chicago office, informed Fred Schomer that the Polish government was inviting bids for the acquisition of Alima S.A., a food processing plant located in the southeastern town of Rzeszow.[9] Simpson did not know a lot about the plant, but he knew that it was considered one of Poland's best businesses and that one of its products was baby food. Quickly Schomer called a meeting with Piergallini and senior managers from Gerber's International Division. After a brief strategy session they all agreed that the offer was intriguing but that they needed to learn much more about Poland and Alima before they went any further.

Country Risks: The Political Economy of Poland

Macroeconomics and the leap to the market. In January of 1990, the Polish government had launched an unprecedented program of economic reform. Under the leadership of Leszek Balcerowicz, the country's controversial Finance Minister, Poland had attempted to "leap to the market," moving as quickly as possible to stabilize its inflationary economy and establish the foundations of a market economy.[10] On the morning of January 1, the government had simultaneously lowered trade barriers, declared a convertible currency, and eliminated virtually all domestic price controls. Soon thereafter, it also announced an increase in taxes and a substantial decrease in the existing consumer subsidies.

---

[8]Since 1989, Poland had been involved in a series of trade negotiations with the European Community. Early on, both sides had agreed to the elimination of most tariffs within five years. In December 1989, the EC extended its Generalized System of Preferences to Poland, waiving import duties for a broad array of goods. In December 1991, Poland was officially granted association status with the EC. Under the association agreement, tariffs on most Polish goods were substantially reduced. See Kalypso Nicolaïdis, "East European Trade in the Aftermath of 1989: Did International Institutions Matter?" in Robert O. Keohane, Joseph S. Nye and Stanley Hoffmann, eds., *After the Cold War. International Institutions and State Strategies in Europe, 1989–1991* (Cambridge: Harvard University Press, 1993), pp. 196–245.

[9]Pronounced Zhes-hoff.

[10]For more detailed account of these changes, see Debora Spar, *Poland 1989,* Harvard Business School Case No. 792–091 (Boston: Harvard Business School, 1992).

The logic of the plan was tough but straightforward: to push Poland away from centralized control of its economy and towards the rigors of the market. Once wage and price controls were removed and the zloty allowed to trade openly on world markets, prices in Poland would converge gradually with those prevailing elsewhere. Likewise, once the government stopped subsidizing Polish consumers and financing industry, market mechanisms would have to develop in order to serve these needs. And once realistic prices and financial institutions were in place, the government could advance to the next stage of reform—the mass privatization of Poland's state-owned economy.

After nearly two years of austerity, though, Balcerowicz's plan had still not achieved all that its proponents had expected. On some fronts, the results were promising. The long lines and empty shelves of communism had disappeared, replaced by new establishments selling everything from personal computers to designer fashion. Restaurants and office buildings had sprouted up across Warsaw and a farmer's market flourished in the shadows of the former Ministry of Culture. Polish exports were faring well on world markets and inflation, which had been 54% a month in 1989, had declined to a manageable 3%.

But other areas were disappointing. While the stores were stocked with luxury items, few Poles could afford to buy any of the merchandise because their savings had been deflated so severely by the currency conversion. Even basic items such as food and rent had become prohibitively expensive after the lifting of price controls. Energy prices alone had risen by 500% and government deficit rose to US$400 million and was predicted to soar to $1 billion by 1993. Meanwhile, Poland's traditional industrial base was struggling to deal with the triple burdens of global competition, a cessation of government support, and the loss of their Eastern European market. Industrial production fell 30% in 1990, many smaller firms were forced out of business, and unemployment, which was virtually unknown under communism, was predicted to climb to 12% by early 1993. Most dramatically perhaps, the country was still critically short of the capital it needed to import technology and modernize its industrial base. The government was able to raise some funds on international markets and through institutions such as the World Bank and European Bank for Reconstruction and Development. But these sources were limited. Poland's outstanding debt of $41 billion in 1989 made it a poor risk for international lenders, and its lack of an adequate financial infrastructure made even the most generous donors wary of advancing much money. In the shortrun, at least, the transformation of Poland's economy depended on the capitalization of industry. And the capitalization of industry depended on foreign investors.

The climate for investment.   In many ways, the new Poland was an ideal target for foreign investment. There was a domestic market of nearly 40 million people, decades of pent-up demand, and a government desperate for hard currency and eager to sell its aging industrial assets. Because the Poles needed Western capital so badly, they were apparently willing to negotiate with anyone who offered and willing to make whatever concessions were necessary to attract potential investors.

Unlike the other countries of Central Europe, moreover, Poland had a relatively strong history of foreign investment. Officially, Poland had been open to foreign investment since 1976, when the Council of Ministers passed a regulation permitting the establishment of small-scale enterprises.[11] Then, in 1982 the Sejm had loosened the rules even further, formally recognizing the legal basis for foreign investment and creating a state guarantee for the invested capital.[12] The laws were liberalized again in 1986 and 1988 until, with the passage of still more legislation in 1991, the country had abolished virtually all legal restraints on foreign investment. There was no minimum set on the amount of the initial investment and permits were required only for a handful of industries such as defense, air and sea ports, real estate, and wholesale trade in imported goods. Foreign companies were allowed to repatriate all of their capital, including capital gains, and to remit full profits and dividends. For companies that made large investments (ECU two million or more) or large exporters (exporting 20% of their production), additional tax relief could be obtained. Foreigners were given full national treatment as well as investment guarantees, tax credits, and capital export allowances, which arguably were not available to the average Polish investor.

In effect, the Polish laws had placed foreign direct investment beyond the realm of government regulation. Foreigners were free to engage in any business they desired, as long as they paid their taxes and brought hard currency with them. But still there were problems. Outside the government, many Poles were adamantly opposed to foreign investment, seeing it as just another form of foreign control over Poland's economic development. As of 1991, the opposition was relatively quiet, since even the most vehement opponents of investment recognized the country's desperate need for capital. If foreign investment grew too large however, or if it was seen as contributing in any way to the country's economic woes, then the critics would undoubtedly become louder, and bring their discontent directly into the political process.

Alima S.A.

The Alima food processing plant was located in a small Polish town that bore a certain resemblance to Gerber's headquarters in Fremont. Like Fremont, Rzeszow was an agricultural center, surrounded by thousands of farmers whose families had been selling fruits and vegetables to Alima for two or three generations. As was the case in most of Poland, the plots around Rzeszow had never been successfully collectivized, and thus their farmers tended to be more independent and financially better off than

---

[11] Under these laws, however, the investors were significantly constrained both in the scale of their operations and in their potential profitability. They were not eligible, for instance, for credit at any Polish banks; they had to make an advance deposit of 30% of their projects cost to a Polish bank; and they were allowed to transfer 50% of their export profits out of the country. Under these conditions, only nine major firms chose to invest in Poland during the six years those regulations were in place.

[12] This section draws heavily on Debora Spar, "Foreign Direct Investment in Eastern Europe," in Keohane, Nye and Hoffmann, eds., *After the Cold War*, pp. 286–309.

the rest of the population. The farmers were also technologically quite advanced, since they benefitted from an extensive system of university support for agriculture.[13] The crops around Rzeszow were not exactly what Gerber would want to use in the future—the apples were too tart and the carrots not right for baby food—but as long as the plant had a good relationship with the farmers, which seemed to be the case, Gerber believed it could work with the farmers to ensure that the right changes were made.

Physically, the Alima plant bore the strong imprint of centralized planning. It was an odd amalgamation of facilities and businesses lumped together by planners who had simply assigned them to the Alima site. Thus Alima produced everything from pickled beets to pureed raspberries. Baby food accounted for only about 10% of its total production, while 60% was composed of various fruit juices and nectars sold domestically under the "Bobo" label. The remainder of the plant's production was a random and varying mix of whatever the farmers had grown that year. In addition, Alima's facilities included a set of apartment complexes and a separate enterprise, Borek Stary, which specialized in the production of liquored peaches and "fortified" (alcoholic) fruit beverages.

Technically, Alima was rather up-to-date. While some of its equipment dated from the 1920s, the baby food lines contained state of the art machinery imported from Italy in 1985. The lines lacked some key parts and were not perfectly aligned, but they still produced 300 to 400 jars of baby food per minute. This was far below Gerber's rate of 1,300 jars per minute, but still quite acceptable. Alima also had a stable source of high-quality glass jars, a crucial input for any baby food manufacturer. Located just 50 miles down the road, the Jaroslaw glassworks had supplied Alima for decades. Jaroslaw was well-run, technically proficient, and unusually fuel efficient, since it produced 50% of its fuel from a local gas well. Like most of Poland's state-owned enterprises, Jaroslaw was in transition and slotted to be sold as part of the government's privatization program. Until the sale took place, however, the plant would continue to provide Alima with glass jars.

Alima's final asset was its manager, Maria Potocka-Bielecka. Potocka-Bielecka had been chosen by a national search for the Alima position and knew her business well. By all accounts, she was extremely intelligent, flexible, and adept at heading off worker strikes.

Despite Potocka-Bielecka's skills, though, business at Alima still operated haphazardly. No one paid much attention to accounting procedures or financial reports, and orders were placed on an ad hoc basis: if raspberries had been delivered in the previous year, then Alima would order and process raspberries again, even if there was no demand for the fruit. Similarly, the plant had no sales force. It simply waited for requests to come by phone or during Poland's quarterly food processing fair. It never marketed its production in any way since Poland's "economy of shortage" had always meant that buyers would take whatever was available.

Though awkward by Western standards, this system had served Alima well.

---

[13]In the words of one Gerber official, the farmers of Rzeszow "have the book on the shelf and actually use it."

With $20 million in sales, Alima was one of the most successful enterprises in Poland. It employed 1,200 people, bought produce from thousands of farmers and produced one of Poland's most popular beverages. The question, though, was whether Alima could survive the transition to capitalism, and whether Western capitalists could ever make Alima worth their efforts.

Evaluation and Assessment

For Gerber, the evaluation process began in May of 1991, only days after Schomer had received the first phone call from Wasserstein Perella. In order to compete for Alima, Gerber had to meet the government's deadline for entering bids. That gave the company's executives two weeks to investigate everything from politics to radiation poisoning.

Right from the start, the Gerber team saw the logistical difficulties of doing business in Poland. First, Wasserstein Perella had never closed a deal in Poland. While they had done some previous work in Central Europe, this acquisition involved new issues and a very new territory. Second, few law firms were suitable to represent Gerber's interests. The Polish firms that Steve Clark interviewed did not really understand Western style practices or the legal language that Gerber and its advisors would rely upon. And Gerber's lawyers in the United States were completely unfamiliar with Poland's changing investment laws. Finally, Gerber settled on the London office of Skadden, Arps, Meagher & Flom since they were representing the Polish government in several deals and at least knew the government officials.

In the meantime, teams of Gerber specialists flew to Poland to check into plant and environmental conditions. At Alima, they were mostly pleased with what they saw. Gerber's engineers found that while the plant lacked some technical expertise, it was basically sound. They confirmed that the equipment was in good repair and of top quality. As expected, they also reported that the plant had too much equipment and a number of auxiliary operations that would have to be jettisoned. The engineers also investigated the glassworks at Jaroslaw and judged it to be adequate for meeting Alima's short-term needs. Once the manufacturing process at Alima was brought up to Western speeds, the glass would have to be stronger, but until then Jaroslaw would be fine.

On the environmental front, Gerber's first priority was to ensure that the soil around Rzeszow had not been in any way contaminated by fallout from the 1987 disaster at Chernobyl. And on this score, they were lucky: after extensive sampling, consultants from the World Health Organization confirmed that the soil was completely clean. Simultaneously, however, Gerber's own engineers uncovered a number of potential environmental problems. First, the farmers were using too many pesticides for Gerber to accept their produce as "pure and natural." Second, the solid waste disposal system at the Alima plant was faulty and would need at least $3 million worth of repairs. And third, Alima's management permitted some practices—such as smoking on the production line—that simply violated existing EC and U.S. regulations. Still, Gerber's engineers did not consider these problems insurmountable. They would cost money and take time, but they could be solved.

A more troubling issue was how to evaluate the broader context of the Alima deal. Gerber's management knew that Poland was changing, but they had little sense of how specific changes might occur and what impact they could have on a Western investor. To learn more, Gerber's managers consulted with a number of academic specialists. They inquired into Poland's history, its culture, and its experience under communist rule. No one, of course, could predict how Poland would emerge from this period of transition, but the academics pointed out several trends and practices that gave Gerber reason for optimism. First, unlike some of its neighbors in Central Europe, Poland had a tradition of commercial life that extended back to the Middle Ages. Even under communism, the Poles had retained a certain spirit of free enterprise. Polish farmers had never been collectivized and Polish laborers went on strike far more frequently than their counterparts in other countries of the Soviet bloc. Second, most Poles had always detested the communist regime that was thrust upon them after World War II. They always saw it as a foreign intrusion and thus had never developed an indigenous ideology or a hard-core band of devotees. Thus, no matter how badly the economy deteriorated during the transition to a free market, it was unlikely that the Poles would choose to return to communism.

Finally, the academics underlined the importance of Poland's bid to enter the European Community. With 1992 fast approaching, most Poles wanted desperately to join the common market and register their status as full-fledged Europeans. Realistically, of course, membership in the EC was still many years away. But the desire to conform to European standards would act as a powerful constraint on the Poles, forcing them to acquiesce whenever possible to existing norms.

Forecast and Conclusions

While Schomer, Clark, and others from the Gerber team were interviewing the experts and visiting the Alima site at Rzeszow, Martin Lasher was back in Fremont trying to piece all the data together. As Director of Corporate Planning, Lasher's job was to evaluate the overall prospects of the Alima deal, and to recommend how much—if anything—Gerber should pay for this acquisition.

To arrive at this calculation, Lasher in conjunction with Wasserstein Perella constructed a basic capital budget model and tried to estimate the relevant variables as closely as possible (see **Exhibit 11**). In some cases, Lasher was able to derive his numbers from the usual sources. He projected revenues on the basis of current sales of Bobo fruit. Gerber expected to have sales of baby food in Poland and France, and future exports to Central and Eastern European markets. He based labor costs on existing wages plus expected inflation and used prevailing international prices to figure the cost of key inputs such as jars, caps, and labels. In all of these calculations Lasher was conservative, basing his assumptions on a worst case scenario.

Input prices, however, were the easy part. Lasher's real challenge lay in fore-casting broader variables such as interest rates, inflation rates, and any tax credit that the government might allow under current conditions in Poland. These economic factors were liable to swing quickly and significantly, even over a short period. Unlike the financial variables, moreover, these factors were also particularly vulnerable to any shift in government policy. If popular pressures mounted against Balcerowicz's program of economic reform, for example, the government might be forced to reinstitute price controls or revalue the zloty. If foreign investors came under particular attack, the government might try to revoke any special privileges it had bestowed upon Gerber.

Thus, on all fronts, the Alima deal faced tremendous uncertainties. But somehow Marty Lasher had to convert these uncertainties into numbers and plug them into his model. So, as conservatively as he could, he guessed. The existing assets at Alima were valuable, but the other warehouses filled with old equipment were useless to Gerber and would have to be scrapped. Lasher then gathered current and predicted sales information, reduced the numbers, and then put them into his model. He assumed that the devaluation of the zloty would roughly keep pace with the inflation rate, and that both would stabilize over the next five years, eventually reaching levels similar to those of Spain, another agrarian-based European economy. He also assumed that Gerber would price its exports in foreign currencies, borrow locally to meet its Polish capital requirements, and export its profits in the form of quarterly dividends. Finally, he assumed that the Polish government would give Gerber a significant tax credit during the first few years of its investment. With these assumptions in place, Lasher ran the model repeatedly, tinkering with the various numbers and running sensitivity analyses on the key political and economic variables. Each time the project produced a robust internal rate of return and a positive net present value. Barring political or economic catastrophes, Alima seemed like a very good deal.

On the basis of these calculations, Gerber entered its bid. It offered to purchase 60% of Alima's stock for an up-front purchase price of $11 million, and then to spend another $14 million over the next three to five years in reengineering the existing facility and upgrading its waste disposal system. The Gerber officials knew that their total capital commitment of $25 million was somewhat less than the Polish government had hoped for. But, combined with their technological expertise and their position in the industry, they thought it was a reasonable offer.

Anatomy of a Deal

Luckily for Gerber, the Ministry of Privatization also agreed that theirs was a reasonable offer and selected the company from among its 19 competitors. After Gerber's bid was accepted, negotiations began in earnest.

The government was clear in laying out its own objectives. It wanted to ensure that it got a reasonable selling price for Alima and a guaranteed level of future investment. It also wanted guarantees that Gerber would not immediately reduce employment at the Alima plant and that it would continue to purchase fruits and vegetables from its current suppliers. The government also wanted to make certain that the workers at Alima received some means by which to participate in the management of their new venture.

The Gerber negotiators accepted these demands unconditionally. They agreed to keep all employees for at least 18 months and to allow the Ministry of Privatization to reserve 40% of the new enterprise's stock for sale to Alima's employees and suppliers. Informally, Gerber also told the government that they intended to give the employees a considerable raise at the time of purchase and establish programs to teach these people how the stock market operated. As the negotiations progressed, Gerber made the stock option even more attractive by promising to subsidize purchases made by their new employees and to match up to certain levels the money employees spent for shares on a one-for-one basis.

Thus the government and Gerber amicably settled the core issues of the Alima deal. But still there were differences. Three points in particular became Gerber's grounds for negotiations:

The Borek Stary facility.   The Gerber officials expressly did not want this facility since its production of alcoholic beverages would not sit well with the company's predominant image as a "pure and natural" baby food manufacturer. In addition, Gerber's engineers had uncovered some environmental problems at the plant that were potentially quite complicated and expensive. If Gerber took possession of the plant even briefly, it risked being held responsible for any capital improvements that had to be made, including any environmental clean up. In an effort to avoid this additional burden, Gerber had requested that the Polish government sell Borek Stary independently. The government consented, and committed itself to the sale of Borek Stary under the terms of the October 1 Purchase and Sale agreement. Soon after the agreement was signed, however, it became clear that the government would not fulfill this commitment. The problem, it seemed, was that the people with whom Gerber was negotiating simply did not have the power to do as they had promised. They were not in a position to negotiate a separate deal for Borek Stary, and they had no authority over the *wojwewoda*, the local authority entrusted to handle these matters.

Property rights.   A broader and even riskier source of contention concerned the status of property rights at the Alima facility. Formally, of course, the land and the plant belonged to the state, and thus to the Ministry of Privatization that had been entrusted with its sale. Potentially, though, the land could be claimed by any of the thousands of people whose ancestors had farmed it sometime during Poland's past. One of the likeliest claimants, moreover, was a Catholic church that sat right beside the Alima plant and had historically owned a swath of land that ran directly through the middle of the facility.

For months Clark and the legal staff at Fremont had pored over maps of the property, trying to figure out who the claimants were and where their various slices of the property were located. Eventually, they decided not to wrestle with the ownership issue directly and to settle instead for a 99-year lease. Still, they were concerned that any lease signed with the federal government could be contested and even invalidated at the regional level, especially if the *wojwewodas* began to draw power away from the center.

Again, though, the Gerber team agreed to sign the Purchase and Sale agreement before the issue of ownership was completely resolved. It trusted that the Ministry officials would soon be able to secure the lease and protect it from any competing claims or regional interference.

Taxation.   For Gerber, the most important unresolved issue was taxation. According to the numbers generated by Marty Lasher's model, Alima's total long term return depended significantly on the taxes it paid. If Gerber were granted the kind of tax credit that the Polish government had initially offered to foreign investors, it would enhance the potential return of the Alima deal. Thus the Gerber team was determined to secure a favorable tax break. Specifically, they wanted the Polish government to grant them a dollar-for-dollar exemption for all capital invested in the country over a three-year period. The government officials balked at these terms but eventually agreed. In the letter of intent, however, the specifics of the tax credit were left open. Negotiators agreed to work out the financial details as quickly and as amicably as they could.

Gerber's Choice

Gerber's plans were derailed, however, by the political events that unfolded in October. For several weeks after the elections, policymaking effectively came to a halt in Poland as the new deputies scrambled to form a government and assemble a cabinet. Work in the ministries ground to a halt as bureaucrats waited for their instructions and newly appointed officials groped to learn the outline of their responsibilities. None of this boded well for Gerber, since it still needed the government officials to iron out the critical details of the Alima deal.

The Polish media, meanwhile, was making matters even worse. Emboldened by the nationalist bent of the elections, many of Warsaw's 70 papers were targeting foreigners as the source of Poland's economic problems. Because the Alima deal was so big, and because the enterprise was already quite successful, the press attacked Gerber with a particular vengeance. Critics charged that the Ministry of Privatization had blundered the deal, that the government was "giving away a crown jewel," and that Gerber intended to fire the workers, close the Alima facility, and import its own products from the United States. The charges were false, but in the political turmoil that surrounded the elections, the Gerber officials had no chance to refute them.

More importantly, the Gerber team also no longer had any relationship with high-ranking members of the Polish government or the Ministry of Privatization. All Gerber knew was that the new government was more conservative than its predecessor, it was under tremendous public pressure not to sell Poland's assets to foreigners, and that it had already considered abrogating the Alima deal entirely.

And thus Schomer and Clark were back in the Warsaw Marriott, reviewing the deal and wondering what to do with it. On the one hand, the Gerber officials felt that any Polish government would want to comply with normal contract laws and honor their contractual commitments. As long as Poland intended to move closer to the European Community it behooved the government to adhere as closely as possible to the norms of Western business. On the other hand, though, Schomer and Clark felt certain that political pressures in Poland would force the government to renegotiate the Alima deal and revoke the specific guarantees of nonexpropriation and repatriation that the previous government had extended. If the government went any further, slowing economic reform or introducing price controls, Gerber's acquisition of Alima could quickly become a financial disaster. In addition, the turmoil that surrounded the deal made it increasingly unlikely that the Polish government would find a buyer for Borek Stary, clarify the remaining issues of ownership, or grant the type of tax credit that Gerber had requested. Finally, inflation was also beginning to rise again in Poland and the government's deficit was mounting.

By the same token, Schomer and Clark still felt that the fundamentals of their deal were sound. The plant was good, the price was reasonable, and if Gerber walked away they risked losing their potentially lucrative markets of Central Europe to one of their traditional competitors. With flat birth rates in their core U.S. market and strong competition in Western Europe and Canada, Gerber's management clearly wanted to establish the company in Central Europe. But now they had to decide if the rewards of investment in Poland were worth the risk.

EXHIBIT 1   Gerber Products Company and Subsidiaries—Consolidated Balance Sheet, 1990–1991 (thousands of nominal dollars)

	1990	1991
ASSETS		
Current Assets:		
Cash and cash equivalents	$ 32,097	$ 99,195
Short-term investments	19,941	29,892
Trade accounts receivable, less allowances	110,355	120,960
Inventories:		
Finished products	101,140	116,465
Work-in-process	37,835	30,691
Raw materials and supplies	59,428	44,667
Current assets of discontinued operations	2,574	
Total Current Assets	$363,370	$441,870
Other Assets:		
Investments held by insurance operations	$ 57,325	$ 66,794
Deferred policy acquisition costs	33,578	38,790
Prepaid pension costs	37,046	44,161
Miscellaneous other assets	22,405	31,891
Intangible assets, less accumulated amortization		
of $4,744	7,653	
Land, Buildings, and Equipment:		
Land	4,036	4,148
Buildings	88,670	89,133
Machinery and equipment	220,525	234,285
Construction in progress	19,278	21,502
Allowances for depreciation	(140,714)	(145,238)
Fixed assets of discontinued operations (net)	41,561	
Total Assets	$754,733	$827,336
LIABILITIES AND SHAREHOLDERS' EQUITY		
Current Liabilties:		
Short-term borrowings	$ 7,032	$ 475
Trade accounts payable	59,868	56,770
Salaries, wages, and other compensation	36,634	43,992
Local taxes, interest, and other expenses	51,863	58,302
Income taxes	10,460	20,567
Policy claims and reserves	7,343	10,884
Current liabilities of discontinued operations	8,656	
Current maturities of long-term debt	424	1,117
Total Current Liabilities	$182,280	$192,107
Long-term debt	146,221	164,491
Deferred income taxes	26,941	20,507
Future policy benefits	47,486	55,674

(continued)

EXHIBIT 1 Gerber Products Company and Subsidiaries—Consolidated Balance Sheet, 1990–1991 (thousands of nominal dollars) (*Continued*)

	1990	1991
LIABILITIES AND SHAREHOLDERS' EQUITY (*CONTINUED*)		
Current Liabilties:		
Shareholders' equity:		
Common stock, par value $2.50 a share—		
authorized 200M shares: (1992—37,196,959		
shares, 1991—37,392,560 shares)	104,134	93,481
Paid-in capital	6,390	5,382
Retained earnings	377,768	322,121
Foreign currency translation	(2,190)	(3,598)
Unearned stock comp.	(269)	(3,115)
Unearned ESOP compensation	(20,300)	(19,714)
Cost of common stock in treasury:		
(1990—3,956,768 shares)	(113,728)	
Total	$754,733	$827,336

Source: *Gerber Annual Report*, 1991, pp. 24–25.

EXHIBIT 2   Gerber Products Company and Subsidiaries—
Consolidated Statement of Operations (thousands of nominal dollars)

	1990	1991
Net sales and revenue	$1,136,436	$1,178,942
Interest, royalties, and other income	14,366	24,264
Total income	$1,150,802	$1,203,206
Deductions from income:		
Cost of products sold, services provided	$ 678,216	$ 691,527
Marketing, distribution, administrative		
and general expenses	285,223	291,786
Restructuring charges	16,500	19,000
Interest expense	16,487	17,543
Total deductions	$ 996,426	$1,019,856
Earnings from continuing		
operations before income taxes	$ 154,376	$ 183,350
Income taxes	59,822	70,532
Loss from discontinued operations	(479)	
Net earnings	**$ 94,075**	**$ 112,818**
Net earnings per share	**2.49**	**3.00**

Source: *Gerber Annual Report*, 1991, p. 23.

EXHIBIT 3   Poland—National Income Accounts, 1985–1990 (billions of 1987 zlotys)

	1985	1986	1987	1988	1989	1990
Gross domestic product	15,803	16,585	16,940	17,626	17,675	15,630
Government consumption	1,560	1,508	1,516	1,445	1,056	1,160
Private consumption	9,752	10,137	10,157	10,063	9,145	8,431
Gross fixed capital formation	3,370	3,631	3,821	3,964	2,891	2,982
Increase in stocks	1,034	1,159	1,063	1,781	3,911	1,769
Exports	2,898	3,019	3,625	4,013	3,372	4,024
Imports	−2,672	−2,784	−3,218	−3,530	−2,630	−2,749

Source: IMF, *International Financial Statistics Yearbook*, 1992, p. 581; World Bank, 1992, p. 493.
Figures may not add due to rounding.

EXHIBIT 4   Poland—Balance of Payments, 1985–1990 (millions of 1985 $US)

	1985	1986	1987	1988	1989	1990
A. Current Account						
Exports (fob)	10,945	11,612.5	11,3454.3	12,587.3	11,200.2	13,241.6
Imports (fob)	10,599	11,157.7	10,600.0	11,597.3	11,159.3	10,240.8
Trade Balance	347	454.7	745.3	990	40.9	3,000.8
Services, credit	2,104	1,962.0	2,090.6	2,247.3	2,785.9	2,675.6
Services, debit	1,846	1,959.1	1,913.2	2,185.5	2,657.1	2,380.4
Services, net	258	2.9	177.4	61.8	128.8	295.2
Interest and dividends, credit	173	183.1	204.7	246.4	356.8	504.2
Interest and dividends, debit	2,730	2,785.8	2,954.7	2,932.7	3,153.2	3,335.3
Interest and dividends, net	−2,557	−2,602.7	−2,750	−2,686.4	−2,796.3	−2,831.1
Private transfers	970	1,068.2	1,469.8	1,537.3	1,323.8	1,844.5
Official transfers					76.6	255.1
Transfers, net	970	1,068.2	1,469.8	1,537.3	1,400.3	2,099.5
Current account balance	**−982**	**−1,076.9**	**−357.5**	**−97.2**	**−1,226.2**	**2,564.4**
B. Direct Investment	14	−5.8	3.4	−6.4	−6.1	74.4
C. Other Capital						
Resident official sector	−827	−799.4	−2,229.3	−423.6	−1,019.2	5,418.1
Deposit money banks	−797	−2,887.1	469.8	−1,851.8	−426.5	−2,880.4
Other sectors	134	21.4	−250.9	−398.2	−111.4	−5.8
D. Errors and Omissions	118	771.8	85.8	−242.7	−95.7	111.2
E. Reserves and Related Items						
Change in reserves	236	168.5	−751.8	−510	−225.4	−2,021.7
Exceptional financing	2,104	3,867.6	3,030.2	3,511.8	3,110.5	−3,685.6
Use of fund credit and loans						425.6

Source: IMF, *International Financial Statistics Yearbook*, 1992, p. 581.

EXHIBIT 5   Prices, Production, and Employment, 1985–1991 (1985 = 100)

	1985	1986	1987	1988	1989	1990	1991
Producer prices	100	117	149	238	745	5,385	7,976
Consumer prices	100	117	147	236	828	5,684	9,680
Wages:							
Average nominal earnings	100	121	147	270	1,035	4,817	7,696
Industrial production	100	104	107	112	111	82	69
Industrial employment	100	100	99	98	95	83	83

Source: IMF, *International Financial Statistics Yearbook*, 1992, p. 581.

EXHIBIT 6   Monthly Inflation
and Exchange Rates

Year and Month	CPI Inflation	Nominal Exchange Rate (zloty/$)[a]
89:1	11.1	505.8
89:2	7.9	525.9
89:3	8.1	566.9
89:4	8.9	631.3
89:5	7.2	746.2
89:6	6.1	848.7
89:7	9.5	836.2
89:8	39.5	988
89:9	34.4	1339.5
89:10	54.8	1970.3
89:11	22.4	3076.7
89:12	17.7	5235.5
90:1	79.6	9500
90:2	23.8	9500
90:3	4.3	9500
90:4	7.5	9500
90:5	4.6	9500
90:6	3.4	9500
90:7	3.6	9500
90:8	1.8	9500
90:9	4.6	9500
90:10	5.7	9500
90:11	4.9	9500
90:12	5.9	9500
91:1	12.7	9500
91:2	6.7	9500
91:3	4.5	9500
91:4	2.7	9500
91:5	4.9	10290
91:6	.1	11498
91:7	.6	11523
91:8	4.3	11301
91:9	4.3	11039
91:10	3.2	11222
91:11	3.2	11224
91:12	3.1	10967
92:1	7.5	11483

Source: Data from the Polish Central Statistical Office.

[a]The zloty was declared convertible on January 1, 1990 and was fixed until May 17, 1991, at which time it began following a crawling peg.

Shock Treatment
Consumer price
% incease on previous month

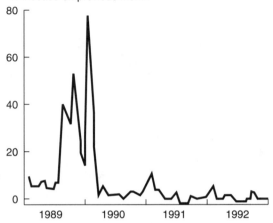

EXHIBIT 7   Poland—Consumer Prices, 1989–1992
Source: *The Economist*, January 23, 1993, p. 21.

Convalescing
Industrial production
January 1989=100

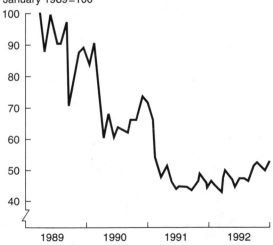

EXHIBIT 8   Poland—Industrial Production,
1989–1992
Source: *The Economist*, January 23, 1993, p. 21.

EXHIBIT 9   Poland—Percent Share of the Private Sector, 1989–1991

	1989	1990	1991
GDP	29	31	42
Employment, incl. private agriculture	44	46	51
Employment, excl. private agriculture	22	23	27
Exports	—	5	22
Imports	—	14	50
Investment	35	42	41
Industrial production	16	18	24
Construction	33	32	55
Commerce	60	64	83
Transport	12	14	24

Source: *The Economist*, January 23, 1993, 22.

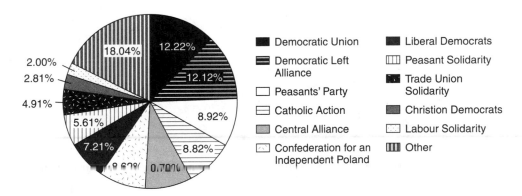

EXHIBIT 10   The Lower House of the Sejm, November 1991

Source: "How many Polish parties does it take to make a cabinet?", *The Economist*, November 2, 1991, p. 43.

EXHIBIT 11 Gerber's Capital Budgeting Model: Volume, Price, and Revenue Forecast

	1992	1993	1994	1995	1996	1997	1998	1999	2000	2001
Volume:										
Bobo nectar business (dozens mn's)										
Domestic	8.0	8.0	8.0	8.0	8.0	8.0	8.0	8.0	8.0	8.0
Export	0.0	0.0	0.0	0.0	0.0	0.0	0.0	0.0	0.0	0.0
Gerber jar business (dozens mn's)										
Domestic	0.0	1.2	1.8	2.4	3.0	3.6	4.2	4.8	5.4	6.0
Export	0.0	5.0	7.0	9.0	11.0	13.0	15.0	17.0	17.0	17.0
Industrial products (tons 000's)										
Domestic	0.0	0.0	0.0	0.0	0.0	0.0	0.0	0.0	0.0	0.0
Export	10.0	13.8	17.51	21.3	25.0	28.8	32.5	36.3	40.0	43.8
Total Bobo & Gerber jar volume (dozens mn's)										
Domestic	8.0	9.2	9.8	10.4	11.0	11.6	12.2	12.8	13.4	14.0
Export	0.0	5.0	7.0	9.0	11.0	13.0	15.0	17.0	17.0	17.0
Prices:										
Bobo nectar business ($/dozen)										
Domestic	$1.91	$1.91	$1.91	$1.91	$1.91	$1.91	$1.91	$1.91	$1.91	$1.91
Export	0.00	0.00	0.00	0.00	0.00	0.00	0.00	0.00	0.00	0.00
Gerber jar business ($/dozen)										
Domestic	2.56	2.56	2.56	2.56	2.56	2.56	2.56	2.56	2.56	2.56
Export	2.12	2.12	2.12	2.12	2.12	2.12	2.12	2.12	2.12	2.12
Industrial products ($/ton)										
Domestic	0.00	0.00	0.00	0.00	0.00	0.00	0.00	0.00	0.00	0.00
Export	400.00	400.00	400.00	400.00	400.00	400.00	400.00	400.00	400.00	400.00
Total Revenues ($ MN's):										
Bobo nectar business										
Domestic	$15.3	$15.3	$15.3	$15.3	$15.3	$15.3	$15.3	$15.3	$15.3	$15.3
Export	0.0	0.0	0.0	0.0	0.0	0.0	0.0	0.0	0.0	0.0
Gerber jar business										
Domestic	0.0	3.1	4.6	6.1	7.7	9.2	10.8	12.3	13.8	15.4
Export	0.0	10.6	14.9	19.1	23.3	27.6	31.8	36.1	36.1	36.1
Industrial products										
Domestic	0.0	0.0	0.0	0.0	0.0	0.0	0.0	0.0	0.0	0.0
Export	4.0	5.5	7.0	8.5	10.0	11.5	13.0	14.5	16.0	17.5
Total Revenues	$19.3	$34.5	$41.8	$49.0	$56.3	$63.6	$70.9	$78.1	$81.2	$84.2

EXHIBIT 11 Gerber's Capital Budgeting Model: Volume, Price, and Revenue Forecast (*Continued*)

	1992	1993	1994	1995	1996	1997	1998	1999	2000	2001
Variable Costs ($ dozen):										
Bobo nectar business										
Ingredients	$0.36	$0.36	$0.36	$0.36	$0.36	$0.36	$0.36	$0.36	$0.36	$0.36
Jars/containers	0.45	0.45	0.45	0.45	0.45	0.45	0.45	0.45	0.45	0.45
Lid/caps	0.05	0.05	0.05	0.05	0.05	0.05	0.05	0.05	0.05	0.05
Cases_overwrap	0.06	0.06	0.06	0.06	0.06	0.06	0.06	0.06	0.06	0.06
Labels	0.06	0.06	0.06	0.06	0.06	0.06	0.06	0.06	0.06	0.06
Direct manufacturing overhead	0.08	0.08	0.08	0.08	0.08	0.08	0.08	0.08	0.08	0.08
Total Bobo Nectar Variable Costs (dz. jars)	$1.05	$1.05	$1.05	$1.05	$1.05	$1.05	$1.05	$1.05	$1.05	$1.05
Gerber jar business										
Ingredients	$0.28	$0.28	$0.28	$0.28	$0.28	$0.28	$0.28	$0.28	$0.28	$0.28
Jars/containers	0.65	0.65	0.65	0.65	0.65	0.65	0.65	0.65	0.65	0.65
Lid/caps	0.33	0.33	0.33	0.33	0.33	0.33	0.33	0.33	0.33	0.33
Cases_overwrap	0.06	0.06	0.06	0.06	0.06	0.06	0.06	0.06	0.06	0.06
Labels	0.06	0.06	0.06	0.06	0.06	0.06	0.06	0.06	0.06	0.06
Direct manufacturing overhead	0.08	0.08	0.08	0.08	0.08	0.08	0.08	0.08	0.08	0.08
Total Gerber Variable Costs (dz. jars)	$1.46	$1.46	$1.46	$1.46	$1.46	$1.46	$1.46	$1.46	$1.46	$1.46
Total Variable Costs ($MN's):										
Bobo nectar business										
Ingredients	$2.9	$2.9	$2.9	$2.9	$2.9	$2.9	$2.9	$2.9	$2.9	$2.9
Jars/containers	3.6	3.6	3.6	3.6	3.6	3.6	3.6	3.6	3.6	3.6
Lid/caps	0.4	0.4	0.4	0.4	0.4	0.4	0.4	0.4	0.4	0.4
Cases	0.5	0.5	0.5	0.5	0.5	0.5	0.5	0.5	0.5	0.5
Labels	0.5	0.5	0.5	0.5	0.5	0.5	0.5	0.5	0.5	0.5
Direct manufacturing overhead	0.6	0.6	0.6	0.6	0.6	0.6	0.6	0.6	0.6	0.6
Bobo Nectar Variable Costs	$8.4	$8.4	$8.4	$8.4	$8.4	$8.4	$8.4	$8.4	$8.4	$8.4
Gerber jar business										
Ingredients	$0.0	$1.7	$2.4	$3.2	$3.9	$4.6	$5.3	$6.1	$6.2	$6.4
Jars/containers	0.0	4.0	5.7	7.4	9.1	10.8	12.5	14.2	14.6	15.0
Lid/caps	0.0	2.1	2.9	3.8	4.7	5.5	6.4	7.3	7.5	7.7
Cases	0.0	0.4	0.5	0.7	0.8	10.0	1.1	1.3	1.3	1.4
Labels	0.0	0.4	0.5	0.7	0.8	10.0	1.1	1.3	1.3	1.4
Direct manufacturing overhead	0.0	0.5	0.7	0.9	1.1	1.3	1.5	1.8	1.8	1.9
Gerber Jar Variable Costs	$0.0	$9.1	$12.9	$16.7	$20.5	$24.3	$28.1	$31.9	$32.7	$ 33.0
Industrial variable costs (assume _0% margin)	3.6	5.0	6.3	7.7	9.0	10.4	11.7	13.1	14.4	15.8
Total Variable Costs	$12.0	$22.4	$27.6	$32.7	$37.9	$43.0	$48.2	$53.3	$55.6	$57.8

287

Xerox and Fuji Xerox

We are committed to strengthening the strategic and functional coordination of Xerox and Fuji Xerox so that we will compete effectively against strong and unified global competitors.

—Paul Allaire, President and CEO of Xerox Corporation
—Yotaro Kobayashi, President and CEO of Fuji Xerox

Fuji Xerox, the joint venture between Xerox and Fuji Photo Film, was at a pivotal point in its 28-year history in 1990. Many considered it the most successful joint venture in history between an American and a Japanese company. Originally a sales organization for Xerox products in Japan, Fuji Xerox had evolved into a fully integrated operation with strong research, development, and manufacturing capabilities. As its sales and capabilities evolved, so did its importance within the Xerox Group: its 1989 revenues of $3.6 billion represented 22% of the Xerox Group's worldwide revenue.[1] Furthermore, Fuji Xerox supplied the rest of the Xerox Group with low- to mid-range copiers. In Japan, the home country of Xerox's major competitors, Fuji Xerox held 22% of the installed base of copiers and 30% of revenues in the industry.

Yotaro "Tony" Kobayashi, Fuji Xerox's president and CEO, ascribed a good deal of the company's success to the autonomy that the joint venture had enjoyed

Research Associate Krista McQuade and Professor Benjamin Gomes-Casseres prepared this case as the basis for class discussion rather than to illustrate either effective or ineffective handling of an administrative situation.

[1] The Xerox Corporation (XC) is referred to in this case simply as Xerox. The combination of Rank Xerox (RX), Fuji Xerox (FX), and the xerox Corporation is referred to as the Xerox Group. The revenues of Rank Xerox were consolidated into those of Xerox Corporation, but Fuji Xerox revenues were not. As described below, Xerox Corporation received 66% of RX earnings, which in turn included half of FX earnings.

from the beginning. Fuji Xerox was not "the norm" for joint ventures, he contended, adding that "the degree to which Xerox let us run was very unusual." Yet, paradoxically, as the company grew to represent a larger portion of Xerox's worldwide business (**Exhibit 1**), this situation seemed to be changing. "We have to begin to pay more attention to what our actions mean to Xerox," explained Kobayashi.

Paul Allaire, Xerox's president and CEO, added that Fuji Xerox's autonomy had been an important factor not only in its own success, but also in its growing contribution to the Xerox Group:

> The fact that we had this strong company in Japan was of extraordinary importance when other Japanese companies started coming after us. Fuji Xerox was able to see them coming earlier, and understood their development and manufacturing techniques.

> We have excellent relationships with Fuji Xerox at the research, development, manufacturing, and managerial levels. Yet, because of this close relationship, there is a greater potential for conflict. If Fuji Xerox were within our organization, it would be easier, but then we would lose certain benefits. They have always had a reasonable amount of autonomy. I can't take that away from them, and I wouldn't want to.

Over the years, Fuji Xerox saw its local competitors grow rapidly through exports. The terms of its technology licensing agreements with Xerox, however, limited Fuji Xerox's sales to Japan and certain Far Eastern territories. As Canon, in particular, grew to challenge Xerox worldwide in low-end copiers, laser printers, and color copiers, Fuji Xerox began to feel constrained by the relationship. "Fuji Xerox has aspirations to be a global company in marketing, manufacturing, and research," explained Jeff Kennard, who had managed the relationship between Xerox and Fuji Xerox since 1977. Kobayashi elaborated:

> The goals of Xerox and Fuji Xerox can be described as mostly compatible and partly conflicting. There *are* serious issues facing us. We often compare our situation with that of Canon or Ricoh, companies that have a single management organization in Japan. Are we as efficient and effective in the worldwide management of our business as we could be?

> Some of Fuji Xerox's products, such as facsimile machines, are managed like Canon's—with single-point design and manufacturing. But now there are external conditions in the United States and Europe that call for local manufacturing and development. Rank Xerox and Xerox are able to reach efficient volumes in their marketplaces. If Fuji Xerox manufactures only for Japan and adjacent markets, our volume will be too small, but Xerox is insisting on this. It is a tough challenge that we have to face together.

How should Fuji Xerox's aspirations be managed within the context of the Xerox Group? This was one of the questions facing the Codestiny Task Force commissioned in 1989 to review the capabilities and goals of Xerox and Fuji Xerox. Composed of senior managers from both companies, the task force would seek ways to enhance the strategic relationship between Xerox and Fuji Xerox for the 1990s. This was the third such review; Codestiny I (1982) and Codestiny II (1984) had both resulted in changes in contracts and agreements between the firms. With the basic technology licensing contract between Xerox and Fuji Xerox due to be renegotiated in 1993, participants in Codestiny III knew that their analysis could well lead to a substantial restructuring of the strategic relationship between the companies.

Xerox's International Expansion

When Chester Carlson tried to sell the rights to the revolutionary xerographic technology that he invented in 1938, GE, IBM, RCA, and Kodak all turned him down. Instead, the Haloid Corporation—a small photographic paper firm in Rochester, NY—agreed in 1946 to fund further research, and 10 years later acquired the full rights to the technology. By the time the company introduced its legendary 914 copier in 1959, xerographic products had come to dominate its business; in 1961 Haloid's name was changed to Xerox Corporation. The 914 was the world's first automatic plain paper copier (PPC), and produced high-quality copies four times faster than any other copier on the market. These advantages, coupled with an innovative machine rental scheme, led Xerox to dominate the industry for nearly 20 years. Company revenues rose from $40 million in 1960 to nearly $549 million in 1965, and to $1.2 billion in 1968, breaking the American record for the fastest company to reach $1 billion in sales. Net income grew from $2.6 million in 1960 to $129 million in 1968. In a mere decade, the name Xerox had become synonymous with copying.

Xerox moved quickly to establish an international network. Lacking the funds to expand alone, it formed a 50/50 joint venture in 1956 with the Rank Organization of Britain. Xerox would be entitled to about 66% of the profits of Rank Xerox. Rank operated a lucrative motion picture business and was seeking opportunities for diversification. Rank Xerox (RX), the new joint venture, was to manufacture xerographic products developed by Xerox and market them exclusively worldwide, except in the United States and Canada. By the early 1960s, Rank Xerox had established subsidiaries in Mexico, Italy, Germany, France, and Australia. In 1964, Xerox bought back the right to market xerographic products in the Western Hemisphere.

Japanese firms immediately inquired about obtaining xerography licenses from Rank Xerox, but they were refused on the grounds that the technology was not commercially mature. By 1958, however, RX executives had turned their sights to the Japanese market. Aware of Japanese government regulations that required foreign firms to sell through local licensees or joint ventures, they sought a strong partner. Twenty-seven Japanese firms jockeyed for the position; Fuji Photo Film (FPF) was the only nonelectronics firm in this group. Still, the company was chosen, partly because of the personal relationship and trust that had developed between RX President Thomas Law and FPF Chairman Setsutaro Kobayashi.

Fuji Photo Film was a manufacturer of photographic film since the early 1930s and second only to Kodak in that field. The company was trying to diversify its business away from silver-based photography, and was convinced that its technical expertise was well suited to the requirements of xerography. Under the direction of Nobuo Shono, the company had already begun experimenting with xerography; by 1958, it had invested six million yen in research and manufacturing facilities for the copiers that it hoped to license from Rank Xerox. As negotiations between the two companies intensified, Rank Xerox insisted on a joint venture instead of simply a license to Fuji Photo Film.

The Establishment of Fuji Xerox

Fuji Xerox, the 50/50 joint venture established by Fuji Photo Film and Rank Xerox in 1962, was originally intended to be a marketing organization to sell xerographic products manufactured by Fuji Photo Film. When the Japanese government refused to approve a joint venture intended solely as a sales company, however, the agreement was revised to give Fuji Xerox manufacturing rights. Fuji Xerox—not Fuji Photo Film—then became the contracting party with Rank Xerox, and received exclusive rights to xerographic patents in Japan. Fuji Xerox, in turn, subcontracted Fuji Photo Film to manufacture the products. As part of its technology licensing agreements with Rank Xerox, Fuji Xerox had exclusive rights to sell the machines in Japan, Indonesia, South Korea, the Philippines, Taiwan, Thailand, and Indochina. In return, Fuji Xerox would pay Rank Xerox a royalty of 5% on revenues from the sale of xerographic products. Rank Xerox would also be entitled to 50% of Fuji Xerox's profits.

Nobuo Shono became Fuji Xerox's first senior managing director, and Setsutaro Kobayashi, its president. Shono and Kobayashi drew their core executive staff, later known as the "Seven Samurai," from the ranks of Fuji Photo Film. A board of directors consisting of representatives from Rank Xerox and Fuji Photo Film was established to decide policy matters, while day-to-day operations were left to the Japanese management. The Xerox Corporation itself was to have no direct relationship with Fuji Xerox, and would participate in the profits of the joint venture only through its share in Rank Xerox.

Although Fuji Xerox adopted a number of business practices from Xerox, including organizational structure and the rental system, it remained distinctly Japanese throughout its history. Hideki Kaihatsu, managing director and chief staff officer at Fuji Xerox, explained:

> Employees are typically rotated through many functions before rising to the level of general management, and compensation and lifetime employment practices are similar to those of other Japanese firms. We emphasize long-term planning, teamwork, and we follow bottom-up decision making, including the "ringi" system. Furthermore, in procuring parts we follow the Japanese practice of qualifying a small group of vendors and working closely with them.

The Development of Fuji Xerox's Capabilities

Well before negotiations for the joint venture were finalized, engineers at Fuji Photo Film geared up for the production of Xerox copiers. Xerox machines were disassembled and studied to determine the equipment and supplies necessary for production. Three FPF engineers spent two months touring Xerox and Rank Xerox production facilities. At the establishment of the joint venture, a specific schedule was agreed upon, calling first for the sale of imported machines, then the assembly of imported knocked-down kits, and finally the domestic production of copiers. Import restrictions in Japan and government pressure to source locally accelerated this schedule, and the first Japanese-produced Xerox 914 was completed in September 1962; by 1965, 90% of the parts for the 914 came from local suppliers.

Fuji Xerox's first sales plan targeted financial institutions, large manufacturing corporations, and central government agencies. At the time of the introduction of the 914, 85% of the market was held by the inexpensive diazo type of copier. Although these copiers were difficult to operate and produced poor quality copies, they had been enormously successful in Japan, as the large number of characters in the Japanese language made typewriters difficult to use, and made copiers essential even for small offices. Ricoh, Copyer, and Mita had sold diazo copiers since the 1940s. By the early 1960s, Ricoh held an estimated 75% share of the market. A diazo copy was often referred to as a "Ricopy" in Japan.

Though Fuji Xerox had intended to sell the 914 copier outright, at Rank Xerox's insistence it implemented Xerox's trademark rental system. Within a year, the back-order list for the copier was five months' long. Output rose fivefold in five years, and Fuji Photo Film soon built a second production facility. In 1967, Fuji Xerox's sales passed those of Rank Xerox's French and German subsidiaries. Fuji Xerox's product line expanded to include other models, including a faster version of the 914, and a smaller, desktop model. The 2400, capable of making 40 copies per minute (cpm),[2] was introduced in 1967. Sales subsidiaries were established throughout Fuji Xerox's licensed territory.

By the late 1960s, Fuji Xerox dominated the high-volume segment of the Japanese copier market. Ricoh, however, had made great inroads into the middle segment with an electrostatic copier based on an RCA technology, and was squeezing Fuji Xerox's market from below. In addition to the threat of substitute technologies, Fuji Xerox faced the end of its monopoly in plain paper copying; some of Xerox's core patents were scheduled to expire between 1968 and 1973. FX managers were already aware of efforts by several Japanese firms to develop plain paper copiers. In response to these pressures, Peter McColough, Xerox's president and CEO at the time, pro-

---

[2]The copier market was typically divided into low-, mid-, and high-volume segments. In the 1960s, the 2400 was considered a high-volume model; the original 914 copier made seven copies per minute. In the 1980s, copiers making less than 25 cpm were generally considered low-volume, while those making over 90 cpm were considered high-volume.

posed to transfer the manufacture of copiers from Fuji Photo Film to Fuji Xerox, and in this way combine manufacturing and marketing activities under one roof. Mc-Colough described the rationale for this decision:

> Fuji Xerox had to develop its own manufacturing capability. It had built up a good marketing organization, but had no assured source of supply. That left the company vulnerable. Fuji Photo Film initially resisted this idea because it would lose manufacturing volume and product revenues. They realized in the end that the issue went to the heart of the joint venture. Looking back, that was the most difficult period in our relationship.

In 1971, Fuji Photo Film transferred its copier plants to Fuji Xerox. That same year, Fuji Xerox completed the construction of a 160,000 square-foot manufacturing and engineering facility. From then on, Fuji Photo Film had little direct role in Fuji Xerox's operations. Yoichi Ogawa, senior managing director at Fuji Xerox in 1989 and one of the Seven Samurai, explained why Fuji Photo Film remained a passive partner after 1971:

> According to Fuji Photo Film's agreement with Xerox, the company, as a shareholder, could collect information from Fuji Xerox, but it could not use it in its own operations. In addition, a technology agreement between Fuji Xerox and Xerox provided that any technology acquired by Fuji Xerox from outside sources (including from Fuji Photo Film) could be freely passed on to Xerox.

In a separate development, Rank Xerox also lost much of its direct role in Fuji Xerox's operations. In December 1969, Xerox bought an additional 1% share of Rank Xerox from the Rank Organization, giving it 51% control of that joint venture. From then on, Rank Xerox would be managed as a Xerox subsidiary. Moto Sakamoto, an FX resident at Rank Xerox at the time, noticed an immediate change: "Things changed instantly as the Americans started coming in . . . gone was the old British style of management." Sakamoto was transferred to Xerox's main facility in Rochester, NY, as Fuji Xerox began to deal directly with Xerox. Rank Xerox's ownership share in Fuji Xerox remained at 50%, and the Xerox Corporation continued to receive 66% of Rank Xerox's profits, and therefore 33% of Fuji Xerox's.

Product Development at Fuji Xerox

The transfer of production facilities to Fuji Xerox and the direct relationship established between Fuji Xerox and Xerox contributed to a continued strengthening of FX technical capabilities. Fuji Photo Film engineers had already been making modifications to Xerox designs in order to adapt the copiers to the local market; Japanese offices, for example, used different sized paper than American offices. Nobuo Shono, however, advocated the development of long-term R&D capabilities that would enable the company to develop its own products. In particular, he envisioned a high-performance, inexpensive, compact machine that could copy books. At the time, Xerox's priorities were different. Tony Kobayashi explained:

> We had been insisting that the Xerox Group needed to develop small copiers as an integral part of its worldwide strategy. However, Xerox's attitude was that the low end of the market was not a priority. . . . On the other hand, we were seeing rising demand for small copiers in Japan.[3]

Shono's development group produced four experimental copiers, each with projected manufacturing costs approximately half those of Xerox's smallest machine. When they first heard of the effort, engineers at Rank Xerox and Xerox doubted that these models could become commercially viable. Shono persisted, and in 1970 took a working prototype to London, where its performance amazed Rank Xerox executives. The machine was slow (5 cpm), but substantially smaller and lighter than comparable Xerox models. This demonstration immediately boosted Fuji Xerox's technical reputation within the Xerox Group, and for the first time Xerox allowed Fuji Xerox a small budget for R&D. In 1973, the FX2200—the world's smallest copier—was introduced in Japan with the slogan: "It's small, but it's a Xerox." The speed of the FX2200 was doubled in 1977 by the FX2202, and the basic model was improved further by the FX2300 and the FX2305.

Mushrooming Competition

The FX2200 appeared just in time to face an avalanche of new and serious competition. Canon was the first Japanese company to enter the plain paper copier market, introducing its low end "New Process" copiers in 1970; these machines were developed in-house and did not infringe on any Xerox patent. Ricoh and Konica, Fuji Photo Film's chief Japanese rivals in film, followed with their own technologies. In 1972, Canon made another major move by introducing copiers using liquid instead of dry toner. This technology was later licensed to Saxon, Ricoh, and Copyer. Liquid-toner copiers had the advantage of being smaller and less expensive to manufacture than dry-toner copiers like Xerox's, but they were cumbersome to use. They were introduced as a cheap alternative to Xerox dry copiers. Minolta, Copia, Mita, Sharp, and Toshiba also entered the plain paper copier industry; by 1975, eleven companies competed in the Japanese market.

In addition to developing small machines for its local market, Fuji Xerox tried to stem the competitive onslaught with more aggressive sales strategies. The company began to offer two- and three-year rental contracts as well as its standard one-year contract, and provided price incentives that were tied to contract length. It also began to offer three of its new low-priced copiers for outright sale, as the competition

---

[3]Quoted in "Fuji Xerox Company, Ltd." Translation of a case study prepared by the Nomura School of Advanced Management in Tokyo.

had been doing. Matazo Terada, one of the Seven Samurai, recalled that when the company tried to sell copiers before, Xerox management resisted:

> Xerox insisted on uniform policies—every country had to be managed like the U.S. firm. That was successful only while we were protected from competitors because of our monopoly. If Xerox had been more flexible from the beginning, we might have captured a larger market. That was a lost opportunity.

By 1977, Ricoh accounted for 34% of the number of copiers installed in Japan. Fuji Xerox followed with 25%, Canon with 15%, and Konica with 10%. In terms of copy volume, however, Fuji Xerox led the competition with more than 50% of the market, followed by Ricoh with 20%, and Canon and Konica with 10% each. In the low end of the market, Ricoh accounted for 50% of copy volume, compared to 10% for Fuji Xerox.

Fuji Xerox's TQC Movement

Partly as a response to the new competition of the 1970s, as well as the oil shock and recession of 1973–1975, Fuji Xerox launched a Total Quality Control (TQC) program. Fuji Photo Film had operated a successful statistical quality control program, and in 1956 won the prestigious Deming Prize, awarded to companies that had shown outstanding quality management throughout their organization. Fuji Xerox's New Xerox Movement had three primary aims: to speed up the development of products that matched customer needs; to reduce costs and eliminate waste; and to adopt aggressively the latest technologies.

The focal point of the campaign was the development of "dantotsu," roughly translated as the "Absolute No. 1 Product." Company executives challenged the marketing and engineering departments to develop a product fitting this description in less time and at a lower cost than the competition. For six months, project proposals were turned down until the basic concept for the new product emerged in 1976: a compact, 40 cpm machine manufactured for half the price of any comparable machine, with half the number of parts of previous models, and developed in two years, compared to Xerox's typical four. Setsutaro's son, Tony Kobayashi, who became FX president in 1978 after his father died, explained:

> This was the first time Fuji Xerox had developed a copier based on our own design concept. The FX2200 copier we previously developed was an improved adaptation of a model developed in the United States. The American system of development was well established in our company. However, the U.S. way of developing new products on a step-by-step basis was too time consuming for our dynamic environment. The competition in the Japanese market required us to study the development systems of our rivals. . . . We found that we had been spending too much time in development. That is why we formulated the design concept for

the new model and committed the entire company's resources to its development within a very limited timetable.[4]

The FX3500 was indeed introduced two years later, and by 1979, it had broken the Japanese record for the number of copiers sold in one year. Ricoh and Canon rushed to develop copiers that could compete in the FX3500's market segment. Largely because of Fuji Xerox's effort to develop the FX3500, the company won the Deming Prize in 1980. In addition, the FX3500 firmly established Fuji Xerox as a technologically competent member of the Xerox Group. David Kearns, who would become Xerox's president in 1977, was amazed when he first saw a demonstration of the FX3500 prototype, and spontaneously broke out in applause.

Later, some observers labeled the FX3500 Fuji Xerox's "declaration of independence." The FX3500 project came after Xerox canceled a series of low- to mid-volume copiers on which Fuji Xerox was depending. Code-named SAM, Moses, Mohawk, Elf, Peter, Paul, and Mary, they were each canceled in mid-development, even though Fuji Xerox had gaps in its product range in the Japanese market. Jeff Kennard remembered that when Tony Kobayashi was told about the cancellation of Moses, he was also asked to stop work on the FX3500 project. "Tony refused," Kennard recalled, adding that Kobayashi said, in effect, "As long as I am responsible for the survival of this company, I can no longer be totally dependent on you for developing products. We are going to have to develop our own."

Xerox's Lost Decade

During the 1970s, competition in the U.S. and European copier markets changed radically. Prior to that period, Xerox had had a virtual monopoly because of its xerography patents. But beginning in 1970, one competitor after another entered the industry, often with new and improved PPC technologies. The Xerox Group share of worldwide PPC revenues fell from 93% in 1971 to 60% in 1975, and 40% in 1985 (**Exhibit 2**). This was Xerox's "lost decade"—an era of increasing competition, stagnating product development, and costly litigation.

New Competition High and Low

The proliferation of PPC vendors that started in Japan in the early 1970s soon appeared in the United States and Europe. By 1975, approximately 20 PPC manufacturers operated worldwide, including reprographic companies (Xerox, Ricoh, Mita, Copyer, A. B. Dick, AM, and 3M), paper companies (Dennison, Nashua, and Saxon),

---

[4]Quoted in "Fuji Xerox Company, Ltd."

office equipment companies (IBM, SCM, Litton, and Pitney Bowes), photographic equipment companies (Canon, Konica, Kodak, and Minolta), and consumer electronics companies (Sharp and Toshiba).

Canon's New Process copiers were the first to hit the U.S. market, followed by a wave of liquid-toner copiers. The new Japanese machines were priced aggressively, and sold outright through independent dealers. On average, these machines broke down half as often as Xerox copiers. Canon sold under its own brand name, taking advantage of its reputation for quality photographic products, and supported its dealers through extensive financing, and sales and service training. Ricoh sold its machines through Savin Business Machines and the Nashua Corporation. Savin, primarily a marketing company, had funded the Stanford Research Institute's development of a liquid-toner copier, and subsequently had licensed Ricoh to manufacture the machines. The first Ricoh machines using this new technology were introduced in 1975 and were an instant success. Konica, Toshiba, Sharp, and Minolta, entered the U.S. market through OEM relationships, as well as with their own brands.

Despite the entrance of so many Japanese competitors into the U.S. market, Xerox initially did little to respond to them. These competitors targeted the low end of the market, leaving Xerox's most important segments seemingly unaffected. Furthermore, Xerox continued to dominate the world copier market, with revenues that rose each year by more than Savin's total copier sales. Xerox executives were more concerned by the entrance of IBM and Eastman Kodak into the copier industry, as these companies targeted the mid- and high-volume segments. (See **Exhibit 3.**)

IBM's introduction of its Copier I in 1970 signaled the end of Xerox's monopoly in its home market. Although IBM's first model was not successful because of a combination of high price and performance problems, the Copier II, introduced in 1972, began to take market share away from Xerox. These machines were marketed by IBM's office products sales force on a rental basis, supported by heavy advertising. IBM introduced the Copier II in Europe and Japan in 1975, and by 1976 had installed 80,000 copiers worldwide, against Xerox's estimated 926,000. IBM's high-volume Copier III came out in 1976, but was withdrawn because of reliability problems. It was reintroduced as a mid-volume machine early in 1978, but IBM's copier business suffered permanently from the setback.

Eastman Kodak's main facilities were located across town from Xerox's in Rochester, NY. Kodak's success as a high-technology, chemistry-based, American firm had been a model for Xerox's founders and early leaders. When Kodak introduced the high-end Ektaprint 100 copier in 1975, however, admiration quickly turned to intense rivalry. Unlike the IBM Copier I, Kodak's first machine was extremely innovative. In particular, it featured a microcomputer that monitored the performance of the copier and alerted operators to problems through a digital display. A central computer at Kodak monitored the trouble signals and dispatched service people to a machine before breakdown. The machines were also capable of excellent reproduction. The Ektaprint series was well accepted in the marketplace, and quickly gained a reputation for the highest-quality image reproduction in the field.

Xerox's Stagnation

In its first competitive actions against IBM, Kodak, and the Japanese entrants, Xerox could not come up with a winning strategy. It focused R&D on developing a super high-speed copier and field-tested its first color copier in 1971; neither became a commercial success. Xerox's mid-volume 4000 and 3100 series, introduced in the early 1970s, suffered from reliability problems and were also commercial failures. Even when the price of the 3100 was slashed from $12,000 to $4,400, it did not sell well. Ricoh/Savin became the top seller in the U.S. market in 1976, and Xerox's market share in the United States continued to fall. However, the seriousness of Xerox's situation was slow to sink in, according to David Kearns:

> . . . we dominated the industry we had created. We were convinced that we were providing the world with high-quality machines, and our convictions were reinforced by the broad acceptance of Xerox products by our customers. We had always been successful, and we assumed that we would continue to be successful. Our success was so overwhelming that we became complacent.[5]

About 1978, Fuji Xerox offered to sell its FX2202 copier to Xerox and Rank Xerox to help them counter Japanese competition in the United States and Europe. Rank Xerox purchased 25,000 of the machines, but Xerox Corporation refused to buy any.[6] Bill Glavin, the managing director at Rank Xerox at that time, noted:

> We had never placed such a large order before and expected to sell them in 12 months. Two thousand machines per month was an incredible rate of sales, but we did it. For Tony Kobayashi, that order must have represented a substantial part of his production that year. We worked closely with them, and they gave us top-notch support.

This first successful cooperation led Rank Xerox to import more of the FX machines. In addition, Kodak had delayed its entry into Europe by two years, giving Rank Xerox time to formulate a defensive marketing strategy for the high end. As for IBM, its excellent distribution network and reputation in Europe could not make up for a generally inferior product. As Wayland Hicks, the general manager of Rank Xerox's U.K. operating company in the late 1970s, noted, "If IBM had Kodak's product, Xerox would have been dead." Rank Xerox was able to defend its market share while Xerox's U.S. share continued to decline.

In 1979, largely because of Rank Xerox's success with the FX product, Xerox began to import the FX2202, and later the FX2300 and the FX2350. Typically, in the year that the products were introduced in the U.S. market, the machines were assem-

---

[5]David T. Kearns, "Leadership Through Quality," *Academy of Management Executive,* vol. 4 (1990): 86–89.

[6]Although Xerox had acquired equity control of Rank Xerox in 1969, the line operations of the two firms were not integrated until 1978. Rank Xerox could thus make this decision in relative autonomy.

bled by Fuji Xerox before export. Then, acceding to union demands in the United States, Fuji Xerox exported them as knock-down units to be assembled at Xerox. "Some of our people had been reluctant to import FX machines," recalled Peter Mc-Colough. "Our engineers felt that they had developed xerography, and that the first FX machines weren't good enough."

Courtroom Battles

Xerox became involved in the 1970s in a series of courtroom battles. Immediately after IBM came out with its Copier I in 1970, Xerox sued for patent infringement, and IBM countersued. The companies argued 12 separate counts in the United States and Canada. Xerox won some of these suits and the rest were settled in 1978, when the firms agreed to an exchange of patents covering all information-handling products and to a $25 million payment to Xerox. Two other American firms, the SCM Corporation and Van Dyk Research, sued Xerox for alleged antitrust violations in 1973 and 1975, respectively, each claiming $1.5 billion in damages. Both lost their suits in 1978–1979.

More damaging still, the Federal Trade Commission (FTC) initiated action against Xerox in 1973, charging that the firm controlled 95% of the plain paper copier industry, and that its pricing, leasing, and patent-licensing practices violated the Sherman Antitrust Act. The FTC demanded that Xerox offer unrestricted, royalty-free licenses on all its copier patents, that it divest itself of Rank Xerox and Fuji Xerox, and that it allow third parties to service, maintain, and repair copiers leased from Xerox. In 1975, Xerox settled out of court by signing a consent decree with the FTC, in which it agreed to license more than 1,700 past and future patents for a period of 10 years. Competitors were permitted to license up to three patents free of royalties, to pay 0.5% of revenues on the next three, and to license additional patents royalty free. Xerox also agreed to forgive past patent infringements, to cease offering package-pricing plans on machines and supplies, and to begin outright sales of machines.

Kodak, IBM, Canon, Ricoh, and other Japanese firms were among the firms to secure Xerox licenses under this arrangement. At this point, the Japanese firms that had entered the market with liquid-toner copiers switched to Xerox's dry-toner process.

Adjusting the Relationship between Xerox and Fuji Xerox

As Fuji Xerox's business grew and Xerox's came under increasing pressure at home, the relationship between the two companies changed. The original joint venture and technology assistance agreements of the early 1960s were updated in 1976 and in 1983, and numerous interim agreements were signed to adjust policies on such issues as procurement and relations to third parties (**Exhibit 4**). Bob Meredith, a lawyer by training and Xerox's resident director in Tokyo, described the role of these contracts:

The legal contracts are flexible. We don't follow an adversarial, arm's-length approach, where you might try to gain short-term advantage or act opportunistically. The equity commitment focuses our relationship on one main objective: What is the profit-maximizing thing to do?

Technology agreements and other contracts between Xerox and Fuji Xerox provided guidelines for the relationship. In addition, the contracts specified royalties and transfer pricing procedures. In 1976, a Technology Assistance Contract (TAC) had been signed by Xerox and Fuji Xerox, which maintained the 5% royalty that Xerox received from Fuji Xerox's xerographic sales, and that was to last 10 years. During the Codestiny I discussions, however, the royalty structure of the contract was revised. The 1983 TAA established a basic royalty on Fuji Xerox's total sales, representing Fuji Xerox's right to use the Xerox tradename and technology in its licensed territory. The royalty on xerographic sales, however, was set to decline annually between 1983 and 1993. In addition, for the first time Fuji Xerox would begin receiving a manufacturing license fee (MLF), designed to compensate it for its development and manufacturing investments. In particular, an MLF of up to 20% could be added to the unit costs of FX machines exported in knocked-down form and assembled and sold by Xerox.

These and other subtle changes in the relationship between the two firms tended to reinforce Fuji Xerox's autonomy. David Kearns recalled how he worked to "unfetter" Fuji Xerox in the late 1970s:

Xerox was attempting to control so many aspects of Fuji Xerox's operations. We were reviewing their marketing strategies, what products they were going to develop, and so on. But it didn't make sense to me to try to run the business from thousands of miles away. So, I encouraged them to pursue their own strategies and develop their own products. Of course, they were moving in that direction anyway.

Turning Around Xerox

In 1979, Xerox began to formalize a strategy based on the reality of its declining position in the copier industry. Kearns recalled the initial shock of the necessity to do so:

The Japanese were selling products in the United States for what it cost us to *make* them. We were losing market share rapidly, but didn't have the cost structure to do anything about it. I was not sure if Xerox would make it out of the 1980s.

One of Xerox's strategies was to diversify out of copiers by acquiring a number of financial services companies between 1983 and 1988. Financial services, Kearns believed, would provide "an anchor in a nonmanufacturing business, and one in which Japanese companies were not active overseas." Before the financial services industry went sour at the end of the decade, this line of business was a steady source of earnings for Xerox, providing more than $2 billion in profits in five years. In 1989, however, financial services' earnings declined significantly and substantial assets were written off.

Kearns also began to take a closer look at the strategies of Fuji Xerox and other Japanese companies. Upon importing the first FX products, Xerox engineers had been amazed by a reject rate for parts that was a mere fraction of the American rate, and by substantially lower manufacturing costs. Visits to FX facilities introduced Xerox executives to the practice of "benchmarking," or systematically tracking costs and performance in all areas of operations against those of the best in the field. The findings from Xerox's own benchmarking efforts helped fuel Kearns's efforts to infuse his organization with new vision and determination.

In 1981, Kearns announced a companywide initiative for "business effectiveness," and two years later formally launched Xerox's Leadership Through Quality program. Xerox's program was based on the experience of Fuji Xerox, and throughout the effort, Kearns called upon Kobayashi and others at Fuji Xerox for help. Xerox hired Japanese consultants recommended by Fuji Xerox, and some 200 high-level Xerox and Rank Xerox managers visited Fuji Xerox in later years to learn first-hand about its TQC management and philosophy. The Leadership Through Quality program emphasized high employee involvement in attaining five major goals: (1) increased market research and competitive benchmarking; (2) just-in-time manufacturing to decrease costs; (3) faster product development; (4) development of state-of-the-art technology; and (5) a devotion to quality in all areas.

The rallying point for Xerox's quality movement was the development of the 10 Series, a new family of copiers. Wayland Hicks, in charge of this development effort, stated: "The Xerox turnaround started on September 22, 1982, at the announcement of the 1075 in New York." Led by this mid-volume machine, the 10 Series became the most successful line of copiers in Xerox history, and served to restore the company's finances and morale. The series—dubbed the "Marathon" family of copiers—represented a new generation of machines aimed primarily at the mid-volume segment of the market. Altogether, some fourteen models were introduced between 1982 and 1986, six of which were still sold in 1990. Fuji Xerox designed and produced the low end models in the 10 Series—the 1020, 1035, and the 1055, the latter drawing on basic technologies developed for the FX3500. The 1075 became the first American-made product to win Japan's Grand Prize for Good Design. Because at that time Xerox's Japanese competitors were not strong in mid-volume copiers, the 10 Series forestalled their move into that segment of the market and helped Xerox win back market share. The company regained 2–3 percentage points in 1983, and 12 points in 1984. By the end of 1985, more than 750,000 10 Series machines had been rented or sold, accounting for nearly 38% of Xerox's worldwide installed base.

Throughout the 1980s, Xerox continued to change the way it did business. For example, over 100,000 employees went through three days of off-site training to unite the entire organization behind the quality effort. The program achieved significant improvements in Xerox operations. After reducing its supplier base, the company reduced its purchased parts' costs by 45% and their quality was improved dramatically. Xerox's average manufacturing costs were reduced by 20% and the time-to-market for new products was cut by 60%. Xerox's progress was recognized by the U.S. Commerce Department in 1989, when the company's Business Products and Systems division received the Malcolm Baldrige National Quality Award for its "preeminent quality leadership." (Xerox's 1980s financial results are in **Exhibit 5**.)

Xerox and Fuji Xerox in the 1990s

The Canon Challenge

A number of factors were expected to continue to draw Fuji Xerox and Xerox closer to each other in the 1990s. One was the continuously rising capabilities of the Xerox Group's competitors, particularly Canon. While Xerox's precipitous decline in the 1970s had been stemmed and many of the competitors from that decade had faded away, Canon's copier business continued to expand. From 1980 to 1989, Canon's total sales grew from $2.9 billion to $9.4 billion, a growth rate of 14% per year. Canon's R&D spending grew even more rapidly at 24% per year, from $77 million to $525 million. By 1989, Canon was no longer primarily a camera company—40% of its revenues came from copiers, and 20% from laser printers.

In the second half of the 1980s, Canon developed a dominating presence in the low end laser printers that were becoming ubiquitous companions to microcomputers. Laser printing technology was closely related to plain paper copying technology, and as digital copying systems were introduced, the importance of laser printing in the PPC market was bound to increase. Canon's laser printing engines were the core of the highly successful Hewlett-Packard Laserprinter series, which accounted for about 50% of laser printer sales in the United States. This OEM business was thought to yield Canon some $1 billion in revenues. In the rest of the world, Canon sold printers under its own brand name.

In copiers, Canon was strong in the low end of the market, and had recently developed a growing business in color copiers, where it held 50% of the market by 1989. Analysts pointed out that Canon was introducing twice as many products as the Xerox Group, although it spent less than $600 million on R&D annually, compared to Xerox's $800 million and Fuji Xerox's $300 million. Canon's goal was to become a $70 billion company by the year 2000, implying a 22% annual growth rate in the 1990s. A significant portion of this growth was projected to come from Xerox's heartland—high- and mid-volume copiers and printers.

Xerox, however, was determined to be aggressive in its response. Hicks, who in 1989 had become the executive vice president for worldwide marketing at Xerox, hung a framed blow-up of a 1984 *Fortune* article on Canon in his office. It was entitled "And Then We Will Attack;" below it Hicks hung a sign that read: "And Then They Will Lose."

   Xerox Group strategists saw the relationship between Xerox and Fuji Xerox as a critical element in competing worldwide against Canon. Canon had a strong presence in all major world markets, as did the Xerox companies (**Exhibit 6**). But Xerox CEO Paul Allaire highlighted a major difference in the two firms' global networks: "When we negotiate with Fuji Xerox, we can't just represent ourselves. We need to find what is fair and equitable to essentially three partners. Canon is 100% owned by one company."

The Fuji Xerox Challenge

Another trend drawing Fuji Xerox and Xerox closer was the growth of Fuji Xerox itself (**Exhibit 7**). Fuji Xerox's dollar revenues grew faster than Xerox's in the 1980s, and represented a more significant portion of the Xerox Group's worldwide revenues than it had previously. Fuji Xerox's financial contribution to Xerox's net earnings in the form of royalties and profits had also grown sharply—from 5% in 1981 to 22% in 1988. And throughout the decade, Fuji Xerox had been an important source of low-end copiers for Xerox. Between 1980 and 1988, Fuji Xerox's sales to Xerox and Rank Xerox grew from $32 million to $620 million (**Exhibit 8**). "Fuji Xerox is a critical asset of Xerox," concluded Allaire.

   Fuji Xerox developed its technological capabilities further in the 1980s, investing heavily in R&D (**Exhibit 9**). While it continued to rely on Xerox for basic research on new technologies, by the late 1980s very few of the models sold by Fuji Xerox in Japan had been designed by Xerox (**Exhibit 10**). For the most part, they were high-end models, working at speeds of above 120 cpm. Heavy investment by Fuji Xerox during the late 1980s had produced many low-end models, and even a few in the 60–90 cpm range. Many of these were exported to or manufactured by Xerox and Rank Xerox. In 1980, 70% of the low-volume units sold by Xerox and Rank Xerox were of their own design, and 30% were of Fuji Xerox design; by 1987, 94% were of Fuji Xerox design. Even in 1989, however, all of Xerox and Rank Xerox's mid- and high-volume copiers were of their own design.

   All these factors led Fuji Xerox and Xerox to intensify their cooperation on research, product development, manufacturing, and planning in the 1980s. Bill Glavin and Jeff Kennard worked together to launch "strategy summits." Glavin described why:

> We needed the senior management of research, engineering, manufacturing, and planning from both companies to come together, and begin discussing the issues that affected them jointly. The talks included people from all product lines—copiers, printers, and systems. We tried to agree on common strategies and allocate who should do what.

   These top management summits were held about twice a year during the 1980s, and led to further meetings between the functional organizations on each side. Fuji Xerox's organization mirrored Xerox's: a corporate research group did basic and applied research; machines were designed and built by the development and manufacturing organization; and products were sold and serviced by the marketing organization. Collaboration between Xerox and Fuji Xerox seemed to be most successful in research, and harder to implement in development and manufacturing; there was no coordination at all between marketing groups, as each had a different licensed territory. Of course, there was some tendency to protect traditional turfs. "On both sides you cannot totally dismiss the NIH syndrome," commented Tony Kobayashi. "It is another form of parochialism." Still, where the incentives for collaboration were high, the companies launched joint projects, agreeing on who would take "lead" and "support" roles and eliminating overlapping activities. Bill Spencer, Xerox vice president of technology at the time, described the rationale behind one of these joint research projects:

> It is an attempt to combine American ingenuity with the manufacturing skills of the Japanese. Xerox has excellent basic research and software capabilities, and Fuji Xerox is good at development and hardware design. Together, we should be able to develop better products quicker than alone.

The functional collaboration between the companies was reinforced by exchanges of personnel and by an evolving communication process. Since the 1970s, personnel from Fuji Xerox had spent time as residents at Xerox, and engineers from both companies had frequently crossed the Pacific to provide on-the-spot assistance. These personnel exchanges had, in fact, been an important channel for the transfer of technology from Xerox to Fuji Xerox. By 1989, an estimated 1000 young, high-potential FX employees had spent three years each as residents at Xerox, and some 150 Xerox people had done this at Fuji Xerox. These residents were directly involved in the work of their host companies. Every year there were also some 1000 shorter visits by engineers and managers. These exchanges and the summit meetings contributed to a constructive relationship. "Whenever a problem came up, we established a process to manage it," explained Jeff Kennard. "The trust built up between the companies has been a key factor in the success of this relationship. It enables one to take on short-term costs in the interest of long-term gains for the group."

By the mid-1980s, most Xerox managers also had mixed feelings of challenge and admiration toward Fuji Xerox, which were echoed by Kennard:

> It seems that every time Xerox blinks and retracts, Fuji Xerox forges ahead. Fuji Xerox continues to be the agent for change. They have great corporate vision and they target what is strategically important. Then they take tough decisions and make the needed investment.

The Management Challenge

In this context, Allaire and Kobayashi commissioned the Codestiny III Task Force, charging it with developing a framework for cooperation between the two companies in the 1990s. The task force consisted of top planners in each company and was to report to the two CEOs within a year of its formation. Roger Levien, Xerox's vice president for strategy and head of the Codestiny III talks, described the motivation for the project:

> Fuji Xerox had certain issues they wanted to discuss, and we agreed to do so in the Codestiny process. One of their desires was to get the worldwide market for the low end. They also wanted to develop a more symmetric relationship with us. We wanted to spell everything out, identify all of the alternatives, and leave the final decision to top management.

One of the issues to be addressed by the Codestiny team was Fuji Xerox's aspirations to expand its markets in Asia. Under the existing technology licensing contracts, Fuji Xerox had the right to sell in Indonesia, South Korea, the Philippines, Taiwan, and Thailand (total GDP in 1989: $570 billion), and it had indeed established sales subsidiaries in each of these markets. But Rank Xerox in London was responsible for managing sales in what it called the South Pacific Operations—Australia (1989 GDP: $280 billion), New Zealand ($45 billion), Singapore ($28 billion), Malaysia ($37 billion), China ($420 billion), and Hong Kong ($63 billion). Since the early 1980s, Fuji Xerox had argued that this arrangement led to inefficiencies in serving the South Pacific markets. At that time, knock-down kits were sometimes shipped from Fuji Xerox to Britain for assembly, and then shipped back to Asia for sale. Furthermore, Rank Xerox followed a very different marketing strategy in these markets than Fuji Xerox did in its neighboring Asian markets. Rank Xerox emphasized high profit margins and sales of high-end machines, whereas Fuji Xerox put greater emphasis on market share and low-end products. As a result, when Fuji Xerox urged Rank Xerox in the late 1970s to adopt a more aggressive sales strategy in Australia before Canon entered that market, Rank Xerox refused. Although Rank Xerox managed the South Pacific countries out of a regional office in Hong Kong, Fuji Xerox's sales subsidiaries were usually joint ventures with local partners, and so drew more on local management talent.

Another key issue for the Codestiny team was how the Xerox Group should manage the low-end laser printer business in the United States. This market segment was receiving renewed attention in 1989, following the appointment of Bill Lowe as Xerox's executive vice president for development and manufacturing. Lowe came to Xerox from IBM, where he had been in charge of the personal computer business. Soon after arriving at Xerox, he began to focus on the problems in the low-end copier and printer businesses, where Fuji Xerox typically developed and manufactured products sold by Xerox.

> Both companies were trying to get full profit out of it, even though the margins were slim. Fuji Xerox's policy was to mark up costs; Xerox's was to get an acceptable gross profit. Furthermore, each product had a different mark-up scheme, and many sideline deals confounded the issues. This fostered sharp dealings between the partners. So, most of our energy was focussed on each other, not on Canon. We were pointing fingers and frustrating ourselves.

The Codestiny team analyzed these specific issues within a broad framework, and began by outlining the various options available for cooperation in marketing, research, and development and manufacturing (**Exhibit 11**). The team considered the advantages and disadvantages of each of these options and began to develop possible strategies for the South Pacific Operations and for the low-end printer business in the United States.

But there was much more at stake than decisions in these two areas. The central question facing Xerox and Fuji Xerox was: How should the relationship between the two companies be structured and managed in the new global environment of the 1990s?

Xerox and Fuji Xerox Revenues

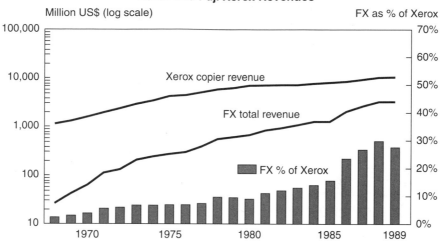

Xerox and Fuji Xerox Earnings

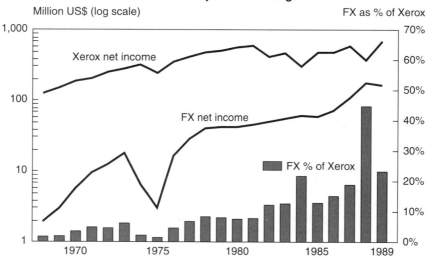

EXHIBIT 1 Growth of Xerox Corporation and Fuji Xerox, 1968–1989

Source: Xerox and Fuji Xerox annual reports.

Notes: Top: The Xerox revenues shown include Rank Xerox but not Fuji Xerox.
Bottom: Xerox earnings include 33% of FX earnings.

EXHIBIT 2   Copier Sales of Leading Vendors Worldwide,
1975–1985 (in millions of US$)

	1975	1980	1985
Xerox Group	$3,967	$7,409	$8,903
U.S. and Americas	2,340	3,866	4,770
Rank Xerox	1,350	2,856	2,400
Fuji Xerox	277	687	1,733
Canon	87	732	2,178
Ricoh	290	1,092	1,926
Kodak	1	300	900
IBM	310	680	700
Minolta	25	387	743
3M	380	575	400
Oce	178	680	600
Savin	52	430	448
Konishiroku	85	302	470
Nashua	155	401	278
Agfa	115	268	200
Pitney Bowes	52	129	204
A.B. Dick	35	55	60
Saxon	56	127	20
AM International	59	23	10
Other Japanese	155	1,220	2,846
Other	596	792	1,115
Total	**$6,598**	**$15,602**	**$22,001**
Shares of Leading Firms in World Total			
Xerox Group	60%	47%	40%
Americas	35	25	22
Rank Xerox	20	18	11
Fuji Xerox	4	4	8
Canon	1	5	10
Ricoh	4	7	9
Kodak	0	2	4
IBM	5	4	3
Minolta	0	2	3

Source: Donaldson, Lufkin & Jenrette, Inc.

EXHIBIT 3 Copier Unit Placements of Xerox and Major Competitors

	Thousands of units placed by market segment (net)[a]					Share of net placements in each market segment[a]				
	PCs	Low	Mid	High	Total	PCs	Low	Mid	High	Total
In the United States:										
Xerox										
1975	—	9	−8[b]	1	2	—	29%	—	100%	6%
1980	—	34	6	6	46	—	11%	22%	52%	13%
1985	—	66	27	15	108	0%	10%	21%	53%	10%
1989	12	101	53	13	179	5%	14%	27%	45%	15%
Kodak and IBM										
1975	—	—	10	—	10	—	0%	213%	0%	27%
1980	—	—	5	5	11	—	0%	20%	48%	3%
1985	—	—	2	13	14	0%	0%	2%	46%	1%
1989	—	—	5	9	13	0%	0%	2%	31%	1%
Canon										
1975	—	3	—	—	3	—	10%	0%	0%	8%
1980	—	46	4	—	50	—	15%	14%	0%	14%
1985	176	107	17	—	300	86%	16%	13%	0%	29%
1989	141	106	19	4	270	62%	15%	10%	13%	23%
Others										
1975	—	19	3	—	22	—	61%	55%	0%	59%
1980	—	237	12	—	249	—	75%	44%	0%	70%
1985	30	514	81	—	625	14%	75%	64%	0%	60%
1989	75	513	123	3	714	33%	71%	61%	11%	61%
Total for All Vendors										
1975	—	31	5	1	37					
1980	—	317	27	11	355					
1985	206	687	126	28	1,047					
1989	227	710	200	29	1,176					
In Western Europe:										
Rank Xerox										
1980	—	40	4	4	48	—	11%	22%	100%	13%
1984	—	54	19	9	82	0%	9%	25%	74%	10%
1989	18	73	49	4	144	7%	10%	29%	34%	12%
Kodak										
1980	—	—	4	—	4	—	0%	22%	0%	1%
1984	—	—	—	3	3	0%	0%	0%	26%	0%
1989	—	—	2	2	3	0%	0%	1%	13%	0%
Canon										
1980	—	36	4	—	40	—	10%	21%	0%	11%
1984	115	81	8	—	204	90%	15%	10%	0%	26%
1989	130	110	25	3	268	49%	15%	15%	26%	22%
Total for All Vendors										
1980	—	331	19	4	374					
1984	128	578	76	12	794					
1989	268	752	168	11	1,199					

(continued)

EXHIBIT 3   Copier Unit Placements of Xerox and Major Competitors (*Continued*)

		Thousands of units placed by market segment (net)[a]					Share of net placements in each market segment[a]			
	PCs	Low	Mid	High	Total	PCs	Low	Mid	High	Total
In Japan:										
Fuji Xerox										
1986					112					20%
1989					142					21%
Canon										
1986					138					25%
1989					195					28%
Others[c]										
1986					311					55%
1989					354					51%
Total for All Vendors										

[a]"Net Placements" are sales and new rentals minus old rentals returned to the vendor. Volume segments are defined as follows:

   PC = less than 12 cpm (average price about $1,000)
   Low = 12 to 30 cpm (average price about $3,000)
   Mid = 31 to 69 cpm (average price about $8,500)
   High = over 70 cpm (average price about $55,000)

[b]Indicates that, on balance, 8,000 rental units were returned.

[c]Ricoh was particularly strong in Japan, with a 32% share in 1989.

Source: Dataquest Incorporated.

EXHIBIT 4   Major Agreements Between Xerox and Fuji Xerox

1960 Joint Enterprise Contract and Articles of Incorporation (1962)
- Established equal ownership of FX by Rank Xerox and Fuji Photo Film
- Defined FX's exclusive license to Xerography in its territory: Japan, Taiwan, Philippines, the Koreas, Indonesia, Indochina
- FX nonexclusive license to nonxerographic products in territory
- Specifies terms of technology assistance
  -Royalty due Rank Xerox: 5% of net sales of xerographic products

1976 Joint Enterprise Contract (JEC)
- Agreement between Rank Xerox and Fuji Photo Film, updating 1960 JEC
- Specified Board of Directors composition
- FX Management to be appointed by Fuji Photo Film
- Agreements on technology transfer, royalties, and transfer pricing
- Identified matters requiring Xerox concurrence, including:
  -Financial policy, including major capital expenditures
  -Business and operating plans
  -Relations with third parties
  -Sales outside of FX licensed territory

1976 Technological Assistance Contract (TAC)
- 10-year agreement between Xerox and Fuji Xerox
- Revised technology assistance agreements of 1960, 1968, and 1971
- Maintained 5% royalty on xerographic products

1978 R&D Reimbursement Agreement
- Defines reimbursement to FX for R&D on FX products marketed by Xerox
  -100% to 120% of design cost

1983 Technology Assistance Agreement (TAA)
- 10-year agreement between Xerox and Fuji Xerox
- Replaced 1976 technology transfer agreements
- Revised royalty rates:
  -Basic Royalty on **total** FX revenue, plus
  -Royalty on **xerographic** revenues to decline annually from 1983 to 1993

1983 Product Acquisition Policy
- Provided guidelines for intercompany transfer pricing
- Established concept of reciprocal Manufacturing License Fee (MLF), designed to reimburse FX for development and manufacturing costs:
  -Up to 25% mark-up on assembled machines supplied by FX
  -Up to 20% mark-up on unit cost for FX machines assembled by XC
  -Specific designs and services required by Xerox reimbursed 100%

1985 Procurement Policy
- Provided guidelines for Xerox procurement in FX licensed territory:
  -FX right to bid first
  -Procurement from third party to be coordinated with FX

1986 Arrangements Strategy Agreement
- Defined parameters for negotiating alliances with third parties.

Source: Compiled from Xerox Corporation documents

EXHIBIT 5 Key Financial Data for Xerox and Fuji Photo Film (in millions of US$)

	1971	1976	1981	1982	1983	1984	1985	1986	1987	1988	1989
XEROX CORPORATION											
Total revenues	1,954	4,515	8,180	8,073	10,463	11,400	11,994	13,287	15,108	16,441	17,635
Document processing			8,013	7,895	8,223	8,714	9,068	9,744	10,834	11,688	12,431
Financial services			167	178	2,240	2,686	2,926	3,543	4,274	4,753	5,204
Operating income	785	1,486	2,071	1,654	1,444	1,557	1,502	1,327	1,376	2,154	2,031
Net income	213	365	598	424	466	291	475	465	578	388	704
Total assets	2,250	4,959	7,674	7,668	14,064	15,154	16,838	19,050	22,450	26,441	30,088
Long-term debt	425	1,000	870	850	1,461	1,614	1,583	1,730	1,539	5,379	7,511
Stockholders' equity	1,052	2,179	3,728	3,724	4,664	4,543	4,828	5,129	5,547	5,667	6,116
R&D expenses	96	226	511	541	529	555	597	650	722	794	809
Employees (millions)	66	100	112	103	108	111	113	112	112	113	111
Earnings/Share ($)	2.85	4.35	6.25	4.06	4.5	3.26	3.42	4.48	5.3	3.49	6.56
Dividend/Share ($)	0.80	1.10	3.00	3.00	3.00	3.00	3.00	3.00	3.00	3.00	3.00
Document processing revenues as share of total	a	a	98%	98%	79%	76%	76%	73%	72%	71%	70%
Operating income/Revenue	40%	33%	25%	20%	14%	14%	13%	10%	9%	13%	12%
Operating income/Assets	35	30	27	22	10	10	9	7	6	8	7
Operating income/Equity	75	68	56	44	31	34	31	26	25	38	33
Net income/Revenue	10.9%	8.1%	7.3%	5.3%	4.5%	2.6%	4.0%	3.5%	3.8%	2.4%	4.0%
Net income/Assets	9.5	7.4	7.8	5.5	3.3	1.9	2.8	2.4	2.6	1.5	2.3
Net income/Equity	20.2	16.8	16.0	11.4	10.0	6.4	9.8	9.1	10.4	6.8	11.5
R&D expense/Revenue	4.9%	5.0%	6.2%	6.7%	5.1%	4.9%	5.0%	4.9%	4.8%	4.8%	4.6%
Long-term debt/Assets	19%	20%	11%	11%	10%	11%	9%	9%	7%	20%	25%
Equity/Assets	47	44	49	49	33	30	29	27	25	21	20
Dividends/Earnings	28	25	48	74	67	92	88	67	57	86	46
FUJI PHOTO FILM											
Total revenue							3,136	4,504	5,636	6,833	6,732
Net income							600	801	1,030	1,217	1,210
Dividends							21	30	35	41	36
Net income/Revenue							19%	18%	18%	18%	18%
Dividends/Earnings							3.5%	3.7%	3.4%	3.4%	3.0%

aPractically 100%.

Source: Company annual reports.

EXHIBIT 6   Global Configuration of Xerox Group and Canon in 1989

	UNITED STATES	JAPAN	WESTERN EUROPE	OTHER
Share of world GNP	26%	14%	21% (4 largest countries)	39%
Share of world PPC market (units)	33%	20%	34%	14%

XEROX GROUP

	UNITED STATES	JAPAN	EUROPE	AMERICAS
Revenues	$6.6 billion	$3.5 billion	$4.0 billions	$1.7 billion
Employees	54,000	19,600	29,000	16,000
Production				
PPC	149,000	180,000	176,400	39,100
Printers	15,000	60,000	15,700	—
Systems	8,000	18,000	1,900	—
Faxes	—	95,000	—	—
% of Market (units)				
PPCs	15%	22%	12%	
R&D centers	2	1	1	1
Alliances	—	Fuji Photo Film	Rank Organization	

CANON

	NORTH AMERICA	JAPAN	EUROPE	OTHER
Revenues	$2.9 billion	$2.9 billion	$2.9 billion	
Employees	4,500	27,500	6,500	
Production:				
PPC	60,000	700,000	370,000	
Other	Laser printers and engines	Cameras, printers		Cameras in China
% of market (units)				
PPCs	23%	26%	23%	
Laserprinting	70			
Color PPCs	50			
R&D centers	0	1	0	
Alliances	HP ($1B OEM) Kodak, NeXT		Olivetti	

Source: Xerox and industry sources.

EXHIBIT 7 Key Financial Data for Fuji Xerox (in millions of US$) (at yearly average exchange rates)

	1971	1976	1981	1982	1983	1984	1985	1986	1987	1988	1989
Revenues	107	307	872	962	1,111	1,282	1,456	2,303	2,955	3,570	3,554
Operating expenses	79	259	754	813	970	1,125	1,304	2,093	2,673	3,197	3,180
R&D	—	13	49	47	84	109	117	151	194	242	292
S,G, and A	38	119	308	333	399	443	507	801	1,041	1,296	1,324
Operating income	27	47	117	150	141	157	152	210	282	373	374
Net income	10	17	46	50	56	61	59	71	106	173	162
Total assets	176	405	897	931	1,046	1,199	1,276	1,883	2,457	3,186	3,093
Total equity	49	121	324	325	388	440	487	744	959	1,237	1,285
Retained earnings	33	84	270	277	338	390	439	680	885	1,154	1,131
Depreciation and amortization	16	63	131	113	130	155	153	218	266	271	278
Capital expenditure	65	64	196	178	230	217	244	296	284	297	512
Employees (thousands)	4.9	7.7	9.8	11.3	12.6	13.9	15.1	16.5	17.2	18.0	19.6
Dividends paid out	1	7	9	8	8	8	8	12	14	18	30
FINANCIAL RATIOS											
Operating income/Revenues	25%	15%	13%	16%	13%	12%	10%	9%	10%	10%	11%
Operating income/Assets	15	12	13	16	13	13	12	11	11	12	12
Net income/Revenues	9.1%	5.6%	5.3%	5.2%	9.1%	4.8%	4.1%	3.1%	3.6%	4.9%	4.5%
Net income/Assets	5.5	4.3	5.1	5.3	5.4	5.1	4.6	3.7	4.3	5.4	5.2
Net income/Equity	19.9	14.3	14.2	15.3	14.6	13.8	12.2	9.5	11.1	14.0	12.6
R&D expense/Revenues	—	4.4%	5.6%	4.9%	7.6%	8.5%	8.0%	6.5%	6.6%	6.8%	8.2%
Capital expenditure/Revenues	61.2%	20.9%	22.5%	18.5%	20.7%	16.9%	16.8%	12.9%	9.6%	8.3%	14.4%
Total equity/Assets	28%	30%	36%	35%	37%	37%	38%	40%	39%	39%	42%
Dividends paid/Total equity	1.6%	6%	3%	2%	2%	2%	2%	2%	1%	1%	2%
Dividends/Earnings	8.2%	41%	20%	16%	14%	13%	14%	17%	13%	10%	19%
Average exchange rate (yen per US$)	348	297	221	249	238	238	239	169	145	128	138

Note: FY ending October 20.

Source: Fuji Xerox annual reports; exchange rate from the IMF.

Fuji Xerox Trade with Xerox Group

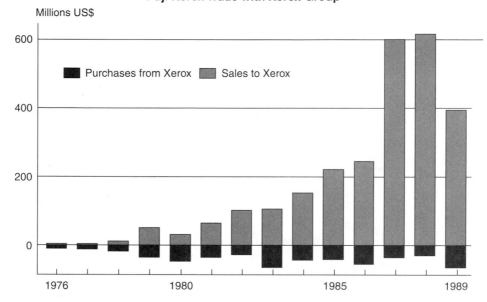

Japan – US Trade in Copiers

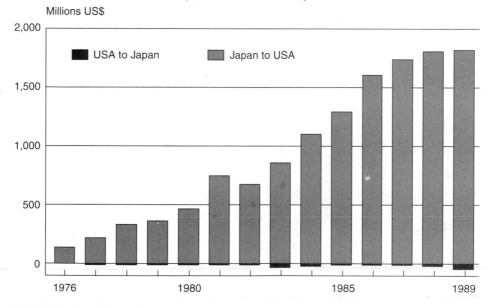

EXHIBIT 8   Intra-Firm and Bilateral Trade in Copiers

Notes: Top: Includes finished machines, parts, and knock-down kits. Bottom: Includes copiers (SITC 75182) and copier parts and accessories (SITC 75919).

Source: Fuji Xerox annual report and United Nations, *SITC Trade Data Base*.

FX Technology Spending and Receipts

Share of Total FX Revenue

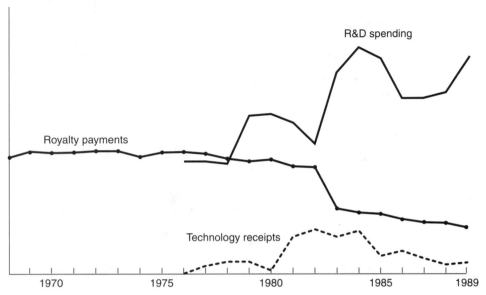

EXHIBIT 9   Fuji Xerox Technology Spending and Receipts, 1968–1989

Note: Technology receipts represent reimbursement to Fuji Xerox for special design and customization work on machines sold by XC and RX.

Source: Fuji Xerox annual reports

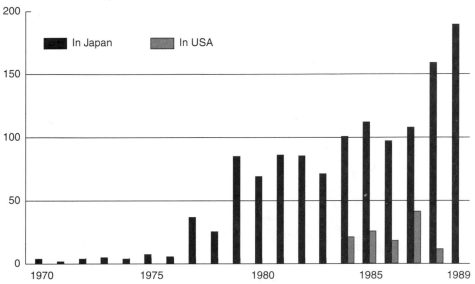

EXHIBIT 10   Growth of Fuji Xerox's Technical Capabilities, 1970–1989

Notes: Top: Utility models included in Japan. Bottom: Based on product introductions, assuming that every product has a commercial life of four years.

Source: Fuji Xerox

MARKETING

A. Independent and overlapping

Act as two separate companies serving the world market, with some coordination on business direction and strategy. No geographic constraints.

B. Independent and separate

Concentrate efforts on licensed territories for core products, with multinational business as required.

C. Separate with exceptions

Same as B, but with joint or overlapping activities across territorial boundaries on case by case basis.

D. Coordinated global product mandates

Worldwide and exclusive responsibility for products or product ranges manufactured under special licenses.

RESEARCH

A. Independent

Each pursues own interest and becomes self-sufficient.

B. Coordinated

Coordinated group research programs of XC and FX, with both self-sufficiency and overlap.

C. Joint

Single research organization without overlap.

D. Complementary

Separate organizations operating on exclusive projects.

EXHIBIT 11   Relationship Options Identified by Codestiny Task Force

Source: Compiled from Xerox documents.

DEVELOPMENT AND MANUFACTURING

A. Independent

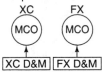

Each development and manufacturing (D&M) organization supplies its own marketing organization (MCO).

B. Complementary without overlap

Assign development roles to each organization, with no overlap allowed in development projects.

C. Complementary with overlap

Same as B, but with overlap in development projects.

D. Joint

Single development and manufacturing organization with individual projects targeted to needs of separate marketing organizations.

EXHIBIT 11   (*Continued*)

Shell Brasil S.A.:
Performance Evaluation
in the Oil Products Division

In early March 1986, Roberto Boetger, vice president of the Oil Products Division of Shell Brasil S.A., was considering a major change in the control systems in his division. The previous week the Brazilian government had announced the Cruzado Plan, which introduced far-reaching economic and financial reforms, including a change in the national currency and a general one-year price freeze. The government plan, which took the country by surprise, intended to reduce annual inflation rates from 255% to less than 10%. Boetger felt that, with the Cruzado Plan in place, it might now be feasible to evaluate managers more objectively, based on financial measures of performance, instead of relying on subjective evaluations.

"Up to now, it has been relatively difficult to hold people responsible for not meeting the budget, because of the 'masking effects' of many factors that are outside the manager's control, such as widely fluctuating inflation and exchange rates. If the Cruzado Plan is successful and inflation rates drop to 20% or less and stabilize, the budget targets will be much more meaningful. We could use actuals vs. budget comparisons for evaluating managerial performance and, possibly, for providing managerial incentives. The problem is that we can still expect some residual effects of inflation and exchange rates to influence performance significantly in the future. Can we really tell, then, by comparing budget vs. actual, if a manager has done a good job?"

This case was prepared by Research Assistant Lourdes Ferreira, under the supervision of Associate Professor Kenneth A. Merchant, as a basis for class discussion rather than to illustrate either effective or ineffective handling of an administrative situation.

Company Background

Shell Brasil S.A. was the largest private company in Brazil and a wholly owned subsidiary of Royal Dutch/Shell Group, the largest corporation in the world outside the United States. The parent group had operating companies in over 100 countries in businesses such as oil and natural gas, chemicals, metals, and coal. In 1985 the group reported earnings of $3.9 billion in the oil business only, making it the largest oil company worldwide.

Shell Brasil was organized into three main divisions: oil products, chemicals, and metals (see **Exhibit 1** for the organization chart). Besides these businesses, Shell had recently diversified into what it called "non-traditional businesses," such as asphalt, motels (situated along highways, close to some of Shell's gas stations in the countryside), and a joint venture in forestry dedicated to growing eucalyptus and pine trees, which could be used for wood pellets, an alternative source of energy.

The oil business was subject to extensive government control. The government oil company, Petrobras, had a monopoly on oil exploration, and regulations also restricted oil distribution. For example, gas stations were not allowed to open during weekends since the oil price shocks; the location of gas stations was limited to certain areas; and distributors had to order oil supplies from Petrobras according to quotas, with lead times of up to three months. The government also set retail prices, which were updated periodically, according to cost information provided by all oil companies operating in Brazil.

Shell Brasil competed in the distribution of various oil products, acting both as a wholesaler to large clients (such as aviation companies) and as a retailer, through a network of 3,500 gas stations spread around Brazil, of which Shell owned about 30%, the rest belonging to franchisers. In the parts of the oil industry where the government allowed private investments, Shell also operated as a manufacturer. In the production of lubricants, for example, the market leader was the government enterprise, Petrobras, with 23% market share, followed closely by Shell, with 21% market share. The Oil Products Division thus had a manager in charge of supplies and distribution of all of Shell's oil products, and an operations manager, responsible for manufacturing. The Oil Products Division had succeeded consistently, generating 60% of Shell Brasil's total sales volume and 70% of its profits. Despite price controls that limited operating margins in gasoline distribution to 2.5%, the oil business was a great cash generator with practically no credit sales.

At corporate, several services were provided to the operating divisions, as can be seen in **Exhibit 1**. In the Finance Division, the legal department was responsible for relations with shareholders, for taxes, and for legal support to the personnel functions at the operating levels. The treasury was a critical department for Shell Brasil, since it centralized the management of cash from all the different businesses. Daily this department dealt with about US$7 million, as a result of cash sales from the oil and chemical divisions. To keep idle cash to a minimum, the treasury department kept tight controls over the operations and maintained accounts with 18 different banks with branches all over Brazil.

Planning and Budgeting

The planning cycle at Shell Brasil consisted of three main stages: strategic planning, long-term financial planning, and operational budgeting. Strategic planning involved forming macroeconomic scenarios for the next 20 years and preparing the Country Plan Documentation (CPD). CPD focused on a time horizon of three years, and had the objective of quantifying the strategies necessary to meet the corporate goals. However, at this first stage management could not quantify some strategies in detail, so they presented targets such as "maintain market share" or "the Oil Products Division has to be a cash generator."

Targets were often differentiated according to geographical characteristics. For instance, within the Oil Products Division targets varied depending on whether the unit was located in a metropolitan region or in the countryside. In the large cities, service levels and sales volume were key targets, while in the countryside the emphasis was on building new gas stations as fast as possible to guarantee future market share in a fast-growing segment. The Strategic Plan was approved by the parent group, generally around the end of August.

The Long-Term Financial Plan involved a review of the total resources the company would provide or need in the next five years. In recent years, Shell Brasil had consistently needed more resources than what it provided. The Long-Term Financial Plan was sent for approval to the parent group in November.

Operational budgeting, which started in December, began at the operating division level. Each manager presented revenue targets (based on forecasts for each customer account) and cost estimates for the upcoming year for each of the various businesses. By year end the three operating Vice Presidents (Oil Products, Chemicals and Metals divisions) and the finance and personnel vice presidents met with the President to discuss and approve the budget.

Once the budget was approved, any changes had to be approved at the vice president level. In situations where the forecasts proved to be very far from reality, the division could ask for a budget review, subject to direct approval by the President. Only a major disruption, however, such as a variation of 200% in the expected inflation rate, would cause a change in the plans. As John Beith, in charge of corporate planning, explained, "Variances are an essential part of any planning effort. In fact, one of the few things we can be sure about when putting a plan together is that we'll miss it! Brazilians sometimes tend to have a lot of expectations about the numbers in their plans, and later, when they find, year after year, that they missed the plan because of some unforeseen circumstances, they get so disappointed that some people simply lose their confidence in any plan."

Performance Measurement

The operating divisions at Shell Brasil were evaluated on the basis of return on investment. Return was measured as profit after taxes and interest rates. The budget contained targets defined for three levels of profitability, called Margin I, Margin II, and Margin III, as shown in **Exhibit 2**. Margin I was a gross profit number. Margin II was division profit before allocations of indirect costs. Margin III was a fully allocated profit number, net of taxes. When computing the return on investment, Margin III was divided by total assets employed (defined as net working capital plus fixed assets). When Margin III was negative, management had to use Margin II to compute the return on investment. This happened in 1984 and 1985, but generally Margin III was the ultimate criterion for measuring profits. Despite continuous efforts by top management to find the best possible bases for allocating corporate costs at the division level, many managers still considered Margin III an unreliable indicator of the true contribution of the profit center to the performance of the whole company, because it depended on many factors outside the manager's control.

During the year each operating division prepared special reports for monthly, quarterly, and semiannual reviews. These reports compared actual results with the plans. Managers had to provide detailed explanations of the causes for variances only when failing by more than 5% to meet profitability targets. Managers often felt that it was much harder to explain unfavorable variances, so most of them preferred to set conservative targets.

Performance evaluation meetings were held every six months. Division managers had to rank all their subordinates according to how well they had met financial targets and other objectives, such as participating in leadership training programs, increasing sales volume, or opening new gas stations. In a first round, all employees in a division had to rank their peers (other employees at the same job level), and then each boss would review and consolidate the rankings of the subordinates. The personnel division collected these rankings with individual evaluation reports. The data were used for career planning, management succession, training, and internal transfer programs, as well as merit wage increases. Managers at all levels had to conduct interviews for preparing evaluation reports with each subordinate. Together they identified the factors that facilitated or prevented the achievement of each goal, including those that could not be quantified. The boss was also expected to serve as a counselor on career plans and to provide alternatives for improving performance.

Shell had attempted to reduce subjectivity in the evaluation process by setting performance targets at the beginning of each year and by quantifying the performance measures as much as possible. Some managers still felt uncomfortable, however, about giving a bad evaluation to their subordinates. In some instances managers ranked half of their subordinates as "perfectly acceptable" and the other half as "very good." The problem was aggravated when the manager had to justify why his or her unit performed poorly if all subordinates had done such a good job.

Isolating Uncontrollables

In 1985 top management made some attempts to separate controllables from uncontrollables in the performance measures. Ian Wilson, corporate controller, commented:

"Uncontrollables are outside factors that make you realize that you can't rely only on your own resources. Managers should be evaluated solely on their individual contribution." Unfortunately, however, management had difficulty in defining what was "controllable."

For example, in the Oil Products Division, if a manager was responsible for opening new gas stations in the countryside, and despite all efforts in developing good plans for this operation, government officials decided not to grant the necessary authorization, then the manager would not be held responsible for failing to open the new stations. But if the manager disrupted some relationships with government officials because proper authorization was denied for the new gas stations, then the manager could be demoted, perhaps even fired.

Another example would be the frequent oil price increases. Approximately once a month the government determined price increases for different oil products, including gasoline. If a manager could forecast more or less accurately when the price increase would come, he or she could maximize inventory just before that day, and then sell everything later at the greater price. This gain could amount to a boost of about US$20 million in profits for a company as large as Shell.

To take advantage of these gains, some of Shell's competitors adopted various procedures not to sell just before the price increase was expected. For example, they would allege that delivery trucks had broken down or that the pumps were out of order in some gas stations, or they would intentionally reduce service levels to create large lines of customers. As a manager in the Oil Products Division commented, "We at Shell consider such procedures unethical. However, there are some ordinary business steps that a manager can take to maximize the gains with the oil price increases. For instance, a manager could anticipate purchases to maximize inventory around the time when he or she expects the price increase to occur. Should we reward such a manager even if the underlying cause for the large gains—the price increase announced by the government—was outside the manager's control?"

Two "uncontrollable" factors, inflation and the fluctuation in exchange rates, typically had a particularly significant impact on performance measurement, sometimes with opposite effects. This led management to consider explicitly these effects in computing Margins II and III.

A. Inflation:

Brazilian inflation rates, as high as 250%, caused major distortions in financial statements. Nevertheless, government regulations limited the adjustments that companies could make to account for inflation, allowing adjustments in just a few accounts, such as fixed assets. Due to other restrictions in the tax laws, companies in Brazil tended to use the same reporting system for tax and financial purposes. Thus, a large part of the reported results depended on the relative changes in prices over the period. In the Oil Products Division, for instance, management estimated that about 50% to 60% of reported profits were caused merely by inflation. For internal purposes, management prepared "what if" reports, that showed actual results adjusted for what they would have been, had inflation been just as expected. Even so, few people could understand the effects of inflation on various accounts. Some managers could enumerate between 20 and 30 effects of inflation with different magnitudes and which could have a positive or negative impact on the various line items in the budget. It was very hard to assess what their net result would be. The hardest effects to predict were changes in relative prices (e.g., how would the price of a finished product vary, compared with the variation in the price of one or more of its inputs).

As an approximation, management computed an "inflationary loss" estimate, according to the formula:

$$\text{Inflationary Loss} = \text{Inflation Adjustment} \times \text{Net Working Capital}$$

where:

Inflation Adjustment – Percent adjustment that the government allowed for accounting for inflation during the period.

Net Working Capital – Balance, in U.S. dollars, outstanding at the beginning of the period.

Margin I, less the Inflationary Loss and Direct Costs, resulted in what was called Margin II. From Margin II the divisions deducted the Indirect Costs, and the result (Profit Before Taxes) was the basis for computing tax liability or savings. The total tax liability or savings for the company arose from consolidating the above computations supplied by each division.

B. Exchange Rate Changes:

Shell Brasil set budgets in dollars for all the different businesses, and used the targets contained in those budgets to control the performance of its general managers. Top management believed that results in dollars, rather than cruzeiros, better reflected real performance. One reason was that targets expressed in dollars would not be subject to the effects of the inflation of the cruzeiro, only to the inflation in dollars, which had been comparatively much smaller. Another reason was that the use of profitability measures denominated in dollars facilitated comparisons with the international competitive environment. Some managers, however, wondered why they should be held responsible for fluctuations in the exchange rates. They argued that they did their business in cruzeiros and had no control over exchange rates that were periodically established by the Brazilian government.

Besides the effects of changes in the value of the cruzeiro regarding the dollar, financial performance at Shell Brasil was also influenced by fluctuations in the exchange rate between cruzeiros and British pounds. The Dutch-British parent group required that Shell Brasil report its financial statements in British pounds to consolidate the corporate accounts worldwide. And when the president of Shell Brasil went to London to discuss budget reports, he would present the numbers, taking into consideration explicitly the effects of fluctuations in the exchange rates.

Devaluations of the cruzeiro concerning foreign currencies generally had a net negative effect on performance. Each time the Brazilian government established a new exchange rate, usually to devalue the cruzeiro, companies received more cruzeiros for their exports, but meanwhile they needed more cruzeiros to pay their foreign debt. Shell Brasil, like many other companies, had a substantial part of its current liabilities denominated in dollars and only a small percentage of revenues derived from exports. Because the government also controlled prices of many of Shell's products, the end result was that the frequent devaluations of the cruzeiro had a significant negative impact on performance of the different businesses at Shell.

For internal reporting purposes, the effects of variations in the exchange rates were computed by the Difference in Exchange (DIE) formula, as follows:

$$\frac{\text{Net Working Capital (NWC)}}{\text{Beginning Exchange Rate}} - \frac{\text{Net Working Capital}}{\text{Ending Exchange Rate}} = \frac{\text{Beginning Loss}}{\text{in Dollars (BLD)}}$$

$$\text{BLD} + \frac{\text{Variation in NWC}}{\text{Average Exch. Rate}} - \frac{\text{Variation in NWC}}{\text{Ending Exch. Rate}} = \text{DIE}$$

where:

Net Working Capital – Beginning Balance, in cruzeiros.
Variation in NWC – Difference between Net Working Capital of two consecutive periods.
Exchange Rate – Expressed as how many cruzeiros one needed to buy U.S. $1.

The DIE was deducted from Margin I, along with the direct costs, and the final result was Margin II. This Margin II could be very different from the Margin II calculated as Margin I minus direct costs and the Inflationary Loss, as explained above. If one considered the inflationary loss only, and not DIE, one would have a measure of what contribution the division made to the overall profit of the company, translated from cruzeiros to dollars at the current exchange rate at the end of the period. Yet, if one considered DIE only, and not the inflationary loss in cruzeiros, one would have a measure of the division's performance in dollars, allowing for the effect of the changes in the cruzeiro's value concerning the dollar during the period being evaluated. Management had to report the budget variances according to both criteria for computing Margin II (and, consequently, Margin III).

Exhibit 3 illustrates the evolution of the inflation rates of the cruzeiro and the dollar, and compares it with the changes in the exchange rate of the cruzeiro regarding the dollar, for the period 1981–1985. Respecting performance evaluation, these large variations in the inflation and exchange rates caused major uncontrollable variances from budget estimates. As a corporate manager explained, "When you receive a budget report that shows a big loss in dollars due to a major devaluation of the cruzeiro, or a loss in cruzeiros due to a jump in inflation, you often feel like you can't penalize the manager for missing the budget. However, you would expect that the manager would have reacted to these outside factors in some way, to offset some of these negative variances."

Compensation Policies

Labor expenses at Shell Brasil accounted for over 50% of the company's total operating expenses, or about US$50 million per year. Shell compensated its managers on a salary basis, at levels designed to be competitive with total compensation (salary plus bonuses) packages offered by some large companies surveyed annually.

By 1986 an estimated 55% of the major companies in Brazil would be paying incentive bonuses. Part of Shell's reluctance to pay bonuses or other forms of compensation based on performance stemmed from the tradition among European companies against incentive plans. As a Shell executive explained, "We don't want our managers to be in a situation where one year they can earn a big bonus but then earn nothing the following year."

On some rare occasions, a small number of Shell managers (usually less than 5% of the total management team) would be eligible for either merit increases in salary (often associated with promotions) or cash bonuses, subject to approval by the Board of Directors. In its evaluation the Board emphasized two aspects—individual contribution and consistency. The individual contribution was defined as outstanding performance in relation to individual budget targets. Consistency, however, referred to long-term trends in performance. It was not enough to meet budget in any given year, because the Board was also looking for a consistent pattern of superior performance over a longer period, such as three to five years. The Board also used consistency to grant merit increases or bonuses to a manager who had "exceptional performance," even if his or her division had not met budget in the current year. An obstacle to assessing "consistent performance" was that Shell frequently transferred people across functional departments and divisions to give high-potential employees varied experiences. Therefore, managers often had to change positions every two or three years.

Another problem with bonus payments was that managers received them only after the previous year's results had been thoroughly evaluated. This often delayed the delivery of bonus payments to midyear. By that time managers were already worried about meeting the current year's targets.

The Cruzado Plan

The Cruzado Plan, which took effect on March 1, 1986, was a government attempt to eliminate one of the factors believed to be a root cause for inflation: the expectations of future inflation based on past price increases. So far the Brazilian economy had operated with an "indexation system" in which most prices were automatically raised according to variations in price indexes computed by the government. For some products, these price increases could occur weekly. The Plan introduced two major reforms addressing this problem—all prices were frozen as of February 28, 1986, and a new monetary unit was created, the cruzado, equivalent to 1,000 old cruzeiros. The currency change was intended to erase inflationary memories.

The Cruzado Plan raised many questions about how to implement the generalized price freeze. A major concern was that, without the Plan, wages would have been readjusted on March 1st to account for inflation (wages in Brazil used to be adjusted twice a year, in March and November). Recognizing this, the Plan determined that wages should now be frozen at their average *real* value from the last six months. To this average, the government decided to add an 8% bonus. Furthermore, the Plan established a sliding scale mechanism that allowed automatic wage raises if the annual inflation rate reached 20%. The Plan also introduced unemployment benefits for the first time in Brazil. But no one knew how the labor unions would respond.

Another major problem with implementing of the price freeze was the required revisions in current long-term contracts. These contracts usually established adjustments in the periodic payments according to variations in the inflation or the exchange rates. Now the Plan prohibited any contracts (including investments) from having such provisions. Nevertheless, it was still reasonable to expect some residual inflation, even with the new price freeze. The Cruzado Plan considered this expected residual inflation by establishing a "conversion calendar," that translated old cruzeiros into cruzados for every day of the year until March 1, 1987. Each day one needed more old cruzeiros to buy one cruzado. For example, on March 1, 1986, one cruzado was set as equivalent to 1,000 cruzeiros; six months later, one cruzado would be equivalent to 2,997.39 cruzeiros. This conversion calendar allowed for conversions into the new currency for payments established in cruzeiros in long-term contracts signed before the Plan. Another example was that if one had agreed before the Plan to pay 5 million cruzeiros on February 28, 1987, now one would have to pay about only 1,000 cruzados at that same date.

The Cruzado Plan's Effect on Shell's Management

A wave of optimism about the promised stronger economy swept Shell the day the Plan was announced, but uncertainty lingered concerning the repercussions that the Plan would trigger. For example, how long could the government enforce the price freeze? After over twenty years of military government, the first elected president—a civilian—had certainly strong popular support, which would provide the much needed help to implement the Cruzado Plan. Coming elections for the Congress in November, however, could change the political scenario substantially, especially because the new Congress would vote on a new constitutional reform. It seemed that there was more uncertainty about the next year than about the nineties. Despite all uncertainties, Shell had to continue to set prices and renegotiate contracts with suppliers, banks, and insurance companies. Top management had to act quickly to send instructions to all managers, spread out over the whole country, for the adoption of coherent policies that might change practically every aspect of the way they operated in their different businesses.

The Cruzado Plan particularly affected the distribution business. Manufacturers used to sell to wholesalers offering deferred payment terms (generally between one to three months) that incorporated an inflation forecast. Now, according to the new conversion calendar, which converted cruzeiros into cruzados at different rates daily, wholesalers and retailers would face increasing costs. This situation, combined with the price freeze, caused many managers in the distribution business to doubt whether they would be able to keep earning their expected returns. Some people even speculated about a crisis in supplies and the creation of an underground economy.

Luiz Fortes, Treasurer, perceived an increasing pressure to meet performance targets: "The Cruzado Plan forces us to look at real returns. For example, we are all used to thinking about returns in nominal terms, with a large inflationary component built-in. Now only the really best performers will be able to generate significant real returns and beat competition." Ian Wilson, the corporate controller, predicted some positive effects of the Plan: "It'll be much easier now to compare budget with actual results. We can be more confident about our forecasts. It's a good opportunity to implement tighter cost controls and to hold people accountable for financial targets. We'll be able to ask good questions when somebody misses the budget. We won't have all those masking effects any more." Some people at corporate, however, remained uncertain about how the Plan would change the role of budgets in the performance evaluation process. Some managers argued that criteria such as meeting targets for Margin III, for instance, would be more reliable in the future, because then costs and other factors would be estimated much more precisely. However, others argued that with frozen prices managers would have less control over their results, so that even simpler criteria, such as Margin I, would not capture the "real effort" that each person made to accomplish his or her goals.

William Mills, the vice president of personnel, agreed that it was time to review some control policies: "We may now have a unique opportunity to introduce some performance-based compensation plans. There are several alternatives for careful examination. For instance, should we tie compensation to the performance of the profit center only? To what extent should we measure performance over a longer period of time—say, five years?"

The planning department at corporate would have to revise most of its macroeconomic premises, especially about inflation and exchange rates. If the inflation rate exceeded the devaluation rate of the cruzado concerning the dollar, Shell Brasil could possibly end up with losses in cruzados but profits in dollars.

An Example: Evaluation of Performance in the Lubricants Business

Roberto Boetger, vice president of the Oil Products Division, had just received the latest budget forecasts for the lubricants business (**Exhibit 5**) accompanied by a review of the performance of this business in the last two years (see **Exhibits 4A** and

4B). The lubricants business, which required large amounts of working capital, was representative of how the inflation and exchange rate effects could alter the financial results substantially. As shown in **Exhibits 4A** and **4B,** the lubricants business missed its budget targets for Margins II and III in 1984, but did better than budget in 1985. In both years, management had underestimated sales volume. This was consistent with a conservative attitude that some managers at Shell adopted when preparing budget estimates. In both 1984 and 1985 management had also underestimated inflation, so the actual inflationary loss produced negative variances in both years.

Following the other criteria for measuring Margins II and III, that is, taking into consideration DIE, both in 1984 and 1985 the actual variation in exchange rates was much higher than expected. This led to a bottom line (Margin III) loss of $8 million dollars in 1984. However, in 1985 the actual variation in exchange rates was lower than inflation, causing substantial savings in direct costs. Thus, the bottom line (Margin III) for 1985 resulted in neither gains nor losses for the lubricants business.

Now, when reviewing the budget for the following years, corporate planning expected both the DIE and the inflationary effects to be much smaller. Yet, they also expected that the spread between the variation in exchange rates and inflation would increase substantially. In particular, for 1987 top management estimated that the effect of inflation would be much smaller than the DIE, so that lubricants would report profits in cruzados (and a consequent payment of taxes), but losses in dollars. In 1988 management expected these results to reverse. These forecasts and their underlying assumptions appear in **Exhibit 5.**

Even assuming that the forecasts for the next couple of years were reasonably accurate, top management at Shell Brasil still had to decide what criteria should be used to assess management performance. Should they leave the system unchanged and continue to depend on more subjective judgements? Or should they rely primarily on budget standards? If so, should performance be measured in cruzados, in dollars, or in British pounds? Should managers be held responsible for the three levels of profitability—Margins I, II, and III? What criteria should be used to compute the profitability margins?

Organization Chart

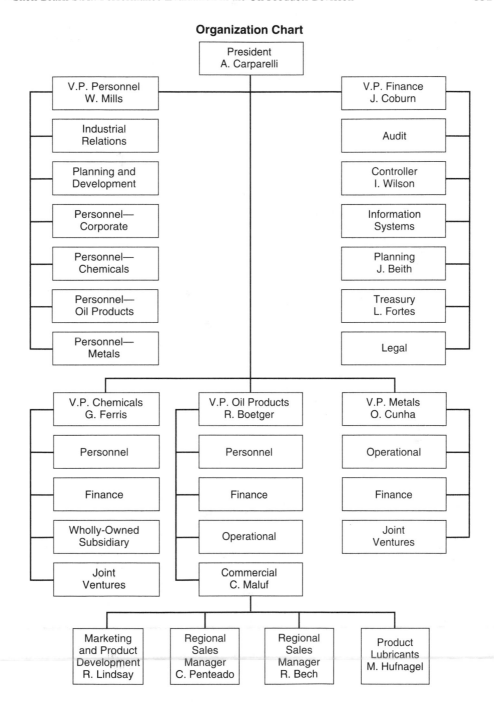

EXHIBIT 1   SHELL BRASIL S.A. *Organization Chart*

EXHIBIT 2   Shell Brasil S.A. *Format for Evaluation of Profitability Levels*

	Budget			Actual		
Net Revenues						
Less:						
Cost of Goods Sold		_____			_____	
Margin I						
Less:						
Plant costs						
Administrative expenses						
Depreciation						
Freight costs						
Interests						
Sales and distribution						
Other direct costs						
Total direct costs		_____			_____	
Contribution						
Less:						

	DIE	Inflationary Loss		DIE	Inflationary Loss
	—	_____		—	_____
Margin II					
Less:					
Corporate overhead					
Publicity and other					
sales expenses					
Other allocated costs[a]					
Total indirect costs	—	_____		—	_____
Profit before taxes					
Less:					
Income taxes					
	—	_____		—	_____
Margin III					

[a]Examples include corporate services such as legal assistance, computer support, and auditing.

EXHIBIT 3   Shell Brasil S.A. Performance
of Brazilian Economy

Year	Annual Inflation Rates (%) of: CR$[a]	US$[b]	Exchange Rates: Yearly Averages (CR$/US$)	% Change in Yearly Average Exchange Rate
1981	88.0	8.9	98.12	—
1982	99.7	3.9	193.56	97.3
1983	211.0	3.8	629.64	225.3
1984	223.8	4.0	2,132.00	238.6
1985	235.1	3.8	7,037.50	230.0

[a]Computed as percent change of the Generalized Price Index, from December of the previous year through December of the current year. Source: Conjuntura Economica.

[b]Computed as percent change of the Cost of Living Index—Total, from December of the previous year through December of the current year.

Source: U.S. Bureau of Labor and Statistics.

EXHIBIT 4A   Shell Brasil S.A. *Variance Analysis of the Lubricants Business—1984* (U.S.$ millions)

	BUDGET With DIE	With Inflation	ACTUAL With DIE	With Inflation
Net Revenues	128	128	160	160
Less:				
Cost of Goods Sold	84	84	111	111
Margin I	44	44	49	49
Less:				
Direct Costs	6	6	4	4
DIE Effect	34	—	43	—
Inflationary Loss	—	33.1	—	43.4
Margin II	4	4.9	2	1.6
Less:				
Indirect Costs	16	16	17	17
Profit (Loss) Before Taxes	(12)	(11.1)	(15)	(15.4)
Less:				
Income Tax Savings	5	5	7	7
Margin III	(7)	(6.1)	(8)	(8.4)

Other Data:

	BUDGET	ACTUAL
Sales Volume (1,000 m3)	140.5	168.0
Inflation (%)	200.0	223.8
% Variation in Exchange Rates (Cr$/US$)	210.0	238.6

EXHIBIT 4B   Shell Brasil S. A. *Variance Analysis of the Lubricants Business—1985* (US$ millions)

	BUDGET		ACTUAL	
	With Die	With Inflation	With DIE	With Inflation
Net Revenues	133	133	169	169
Less:				
Cost of Goods Sold	91	91	111	111
Margin I	42	42	58	58
Less:				
Direct Costs	12	12	7	7
DIE Effect	36	—	39	—
Inflationary Loss	—	38	—	39
Margin II	(6)	(8)	12	12
Less:				
Indirect Costs	12	12	12	12
Profit (Loss) Before Taxes	(18)	(20)	0	0
Less:				
Income Tax Savings	9	9	0	0
Margin III	(9)	(11)	0	0

Other Data:

	BUDGET	ACTUAL
Sales Volume		
(1,000 m3)	140.5	173.0
Inflation (%)	230.0	235.1
% Variation in Exchange Rates (Cr$/US$)	220.0	230.0

EXHIBIT 5   Shell Brasil S. A. *Forecasts for 1987/1988—Lubricants*:

	1987		1988	
Assumptions:	Beginning	Ending	Beginning	Ending
Net Working Capital (Cz$ millions)	447.0	851.2	851.2	914.6
Exchange Rates (Cz$/US$)	15.0	23.0	23.0	37.0
DIE Effect (US$ millions)	14.1		14.4	
Inflation Adjustment (%)	21.5		53.2	
Inflationary Loss (US$ millions)	6.4		19.7	

	1987		1988	
Forecasts(US$millions):	With DIE	With Inflation	With DIE	With Inflation
Margin I	47.9	47.9	49.8	49.8
Less:				
Direct Costs	16.1	16.1	16.3	16.3
Inflationary Loss	—	6.4	—	19.7
DIE	14.1	—	14.4	—
Margin II	17.7	25.4	19.1	13.8
Less:				
Indirect Costs	13.0	13.0	13.0	13.0
Profit Before Taxes	4.7	12.4	6.1	0.8
Less:				
Income Tax (45%)	5.6	5.6	0.4	0.4
Margin III	(0.9)	6.8	5.7	0.4

The Global
Computer Industry

The computer industry's importance in the global economy has been remarkable, especially given its short history of four decades. During this time, it evolved from being the province of U.S. academia and government to permeating every aspect of modern life. Computers became critical to firm and national competitiveness in numerous sectors. In 1990 the industry represented more than $300 billion in sales annually—the largest in the information technology (IT) sector. Electronic data processing equipment accounted for 50% of the $660 billion in IT revenues worldwide. The next largest segments were software and services ($140 billion, or 21%), and telecommunication equipment ($120 billion, or 18%).

As computers were revolutionizing the business world, the industry itself was undergoing radical changes. Foremost among these were the appearance of new firms and massive shifts in patterns of international trade and competition. An industry dominated by the United States and by a handful of U.S. firms evolved into a truly international industry with intensive competition among diverse firms. Technological change, firm strategies, national development, and government policies all played a part in this evolution.

Research Associate Maryellen C. Costello and Associate Professor Benjamin Gomes-Casseres prepared this note as the basis for class discussion rather than to illustrate either effective or ineffective handling of an administrative situation.

Industry Characteristics

Size and Scope

The computer hardware industry comprised the manufacture, sale, and maintenance of data processing equipment, including related peripherals such as printers and disk drives. It was closely linked to related sectors of the semiconductor and telecommunications equipment industries.[1] The United States has been the largest DP market, although demand in Asia and Europe has been growing rapidly (see **Exhibit 1**). The top 100 firms in the industry employed almost 2 million people worldwide, with about 1.2 million in the United States, 270,000 in Asia, and the rest in Europe.

The industry could be segmented in a number of ways, and its economics varied between segments. Peripherals could be separated from central processing units (CPUs), which in turn could be classified by size and cost. Sales of mainframe systems and personal computers (PCs) each accounted for 22% of the total in 1988, but the latter was growing two to four times as fast as the former. Sales of peripherals, such as disk drives and printers, also grew rapidly, partly because they were used with PCs. Peripherals represented about one-third of the total. Since about 1982, the minicomputer segment (14% of total) had been squeezed between booming PC sales and continued strong mainframe sales.[2]

IBM and Early Development of the Industry

While there had been research in the 1940s on electronic digital computers and production of a few one-of-a-kind machines, the commercialization of computers really got underway after the Second World War. Through the 1960s, U.S. firms, led by IBM, turned out increasingly sophisticated machines and dominated almost every market in the world. By 1971, IBM had a 62% share of the world computer market, other U.S. manufacturers combined had a 30% share, while European and Japanese producers had 4.1% and 3.4%, respectively. Europe's most important computer firm, the British ICL, had a 2.6% share and Japan's top two companies, Fujitsu and NEC, each had about 1%.

Despite many innovative management policies, analysts in the 1950s viewed IBM as a technologically conservative company, and its competitors regularly an-

---

[1]See David B. Yoffie and Alvin G. Wint, "The Global Semiconductor Industry, 1987," Harvard Business School case number 9–388–052 and Julie Herendeen, Willis Emmons, Richard H.K. Vietor, and David B. Yoffie, "The Global Telecommunications Equipment Industry," Harvard Business School case number N9–391–020.

[2]In 1988, *Electronics* defined PCs as systems costing under $5,000, and mainframes as systems between $400,000 and $5 million. Minicomputers cost between $20,000 and $1 million.

nounced new and superior technology. At the time, IBM sold six different and incompatible computer lines. This meant that software written for one machine could not be used on another; software represented about 40% of development costs for a new machine at the time. Also, different machines were designed specifically for scientific or business use.

To address these issues, IBM announced its System/360 line of computers in 1964. Named for the 360 degrees in a circle, it was designed to encompass all computing needs. For the first time, a broad "family" of compatible, multi-purpose computers was available, enabling users to upgrade without having to replace their existing databases or programs. This was also the first time transistors were used in computers, representing a leap forward from vacuum-tube and magnetic-core technologies. IBM took a big risk in launching this system—*Fortune* called it "IBM's $5,000,000,000 Gamble"—because of the enormous cost of engineering and producing it. After initial startup problems, the gamble paid off in increasing market share and profits. By 1970, IBM computers comprised 70% of the installed base of equipment in the United States. When IBM launched the System/370 in the early 1970s, its lead seemed insurmountable to General Electric and RCA, which soon abandoned their mainframe computer businesses. Across the Pacific and Atlantic, however, firms and governments launched aggressive programs to catch up with IBM.

Technological Change and Standards

The explosive growth of the industry occurred because of the technologies that reduced both the size and cost of computers. In the large systems era of the 1960s and 1970s, when mainframes were the norm, computers were built from the ground up with proprietary hardware architectures and unique components. New, standardized semiconductors introduced in the late 1970s were more reliable, smaller, faster, cheaper, and more powerful than earlier components. Through "downsizing," wholly new industry segments were created and came to threaten sales of the large systems. Minicomputers came to do the work of mainframes in the 1970s, and PCs and workstations (which in many cases could be made from readily available components) began to replace minis in the 1980s.

The large systems era was also the heyday of proprietary operating systems.[3] Originally, IBM and other mainframe vendors sold the operating system software bundled in with the hardware. As pressure from the U.S. Justice Department mounted, IBM began to sell unbundled hardware and software after 1969. This opened the door for other firms to produce and sell IBM-compatible hardware, so-called plug-compatible machines (PCMs). Even after 1969, however, IBM software was written specifically for a particular hardware architecture—in the case of Sys-

---

[3]An operating system was the software interface between the computer's hardware and the application programs. It managed files, memory, input and output, and other functions. For example, MS-DOS was the most popular operating system for PCs in the 1980s.

tem/360 for the whole family of computers. Although IBM's PCM competitors began to carve into its hardware market, IBM's architecture and operating system continued to dominate the large systems market.

The minicomputer industry also had proprietary operating systems, but while the most prominent was Digital's VMS, none was as dominant as IBM's in mainframes. The microcomputer revolution of the 1980s gave rise to "open systems," which allowed various hardware and software firms to make and sell products that would be compatible with each other. To achieve this, the operating system producers—Microsoft for MS-DOS and AT&T for UNIX—licensed to others to make compatible products. Furthermore, the PC hardware standard was open, too, since IBM—which introduced it in 1982—used off-the-shelf components and readily available Intel microprocessors. Apple's architecture and operating systems, however, remained proprietary and "closed": other than Apple itself, very few vendors were licensed to make compatible equipment or software.

Because of the "portability" of software applications resulting from open standards and the availability of standard components, some segments of computer hardware have become close to commodity businesses. According to *The Wall Street Journal*, "the [hardware] industry is condemned to ceaseless innovation, price cutting, and product cycles that are nasty, brutish and short.[4]

Production, Marketing, and R&D

The economics of the industry varied by segment and over time. The cost of goods sold was proportionately higher in PCs and peripherals than in mainframes. But selling expenses were lower for PCs and peripherals because they were usually sold through indirect channels. Mainframes required direct sales and substantial after-sales service. On average, about one third of the employees in leading computer firms worked in manufacturing, one quarter in sales, one tenth in research, and almost one fifth in maintenance and repair. Labor costs were not critical to competitiveness, though they could be important in the production of components. Even in PCs, direct labor accounted for less than 5% of total variable cost, and overhead for another 10%. More important were costs of components, such as semiconductors, printed circuit boards, and disk drives, which accounted for about three-quarters of variable costs.

From the outset, IBM leased its mainframe systems, setting the industry norm through the late 1970s. Leasing reduced the up-front cost to users and facilitated upgrading, while tying them to IBM service and support. This practice made entry difficult for firms too small to fund the up-front costs and strengthened the position of firms with large installed bases. But this pattern changed over time. At the U.S. government's insistence, IBM made equipment available for outright purchase in the late 1950s. Thus, when third-party leasing companies entered the market in the early 1970s, they were able to do so with IBM's machines. Digital Equipment Corporation

---

[4]*The Wall Street Journal*, September 5, 1991, p. 1.

(DEC) began selling minicomputers outright to the scientific and academic communities in the 1960s. By the late 1970s, IBM itself started emphasizing purchases over leasing. By the 1980s, PCs were being sold by mass-market retailers and mail-order discounters.

Aside from production costs and marketing, R&D was critical to competitiveness in computers, as it determined product features and computing power. Leading computer firms invested almost 10% of revenue annually in R&D, and another 10% in capital expenditures on new plant and equipment. Not surprisingly, PCs and mainframes were on opposite ends of this spectrum, too. Developing a new mainframe cost about $500 million and took five years; PCs required significantly less time and money, and designs of one firm could often be copied within months by others.

International Trade and Competitiveness

Demand and costs of production influenced the location of plants and sales worldwide, and thus the pattern of trade. These factors changed over time, and so accounted for some of the competitive shifts in the industry.

Early Trade Patterns

From the early 1960s, the United States was the largest exporter of computer products. Still, non-U.S. production grew quickly and major markets in Europe and Japan soon came to be served primarily by local production. Much of this local production, however, as well as what few exports these countries had, bore the logo of IBM. In 1960, IBM was already operating in 87 countries, had 19 manufacturing plants abroad, and employed 30,000 people outside of the United States. By 1972, IBM World Trade was active in 126 countries, with 22 manufacturing plants and 115,000 employees. Between 1967 and 1972, IBM World Trade's revenues had grown at 22% per year and represented 44% of IBM's total volume.

The pattern of trade in the 1960s and early 1970s, therefore, reflected IBM's international production strategy. Starting in the mid-1960s, the company pursued a goal of balanced trade in North America, Western Europe, and Japan.[5] IBM's booming foreign sales grew largely through local (or regional) production rather than by exports from the United States. IBM reportedly accounted for all of Japan's exports in 1972 and cross-shipments among IBM plants in Europe were thought to account for the bulk of exports registered by European countries in the mid-1960s. At this

---

[5]No region was meant to be self-sufficient. Rather, the aim was to balance any imports against exports. In fact, IBM Japan exported about 25% to 30% of its production and IBM Europe produced 90% of its sales in the region, implying imports of 10% of sales.

time, IBM accounted for three-quarters of the markets in West Germany, Italy, and France, half of the market in the United Kingdom, and about two-fifths in Japan.

Shifting Competitive Advantages

Overall, in 1990, world trade in data processing equipment and parts[6] amounted to about $70 billion, or one-quarter of consumption. The share of imports and exports in consumption varied over time and across regions, as did the composition of finished goods and parts (see **Exhibit 2**).[7] While U.S. imports and Asian exports grew robustly during the late 1970s and the 1980s, Europe remained the most dependent on imports and the least successful in exports. The difference in trade pattern between Japan and Europe has become more pronounced, as the trade balances in **Exhibit 3** show. While the United States continued to run a surplus in the industry, this surplus fell from $3.5 billion in 1978 to $2.5 billion in 1990, and as a share of total computer exports it declined from 80% to 10%.

The underlying theme in these trends is the rapid development of Japan, and to a lesser extent the newly industrializing countries (NICs), into successful exporters of computers. At the same time, the position of the United States declined. A world industry dominated by U.S.-based production in the early 1970s had become one where the United States and Japan held more similar positions. The slow decline of Europe as a production site was less dramatic than that of the United States, since Europe never held a dominant position in the industry (see **Exhibit 4**).

Factor costs were only partly responsible for these shifts. First, wages were a small component of production cost. Second, electronics wage differentials between Japan, the United States, and Europe had all but vanished by 1990. From the mid-1970s to the mid-1980s, Japanese wages were half those in the United States, but this gap had closed. European wages fluctuated around the U.S. level over most of this period. Labor costs remained low only in the Asian NICs, even though these too rose from about one-sixth to one-half those in the United States.

Only the Asian NICs have been successful in segments where labor costs were important. Most of the major computer firms have manufacturing plants there for labor-intensive components such as keyboards, printers, disk drives, and tape drives. In 1990, Taiwan alone exported $5.2 billion in computer products, making it the second largest Asian exporter behind Japan. Its exports represented 66% of world exports of PC system boards and 20% to 40% of monitors, power supplies, keyboards,

---

[6]"Parts" here excludes generic semiconductor and other components, but includes semi-finished equipment, printed-circuit boards, disk drives, and other electrical and mechanical components intended specifically for computers.

[7]Unless otherwise noted, the trade data for Europe exclude trade *among* Belgium, France, the Netherlands, the United Kingdom, West Germany, Italy, and Sweden; they thus represent an estimate of European trade with non-European countries. The data shown for NICs include only Hong Kong, Singapore, and South Korea; no comparable data were available for Taiwan.

graphics cards, and scanners. Thirty percent of these exports were made by sub-sidiaries of foreign firms, and 47% were sold by Taiwanese firms on an OEM basis to foreign firms.

The rise of Asian production and exports was also related to other factors. The volume and sophistication of demand for computers grew fast in Japan, and many of the leading-edge technologies (e.g., laptop computers) become popular there first. Related industries that fed directly into the computer industry, such as semiconductors, consumer electronics, and office printing and copying, blossomed in Japan. Japanese universities turned out large numbers of electronic engineers, and government as well as firms invested heavily in R&D.

The conditions behind the rising competitive advantage of the Asian NICs were somewhat different. Domestic demand was less important, and technology was usually acquired from the outside through licensing or foreign direct investment. But here, too, related industries played important roles, as skills first applied in simple consumer electronics were transferred to assembly of computer products. While they remained dependent on Japan and the United States for key components such as microprocessors and liquid-crystal display screens, the Asian NICs invested heavily in production of commodity semiconductors.

The destination of exports and the origins of imports—as distinguished from overall trade volumes—also developed in distinct ways since the late 1970s, as shown in **Exhibit 5**. In short, the United States became the premier importer of Japanese and NIC goods and the dominant exporter to Europe and the rest of the world. By 1990, the United States ran $4 billion trade deficits with both Japan and the NICs, and an equally large surplus with the rest of the world. Japan, in turn, ran trade surpluses with all the regions, with Europe and the United States each taking $4 billion in net exports. The Asian NICs depended even more on the United States as a destination for their exports, and ran deficits only with Japan.

Trade, Foreign Investment, and International Strategy

One reason for this pattern lay in the role of firm-level strategy and competition in determining trade flows. From the Japanese firms' point of view, the United States was a larger, more accessible market than Europe, partly because these firms had experience exporting consumer electronics to the United States. Europe had traditionally been more closed to Japanese imports and internally fragmented. Several other factors made a presence in the U.S. market more important to these firms than a presence in Europe: the United States had more sophisticated demand, more advanced technology, and was home to the leading firms in the industry. This pattern changed during the 1980s, as Europe slowly became a more important destination for Japanese exports.

For the U.S. firms, Europe and Latin America were the traditional destinations of exports and foreign investment. The Japanese market was relatively closed to U.S. firms; IBM was strong in Japan only by virtue of its local production. As a result, more than 32% of the total sales of U.S. data-processing firms were in Europe in 1990, compared with 11% in Asia (see **Exhibit 6**).

Not all U.S. computer firms followed such foreign investment strategies, and those that did not often failed in foreign markets. Some entrants, like RCA and GE, never made a substantial commitment to foreign markets, preferring instead to export or license technology. Neither established a presence abroad, and both exited the business in the 1970s. Sperry invested more in foreign markets, including an early marketing joint venture in Japan that led to Nihon Unisys's strong position there. DEC's European production strategy was similar to IBM's: it produced most of what it sold in the region, and became a strong contender there.

Overall, U.S.-based computer firms were disproportionately active abroad. The assets of their foreign affiliates were $58 billion in 1986, or fully 20% of the total foreign assets of U.S. manufacturing firms. These assets represented 58% of the total assets of the parent firms, a higher share than for any of the other major industrial categories tracked by the U.S. Commerce Department. Furthermore, just over half of the foreign assets of U.S. computer firms were in Europe in 1986, down from 66% in 1982.

The role of foreign investment in supplying regional markets could be estimated by taking total consumption, and subtracting (a) sales in the local market by domestic firms and (b) imports from foreign firms abroad. The residual could be ascribed to local production by foreign firms. By this method, in 1990 local production by foreign firms accounted for only 6% of U.S. consumption, but 21% of Asian consumption, and 48% of European consumption. In both Japan and Europe, local production by foreign firms was twice as large as imports.

Government Policies

In addition to economic and technological trends, the policies of national governments affected the development of the industry worldwide. The large foreign investment by U.S. computer firms, for example, was partly motivated by host government pressure. Jacques Maisonrouge, CEO of IBM World Trade, said in 1973: "Political power is stronger than economic power when the two collide."[8] In accordance with this motto, IBM traded off responsiveness to local political constituencies for global efficiency: it continued to expand local production and R&D in Japan and the major European countries, even when exports from the United States or from a smaller number of plants might have been more efficient. In theory, competitive bidding among IBM plants determined the allocation of production, but a study by a former IBM manager noted: "The balancing act involved in assigning new production re-

---

[8]Quoted in Nancy Foy, *The Sun Never Sets on IBM* (New York: Morrow, 1974), p. 158.

quirements often revolves around political factors that are little related to economics."[9]

Government policies affected competition in other ways as well. In particular, they often supported domestic firms against foreign competitors or encouraged technology development and diffusion. While American, European, and Japanese governments all influenced the development of the industry, the nature and effects of their policies differed.

Defense Spending and Antitrust in the United States

The U.S. military's support began in World War II and continued through the Cold War until the late 1960s, when the Vietnam War diverted funds. Most of the innovations in computer design and component technologies in the 1960s stemmed directly from government-supported R&D. The military funded the early, experimental, one-of-a-kind computers of the 1950s and continued funding leading-edge research through the 1980s. Between 1967 and 1975, the defense department and other agencies spent an average of $280 million (1982 dollars) annually on research in mathematics and computer science; this average rose to $380 million in 1975–1986. While government assistance often provided the early spark, private R&D targeted to the commercial market became the norm in the 1970s and later. For example, IBM's annual expenditure of internal funds on R&D climbed steadily from $676 million in 1972 to $4.1 billion in 1984, and $6.2 billion in 1990.

Through the 1970s and 1980s, 40% of U.S. government math and computer research budgets went to support work in universities. The Defense Advanced Research Projects Agency (DARPA) led this effort, but the Department of Energy (DOE), the National Science Foundation (NSF), the National Aeronautical and Space Administration (NASA), and the National Institutes of Health (NIH) also participated. The NSF alone spent $200 million (1982 dollars) from 1956 to 1970. These programs were in addition to military and government procurement, the second most significant source of support for the industry. In 1953, federal agencies used an estimated 54% of the stock of general purpose computers; even by 1961, 15% of IBM's revenues and more than 50% of Control Data's came from sales of special products and services to U.S. government agencies. However, by the 1970s, federal installations accounted for only about 5% of the stock of computers in the United States, as the commercial market had grown dramatically. Still, through the 1980s, the federal government continued to buy about half the supercomputers made in the United States.

U.S. government policies also regulated domestic competition. The Justice Department initiated three major antitrust suits against IBM, which had important implications for the evolution of the industry. In 1956, IBM signed a consent decree that restricted its marketing practices and affected the dissemination of computer technol-

[9]David Mercer, *The Global IBM: Leadership in Multinational Management* (New York: Dodd, Mead, 1987), p. 168.

ogy. In 1969, the company agreed to "unbundle" hardware and software. There was also much discussion in the early 1970s of whether and how to break up IBM as a remedy for its alleged monopolistic power. The biggest thorn in IBM's side was the suit beginning in 1969 that the Reagan administration finally determined was without merit in 1982. This suit was "stressful" for IBM, according to Thomas Watson, Jr., the company's CEO from 1956 through 1971:

> The government objected to virtually our entire way of doing business, from our use of total system sales—supplying customers with complete installations including hardware, software, engineering help, training, and maintenance—to the big discounts we gave universities. Strangely, none of these practices was illegal *per se* . . . Nothing in my experience prepared me for how treacherous the legal process can be when it gets out of hand.[10]

Industrial Policy in Japan

While Japanese research into computing began in the 1930s, governmental involvement remained minimal until MITI was granted extensive power over the computer industry in 1957. Over the next quarter century, Japanese computer firms benefitted from government efforts to spur technology cooperation, R&D, and domestic demand, while being protected from foreign competition. As *Forbes* put it in 1977: "Systematically, doggedly, as they did in cameras, cars and TVs, the Japanese are mounting an attack on the worldwide computer market."[11]

The primary target of the Japanese government's actions in information technology was IBM Japan. In the late 1950s, IBM requested permission from MITI to produce computers locally. After three years of negotiations, IBM gained MITI's approval, but only in exchange for licenses to its basic computer patents as part of a cross-licensing agreement. In addition, IBM's local business was to be limited; MITI restricted the number and type of machines manufactured and IBM's market share, and required the firm to export about one third of its Japanese production. "The government really put some clamps on us that legislated against our progress," according to George Conrades, head of IBM Asia/Pacific Group.[12]

During the 1960s, Japan also imposed import duties of between 15% and 25% on computers, as well as import quotas. As part of a "Buy Japanese" program, prospective purchasers of computers from non-Japanese firms were subjected to government interrogation and social ostracism. The government also encouraged domestic demand through the Japan Electronic Computer Company (JECC). This leasing company used government money and low-cost loans to finance rentals of machines

[10]Thomas Watson, Jr., *Father, Son & Co.: My Life at IBM and Beyond* (New York: Bantam Books, 1990), p. 376.

[11]"The Coming Japanese Computer Push," *Forbes,* May 15, 1977, p. 59.

[12]Quoted in Robert Sobel, *IBM vs. Japan: The Struggle for the Future* (New York: Stein and Day, 1986), p. 152.

from Japanese manufacturers. Japanese customers would place orders with JECC, which would then buy machines from the Japanese vendors and lease them to customers at competitive rates.

NTT, Japan's telephone monopoly since 1952, acted in concert with MITI in supporting domestic computer manufacturers. It did early research on computers and funded several major joint R&D projects from the 1970s through the 1990s. It bought only Japanese computers for its own operations, and had to approve any equipment linked to its communication network. These programs were funded partly through consignment fees and low-interest loans from the government.

But even with this government support, in the 1960s Japanese companies were dependent on American firms for technology. In 1961, Hitachi signed a technology transfer arrangement with RCA; NEC linked up with Honeywell in 1962, as did Mitsubishi with TRW; Sperry Rand was forced by MITI into a joint venture with Oki Electric in 1963; and Toshiba signed with General Electric in 1964. Only Fujitsu did not manufacture machines designed by a foreign partner; it was also the only one with a sizable research department. When IBM announced its System/360 line, Japanese computers were still far behind in technology, performance, quality and price; thus, MITI delayed production of the 360 series in Japan until 1966 and limited production volume.

IBM's announcement of the System/370 in 1970 was traumatic for the Japanese. Since most of their American partners exited the industry, the Japanese firms were in a quandary. MITI then formed three pivotal joint research projects, which were to shape the rise of the Japanese industry. One project involved Fujitsu and Hitachi, and was aimed to develop IBM-type mainframes and to challenge IBM's position directly. The second, between Toshiba and NEC, was to develop mid-size computers. The third, between Mitsubishi and Oki, was to focus on smaller computers and peripherals. This work was subsidized by MITI, whose contribution to industrial R&D in computers rose dramatically from 7% in 1970 to 84% in 1974. All together, the value of Japanese government subsidies, tax benefits and loans to the industry amounted to an estimated average $60 million annually between 1961 and 1969, $310 million annually between 1970 and 1975, and $635 million annually between 1976 and 1981.[13]

By the time the Japanese market was "liberalized" in 1975, domestic firms had gained a substantial share of the market and were moving to compete on a world scale. In addition, there remained strong incentives for domestic production: the government, which represented a quarter of the total demand, was still required to buy Japanese products. IBM was among the first to recognize the future role that Japanese firms would play in global competition. IBM World Trade's Management Committee warned in 1972:

---

[13]These values were equivalent to 188%, 168%, and 93% of the amount that the firms invested in R&D and plant and equipment during the same period, respectively.

[T]he Japanese manufacturers have demonstrated commitment to an overseas marketing strategy. . . . In light of the Japanese Government's demonstrated support of this exporting strategy for computers, the effect of our action programs in Japan will be at best to delay the inevitable schedule by perhaps one year.[14]

Through the rest of the 1970s and the 1980s, MITI's role in the computer industry remained significant but declining. This was due in part to the opening of the Japanese market: although informal restrictions were still in place, continued overt protectionism and subsidies would not be tolerated overseas. The improving market position and financial strength of Japanese firms also created a shift in the balance of power towards the firms and away from MITI. MITI's objective shifted in the late 1970s to focusing Japanese firms on developing advanced semiconductor technology, so they could anticipate and compete with IBM's future offerings rather than imitate them. Other government-backed projects of the 1980s, including the Supercomputer and Fifth Generation projects, sought to end Japanese dependence on foreign technologies and software standards.

National Champions and Technology Collaboration in Europe

Aware of their lagging status even as early as the 1960s, European governments, individually and later in concert, attempted to close the gap in information technology. In addition to funding R&D, they created "national champions" to achieve economies of scale in local markets. These firms were favored in government procurement and received subsidies in various forms. As late as 1992, there was controversy over the $1 billion that the French government was considering injecting into ailing Groupe Bull. But major scale economies were elusive—each nation supported its own champion, so that none was able to establish strong market positions across the whole region. Bull was strong only in France, Siemens in Germany, Olivetti in Italy, and ICL in Britain. And European markets were generally open to foreign investment and trade, allowing American firms to establish important positions everywhere.

European countries supported their firms with research funds as well. Average annual expenditures on computer and microelectronics programs in France, Germany, and Britain rose from $184 million in 1967–1975 to $356 million in the late 1970s. Until the 1980s, these national governments usually acted alone, and with differing philosophies. The "mission-oriented" countries—Britain and France—followed focused, centrally directed programs aimed at well-defined national goals and often tied to the military. The policies of "diffusion-oriented" countries–Germany and Sweden–were less targeted and attempted instead to spread technologies widely through product standardization and cooperative research.

---

[14]Minutes of February 28, 1972, quoted in Leo A. Morehouse and John W. Rosenblum, "IBM World Trade Corporation," Harvard Business School case number 374–303 (1974).

While European countries had long cooperated in steel, aviation, and space, it was not until the early 1980s that the various governments began to act jointly on information technology. Prior to this time, most intra-European collaboration was driven by the private sector. One notable case was Unidata, a 1973 joint venture between Siemens, Philips, and the French CII (a predecessor of Bull's). It fell apart after only two years when the French decided to seek American partners. The three firms had been unable to resolve differences over technology and markets.

In 1982, the European Community (EC) launched the European Strategic Project on Information Technology (ESPRIT), a ten-year, multi-billion dollar program to promote cooperative R&D. It offered partial government funding for approved "pre-competitive" joint R&D projects among European firms. Results of this research were to be licensed on reasonable terms to all other ESPRIT participants and at no charge to a firm's partners on the project. Local subsidiaries of foreign firms could participate, but on limited terms, in these projects. However, ESPRIT innovations were to be applied only within Europe. By 1986, ESPRIT was funding 200 projects, involving 240 partners and 2,900 researchers, and had exhausted nearly its phase-one budget of $1.3 billion, half of which came from the EC.

Another cooperative research program was the European Research Coordination Agency (EUREKA), which targeted energy, new materials, and biotechnology, in addition to information technologies. This was not an EC program, but involved nineteen Western European countries. It funded cooperative R&D with commercial applications rather than basic research. After receiving qualification as a EUREKA project, the participants would negotiate with their national governments, who agreed to provide funds for approved projects. By the end of 1987, 600 companies were participating in 165 projects costing $4 billion, about 40% of which was public funding. About a quarter of this amount was for information technology.

Competition Among Firms

The economics of the industry led to a classic oligopolistic structure. The mainframe segment was much more concentrated than others; its top four firms sold 77% of the world total in 1990, compared to 51% for microcomputers and 30% for peripherals. IBM alone accounted for 51%, 24%, and 10% of the sales in these segments. These shares were somewhat lower in the 1970s, but not by much. They indicate the great extent of the barriers to entry facing new firms.

U.S. firms dominated the world computer industry almost since its inception. Even in 1990, U.S. firms accounted for 64% of world computer sales and 88% of U.S. sales. Their position in Europe (62% of market) and in Asia (28%) was stronger than that of U.S. firms in most other comparable industries (see **Exhibit 6**). These foreign markets were, in turn, critical to the U.S. firms. The share of foreign sales in IBM's total, for example, grew steadily from 20% in 1960 to a peak of 54% in 1979; after that it declined and rose again to 59% in 1989.

The way computer firms chose to deploy their resources internationally could be crucial to their performance. The dominant U.S. firms in the 1970s organized themselves differently, pursued different strategies, and developed different capabilities (see **Exhibit 7**). While the European and, especially, the Japanese firms were still in their infancy, it took no exceptional strategies and management for U.S. firms to penetrate foreign markets. But by the mid-1970s, foreign firms gained capabilities and market position, first in their home country, and later, abroad.

When the Japanese government identified computers as a strategic industry, domestic manufacturers held less than 7% of their home market. Even by 1975, none of the world's top ten computer manufacturers were Japanese. However, by 1990, Japanese firms held 69% of the Asian market, and 23% of the world market, up from 12% in 1984. By then, four were among the world top fifteen firms (see **Exhibit 8**). Competition in Japan developed differently than in the United States or Europe. Although IBM had the largest sales before 1979, the top tier of the Japanese market was split four ways, and by 1989, Fujitsu, NEC, IBM and Hitachi each held between 12% and 15% of the market. By contrast, in the United States and Europe IBM led with about a 25% share, followed by a group of firms each with between 3% and 5%.

Thus, by the late 1970s, U.S. and Japanese firms dominated their home markets. The Europeans, on the other hand, were weak in their own region, with only 30% of the regional market in 1990. American firms, led by IBM, had established positions in these markets that could not be overcome easily by the smaller European firms, or, for that matter, the rising Japanese firms. Furthermore, the fragmented nature of the European market made it difficult for them to develop regional scale to challenge the substantial world scale of American firms.

The Role of International Alliances

A distinct feature of competition in the computer industry was the increasing importance of international alliances (see **Exhibit 9**). These alliances helped transfer technologies across national borders, facilitated market entry by new firms, and became competitive tools in battles over standards and market share. They were, at the same time, signs of the narrowing gap between the capabilities of firms from different nations and direct contributors to this trend.

A survey of press reports of the major international alliances formed by 24 top computer firms between 1975 and 1990 identified 226 deals.[15] These partnerships covered a range of structures and activities falling in the grey area between open-market purchases and internal company transactions. Forty-six percent of the deals were structured as supply agreements, 19% as technology licenses, 20% as joint R&D projects, and 21% as equity joint ventures or equity investments.

In the early 1980s, the computer industry was already third among a large group

---

[15]For further details, see Benjamin Gomes-Casseres, "International Trade, Competition, and Alliances in the Computer Industry," Harvard Business School working paper number 92–044, (Rev. 1992).

of industries in its use of alliances. After that came a rapid increase in the formation of alliances in computers, from fewer than four a year before 1980 to an average of 26 per year in 1985–1989. This rise was double that in world consumption of DP equipment, which rose from about $50 billion in 1980 to an average of $150 billion in the same period.

Computer firms used alliances in all parts of the value chain. About one-third were devoted to trading goods and components, another third to technology development and transfer, and about one-fifth to manufacturing. Over time, however, the role of technology development and transfer in alliances tended to increase; before 1984, 29% of the alliances were structured as joint R&D and technology licenses, compared with 37% in 1985–1989 (see **Exhibit 9**).

The alliances also varied by the contributions of the partners. Sometimes the partners exchanged technology for technology, at other times one contributed technology and the other a market, and so on. There seemed to be some systematic differences across regions in the types of contributions made and sought by national firms (see **Exhibit 10**).

Selected Competitors

IBM.   IBM has been unique in the computer industry because of its size and early dominance. It was traditionally a mainframe producer, although it became highly successful in PCs and also in minicomputers in the 1980s. It had the reputation of being more marketing-oriented than its competitors and of excelling at customer service. Many also argued that IBM's secret lay in its corporate culture, which, until the 1990s, included virtual lifetime employment and great employee loyalty. In 1991, it suffered its first annual loss ever, as it was rocked by recession and overcapacity in the industry. But it still held number one positions in a number of segments, including personal computers and mainframes. IBM attained its leadership through creative technology management in the 1960s, aggressive marketing, sheer financial clout, and by extensive foreign production and sales. In 1991, it began a radical reorganization intended to decentralize operations and encourage greater market responsiveness in its businesses.

In foreign countries, IBM traditionally operated through wholly-owned subsidiaries. This approach was not always welcomed by host governments. In 1978, IBM pulled out of India rather than give in to the government's demand for a joint venture. In the 1980s, the company softened its insistence on whole ownership, and, in fact, became an active user of inter-firm alliances. This change stemmed from the gradual erosion of its market position in Japan and Europe, where local firms were aggressive in the new microcomputer segments (e.g., Olivetti in Europe) or had simply reached a stage where their products were good enough to challenge IBM's (Japanese firms). In response, the firm began to pursue alliances with local firms. In 1982–1984, IBM Japan formed only four alliances with local firms involving some equity investment; in 1987–1989, it formed 25 such alliances. Following this example, IBM Europe expanded its stock of equity-based alliances from six in 1987 to 150 in 1990. In the early 1990s, IBM even formed joint ventures in India and China.

Other U.S. mainframe firms.   The BUNCH group of companies comprised a second-tier of mainframe firms in the 1960s and 1970s—Burroughs, UNIVAC, NCR, Control Data, and Honeywell. This group plus GE and RCA (before they dropped out of the industry) had previously been known as the Seven Dwarfs and were the key challengers to IBM through the 1960s. On the whole, what was left of this group of once formidable potential has suffered declining performance and market share. In the 1980s, Burroughs and Univac merged to form Unisys, Honeywell Information Systems was acquired by France's Bull, and in 1991 NCR was acquired by AT&T.

Aside from these broad-line firms, there were niche players in mainframes. In high-end mainframes, Control Data and Cray Research became the market leaders in scientific supercomputers. The manufacturers of PCMs were more direct competitors in IBM's heartland. Since 1975, Amdahl had been the most important player in this market. Gene Amdahl had been a lead engineer on IBM's System/360 and /370 projects, and set out on his own in the early 1970s, with the financial support of Fujitsu. In 1990, Fujitsu owned about 43% of Amdahl, and the two firms developed and produced computers together.

U.S. minicomputer firms.   Digital Equipment Corporation, the strongest minicomputer maker in the 1970s and 1980s and the segment's pioneer, was started in 1957 by Kenneth Olsen (still the CEO) and Harlan Anderson. As a result of their favorable price/performance ratios, DEC's machines provided substantial competition to IBM's low-end mainframes. By the 1990, DEC was the second largest U.S. computer manufacturer, with operations around the world; it was most successful with scientific and academic users, but less so with the business community.

Each minicomputer specialist—DEC, Data General, Hewlett-Packard, NCR, Prime, and Wang—had its own proprietary system architecture, and together they eclipsed IBM's share in this segment. But in the 1980s and 1990s they were all being threatened from below by workstations using open UNIX systems. Except for IBM and DEC, all more or less abandoned their proprietary systems by 1990 and were moving toward the less profitable open systems. Wang was hurt the most by this trend, and in 1991 began selling IBM hardware. Others had to downsize their operations and cut their workforces. In 1991, DEC suffered the first loss in its history.

U.S. microcomputer firms.   After IBM, Apple was the most important microcomputer maker in the United States. Its Macintosh system, introduced in the mid-1980s, pioneered the marketing of a friendly graphical user interface. Most other microcomputer producers sold "clones" of IBM's PC, using Intel X86 processors and Microsoft's MS-DOS operating system. The clone makers used marketing strategies and time-to-market advantages for differentiation in a cut-throat business. Compaq, established in 1982 and soon among the *Fortune 500*, was first to undercut IBM's prices, while still claiming a premium product. Dell, AST, Northgate, and Gateway grew rapidly in the late 1980s by selling exclusively through direct mail, cutting costs to the bare minimum.

U.S. workstation firms.   Sun Microsystems was the archetypical workstation vendor of open systems. By contrast, workstation pioneer Apollo was taken over by Hewlett-Packard in 1989 after missing opportunities in open systems. Sun makes its own chips, but makes extensive use of alliances and liberal licensing to promote use of its RISC[16] design called SPARC. Sun produces systems and sells them under its own name through an aggressive sales force, while selling through so many OEM vendors in Japan (including Fujitsu, Toshiba, and Oki) that none is reportedly making any money on the business. Sun also invites clones, in another attempt to maximize the number of SPARC-based machines on the market.

American firms already well established in the computer industry—Hewlett-Packard, DEC and IBM—also used alliances in the workstation field, often to promote their own RISC architectures. DEC was an important ally of RISC designer MIPS Computer Systems, which in turn had a large network of partnerships. These firms joined Compaq, Microsoft, and others in the Advanced Computing Environment (ACE) consortium, formed to bring the MIPS architecture to the commercial desktop market. Hewlett-Packard, which had merged with Apollo, also began to push its PA-RISC architecture actively in the 1990s. Perhaps the most surprising, and potentially formidable, RISC alliance was that formed in 1991 by IBM, Apple, and Motorola. Together, these firms intended to promote a new "Power PC" based on IBM's RISC architecture, Motorola's microprocessor manufacturing expertise, and Apple's software capabilities.

Fujitsu and Hitachi.   In the MITI-sponsored projects of the mid-1970s, Fujitsu and Hitachi focused on challenging IBM's position in mainframes, partly through development of PCMs. Fujitsu was aided in this by its alliance with the U.S.'s Amdahl Corporation. Short of cash and unable to raise funding at home, Amdahl struck a deal with Fujitsu in 1972, taking in a 24% equity investment and providing technology and the permission for Fujitsu engineers to "look over the shoulder" of engineers at Amdahl. Amdahl began shipping its first plug-compatible CPU in 1975; two years later, Fujitsu announced that it would begin manufacturing the machines for Amdahl to sell in the United States.

By 1990, Fujitsu had the leading market share in Japan (23%) and was an important supplier of large computer and telecommunications systems to government and industry. It moved ahead of DEC in 1990 to become the second largest firm in the world when it acquired 80% of Britain's ICL. This climax to a ten-year technology sharing arrangement increased Fujitsu's overseas sales from 25% to 40% of its total.

---

[16]Reduced Instruction Set Computing (RISC) was a new type of processor design that yielded greater power than traditional designs.

Hitachi, which produced a broad spectrum of electronics products, was the third largest Japanese computer company. Hitachi was stung in 1982 by the FBI in an embarrassing corporate espionage case. Its employees attempted to fill "a long shopping list of IBM technologies" using "cloak-and-dagger" methods.[17] After this case came to light, Hitachi settled a suit with IBM and the two developed cross-licensing arrangements. Following a long dispute over intellectual property rights to IBM software, Fujitsu and IBM, too, reached an agreement in 1987 to allow Fujitsu to use IBM software under restricted conditions and pay IBM $833 million plus an annual fee.

NEC and Toshiba.   With their greater capabilities in consumer electronics, NEC and Toshiba focused on small machines and peripherals. Production cost was relatively more important in these segments than in the others, so these companies could enter and compete on low-cost strategies. In the early 1990s, these two firms still excelled in small computers, although NEC also competed in mainframes and supercomputers. NEC developed a proprietary microcomputer standard that grew to dominate the Japanese market with a 50% share in 1990. NEC had a long-standing relationship with Honeywell Information Systems, and came to own 5% of Groupe Bull after Bull bought Honeywell's business. NEC's strategy has been to focus on "C&C"—computers and communications. Toshiba was the fourth largest Asian computer firm. It was particularly strong worldwide in laptop and notebook machines, with 14% of the portable computer market in the United States in 1991.

European firms.   European computer manufacturers were not much of a threat on a global scale. Even the largest, the merged Siemens-Nixdorf, was ranked eighth in the world in 1990. While European firms have some presence in the United States, they are negligible factors in Asia.

France's Bull and Britain's ICL were created through mergers of smaller firms to be their governments' national champions. Bull ended up with several incompatible product lines and with little incentive to be efficient. It attempted to expand internationally in the late 1980s by buying Honeywell Information Systems and Zenith Data Systems. Both moves gave it a strong U.S. presence and helped it move away from minis and mainframes toward smaller systems. Still, it had massive layoffs in the early 1990s and began reducing the size of its manufacturing operations. In 1992, Bull received a 5% equity investment from IBM, and began to sell IBM hardware through its channels. ICL, which was Europe's only profitable computer maker and excelled in software (particularly UNIX) and services, became a majority-owned subsidiary of Fujitsu in 1990.

The second largest computer maker in Europe after IBM was formed when Germany's two leading computer firms, Siemens and Nixdorf, merged in 1990. Siemens had a strong proprietary mainframe line, and sold heavily in telecommunications

[17]Marie Anchordoguy, *Computers Inc.: Japan's Challenge to IBM* (Cambridge: Council on East Asian Studies, Harvard University, 1989), p. 1, 149.

markets. Unlike Bull, Siemens made its own semiconductors, and had an important joint R&D project with IBM on semiconductor technology. Nixdorf had traditionally sold its own minicomputer systems to banking and small business markets, but had missed the transition to open systems.

Olivetti was the third largest European computer firm, and specialized mostly in PCs. It had several joint ventures with American and Japanese firms to make disk drives, displays, and computer systems. A joint venture with AT&T in the 1980s was shortlived, however, and failed to give the company the boost that it sought in the U.S. market. Finally, the Dutch-based Philips, which had long been a player in the European computer market, sold its computer division to DEC in 1991.

Competitive Conditions in the 1990s

As hardware manufacturers faced maturing markets, recessionary economies, rapid technological change, and excess capacity in the early 1990s, profits in the industry were sluggish or nonexistent. Operating income as a percent of revenue in the industry declined from 14% in 1984 to 8% in 1990 and dropped further in 1991. Turmoil and an uncertain future sent hardware manufacturers seeking solutions, but the crisis in profitability eroded firms' power and options. Foreign vendors continued to face barriers in Japan, which had the second largest market in the world and sophisticated users. While there were exceptions in the hardware segment, software and services showed potentially greater prospects for profit. Growth in these segments was expected to accelerate: spending on software was growing twice as fast as that on hardware, and computer services expenditures were projected by some sources to grow to $1.3 trillion by 1995.[18] While the future for many firms remained uncertain, change was sure to be a part of it. The question was how firms and governments could take action to prepare for it.

---

[18]IBM *Annual Report,* 1990, and "Why EDS Loves a Recession," *The New York Times,* October 20, 1991, Section 3, p. 1.

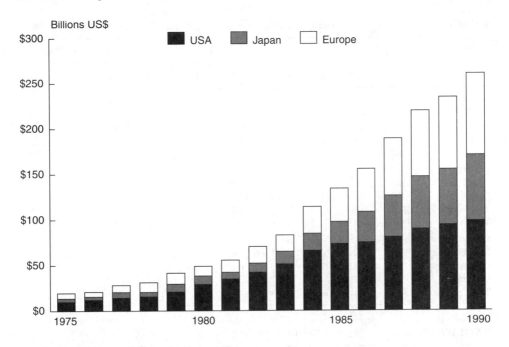

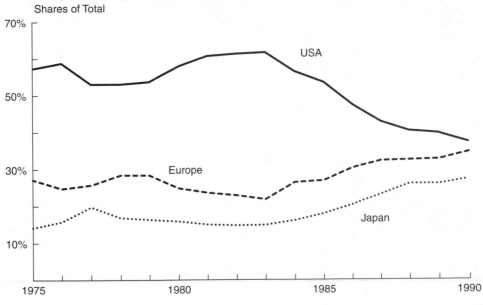

EXHIBIT 1   Consumption of Dataprocessing Equipment, 1975–1990

Sources: Compiled from *Electronics* and Gartner Group, *Worldwide Yardstick.*

EXHIBIT 2A   Trade and Consumption of Computers and Parts, 1978–1990 (billions US$)

	1978	1981	1984	1987	1990	Annual Growth 1978–90	Trade as Share of Consumption				
							1978	1981	1984	1987	1990
Imports											
By USA	0.9	1.8	8.1	15.3	23.4	31%	5%	5%	12%	19%	24%
By Asia	0.8	1.7	3.2	5.2	12.2	25	15	19	17	12	17
By Europe	3.1	6.0	10.2	18.8	27.8	20	33	44	33	30	31
Total	**4.8**	**9.5**	**21.4**	**39.3**	**63.4**	**24**	**15**	**17**	**18**	**21**	**24**
Exports											
By USA	4.4	9.0	14.0	18.8	25.9	16%	26%	26%	21%	23%	26%
By Asia	0.8	2.0	8.5	18.9	33.3	36	16	22	44	42	47
By Europe	1.8	2.9	4.9	9.3	11.8	17	20	21	16	15	13
Total	**7.1**	**13.9**	**27.5**	**47.0**	**71.0**	**21**	**22**	**24**	**24**	**25**	**27**
Consumption											
By USA	17.1	35.0	65.8	82.1	97.8	16%					
By Asia	5.4	8.7	19.2	44.7	71.4	24					
By Europe	9.3	13.7	31.2	61.7	89.7	21					
Total	**31.8**	**57.4**	**116.2**	**188.5**	**258.9**	**19**					

EXHIBIT 2B   Parts as Share of Total DP Trade[a]

Imports					
By USA	57%	61%	55%	52%	33%
By Japan	26	29	30	34	41
By Europe	27	29	31	28	29
By NICs	77	58	50	57	51
Total	**35**	**37**	**42**	**40**	**34**
Exports					
By USA	40%	44%	48%	51%	39%
By Japan	46	35	20	26	36
By Europe	34	36	41	41	33
By NICs	98	89	56	35	30
Total	**41**	**43**	**42**	**40**	**36**

[a]SITC 7599 divided by 752 + 7599

Sources: Trade data from the United Nations (includes SITC 752 plus 7599); consumption from *Electronics* and Gartner Group, *Yardstick Worldwide*.

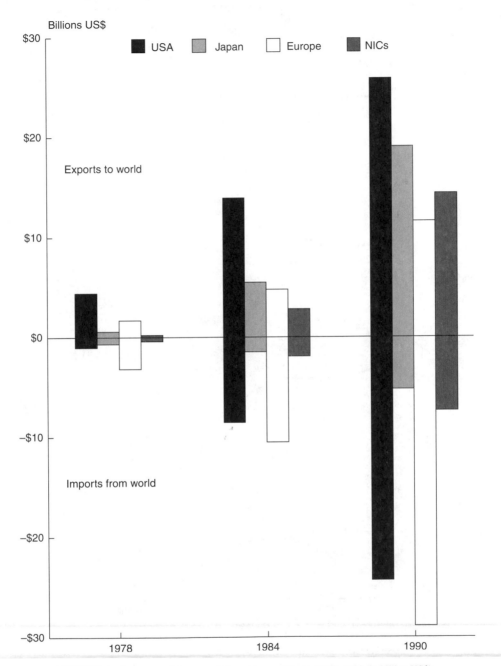

EXHIBIT 3 Imports and Exports of Computers and Parts, 1978–1990 (in billion US$)
Source: Compiled from United Nations data. Includes SITC 752 and 7599.

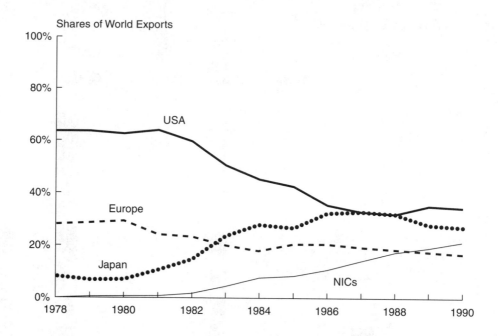

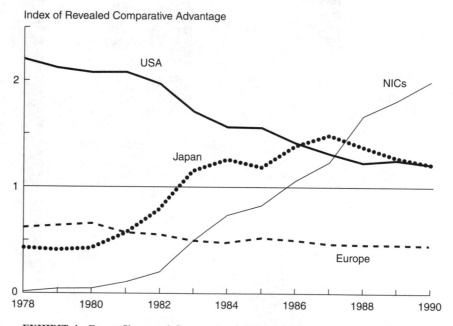

EXHIBIT 4 Export Shares and Comparative Advantage by Region, 1978–1990 (DP equipment only)

Note: Index of revealed comparative advantage calculated using Balassa method—share of computers in total exports for each region divided by share of computers in total world exports. An index greater than one indicates comparative advantage, and less than one indicates disadvantage.

Source: Compiled from United Nations data (includes only SITC 752).

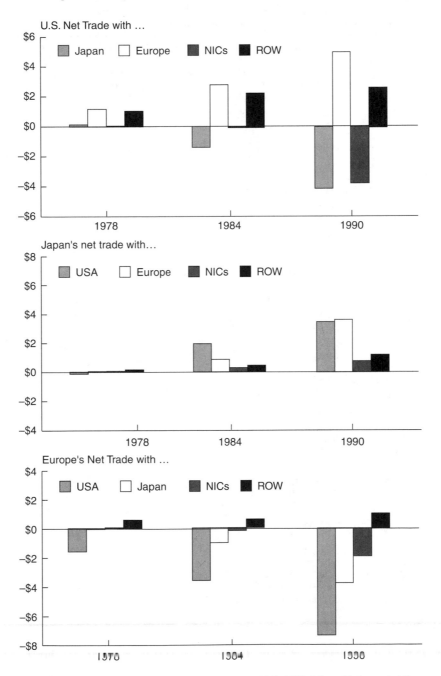

EXHIBIT 5   Computer Trade Balances by Region, 1978–1990 (bilateral balances in billions US$)

Note: ROW = Rest of the world.

Source: Compiled from United Nations data.

EXHIBIT 6   Geographic Positions of Computer Firms, 1984–1990

| Market Shares of Firms in Each Market (By nationality of firm) | | | | Relative Weight of Geographic Markets in Each Firm's Sales (By nationality of firm) | | | |

Total market sizes (billions US$)				Total sales (billions US$)			
	1984	1990	CAGR		1984	1990	CAGR
USA	66	98	6.8%	IBM	43	65	7.2%
Europe	31	90	19.2%	All US	95	175	10.7%
Asia	19	71	24.5%	Japanese	14	64	28.1%
Other	8	16	12.6%	European	15	34	14.9%
World total	124	275	14.2%	Total	124	275	14.2%

Share of US market accounted for by:			Weight of US market in total for:		
IBM	39%	26%	IBM	60%	39%
All US	94%	88%	All US	65%	49%
Japanese	2%	6%	Japanese	10%	10%
European	4%	4%	European	17%	13%
			All	53%	36%

Share of European market by:			Weight of Europe in total for:		
IBM	34%	27%	IBM	25%	38%
All US	63%	62%	All US	21%	32%
Japanese	3%	7%	Japanese	6%	10%
European	34%	30%	European	72%	79%
			All	25%	33%

Share of Asian market by			Weight of Asia in total for:		
IBM	18%	13%	IBM	8%	14%
All US	35%	28%	All US	7%	11%
Japanese	61%	69%	Japanese	81%	77%
European	4%	3%	European	5%	5%
			All	15%	26%

Share of other markets by:			Weight of other markets in totals:		
IBM	41%	38%	IBM	8%	9%
All US	83%	79%	All US	7%	7%
Japanese	6%	11%	Japanese	3%	3%
European	11%	6%	European	6%	3%
			All	6%	6%

Share of world market by:		
IBM	34%	24%
All US	76%	64%
Japanese	12%	23%
European	12%	12%

Source: Compiled from Gartner Group, *Yardstick Worldwide.*

EXHIBIT 7   Product Positions of Computer Firms, 1984–1990

Market Shares of Firms in Each Segment (by nationality of firm)				Relative Weight of Products in Each Firm's Sales (by nationality of firm)			
Total Market Sizes (billions US$)				**Total Sales (billions US$)**			
	1984	1990	CAGR		1984	1990	CAGR
Mainframes	21	36	9.4%	IBM	43	65	7.2%
Minis	19	31	7.9%	All US	95	175	10.7%
Micros	14	43	20.4%	Japanese	14	64	28.1%
Peripherals	22	51	15.0%	European	15	34	14.9%
Software	10	29	20.0%	Total	124	275	14.2%
Other	38	85	14.3%				
Total	124	275	14.2%				
Share of Mainframe Market				**Weight of Mainframes in Total for:**			
IBM	67%	51%		IBM	33%	31%	
All US	85%	66%		All US	19%	15%	
Japanese	11%	28%		Japanese	17%	16%	
European	3%	6%		European	4%	5%	
				Total	17%	14%	
Share of Minicomputer Market				**Weight of Minis in Total for:**			
IBM	21%	21%		IBM	10%	9%	
All US	74%	72%		All US	15%	14%	
Japanese	14%	16%		Japanese	18%	12%	
European	12%	12%		European	16%	10%	
				Total	16%	13%	
Share of Microcomputer Market				**Weight of Micros in Total for:**			
IBM	43%	24%		IBM	14%	15%	
All US	82%	61%		All US	12%	14%	
Japanese	9%	24%		Japanese	9%	16%	
European	9%	13%		European	9%	16%	
				Total	11%	15%	
Share of Peripherals Market				**Weight of Peripherals in Totals:**			
IBM	23%	10%		IBM	12%	8%	
All US	64%	48%		All US	15%	14%	
Japanese	20%	38%		Japanese	30%	30%	
European	17%	13%		European	24%	21%	
				Total	18%	18%	
Share of Software Market				**Weight of Software in Total for:**			
IBM	33%	35%		IBM	7%	15%	
All US	76%	70%		All US	8%	12%	
Japanese	11%	18%		Japanese	7%	8%	
European	13%	11%		European	8%	9%	
				Total	8%	10%	

Source: Compiled from Gartner Group, *Yardstick Worldwide*.

EXHIBIT 8   Top 15 Computer Firms Worldwide, 1975–1990

1975	1985	1990	1990 DP Rev. (billions US$)
IBM	IBM	IBM	64.6
Burroughs	DEC	Fujitsu	16.0
Honeywell	Sperry	DEC	13.1
Sperry	Burroughs	NEC	11.8
CDC	Fujitsu	Hitachi	10.8
NCR	NCR	Unisys	10.1
Bull	NEC	HP	8.3
DEC	CDC	Siemens-Nixdorf	7.0
ICL	HP	Olivetti	6.5
Nixdorf	Siemens	Bull	6.4
NEC	Hitachi	Apple	5.7
Memorex	Olivetti	NCR	5.4
HP	Wang	Toshiba	4.1
TRW	Xerox	Compaq	3.6
Olivetti	Honeywell	Philips	3.3
		Top 100	**275.0**

Source: Compiled from data from McKinsey & Co. and Gartner Group, *Yardstick Worldwide.*

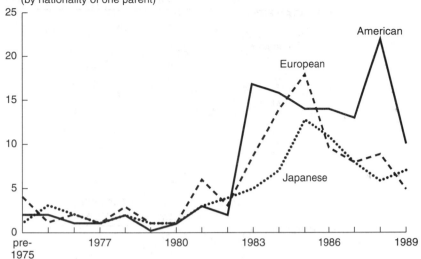

Number of New Alliances Formed each Year
(by nationality of one parent)

American

European

Japanese

pre-1975　1977　1980　1983　1986　1989

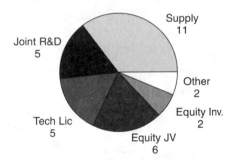

Types of International Alliances

Supply
11

Joint R&D
5

Other
2

Equity Inv.
2

Tech Lic
5

Equity JV
6

Before 1980 (Total: 31)

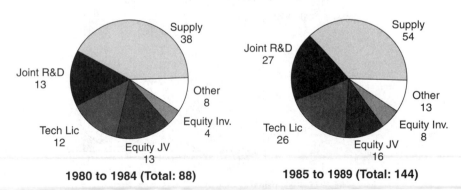

Supply
38

Joint R&D
13

Other
8

Equity Inv.
4

Tech Lic
12

Equity JV
13

1980 to 1984 (Total: 88)

Supply
54

Joint R&D
27

Other
13

Equity Inv.
8

Tech Lic
26

Equity JV
16

1985 to 1989 (Total: 144)

EXHIBIT 9　International Alliances of Leading Computer Firms, 1975–1989

Note: The totals in the bottom panel differ from the total number of alliances reported in
the text (226), because many alliances had more than one structure, and so were
counted more than once in the pie charts.

Source: Survey of press reports; see Gomes-Casseres (1992).

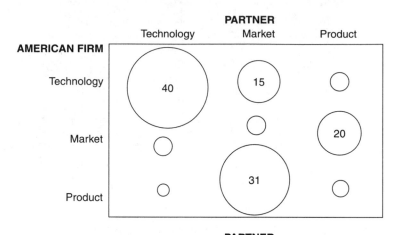

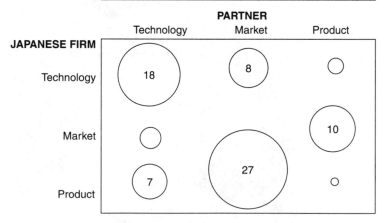

EXHIBIT 10 Contributions of Partners in International Alliances (total number of alliances for 1975–1989, paired as shown)

Note: This chart is to be read as follows: E.g., the top panel shows that in 15 cases American firms contributed technology to an alliance in exchange for market access that was provided by the partner.

Source: Survey of press reports; see Gomes-Casseres (1992).

Collision Course in Commercial Aircraft: Boeing-Airbus-McDonnell Douglas—1991 (A)

You don't succeed in this business by being cautious. If you don't want to play the game, maybe you ought to do something else. . . . The willingness to gamble, whether in product innovation or product introduction, is very important. The worst thing for us is to overreact and get so conservative that we try to live off our past accomplishments. . . .[1]

At various points in the previous two decades, accusations of unfair trade practices had led the United States and the European Community to the brink of trade war in commercial aircraft. Booming demand at the end of the 1980s seemed to signal a respite in the fight between companies and countries on both sides of the Atlantic. The three major manufacturers—Boeing, Airbus Industrie, and McDonnell Douglas—were struggling to produce enough aircraft to satisfy a seemingly unquenchable need for passenger and freight transport around the world.

But the political and competitive battle showed signs of heating up again in mid-1991. Airbus, a consortium of European aircraft manufacturers formed in 1970

Research Associate Eric J. Vayle prepared this case under the supervision of Professor David B. Yoffie as the basis for class discussion rather than to illustrate either effective or ineffective handling of an administrative situation.

Note: This case borrows heavily from "Airbus vs. Boeing (A, B, and C)," HBS Case Nos. 386–193. 388–145, and 388–146 by Research Associates Wendy Coleman and Irene L. Sinrich under the supervision of Professor Malcolm Salter.

[1]Boeing Chairman and CEO Frank Shrontz, interviewed in *Fortune,* October 17, 1989.

and backed by their various national governments, grabbed 30% of new aircraft orders in 1991, largely from McDonnell Douglas (MD). With MD holding only 14% of industry backlog, it was questionable whether MD's commercial operations could stay out of the red. Moreover, Airbus Managing Partner, Jean Pierson, confidently predicted at the Harvard Business School in 1991 that there would "only be two manufacturers in the year 2000," implying that MD was unlikely to be around.

Having proclaimed victory in one competitive arena, Airbus publicly committed to the biggest pie in the industry: intercontinental jumbo jets. This was Boeing's territory, the lucrative Boeing 747 market. When it first introduced them in 1966, Boeing sold 747s for about $18 million each. In 1991, the same airframe (albeit with some improvements and renovations) cost about $150 million apiece. One industry analyst estimated that Boeing's 1991 profit on each 747 sold was about $45 million. (See **Exhibit 1**.) Yet if Airbus wanted to develop a long-range jumbo jet, it would have to invest billions of dollars in research and fixed assets over the next few years. Furthermore, it would not earn any revenues in this segment before the year 2000, and cash flow from continuing operations were grossly insufficient to cover development costs.

The early 1990s would be a watershed for the commercial aircraft industry. McDonnell Douglas had to fend off Airbus to survive; Airbus had to finance its ongoing assault against its American competitors; and Boeing faced the prospect of its first direct threat to its cash cow. At stake for the companies *and* their respective countries was over $600 billion in orders over the coming decade.

The Business of Making and Marketing Airframes

Industry-Government Interaction

In 1917, just 14 years after the Wright brothers took the first manned flight, the U.S. government built a major aeronautics research center in Langley, Virginia. Since that time, the industry had been characterized by close collaboration between the private and public sectors. In the United States, government investment in civil aircraft manufacture was substantial before and during World War II, as the industry mobilized to meet the country's military needs. As a consequence, U.S. manufacturers emerged from the war with a distinct technological and economic advantage over competitors in Europe. The industry continued to be a high government priority after World War II. Governments around the world recognized that nations could benefit from investment in aircraft. When a country had a viable aerospace industry, the economic and technological spillovers created dozens of new industries and thousands of new jobs.

While federal funding in the U.S. was targeted for military aviation, European government support was directly aimed at the commercial sector. Government subsidies were instrumental in creating and sustaining Airbus. Government funds were the sole source of capital for the development of the A300, Airbus's first aircraft, and European subsidies continued to underwrite substantial portions of the R&D for new models. This ongoing government role produced intense pressure on both sides of the Atlantic for government officials to tip the balance of industry economics in the favor of their country's home producers.

Economic Factors

Launch costs. Commercial airframe manufacturers tended to be in the business for the long haul. Years of investment were needed before production began and revenues appeared. Launch investment costs typically fell into three categories: 40% for development, 20% for tooling, and 40% for work-in-process and overhead costs. The total amount, spent over an average five years of development, was necessary to develop and certify the aircraft and set up a production line, all before any assessment of success in the market. Manufacturers tried to book as many launch orders as possible, but in the history of the industry there had never been enough to ensure breakeven profitability before the launch date. As a measure of investment risk, Boeing's combined investment in the 1970s for its new 757 and 767 aircraft totaled more than the company's net worth.

The development period began with an aircraft design known as the "paper airplane," a three-way-view model with estimates of performance and operating costs. The manufacturer used these models to demonstrate new technology and, most important, to assess the response of potential buyers. Typically, manufacturers held discussions with key airlines about adaptations and options to incorporate into the prototype. Often these airlines became launch customers, making initial orders that guaranteed a minimum volume, while sending a signal to the marketplace that the aircraft would likely succeed. A launch customer's reputation was important for subsequent sales.

Once minimum backing was achieved—either through orders received from a group of airlines or financial commitments from government agencies—the program could proceed and full-scale development begin. The design and development phase faced built-in costs, such as regulatory approval and costly and time-consuming flight tests, in addition to prototype construction and assembly.

The majority of the tooling costs were associated with the construction jigs, which were expensive to build and required precise specifications. Work-in-process and general administration costs were large because the manufacturer was required to start production of a new model long before it was government certified; otherwise, there would be a delay of 12 to 24 months (the length of the manufacturing cycle) before any aircraft were delivered. The initial inventory was equivalent to about 40 aircraft, although the costs of the inventory buildup could be offset partly by customer progress payments and subcontractor credits. All in all, launch costs could total up to $20 million per seat, as inferred from estimates of the launch investment of $2.5 billion for Airbus's A-320. In the 1990s, a new development project from scratch was more likely to cost between $4 billion and $5 billion, adding to the sales volume necessary to break even. In addition, any upgrades or derivatives, a normal part of the development phase for long production runs, could add 30% to 40% to the overall investment.

An aircraft's sale price typically included purchased parts, direct expenses (labor and supplies), and the launch investment. With normal 25% gross margins, manufacturers typically reached breakeven (recovered launch costs) at 400 units, 12–14 years after the decision to launch the program. Realizing profits in this industry followed a traditional learning curve. As more were produced, the marginal cost to produce each unit decreased. Yet not every manufacturer faced exactly the same curve. When Airbus decided to produce the A-320, it was more likely that 600 sales were needed to break even. However, only one of the 14 European jetliners that had entered service since 1952 ever reached 300 sales (the A300 in 1991), and only 6 out of 12 American models—the Boeing 707, 727, 737, and 747 and the McDonnell Douglas DC-9 and MD-80—had ever generated over 600 shipments each.

Civil aircraft selling was also a long-term relationship business. A manufacturer's sales force and designers worked closely with engineers at the airlines during the development phase. Customers demanded that manufacturers provide service worldwide, with minimum delay. To obtain operational and maintenance efficiency, airlines did not usually mix directly competitive types of aircraft or engines in their fleets. Neighboring airlines also found it advantageous to have access to one another's spare parts and maintenance services. Thus, an initial order tended to have substantial ripple effects. It established an airline's fleet composition by aircraft or engine type for a decade or more. With an aircraft's normal service life of 22 years, a lost sale could easily have a ripple effect of 15 to 20 years. In addition to the hurdle of launching costs, suppliers faced the challenge of selling several jetliners to a few large customers at the outset, rather than marketing initial units to a large cluster of small airlines, which was far more costly. All of the major competitors in the industry strove to make large sales at the launch, and to maintain their fleets at important airlines. Harry Colwell, an analyst at Chase Manhattan Bank, commented that "the manufacturer feels that he has to win each competition. It becomes so important as to be obsessive—a kind of phobia."[2]

Future demand.   Demand for new aircraft was driven by traffic growth and fleet replacement. At the end of 1990, there were over 7,800 aircraft in service. The industry expected air travel at the end of the century to be nearly double its 1990 level (**Exhibits 2** and **3**). In 1991 dollars, this represented about $600 billion in new orders; of this, about $200 billion was replacement demand, and the rest was new growth. These figures also did not take into account the Soviet Union and Eastern Bloc countries. Hungary, Romania, and Poland had entered into negotiations with Boeing, and Airbus Industrie was completing an application to sell two widebodied planes to East Germany. The Soviet Union's state-run airline, Aeroflot, was the world's largest, and

[2]John Newhouse, *The Sporty Game* (New York: Alfred A. Knopf, 1982), p. 21.

was also considering expanding its fleet in 1991, possibly to include Western aircraft for the first time.

Historically, most non-U.S. carriers had been small, government-owned airlines, which tended to place small orders. However, some European and Asian carriers were approaching the size and scope of U.S. mega-carriers and were placing huge orders. Also, some international carriers had formed purchasing alliances that allowed them to order greater quantities of aircraft.

The rate of aircraft replacement was determined by the airlines' ability to pay for new equipment and the cost of keeping old equipment in service. Other factors that affected the replacement life were the resale value of old aircraft and routes to be served. As of 1984, the average for retiring an aircraft had been 18.5 years. But many airlines continued to postpone aircraft retirement, causing the average aircraft age to climb. By 1990, it had reached 22 years. Postponing aircraft replacement allowed carriers lower depreciation charges and delayed major capital outlays. However, replacement of older jetliners lowered airlines' charges for fuel and maintenance (between them, the lion's share of operating expenses). Newer technology allowed savings on skilled labor (two instead of three in the cockpit), which also represented a substantial portion of operating cost. According to an estimate by Boeing, about 300 planes per year were expected to be retired between 1991 and 2005.

Engine noise restriction was the one aircraft replacement factor that airlines did not control. By 1985, the industry's oldest jetliners (e.g., Boeing's 707) were no longer able to serve U.S. markets due to noise regulations. In 1990, Congress set a timetable for airlines to have Stage 2 aircraft (aircraft built with some noise control, after initial noise restrictions were put into effect) like 727s, 737s, and some 747s from Boeing, and McDonnell-Douglas DC-9s and DC-10s, either retired or modified to further reduce engine noise by the year 2000. These regulations were only for U.S. airports, but similar restrictions existed in Europe and elsewhere.

Although demand for new planes seemed high and steady in 1991, the major players understood that demand in this industry was cyclical and that the risk of an eventual slowdown in orders existed. Industry players faced the challenge of positioning themselves so that they were able to keep up with demand during booming periods, but were not caught with overcapacity during the busts.

The Boeing Company

The Boeing Company, founded in July 1916 in Seattle, Washington, was the world's largest private commercial aircraft manufacturer and America's largest exporter. In 1990, Boeing delivered 385 airplanes while taking new orders for 543 aircraft. Boeing also produced military aircraft and products for NASA and other aerospace organizations.

During the 1970s and 1980s, Boeing's stated goal was to be the dominant competitor in every segment of the commercial transport market. To accomplish its goal,

Boeing identified several strategies. First, it had to be a technological leader, spending between 4% and 9% on research and development programs for commercial aircraft. Boeing was nearly pushed into bankruptcy in 1971, for example, because of the large expense of developing the 747. It had been forced to take measures as drastic as cutting its work force by over 60% at that time, but Boeing had expanded tremendously since 1971. By 1990 its manufacturing capacity was over 430 planes per year—about 70% of worldwide demand.

The military aircraft and space product programs at Boeing and McDonnell Douglas also helped promote the development of new technology and commercial products. By absorbing the heavy research and development costs for jet engines, jumbo airframes and wings, and advanced avionics, federal military grants enabled Boeing to move down the learning curve on commercial planes with far smaller investments of their own capital. In the 1960s, for example, the U.S. military ordered 600 KC-135 military transports from Boeing. Because the 707 was such a close derivative of the KC-135, its initial profitability was ensured before production commenced. Similarly, development work on airframes and engines for the Air Force's giant C-5 transport led to commercial jumbo jets like the Boeing 747 and McDonnell Douglas's DC-10.

Boeing also developed a family of basic models for a wide variety of flight ranges and passenger capacities. From these, derivatives could be developed to expand markets and to extend product life cycles (see **Exhibit 4**). In 1991, Boeing's airframe families included the 727 and 737, both short-range aircraft; the 757 and 767, both larger, medium-range craft; and 747, a massive widebody airplane that held 400 passengers and could fly farther than any other commercial airliner. Until 1987, Boeing had planned to offer a short-range, 150-seat plane called the 7J7 starting in 1992. It had so much difficulty finding launch customers for the plane, given competitive products by Airbus already available to airlines, that it repeatedly postponed and eventually canceled the project. It transferred some of the 7J7's technical innovations to development of the 777, a medium-to long-range widebody aircraft that Boeing expected to deliver in 1995.

Cancellation of the 7J7 development program strengthened Boeing's cash position and helped its strong, well-coordinated marketing team to sell planes more aggressively on a global scale. Salespeople endeavored to identify potential sales earlier than competitors when possible. Without the costs of 7J7 development, Boeing had better financial wherewithal to compete on the basis of price as well. While the team attempted to sell to all airlines and aircraft-leasing companies worldwide, it targeted certain carriers that it refused to relinquish as customers at any price. These tended to be the world's largest, best-capitalized carriers, such as United Airlines, Lufthansa, British Airways, Air France, and Japan Airlines. United, for example, placed a $22 billion order for new aircraft in 1990, calling for 128 planes to be delivered between 1991 and 2004. The entire order was for Boeing aircraft; not only was this the largest order in aviation history but it would also make United an all-Boeing carrier. According to James Bryan, president of Airbus North America, "There was no way that Boeing was going to let Airbus into United. They would have given away the airplanes if it had come to that."

Boeing also developed a reputation for providing rapid, worldwide service and parts replacement for its customers. By 1991, Boeing boasted an enormous customer base: nearly 6,300 commercial aircraft had been delivered to more than 450 owners and operators. Boeing's range of products made it the only civil aircraft producer that met the demands of most large continental and intercontinental carriers.

Airbus Industrie

Airbus Industrie was formed in 1970 as a GIE (Groupement d'Intérêt Economique), an entity of French origin under which separate companies pooled their interests and activities for mutual gain. The GIE itself, however, did not exist to make a profit. All of the financial accounts associated with the Airbus programs were incorporated into the partners' own accounts, and the GIE did not report its financial results. Each participant's profit depended upon its own costs, and the costs of one participant were not borne by the others. In effect, profits (and losses) were not shared.

A major reason for Airbus's existence was the desire of several European governments to have a viable aerospace industry. Although European competitors had existed in the industry from its outset, they had historically comprised a minute portion of high-capacity aircraft sales. In 1970, the consortium was formed. Its initial two members were France's Aérospatiale and West Germany's Deutsche Airbus. Later, British Aerospace and Spain's CASA would join as well. Discussions on cooperation stemmed from perceived opportunities in the short- to medium-range market. At that time, over 60% of the world's airline traffic flew routes less than 2,500 nautical miles and the short- to medium-range airliner market was virtually untapped.

The partners focused their discussions around the development of the A-300, the world's first twin-engine widebodied aircraft, seating 240 to 345 passengers with a range of 2,000 to 4,000 nautical miles. Airbus Industrie was responsible for managing the development, production, marketing, and after-sales service of the aircraft. Functions specifically associated with the engineering, production, and program finance, while coordinated by Airbus Industrie, were primarily executed by the partner companies.

In 1974, the first A-300s were delivered. The consortium's second effort was the A-310, a smaller and longer-ranging widebody, which began delivery in 1983. Recognizing the importance of having a range of aircraft "families" available to fill various niches for customers in the 1980s, Airbus followed these with the A-320, a small-capacity, short-range craft in 1988. This craft was built to accommodate two new trends in the industry. First, many new airlines had appeared since deregulation in the United States and Europe in the 1980s. These new carriers operated at lower cost, offered discounted fares, and required smaller seating capacity. Second, flight scheduling focused around the hub-and-spoke pattern, under which short-haul routes fed into major airports for connection with longer-haul segments of the trip. During the late 1980s, the company began taking orders for two new airframes, the A330 and A340, to compete with the MD-11 and 747 on medium- to long-range routes. They were built to access the expected increase in intercontinental (especially trans-Pacific) travel and were expected to be ready for delivery in 1993.

Airbus aircraft boasted technological advances over U.S. planes. Technological firsts for Airbus on the A-320 and the A-330 and A-340 included, among other features, active controls, variable camber wing, fly-by-wire, digital auto-flight system, side-stick controllers, and advanced composite materials in the aircraft's structure. Several of these technologies would be incorporated into new Boeing and MD designs like the 777 and MD-11.

Between 70%–90% of R&D costs for Airbus's technological development were financed by money from the participant nation governments. According to a 1990 consultant's report commissioned by the U.S. Department of Commerce, over $13 billion in government subsidies for development and production had been granted to Airbus partners since its inception. If that money had been borrowed at commercial rates, Airbus would owe more than $25 billion. The report continued that further aid would be available to Airbus, as needed for future development projects. Airbus claimed that government "launch aid" consisted only of loans, which were repaid by an agreed-upon share of the proceeds of each aircraft sale, transferred by Airbus Industrie to the partners. Evidence suggested that interest rates on these loans were below market rates, and that interest was sometimes forgiven altogether. Some government assistance was also provided to offset currency difficulties faced by subsidiaries: Airbus was paid in U.S. dollars for its deliveries, and in turn paid its member companies in dollars. The subsidiaries paid their expenses in local currencies. In 1989, the German government sold Deutsche Airbus to MBB, a German heavy manufacturing conglomerate. The sale was accomplished only with the stipulation that the German government would reimburse MBB for profit shortfalls caused by any exchange rate losses.

McDonnell Douglas Corporation

The industry's third major manufacturer was McDonnell Douglas (MD). MD had been making commercial airliners since 1920, and MD's Douglas Commercial (or DC) line of planes had been in service for over half a century. The majority of McDonnell Douglas's revenues came from U.S. government orders in 1991. MD was the largest defense contractor in the United States, producing about $10 billion worth of combat aircraft, helicopters, missiles, and defense electronic systems for the U.S. Armed Forces in 1990. During the 1960s and 1970s, the Commercial Aircraft Group at MD developed two major airframe designs that would become the backbones of its modern fleet. They were the DC-9, a narrow-body, short-range craft seating about 150 passengers, and the DC-10, a widebody, medium-range jet seating 250–350.

McDonnell Douglas was in financial disarray in 1990. Both its government sector business and its commercial business were faced with strong competitors and rapidly dropping demand for its products. Despite combat in the Persian Gulf, the defense sector underwent a major downturn in research and procurement during the late 1980s and early 1990s. Amidst the general slowdown, McDonnell Douglas's military group faced particularly serious setbacks due to the cancellation of the $4.8 billion A-12 Stealth attack plane in early 1990.

The company's transport aircraft sector had faced financial difficulties since the early 1980s. Competition between MD's DC-10 and Lockheed Corporation's L-1011 had cost the commercial division precious profitability in the late 1970s, and the strong emergence of Airbus squeezed MD's market share (see **Exhibits 5** and **6**). In 1985, MD's fleet comprised 28% of aircraft in service. By 1989, MD had only 26% of the worldwide fleet. In an attempt to revive lagging profits, MD undertook a massive restructuring in 1989. Personnel in production and other departments were cut by 8,400 jobs. Managers were required to interview for their own jobs. The restructuring, while having little effect on the division's profitability, was a devastating blow to employee and management morale. In 1990, the division lost over $177 million despite the restructuring and an Air Force procurement program for the C-17 transport.

In the late 1970s, McDonnell Douglas had needed to develop a new set of aircraft to replace aging DC-9s and DC-10s. Given its financial difficulties, MD chose to use the basic airframe and wing technologies of the DC-9 to develop the MD-80 series of twinjets, rather than invest in a completely new start-up development program. The MD-80 series, put into service in 1980, was available to carriers in a wide variety of passenger configurations and was MD's biggest seller. By 1990 over 1,600 MD-80s were in service. The MD-90 series, a derivative of the MD-80, was expected to enter service in 1994.

A similar development decision was made with the MD-11 in the late 1980s; instead of being developed from scratch, this tri-engine widebody craft was derived from DC-10 technology, and was put into service in 1990. By March 1991, 377 MD-11s had been ordered, selling out MD's production capabilities through 1995. MD hoped that the launch of the MD-11 would mark the company's turnaround. Instead, the MD-11 was filled with technical and manufacturing difficulties. The first planes off the assembly lines were delivered several months behind schedule and with several engineering deficiencies. As a result, the airplane was incapable of reaching its advertised maximum range when filled to its maximum capacity. Major launch customer American Airlines had inaugurated service from Boston to San Jose to Tokyo with this new craft, and the airplane was unable to make the full journey. American Airlines CEO Robert Crandall was infuriated, claiming he was "unhappy with the single MD-11 [American] has received, and very disappointed with McDonnell Douglas"[3] in January 1991. By May 1991, the craft was still not being used for

---

[3]*Aviation Week and Space Technology,* February 25, 1991, p. 29.

the trans-Pacific portion of the trip. With over 200 MD-80s in its fleet, and with 19 firm orders and 31 options for MD-11s, American was McDonnell Douglas's largest single customer.

While in the midst of MD-11 development in 1988, McDonnell Douglas approached Airbus about potential joint ventures. An alliance between the two would have made them equal to, if not larger than, Boeing in terms of market share. According to a news report, McDonnell Douglas [was] willing to use spare production capabilities in southern California to help Airbus produce its A-320, and there were "possibilities for joint production of a 100- to 120-seat aircraft [to rival the Boeing 737] and an aircraft in the 400-seat range to compete with the Boeing 747."[4] The two discovered that neither could abandon its current plans for a medium- to long-range craft. "Airbus was proceeding with plans for [its] two new widebody jets, the A-330 and the A-340, to be introduced in 1992,"[5] while McDonnell Douglas adhered to plans to deliver the competing MD-11 by 1990. However, they considered a stretched version of the MD-11, fitted with an Airbus A-330 wing. This "McAirbus" would have had two engines under the wing and a third (McDonnell Douglas style) in the tail. The plane could carry more than 500 passengers and would be the first direct competitor to Boeing's 747. Moreover, with one less engine, the McAirbus would be able to do what a 747 did more cheaply. Negotiations broke down when the companies hit an impasse over which should build the cockpit, the critical portion of the craft. The two broke off all discussions and continued on their separate projects. Talks had not resumed by 1991.

International Collaboration

Despite the lack of an agreement between Airbus and MD, success in the commercial aircraft industry had become dependent upon multinational joint ventures by the mid-1980s, and the industry was expected to become even further globalized as the century ended. Sharing the risks and rewards of development programs reduced market, financial, and technological uncertainties for manufacturers undertaking new projects.

Airbus, in addition to being an international consortium, depended on non-EC suppliers for a substantial portion of each aircraft. The largest of these foreign contributors were General Electric (GE) and CFM, an engine manufacturer that was a joint venture of GE and SNECMA, a French manufacturer. Both of these American manufacturers fitted Airbus planes with engines. In 1987, Airbus ordered $2 billion worth of engines from these companies. (See **Exhibit 7**.)

In the late 1980s, McDonnell Douglas joined forces with Aeritalia to produce over 10% of the MD-11 airframe; other international partners produced substantial amounts as well. In April 1985, McDonnell Douglas also signed an agreement with

[4]*Financial Times,* March 4, 1988, p. 5.
[5]*Business Week,* March 21, 1988, p. 51.

Shanghai Aviation Industry Corporation (SAIC) to co-produce 25 MD-80 twin-jet transports, with an option for 15 more. McDonnell Douglas was forging a long-term relationship in China with an eye toward further collaboration with SAIC.

Boeing contracted with three Japanese heavy manufacturers to build 20% of the airframe of its new 777 twin-engine widebody. In return, the Japanese Aircraft Development Corporation (a subsidiary of MITI, Japan's Ministry of International Trade and Industry) agreed to fund a substantial percentage of the development costs of the project. When asked whether or not Airbus would become similarly involved with Japanese manufacturers, Airbus Managing Partner Jean Pierson replied that Airbus was "considering the opportunity of taking, perhaps, a 15% risk partner. We're examining a new widebody project for 1997 or 1998, and we might bring them in on that." Manufacturers feared cooperating with Japan because MITI had publicly announced its intention to develop the aerospace industry in Japan as it had electronics and automobiles. In 1991, Japanese manufacturers did not have enough expertise to develop whole aircraft, but they had made great strides in that direction.

Pricing Competition

Since Airbus's entry into the world market with the A-300 and A-310, selling competition had increased steadily and substantially among the manufacturers. In a 1978 sale to Eastern Airlines, Airbus offered a financial arrangement known as a "Deferred Seat Plan." Under the plan, 12 of 23 planes were sold as if they had only 170 seats rather than 240. After four years or if Eastern's load factors exceeded a certain level, Eastern would be required to repay the "deferral." By offering to finance about 85% of a 1985 sale to Indian Airlines, Airbus clinched a sale even after the airline had signed a letter of intent with Boeing. To get the sale, Airbus offered to deduct from the sale price the costs of several aircraft that the airline leased while the ordered planes were being built. According to one published report, the French government also intervened in the sale on Airbus's behalf. French officials allegedly proposed offers of assistance to the Indian government, ranging from help in securing loans at the World Bank to accelerating deliveries of French military aircraft to India, to technical assistance in cleaning up the polluted Ganges River.[6]

Another financing package offered by manufacturers was the "walk-away lease." In 1988, American Airlines became the first carrier to utilize such a package when it split an order between the Boeing 767 and the Airbus A-300. Both manufacturers agreed to buy back the jets with as little as 30 days' notice. Another was the "trade-in" of competitor aircraft. All of the competitors had organizations to refurbish and sell used aircraft from competitors, which they purchased in exchange deals for new planes. In one deal, Boeing repurchased three *brand new* A-310s from Kuwait Airways in order to sell 767s to the airline. Tightening profits among the world's airlines made competitive financing increasingly risky for manufacturers in 1991. East-

[6]*International Herald Tribune,* October 31, 1985.

ern went bankrupt in 1991, leaving creditors including Airbus with billions of dollars' worth of uncollectible debt. If losses continued to plague airlines, manufacturers would continue to be stuck with bad debt and airplanes to resell.

Some of the fiercest competition came in the form of underbidding. Prior to 1988, Airbus often forced Boeing and MD to choose between losing a sale or cutting the prices below operating expenses. "We were pricing for market share," admitted Airbus Chairman Alan Boyd, "we had to do it in order to get our feet in the door." The further that Airbus was willing to price its aircraft below what U.S. manufacturers believed its operating costs to be, the more U.S. manufacturers believed Airbus was competing unfairly. U.S. trade officials stepped in to examine whether Airbus was in violation of international trade agreements.

Government Intervention

In the late 1970s, representatives of the United States, EC, and other governments drew up major fair trade agreements for aircraft sales as part of the General Agreement on Trade and Tariffs (GATT). The 1979 GATT Agreement on Trade in Civil Aircraft set forth an international legal framework governing the conduct of trade in civil aircraft. The framework included the elimination of duties and technical barriers for civil aircraft, the avoidance of disruptions in trade (including fair pricing), and a ban on governmental interference on sales or purchases. (**Exhibit 8** highlights the salient points of the GATT Aircraft Agreement.) The Large Aircraft Sector Understanding, signed in July 1985, updated the GATT agreement and sought to remove government financial assistance from the selling process by using interest rates to equilibrate customer financing opportunities among manufacturers.

Through the early 1980s, Airbus's sales were relatively few and American manufacturers were not concerned about competitive pressure from Europe. As Airbus's sales expanded in the mid-1980s and as the consortium developed products to compete in a wide range of market segments, industry officials began to pressure the U.S. Department of Commerce and the Office of the United States Trade Representative to help counter the trend. Government officials lodged protests over actions by European governments that seemed to violate the intent of the trade agreements to which they were signatories. European governments rejected American claims and put forth counter claims about U.S. government involvement in the industry. The diplomatic debate over active and financial involvement raged between them for the rest of 1980s and into the 1990s.

Embassy Assistance

The United States and European Community governments accused one another of intervening to provide "embassy assistance" to their manufacturers in situations where airlines were state-run agencies. In addition to reported French government activities in India, Airbus aircraft sales were also linked to French investments in a Kuwait petrochemical plant and to landing rights in Paris allowed to Korean Airlines. Along the same lines, however, Boeing's Vice President Boris Mishel admitted in 1988 that "U.S. embassy personnel have been extremely helpful in promoting the export of aircraft as well as all other U.S. manufactured goods."

Airbus's three largest partners also offered export credits, loans, and guarantees for the purchase of aircraft outside the consortium countries through institutions owned by their governments. France's Compagnie Française d'Assurance du Commerce Extérieur (COFACE) along with the Banque Française du Commerce Extérieur (BFCE) provided insurance and financing for up to 85% of the total purchase at the interest rates set out by the Large Aircraft Sector Understanding. Great Britain's Export Credit Guaranty Department (ECGD) performed both roles, insurance and banking, under the international guidelines. West Germany's Hermes, a private insurance agency owned by a consortium of large commercial banks but acting on behalf of the government, provided export credit guarantees for Deutsche Airbus. The conditions that were offered were reportedly in accordance with the Understanding.

Government Subsidies

Even more than political interference and export financing, U.S. industry and government officials were concerned about what they considered unfair subsidies provided to Airbus by European governments. McDonnell Douglas Vice President James Worsham encapsulated the U.S. position in the trade dispute: "No private U.S. company in our capital-intensive industry can compete indefinitely with the national treasuries of the most powerful European governments." Bruce Smart, undersecretary for international trade in the Department of Commerce, estimated that "about $12 billion of U.S. value-added [in 1984 dollars] would have resulted from shipments of U.S. rather than Airbus aircraft from 1974 to 1986, [and furthermore, that] translated to about 8,000 U.S. jobs in the aerospace industry and another 24,000 jobs in related industries." U.S. officials reacted skeptically when told that over a billion dollars' worth of commercial loans for the A300 and A310 were forgiven Deutsche Airbus by the German government in 1988. "This confirms," claimed Orvil Roetman, Boeing VP of international Business and Government Affairs, "the commercial insolvency of Airbus."

Airbus countered the charges of subsidization by stating that government assistance was necessary to overcome American monopoly status in the industry. It further claimed that the U.S. government was equally guilty of providing indirect subsidies to manufacturers through development and production contracts for military products with commercial applications. According to one Airbus claim, U.S. aircraft manufacturers (military as well as commercial) received a total of $23 billion in indirect government support between 1960 and 1988.

Conflict and Negotiations

In a 1985 press conference, President Ronald Reagan announced several alleged violations of trade agreements by U.S. trading partners, one of which was Airbus. The press conference resulted in speculation that the U.S. would file a Section 301 case against Airbus.[7] It did not. On June 23, 1987, however, the dispute escalated when the House Subcommittee on Commerce, Consumer Protection, and Competitiveness held its first hearing on competition between Airbus and the U.S. industry. Committee Chairperson James Florio (D-NJ) advocated the use of Section 301 of the U.S. trade law if the continuing negotiations failed to produce a resolution. He declared that "our trade partners should understand . . . that the Congress cannot, and will not, ignore the failure of negotiations to produce an acceptable agreement. The aerospace industry is too important to our nation's trade, economic, and defense interests to allow this situation to continue."

With such high stakes for trade balances and employment on the one hand, and the threat of lost aircraft sales on the other, GATT negotiators were pressed to provide a solution to the lingering civil aircraft trade dispute. On October 27, 1987, U.S. and E.C. negotiators agreed upon a framework of principles to resolve the dispute. Future meetings would aim at resolving embassy involvement and government financial support. Negotiations continued after that meeting, as negotiators attempted to find a diplomatic solution. However, exchanges were frank and often heated. Each side accused the other of violations, and each defended its actions on the basis of economic necessity. Little progress was made before a March 18, 1988, ministerial meeting. Convened in Konstanz, West Germany, U.S. Trade Representative Clayton Yeutter debated the remaining differences in the civil aircraft trade dispute with his counterparts from Britain, France, Germany, and the EC. They sought to resolve misunderstandings about direct government procurement, mandatory subcontracts and inducements, and issues concerning government support, both direct and indirect. The meeting, like its predecessors, yielded little progress. The parties agreed to eliminate state funding of *production*, as opposed to *research* and *development*, and agreed that both direct and indirect production funding would be covered by the agreement. However, as the meeting drew to a close, it was apparent that principles, and not details, were agreed upon. Progress had not led to resolution.

Between 1988 and 1991, U.S. Trade Representatives threatened four times to take trade action against the EC and Airbus. American government officials were concerned about maintaining the U.S. position in aerospace because it was one of the few shining stars in the U.S. trade balance: in 1989, for example, American aerospace companies exports totaled more than $23 billion (about 6.5% of total U.S. exports), and the sector's trade surplus stood at nearly $18 billion. In contrast, the United States overall trade deficit was $104.2 billion in 1989. Yet retaliation never material-

---

[7]Section 301 refers to the sections of the U.S. Trade Act of 1974, in which the president was empowered to take action to enforce the rights of the United States under any trade agreement and to eliminate unfair trade practices by a trading partner.

ized since "satisfactory progress" was made at preliminary meetings. By 1991, trade negotiators had agreed to limit Airbus government subsidies to 45% of total costs, down from 75% in the past. American negotiators still hoped to lower the amount to 25%. Beyond that issue, negotiations were at an impasse. Requests for financial transparency, an opening of the accounting books on both sides, were denied. European negotiators refused to disclose the true amount of subsidization until American negotiators disclosed the amount of indirect support available to American producers through military and NASA contracts. In 1991, the political situation appeared to be intensifying again. Aerospatiale's president, Henri Martre, urged the EC to harden its stance in subsidy negotiations, calling for "a strong, comprehensive case to defend European interests." This closely followed a claim by Airbus Managing Partner Jean Pierson that the U.S. was "deliberately manipulating [instruments like] the exchange rate to hurt European companies like Airbus Industrie." Alan Boyd of Airbus North America warned that "neither the EC nor Airbus will roll over and play dead" in the face of U.S. pressure.

Funding a New Jumbo

Managing Partner Pierson proudly exclaimed that, counter to the claims of American industry and government officials, "Airbus reached [operating] profitability in 1991, four years ahead of original expectations." Yet it would not be enough to cover development costs of the new craft; government subsidies would be required for the development of any new airframe. Yet in 1991, the government subsidies that had proven necessary in the past were being negotiated away. For Airbus, the key questions were, How do we continue financing our R&D and launch costs? What are our options and how do we frame the arguments?

The 747 was Boeing's last bastion of monopoly, and an Airbus competitor to the 747 could cement the European consortium's position squarely in the thick of the industry as the twenty-first century approached. Creative selling by Airbus had revolutionized the industry already, and American producers were faced with another possible assault. As they watched Airbus gather its political and economic weapons to prepare for the development of a new Airbus jumbo jet, U.S. manufacturers and government officials were faced with a number of questions. Would government-subsidized development of an Airbus competitor to the 747 be unfair or in violation of the GATT agreement? If Airbus could sell airlines directly competitive to the 747, what would that do to the industry structure? How should Boeing and MD respond to Airbus's relentless drive for market share?

EXHIBIT 1   Manufacturers' Operating and Financial Statistics

	1990	1989	1988	1990	1989	1988
	TRANSPORT AIRCRAFT[1]			TOTAL OPERATIONS[2]		
McDonnell Douglas						
Revenues	$5,812	$4,511	$4,637	$16,246	$14,581	$14,435
R & D				620	617	562
Oper Income	(177)	(167)	110	185	250	737
Depreciation	140	116	96	581	542	538
Net Income				275	(37)	372
Cash & Equivalents				226	119	107
Assets	5,432	4,030	2,949	14,965	13,397	11,783
LT Debt				5,584	4,935	3,626
Equity				3,514	3,287	3,186
Cap'l Exp	146	213	219	406	582	619
Rtn on Sales				1.7%	−0.3%	2.6%
Rtn on Avg. Equity				8.1%	−1.1%	12.1%
Boeing						
Revenues	$21,230	$14,305	$11,369	$28,043	$20,623	$17,340
R & D				827	754	751
Oper Income	2,189	1,165	585	1,972	922	820
Depreciation	349	280	264	672	622	563
Net Income				1,385	973	614
Cash & Equivalents				3,326	1,863	3,963
Assets	6,267	6,675	4,558	14,591	13,278	12,608
LT Debt				311	275	251
Equity				6,973	6,131	5,404
Cap'l Exp	1,001	612	326	1,586	1,362	690
Rtn on Sales				5.0%	3.3%	3.6%
Rtn on Avg. Equity				19.9%	11.0%	11.4%

[1]Transport Aircraft operations at McDonnell Douglas include production of the C-17, a military transport aircraft. Transport aircraft operations at Boeing are exclusively commercial.

[2]Non-transport aircraft operations for these two companies include the manufacture of military aircraft and other aerospace products.

Source: Boeing and McDonnell Douglas Annual Reports.

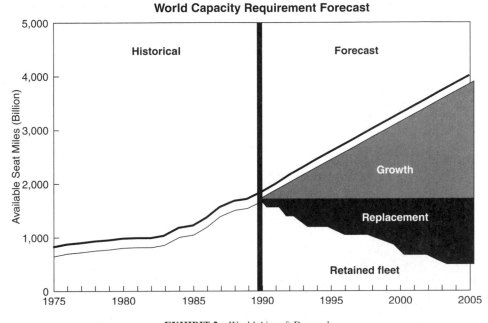

EXHIBIT 2   World Aircraft Demand

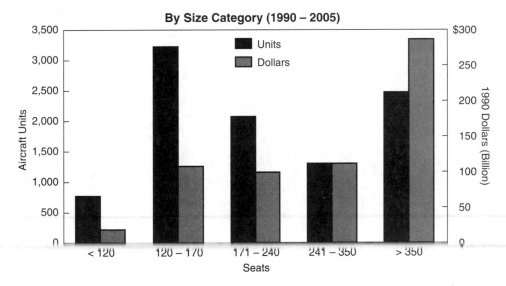

EXHIBIT 3   Aircraft Delivery Forecast
Source: *1991 Current Market Outlook*, The Boeing Company, 1991.

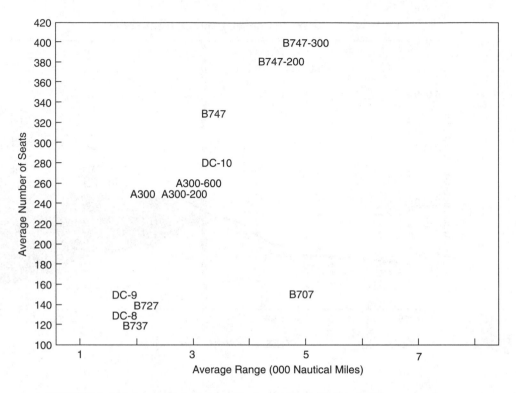

EXHIBIT 4   Existing Airframe Models of Boeing, Airbus, and MD in 1975

Source: R. Moriarty "The Airframe Industry (M)," Harvard Business School Case no. 582–013, 1982.

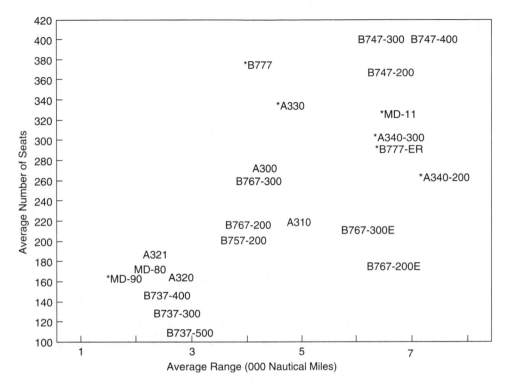

EXHIBIT 4   (*Continued*)

Source: Boeing *1991 Current Market Outlook*, Airbus and MD documents.
*PROPOSED MODELS ARE PRECEDED BY AN ASTERISK.

EXHIBIT 5 Market Share of Orders, 1974–1990

	1974	1975	1976	1977	1978	1979	1980	1981	1982	1983	1984	1985	1986	1987	1988	1989	1990
Boeing	70%	69%	72%	67%	68%	68%	81%	57%	62%	56%	50%	61%	47%	53%	57%	53%	45%
Airbus	1%	4%	5%	5%	14%	15%	6%	29%	13%	0%	22%	9%	25%	28%	15%	24%	34%
MD & Others	29%	27%	23%	28%	18%	17%	13%	14%	25%	44%	28%	30%	28%	19%	28%	23%	21%

EXHIBIT 6 Forecast of Aircraft Deliveries

	91	92	93	94	95	96	97	98	99	2000	TOTAL
Boeing											
B737	210	210	210	142	104	106	81	78	46	38	1,225
B747	67	72	72	73	60	60	50	51	40	38	583
B757	96	96	94	96	86	74	74	80	78	84	858
B767	60	60	60	55	54	27	27	18	20	8	389
B777	0	0	0	1	16	46	50	67	57	60	297
Airbus											
A300	37	39	18	15	8	0	0	0	0	0	117
A310	25	24	15	13	8	0	0	0	0	0	85
A320	110	100	88	65	40	30	20	20	14	20	507
A321	0	0	2	15	36	50	60	60	48	50	321
A330	0	2	13	35	66	52	37	43	59	64	371
A340	2	11	22	25	33	22	22	22	22	17	198
McDonnell Douglas											
MD-80	140	119	101	71	30	5	12	0	0	0	478
MD-90	0	1	14	38	39	48	58	80	80	84	442
MD-11	44	63	68	44	35	30	23	22	14	10	353
MD-12	0	0	0	0	2	20	20	20	23	37	122

Source: Forecast International/DMS Market Intelligence Report, May 1991.

A Typical "European" Aircraft Program

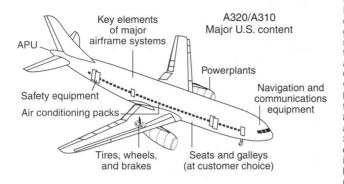

Key elements of major airframe systems

APU

A320/A310
Major U.S. content

Powerplants

Safety equipment

Navigation and communications equipment

Air conditioning packs

Tires, wheels, and brakes

Seats and galleys (at customer choice)

Over 500 U.S. companies participate in the Airbus Industrie industrial programs. In terms of initial investment, every Airbus aircraft sold generates approximately the same amount of business for the U.S. Manufacturing industry as an MD-80.
Over a 15-year cycle each Airbus widebody generates more business for the United States than a 727.
88% of all maintenance items are U.S. manufactured.
Since 1979, Airbus Industrie contracts with the U.S. aerospace industry have exceedd $3.5 billion — an average of $1.2 million per day for 8 years.

A Typical "American" Aircraft Program

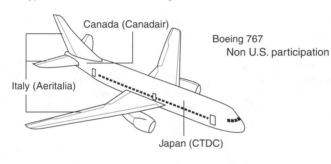

Canada (Canadair)

Boeing 767
Non U.S. participation

Italy (Aeritalia)

–Well over 30% of the 767 is manufactured outside the U.S.
–Because of the scale of resources required the same situation will apply for any new front-line airplane, from whatever primary source.

Japan (CTDC)

MD-80 Airframe Team
McDonnell Douglas – 51.9%
   Douglas Aircraft – 34.5%
   Other locations – 17.4%

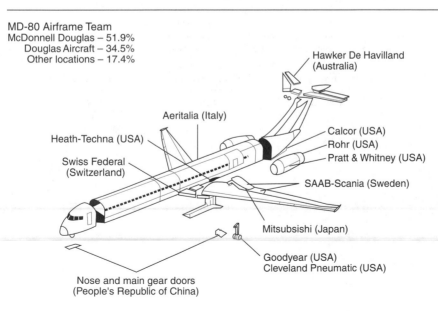

Hawker De Havilland (Australia)

Aeritalia (Italy)

Heath-Techna (USA)

Calcor (USA)
Rohr (USA)
Pratt & Whitney (USA)

Swiss Federal (Switzerland)

SAAB-Scania (Sweden)

Mitsubsishi (Japan)

Goodyear (USA)
Cleveland Pneumatic (USA)

Nose and main gear doors
(People's Republic of China)

EXHIBIT 7   Examples of International Cooperation
Source: Airbus Industrie company document.

EXHIBIT 8   Highlights of the GATT Agreement on Trade in Civil Aircraft

Signatories:

Austria, Belgium, Canada, Denmark, EEC, West Germany, France, Ireland, Italy, Japan, Luxembourg, Netherlands, Norway, Romania, Sweden, Switzerland, United Kingdom, United States

Purpose:

1. Achieve expansion and ever-greater liberalization of world trade through the progressive dismantling of obstacles to trade;
2. Maximize freedom of world trade;
3. Promote technological development;
4. Ensure fair and equal competitive opportunities;
5. Affirm importance in civil aircraft sector;
6. Recognize aircraft sector as a particularly important component of economic and industrial policy;
7. Eliminate adverse effects on trade in civil aircraft resulting from governmental support in civil aircraft development, production, and marketing, while recognizing that such government support, of itself, would not be deemed a distortion of trade;
8. Accept that civil aircraft activities operate on commercially competitive bases, and government-industry relationships differ widely among them;
9. Provide for international notification, consultation, surveillance, and dispute settlement procedures;
10. Establish an international framework governing conduct of trade.

Highlights of Articles Agreed to by Signatories:

1. Ensure airlines' freedom from governmental pressures to select suppliers on basis of commercial and technological factors; purchase of products covered by this Agreement should be made only on a competitive basis; avoid attaching inducements of any kind to the sale or purchase of civil aircraft from any particular source which would create discrimination against suppliers from any signatory.
2. No application of trade restrictions such as import quotas, import licensing requirements, or export licensing to restrict imports or exports.
3. Avoid adverse effects on trade in civil aircraft and take into account the special factors which apply in the aircraft sector, in particular the widespread governmental support in this area, their international economic interests, and the desire of producers of all signatories to participate in the expansion of the world civil aircraft market; pricing should be based on a reasonable expectation of recoupment of all costs, including nonrecurring program costs, identifiable and prorated costs of military research and development on aircraft, components, and systems subsequently applied to the production of such civil aircraft.

The agreement was signed April 12, 1979, in Geneva and went into effect January 1, 1980.

Source: GATT Agreement on Trade in Civil Aircraft.

Volkswagen de Mexico's North American Strategy (A)

Obviously a North American Free Trade Agreement gives security to our decisions. It puts strong pressure on our plant and on our suppliers to be competitive. Even without the agreement, we would still have to be competitive in order to export.[1]

Martin Josephi, President, Volkswagen de Mexico

On June 24, 1992, Volkswagen de Mexico celebrated at the presidential residence in Mexico City the production of VW's 21 millionth Beetle. VW de Mexico President Martin Josephi Wellman, a Mexican national of German descent, recounted the company's accomplishments since it started manufacturing in the country 28 years before and discussed the future challenges of North American free trade. With both President Carlos Salinas de Gortari and Gaspar Bueno Aguirre, the secretary-general of VW's labor union, at his side, he also pledged the commitment of the company and its workers to the National Accord for the Increase of Productivity and Quality, which had been recently signed by Mexico's major firms and labor federations.

VW's facility in the city of Puebla, the company's only production site in North America, seemed well-positioned to maintain its dominance of the Mexican car mar-

Research Associate Gordon Hanson and Professor Helen Shapiro prepared this case, with the assistance of Research Associate Ricardo Dominguez, as the basis for class discussion rather than to illustrate either effective or ineffective handling of an administrative situation.

[1]Interview with Martin Josephi, President of Volkswagen de Mexico, Puebla, June 17, 1992.

ket and to adjust to the gradual opening of the Mexican car market under the terms of the North American Free Trade Agreement (NAFTA). Unit sales had exploded by over 250% from 1987 to 1991, and VW was in the midst of a US$1 billion, five-year investment program to modernize and expand capacity. VW also was gearing up to reconquer the U.S. market with the introduction of Mexican-made Golfs and Jettas in September 1992.

Over that summer, the NAFTA was initialed by the leaders of Mexico, Canada, and the United States, and its ratification by each country's legislature seemed imminent. However, the VW plant was shut down by a bitter and unexpected labor dispute after the union leadership had agreed to a Japanese-style shop floor reorganization without fully consulting the rank and file. A lengthy disruption had the potential of costing the company lost sales and delaying the introduction of new models to the United States.

The Rise and Fall of Volkswagen's North American Fortunes

From the late 1950s, Volkswagen experienced a string of single-product successes in the U.S. market. The Beetle, which achieved almost cult status among U.S. consumers in the 1960s, was followed by the Rabbit (called the Golf in Europe), a fuel-efficient car that enjoyed instant popularity in the energy-conscious 1970s and early 1980s. All vehicles sold in the United States and Canada were imported from the company's central production facility in Wolfsburg, West Germany.

During the 1970s, the appreciation of the deutsche mark against the dollar threatened to price VW's cars—most of which were low- or mid-range models—out of the market. In early 1975, VW was losing money on every car sold in the United States, and falling sales threatened to break up its U.S. distribution network as dealers began to defect, particularly to Japanese firms.[2] The company sought a U.S. base of operations to insulate its sales prices from further exchange-rate volatility. In 1976, it acquired an unfinished manufacturing facility in Westmoreland, Pennsylvania from Chrysler, and the first U.S.-produced Rabbits appeared in 1978. Predating the Japanese transplants, this new subsidiary represented the first modern attempt by a foreign auto maker to produce cars in the United States. At the time, it was only Volkswagen's fourth manufacturing plant outside of Germany. (See **Exhibits 1 and 2** for VW worldwide operations.) The locally produced Rabbit's initial success prompted Volkswagen America to install a second production shift at Westmoreland during its first year of operation, bringing employment to 5,000 workers. The car's quality was considered to be as high or even higher than its German-made counterpart. A diesel Rabbit, introduced in 1979 at the height of the decade's second oil crisis, was so pop-

---

[2]Steven Tolliday, "Rethinking the German Miracle: Volkswagen in Prosperity and Crisis, 1939–1992," mimeo, Harvard Business School, 1991, pp. 29–30.

ular that the company initiated plans to build a second assembly plant in Sterling Heights, Michigan.[3]

The Rabbit's fortunes proved to be short-lived. (See **Exhibit 4** for Volkswagen sales in the United States.) The 1982 recession, the drop in oil prices, and the declining popularity of hatchbacks brought the Rabbit's run to a halt. U.S. sales of domestically built cars declined from a peak of 177,140 in 1980 to 85,045 in 1983, prompting Westmoreland to return to a single shift. Facing stiff competition from Japanese cars, VW was no longer the low-cost producer. Some analysts argued at the time that VW had failed to keep up with U. S. consumers' ever-changing demands. According to Maryann Keller, an auto industry analyst, "VW had it all 20 years ago. VW had a generation of lovers and lost them. They allowed the Japanese to seduce this generation. The VW product line is tired and old."[4]

By 1987, the Westmoreland facility was running at only one-third capacity. U.S.-made content dropped below 50% of each vehicle produced with the June 1987 closing of VW's West Virginia stamping plant. The stamping machinery, which had been tooled to supply two shifts at Westmoreland as well as the planned Michigan plant, was transported to Mexico where the same cars were being built. Despite the appreciation of the mark and the subsequently higher dollar costs of components imported from Germany, the stamping plant's low level of capacity utilization made it increasingly inefficient to keep open; volume was too low to justify its survival.

During the rise and fall of Volkswagen America, Volkswagen de Mexico remained a bit player in the company's global production network. Before the opening of the Westmoreland plant, Mexico had not been considered as an alternative production site for the U.S. market because of poor infrastructure, low domestic volumes, and country risk. Volkswagen de Mexico's car sales topped 100,000 in 1981, but the ensuing debt crisis and world recession drove Mexico into its worst economic crisis since the 1930s. Volkswagen's Mexican car sales fell by more than 40% from 1982 to 1983 and remained stagnant for the next six years. In 1987, its Puebla facility was still running at less than half capacity.[5]

With both its North American plants operating with excess capacity, Volkswagen decided to close one down. The U.S. plant enjoyed higher output per person hour, but the Mexico plant made up for it with lower wages. As VW President Josephi explained, "We compared costs in the U.S. and costs in Mexico. We compared quality in the U.S. and quality in Mexico. On balance, there was possibly a slight advantage for Mexico."[6] Moreover, projections for increasing cost efficiencies and volume growth in the medium term were better for Mexico than for the United States; VW was the market leader in Mexico, while its already small U.S. market share was declining further.

---

[3]*Automotive News,* November 23, 1987.

[4]*Automotive News,* November 30, 1987.

[5]Volkswagen Mexico also assembles vans for the Mexican market, but van sales account for less than 10% of the subsidiary's total vehicle sales.

[6]Interview, Puebla, June 17, 1992.

TABLE A   Volkswagen de Mexico Sales of
Passenger Cars, 1980–1991 (number of vehicles)

Year	Volkswagen de Mexico	Total Mexico Car Sales
1980	94,927	286,041
1981	133,048	340,363
1982	110,052	286,761
1983	63,195	192,052
1984	77,508	217,350
1985	76,364	242,187
1986	54,865	160,670
1987	50,631	154,152
1988	53,802	210,066
1989	77,021	274,505
1990	134,823	352,608
1991	148,646	392,110

Source: Compiled from data in *Balance de la Industria Automotriz*, Associación Mexicana de la Industria Automotriz, various editions.

These factors notwithstanding, the decision to close Westmoreland in 1988 was
ultimately dictated by Mexican trade policy. In the United States, it was possible to
import vehicles, but in Mexico it was not. Josephi continued: "The key was, it was
possible to close the plant in the U.S. and export to the U.S. from Mexico. The reverse was not true. The decision was clear. Closing the Mexican plant would have
meant abandoning the Mexican market."[7]

Rising to the Challenge: The Evolution of Volkswagen de Mexico

Auto Production Under Import Substitution

For Volkswagen de Mexico, adapting its operations to changing conditions was nothing new. Over more than three decades, the subsidiary had faced dramatic shifts in
Mexican trade and industrial policy. During the 1950s, VW started to export wholly
assembled vehicles to Mexico. The U.S. Big Three—Chrysler, Ford, and General
Motors—had already been assembling knocked-down kits in Mexico for several
decades. There was also a variety of Mexican-owned auto makers assembling in
small quantities.

In 1962, a new auto decree presented foreign auto makers with a choice: either
move beyond simple auto assembly to manufacture in Mexico or abandon the market.
The new trade policy was part of Mexico's emerging strategy of import-substitution

[7]Interview, Puebla, June 17, 1992.

industrialization, whose goal was to restrict reliance on imports by developing a domestic manufacturing base. According to the 1962 decree, 60% of a car's direct production costs had to be manufactured in Mexico by 1964. The power train (the engine and transmission) was to be included in this percentage. Production quotas, though loosely enforced, limited the number of vehicles that foreign auto makers could assemble. Automobile manufacturers were exempted from Mexico's standard foreign investment regulations, which restricted foreign firms to minority ownership positions, but they were limited to a 40% equity stake in supplier firms. In addition, firms were restricted to assembling vehicles, machining engines, and manufacturing components that they had produced prior to the decree; further vertical integration was prohibited.

In response to the decree, Volkswagen created Volkswagen de Mexico, S.A., a wholly owned subsidiary, and constructed a plant in Puebla, a medium-sized city (1965 population: 338,685; 1990 population: 1,057,454) located 60 miles east of Mexico City. The manufacturing facility had two parts: an auto-body stamping facility and an auto-assembly plant. Much of the machinery was second-hand, imported from Volkswagen's main plant in Wolfsburg.[8] Volkswagen lured German auto parts producers to form joint ventures with domestic firms to supply the Puebla facility, but the subsidiary continued to import key inputs, such as brake parts, suspension components, and fuel tanks, from Germany.[9] Volkswagen appointed Mexican nationals to top-management positions and, in contrast to its U.S. counterparts, assigned the German executives who were sent to Puebla for extended stays.

The Big Three, along with Nissan and Renault, also expanded their manufacturing facilities (see **Exhibit 5**). The domestic auto parts sector grew, but an unintended shake-out took place among the terminal producers. Most national auto makers folded in the 1960s, leaving auto production concentrated among foreign auto companies. The Mexican motor vehicle industry grew at an average annual rate of 17.6% from 1962 to 1974, almost twice as fast as the manufacturing sector as a whole.

Trade Deficits and Trade Barriers

In the 1970s, Mexico again saw sweeping changes in the policies regulating the auto industry. Mexico's difficulties in adjusting to the 1973 oil shock led to increasing economic disequilibrium and a balance-of-payments crisis. (**Exhibit 6** provides data on Mexico's economic performance.) In 1976, the peso was devalued, for the first time since 1954, by 50%, and austerity measures were adopted. The domestic recession hit the auto industry particularly hard.

---

[8]The government allowed Volkswagen to circumvent the restriction on motor imports in exchange for building the stamping facility (Barbara Samuels II, *Managing Risk in Developing Countries* [Princeton: Princeton University Press, 1990], p. 139).

[9]Ibid. By 1982, approximately 20 joint ventures had been formed by German and Mexican supplier firms, and 40–50 Mexican firms were operating with German licenses.

TABLE B   Mexico Automotive Exports, 1965–1990 (US$ millions)

	Vehicles	Exports Auto Parts	Engines	Vehicles[a]	Imports Auto Parts	Trade Balance
1965	0.1	0.8	0.0	131.7	50.9	−181.7
1970	0.2	26.4	0.0	166.4	53.3	−193.1
1975	9.6	139.0	35.4	189.6	617.6	−623.3
1980	128.7	204.8	32.7	657.7	1,239.0	−1,530.4
1985	140.7	246.9	1,039.2	135.0	858.2	433.5
1990	2,691.0	465.7	1,478.4	345.3	4,591.5	−301.8

Source: Steven Berry, Vittorio Grilli, and Florencio Lopez-de-Silanes, "The Automobile Industry and the Mexico-U.S. Free Trade Agreement, NBER Working Paper No. 4152, August 1992.

[a]An exception to the ban on imported vehicles was made for the border region. Annual quotas were established for the importation of used cars.

The government targeted the auto industry to turn the country's trade balance around. Despite the domestic content requirements of the 1962 decree, the auto industry was running a substantial trade deficit. Exports were insufficient to compensate for the sector's imports, which, due to its relatively low domestic content requirements, increased along with production volumes. Government resolutions issued in 1969 and 1972 tried to address the issue by rewarding exporting firms with larger production quotas, but they failed to bring the sector's trade into balance.

A new 1977 decree required auto makers to attain a positive overall trade balance by increasing either domestic content levels (set at a minimum of 50%) or exports. In an attempt to modernize the domestic supplier industry, at least 50% of a firm's export requirement had to be provided by local auto parts producers. Firms that failed to balance their trade sacrificed various subsidies and tax exemptions and risked the loss of market share through reduced access to imports. The expressed goal of the decree was to encourage auto makers to export finished vehicles, which would provide indirect access to new markets for the Mexican auto-parts industry.[10]

To comply with the new export requirements, Volkswagen de Mexico built an engine plant at Puebla, which also required the construction of an aluminum foundry. The engine plant increased both the domestic content of Puebla's vehicle production as well as exports by supplying the new Westmoreland plant. Volkswagen already had been producing at higher levels of local content and had smaller trade deficits than its U.S.-based competitors; it had started stamping in Mexico even before building engines. Its concentration on a single passenger car model, and its distance from its parent company, also worked in favor of higher domestic content. The combined investments gave Volkswagen the most integrated manufacturing facility in the country.

The Puebla facility began to export engines in 1981. After Westmoreland closed, Puebla continued exporting engines to Volkswagen plants in Germany.

[10]Juan Carlos Moreno Brid, "Mexico's Motor Vehicle Industry in the 1980s," World Employment Program working paper no. 21, International Labour Organization, Geneva, 1988, pp. 12–14.

TABLE C Volkswagen de
Mexico Engine Exports,
1981–1990
(number of engines)

Year	Engine Exports
1981	15,444
1982	40,320
1983	82,963
1984	146,337
1985	219,828
1986	237,651
1987	239,879
1988	211,248
1989	336,820
1990	338,145

Source: Unpublished data, Volkswagen de Mexico

The other auto firms also complied with the decree by building new engine capacity for export. (See **Exhibit 5**.) All together, the new plants increased Mexico's annual productive capacity to almost 2 million units. In contrast to VW, which concentrated all facets of production in its Puebla facility, the other firms built their new engine plants in north or north-central Mexico, far away from their original manufacturing operations near Mexico City (see **Exhibit 5**). All of the engines were aimed at the U.S. market, except for Nissan's, which were divided equally between the United States and Japan.

The announcement of vast oil reserves in 1977 and, with it, easy access to foreign loans promised to eliminate any balance-of-payments constraint on future economic growth. With real GNP growing at an annual average rate of 8.4% from 1978–1981, prospects for the domestic auto market brightened considerably. While the sector's new export capacity was coming on-stream, its overall trade deficit skyrocketed along with domestic sales, hitting US$2.1 billion in 1981. This represented 58% of Mexico's total trade deficit and made the automotive industry the largest private sector contributor to the country's trade imbalance. In 1981, the government insisted on stricter compliance with the 1977 decree, but to little avail.

The Debt Crisis and the Rise of Export Promotion

The 1980s brought new trauma to the Mexican economy (see **Exhibit 6**). The government, on the back of Mexico's oil bonanza, had borrowed its way out of the 1970s foreign exchange crunch, leaving the country with a foreign debt that exceeded the value of the gross domestic product. When interest rates entered the stratosphere in the early 1980s, Mexico was unable to meet the obligations on its external debt. Adjustment to the ensuing debt crisis required massive cutbacks in government spending and a series of peso devaluations. The country suffered a severe economic contraction in 1982, from which it did not recover until 1989. Car production fell by 15% in 1982 and another 30% in 1983. Renault abandoned the Mexico vehicle market in 1986; Ford and GM seriously considered pulling out as well.

To combat the country's economic woes, President Miguel de la Madrid (1982–1988) instituted a sweeping overhaul of Mexico's development policy. The new Mexico was to have less state intervention, an open economy, and a vibrant private sector dedicated to the export of manufacture goods. The auto industry was central to the country's new export-promotion strategy.

De la Madrid's automotive decree of 1983 required firms to generate their own foreign exchange to cover all imports and service payments by 1987. They also had to reduce their product lines to one make and five models. Additional makes were allowed only if they were self-sufficient in foreign exchange. Moreover, the decree prohibited the production of V-8 automobiles for the domestic market as well as the importation of components for luxury cars. This limitation hit U.S. firms especially hard, since it placed severe limits on their ability to compete via product diversification. In addition, their fastest-growing and most profitable lines had been in luxury and sports cars during the oil boom. From 1983 to 1988, the industry overall showed a trade surplus for the first time, due initially to the reduced demand for imports in the face of severe contraction in domestic vehicle production and subsequently to export growth.

In 1989, the new government of Carlos Salinas (1988–1994) issued its own automotive decree, which mirrored more general moves to liberalize further the economy. Restrictions were removed on product lines, and for the first time, the government allowed auto firms manufacturing in Mexico to import finished vehicles. To do so, a firm had to generate a trade surplus of US$2.5 for every dollar spent on imported vehicles. Over time, the ratio was to be reduced. Local content requirements were cut to 36% of a car's value added, and import restrictions on individual components were eliminated. Auto makers could now choose which parts to import and which to source domestically, as long as they met the content requirement.

Just as some auto makers were about to leave the Mexican domestic market for dead, auto sales rebounded by over two-and-a-half times between 1987 and 1991. Volkswagen led the way (see **Exhibit 7**). The company firmly consolidated its leadership position in 1990 and 1991, when it outsold Nissan, its nearest competitor, by nearly two-to-one, and captured 38% of the new car market.

The Inexorable Beetle

Volkswagen's surge in sales was largely due to the continued popularity of the Beetle. (**Exhibit 8** gives Volkswagen de Mexico's sales by model from 1988 to 1991.) Two factors contributed to the Beetle's success. The first was the government's "*Auto Popular*" decree in 1989, which granted tax exemptions to cars with a low purchase price. The initiative was part of the government's concerted anti-inflation effort. VW cut the Beetle's price by 20% to qualify for the scheme; no other auto maker followed suit. The resulting sales price of US$6,700 made the Beetle by far the cheapest model on the market; its nearest competitor was priced at about US$10,000.[11] The move reduced the car's profit margins but sales more than doubled between 1989 and 1990. Mr. Josephi commented, "It's not our most profitable car, but I would also not say we are losing money."[12]

The second factor that spurred Beetle sales was new pollution controls in Mexico City. A 1990 government decree required all new vehicles to have catalytic convertors. To reinforce the decree, the government offered taxi drivers incentives to trade in their old vehicles. In 1991, Volkswagen launched a catalytic convertor-equipped Beetle, and by 1992, the Beetle accounted for 95% of all taxis operating in Mexico City.[13]

Many observers questioned the wisdom of continuing to push the Beetle. They argued that with rising incomes, Mexican consumers would inevitably move toward larger, safer vehicles, as they had in the United States and elsewhere. Subcompacts still accounted for most Mexican car sales, but compacts were gaining ground fast (see **Exhibit 9**). VW, while surprised by the Beetle's continued success, had no plans to scrap the car. Eric Paul, the director of Technical Development at Volkswagen de Mexico, foresaw strong demand for the Beetle through the year 2000, stating flatly, "We are prepared to continue production of the Sedan for as long as the market wants."[14] Josephi pointed out that the Beetle's real competition came from used cars: "Many people prefer to have a new Beetle than a three-year old Topaz, Cavalier, or Golf."[15]

Volkswagen's New North American Strategy

Consolidation

The consolidation of North American production in Puebla converted Volkswagen de Mexico from a small-time, developing-country subsidiary to a major player in VW's global strategy. Puebla was to become the main supplier to the U.S. market, which had been supplied from Germany since the 1987 closure of the Westmoreland plant. The shift was necessary to compensate for the lack of capacity in Europe, where VW's sales were booming. The weak dollar had also hurt VW sales in the United States; at 1991 exchange rates, Mexican production was cost-competitive with Germany's. In contrast to VW's domination of the European market, its U.S. sales had collapsed.

[11]*Automotive News,* March 9, 1992.

[12]*Automotive News,* March 9, 1992.

[13]*El Financiero International,* February 24, 1992.

[14]Interview, Puebla, June 18, 1992.

[15]*Automotive News,* March 9. 1992.

Consolidation implied a massive modernization program for Volkswagen de Mexico. The plant had never been oriented toward vehicle exports, but rather toward relatively small production runs for the Mexican market. James Womack, an international automotive consultant, estimated the minimum-efficient scale for auto production to be 240,000 vehicles a year.[16] Volkswagen de Mexico's largest production runs were of the Beetle, which had sales of 85,681 cars in 1991—an all-time record. Josephi stated, "Before Mexico can become internationally competitive in the motor vehicle industry we have to change the very nature of production because we don't have economies of scale."[17]

The real challenge facing Volkswagen de Mexico, therefore, was not the 1989 decree's export requirement, which actually complemented Volkswagen's North American strategy, but restructuring the Puebla facility for production of a new generation of Golfs and Jettas for the domestic market and for export to the United States and Canada. In 1989, Volkswagen de Mexico initiated a wholesale reorganization of the Puebla facility, committing investments totaling US$1 billion. Part of the investment went toward acquiring new plant and equipment, which was needed to replace the decades-old machinery from Wolfsburg, and to retool the assembly line for the new models. But the most basic task was to increase capacity.

In Josephi's view, recapturing the U.S. market was critical for the future, not just of VW de Mexico but the company as a whole:

> It is important for Volkswagen to be present in all major markets to gain scale economies in R&D and marketing. But most important, VW will face the same challenges in Europe in 10 years that we are facing now. Up until now, the European market has been relatively protected from imports, so headquarters doesn't always understand the need for competitiveness in Mexico. That is why the United States is so important. If we cannot make it there, VW won't survive in Europe either.[18]

The company predicted that it would have to sell 250,000 to 300,000 cars a year in the United States to cover its development and marketing costs.

Product Mix

To regain its position in the U.S. market, Volkswagen was counting on the new generation of Golfs and Jettas which had led its success in Europe. It planned to introduce these models to the United States and Mexico in the fall of 1992. The Golf and

---

[16]James P. Womack, "A Positive Sum Solution: Free Trade in the North American Motor Vehicle Sector," in M. Delal Baer and Guy F. Erb, eds., *Strategic Sectors in Mexican-U.S. Free Trade* (Washington, D.C.: Center for Strategic and International Studies, 1991), p. 46.

[17]"Face to Face: With the Vehicle Manufacturers of Mexico," *Economist Intelligence Unit International Motor Business,* April 1992, p. 13.

[18]Interview, Mexico City, November 16, 1992.

Jetta were considered part of a single line because both cars were similarly engineered and used many of the same parts. The new line had a more aerodynamic exterior, roomier interiors, and a more performance-oriented engine than the second generation Golf/Jetta it replaced.

Volkswagen, unlike Japanese and U.S. auto makers, introduced new versions of a given model with relative infrequency. While Honda, for example, introduced a new version of the Accord every three or four years, the 1992 Golf/Jetta was only the second time Volkswagen had changed the line since its introduction in 1974. The Golf/Jetta, though far safer and more sophisticated in engineering than the old Beetle, embodied the same basic principle Volkswagen had followed since the end of World War II: to mass-produce a single product using highly standardized parts.[19] It was on this principle that Volkswagen first conquered the U.S. market. So important was the United States to Volkswagen that by 1968 the market accounted for 40% of the company's global sales.[20]

As a result of this shift in production location, VW de Mexico planned to produce more Golfs and Jettas than Beetles for the first time in 1992. The subsidiary expected to produce a daily average of 400 Beetles, 700 Golfs/Jettas (340 for Mexico, 360 for export), and 65 vans.[21] Annual production was to reach 300,000 vehicles in 1992, and 350,000 by 1993. Planned exports of 90,000 vehicles in 1992 would nearly double 1991 levels. (**Exhibit 11** provides exports of passenger cars by auto maker in Mexico from 1986 to 1991.) Though Volkswagen de Mexico's exports had grown from practically nothing in the mid-1980s, domestic sales still dwarfed exports, in contrast to the Big Three.

VW de Mexico was not the only supplier of VWs to the U.S. market. Table D provides Volkswagen's U.S. passenger car sales by model for 1990 and 1991:

TABLE D Volkswagen U.S.
Car Sales by Model, 1990–1991
(number of vehicles)

Model	1990	1991
Cabriolet	7,615	5,401
Corrado	5,675	4,331
Jetta	58,314	38,017
Golf/GTI	17,122	14,340
Passat	18,274	16,134
Fox	22,640	13,463
Total	129,705	91,688

Source: Compiled from data in *Automotive News Market Data Book*, various years.

---

[19]Tolliday, "Rethinking the German Miracle: Volkswagen in Prosperity and Crisis, 1939–1992," p. 21.

[20]Ibid., pp. 27–29.

[21]Unpublished data, Volkswagen de Mexico.

The Brazilian-made Fox (1992 price, $7,995–$8,995) remained the company's sole entry-level vehicle; the Golf (1992 price, $9,640–$13,910) competed at various levels in the compact market; the Jetta (1992 price, $11,370–$15,480) was a low- to mid-range sedan; the Passat (1992 price, $14,950–$17,970) was Volkswagen's entry in the high-end sedan market; and the Cabriolet ("convertible") and the Corrado were high-priced sport models.[22]

While Volkswagen was moving into high gear for sales of the new Golf/Jetta, it did not appear to have fixed plans for the other models. The Fox was made in Brazil, where high inflation and an increasingly overvalued exchange rate were seriously affecting the profitability of this price-sensitive export. Autolatina, the holding company formed by Volkswagen and Ford in Brazil and Argentina in 1987, was in the process of phasing out all Fox exports to the United States, which would leave Volkswagen without an entry-level model. In the longer term, a similar fate could await the Passat. Volkswagen continued to produce the car in Germany, where the Passat's profitability remained subject to the same exchange-rate risk that had plagued the company since the 1970s. There were no plans to export cars from VW's Spanish facilities, which had been in operation since the mid-1980s and were already stretched to meet European demand.

The Challenge of North American Free Trade

NAFTA

On August 14, 1992, the leaders of Mexico, the United States, and Canada signed a North American Free Trade Agreement (NAFTA) that would eliminate most tariff barriers among the three countries over a 10-year period. The treaty's terms with respect to the auto industry were as follows:

1. **Imports and trade** Mexico's 20% tariff on imported cars and light trucks would immediately be reduced by half and fall to zero over a 10-year period. Within 5 years, duties on three-fourths of all parts exports to Mexico would be eliminated. The trade-balancing requirements would be phased out over 10 years. The United States would immediately eliminate its average 2.5% tariff on passenger cars. Its 25% tariff on light trucks would immediately be reduced to 10% and be completely phased out over 5 years. Canada would eliminate its tariffs on vehicles imported from Mexico on the same schedule that Mexico followed for imports from Canada and the United States.
2. **Domestic content** NAFTA stipulated that "Mexico may not require that an enterprise attain a level of national value added in excess of 20% of total sales as a

---

[22]*Automotive News Market Data Book* 1992.

condition to qualify as a national supplier or enterprise in the auto parts sector."
For an auto manufacturer, the required percentage of national value added could
not be greater than 34% from 1994–1999, would have to drop to 29% by 2003,
and ultimately would fall to zero. In addition, purchases from certain in-bond
production facilities (*maquiladoras*) could be counted towards domestic content.

3. **Regional content** NAFTA would introduce *regional* domestic content requirements. Within 8 years, all vehicles would have to contain 62.5% North American content to qualify for preferential tariff treatment.
4. **Used cars** As of the year 2009, Mexico could not restrict imports of used vehicles that were at least 10 years old; by 2019, no restrictions would be allowed
   on used cars of any age.
5. **Foreign direct investment in parts** "NAFTA investors" would be permitted to
   hold a majority interest immediately in new auto parts firms and in five years in
   existing firms. (Prior to NAFTA, the government allowed majority or total
   ownership only in "exceptional" cases.)

During the NAFTA negotiations, Ford and Chrysler proposed a 70% regional
content requirement; GM suggested 60%. Nissan and Volkswagen preferred the 50%
required by the U.S.-Canada Free Trade Agreement, as did Honda and Toyota.

According to Josephi, a rapid trade opening was in no one's interest in Mexico,
least of all the U.S. companies. It would have been like:

> . . . giving the cake to the Japanese firms and letting them divide it among themselves. The
> real point of contention was regional content. The U.S. wanted regional content of 70%—this
> isn't free trade. It's protectionism . . . Who is going to win with NAFTA? In any situation
> where two parties negotiate, there is a winner and a loser. For that reason we can speak of a
> winner of the NAFTA: the United States. The more Mexico opens, the easier it will be to
> close one plant in Mexico and keep one open in the U.S.

Nevertheless, the free trade challenge was one the company had already assumed for itself. Julio Moctezuma, Volkswagen de Mexico's chief of Materials Purchases, stated, "With or without a free trade agreement, we must be internationally
competitive."[23] NAFTA nevertheless imposed a deadline by which time Volkswagen's North American strategy had to bear fruit.

Volkswagen was not alone in reorganizing its Mexican operations. The other foreign auto makers in Mexico had also built new capacity for export in response to the
government's new export requirements. Ford exported the Escort and Tracer to the
United States from its new plant in Hermosillo, and General Motors sent the Buick
Century and Chevrolet Cavalier north from its new plant in Ramos Arizpe. Chrysler
was readying its Toluca plant to export the Shadow and the Spirit, and Nissan had built

---

[23]Interview, Puebla, June 18, 1992.

a massive complex in Aguascalientes to ship cars to Japan.[24] The Big Three were also expanding their *maquiladora* operations along the Mexico-U.S. border, where General Motors already assembled most wire harnesses, seat covers, and interior trim.

A North American Supply Network

Under Mexico's auto decrees, all companies faced the same poor quality and high costs that came with a protected, low-volume, domestic auto-parts industry. NAFTA's regional content requirements, however, gave the Big Three's Mexican subsidiaries access to their parent companies' extensive supply networks in the United States and Canada. The same would not be true for Volkswagen de Mexico (or for Nissan). NAFTA's 62.5% regional content requirement was far more restrictive than Mexico's 1989 decree's national content requirement of 36% and meant that VW de Mexico would have to extend its North American supply base.

In 1992, Volkswagen acquired 50% of the materials it used from Germany, 40% from Mexico, and 10% from the United States.[25] Overall sourcing levels hid the fact that different models had vastly different German-content levels. Over 80% of materials used in the Beetle were of Mexican origin. Mexico was the only country where Volkswagen still made the Beetle. The car's suppliers in Germany and elsewhere had long since gone on to other endeavors. For the third generation Golf/Jetta, the situation was much different. As much as 90% of the materials for the model were imported from Germany. With the model less than a year old, Puebla had yet to find suppliers in North America. Roughly 1,000 parts in the new Golf/Jetta were different from those in the previous model.

According to VW managers, the decision to form North American supply linkages was made before anything was known about a free trade agreement. Their goal was to source 40% from the United States, 40% from Mexico, and 20% from Germany. VW de Mexico President Josephi estimated that it would take at least 10 years to develop an adequate supplier base to compete with U.S. auto makers. Toward this end, VW de Mexico renewed contact with the parts producers that had supplied the old Westmoreland facility. Puebla found that many had not kept pace with changing German technology. When Westmoreland closed, it was producing the second generation Golf/Jetta. Many suppliers were unequipped to accommodate the new model. VW nevertheless remained optimistic that it could attract world class suppliers. The key, management felt, was volume. Josephi stated:

> Economies of scale have allowed us to change the structure of our purchases. When we began to produce not 200 vehicles a day but 700, we were able to change our source of purchases from Germany to the United States and Mexico.[26]

---

[24]*Newsweek,* March 16, 1992.

[25]*Automotive News*, January 20, 1992.

[26]Interview, June 17, 1992.

In Mexico, when production of a part required foreign technology, the company encouraged joint ventures with German or U.S. suppliers. In November 1992, VW also inaugurated a new industrial park in Puebla that was expected to accommodate about 20 new supplier firms from around the world. For example, a Canadian supplier of bumpers was expected to relocate in Mexico to save on transport costs and to allow for the bumper to be painted from the same batch as the car body. Josephi emphasized that not only were some non-German firms first rate, but that not all German companies were "lean." Although there were limits to "Just in Time" supplier networks because the designs were from Germany, "Just in Time" was not important for all parts. For some, VW would seek out the cheapest supplier in the world. In addition to VW's planned expansion, firms were also encouraged by new Mexican laws that allowed them to hold majority interests in new parts firms. These new firms would join or replace VW's current 500 parts suppliers, which employed about 50,000 people.

Labor Reorganization

VW accounted for the largest share of manufacturing employment in Puebla. In 1989, employment at Puebla stood at 19,000 workers, reaching the administrative limits of a single management team. Volkswagen de Mexico had sought to increase capacity without increasing employment by applying "lean production" techniques. Previously, the organization of work had been a textbook application of mass-production techniques. The assembly line was divided into a number of work stations responsible for specific operations. Activities at each work station were further divided among individual workers, each of whom had a rigidly defined task. The pace of work was controlled by preset guidelines. Auto assembly proceeded in a continuous line from start to finish, so that a worker who encountered a delay threatened to slow down the entire process. Conversely, a worker who finished a task early was constrained by specific job categories from helping others.

The new organization was based on work groups. Production was divided into subassembly operations—such as putting together doors, creating front-ends, and crafting interiors—which were carried out separately from the final assembly line. Each subassembly operation was assigned to a specific work group, whose members decided how to complete given tasks. There were no individual job descriptions. Workers engaged in a variety of activities and often worked jointly.

As of June 1992, VW de Mexico had completed the first phase of implementing these production techniques. Work groups were first tried in production of the van, known as the Combi in Mexico, whose small production runs made it a natural test case. With the same number of employees working a single shift, van production increased from 50 to 65 vehicles a day. Work groups were next tried on the Beetle, which under mass production required three shifts to make 450 vehicles a day. Works groups allowed Puebla to cut back to two shifts, and still produce 400 vehicles a day. With full implementation of work groups, VW expected to produce 440 Beetles a day with just two shifts. The final stage of work-group implementation was to occur in the assembly of the new Golf/Jetta. By the end of 1992, modernization was expected to expand annual capacity from 200,000 to 350,000 vehicles, or more than double the number produced in 1991.[27]

Rather than only retrain the existing work force for these new tasks, Volkswagen de Mexico hired and trained new workers. General assembly-line workers received a six-week training course, while trainees for high-skill jobs received a three-year course in the plant. Each year, 100 trainees were chosen from a pool of over 1,000 candidates. The trainees, most of whom were recent junior high school graduates, received a stipend during their education, but did not become full-time employees until they completed the program.[28]

Volkswagen de Mexico also sought to trim its full-time work force in the aftermath of the 1980s economic slump. In 1988, it cut 1,800 permanent assembly-line jobs. When demand picked up the following year, the plant hired many of the workers back, but on a temporary basis. Temporary employees were not covered by the union collective bargaining agreement and could be hired and fired at will. Puebla also began to subcontract many non-production tasks, such as cleaning, maintenance, and security, which were previously done by full-time employees. Subcontractors, who were also non-union, did not receive the Volkswagen benefits package.[29] These efforts allowed Puebla, in the midst of expanding capacity, to cut its work force to 17,800 in 1992. As a company, VW still accounted for the largest share of manufacturing employment in the region.

Union Politics

The Independent Union of Automotive Industry Workers, Volkswagen de Mexico (SITIAVW) had been relatively flexible in regard to these changes on the shop floor. Though independent from any broad trade union federation and the PRI since 1981, it had been affiliated with the Union of Independent Workers (UOI) for the previous 10 years. The UOI's focus on national political issues ultimately led to conflict with VW's union, whose main priority was local factory issues.

While affiliated with the UOI, the SITIAVW introduced a policy that restricted the union's executive committee to a three-year term in office, after which it had to leave the plant altogether. This requirement was atypical to most Mexican unions, in which leaders often remained in their posts for decades or used their positions as springboards to union politics at the national level. While in office, the secretary general and the executive committee of the SITIAVW received the highest salary and no

[27]Interview with Marco Antonio Ramirez Barrera, Chief of Production Planning, Volkswagen de Mexico, Puebla, June 18, 1992.

[28]Interview with Jesus Landa, Chief of Training, Volkswagen de Mexico, Puebla, June 18, 1992.

[29]Graciela Bensusán and Carlos García, *Cambio en las Relaciones Laborales: Cuatro Experencias en Transición* (Mexico City: Fundación Friedrich Ebert, 1990), pp. 23–25.

longer worked on the shop floor; they left VW with an attractive financial package as well. This policy was designed in part to give the UOI greater control of the union. However, it was also during this period that the VW union solidified a collective bargaining agreement that was considered one of the "best in the industry."[30]

The company's relationship with the union was not totally without conflict, but previous protests centered mostly around salaries, benefits, and layoffs, rather than the organization of work or the hiring of temporary workers. The work force had a tradition of resorting to wildcat strikes, particularly when dissatisfied with contracts negotiated by the union leadership. For example, in September 1988 the plant was paralyzed for four days, during which time two men were reported killed and others injured while fleeing from state riot police and their dogs, who were trying to prevent hundreds of ex-VW workers from blocking the plant entrance. The conflict started when the union secretary general had asked employees to participate in a voluntary layoff program that included over 1,000 workers without consulting the rank and file. Workers claimed that they had been pressured by the union to resign. The secretary general was ousted from his position, but most workers were not rehired. At the time, Josephi said that VW was not involved in the union conflict, but acknowledged that the company had asked the state government to "find a solution to the problem."[31]

1992 Summer of Strife

VW's North American strategy was seriously challenged by unforeseen labor conflict during the summer of 1992. The company's contract with its work force expired on July 1, 1992. After rejecting VW's proposed 12% wage increase, the union leadership called a strike. Workers were back on the job two days later, after the union's secretary-general Gaspar Bueno and its executive committee had approved a total increase of 20% (18% wages, 2% benefits).

Over the next three weeks, however, uneasiness spread among the rank and file as it learned about an accord that had been signed in tandem with the collective bargaining agreement. This so-called covenant included plans to expand the application of Japanese-style production teams to the shop floor. It also made pay scales and job assignments primarily dependent on productivity rather than on seniority. The union's executive committee posted a brief bulletin summarizing the covenant, but it communicated poorly the results of the negotiations. The covenant itself was ambiguous, especially with respect to the calculation of wage increases and the reallocation of personnel within the plant.

On July 21, a group of union dissidents called a walkout and held an impromptu general assembly at the plant to unseat the executive committee. It accused Gaspar Bueno of selling out the workers and of not fully divulging the content of the new ac-

---

[30]*EIF International,* August 24, 1992.

[31]*Automotive News,* October 10, 1988.

cord. Shop stewards were particularly concerned about their future in the plant restructuring. The dissidents gathered 9,000 signatures (of a union membership of 16,000) on a petition to disavow the productivity agreement and to recall the union leadership. They took their appeal to the authorities in Mexico City. The company estimated that the work stoppage could cost as much as US$10 million a day.

Bueno claimed that the walkout was provoked by his opponents within the union who had been unable to defeat him in the previous election. That election had been especially contentious and fractious. Seventeen different slates of candidates had run, and only 70 votes separated Bueno from the dissident group now challenging his authority.

EXHIBIT 1 Auto Companies' Production—Location

General Motors	1990 Passenger Cars	1990 Total
G. M.—United States	2,755,284	4,222,533
G. M.—Canada	462,277	791,426
Opel—W. Germany	1,029,955	1,048,772
Lotus—U.K.	2,142	2,142
Vauxhill—U.K.	256,293	275,966
G. M.—Spain	386,832	386,832
G. M.—Brazil	164,198	203,334
G. M.—Mexico	73,775	136,086
G. M.—Holden—Australia	77,465	77,465
Total	**5,208,221**	**7,144,556**
Nissan		
Nissan—Japan	2,020,523	2,417,010
Nissan Diesel—Japan	0	61,693
Nissan—Mexico	98,690	137,568
Nissan—Australia	57,918	57,918
Nissan Motor Iberica—Spain	0	79,662
Nissan—U.K.	76,190	76,190
Nissan—United States	95,844	235,248
Total	**2,349,165**	**3,065,289**
Fiat		
Fiat—Italy	1,325,414	1,333,264
Lancia—Italy	168,702	168,702
Autobianchi—Italy	144,464	144,464
Iveco—Italy	0	98,040
Sevel Fiat—Italy	0	72,645
Ferrari—Italy	4,292	4,292
Fiat Vehiculos—Argentina	0	574
Fiat—Brazil	162,577	223,668
Iveco Unic—France	0	0
Iveco—Margirus—W. Germany	0	14,881
Iveco Ford—U.K.	0	8,792
Total	**1,805,449**	**2,069,322**

Ford	1990 Passenger Cars	1990 Total
Ford—United States	1,377,351	2,762,428
Ford—Canada	385,232	516,664
Ford—W. Germany	594,330	594,330
Ford—Belgium	311,803	385,263
Ford—U.K.	329,597	470,233
Ford—Spain	334,418	334,418
Ford—Brazil	99,055	146,932
Ford—Mexico	134,591	170,494
Ford—Australia	123,856	135,238
Ford—Argentina	13,413	19,285
Total	**3,703,646**	**5,535,285**
Volkswagen		
V.W.—W. Germany	1,508,818	1,598,346
V.W.—Audi—W. Germany	421,378	421,378
V.W.—Argentina	7,893	8,173
V.W.—Brazil	249,853	288,813
V.W.—Mexico	180,589	190,884
Seat—Spain	505,338	505,338
Total	**2,873,869**	**3,012,932**
Renault		
Renault—France	1,316,930	1,616,104
Renault—Argentina	24,942	26,696
Renault FASA—Spain	324,562	324,562
Renault RVI—Spain	0	2,853
Renault—U.K.	0	1,207
Mack—United States	0	15,243
Mack—Canada	0	1,742
Total	**1,666,434**	**1,988,407**

Toyota	1990 Passenger Cars	1990 Total
Toyota—Japan	3,345,885	4,212,373
Toyota—United States	321,523	321,523
Toyota—Canada	60,793	60,793
Toyota—Australia	71,528	71,528
Toyota—Brazil	192	5,091
Total	**3,799,921**	**4,671,308**
Peugeot—Citroen		
Peugeot—France	1,287,920	1,369,359
Citroen—France	689,965	783,224
Sevel Peugeot—Italy	0	67,124
Peugeot Talbot—Spain	142,846	142,846
Citroen—Spain	221,860	221,860
Peugeot/Talbot—U.K.	116,548	116,642
Total	**2,459,139**	**2,701,055**
Honda		
Honda—Japan	1,223,389	1,383,711
Honda—Canada	105,949	105,949
Honda—United States	435,437	435,437
Total	**1,764,775**	**1,925,097**
Chrysler		
Chrysler—United States	726,742	1,253,244
Chrysler—Canada	24,676	393,089
Chrysler—Mexico	107,827	166,960
Total	**859,245**	**1,813,293**

Source: World Motor Vehicle Data 1992, pp. 20–22.

EXHIBIT 2 Volkswagen Figures, 1980—1990

VW Group	1980	1981	1982	1983	1984	1985	1986	1987	1988	1989	1990
Sales (DM millions)	33,288	37,878	37,434	40,089	45,671	52,502	52,794	54,635	59,221	65,352	68,061
% domestic	36	32	32	36	32	31	36	41	38	36	40
% foreign	64	68	68	64	68	69	64	59	62	64	60
Vehicle sales (thousand units)	2,495	2,279	2,120	2,127	2,145	2,398	2,758	2,774	2,854	2,941	3,030
% domestic	32	32	32	35	33	30	30	33	30	29	31
% foreign	68	68	68	65	67	70	70	67	70	71	69
Production (thousand units)	2,574	2,246	2,130	2,116	2,148	2,398	2,777	2,771	2,848	2,948	3,058
% domestic	58	63	65	67	69	68	60	60	59	60	59
% foreign	42	37	35	33	31	32	40	40	41	40	41
Work force (thousands)	258	247	239	232	238	259	276	260	252	251	261
% domestic	62	65	66	67	67	66	61	65	65	64	64
% foreign	38	35	34	33	33	34	39	35	35	36	36
Capital Investment (DM millions)	4,279	4,851	4,892	4,858	2,782	3,388	6,371	4,592	4,251	5,606	5,372
% domestic	74	64	75	72	68	74	60	87	83	80	56
% foreign	26	36	25	28	32	26	40	13	17	20	44
Net earnings (DM millions)	321	136	-300	-215	228	596	580	598	780	1038	1086
Increase in Reserves	121	—	—	—	—	—	—	—	—	—	—
Depreciation and Writedown	2,102	2,934	3,038	3,689	2,961	3,411					
Cash Flow (DM millions)	3,141	3,936	3,452	5,207	4,081	4,558	4,285	4,874	5,018	5,412	5,701
Dividend VW AG (DM millions)	192	120	0	0	120	240	306	306	306	336	369

Source: "Rethinking the German Miracle: Volkswagen in Prosperity and Crisis, 1939–1992," Steven Tolliday, mimeo, Harvard Business School, November 4, 1991.

EXHIBIT 3   West European New Car Market, 1990–1991

A. Leading Shares

	1990 %	1991 %	1991 (thousands)
VW group	**15.5**	**16.0**	**2,157**
Fiat group	14.2	12.9	1,739
PSA	13.0	12.1	1,632
GM	11.9	12.1	1,632
Ford	11.6	11.9	1,605
Renault	9.9	10.0	1,348
Japanese	11.6	12.3	1,658
Others	12.3	12.7	1,713
Total	100.0	100.0	13,484

B. Sales of Leading Suppliers by Major Market (thousands)

	Germany	Italy	France	U.K.	Spain
VW group					
1990	820	304	237	135	200
1991	1,107	301	170	104	165
Fiat group					
1990	152	1,240	163	62	83
1991	195	1,093	143	40	72
PSA					
1990	131	181	765	185	179
1991	183	183	673	169	163
GM					
1990	531	106	114	323	135
1991	729	105	108	249	107
Ford					
1990	302	182	160	518	142
1991	431	260	175	392	120
Renault					
1990	107	159	639	68	164
1991	223	190	540	63	163
Japanese					
1990	483	45	76	235	23
1991	613	63	83	185	28

Source: Economist Intelligence Unit International Motor Business, "Short-Term Prospects for the West European Motor Industry," April 1992.

EXHIBIT 4 U.S. Sales of Passenger Cars, 1980–1991 (Units)

	1980	1981	1982	1983	1984	1985	1986	1987	1988	1989	1990	1991
Sales of Domestically-Built Passenger Cars (Number of vehicles)												
Chrysler	625,463	729,873	691,703	844,522	986,998	1,139,936	1,173,463	962,057	1,062,782	917,506	795,096	636,994
Ford	1,445,988	1,380,600	1,345,698	1,571,321	1,979,317	2,070,392	2,066,507	2,019,783	2,205,336	2,041,807	1,845,895	1,527,168
General Motors	4,065,769	3,796,696	3,515,660	4,053,561	4,587,508	4,607,458	4,532,796	3,555,538	3,641,542	3,276,941	3,141,157	2,783,962
Honda	—	—	50,402	133,601	145,976	235,247	316,618	375,625	389,472	464,118	482,097	112,800
Nissan	—	—	—	—	—	39,794	55,602	119,678	112,125	103,134	109,575	332,623
Toyota	—	—	—	—	—	—	7,281	44,853	72,354	212,388	348,540	—
Volkswagen	177,140	162,445	91,166	85,045	73,838	77,716	73,911	61,064	24,939	—	—	—
Total Sales	**8,760,937**	**8,531,514**	**7,977,570**	**6,795,302**	**7,951,517**	**8,204,721**	**8,214,662**	**7,081,262**	**7,501,095**	**7,014,850**	**6,842,733**	**6,072,255**
Sales of Imported Passenger Cars (Number of vehicles)												
Honda	375,388	370,705	365,865	350,670	374,819	406,413	405,399	312,218	265,122	251,569	252,377	177,562
Hyundai	—	—	—	—	—	—	166,882	263,610	264,282	183,261	137,448	177,630
Mazda	161,623	166,105	163,150	173,388	169,666	211,093	222,716	206,354	224,719	184,583	153,055	144,287
Nissan	516,890	464,805	470,246	521,902	485,296	535,372	493,549	405,996	360,745	396,202	312,406	264,698
Toyota	582,204	576,491	530,246	555,766	557,961	620,047	640,155	583,809	616,529	448,249	367,134	338,192
Volkswagen	90,923	82,173	87,352	77,009	103,479	140,505	143,318	130,641	143,861	128,503	129,705	91,668
Total Imports	**2,396,934**	**2,326,376**	**2,220,911**	**2,396,064**	**2,441,341**	**2,541,063**	**3,248,430**	**3,144,054**	**3,068,738**	**2,757,077**	**2,452,948**	**2,103,759**

Source: Compiled from data in *Automotive News Market Databook*, various years

Company	Location	Date	Activities	Markets
△ Chrysler	Toluca	1964	Car Assembly, engine plant	Mexico, U.S.
	Mexico City	1941	Truck assembly	Mexico, U.S.
	Ramos Arizpe	1981	Engine plant	U.S., Canada
■ Ford	Cuautitlán	1964	Car and truck assembly	Mexico
	Chihuahua	1983	Engine plant	Export
	Hermosillo	1986	Car assembly, stamping	U.S.
● General Motors	Mexico City	1935	Truck assembly, engine assembly	Mexico
	Ramos Arizpe	1981	Car assembly, engine plant	U.S., Mexico
◇ Nissan	Cuernavaca	1965	Car assembly	Mexico, export
		1975	Truck assembly	
	Lerma	1978	Engine assembly	
	Aguascalientes	1965	Engine plant	Mexico
		1983	Engine plant, stamping	U.S., Japan
○ Volkswagen	Puebla	1966	Car assembly, stamping	Mexico
		1980	Engine plant	Mexico, U.S.
		1989	Plant conversion	Mexico, U.S.

EXHIBIT 5   Major Operations of Foreign Auto Makers in Mexico

Source: Compiled from data in Cornelius, Wayne and Craig, Ann, *The Mexican Political System in Transition* (San Diego: Center for U.S.-Mexican Studies, 1991) (map); *Ward's Automotive Yearbook,* Fifty-fourth edition, 1992, p. 112; and Womack, James "Seeking Mutual Gain: North American Responses to Mexican Liberalization of its Motor Vehicle Industry" (Cambridge: Massachusetts Institute of Technology, 1989), p. 19 and 23.

EXHIBIT 6 Mexican Economy 1975–1990

	% Change in Real GNP per Capita	Inflation (January to January)	Exchange Rate (Pesos per Dollar)	Trade Surplus Exports–Imports (1970 US$ billions)
1975	2.5	17.8	12.5	−3.65
1976	1.4	12.1	15.4	−2.64
1977	0.4	28.6	22.6	−1.05
1978	5.9	19.6	22.8	−1.86
1979	6.7	17.6	22.8	−3.16
1980	5.9	21.6	23.0	−3.39
1981	6.2	27.8	24.5	−3.85
1982	−2.9	30.8	56.4	6.79
1983	−10.3	110.1	120.1	13.76
1984	1.4	73.4	167.8	12.94
1985	0.4	60.7	257.0	8.45
1986	−2.0	65.9	611.4	4.60
1987	−4.1	104.3	1,366.7	8.43
1988	−0.6	176.8	2,250.3	1.67
1989	1.1	34.6	2,453.2	−0.65
1990	2.3	22.5	2,810.2	−1.10

Source: Compiled from *La Economía Mexicana en Cifras 1990* (Mexico City: Nacional Financiera, 1991), and *Indicadores Económicos*, Banco de Mexico, May 1992.

EXHIBIT 7 Mexico Sales of Passenger Cars, 1985–1991

Company	1986	1987	1988	1989	1990	1991
Chrysler	27,666	23,464	48,732	56,952	52,580	64,681
Ford	19,516	16,524	32,001	47,801	52,352	56,460
General Motors	11,365	14,444	15,284	22,876	32,351	42,970
Nissan	43,291	49,064	60,247	69,855	80,502	79,353
Volkswagen	54,865	50,631	53,802	77,021	134,823	148,646
Total Sales	**160,670**	**154,152**	**210,066**	**274,505**	**352,608**	**392,110**

Source: Compiled from data in *Balance de la Industria Automotriz*, Associación Mexicana de la Industria Automotriz, various editions.

EXHIBIT 8 Volkswagen de Mexico Vehicle Sales by Model, 1988–1991

Domestic	1988	1989	1990	1991
Beetle	19,348	32,545	82,245	86,353
Golf	16,988	25,199	27,948	38,485
Jetta	12,293	18,757	21,390	23,736
Other car	5,173	520	111	12
Van/Truck	6,903	9,008	10,248	11,965
Import				
Passat	0	0	1,129	60

Source: Compiled from data in *Balance de la Industria Auto-motriz*, Associación Mexicana de la Industria Automotriz, various editions.

EXHIBIT 9 Mexico Sales of Passenger Car by Class, 1986–1991

Year	Subcompact	Compact	Luxury	Sport
1986	93,466	51,199	11,565	4,460
1987	92,939	45,237	13,230	2,746
1988	110,053	78,916	17,209	3,888
1989	146,591	104,322	19,936	3,656
1990	213,590	110,213	19,569	5,431
1991	226,264	132,488	24,308	3,859

Source: Compiled from data in *Balance de la Industria Auto-motriz*, Associación Mexicana de la Industria Automotriz, various editions.

EXHIBIT 10   Mexico: Vehicle Exports by Destination, 1981–1990 (units)

Year	North America	Central America	South America	Africa	Asia	Europe	Total
1981	3	697	4,144	1	385	9,198	14,428
1982	623	711	56	—	845	13,584	15,819
1983	203	3,600	133	1,520	269	16,730	22,455
1984	13,448	3,645	624	—	798	15,120	33,635
1985	47,197	6,845	1,129	—	99	3,153	58,423
1986	60,466	8,419	2,490	—	707	347	72,429
1987	145,658	12,621	4,047	—	377	370	163,073
1988	153,040	11,187	8,513	92	4	311	173,147
1989	170,270	9,698	14,443	125	717	746	195,999
1990	251,350	10,641	12,735	289	1,445	399	276,859

Source: Economist Intelligence Unit, *Mexico's Motor Vehicle Industry*, Special Report No. R301, November 1991

EXHIBIT 11   Mexico Exports of Passenger Cars, 1986–1991

Company	1986	1987	1988	1989	1990	1991
Chrysler	15,499	41,037	28,495	45,643	55,355	67,805
Ford	0	51,773	66,361	39,580	88,604	111,983
General Motors	18,672	32,272	36,506	40,376	40,993	81,231
Nissan	5,965	10,325	12,319	17,228	18,737	23,298
Volkswagen	80	74	436	23,057	46,232	50,432[a]
Total Vehicle Exports[b]	**72,492**	**163,073**	**173,147**	**195,999**	**276,869**	**358,666**

Source: *Balance de la Industria Automotriz*, Associación Mexicana de la Industria Automotriz, various editions.

[a]Approximately 80% of these exports went to the United States; most of the rest went to Canada.

[b]Total includes passenger cars and trucks, but company totals are for passenger cars only.

EXHIBIT 12   Hourly Compensation for Motor Vehicle Production Workers, 1980–1990 (US$)

Country	1980	1982	1984	1986	1988	1990
United States	15.88	17.99	18.92	19.97	21.11	21.93
Canada	10.63	12.30	13.05	13.38	16.56	19.23
Mexico	4.38	3.56	2.55	2.03	—	2.75
Brazil	2.01	2.47	1.59	—	—	—
Japan	6.97	7.21	7.90	11.80	16.36	15.77
South Korea	1.33	1.55	1.87	2.00	3.41	5.73
Germany	15.56	13.03	11.92	16.83	23.00	27.12
Spain	7.11	6.69	5.35	7.74	10.85	—

Source: *Ward's Automotive Year Book*, 1992 p. 64.

EXHIBIT 13　Selected Volkswagen de Mexico Wages, August 1992–
August 1993 (as stipulated in the August 1992 Collective Bargaining Agreement)

A. Working Groups in the machinery areas of automatic lathes, engine parts, brake drums and brake discs,
rear-axle parts, semiaxis, and in stamping.

Technician Level	Daily Salary (Current Mexican Pesos)	Daily Salary (Equivalent in U.S. Dollars[a])
A	38,054.64	12.32
B	39,767.10	12.87
C	41,705.60	13.50
D	43,540.65	14.09
E	45,535.82	14.74
F	48,632.25	15.74
G	52,184.63	16.89

B. Working Groups in the machinery areas of body parts; painting, vehicle assembling; machinery (except
automatic lathes, engine parts, brake drums and brake discs, rear-axle parts, and semiaxis); axle assembly,
engine assembly; extra-parts assembly.

Technician Level	Daily Salary (Current Mexican Pesos)	Daily Salary (Equivalent in U.S. Dollars)[a]
A	38,054.64	12.32
B	39,767.10	12.87
C	41,705.60	13.50
D	43,540.65	14.09
E	45,535.82	14.74
F	48,632.25	15.74
G	52,184.63	16.89
H	55,263.50	17.00
I	58,663.56	18.98
J	61,530.07	19.92
K	64,693.84	20.94

Source: Volkswagen Union Contract

[a]Average August-September 1992 exchange rate: 3,090 pesos = 1 U.S. dollar.

The Foreign Exchange Market: Background Note and Problem Set

International finance plays a large though often hidden role in all of our lives. Whether we are driving to work in a Japanese car, wearing clothes tailored in Hong Kong, or having a German beer before dinner, we are using products originally purchased with currencies traded through the foreign exchange market. An understanding of this market is essential to firms that operate globally because they are exposed to foreign currency fluctuations. Moreover, the market has grown substantially in recent years because of floating exchange rates, deregulation, and the advancement of communication technology. Though it is difficult to measure the size of the foreign exchange market, in 1985 the Group of Thirty research organization estimated the *daily* foreign exchange turnover at $150 billion. By 1986, however, a survey of the central banks from the United States, the United Kingdom, and Japan reported that daily turnover in the top three centers alone was $188 billion. Continued reform will make the foreign exchange market an increasingly innovative and exciting arena in which to participate.

Research Associate Richard P. Melnick and Professor W. Carl Kester prepared this case as the basis for class discussion rather than to illustrate either effective or ineffective handling of an administrative situation.

Market Participants

The foreign exchange market involves participants buying and selling currencies all over the world. Elaborate communication systems, including telephones, telexes, computers, and news wires, link individuals worldwide. Trading takes place throughout most of each day, starting in Tokyo; moving west to Singapore and Hong Kong; continuing to Zurich, Frankfurt, and London; and then ending in New York, Chicago, and San Francisco.

Participants in the market include individuals, corporations, commercial banks, and central banks. Each has different motives for transacting. Commercial banks with large foreign exchange sales and trading departments act as dealers when they buy and sell foreign exchange for clients. Their clients, usually corporations, need to transfer purchasing power to and from other countries in order to buy foreign goods and services and to invest in foreign assets. Commercial banks profit from the spread between buying currencies low at a "bid" price and selling them at a higher "ask" or "offer" price. Individual speculators profit when there is a change in general price levels, and they have predicted the change better than the market. Individuals, including tourists, importers, and exporters, use the foreign exchange market to conduct trade or investment transactions.

Central banks have two official reasons for participating in the foreign exchange market: 1) to monitor the market; and 2) to intervene for purposes of policy implementation. A central bank might intervene, for example, to smooth out extreme currency fluctuations or to meet obligations under formal agreements such as the European Monetary System (EMS).[1] A striking example of the central banks' ability to influence the market was the Group of Five's effort to depreciate the dollar in September 1985. Through the sale of billions of dollars, the dollar depreciated 35% in ten months. Intervention on this scale was unprecedented.

Profiting on their currency reserves has increasingly become an additional motive for some central banks to enter the foreign exchange market. The Soviet Union, acting through their Vneshtungbank trade bank, reportedly has been so profitable in its foreign exchange dealings that many suspect information leaks from the U.S. Commerce Department and the German Bundesbank.[2]

Central banks can act discreetly or conspicuously, and they often exploit the market power derived from their mere threat of action. The Bank of England is reported to be the most professional bank and has cleverly used the market to discour-

---

[1]The European Monetary System is an organization composed of all the European Economic Community members. It was founded in 1979 to stabilize exchange rates among the European countries. Their currency basket, called the European Currency Unit (ECU), is composed of a predetermined quantity of each currency, where the components reflect each member's relative size. Each nation's currency may not deviate from the ECU by more than 2.25% (the British pound does not follow the ECU restrictions), but the ECU itself floats against the rest of the world.

[2]Henry Sender, "Games Central Banks Play with Currencies," *Institutional Investor* (November 1985): 100–110.

age speculation against sterling. The German Bundesbank is considered sophisticated, but with a somewhat tarnished reputation as it has been thought to give domestic banks advantageous information. By telling their national banks outright what to
do, the Bank of Japan acts aggressively without trading directly. Traders generally
like to avoid the U.S. Federal Reserve Bank whose intervention is often thought to be
clumsy and inept.[3]

A 1986 survey of the United States, United Kingdom, and Japanese central
banks shows that London, New York, and Tokyo, with $90 billion, $50 billion, and
$48 billion, respectively, in estimated *daily* turnover are the leading foreign exchange
centers. London is the world's largest foreign exchange center because it has several
advantages: history, geography, and a healthy regulatory environment. Expertise and
tradition go back to the days when the pound was the most widely traded currency.
More important, however, is the fact that London can trade with Tokyo and Hong
Kong in the morning and New York in the afternoon, as well as Frankfurt and Zurich
continually. Trading has increased substantially since 1979 when foreign exchange
regulation decreased and banks were permitted to trade directly rather than through
brokers.

Tokyo's foreign exchange market has grown dramatically from an estimated
daily turnover of only $8 billion in 1985. Under pressure from the United States, the
Japanese have also decreased market regulation and have thereby surpassed Hong
Kong and Singapore in average daily turnover.

New York's foreign exchange system grew during much of the early 1980s, but
suffered under the weak dollar of 1986 and the increased power of European central
banks. Nonetheless, the greatest volume occurs in the European afternoon when New
York is open. Because of the deep market, this is the safest time to execute large
transactions.

The Spot Market

The *spot* exchange rate allows for the buying and selling of foreign exchange with
settlement in two business days, known as the *value date*. According to the aforemen-
tioned central bank survey, spot transactions accounted for 73% of all business in
London and 63% in New York. Spot rates are quoted in terms of both currencies in
the *Wall Street Journal*, one just being the reciprocal of the other. On September 2,
1986, for example, the spot rate for Swiss francs against U.S. dollars was SF =
$0.60994, and the cost of the U.S. dollars was therefore 1/.60994 or 1.6395 Swiss
francs.

Quotes are said to be direct or indirect. A *direct* quote is the price of a foreign
currency unit in terms of the home currency. According to the previous example, the
direct quote for Swiss francs in the United States was $0.60994. An *indirect* quote is

---

[3]*Ibid.,* 108.

the price of a unit of home currency measured in the foreign currency. Thus, the indirect quote for Swiss francs in the United States is SF1.6395.

With this system, a quote's definition depends on the country of reference. To clarify this ambiguity, New York bankers established the *European terms* convention, which uses the U.S. dollar as the common denominator. Thus, traders in the United States, Switzerland, or any other country would all quote Swiss francs as SF1.6395/$. The exceptions to this rule are British sterling and the currencies of several former Commonwealth countries including Australia and New Zealand. The exceptions exist because the pound was formerly not a decimal currency and it was easier to quote sterling in terms of other currencies. Today, these currencies are still quoted around the world in "American terms," which is the number of dollars per unit of their currencies.

Cross Rates and Triangular Arbitrage

If a Swiss bank wants German marks, it could get a rate of Swiss francs per deutsche mark from a German bank. From the perspective of dealers in a dollar-based market, this quote would be a *cross rate*. These rates can be given with either currency serving as denominator and they are most common among the Western European currencies. These cross rates are typically used by central banks of countries in the EMS trying to determine when they need to intervene.

Cross rates should equal the rates resulting from conversion to and from U.S. dollars (except for small differences attributable to transactions costs). Before using a cross rate, it is useful to see if transacting through dollars as an intermediate currency yields a different rate. For instance, if a dealer offers a dollar for 6.6625 French francs or 2.0320 deutsche marks, then the cross-offer rate should be 3.2788 French francs per deutsche mark. With bids of FF6.6575 and DM2.0310 per dollar, the corresponding cross-bid rate would be 3.2779. If the cross-bid rate were actually 3.3000 French francs per deutsche mark, traders could engage in "*triangular arbitrage*" to devalue the cross rate and push the system into equilibrium. Traders would take the following three steps: 1) sell DM1,000,000 (the "overpriced" currency) for French francs at a cross rate of 3.300 French francs per deutsche mark and receive FF3,300,000; 2) sell French franc holdings against dollars at a spot offer rate of FF6.6625 per dollar and receive $495,310; and 3) sell U.S. dollar holdings against deutsche marks at a spot rate of 2.0310 deutsche marks per dollar and receive DM1,005,975. The potential for this profit of DM5,975 would erode quickly as deutsche marks are sold against French francs at the overvalued cross rate.

Newspapers usually give only the bid rates or estimates at the midpoint of dealer spreads under European terms (except for sterling), while actual dealers give buying and selling quotations. "Offer" or "ask" rates under European terms will be higher than bid rates since dealers will want to sell dollars at a higher price than that at which they buy dollars. The difference between the two rates is usually quite small. For example, Citicorp could buy French francs (sell dollars) at FF6.6675 per U.S.

dollar and sell francs (buy dollars) at FF6.6625 per U.S. dollar. The spread is FF0.0050 or 50 points, where a "point" refers to the quote's last digit.[4] Though the bank's spread might be as small as 0.0005 of the transaction value, this is how banks profit in the foreign exchange market. With a more typical 10-point spread, bank revenues on $1 billion of transactions could be $1 million. The spread travellers experience can be ten times as high because executing their many small transactions requires higher inventory carrying costs and virtually the same amount of paperwork as that of large transactions.

The Forward Market

When business deals require individuals and corporations to pay or receive foreign currency in the future, they often prefer to transfer the risk that currency values will change. The *forward market* allows corporations to establish the exchange rate between the two currencies for settlement at a fixed future date. This is known as hedging or covering foreign currency exposure. The *forward rate* is fixed at the time the contract is made, but payment and delivery are not made until the value date. Forward contracts are often negotiated against dollars, though European traders also exchange domestic European currencies against each other. The most frequent forward contracts are for one, two, three, six, or twelve months. Banks actively trade in these markets both for their customers and for themselves. "Odd dated" forward contracts (i.e., maturities other than the most common ones) are possible, but they are more expensive because of the thinner market. Long-dated forwards and special quotes can be arranged for up to ten years with major currencies.

The ratio at which two currencies will be exchanged on a future date is known as the *outright* forward rate. These rates are usually printed in newspapers and are used by banks when dealing with their clients. Foreign exchange traders like to abbreviate, however, and quote forward premiums or discounts in terms of points.[5] A *dollar premium* implies that forward dollars are at a premium over spot, and the French, for example, need more French francs to buy dollars forward than to buy dollars spot. Similarly, a *dollar discount* means one needs fewer units of foreign currency to buy dollars forward than to buy dollars spot.

In order to tell if a currency is at a premium or a discount, compare the size of

---

[4]A "point" or "pip" can refer to 2, 4, 6, or any number of decimal places. If the Japanese yen were quoted in American terms with an ask of $0.001235 and a bid of $0.001230, this would still be considered a 5-"point" spread.

[5]Dealers often do not use the decimal point for forward bid-offer points. Whether talking on the phone or placing quotes on a screen, traders give the complete first bid of the spot quote (e.g., FF6.6575). All that is given for the ask, however, are the digits that differ from the bid (i.e., 75). A slash (/), communicated orally by the word "to," separates the bid and ask quotes. Thus a spot quotation for the French franc might appear on a screen as 6.6575/625, implying an offer rate of 6.6625, and the corresponding three-month forward rate would be represented as 263/296. One adds these points to the *last* three digits of the spot rate to get the outright forward quote.

the forward bid points with the forward ask points for a given maturity. If the forward bid points are higher than the forward ask points, the U.S. dollar is at a forward discount. For example, if the three-month forward points for deutsche mark are 38/35, then the forward bid points of DM0.0038 are greater than the forward ask points of DM0.0035 and the forward market is at a dollar discount. Similarly, if the three-month forward points on French francs are 50/55, the bid is smaller than the ask, and the dollar is at a forward premium.

To calculate the outright forward rate, one needs to know if the U.S. dollar is at a premium or a discount. Looking at the forward bid-offer points, if forward bid points are greater than the offer points, the currency is at a U.S. dollar discount, and the trader should *subtract* the forward bid-offer points from the quoted spot rates. If the forward bid points are less than the forward offer points, the currency is at a dollar premium, and the trader should *add* the forward points to the respective spot points.

Forward quotes can also be presented as a percent-per-annum deviation from the spot rate. By convention, the formula for calculating forward premiums and discounts as percentages using European terms, with n equal to the number of months in the contract, is:

$$\text{Forward premium or discount (\% p.a.)} = \frac{\text{spot rate} - \text{forward rate}}{\text{forward rate}} \times \frac{12}{n} \times 100$$

Using spot and three-month forward quotes for deutsche marks of 2.2605 and 2.2406, respectively, we would have:

$$\frac{2.2605 - 2.2406}{2.2406} \times \frac{12}{3} \times 100 = 3.55\%$$

When using American terms, the formula changes as follows:

$$\text{forward premium or discount (\% p.a.)} = \frac{\text{forward rate} - \text{spot}}{\text{spot}} \times \frac{12}{n} \times 100$$

Thus, in the above example we would have :
$$\frac{.4463 - .4424}{.4424} \times \frac{12}{3} \times 100 = 3.53\%$$

This differs from the percentage using European terms only by a rounding error.

Covered Interest Arbitrage

Many factors explain the changing values of foreign currencies relative to the U.S. dollar. Spot rates can be quite volatile, influenced by news, rumors, speculation, supply and demand imbalances, and central bank intervention. Over the long run, spot rates are affected by relative interest rates and inflation rates, trade imbalances, and purchases or sales of foreign assets.

Perhaps the dominant factor influencing the forward rate of a currency relative to its spot rate is the difference between nominal interest rates on foreign currency-denominated investments and comparable U.S. dollar investments. Investors will compare interest rates around the world in pursuit of the best possible return for a given level of risk. Large banks and corporations seeking short-term use of cash will generally look at Eurodeposit rates since such deposits are quite accessible, secure, and competitively priced because of the less-regulated nature of the Eurodeposit market.

However, the highest nominal Eurodeposit rate does not necessarily imply the highest expected yield in home currency terms. If the currency in which the deposit is made depreciates against the home currency, then the actual yield on the deposit in home currency terms will be less than the quoted nominal yield. For example, a one-year Eurofranc deposit may offer a yield of 11 5/8% compared to a one-year Eurodollar deposit offering 7 7/8%. But if the franc depreciates by 3.36% or more, the interest rate difference favoring the franc will have been completely offset from a U.S. dollar perspective. The depositor could hedge this risk by selling francs (purchasing dollars) forward at the prevailing market exchange rate, thus locking in the future rate at which the principal plus interest can be converted to dollars. In principle, assuming an efficiently operating foreign exchange market, the prevailing one-year forward contract rate for French francs will reflect the market's collective judgment about what the spot rate will be one year later. In other words, the current forward rate should be an unbiased predictor of the future spot rate, a condition known as *forward parity*.

Because money can flow quickly and in large volume from one Eurocurrency deposit to another, and because forward rates may be thought of as unbiased predictors of future spot rates, Eurodepositors aggressively seeking the highest *effective* return (including expected exchange rate movements) should drive Eurodeposit rates, spot exchange rates, and forward exchange rates into an interdependent relationship in which expected yields are identical across currencies. This condition is known as *interest rate parity*. It can be expressed notationally by the following equation:

$$F = S\frac{(1+R_F)}{(1+R_\$)}$$

where,

F	= the forward exchange rate expressed as units of foreign currency per dollar (European terms);
S	= the spot exchange rate expressed as units of foreign currency per dollar;
$R_\$$ and R_F	= the Eurodollar deposit rate and the other Eurocurrency deposit rate, respectively.

If this condition is violated, a *covered interest arbitrage* opportunity will present itself (for this reason, the above equation is also frequently referred to as the "covered interest arbitrage" condition). For example, consider the terms presented in Table 1.

TABLE 1

	Spot	3-Month Forward
French Franc	7.7150/200	300/425
3 Mo. Eurofranc Deposit Rate	11 5/8–11 3/4%	
3 Mo. Eurodollar Deposit Rate	7 7/8– 8%	

The French franc is selling at a forward discount against the dollar. Using the midpoints of the quotes, the discount is 1.88% on an annualized basis. This is smaller in absolute terms than is theoretically justified on the basis of differences in interest rates:

$$3.68\% = \{[(1+11.6875/400)\,/(1+7.9375/400)\,]-1\}\times4\times100$$

Consequently, an arbitrageur could profit risklessly by taking the following steps:
1. Borrow 1,000,000 Eurodollars for 3 months at 8%.
2. Purchase FF7,715,000 at the spot bid rate.
3. Invest the francs for 3 months at the Eurofranc deposit rate of 11-5/8%.
4. Simultaneously sell francs (buy dollars) forward at the forward offer rate of 7.7625. The amount of the forward sale should equal the total amount of franc proceeds at the deposit's maturity, or FF7,939,217 [FF7,715,000 × (1 + .11625/4)].

In three months, the arbitrageur would receive the Eurofranc deposit with interest, execute the forward contract, and obtain $1,022,765 [FF7,939,217/7.7625]. This could be used to repay the Eurodollar loan with interest amounting to $1,020,000 [$1,000,000 × (1 + .08/4)], leaving a gain of $2,765. Assuming total transaction, brokerage, and cable cost of 0.25%, or $250 on the $1,000,000 deal, a net profit remains of $2,515. Note that this was obtained risklessly and without any equity directly committed by the arbitrageur. As many people try to exploit this opportunity in volume, interest rates and exchange rates will adjust until parity is restored and riskless profit opportunities are eliminated.

Interbank Trading

The vast bulk of foreign exchange transactions takes place in the *interbank market* where banks and foreign exchange brokers determine exchange rates. Dealers try to develop a sense for where the market is going and then buy or sell currency either for their clients or for their own portfolios. After dealer A decides what he wants to buy or sell, he calls foreign exchange dealers at other banks and "asks for the market." He wants to know whether the dealers' rates are competitive and doesn't say whether he intends to buy or sell. Foreign exchange dealer B (being called now) must use her intuition to determine what caller A wants to do before offering a quote. Many techniques are used in an effort to get the best rate. For example, if the first caller wants to buy deutsche marks, he might first ask for the market in pounds to confuse the dealer and only later ask for deutsche marks.

Aside from figuring out what the caller wants to do, dealer B must also devise a strategy that meets her goals. If dealer B wants to *sell* deutsche marks (buy dollars), she might present a bid of DM2.5235 per dollar, two points higher than other banks', which are at 2.5233. The dealer must also quote an offer, and this should not be better than the market since she does not want to own deutsche marks. Convention holds that the caller can choose either rate and any amount within one minute after the quotes. After the minute, dealer B can change her quotes. When a difference in the fourth decimal place can represent thousands of dollars on a big transaction, good judgment and fast thinking are vital.

The parties exchange confirmation papers after a deal has been arranged over the phone. Settlement occurs on the value date as the currencies are exchanged through the banks' clearing accounts. Client rates are generally determined in the retail bank draft market, while the interbank rate is determined in the wholesale market. The largest corporate clients get rates similar to those offered to other banks.

Sometimes banks cannot make markets among themselves. When a private deal cannot be arranged, foreign exchange brokers are used as intermediaries. Banks call brokers and tell them how much foreign currency they want to buy or sell and at what rate they will do the transaction. The broker then takes many requests to buy or sell and tries to find banks with complementary goals. If two banks' exchange rate terms can be matched, a trade is made. The banks only learn of each other's identities after a contract is settled. Following the contract's consummation, the broker receives a fee from each bank. Banks always prefer to make their own market since the broker's fee makes the same transaction more expensive.

Other Foreign Exchange Instruments

As indicated, the foreign exchange market allows individuals and corporations to transact in the spot market for immediate delivery and in the forward market for settlements in the future. Other foreign exchange vehicles and markets are also appearing. Although they accounted for less than 1% of total foreign exchange transaction volume in 1986, their importance is likely to grow.

While forward rates are quoted by commercial banks, *foreign currency futures* are homogeneous contracts traded in physical market places such as the International Monetary Market (IMM) in Chicago. Buyers and sellers of foreign currency futures deal through the exchanges rather than directly. Advantages of these contracts are that they are relatively small, and because of their homogeneity, are highly liquid. However, homogeneity also implies inflexibility, and there are high costs on large futures transactions.

Though complicated, expensive, and relatively illiquid, *foreign currency options* are becoming an attractive transaction alternative. Options allow a company to hedge against foreign exchange losses, but they also provide opportunities for bold speculation in the market. Unlike futures contracts, options represent the right, but not the obligation, to buy or sell a specific amount of currency at a fixed price on or before some future date. Since the option holder can always avoid exercising the option if it is uneconomical to do so, options make possible large upside gains while limiting downside losses. Costing an average of 5–6% of the underlying contract amount, options are expensive compared to the spreads on interbank forward contracts. Though options are not for everyone, more companies are using them to make a profit and hedge risk in times of volatile exchange rate fluctuations.

A common tool used to hedge foreign currency risk is a *foreign currency swap*. A foreign currency swap allows one party to swap principal and interest in one currency for principal and interest in another. Usually the participants borrow different currencies, exchange the receipts, and then service each other's debt. This arrangement eliminates exchange risk for the transaction and makes future currency fluctuations irrelevant. Sometimes a domestic company is able to borrow funds at a cheaper rate than a foreign company could. Swaps provide cost savings when two companies with complementary needs and desires get together. The World Bank is a frequent participant in these swaps and arranged the first important swap with IBM in 1981. Interest rate swaps, developed in 1982, allow a company with a fixed rate asset or liability to convert the security into a floating rate obligation or vice versa. Since then, foreign currency and interest rate swaps have typically been used together. Further details concerning swaps are provided in the note, "Foreign Currency Swaps" (Harvard Business School, 286–073, Rev. 3/89).

Exchange Rate Problems

The mechanics of exchange rate arithmetic, though fundamentally simple, can be confusing for those not using it on a regular basis. The questions below are designed to provide practice in the more common manipulations. They are of low to moderate difficulty with the easiest problems occurring first. **Exhibits 1–3**, along with general background information provided in this note, are sufficient to solve the problems.

1. Are the dealer quotes shown in **Exhibit 1** direct or indirect? If DM1,000,000 were sold spot how many dollars would be received? When would settlement normally take place?
2. Examine the cross-spot rates shown in **Exhibit 2**. Are there any triangular arbitrage opportunities among these currencies (assume deviations from theoretical

cross rates of 5 points or less are attributable to transaction costs)? How much profit could be made on a $5 million transaction?

3. What would be the $/SDR bid if the SDR appreciates 15% against the dollar? What would be the *SDR/$* offer rate if the SDR appreciates 15%?

4. Which currencies are at a dollar discount and which are at a dollar premium? What are the outright forward rates for the pound? For the French franc? Using the midpoints of bid-ask spreads, what are the forward premia or discounts on an annualized percentage basis for both these currencies?

5. A private speculator expects the yen to depreciate 7% against the dollar over the next three months. How can the speculator try to profit on these expectations through a) spot market transactions only, and b) forward market transactions only (assume no margin requirements or restrictions on transactions in credit markets)? What will be the expected dollar profit on a $1 million position in each case? What other considerations should factor into the speculator's choice between the spot and forward markets for purposes of profiting on future movements of the yen?

6. A U.S. corporate treasurer will receive a 2 million payment in 30 days from a British customer. The treasurer has no strong opinion about the direction or magnitude of changes in the sterling spot rate, but would like to eliminate the uncertainty surrounding such movements. Within the context of the rates shown in **Exhibits 1** and **3**, what options are available to the treasurer for hedging the foreign exchange risk associated with the sterling payment? What is the expected cost (expressed as an annualized percentage) of each alternative? Which alternative should the treasurer pursue? How would your answers to the above questions change if the treasurer believed very strongly that sterling would trade at $1.45?

7. Compare the one-year forward premium or discount on the French franc to the one-year Eurodollar and Eurofranc interest rates shown in **Exhibit 2**. How can this situation be arbitraged?

8. Examine the spot rate and the six-month forward rate for the British pound. Suppose a speculator anticipates that the pound's spot rate and the six-month Eurodollar deposit rates will be unchanged from their present levels in six months time. However, at that future date, the six-month Euro-sterling deposit rates will have changed to 10.0000–10.0625% per annum. What should be the new six-month forward rate for the pound if covered interest arbitrage opportunities are to be avoided half a year from now? How can the speculator profit from the expected change in the interest rate difference while remaining in a "square" position (i.e., offsetting foreign exchange purchase contracts with sales contracts) at all times? What will be the expected dollar profit per pound? How will this expected profit change if the spot rate six months later does not remain constant but changes to 1.5500/10? To 1.4500/10? What circumstances might cause the speculator to realize a loss rather than a gain?

EXHIBIT 1   Spot and Forward Exchange Rates

Currency	Spot	1 Month	3 Months	6 Months	12 Months
Sterling[a]	1.4890/00	55/52	160/156	302/289	560/523
Deutsche mark	2.0310/20	22/18	64/54	128/105	277/228
French franc	6.6575/625	73/86	263/296	505/590	1194/1351
Yen	154.20/30	8/6	33/27	75/62	164/137
SDR[a]	1.2141/43	5/3	12/8	18/11	24/12

[a]U.S. dollars per unit of currency.

EXHIBIT 2   Cross-Spot Exchange Rates[a]

	DM	FF	Yen
DM	—	.3050/51	1.3169/71
FF	3.2779/88	—	4.3365/84
Yen	75.9232/350	23.1595/618	—

[a]Quotes should be interpreted as units of the currency represented in the left-hand column per unit of currency shown in the top row. Quotes for the DM/yen and FF/yen are expressed in units per *100 yen*.

EXHIBIT 3   Eurocurrency Interest Rates

Currency	1 Month	3 Months	6 Months	12 Months
U. S. Dollar	5.6875–5.8125	5.5000–5.6250	5.5000–5.6250	5.6250–5.7500
Sterling	10.0625–10.1875	9.8750–9.9375	9.6875–9.7500	9.6250–9.7500
Deutsche mark	4.4375–4.5625	4.3125–4.4375	4.3125–4.4375	4.3125–4.4375
French Franc	7.1250–7.2500	7.1875–7.3125	7.1875–7.3125	7.2500–7.3750
Yen	5.1250–5.1875	4.7500–4.8125	4.6250–4.6875	4.6250–4.6875
SDR	5.9375–6.0625	5.8125–5.9375	5.7500–5.8750	5.8125–5.9375

CIBA-GEIGY AG:
Impact of Inflation and Currency Fluctuations

On February 18, 1988, Dr. Hans-Peter Schaer, member of the Konzernleitung (Executive Committee usually referred to as KL), presented the preliminary 1987 results to the Ciba-Geigy board of directors. For the second year in a row sales and profits reported in Swiss francs had declined. (See **Exhibit 1** for Ciba-Geigy's financial results.) Yet, when expressed in local currencies, Ciba-Geigy sales had increased by 9%, of which only 1% was accounted for by acquisitions (see **Exhibit 2**).

Ciba-Geigy in 1988 was the second largest Swiss industrial company, being ranked as No. 50 on Fortune's International 500 list. At that time corporate activities were organized in four divisions and three groups. The four divisions accounted for 90% of 1987 sales divided as follows: Dyestuffs and Chemicals, 15%; Pharmaceuticals, 30%; Agricultural, 22%; and Plastic and Additives, 23%. The three groups were Electronic Equipment, 5%; Ilford, 3%; and Cibavision, 2%. **Exhibits 3** through **7** provide financial information on Ciba-Geigy contained in the 1987 annual report.

As was traditional at the February board meeting, the four divisions presented their budgets for 1988. In terms of budgeting, 1988 was a particularly difficult and interesting year because of the uncertainty resulting from the stock market crash of October 1987. At the time of the February meeting it was still unclear what impact, if any, Black Monday would have on the economic outlook for 1988. Nevertheless, in

Professor Hugo Uyterhoeven prepared this case as a basis for class discussion rather than to illustrate either effective or ineffective handling of an administrative situation.

spite of Black Monday, all four divisions were very optimistic in their budgets, expecting substantial increases in sales and divisional contribution. However, when the Chairman of the KL, Mr. Heini Lippuner, pulled all the optimistic divisional and group budgets together into the corporate Swiss franc budget, 1988 would become the third consecutive year of declining profits and sales. Increasing divisional and group budgets added up to a declining corporate budget because budgeted exchange rates predicted a further strengthening of the Swiss franc vis-à-vis a number of other currencies. This applied particularly to the U.S. dollar for which the 1988 budgeted rate was SFr 1.30 = $1 vs. the actual average rate of SFr 1.49 = $1 for 1987. For Ciba-Geigy, each 10 centime decline in the dollar exchange rate resulted in a profit decline of over 100 million Swiss francs.

This discrepancy between the divisional and corporate budgets gave rise to a lengthy debate among members of the board. Some members expressed concern about Ciba-Geigy's competitive position. Even though only 2% of its sales were in Switzerland, 46% of its manufacturing and 58% of its R&D activities were conducted there. Thus, the question was raised whether Ciba-Geigy as well as other Swiss companies could continue to compete in the world market from their Swiss home base with a continuously stronger Swiss franc. Or, would major relocations for manufacturing and R&D activities be required to remain competitive? The question was raised whether Ciba-Geigy could do more to protect its financial statements from these adverse currency developments. It was also pointed out that the 1986 and 1987 developments had to be viewed in a long-term context. The U.S. dollar, which stood at SFr 1.65 = $1 in 1980 had risen continuously until it reached SFr 2.46 = $1 in 1985 only to decline to SFr 1.49 = $1 in 1987 (see **Exhibit 8**). Thus, during the early 1980s Ciba-Geigy's sales and profits benefited from the rising dollar. It was only inevitable that the opposite would happen. Another board member raised the question whether, with only 2% of its sales in Switzerland, it made sense for Ciba-Geigy to consolidate in Swiss francs. It was mentioned that ABB, resulting from the recent merger of ASEA and Brown Boveri, had chosen to consolidate in U.S. dollars rather than in either Swedish krona and/or Swiss francs as the respective currencies of the parent companies. One board member worried about the impact of declining Swiss franc sales results on employees and the public at large, who might perceive the company as a poor performer while in reality it had been growing rapidly. At the end of the discussion, the chairman of the board, Dr. Alex Krauer, promised to return to the topic at a subsequent board meeting.

In early June of 1988, in preparation for this board discussion on the impact of exchange rates, Dr. Krauer again reviewed this topic. First of all, he was wondering whether it retained the same sense of urgency as when it had been discussed at the February board meeting. The June exchange rates were slightly above the SFr 1.41 = $1 rate that had prevailed in February. Thus, the budgeted decline to SFr 1.30 = $1 had not yet occurred. In fact, the dollar had strengthened slightly.

Dr. Krauer began by pulling out of his files remarks he had made at the May 1978 annual meeting when he was still the KL member in charge of corporate control.

Consolidated Group Accounts - a useful instrument of management or a numbers game?

Happy for those for whom "spring" denotes lilac blossom and balmy moonlit nights! In the spring a company controller's fancy, in contrast, lightly turns to thoughts of the Accounts, of joyous tidings expressed in figures, of a strong balance sheet.

Which brings us right into the middle of our theme.

I mean, you don't normally expect much disagreement on whether lilac is in bloom or on the degree of balminess of a moonlit night. But when it comes to accounts there is a lot more difficulty in deciding whether profit is high or low, or how performance compares with competitors', and disagreement is that much more likely.

420 million francs—100 million francs more than in 1976—is the Ciba-Geigy Group profit figure for 1977.

Is this much or little? Good or bad?

Up to the early nineteen-seventies there was no problem in assessing the financial performance of an industrial enterprise or in comparing figures from different years or from competitor companies.

The scene had something in common with the football league tables: the company to which the finance analysts, investment advisers and financial journalists gave the highest aggregate of points came out head of the league. Its managers were held up as shining examples, while the managers of the company at the bottom of the league were having sleepless nights.

Oh the good old days! How so?

In order to measure anything properly, you need a reliable measuring instrument. Since profit is expressed in terms of money, the measure used for it is the value of money. Stability of the value of money is therefore essential for the proper measurement and assessment of profit.

The stability of monetary value—and thus the prerequisite for the proper measurement and assessment of profit—has for some years past been undermined from two directions: by inflation, which erodes the internal value of money, and by the volatility of the foreign exchange market, which distorts the external value of money.

Two examples will serve to demonstrate how severe the effect of these two intrusive factors on published profit can be:

The British chemical giant ICI published a trading profit figure for 1977, arrived at by conventional accounting methods, of approximately 550 million pounds. Restated for inflation, in a special statement incorporating inflation adjustments designed to give a truer picture on the basis of current costs, trading profit is reduced by 250 million pounds to 300 million pounds. In other words, nearly half the conventional published profit is paper profit due to inflation.

How exchange-rate fluctuations can distort the external value of money can be illustrated by reference to the Ciba-Geigy Accounts: 100 million francs were wiped off the Group profit figure in 1977 solely by the appreciation that took place in the Swiss franc in comparison with the 1976 mean rates.

What lessons can be drawn from the foregoing remarks and from our two examples? Must we resign ourselves to the thought that the measurement and assessment of the performance of internationally operating concerns is no longer feasible? Have consolidated accounts had their day, and do they belong on the rubbish-heap of management science?

The answer to these provocative questions is a clear and unequivocal *no*!

Since our Group is an economic entity and is managed as such, we cannot, now or in the future, do without an accounting system that gives a complete picture of the results and performance of the whole Group by bringing together and combining, or as we say consolidating, the results and performances of all the parts. In view of the manifold commercial and financial interconnections between the parts of our Group—we have companies in more than sixty countries—the local results of the individual operating units are, moreover, only to a limited extent suited to the measurement and assessment of economic performance.

Thus we cannot solve the problem by doing away with consolidated accounts. Instead, they need careful presentation and interpretation. Consolidated figures not overboard but more informative and easier to understand is the watchword. This requires the development and application of aids to interpretation. I should like to explain what is meant by this by means of some examples from our 1977 Accounts.

An important measure and assessment criterion is sales performance in the markets. Have we managed to maintain or improve our market share? Does an increase in sales value really express increased sales volume, or merely increased prices due to inflation in the country concerned? For answering these questions the sales figure in terms of Swiss francs is useless, since distortions due to parity changes will have been introduced in the process of converting local into Swiss currency figures. For this reason our Annual Report, as an aid to interpretation, supplements the Swiss franc figures with a Table [see table below from the 1987 Annual Report] of the sales achieved in the individual countries in terms of the local currency. These local figures, in their turn, can be examined in the light of local inflation to determine how far sales have risen or fallen in real terms.

Last year, for example, sales-weighted inflation in our market countries was running at an average of 10%. Sales growth in local currencies was 11%, i.e., growth marginally exceeded inflation.

More complex than in the case of sales is the basis for understanding Group profit. Let me remind you first of all that Ciba-Geigy's published Group profit is arrived at on what is called the "current value principle." This means that long-term asset valuations are adjusted year by year to take account of inflation, and depreciation charges are calculated on these current values and not on the historical cost of the asset. By this method depreciation charges for 1977, for example, were some 120 million francs higher than they would have been on a historical cost basis. Furthermore, our current value accounting contains no valuation gains or losses that would distort the trading figures.

In order to be able to compare our Group profit with the profit published by other companies—another form of measurement and assessment, and my second example of an aid to interpretation—we must take account of the different valuation principles adopted from company to company. If, for this purpose, we convert our current-value 1977 profit to a nominal profit of the type published by other companies, we arrive at a figure enhanced by more than 100 million francs, i.e., 530 instead of 420 million francs.

This supplementary calculation is not intended to give the impression of being more than we

Sales in the principal local currencies[1]

Country	Currency Unit	1987 Millions	1986 Millions	Change, %	Average Inflation-Rate,[2] %
U.S.A.	$	2,731	2,434	+ 12	4
West Germany	DM.	1,917	1,811	+ 6	0.2
U.K.	£	373	335	+ 11	4
France	Franc	4,325	4,113	+ 5	3
Italy	Lira	812,859	746,562	+ 9	5
Japan	Yen	100,947	94,752	+ 7	−0.3
Spain	Peseta	31,576	26,822	+ 18	5
Canada	$	334	293	+ 14	4
Brazil	Cruz.	12,910	4,441	+191	230
Switzerland	Franc	316	311	+ 2	2
Mexico	Peso	181,702	65,003	+180	132
Australia	$	200	168	+ 19	8
Netherlands	Guilder	440	406	+ 8	−0.5
Belgium/Lux.	Franc	5,195	4,897	+ 6	0.8

[1] Sales by or on behalf of local companies (excluding inter-company shipments).

[2] Movement of retail price index, 1987. Source: O.E.C.D., *Main Economic Indicators*, February 1988. (Brazil and Mexico percentages estimated.)

are or of putting ourselves above other companies. It is not merely a useful, but rather an essential tool for making cross-comparisons.

With the same purpose in view I should like to develop a further profit-related aid to interpretation.

The current value principle makes it possible to correct the falsification of Group profit by inflation; but it does nothing to remove the distortions caused by exchange-rate fluctuations.

On the one hand the appreciation of the Swiss franc reduces the Group profit figure. From the viewpoint of a Group like Ciba-Geigy, 98% of whose earnings derive from abroad and about 50% of whose costs are incurred in Switzerland, this statement will come as no surprise. Exchange-rate fluctuations reduced Ciba-Geigy profit for 1977 by some 100 million francs. The first step is to recognize this as a pure book loss arising when revenue and expenditure are, for the purposes of the accounts, converted from foreign currencies into Swiss francs at the average exchange-rates prevailing in 1977 as against 1976.

Now, how much of this book loss represents a loss in real terms, in other words one due not to the method of consolidation but, for example, to the transfer of the proceeds of a sale of goods from the currency area of the sale to the currency area of manufacture?

In order to pass from the book effect to the actual effect of franc appreciation on Group profit, we again make use of an aid to interpretation. Its purpose is to show what positive exchange effects can be set against the book losses.

A first positive corrective factor lies in the fact that the appreciated Swiss franc makes raw materials and intermediates bought from abroad cheaper. However, in 1977 this advantage was scarcely of practical significance to us, because about half of our feedstock imports come from West Germany, whose currency was exceptional last year in not easing against the Swiss franc but appreciating (by about 4%). But previous years brought us useful savings from this source, and the same will be the case in 1978.

Another positive corrective factor is represented by the increased purchasing power of our profit brought by the appreciation of the Swiss franc. There is no need to tremble for "the franc in your pocket." For both the shareholder and the enterprise, a franc is worth more in international purchasing power in 1977 than in 1976. Just how useful this fact is depends on where the shareholder spends his dividend or the Company spends its retained profit. Spent inside Switzerland, the gain is nullified. In the case of the Company's retained profit we can assume that it will be used—in pursuit of a policy of self-financing—as a source of finance for investment projects or acquisitions. Since about 60% of our investment spending and virtually all acquisitions take place abroad, the benefit accruing to Ciba-Geigy from the appreciation of the Swiss franc in 1977 can be estimated at about 50 million francs. This means that, of last year's book loss of some 100 million francs, only about half remains as a real drop in Group profit caused by the appreciation of the Swiss franc.

There is also, providing we are willing to look behind the scenes of the consolidated Accounts for it, an answer to the frequently heard question as to how we managed to make an almost equally large profit in 1977 with the U.S. dollar at SFr. 2.40 as three years earlier when it was SFr. 3.—. We then observe that it has been possible in recent years to offset at least part of the negative effect of Swiss franc appreciation by means of measures designed to increase revenue on the one hand (higher sales volume, price-increases to compensate for cost inflation, successful new products) and to reduce expenditure on the other. Had we omitted to take such measures, and had we in consequence remained at the sales and costs levels of 1974, we should indeed be in the red today.

I bring my remarks to a close in the firm conviction that I have succeeded in confusing you sufficiently for the present. It is, for one thing, a complicated subject; you will, secondly, I hope make allowances for the speaker; and thirdly it was not quite unintentional. It was, I may confess, my intention to confound those who expected a neat, ready-made solution.

For those, in contrast, who are prepared to consider discriminating answers to complex questions, I hope I may have succeeded in pointing out some lines of approach to a better understanding of consolidated accounts.

In principle it is a matter of ceasing to be hypnotized by the last figure of the profit and loss account. It always was difficult, and has nowadays become impossible, to grasp and assess the performance of a complex organization like Ciba-Geigy in a constantly changing environment on a single figure, the net profit. Consolidated accounts and their profit figure should instead be understood as an information base from which we must extract the relevant data specifically and discriminatingly as required. A mass of qualitative and quantitative information is available as an aid to interpretation.

But there must always be a readiness on the part of the reader to recognize and understand the economic facts and influences that lie behind such accounts, to take the trouble to analyze the information carefully, to sift and utilize it—a demanding job, admittedly, but not an impossible one.

[translated from the German originals]

Also, Dr. Krauer reviewed some of the worksheets on the impact of inflation and currency changes which were used in 1987 at the company's annual General Management Meeting (GMM), at which the top 40 executives from all over the world participated. At that meeting the participants analyzed and discussed the impact of inflation and currency changes on management decision making and corporate financial performance. The first question which was asked at this meeting was why Ciba-Geigy's current-value operating profit and its historical-cost profit moved in opposite directions during 1985 and 1986. (See **Exhibits 7** and **9** for the relevant data from the 1985 and 1986 annual reports and **Exhibit 10** for Worksheet 1.) The participants were also asked to fill out Worksheet 2 (see **Exhibit 11**) using annual report data (see **Exhibit 4**) and to answer the following two questions: "To what extent are the valuation adjustments similar or different from those used in Worksheet 1?" and "Why are these adjustments made?" A third worksheet was given to the GMM participants (see **Exhibit 12**) with these questions: "From the point of view of a Ciba-Geigy shareholder, do the additional adjustments on the attached worksheet make sense?" and "Which figure best reflects Ciba-Geigy's performance?"

Dr. Krauer furthermore reread a paper prepared by Mr. Walther Zeller, head of the corporate finance function (roughly equivalent to the job of treasurer) which was written in preparation for the 1987 GMM meeting.

Some ideas on how to possibly structure a discussion on what can be realistically expected from hedging operations

1. *We state that in 1986 exchange rates have had a negative impact* of
   SFr. 2,813 millions on our sales
   SFr. 662 millions on our profit
   Moreover, we show currency losses charged directly to equity of
   SFr. 965 millions on fixed assets
   Sfr. 50 millions on other long-term assets, current assets and liabilities
   Questions: Could the damage not have been avoided or at least much reduced through hedging operations? Did our Finance sleep, in contrast to, e.g., Sandoz who repeatedly stated that "they have the $-problem under control"? Similar questions are often asked by bankers: Why do you not solve your problem by invoicing in SFr., or by making use of the modern hedging tools available (options, swaps, etc. besides forward contracts)?
   The *fact* is: we did an unprecedented amount of hedging from the middle of 1985 through the end of 1986 (over $500 million), and we did use a variety of instruments (debt in local currency, forward contracts, options). On the contracts maturing until the end of 1985 we realized gains of over SFr. 300 million. It seems, however, that the problem is more complex than some people think.

2. *What do the above-mentioned figures mean?*
   2.1 *The impact on our P&L*
      The above figures show what additional sales and profits would have been realized if all 1986 figures would have been converted into SFr. at 1985 ex-

change rates. The rates serving for comparison are monthly rates for sales (conversion at the time of invoicing) and quarterly rates for costs/expenses. Note that this is a theoretical approach. It is a very useful tool for analysis, but it does not take into account what is commonly called "economic exposure": the effects of exchange rates on volume/mix, on our competitors' sales prices and ours, nor managerial action to cope with the new situation. The results of hedging transactions are not included, either.

2.2 *The impact on our Balance Sheet*

All assets and liabilities are converted at year-end rates and compared to the SFr. values a year ago.

The resulting "profits or losses" are not cash but valuation differences. The exchange risk on the balance sheet items is referred to as "translation exposure." In other words, we have invested our equity partly in foreign currencies, so the equity value changes with exchange rate fluctuations.

There is one element of realized exchange differences included, however: since revenues are translated into SFr. and credited to the P&L immediately when invoiced, differences can accrue until payment is received, and until a part of the receipts is actually transferred ("transaction exposure"). The transaction risk lends itself to hedging operations: the Swiss exporter who is satisfied with the SFr. countervalue of a sale made in $ can sell the $ invoice amount forward until he receives payment (he actually finances the merchandise credit in $ at a $ interest rate).

3. *How do we assess the exposure as a basis for considering whether to hedge?*

3.1 *Balance Sheet*

We have just discussed the balance sheet exposure. However, should we consider hedging everything?

Fixed assets will in all probability never be liquidated and converted into SFr. for repatriation. Moreover, they are periodically revalued in local currencies, and since inflation rate differentials are still a factor determining exchange rates (at least in the long run, although much less so short term) there is a built-in compensation. As a matter of fact, revaluation gains have more than matched currency translation losses from 1974 up to the present. We, therefore, feel that hedging fixed assets should normally be unnecessary.

On the other hand, we think we should consider all monetary assets (liquid funds, receivables) as fully exposed. Monetary liabilities (payables, financial debt) can be deducted, so it is the net balance that counts.

What about inventory? In principle, we have a similar situation as with fixed assets, but since we know from experience that only about half the inflationary revaluation gains can be realized (through sales price increases), we consider—somewhat arbitrarily—50% of the inventory as exposed also.

3.2 *Cash Flow*

We look at the cash flow expected to be generated in each foreign currency during the forthcoming 12 months (sales minus costs/expenses except depreciation of fixed assets). Then, for the same reasons as explained above, we deduct the portion which will be invested into fixed assets as well as 50% of the expected investment (increase) in inventory. The remaining amount will be used for transfers into SFr. (mainly payment for merchandise) or invested in monetary assets and is, therefore, to be considered as exposed.

Please notice that this is a global, consolidated calculation of foreign exchange exposure. Intercompany merchandise transactions and their currency denomination do not alter the total picture; they merely determine whether a particular exposure rests with the group company or with the parent company. Intercompany financial transactions (share capital, loans and merchandise credit) do not alter the asset side but they will cause local debt (which is a natural hedge) to be higher or lower.

4. *So we have our exposure figures now, but what to do?*
   Supposing you agree with our method of assessing the exposure (and thus eliminating a good part of the mathematical exposure, namely, fixed assets and 50% of the inventory), should we automatically and always hedge? We see the following main problems:

   4.1 *Hedging involves costs.* Therefore, every decision to hedge means that we are willing to pay a price which can be substantial. For forward contracts or borrowing in local currencies, the price corresponds to the interest rate differential between the respective currency and the SFr. Since this would amount to several SFr. 100 million a year, paying the price is only attractive if the risk for the respective currency is considered higher.

   4.2 Moreover, *hedging locks in the respective rate* (minus hedging costs). Especially when hedging over a long time horizon, we might put ourselves at a competitive disadvantage, or just look foolish if the market moves the other way (Lufthansa case: they bought $ at a high rate in 1985 when they made their investment decision to buy airplanes and were later on blamed for "losing" hundreds of millions DM.)

   With options you do not lock yourself in, it's more like paying an insurance premium. On the other hand, you buy a safety net at a higher cost and/or at a lower level. Options may be attractive in certain situations. We have, e.g., this year made use of an interesting technique: when the $ stood at SFr. 1.50 you could buy a put-option at SFr. 1.40 while selling a call-option at slightly over SFr. 1.50, at no cost on balance. A forward contract would have locked us in at around SFr. 1.45. So we kept a certain upward potential, but had to accept a lower floor for the hedge.

   4.3 *When should we hedge, and for how long?*
   Easy: sell when the $ is high, buy it back when it is low! Supposing one knows. . . . Should we hedge continuously as sales progress and are credited to the P&L? Or should a budget result (assuming it is acceptable at the

prevailing forward rates) be protected against currency risks and opportunities (as a few group companies sometimes tend to favor)?

As it is, we try to evaluate the exchange rate outlook at frequent intervals and decide to hedge only when the downward risk seems higher than the costs involved.

As to the time horizon, we do not go beyond a year. Perhaps wrongly so; with hindsight it might have been attractive to lock in the $ at above SFr. 2.50 for several years, but I underline with hindsight!

4.4 *Should we try to make short-term profits by trading?*

We *do* some trading, but only by way of increasing our hedge when we consider a currency temporarily high in order to buy it back (reduce our position) later on at a lower level. However, we never increase our exposure. The objective of our hedging policy is to reduce our risk and, hopefully, do better than if we hedged everything at all times. The dangers of a different policy became apparent in the Volkswagen case. The now popular claim that "profits from so-called in-house banking" can easily be made in reality means speculation.

4.5 *Do the results of hedging impact our published financial results?*

This is perhaps not the most important aspect, but it is nevertheless worth realizing that at Ciba-Geigy the results of hedging do not affect the P&L. You heard earlier this morning that the SFr. 334 million net gains from hedging operations were netted with the translation differences on "other long-term assets, current assets and liabilities" and booked directly over equity. So, no hedging operation could prevent the currency impact on our P&L.

Accounting differences incidentally are sure to provide one explanation for Sandoz' claim. We know that they did some hedging (although we do not know whether it was more than we did) and in their case the positive results did improve the published profit.

5. *What conclusions can we draw?*

— If we have mentioned a number of problems, we do not want to imply that we are basically adverse to hedging. On the other hand, we are convinced that it is uneconomical to be fully hedged at all times. Considering the open time horizon and "economic exposure" there is, moreover, no such thing as a "full hedge."

— Selective hedging can be very useful and must always be considered anew, depending on the foreign exchange outlook. However, it does not in itself provide the solution to our foreign exchange problems.

— In particular, the currency structure of our operations (revenues, cost/expenses, new investment) as well as the development of sales prices remain decisive. Long term, we must be able to adapt our business operations to changes in currency values; hedging can at best mitigate the short-term effects.

In addition, Dr. Lorenz Schmidlin, head of the corporate control and management services function (i.e., the corporate controller) had submitted a proposal for a series of slides for possible presentation at the forthcoming June board meeting (see **Exhibits 13–17**). **Exhibit 13** shows the different distribution of sales and costs by currency or currency groups. **Exhibit 14** shows how the foreign exchange loss has been calculated. **Exhibit 15** portrays the profit and loss statement in both Swiss francs and U.S. dollars. **Exhibit 16** indicates how net working capital and fixed assets are distributed by currency or currency groups. **Exhibit 17** indicates where investments in fixed assets and acquisitions were made as well as the positive impact of a stronger Swiss franc in 1987 compared to the 1986 exchange rates.

Dr. Krauer also took the opportunity to review some of the reporting practices of other multinational companies. Unilever, for example, reported its salient figures in eight different currencies (see **Exhibit 18**). Shell also used more than one currency (see **Exhibit 19**). Of particular interest to Dr. Krauer was note 29 in the Shell annual report on the statement of Source and Use of Funds (see **Exhibit 20**). Sandoz used a different reporting format compared to Ciba-Geigy. It did not use any inflation accounting, it translated fixed assets at the historical exchange rate, and it took "translation and exchange rate differences" as an expenditure item directly into the P&L rather than charging them to equity. Also, the Sandoz Annual Report stated: "Gains are carried forward to be offset against any corresponding losses in future accounting periods." As a result, the annual charge in the profit and loss statement would not necessarily reflect the exchange impact of that particular year.

As a board member of Brown Boveri, Dr. Krauer had participated in the recent board meetings concerning the merger with ASEA and the choice of the U.S. dollar as the currency to consolidate the ABB accounts. During one of these board meetings, it was reported that in preparing for the merger some calculations had been made restating ASEA results in Swiss francs and Brown Boveri results in Swedish krona. ASEA, which had reported rapidly growing sales in Swedish krona, became a stagnating company when its results were converted into Swiss francs. In contrast, Brown Boveri, which had been reporting flat sales for years, became a growth company once its results were converted into Swedish krona. One of Dr. Krauer's colleagues on the board had, subsequent to that meeting, recalculated an analysis published in the leading Swiss newspaper which in 1985 had published an article indicating that during the preceding 10-year period Brown Boveri had grown only by 48% while ASEA had grown by 229%. When converting ASEA's Swedish krona results into Swiss francs, this remarkable 229% growth was reduced to 50% because the Swedish krona declined from SKR 1.6 = SFr 1 in 1975 to SKR 3.5 = SFr 1 in 1984. In discussing this ASEA-Brown Boveri comparison with some of his colleagues and board members three questions had been raised:

(1) Do current currency translation practices in presenting consolidated financial results penalize companies domiciled in strong currency countries and benefit those in weak currency nations?

(2) As a result, are sales and profit growth either under- or overstated, creating in-

correct perceptions among managers, employees, and financial analysts as to actual corporate performance?

(3) Are cross comparisons among companies, increasingly relevant in this era of global competition, rendered meaningless by the distortions caused by current translation practices?

EXHIBIT 1   CIBA-GEIGY AG Ciba-Geigy Group of Companies
Summary of Financial Results at Current Value

	1987 SFr.m.	1986 SFr.m.	Change, %
Revenue			
Group sales to third parties	15,764	15,955	− 1
Interest, royalties, and revenue from minority holdings	424	340	+ 25
	16,188	**16,295**	**− 1**
Expenditure			
Raw materials, intermediates and finished products (variable			
product costs, including inward freight and duties)	4,805	4,915	− 2
Wages, salaries, bonuses and welfare benefits	4,842	4,924	− 2
Interest payable	298	317	− 6
Depreciation on fixed assets[1]	858	844	+ 2
Other expenditure,[2] including taxes	4,285	4,134	+ 4
	15,088	**15,134**	**± 0**
Group operating profit	**1,100**	**1,161**	**− 5**
as a percentage of sales	7.0	7.3	
Group operating cash flow	**1,958**	**2,005**	**− 2**
as a percentage of sales	12.4	12.6	

[1]Current-value basis. Book depreciation (historical-cost basis) on fixed assets was:
1987, SFr. 720m.; 1986, SFr. 680m.

[2]"Other expenditure" includes minority profit attributions: 1987, SFr. 14m.; 1986, SFr. 1m.

Translation of foreign currencies

All figures in the consolidated summaries of Financial Results and Financial Status are stated in *Swiss francs*.

In the case of the Group *Summary of Financial Results*, the individual Group companies' sales, expenditure and revenue in local currencies are translated into Swiss francs at the average rates applicable to the accounting period.

In the case of the Group *Summary of Financial Status*, translation has been effected at the rates prevailing at the year-end.

All *exchange-rate differences* arising from translation of individual book items into Swiss francs have been set off direct against Group equity. The Summary of Financial Results therefore contains no valuation differences of this kind.

Application of current value

Inflation and currency fluctuations have for some time past been factors which cannot be ignored in management and financial analysis, and accounting policies must pay due regard to them. We have attempted to do this by applying, Groupwide with a few exceptions, the current value principle.

- In the Summary of Financial Results, both sales on the one hand and expenses and costs on the other are stated at current value. Depreciation at current value assists in the maintenance of physical capital, and the appearance of paper profits in the accounts is avoided.

- The current value principle is applied to the Summary of Financial Status by means of adjustments to the fixed assets and revaluation of stocks.

Source: 1987 Ciba-Geigy Annual Report

EXHIBIT 2   CIBA-GEIGY AG

Increase of Sales and Costs/Expenses in Percent (Currency-Adjusted)

	1981	1982	1983	1984	1985	1986	1987
Sales							
Volume/Mix	5	3	6	13	6	2	6
Sales prices	6	5	3	2	2	1	2
Raw material							
(standard) costs	5	4	2	0	1	−4*)	−2
*) positive deviations of purchase prices included							
Period costs/expenses	7	7	5	12	11*)	6	6
*) 1984 Airwick excluded							
Ø *inflation rates CG group*							
weighted by sales structure	11	10	5	5	$4\frac{1}{2}$	$2\frac{1}{2}$	3
weighted by cost structure	9	8	4	4	4	2	3
inflation rates Switzerland	$6\frac{1}{2}$	$5\frac{1}{2}$	3	3	$3\frac{1}{2}$	1	2

Source: Ciba-Geigy AG, internal document.

EXHIBIT 3   CIBA-GEIGY AG Group Profit by Conventional (Historical-Cost) Accounting

	1987 SFr.m.	1986 SFr.m.	Change, %
Current-value Group operating profit	1100	1161	− 5
Less Revaluation of stocks	17	0	
Add Difference between current-value and historical-cost depreciation on fixed assets	138	164	
Less Valuation differences due to parity changes on the Financial Status item "Other long-term assets", current assets and liabilities	307	50	
Approximate historical-cost Group profit	**914**	**1275**	**− 28**
as a percentage of sales	5.8	8.0	
Add Book depreciation (historical-cost basis) on fixed assets (cf. footnote 1)	720	680	
Approximate historical-cost cash flow	**1634**	**1955**	**− 16**
as a percentage of sales	10.4	12.3	

Source: 1987 Ciba-Geigy Annual Report.

EXHIBIT 4   CIBA-GEIGY AG Ciba-Geigy Group of Companies Movement
of Equity Funds

	1987 SFr.m.	SFr.m.	1986 SFr.m.	SFr.m.
Group equity at January 1		**14,401**		**13,978**
Group operating profit after taxation		**+1,100**		**+1,161**
Adjustment of fixed assets to current value	+381		+412	
Revaluation of stocks	− 17		0	
Valuation differences due to parity changes				
on fixed assets	−756		−965	
on the Financial Status item "Other long-term assets",				
current assets and liabilities	−307		− 50	
Total valuation adjustments		− 699		− 603
Other equity changes		− 414		+ 65
Distribution of profits (dividend and directors' percentages				
of CIBA-GEIGY Limited)		− 200		− 200
Group equity at December 31		**14,188**		**14,401**

Movement of equity funds

The Movement of Equity Funds summary represents an essential supplement to the Summary of Financial Results. The latter expresses the results of the business operations *per se*, while the Movement summary contributes information on all such valuation corrections made to balance-sheet items as are attributable to external factors. These corrections comprise:

- Adjustment of fixed assets to current value.

- Revaluation of stocks as a result of changes in raw material prices (in pursuance of the current value principle).

- Valuation differences due to parity changes on balance-sheet items.

The effects of parity changes are stated separately for fixed assets on the one hand and other long-term assets, current assets and liabilities on the other. The valuation differences arise from foreign-currency balance-sheet items relating to the consolidated Group companies, as a result of the difference between the exchange-rate of the currency concerned at the beginning of the year as against the end, which is the value on which the Group Financial Status summary in Swiss francs is based. Under the heading "Valuation differences due to parity changes on the Financial Status item 'Other long-term assets,' current assets and liabilities" are included all exchange gains or losses booked by CIBA-GEIGY Limited and the Group companies during the course of the year.

Source: 1987 Ciba-Geigy Annual Report

EXHIBIT 5   CIBA-GEIGY AG Ciba-Geigy Group of Companies
Summary of Financial Status

	December 31, 1987		December 31, 1986	
	SFr.m.	SFr.m.	SFrm.	SFr.m.
Current assets				
Liquid funds[1]	5,160		4,663	
Customer receivables	2,733		2,776	
Various current assets	1,061		1,067	
Stocks	3,269	12,223	3,621	12,127
Less Current liabilities				
Suppliers	863		852	
Banks	1,085		993	
Other current liabilities	3,205	5,153	2,981	4,826
Net current assets		**7,070**		**7,301**
Long-term assets				
Fixed assets[2]	8,990		9,035	
Other long-term assets (interests in associated companies, loans and other assets of a long-term character)	945	9,935	1,136	10,171
Total net current assets and long-term assets		**17,005**		**17,472**
Less Long-term liabilities				
Debenture loans and private placements	874		899	
Other loans and long-term liabilities	1,761	2,635	1,989	2,888
Less Minority interests		182		183
Group equity		**14,188**		**14,401**
Balance-sheet total		**22,158**		**22,298**

[1]Of which: Cash/P.O. Giro/   Securities
                     Bank
31.xii.87   SFr. 2,592m.   SFr. 2,568m.
31.xii.86   SFr. 2,580m.   SFr. 2,083m.

[2]Of which: Land and buildings Plant
31.xii.87   SFr. 4,219m.   SFr. 4,771m.
31.xii.86   SFr. 4,395m.   SFr. 4,640m.
Current value. Use of acquisition
value less appropriate depreciation
would give a valuation of:
SFr. 5,138m. at December 31, 1987.
SFr. 4,960m. at December 31, 1986.
Insured value of fixed assets:
SFr. 17,950m. at December 31, 1987.
SFr. 18,270m. at December 31, 1986.

Source: 1987 Ciba-Geigy Annual Report.

EXHIBIT 6   CIBA-GEIGY AG Ciba-Geigy Group of Companies Summary of Financing

	1987 SFr.m.	SFr.m.	1986 SFr.m.	SFr.m.
Sources of funds				
Group operating cash flow		1958		2005
Distribution of profits, CIBA-GEIGY Limited, in respect				
of the preceding year		−200		−200
Self-financing		1758		1805
Decrease in net current assets (except liquid funds)				
Goods in stock (before revaluation)	335		334	
Trade receivables	43		249	
Other current assets	6	384	8	591
Increase in suppliers' accounts payable		11		—
Increase in other current liabilities		224		3
Increse in other long-term liabilities		—		—
Net decrease in interests in associated companies and loans		191		—
Other items, net change		—		—
Total		**2568**		**2399**
Applications of funds				
Capital expenditure		1368		1232
Net increase in interests in associated companies and loans		—		119
Increase in net current assets (except liquid funds)				
Goods in stock (before revaluation)		—		—
Trade receivables		—		—
Other current assets		—		—
Decrease in suppliers' accounts payable		—		17
Decrease in other current liabilities		—		—
Decrease in other long-term liabilities		187		413
Other items, net change		551		99
Total		**2106**		**1880**
Funds surplus		**462**		**519**
Financing measures				
Funds surplus		462		519
New funds				
Debenture loans, private placements	100		82	
Long-term bank debt	—		—	
Short-term bank debt	92		—	
Proceeds of cession of participation certificates	10		421	
Total new funds		202		503
Debt repayment				
Debenture loans, private placements	125		215	
Long-term bank debt	42		28	
Short-term bank debt	—		114	
Total debt repayments		167		357
Increase in liquid funds		**497**		**665**

Source: 1987 Ciba-Geigy Annual Report.

EXHIBIT 7 CIBA-GEIGY AG The Group in Figures, 1978–1987

		1978	1979	1980	1981	1982	1983	1984	1985	1986	1987
Group sales	SFr.m.	8,932	9,891	11,914	13,599	13,808	14,741	17,474	18,221	15,955	15,764
Change in relation to preceding year	%	−10	+11	+20	+14	+1	+7	+19	+4	−12	−1
Group operating profit after taxation	SFr.m.	360	327	305	521	622	776	1,187	1,472	1,161	1,100
Change in relation to preceding year	%	−14	−9	−7	+71	+19	+25	+53	+24	−21	−5
	As % of sales	4.0	3.3	2.6	3.8	4.5	5.3	6.8	8.1	7.3	7.0
Depreciation on fixed assets	SFr.m.	602	630	727	818	836	804	863	897	844	858
	As % of sales	6.8	6.4	6.1	6.0	6.1	5.4	4.9	4.9	5.3	5.4
Group operating cash flow	SFr.m.	962	957	1,032	1,339	1,458	1,580	2,050	2,369	2,005	1,958
Change in relation to preceding year	%	−9	−1	+8	+30	+9	+8	+30	+16	−15	−2
	As % of sales	10.8	9.7	8.7	9.8	10.6	10.7	11.7	13.0	12.6	12.4
Net current assets	SFr.m.	3,695	4,196	4,546	4,727	5,162	5,479	6,847	7,099	7,301	7,070
Change in relation to preceding year	%	−2	+14	+8	+4	+9	+6	+25	+4	+3	−3
Fixed assets (depreciated current value)	SFr.m.	6,861	7,484	8,619	8,585	9,047	9,253	9,972	9,497	9,035	8,990
Change in relation to preceding year	%	−6	+9	+15	0	+5	+2	+8	−5	−5	10
Equity	SFr.m.	9,331	9,844	10,848	11,018	11,537	12,071	13,921	13,978	14,401	14,188
Change in relation to preceding year	%	−2	+6	+10	+2	+5	+5	+15	±0	+3	−1
Research and development expenditure	SFr.m.	762	824	937	1,076	1,175	1,248	1,456	1,674	1,627	1,673
	As % of sales	8.5	8.3	7.9	7.9	8.5	8.5	8.3	9.2	10.2	10.6
Capital expenditure	SFr.m.	554	598	853	875	868	830	1,007	1,213	1,232	1,368
Change in relation to preceding year	%	−13	+8	+43	+3	−1	−4	+21	+20	+2	+11
	As % of sales	6	6	7	6	6	6	6	7	8	9
Personnel costs incl. welfare	SFr.m.	2,845	3,107	3,719	4,095	4,206	4,390	4,893	5,184	4,924	4,842
Change in relation to preceding year	%	−6	+9	+20	+10	+3	+4	+11	+6	−5	−2
Number of employees		75,294	80,223	81,184	80,179	79,413	79,173	81,423	81,012	82,231	86,109
Change in relation to preceding year	%	+2	+7	+1	−1	−1	0	+3	−1	+2	+5

Source: 1987 Ciba-Geigy Annual Report.

EXHIBIT 8   CIBA-GEIGY AG
Swiss Franc-U.S. Dollar
Exchange Rates

	Nominal Rates[a]	Real Rates[b]
1975	2.58	2.58
1976	2.50	2.49
1977	2.41	2.38
1978	1.79	2.21
1979	1.66	2.06
1980	1.68	1.91
1981	1.97	1.82
1982	2.03	1.82
1983	2.10	1.82
1984	2.35	1.78
1985	2.46	1.78
1986	1.80	1.76
1987	1.49	1.73

[a]Average rates.

[b]Nominal rates adjusted for differences in Swiss and U.S. inflation rates, using 1975 as base year.

Source: Company records.

EXHIBIT 9   CIBA-GEIGY AG Group Profit by Conventional (Historical-Cost) Accounting

	Millions of Swiss Francs			Percent Change	
	1984	1985	1986	1984–85	1985–86
Current-value group operating profit	1187	1472	1161	+24	−21
Add Revaluation of stocks as a result of increased raw material prices	80	95	0		
Add Difference between current-value and historical-cost depreciation on fixed assets	155	175	164		
Less Valuation differences due to parity changes on the Financial Status item "Other long-term assets," current assets and total liabilities	56	659	50		
Approximate historical-cost Group profit	1366	1083	1275	−21	+18
as a percentage of sales	7.8	5.9	8.0		
Add Book depreciation (historical-cost basis) on fixed assets	708	722	680		
Approximate historical-cost cash flow	2074	1805	1955	−13	+ 8
as a percentage of sales	11.9	9.9	12.3		

Source: Various Ciba-Geigy Annual Reports.

EXHIBIT 10   CIBA-GEIGY AG Worksheet 1

Worksheet 1:
Please fill in 1986 figures from annual report

	1974–1980	1981	1982	1983	1984	1985	1986
inventory profit	1.202	316	123	250	80	95	
difference between current							
value and historical depreciation	802	238	248	190	155	175	
inflation profit	2.004	554	371	440	235	270	
currency loss (translation of							
current assets, total liabilities,							
and "other long-term assets")	(1.489)	(425)	(291)	(402)	(56)	(659)	
excess of historical cost over							
current value operating profit	515	129	80	38	179	(389)	
current value operating profit	2.396	521	622	776	1.187	1.472	

Source: Ciba-Geigy AG, internal document.

EXHIBIT 11   CIBA-GEIGY AG Worksheet 2

Worksheet 2:
Please fill in 1986 figures from annual report.

	1974–1980	1981	1982	1983	1984	1985	1986	1974–1986
Inflationary gains								
on inventory	1.202	316	123	250	80	95		2.066
on fixed assets	3.708	576	709	524	532	503		6.964
total	4.910	892	832	774	612	598		9.030
Devaluation gains or losses								
on fixed assets	(2.114)	(525)	(159)	(205)	153	(1.062)		(4.877)
on other net assets	(1.489)	(425)	(291)	(402)	(56)	(659)		(3.372)
total	(3.603)	(950)	(450)	(607)	97	(1.721)		(8.249)
Inflationary gains minus								
devaluation losses	1.307	(58)	382	167	709	(1.123)		781
(or plus devaluation gains)								

Source: Ciba-Geigy AG, internal document.

EXHIBIT 12 CIBA-GEIGY AG Worksheet 3

Confidential	1974	1975	1976	1977	1978	1979	1980	1981	1982	1983	1984	1985	1986	1974–1986
Profit after taxes	473	191	320	420	360	327	305	521	622	776	1,187	1,472	1,161	8,135
Dividends	(100)	(100)	(100)	(101)	(101)	(106)	(106)	(106)	(120)	(137)	(156)	(177)	(200)	(1,610)
Retained earnings	373	91	220	319	259	221	199	415	502	639	1,031	1,295	961	6,525
Inflationary loss on equity[a]	(598)	(276)	(111)	(99)	(64)	(462)	(414)	(683)	(577)	(239)	(334)	(426)	0	(4,283)
"Real" retained earnings	(225)	(185)	109	220	195	(241)	(215)	(268)	(75)	400	697	869	961	2,242
Inflation/devaluation adjustment[b]	(116)	530	70	(251)	(470)	480	1,064	(58)	382	167	709	(1,123)	(603)	781
Fixed assets write-off[c]	—	(14)	(22)	(20)	(13)	(13)	(17)	(64)	(52)	(56)	(47)	(99)	(44)	(461)
Net inflation/devaluation adjustment	(116)	516	48	(271)	(483)	467	1,047	(122)	330	111	662	(1,222)	(647)	320
Other adjustments[d]	(90)	(33)	72	55	(29)	(206)	(285)	(98)	(206)	(361)	30	(116)	(312)	(1,579)
"Real" net change in equity	(431)	298	229	4	(317)	20	547	(488)	49	150	1,389	(469)	2	983
New equity[e]	—	15	36	3	53	15	6	17	33	145	127	100	421	971
Total "real" change in equity	(431)	313	265	7	(264)	35	553	(471)	82	295	1,516	(369)	423	1,954

[a] Amount necessary to compensate for the loss of purchasing power suffered in our equity as measured by the Swiss inflation rate.

[b] See Worksheet 2 (Exhibit 11).

[c] Write-off consists of difference between current value and residual book value of retired fixed assets.

[d] "Other adjustments" include goodwill write-offs, restructuring costs, and book gains or losses on divestitures.

[e] Above-par proceeds from newly issued shares.

Items c, d and e are included in "other equity changes" in Exhibit 4.

Source: Ciba-Geigy AG, internal document.

EXHIBIT 13   CIBA-GEIGY AG Sales and Expense Structure according to Currency Areas

Currency Area	Sales Billions Fr.	%	Cost/Expenses Billions Fr.	%	Net Effect Billions Fr.
Swiss Francs	0,3	2	4,2	29	(3,9)
Europ. Currencies excl. sFr.	7,0	44	5,0	34	2,0
Europ. Currencies total	7,3	46	9,2	63	(1,9)
US- and Can. Dollar	4,5	28	3,9	26	0,6
Latin American Currencies	1,3	8	0,6	4	0,7
Yen	1,0	7	0,6	4	0,4
Other Currencies	1,7	11	0,4	3	1,3
Total	15,8	100	14,7	100	1,1

Source: Ciba-Geigy AG, internal document.

EXHIBIT 14   CIBA-GEIGY AG Currency Effect on Profit and Loss Account Analysis of Group Profit and Loss Account 1987 (Mio[a]sFr.)

	1987 at 1986 exchange rates	1987 at 1987 exchange rates	1987 Currency effect	
Sales	17.317	15.764	(1.553)	−9%
Cost/Expenses	15.832	14.664	1.168	−7%
Profit	1.485	1.100	(385)	−25%

[a]Millions

Source: Ciba-Geigy AG, internal document.

EXHIBIT 15   CIBA-GEIGY AG Group Profit and Loss
Account in sFr. and in US$

	1986 Mio sFr.	1987 Mio sFr.	in % of Previous Year not currency adjusted	currency adjusted
			1987	
			in % of Previous Year	
Sales	15.955	15.764	99	109
Cost/Expenses	14.794	14.664	99	107
Profit	1.161	1.100	95	128
in % of Sales	7.3	7.0		
Exchange Rate	1.80	1.49	1.49	
	Mio US$	Mio US$		
Sales	8.864	10.580	119	109
Cost/Expenses	8.219	9.842	120	107
Profit	645	738	114	128
in % of Sales	7.3	7.0		

Source: Ciba-Geigy AG, internal document.

EXHIBIT 16   CIBA-GEIGY AG Currency Effect on Balance Sheet
(Mio sFr.)

Currency Risk on / Currency Area	Net Current Assets 1)	Fixed Assets	Total
Swiss Francs	1,8	5,0	6,8
Europ. Currencies excl. sFr.	1,4	2,2	3,6
Europ. Currencies total	3,2	7,2	10,4
US- and Can. Dollar	0,3	2,1	2,4
Latin American Currencies	0,4	0,5	0,9
Yen	0,1	0,2	0,3
Other Currencies	0,2	0,2	0,4
Total	4,2	10,2	14,4
Currency Losses	(0,3)	(0,8)	(1,1)
Revaluation of non monetary items	—	0,4	0,4
Net Effect on Equity	(0,3)	(0,4)	(0,7)

1) = Current Assets./. Total Debts

Source: Ciba-Geigy AG, internal document.

EXHIBIT 17   CIBA-GEIGY AG Currency Effects on Capital Expenditures and Acquisitions in 1987 (Mio sFr.)

	Cap.Expend.	Acquisitions	Total	Currency Effect
Swiss Francs	613	—	613	—
Europ. Currencies excl. sFr.	308	15	323	+ 5
Europ. Currencies total	921	15	936	+ 5
US- and Can. Dollar	336	466	802	+137
Latin American Currencies	43	—	43	+ 7
Yen	44	—	44	+ 1
Other Currencies	24	—	24	+ 4
Total	1.368	481	1.849	+154

Source: Ciba-Geigy AG, internal document.

EXHIBIT 18   CIBA-GEIGY AG Unilever Salient Figures in Various Currencies

1987 above 1986	Sterling Pounds	Dutch Guilders	Austrian Schillings	Belgian Francs	French Francs	German Marks	Swiss Francs	U.S. Dollars
Rates of exchange £1 = [a]		3.33	20.84	62.01	10.04	2.96	2.39	1.87
		3.23	20.14	59.48	9.47	2.86	2.39	1.48
In millions of currency								
Turnover	**16 550**	**55 111**	**344 896**	**1 026 247**	**166 159**	**48 987**	**39 554**	**30 948**
	17 140	55 363	345 204	1 019 499	162 318	49 021	40 965	25 368
Operating profit	**1 373**	**4 572**	**28 613**	**85 140**	**13 785**	**4 064**	**3 281**	**2 567**
	1 124	3 632	22 643	66 873	10 647	3 215	2 687	1 664
Profit before taxation	**1 327**	**4 417**	**27 644**	**82 256**	**13 318**	**3 926**	**3 170**	**2 481**
	1 143	3 694	23 030	68 015	10 829	3 270	2 733	1 692
Profit after taxation	**793**	**2 640**	**16 526**	**49 174**	**7 962**	**2 347**	**1 895**	**1 483**
	701	2 265	14 118	41 695	6 638	2 005	1 675	1 037
Profit on ordinary activities attributable to shareholders	**756**	**2 516**	**15 747**	**46 855**	**7 586**	**2 237**	**1 806**	**1 413**
	664	2 144	13 369	39 483	6 286	1 898	1 586	982
Ordinary dividends	**270**	**897**	**5 612**	**16 697**	**2 703**	**797**	**644**	**504**
	232	751	4 683	13 831	2 202	665	556	344
Profit of the year retained	**506**	**1 685**	**10 548**	**31 386**	**5 082**	**1 498**	**1 210**	**946**
	427	1 377	8 589	25 365	4 038	1 220	1 019	631
In units of currency								
Earnings per share[b]								
Per Fl. 4 of capital	**269.37p**	**8.97**	**56.14**	**167.04**	**27.04**	**7.97**	**6.44**	**5.04**
	236.73p	7.64	47.66	140.78	22.42	6.77	5.66	3.50
Per 5p of capital	**40.54p**	**1.35**	**8.45**	**25.14**	**4.07**	**1.20**	**0.97**	**0.76**
	31.51p	1.15	7.15	21.12	3.36	1.02	0.85	0.53
Ordinary dividends[b][c]								
N.V. per Fl. 4 of capital	**108.71p**	**3.62**	**22.65**	**67.41**	**10.91**	**3.22**	**2.60**	**2.03**
	94.922p	3.066	19.114	56.464	8.994	2.714	2.270	1.406
PLC per 5p of capital	**12.09p**	**0.40**	**2.52**	**7.50**	**1.21**	**0.36**	**0.29**	**0.23**
	10.232p	0.330	2.060	6.086	0.968	0.292	0.244	0.152

Movements between 1986 and 1987 will vary according to the currencies in which the figures are expressed.

[a] Rates of exchange are respective year-end rates used in translating the combined figures in the various currencies.

[b] The earnings per share and ordinary dividends for 1986 have been adjusted to reflect the sub-division of shares on 29th June, 1987.

[c] The value of dividends received by shareholders in currencies other than sterling or guilders will be affected by fluctuations in the rates of exchange after the year-end.

Source: 1987 Unilever Annual Report.

EXHIBIT 19 CIBA-GEIGY AG Summarized Financial Data, Royal Dutch/Shell Group of Companies

Income data	£ million					US$ million				
	1983	1984	1985	1986	**1987**	1983	1984	1985	1986	**1987**
Sales proceeds										
Oil and gas	55,463	65,802	64,764	48,051	**51,755**	83,942	87,778	83,809	70,415	**84,799**
Chemicals	5,427	6,309	6,716	6,180	**6,608**	8,219	8,453	8,671	9,063	**10,842**
Coal	462	578	609	460	**530**	698	770	783	674	**874**
Metals	790	995	961	772	**862**	1,194	1,331	1,238	1,130	**1,419**
Other	122	122	52	84	**56**	184	160	68	122	**92**
	62,264	73,806	73,102	55,547	**59,811**	94,237	96,492	94,569	81,404	**98,026**
Sales taxes, excise duties and similar levies	8,956	10,264	10,008	11,341	**12,032**	13,564	13,702	13,007	16,643	**19,714**
Net proceeds	53,308	63,542	63,094	44,206	**47,779**	80,673	84,790	81,562	64,761	**78,312**
Earnings by industry segment										
Oil and gas: Exploration and production	2,519	2,880	3,001	1,494	**1,796**	3,813	3,858	3,855	2,179	**2,946**
Manufacturing marine and marketing	710	823	625	993	**674**	1,065	1,101	795	1,464	**1,085**
Chemicals	127	299	205	462	**764**	190	404	256	677	**1,271**
Other industry segments	(135)	(43)	(217)	(39)	**(36)**	(204)	(50)	(277)	(57)	**(56)**
Earnings from operations	3,221	3,959	3,614	2,910	**3,198**	4,864	5,313	4,629	4,263	**5,246**
Corporate items	(104)	(117)	(527)	(340)	**(259)**	(161)	(163)	(685)	(506)	**(415)**
Minority interests	(363)	(194)	(55)	(30)	**(56)**	(548)	(266)	(67)	(43)	**(91)**
Net income for the year†	2,754	3,648	3,032	2,540	**2,883**	4,155	4,884	3,877	3,714	**4,740**

†If the cost of sales of the volumes sold in the period is based solely on the average cost of supplies incurred in the same period (instead of using the first-in first-out (FIFO) method of inventory accounting used by most Shell companies) and allowance is made for the estimated tax effects, earnings on this estimated current cost of supplies basis would be as follows

	1983	1984	1985	1986	**1987**	1983	1984	1985	1986	**1987**
Oil and gas segment	3,369	3,426	3,741	3,270	**2,447**	5,097	4,596	4,846	4,796	**4,015**
Chemical segments	118	293	191	511	**769**	177	396	238	750	**1,278**
Earnings on an estimated current cost of supplies basis	2,885	3,365	3,133	3,372	**2,865**	4,361	4,513	4,055	4,940	**4,731**

EXHIBIT 19 CIBA-GEIGY AG Summarized Financial Data, Royal Dutch/Shell Group of Companies *(Continued)*

	1983	1984	1985	1986	1987	1983	1984	1985	1986	1987
	£ million					US$ million				
Income data										
Assets and liabilities data (at year-end)										
Total fixed and current assets	49,089	59,647	51,848	51,577	**46,252**	71,179	69,190	74,661	76,334	**86,491**
Net current assets	8,156	6,490	5,118	5,230	**5,038**	11,826	7,529	7,370	7,741	**9,421**
Long-term debt	6,825	7,193	5,360	4,218	**3,169**	9,896	8,344	7,719	6,243	**5,925**
Parent companies' interest in Group net assets	19,566	25,483	23,435	25,006	**22,975**	28,371	29,560	33,746	37,008	**42,964**
Minority interests	2,870	1,149	465	476	**439**	4,161	1,333	670	704	**821**
Total capital employed	29,261	33,825	29,260	29,700	**26,583**	42,428	39,237	42,135	43,955	**49,710**
Source and use of funds data										
Funds generated	7,691	8,932	8,815	7,510	**5,314**	11,611	11,906	11,178	11,025	**8,703**
Capital expenditure (including capitalized leases)	3,920	4,609	5,623	3,732	**3,825**	5,930	6,117	7,486	5,470	**6,302**
Dividends paid	872	967	1,091	1,356	**1,546**	1,327	1,294	1,423	2,017	**2,571**
Funds applied	5,124	9,141	7,862	5,236	**5,708**	7,757	12,377	10,372	7,705	**9,445**
Surplus (deficit) before financing transactions	2,567	(209)	953	2,274	**(394)**	3,854	(471)	806	3,320	**(742)**
Increase/(decrease) in cash and short-term securities	1,900	(276)	(763)	1,440	**(949)**	2,871	(599)	(1,200)	2,079	**(1,490)**
Other statistics										
Net income as % of average net assets	15·1%	16·2%	12·4%	10·5%	**12·0%**					
Return on average total capital employed:	12·1%	13·0%	11·1%	10·0%	**11·3%**					
Long-term debt ratio	23·3%	21·3%	18·3%	14·2%	**11·9%**					

Source: 1987 Royal Dutch Petroleum Company Annual Report.

EXHIBIT 20   CIBA-GEIGY AG Shell's Statement of Source and Use of Funds

The statement below is Note 29 in the Shell 1987 annual report. "Movements derived from Statement of Assets and Liabilities" (i.e., Shell's balance sheet) are the differences between the year-end 1986 and 1987 balance sheet items. For example, inventories were L 4,226 million at year-end 1986 and L 3,967 million at year-end 1987. This decline in inventories of L 259 million between the two year-end balance sheets was caused by a translation adjustment of minus L 482 million (caused by stronger sterling exchange rates at year-end 1987 compared to 1986) and an increase in inventories of L 223 million (at average exchange rates as shown on the statement of source and use of funds):

29 Statement of source and use of funds

This Statement reflects the source and use of funds of Group companies as measured in their own currencies translated to sterling at quarterly average rates of exchange.

Accordingly, the movements recorded in the Statement of source and use of funds exclude the currency translation differences which arise as a result of translating the assets and liabilities of non-sterling Group companies to sterling at year-end rates of exchange. These currency translation differences must therefore be added to the movements at average rate in order to arrive at the movements derived from the Statement of assets and liabilities. The amounts involved are as follows:

	Movements arising from currency translation			Movements at average rate	Movements derived from Statement of assets and liabilities
	1985	1986	**1987**	**1987**	**1987**
					£ million
Tangible fixed assets	(5,147)	(81)	**(4,335)**	935	(3,400)
Provisions for deferred taxation and other	984	(85)	**982**	(213)	769
Inventories	(760)	231	**(482)**	223	(259)
Accounts receivable	(1,025)	150	**(935)**	887	(48)
Accounts payable and accrued liabilities	1,008	101	**730**	(368)	362
Taxes payable	358	4	**240**	300	540
Long-term debt	1,121	18	**622**	427	1,049
Short-term debt	293	9	**310**	128	438
Cash short-term deposits and securities	(339)	86	**(291)**	(949)	(1,240)
Other	(380)	77	**(222)**	(20)	(242)
	(3,887)	510	**(3,381)**	1,350	(2,031)

Source: Royal Dutch Petroleum Company 1987 Annual Report.

Pfizer: Protecting Intellectual Property in a Global Marketplace

The biggest single change in management during my career has been the increase in time that managers spend dealing with government.

—Edmund T. Pratt, Jr.
Chairman of the Board
Pfizer Inc.
April 1991

Introduction

In the spring of 1991, top officials at Pfizer were rethinking their strategy for improving the protection of Pfizer's intellectual property around the world. Until recently, Pfizer and other members of a coalition of American companies known as the Intellectual Property Committee (IPC) had focused on achieving an intellectual property agreement in the Uruguay Round of the GATT negotiations. Under the leadership of its chairman, Edmund Pratt, Pfizer had been instrumental in transforming intellectual

Research Associate Michael A. Santoro prepared this case under the supervision of Professor Lynn Sharp Paine as the basis for class discussion rather than to illustrate either effective or ineffective handling of an administrative situation.

property (a category including primarily patents, copyrights, trademarks, and trade secrets) from a lawyer's specialty into an international trade issue of great concern to governments around the world. The IPC had forged an unusual tripartite coalition among European, Japanese, and United States industry to work with their respective governments to secure global protection for intellectual property through the GATT.

Now, however, it was unclear whether an acceptable intellectual property agreement or, indeed, any agreement at all would emerge from the GATT negotiations. Protection of its pharmaceutical patents was critical for Pfizer's long-term strategy and its commitment to innovation. Lou Clemente, Pfizer's general counsel, and Lillian Fernandez, the director of International Affairs in Pfizer's Public Affairs Division, along with Pratt, were considering the possibilities.

A Brief History of Pfizer

Based in New York City, Pfizer was a worldwide company with over 40,000 employees, approximately two-thirds of whom were employed outside the United States. Its principal lines of business were pharmaceuticals, which accounted for approximately one-half of its annual sales, as well as hospital products, consumer products, animal health, specialty minerals, and specialty chemicals. These products were available in more than 140 countries. In 1990, Pfizer was ranked eighth worldwide in dollar volume of sales of pharmaceutical and medical products.[1] Of its six principal R&D centers, four were located abroad: in Sandwich, England; Amboise, France; Nagoya, Japan; and Illertissen, Germany. The company had manufacturing facilities in more than 65 countries. Twenty-one production facilities were located in Less Developed Countries (LDCs).

Founded in 1849, Pfizer was until World War II primarily a manufacturer of specialty chemicals and the leading world supplier of citric acid, a product with many industrial uses. Through the production of citric acid, Pfizer developed fermentation skills which were regarded as among the best, if not the best, in the world. During World War II, these skills enabled Pfizer to develop cost-effective methods for the mass production of penicillin. The company focused on manufacturing bulk pharmaceuticals such as penicillin and other antibiotics and sold very few pharmaceuticals under its own label until the mid-1950s. One exception was Terramycin, the first antibiotic to be discovered by Pfizer scientists and the first to be sold under the Pfizer brand name. Introduced in 1950, Terramycin marked the entry of Pfizer into the ranks of research-based companies.

Pfizer's expansion into international markets began after World War II with the sale of bulk pharmaceuticals, most notably antibiotics, to European nations rebuilding under the Marshall Plan. About this time, Pfizer started manufacturing and selling a variety of over-the-counter and ethical (i.e. prescription) drugs under its own label. In

---

[1] *Medical Advertising News,* "Top 50 Companies," September 1991.

the early 1950s, largely to meet worldwide demand for its new antibiotics, particularly Terramycin, the company began setting up distribution and manufacturing facilities in other parts of the world, including Asia and Latin America. Pfizer was the first major U.S. pharmaceutical company to establish operations in many of these countries, though European companies such as Hoechst, Bayer, ICI, Beecham, Sandoz, and Ciba-Geigy were also expanding operations into developing countries at this time.

From a commercial perspective, LDC markets had never accounted for more than 10%–12% of Pfizer's worldwide sales. But Pfizer had chosen to stay in difficult countries like Bangladesh, Nigeria, and India. Over time, and despite the difficulties, some LDCs had nevertheless provided healthy profit pictures. Moreover many executives felt committed to relationships Pfizer had established in these countries. They had high hopes for the future as well. Similar hopes had propelled Pfizer into major joint ventures in China in 1989 and Hungary in June 1991 when few other companies were going in in such a big way.

With the chairmanship of Edmund Pratt beginning in 1972, Pfizer increased its emphasis on developing new and innovative proprietary drugs. During this period, marked by steady increases in research spending, Pfizer became a major pharmaceutical innovator. A 1990 study of pharmaceutical research by leading companies had ranked Pfizer ninth in total research spending,[2] and by 1991, it had built up a sizable portfolio of new products and drug candidates. Having launched new pharmaceutical products in 37 international markets in major industrialized countries in 1990, Pfizer planned 60 new launches for 1991.[3] To market its products in the United States, Pfizer had hired some 500–600 new salespeople and added an additional sales company, Pratt Pharmaceuticals, named for its chairman.

During Pratt's tenure, Pfizer's sales rose from $1 billion in 1972 to over $6 billion in 1990 (see **Exhibit 1**). Net income increased from $103.4 million in 1972 to approximately $800 million in 1990. Although it was unclear precisely how much growth was due to products manufactured under patent, Pfizer officials viewed patent protection as critical to corporate strategy. One financial analyst estimated that Pfizer products under patent would generate $4 billion in worldwide sales in 1995 and account for 40% of the firm's revenues.[4]

Like other major pharmaceutical companies, Pfizer's return on equity in 1990 was nearly double that of the median return for *Fortune 500* companies.[5] As it entered 1991, Pfizer had just completed the sale of its citric acid business, once the mainstay of the company. The sale reaffirmed Pfizer's commitment to a strategy of innovation.

---

[2]*Medical Advertising News,* "Top 50 Companies," September 1990.

[3]Pfizer Annual Report, 1990, p. 2.

[4]Brian O'Reilly, "Drugmakers Under Attack," *Fortune,* July 29, 1991, p. 60.

[5]*Id.* at p. 48.

TABLE A   International Sales at Pfizer

Region	1990	1989	1988	1987
United States	$3,472.9	$3,096.6	$2,884.2	$2,651.4
Europe	1,503.5	1,190.1	1,176.4	1.051.5
Asia	873.1	876.1	807.5	704.3
Canada/Latin America	419.6	386.2	405.9	399.1
Africa/Middle East	136.9	122.5	111.4	113.5
International	2,933.1	2.574.9	2,501.2	2,268.4
Consolidated	$6,406.0	$5,671.5	$5,385.4	$4,919.8

Source: Pfizer Inc.

The International Pharmaceutical Industry

The international pharmaceutical industry's global sales were estimated at more than $56 billion for 1990.[6] Seventy percent of both production and consumption was concentrated in advanced industrial nations. Companies based in the United States, Japan and Germany accounted for 50% of world production. Of the world's 20 largest firms by worldwide sales in 1990, eleven were based in the United States, two in Switzerland, three in Germany, and three in the United Kingdom.[7] A little over 10% of world production took place in LDCs, mostly in India, Brazil, Mexico, Argentina, Egypt and the Republic of Korea. The largest consumers of pharmaceuticals were the United States, where 21% of the world's pharmaceutical dollars were spent, and Japan, where 14% were spent. LDCs together accounted for approximately 14% of world spending.[8]

Competition was driven by the development of new products and the promotion of existing ones, including brand name products on which patents had expired or never existed. In pharmaceuticals, as in most other knowledge-based industries, the costs of production were a miniscule proportion of the costs of discovering and marketing new products. Drug research required substantial capital and extremely long development time with a substantial risk of failure. Dr. Joseph DiMasi of Tufts University estimated an average cost of $231 million and more than 10 years to bring a new pharmaceutical from the laboratory through the regulatory review process in the United States.[9] Each phase of the lengthy process of bringing a new drug to market—from initial discovery to the development of promising compounds through preclinical and human investigations, to the New Drug Application approval process—was

[6]Pharmaceutical Manufacturers Association, 1989–1991 Annual Survey Report, p. 4.

[7]"Top 50 Companies," *Medical Advertising News*, September 1991.

[8]Unless otherwise noted, all data in this paragraph from Van R. Whiting, Jr., "Mexico's Modernization: Nationalism or Liberalism in Pharmaceuticals," *Business in the Contemporary World*, Spring 1990, p. 45.

[9]Joseph A. DiMasi, "Rising Research and Development Costs for New Drugs in a Cost Containment Environment," paper of Center for the Study of Drug Development, Tufts University, Boston, Mass., 1991.

fraught with expense and uncertainty. Industry representatives estimated that 5,000 to 10,000 promising new substances had to be evaluated for each new drug that reached the market.

The costs of research and development were rising at Pfizer and in the rest of the industry. Pfizer had estimated expenditures of $750 million on research and development in 1991, an increase of 17% over 1990. According to the Pharmaceutical Manufacturers Association, U.S. pharmaceutical firms spent $8.2 billion (representing 16.8% of sales) on research and development in 1990, compared with $5.5 billion (15.8% of sales) in 1987.[10] In other research-oriented industries such as those represented by IBM, General Motors, Sony, and AT&T, research expenditures were in the range of 4%–6% of annual sales.

The Importance of the Patent System

Pfizer depended on the patent system to protect and justify its investment in innovation. Granted by governments, patents gave inventors certain exclusive rights to exploit their inventions for a limited period of time. These rights typically included the right to make, use, and sell the product or process covered by the patent. The world's first patent laws dated to 1474 when the Republic of Venice granted 10-year patents to inventors of new devices. According to United States patent law, "whoever invents or discovers any new and useful process, machine, manufacture or composition of matter" was entitled to obtain a patent.[11] The invention had to be novel and not obvious to a person having ordinary skills in the art to which the patent pertained. In return for disclosing the invention to the public in the patent application, the inventor was granted for 17 years the exclusive right to exploit the invention and/or to license it to others for a fee.

In 1991, nearly all the fully industrialized countries had patent systems similar to that of the United States. The period of protection varied, however, and except for the United States and the Philippines which awarded a patent to the first to invent, the other nations of the world awarded a patent to the first to file for it. There were also variations in the scope of a patent and conditions under which compulsory licenses could be required, as well as differences in the openness or secrecy of the application, the requirements of the application, the period of time needed for approval, and the procedures for challenging a patent. However, not all of these systems had been in place as long as that of the United States. And patents on pharmaceutical products, as distinct from patents on the processes by which they were made, were relatively recent in some industrialized countries (**Exhibit 2**).

Both product and process patents were critical to the research-based segment of the pharmaceutical industry. However, since most drugs could be produced through a

---

[10]David Rutman, "The Price of Doing R&D Soars," *Chemical Week,* June 13, 1990, p. 48.
[11]35 U.S.C. §101.

variety of processes, product patents were particularly important. Unless the product itself was patented, a competitor could legally produce it using a process different from the patented one. Since the costs of developing and marketing drugs were so high relative to the costs of copying and selling them, pharmaceutical companies sought the protection of both product and process patents. Only with both could they achieve an adequate return on their investments and generate resources to subsidize research and development of additional new drugs.

The social justification for patent protection was rooted in several ideas. One was promoting innovation. The United States Constitution, for example, provided for a system of copyrights and patents to "encourage the progress of science and the useful arts."[12] A period of exclusivity provided inventors an opportunity to recoup and profit from their investment in expensive and time-consuming research. By limiting the duration of the patent, governments attempted to achieve an appropriate balance between the social benefits of increased innovation and the increased costs to consumers of patented products.

Sometimes patents were justified as the inventor's "natural right" or proper reward for inventive activity. According to this view associated with the seventeenth-century English philosopher John Locke, the inventor acquired exclusive rights to an invention by virtue of having labored to produce it. Other members of society were morally obligated to recognize the rights of authors and inventors by not copying their creative works without their permission. Still others saw the inventor's rights as a *quid pro quo* for disclosing an invention to the public. One Pfizer executive saw patents as resting on the principles of liberal democracy and reflecting a "social contract among citizens, government, and innovators." In his view, countries like Canada abrogated this social contract when they passed laws taking away intellectual property rights.

Patent Protection at Pfizer

Under Pratt's leadership, Pfizer was aggressive in protecting and defending its pharmaceutical patents. The company employed some 35 patent attorneys and agents in-house, while relying on outside counsel for patent litigation. Pfizer, said Pratt, "probably spent more than its competitors on defending its patents." Although the costs and benefits of this policy could not be measured precisely, Pratt explained that it was something the company had to do "to discourage others from stealing its intellectual property." To be sure, Pfizer had achieved some dramatic and profitable victories in patent litigation in the pharmaceutical area as well as in the medical device area, another of Pfizer's businesses heavily dependent on patents. In 1983, for example, the company won a judgment for $56 million in a patent infringement suit involving

---

[12]U.S. Constitution, Art. I, §8.

doxycycline, an orally administered antibiotic. Similarly, in 1989, Pfizer's subsidiary Shiley recovered $53 million in damages in a suit related to blood oxygenators.

Lou Clemente, Pfizer's general counsel, first became involved in patent issues as counsel to the Pfizer International subsidiaries in the early 1960s. "My initial exposure to international patent protection issues was through enforcement. I would hear from one of our marketing people that our proprietary products were being copied and manufactured in Europe. In one case a manufacturer was not only copying our product but also counterfeiting Pfizer's name on the product. For the most part, the law in these European countries respected patent rights, and eventually, in some cases after very long and expensive legal proceedings, we were able to shut down these illegal operations by obtaining injunctions."

Not all of these enforcement actions went smoothly for Pfizer, however, "Italy was a particularly difficult place to enforce patent rights," said Clemente, "because there was a law which prohibited pharmaceutical patents. Eventually, this law was declared unconstitutional, and we were able to stop the Italian companies that were stealing our technology."

In the 1970s, having solved their patent enforcement problems in Europe, Pfizer's efforts turned to the LDCs. These markets had by then become important for Pfizer, and lack of patent protection had emerged as a problem in countries such as Mexico, Brazil, Argentina, and India. Gone were the days when lack of infrastructure and technical know-how had protected Pfizer's patents in LDC's. Said Pratt: "We were beginning to notice that we were losing market share dramatically because our intellectual property rights were not being respected in these countries."

Intellectual Property Protection in LDCs

Pfizer and other multinational pharmaceutical companies saw serious deficiencies in the intellectual property protection available in many LDCs. Some declined to grant any protection at all for new chemical and pharmaceutical products. Others offered patent protection for the processes used to produce new drugs, but not for the products themselves (**Exhibit 2**).

Another problem in LDCs was the inadequate duration of patents. This was especially important in the case of drugs which, because of lengthy regulatory reviews, could take many years to reach the market. For example, India, which recognized process but not product patents, granted protection for only five years. Along with other countries, India also required that patented products be produced locally and provided, under certain conditions, for compulsory licensing to local producers willing to pay a fee as determined by the government. Even in countries with patent laws, enforcement and penalties for infringement were often inadequate.

Pfizer's experience in Argentina illustrated many of the problems. Even before Pfizer received the approval of the Argentine government to sell the antiarthritic drug Feldene, a generic competitor was manufacturing and selling it. By the time Pfizer was able to bring the drug to market, it faced six competitors manufacturing Feldene without paying any royalties to Pfizer.

The availability of patent protection also influenced strategic decisions of the firm's international division. For years the company had debated whether or not to shut down the manufacturing facilities in India. "The Indian government was forcing us to license our products to local companies," said Pratt, "and the government was also controlling prices." Although other pharmaceutical companies faced with similar erosion in market share shut down many of their international operations, Pfizer, Pratt said, was determined to "hang in there."

The Indian operations had been unprofitable for many years. Pratt continued, "We had a large investment in plant and equipment, but we were not making any profit. Fortunately, we were doing well in our other operations so it didn't affect our overall performance dramatically. Still, there were some within the company who argued that we should shut down the operations and take a write-off. I was not one of those people. For one thing, over 2,000 members of the Pfizer family worked there. We had a responsibility to them and to the community that they were based in, which really needed our products. And there was always the possibility that the situation would turn around, and India remained a very large potential market for us."

Initial Efforts at Changing the World
Intellectual Property Environment

Pfizer's initial efforts, in the late seventies and early eighties, at changing the intellectual property climate were aimed at persuasion. Clemente recalled that "we went everywhere trying to press our position, including the World Bank. We tried to get the State Department interested in the issue, but they were security-oriented rather than business-oriented at this time." Clemente continued, "We were convinced that providing incentives for invention was truly a good thing for developing countries. We tried to persuade leaders of developing countries of this point of view. We tried to enlist the aid of the U.S. Embassies. All of our efforts at persuasion were fruitless." Pratt explained, "Developing countries told us they were too young, too weak, and too poor to have strong patent laws. But my answer to that was that the United States was a developing country when it wrote patent protection right into the Constitution in 1789!"

Pfizer had a particularly difficult time within the World Intellectual Property Organization (WIPO), one of the fifteen "specialized agencies" of the United Nations. WIPO, headquartered in Geneva, was established in 1967 to administer various multilateral treaties dealing with the legal and administrative aspects of intellectual property. The most important of these treaties were the Paris Convention for the Protection of Industrial Property adopted in 1883 (The "Paris Convention") and the Berne convention for the Protection of Literary and Artistic Work adopted in 1886 (The "Berne Convention"). In 1991, 101 nations were parties to the Paris Convention (**Exhibit 3**) and 84 nations were parties to the Berne Convention.

The Paris Convention required each contracting state to grant the same patent protection to nationals of other contracting states as it granted to its own nationals. The Convention also provided for the right of priority, whereby after a patent application was filed in one country, the applicant had 12 months to file for a patent in any of the other contracting states without losing priority. The Paris Convention specified the conditions under which each contracting state could provide by law for compulsory licensing or, in rare instances, the revocation of a patent (unjustified failure to work a patent, for example). Finally, as to matters not covered by the Convention, each contracting state was free to legislate to, for example, exclude certain fields of technology, or fix the duration of patents. There were no specific enforcement mechanisms or dispute resolution procedures under the Paris Convention.

Since the Paris Convention specifically allowed many of the practices Pfizer sought to change, Pfizer approached WIPO to attempt to change the Convention. But Pfizer made no progress at WIPO. "Our approach to WIPO was a disaster," recalls Clemente. "As a UN organization, WIPO works by majority, and, simply put, there were more of them than us. Our experience with WIPO was the last straw in our attempt to operate by persuasion."

Networks of Influence

After the disastrous experience with WIPO, Pfizer sought other avenues for securing adequate patent protection. Under the leadership of Pratt, this effort extended throughout the Pfizer organization and engaged individuals and companies inside and outside the industry. For instance, during the WIPO debate, Barry MacTaggart, then Chairman and CEO of Pfizer International, published in the *New York Times* an op-ed piece entitled "Stealing from the Mind" (**Exhibit 4**). This article reflected a considered decision to take a tough, open position and to name countries with bad patent protection, despite the risk of incurring their displeasure. Public statements like this by company leaders, as well as internal memos directed to key executives and managers, conveyed the message that intellectual property should be treated as a priority issue. The operating plans and budgets developed annually for each operating division also emphasized the importance of public affairs, including intellectual property protection, and identified specific objectives to be accomplished.

As a result, country managers in problem countries such as Mexico, Brazil, Korea, Argentina, Indonesia, Taiwan, Thailand, and India worked to build a consensus in favor of intellectual property protection through involvement with local business, professional, academic, and government groups. This was sometimes easier for expatriates than for local nationals more likely to face special pressures from their governments. Several hundred Pfizer executives around the world spoke up for intellectual property protection through the trade associations and business organizations with which they were affiliated.

Pfizer executives played key roles in many leading business organizations. For example, Gerald Laubach, then president of Pfizer Inc., sat on the board of the *Phar-*

maceutical Manufacturers Association (PMA), as well as on President Reagan's *Council on Competitiveness.* Pratt headed up the *Business Roundtable* of 200 CEOs. Besides his involvement in many legal groups, Clemente was active with the New York-based *U.S. Council for International Business,* along with Mike Hodin, Pfizer's vice president-Public Affairs. Clemente chaired the council's Intellectual Property Committee while Hodin headed up its EC Committee. Pfizer executives were also involved with the *National Foreign Trade Council* and the *U.S. Chamber of Commerce.*

Overseas, Pfizer International's president, Bob Neimeth, was chair of the Trade Committee of the *Business and Industry Advisory Committee (BIAC) to the OECD.* His predecessor, MacTaggart was involved with the *U.S.-India Business Council* of U.S.-based companies with interests in India. Pfizer's vice president of Public Affairs in Japan worked closely with the Japan Pharmaceutical Manufacturers Association *(JPMA).* Other Pfizer executives were involved with similar Business Councils linked to other countries such as Mexico, Brazil, Thailand, Turkey. Still others executives worked with sister PMA organizations in the United Kingdom, France, Germany and other countries.

Early on, Pfizer established links with key organizations such as the EC Committee of the *American Chamber of Commerce in Belgium.* More than just a committee, the group served as a principal contact with the EC from 1985. Pfizer also built connections to think tanks and the academic community connected to leading universities in OECD countries to strengthen the intellectual foundation for its political efforts.

Through this complex network of organizations and relationships, Pfizer worked the intellectual property issue and built interest and support for its position from the early 1980s onward. A number of the organizations issued reports and papers which provided guidance to government officials in the United States and abroad.

Pratt's Role in Forming the IPC

Pratt, himself, was well-placed to promote intellectual property protection at the highest levels of the U.S. government. Appointed by President Carter to the Advisory Committee on Trade and Policy Negotiations (ACTPN) in 1979, Pratt became the organization's chairman in 1981. This group of private sector leaders was charged with reviewing and reporting to Congress on the policies of the United States Trade Representative's (USTR) office, but their primary purpose was to advise the USTR on trade matters.

For six years, Pratt led this committee in pursuing an aggressive trade agenda. He worked on expanding market access for the service sector and on foreign investment. He also promoted intellectual property protection. As head of ACTPN, Pratt was at the forefront of a revolution in thinking about trade and investment. He and others dissolved the conceptual boundaries that had previously separated these two issue areas and supported institutional structures to reflect the new insights. In the early eighties, the USTR created a new position for an Assistant USTR for International Investment and Intellectual Property. Working with the new Assistant and the USTR, Pfizer and the PMA developed a position paper directed to the White House staff which eventually resulted in a Presidential statement on the importance of intellectual property to the United States and led to important changes in Sections 301, 303, and 501 of the U.S. trade law.[13]

Pfizer was not the only company worried about its intellectual property. Other pharmaceutical companies, as well as copyright-based industries such as software, publishing, movie, and sound recordings, were becoming increasingly concerned. In the 1980s, the press began to report that counterfeit copies of luxury goods such as $3,500 Cartier watches could be bought for $20 in countries with weak intellectual property laws such as Korea. It was estimated that software vendors lost $500 million annually in overseas sales because of inadequate intellectual property protection. Annual losses in the agrichemical industry were estimated at $200 million. The most alarming study came from the U.S. International Trade Commission which estimated that inadequate intellectual property protection cost U.S. firms between $43 and $61 billion in 1986 alone.[14]

In the early 1980s, Pratt and IBM Chairman John Opel, who chaired the intellectual property task force of ACTPN, pressed their concerns with William Brock, the U.S. Trade Representative. They circulated proposals for improving intellectual property protection to the USTR, to the President, and to trade officials, and argued vigorously for including intellectual property on the agenda of the upcoming round of the GATT negotiations (the "Uruguay Round"). The General Agreement on Tariffs and Trade (the GATT) was a multilateral agreement adhered to after World War II by the United States and 22 other nations. By 1990, there were 96 "contracting parties" or members of GATT (**Exhibit 5**). Aimed at expanding and liberalizing world trade, the GATT governed many of the trade relations between these nations, and included rules about quantitative trade restrictions and subsidies, as well as antidumping provisions. An important feature of the GATT was the intermittent series of trade negotiation rounds. From 1947 through 1980, there had been seven such rounds, culminating in the Tokyo Round from 1973 to 1979. The Uruguay Round was the eighth GATT round.

Pratt explained the strategy of addressing intellectual property issues through the GATT: "Unlike in WIPO, we thought we could achieve real leverage through GATT. Many of the countries lacking intellectual property protection at least had important trading relations with the United States and the rest of the developed world. Moreover, through GATT we could forge intellectual property standards that were supported by dispute resolution and enforcement mechanisms, both of which were lacking in WIPO."

---

[13]See text below, "Changes in U.S. Trade Law."

[14]Jacques J. Gorlin, "Yo, ho, ho, and a Gucci Bag," *World Paper,* March 1989, p. 2.

According to Pratt, it was not hard to persuade U.S. officials that something should be done to stop the theft of U.S. companies' intellectual property. But getting intellectual property on the GATT agenda posed some difficulty. Traditionally, the GATT negotiations had covered the reduction of trade barriers such as tariffs and subsidies. Many, including some GATT officials, did not believe the GATT was an appropriate vehicle for prescribing national standards for intellectual property protection. Border controls against counterfeit goods, a subject under discussion by a GATT Working Group established at the end of the Tokyo Round in 1979, were one thing. Standards for intellectual property protection, like those sought by ACTPN, were quite another. Moreover, Article XX (d) of the GATT specifically left intellectual property protection to the discretion of the contracting nations, provided their laws were not discriminatorily applied against other nations, or otherwise in conflict with GATT. Opponents of GATT norms on intellectual property also argued that WIPO was the appropriate forum for this discussion. But Pratt and others countered that even if not all intellectual property issues were within the purview of GATT, surely some were. Hence the phrase "Trade-Related Aspects of Intellectual Property Rights" (TRIPS) was coined to describe the new GATT subject.

In 1985 Clayton Yeutter became the U.S. Trade Representative. Although Yeutter favored the proposal, he knew that getting intellectual property on the GATT agenda would require the support of the other industrialized countries. He advised Pratt and Opel to get the word out to their counterparts in the rest of the world so that they, in turn, could pressure their governments to include intellectual property in the negotiations. In March 1986, Pratt and Opel mobilized a group of CEOs from 13 companies in diverse industries such as movies, computers and pharmaceuticals to form the Intellectual Property Committee (IPC).[15] Financed by its members, the IPC undertook to provide private sector input, to monitor the trade negotiations, and to forge alliances with European and Japanese industry in support of better intellectual property protection. Each member company appointed an intellectual property specialist and a trade or government relations specialist to work with the IPC.

The IPC provided a unique opportunity for collaboration between trade and patent experts. In some members companies, specialists from the two areas had never before communicated. The IPC also brought together specialists from various areas of intellectual property—copyright, patent, trademark, and others. As a consultant to the IPC noted, "Once brought together, copyright-based companies and patent-based companies realized that they had been facing the same pirates."

By the summer of 1986, IPC members were talking to their counterparts and to government in Europe and Japan. Building on the network of relationships already in place, the IPC forged a tripartite coalition among the IPC, the European Union of Industrial and Employers' Confederations (UNICE), and the Keidanren, a private feder-

---

[15]The thirteen members of the IPC were: Pfizer, IBM, Merck, General Electric, Du Pont, Warner Communications, Hewlett-Packard, Bristol-Myers, FMC Corporation, General Motors, Johnson & Johnson, Monsanto, and Rockwell International.

ation of economic organizations in Japan. Although the Europeans and Japanese were at first skeptical of the GATT proposal as well as the effectiveness and authority of the IPC, all recognized the need for global protection for intellectual property.

The Tripartite Coalition at Work

The tripartite coalition's members succeeded in convincing their governments that intellectual property should be on the agenda for the GATT negotiations, and the Ministerial Declaration kicking off the Round included intellectual property as a subject of negotiation. As chairman of ACTPN and as official adviser to the USTR, Pratt attended the opening meeting of the Uruguay Round at Punta del Este in September 1986.

From September 1986 through June 1988, the negotiators became mired in debate over the competency of the GATT negotiating group and the scope of the negotiations. The IPC took advantage of this hiatus to develop a tripartite consensus on the substance of the minimum standards to be negotiated and to create a document the negotiators could use as a guide. In November 1986, IPC, UNICE, and Keidanren members met in Brussels to begin this work. The result appeared in June 1988: a 100-page report detailing the minimum standards for an acceptable TRIPS agreement. This document, the "Basic Framework," (summarized in **Exhibit 6**) addressed six categories of intellectual property: patents, copyrights, semiconductor chips, trademarks, industrial designs and trade secrets.

Several areas of difference had to be overcome to achieve the "Basic Framework." One particularly thorny issue was copyright protection for computer programs. Representatives of the Keidanren wanted to treat computer programs as a special category with distinctive principles that would permit "decompilation" (a sort of reverse engineering), rather than fully protecting programs as literary works under copyright. Concerned about opening the door to diluted copyright protection modelled on Japanese law, UNICE and IPC representatives opposed such an approach. On this issue, the IPC and UNICE prevailed and the "Basic Framework" accorded computer programs the same copyright protections as literary works.

Trade secret protection was another area requiring resolution. In the United States, case law and state statutes protected certain types of secret business information. European Community states had more-or-less similar protection for trade secrets. Japan, however, had no such system, and the Keidanren initially resisted including trade secrets in the "Basic Framework." In the end, however, the IPC and UNICE prevailed and the "Basic Framework" contained a section on propriety information. After the release of the "Basic Framework," Japan for the first time in its history passed a trade secret law based on U.S. and German models.

Not all areas of conflict were capable of being resolved. Long-standing disputes over patent law threatened to unravel the coalition. Europe and Japan were particularly concerned about the basic rule of priority. In the United States, unlike in Europe, Japan, and almost every other nation in the world, patents were awarded to the first to invent rather than the first to file a patent application. While Americans argued that the first-to-invent system favored the individual, the Japanese thought it rendered patent rights unduly uncertain. At any time, someone might come forward to challenge the validity of a patent on the grounds of an earlier invention date. Moreover, the Japanese thought their system of public disclosure of patent applications preferable to the American system of keeping applications secret. Under the Japanese system, they said, it was easier to identify and resolve disputes before a patent was granted.

Adding insult to injury from the European and Japanese perspective was American bias in favor of U.S.-based inventive activity. Under U.S. patent law, an inventor who had worked abroad could not establish a date of invention any earlier than the date of first filing a patent application abroad.[16] Hence European and Japanese inventors who had done their inventive work outside the United States felt discriminated against when they filed patent applications or became involved in patent litigation in the United States because they were assigned priority dates based on when they first applied for a patent rather than when they conceived the invention, the priority date assigned to inventors working in the United States.

The Europeans and Japanese were also unhappy with Section 337 of the U.S. trade law which was used to penalize allegedly unfair competitive practices including patent infringement. They believed that foreign patent defendants brought before the U.S. International Trade Commission, which was not a court, received less favorable treatment than domestic defendants who had to be sued in a federal court where they could, among other things, file counterclaims.[17]

Feelings about these and other issues ran high during the negotiations, but in the end the parties agreed that it was not necessary to resolve everything. As several IPC member companies explained, "The breakthrough came when we all realized that it was not our objective to harmonize intellectual property standards through the GATT negotiations. Rather, we only needed to agree on minimum standards for all GATT nations to follow. Harmonization could proceed through WIPO."

The "Basic Framework" was a unique collaboration among the United States, European, and Japanese business communities. According to John A. Young, president and chief executive officer of Hewlett-Packard Company, the "Basic Framework" was "unprecedented . . . the first time that the international business community has jointly developed a document of this magnitude and such substantive detail for presentation to our government negotiators."[18]

While the U.S. government text closely followed the coalition's position, Clemente believed that "the European governments were less willing to adopt these views. Instead, they chose to emphasize the differences between the United States and Europe. The Japanese government was even less responsive to the document. In

[16]35 U.S.C. secs. 104, 119.

[17]In 1989, a Dutch company obtained a ruling from a GATT dispute panel that Section 337 violated GATT principles of national treatment. *Financial Times,* January 30, 1989.

[18]Intellectual Property Committee Press Release, June 14, 1988.

the Japanese culture there is a much different relationship between government and business. In Japan, it is the government which decides what is best for Japan and for Japanese business." Pratt added, "We have had Japanese businessmen visit us, and ask us to describe our lobbying techniques and to explain how we are able to exert so much influence over the government."

Challenges to the Coalition's Views

Shortly after her appointment in 1987 as Director of International Affairs at Pfizer, Lillian Fernandez, a former Congressional staffer in Washington, was challenged to defend the coalition's views. Arthur Dunkel, the Secretary-General of GATT, was unhappy with the inclusion of intellectual property on the Uruguay Round agenda. He was particularly upset about the implications for pharmaceuticals. He spoke frequently about the importance of access to health care in developing countries, the high costs of drugs, and the sovereignty of nations to regulate cost and access to drugs. Fernandez described one memorable occasion:

> When he finished his speech, there was total silence as people at the table looked at me to respond. Three years working on Capitol Hill prepared me for dealing with sticky situations. I calmly explained to Mr. Dunkel that granting patent protection was not the same thing as eliminating price controls for drugs and that many nations in Europe had both patent protection and price controls. I also said that it was inappropriate to single out drugs for the problems of medical access in developing countries, and that it was the lack of a health care delivery system that was the problem. Finally, I asked him to consider whether stealing drugs was any more acceptable than stealing food. We certainly don't condone stealing food as a means of dealing with the hunger problem.

Changes in U.S. Trade Law

While intellectual property protection was being discussed in the GATT negotiations, Congress was strengthening the hand of U.S. negotiators. In 1984, Congress had passed important trade legislation which for the first time authorized the U.S. government—on its own and without a showing of injury by the industry—to take retaliatory action against countries failing to give adequate protection to intellectual property (Section 301). The Trade and Tariff Act of 1984 had also called on the USTR to report on the barriers to trade in countries throughout the world (Section 303), and authorized the President to consider the adequacy of intellectual property protection in deciding whether a developing country should be granted tariff preferences under U.S. Generalized System of Preferences (Section 501).

The 1988 Omnibus Trade and Competitiveness Act pushed the USTR further toward implementing this legislation. It introduced a process for identifying offending countries and pressuring them to improve intellectual property protection. Under the provision known as "Special 301," the USTR was required each year to identify foreign states denying intellectual property protection to U.S. firms and to designate the most important as "Priority Foreign Countries."[19] Within 30 days of identifying "Priority Foreign Countries," the USTR was to begin an investigation to determine whether the foreign practices violated U.S. rights under a trade agreement or were "unreasonable" or "discriminatory."

In May 1989, the USTR declined to name any "Priority Foreign Countries" under Special 301. Instead, the USTR placed 17 countries on a "Watch List" and 8 others on a "Priority Watch List." The Priority Watch List included Brazil, India, Mexico, Peoples Republic of China, Republic of Korea, Saudi Arabia, Taiwan, and Thailand.[20] In November 1989, citing progress made in these countries, the USTR moved Saudi Arabia, Korea, and Taiwan from the Priority Watch List to the Watch List. Mexico was removed from both lists in January 1990 in recognition of its announced plan to strengthen patents.

In April 1991, because of inadequate protection of pharmaceutical patents, the USTR for the first time named three nations—India, China, and Thailand—as "Priority Foreign Countries" under Special 301. According to U.S. figures, all three countries had significant trade surpluses with the United States in 1990. India's annual trade surplus was some $700 million; Thailand's $2.7 billion; and China's $11 billion. Three trading partners—the European Community, Brazil, and Australia—were placed on the Priority Watch List" and 23 others were placed on the "Watch List."

The U.S. Applies Trade "Leverage"

These changes in U.S. trade law increased the leverage available to U.S. officials negotiating intellectual property standards with offending nations. Many, including Clemente, believed that pressure created by possible retaliation under section 301 of the 1984 trade legislation had led to the 1986 bilateral agreement on intellectual property between the United States and Korea.

Leverage was also brought to bear in negotiations with Mexico. When Mexican President Salinas came to Washington in June 1990 to discuss a free trade agreement, U.S. officials were well prepared. IPC members and others had lobbied hard to convince Congress and the Administration of the importance of intellectual property protection. Salinas was advised that it would be necessary for Mexico to pass an adequate intellectual property law as a prerequisite for a trade agreement.

Pfizer and the pharmaceutical industry regarded Mexico's initial proposal as inadequate: it did not include protection for drugs in the "pipeline," those already patented elsewhere but not yet marketed in Mexico. In 1991 the Pharmaceutical Man-

---

[19]19 U.S.C §2242, *et seq.*

[20]The original "Watch List" included: Argentina, Canada, Chile, Colombia, Egypt, Greece, Indonesia, Italy, Japan, Malaysia, Pakistan, the Philippines, Portugal, Spain, Turkey, Venezuela, and Yugoslavia.

ufacturers Association (PMA) said they would not enthusiastically support "fast-track" authorization for Bush to negotiate a free trade agreement with Mexico unless intellectual property protection met higher standards, including "pipeline" protection.[21]

In June 1991, Mexico passed a new patent law which Pratt described as truly world class. Under the new law, pharmaceutical companies could obtain 20 year patents on new drugs including those patented in other countries but not yet launched in Mexico. Compulsory licensing was limited to exceptional circumstances and would not be granted if the patented product, or products made from the patented process, were being imported into Mexico. A PMA official called the new law "an outstanding achievement for any country, let alone a developing country such as Mexico."[22]

The United States was less successful in applying leverage in other countries. For example, Canada's Bill C-22, passed in 1987, gave 20-year exclusive patent protection only to pharmaceuticals researched and discovered in Canada. Otherwise, compulsory licenses were readily available to generic companies willing to pay a royalty fee (typically 4%) to the patent holder. Companies intending to manufacture for export were entitled to exercise the license immediately, while those intending to manufacture for the Canadian market had to wait seven years from the date of regulatory approval. (Companies wishing to import the drug had to wait 10 years to exercise the license.) In addition, an innovator's rights could be further restricted if Canada's Patented Medicine Prices Review Board found the price of a patented drug excessive.

Unhappy with Bill C-22, the PMA, the IPC, and others vowed to press for more stringent patent protection in Canada as talks for an expanded U.S.-Mexico-Canada free trade agreement progressed in 1991. To counter concern that expanded patent protection would increase drug prices, the PMA pointed to a recent report showing that consumer drug prices did not increase as a result of Bill C-22. But debate about the impact on drug prices continued. An official of a Canadian generic drug manufacturer criticized the report for looking at average prices rather than focusing on the price of new drugs.[23]

The United States also encountered resistance in Brazil. Six months after placing Brazil on the Special 301 "Priority Watch List" in May 1989, the United States levied 100 percent tariffs on $39 million of imports from Brazil in retaliation for pirating U.S. drug patents. Rather than yield to U.S. pressure, however, Brazil in 1990 filed a GATT complaint against the United States, citing its enforcement of Special 301. The complaint was later abandoned by Brazil in the context of negotiations with the United States over the reform of Brazil's patent laws.[24]

---

[21]In general, under the "fast-track" procedure, the President was required to present a draft of a trade agreement he intended to sign 90 days before doing so. Congress could either accept or reject the legislation implementing the trade agreement in its entirety, without any amendments.

[22]Linda Diebel, "U.S. Again Beats Drum for Cultural Free Trade," *Toronto Star,* May 25, 1991, p. D1.

[23]*Ibid.*

[24]Interview with USTR official.

Thailand was another country attempting to withstand U.S. trade pressure even though the United States accounted for nearly 25% of its export market. In 1990, unhappy with Thailand's progress on patent protection for pharmaceuticals, the PMA successfully urged the U.S. government to revoke Thailand's benefits under the U.S. Generalized System of Preferences, which allowed exports from many developing countries to enter the United States duty free.

Thailand's experience illustrated the conflicts facing LDC governments confronted with U.S. trade pressure. In May 1988, the eight-and-a-half-year-old Thai government was toppled by a no-confidence vote after it introduced in the National Assembly a compromise bill on patents.[25] Politicians in the Philippines faced similar political dissatisfaction when the Philippine Congress declined to pass a bill removing patent protection from drug products.[26] Mexico's new patent law also met with domestic criticism when it was passed in 1991.[27]

The LDCs' Point of View

Developing countries regarded the decision to give pharmaceuticals patent protection as an exercise of national sovereignty. Accordingly, they viewed international efforts to pressure them into recognizing patents on pharmaceuticals as an unwarranted infringement on their right to self-determination. In both GATT and WIPO negotiations, many took the position that nations were free to exclude or limit patent protection in particular areas, such as pharmaceuticals, on grounds of public interest, public health, nutrition, national development, or social security. These nations defended their power to compel patentholders who did not manufacture their inventions within the nation's borders to license their patents to competing domestic manufacturers for reasonable royalties.

A Chinese official explained his personal views on the difficulties facing developing countries. "Intellectual property protection has everything to do with a country's level of development—its resources, science, technology, and industry. Some African countries cannot afford even an office, let alone the training in law, foreign languages, and technical fields required of patent officials." He described the background of China's patent law.

China's patent law was adopted in 1984, but a patent law in China could not have been imagined before 1979. In those days knowledge was in the public domain. It would have been wrong to grant a patent. Nowadays, the work of intellectuals is more respected and people realize that creative labor is integral to economic development. But many people still look at things the old way and believe it is all right to copy others. We must educate people to under-

[25]"New Thai patent legislation only meets part of PMA's request," *Financial Times,* September 1, 1989.

[26]Ramon Isberto, "Philippines: Senate not likely to remove drug patents," *Inter Press Service,* Manila, May 18, 1991.

[27]Henry Ricks, "Mexico shores up intellectual property control," *Reuters,* Mexico City, July 4, 1991.

stand what a patent is and why it is important for science and industry, and we need to encourage inventive activity in our institutions and universities. Without the right attitudes, patent protection has no basis.

We also need resources to establish more patent offices and to train patent examiners and court officials. Since the implementation of the patent law in 1985, 2000 cases have been brought and 1000 cases decided in Chinese courts. One-hundred seventeen thousand patent applications have been filed in this period, but we only have 400 patent examiners in China. We also lack resources for research and development. We can't yet afford to provide an advanced level of protection. The developed countries need to be realistic. They cannot expect too much in a short time, and they should recognize the progress we have made over the past six years. We are now working on a revision of our patent law and have outlined a program for a transitional period for the next ten years or so. We have an active and positive attitude toward protecting intellectual property and will get it over time.

Pharmaceuticals are currently excluded from our patent law, along with foods, beverages, scientific discoveries, rules and methods for mental activities, methods for diagnosing and treating disease, and plant and animal varieties. We didn't include pharmaceuticals because we were concerned that prices would be too high. We weren't really sure what would happen. We have studied countries like Japan, Italy, and India to see the effects of protecting pharmaceuticals. We want to see more experiences of countries. In the long run, the fields of intellectual property protection will get broader and broader, but we must do it gradually in a country like China. If we set a task that is impossible to achieve, we can't get anywhere. This is realistic.

Gradualism was the watchword among Latin American pharmaceutical manufacturers, too. An official of the Latin American Association of Pharmaceutical Industries (ALIFAR) predicted that product protection for pharmaceuticals would be a reality in five to ten years. "In the meantime," she explained, "protection is not possible because of poor economic conditions in Latin America. It is impossible for us to invest in research because we have no resources, and it is very important for public administrators to buy medicine for the social security system at affordable prices."

Nevertheless, she thought U.S. pressure would force changes in the law. "We accept that there will be changes, but the issue is how. We want to be able to obtain licenses. We want to limit the absolute right of intellectual property. For example, we think the patent law of Canada is a good system. There, people can obtain an automatic license for pharmaceuticals and pay royalties."

Argentina, the headquarters of ALIFAR, was itself waging a difficult battle to sustain local production of drugs. In 1989, Argentine manufacturers controlled 54 percent of a $1.5 billion market. According to a researcher with the Economic Commission for Latin America and the Caribbean, it was the only Latin American nation where more than 15% of the pharmaceutical market was controlled by domestic producers financed with local capital.[28] Despite such a significant pharmaceutical manu-

---

[28]Gustavo Capdevila, "Argentina: Defies U.S. Over Local Pharmaceutical Protection," *Inter Press Service,* Buenos Aires, March 30, 1989.

facturing segment, Argentina still had a $250 million deficit in international trade in pharmaceuticals.

Under Argentine law, patents were recognized only on processes, not on final products. Local manufacturers thus competed with multinational drug manufacturers by developing alternative processes for manufacturing drugs produced under process patents. In early 1989, the Argentine government signed an agreement with the local pharmaceutical companies to encourage the growth of the pharmaceutical sector. Domestic drug manufacturers agreed to contribute three percent from sales revenues to a "medical assistance fund" to benefit the medical needs of the seven million Argentines thought to be living in conditions of extreme poverty. And in November 1990, facing increased pressure from the United States to change its patent law, Argentine drug manufacturers went on the offensive by taking out a full-page advertisement in the *New York Times* which argued that Argentina's patent policy was a necessary short-term solution to make drugs affordable to Argentines living in and near poverty. See **Exhibit 7.** Other voices within Argentina questioned this view and favored a development strategy oriented to international trade with recognition of intellectual property in all areas of economic activity.[29]

India, another opponent of stronger intellectual property protection, had recently assessed the 1970 revisions of its previously strict and comprehensive patent law. The revisions had aimed to encourage domestic production and reasonable prices. The new law granted patent protection to processes only—and not to pharmaceutical products—for a period of five years. Moreover, it allowed the Indian government, three years after a patent was granted, to require a patentholder to license its patent to another company if the patentholder was not manufacturing the product in India and selling it at a reasonable price. A report of the Indian National Working Group on Patent Laws concluded that as a result of the 1970 law, Indian drug prices went from among the highest in the world to among the lowest in 1991, and that the Indian pharmaceutical industry had benefitted to the point where India was nearly self-sufficient in the manufacture of bulk pharmaceuticals.[30] The *Calcutta Business Standard,* however, that "The Indian Patents Act has retarded the development of new drugs in India" and that "the number of applications for patents in general and for pharmaceuticals, food and agrochemicals in particular, is falling year after year."[31]

Pfizer, too, had undertaken to improve health care in the LDCs. In Gambia, Pfizer participated in a program to improve the distribution of pharmaceuticals. Beginning in the mid-1970s, Pfizer worked closely with Brazilian officials to launch a major demonstration project to combat schistosomiasis, a parasitic disease prevalent in Brazil. The firm also prepared multimedia materials to distribute throughout Asia

---

[29]Fundacion de Investigaciones Economicas Latino Americanas (FIEL), "Protection of Intellectual Property Rights, The Case of the Pharmaceutical Industry in Argentina," Buenos Aires, 1990.

[30]Robert Weissman, "Prelude to a new colonialism," *The Nation,* March 18, 1991, p. 336.

[31]Suresh Thakur Desai, "India Patents Act-II: Acting as a Bar to Innovation," *Calcutta Business Standard,* November 22, 1990.

and Latin America to highlight the role sanitation and drugs play in the control of hookworm and roundworm infestations. In addition, Pfizer, in a program sponsored by the World Health Organization (WHO), trained scientists from LDCs in chemical and microbiological control.

The IPC Responds

Acting on behalf of the pharmaceutical companies located within their borders, the governments of the developed nations pressured the LDCs to strengthen their patent protection laws. For example, in 1989, Carla Hills, the USTR, supported linking U.S. help with Brazil's $120 billion debt with Brazil's cooperation on patent protection. She commented: "I think it is fundamentally wrong for Brazil not to protect intellectual property. And it hurts their national interest because investors all around the world will not want to go into Brazil if they believe their intellectual property—their rights in software, books, recordings, patents—are stolen."[32]

The IPC also attempted to convince developing nations to institute patent protection. Such protection, the IPC argued, would encourage pharmaceutical companies to develop new products for their markets, spur the development of local innovation and industry, and encourage multinational corporations to locate manufacturing facilities within their borders. A report commissioned by Pfizer and the PMA concluded that "there is a causal linkage between economic modernization and the presence of efficient property rights, including intellectual property rights."[33] The report recommended that "protecting intellectual property should be a public policy goal of developing countries seeking sustained economic growth."

As for the effect on consumer prices, industry argued that competition among patented products would insure a measure of control. In any event, since 90% of the 250 items on the World Health Organization's Essential Drugs list were off patent, recognition of patents on new products would have little effect on the price of most drugs used in developing countries. Industry also pointed to Eastern European countries such as Poland and Czechoslovakia where the first steps toward privatization and the creation of conditions favorable to democratic capitalism had included good patent laws for pharmaceuticals.

Developing country officials, however, were not entirely persuaded. The ALIFAR official, for example, commented, "It is not enough to protect intellectual property in general, there must be better economic conditions in order to induce foreign companies to invest. Their main objective is to export goods to improve the balance of trade." She doubted that intellectual property protection would help the local pharmaceutical industry. "With protection, it will be very difficult for Latin American

---

[32]Terry Atlas, "Hills backs using Brazil debt in bargaining on patents," *Chicago Tribune*, April 12, 1989, p. B3.

[33]Richard T. Rapp and Richard T. Rozek, "Benefits and Costs of Intellectual Property Protection in Developing Countries," Working Paper #3, National Economic Research Associates, Inc., June 1990.

producers to compete because they will be unable to get licenses. It is not in the interests of foreign companies to give licenses."

Other advocates for the LDCs' position remained concerned about issues of national sovereignty. They argued that it should be their decision whether or not to give broad patent protection, not a mandate forced upon them as a condition of participation in the world trade markets. They pointed out that the United States, in the early stages of its development, had not honored copyrights granted by other nations and that some other industrialized nations like Japan had only fairly recently recognized product patents on pharmaceuticals.[34]

Pratt saw the issue less in terms of sovereignty and more in terms of reciprocity: not "an eye for an eye," but "an eye for a tooth," as he explained. The fact remained that the United States was a very important market for developing countries. In return for access to that market, Pratt thought developing countries should be expected to respect U.S. companies' intellectual property. Pratt believed the U.S. government should assert its own sovereignty by limits, or denying access to the U.S. market to countries that inadequately protected intellectual property.

Brussels: December 1990

When the coalition's "Basic Framework" was released in June 1988, Pratt and others at Pfizer had high hopes for a strong TRIPS agreement. But by late 1990, the prospects had dimmed. At the ministerial meeting in Brussels in the winter of 1990 it became apparent that the Europeans were unwilling to negotiate hard for an acceptable TRIPS accord. The document that emerged from the meeting was not what the IPC or Pfizer had hoped for.

IPC members had various explanations for the European attitudes. Some noted the Europeans' protective tendencies toward former colonies and their reluctance to use bilateral instruments like U.S. 301. Indeed, Europeans generally preferred multilateral approaches and were critical of the United States' use of 301 as they had been critical of the U.S.-Korea agreement of 1986 which had provided preferential treatment for the United States. Other IPC members noted the Europeans' desire to "play the middle" between the United States and the Third World and to appear more reasonable than the United States. The fact that EC members, Spain, Portugal, and Greece, did not yet have adequate protection made the issue somewhat awkward for EC officials.

Moreover, European government officials seemed much less responsive than their American counterparts to the needs of business. As Pratt pointed out, ". . . the U.S. government's Advisory Committee on Trade [and Policy] Negotiations . . . has

---

[34]Rajan Dhanjee and Lawrence Boisson de Chazournes, "Trade Related Aspects of Intellectual Property Rights (TRIPS): Objectives, Approaches and Basic Principles of the GATT and of Intellectual Property Conventions," *Journal of World Trade,* October 1990, p. 5.

no European counterpart."[35] In addition, European patent lawyers were loath to see their technical specialty turned into a political issue handled at the senior executive level.

Recognizing the paramount importance the Europeans (particularly the French) placed on achieving an acceptable agriculture agreement in the Uruguay Round, some feared the European negotiators might be willing to bargain away TRIPS in exchange for a watered-down agriculture agreement. Coincidentally, many of the nations accused of having weak intellectual property protection, Argentina, *e.g.,* were in the best position to profit from a reduction of agricultural subsidies in the European Community.

Brussels was also the occasion of unnecessary misunderstanding between the industry coalition and their various governments. For example, industry and the negotiators disagreed about including the "moral rights" of authors in the negotiations. In many jurisdictions, the author of a literary work had an explicit and legally inalienable "moral right" to control the interpretation of the work. Industry wanted to avoid the issue and to steer clear of any linkage to WIPO and the Berne Convention and to focus, instead, on minimum standards. The negotiators, on the other hand, accepted the idea that the Berne Convention established the starting point for negotiations. In the end, an acceptable compromise appears to have been worked out. But industry representatives from both sides of the Atlantic felt the dispute had been an unnecessary excursion into a wholly "philosophical debate."

Pfizer and the IPC were also concerned about several issues that had emerged as topics of heated debate. The question of how much "pipeline" protection would be adequate had yet to be resolved. In addition, the Brussels draft had contained a provision on "international exhaustion" of patent rights favored by the LDCs. The tripartite coalition was opposed to the concept of international exhaustion which would have meant that once a patent-holder or licensee put products on the market in a given country, the patent-holder could exercise no further control over the flow of those goods anywhere in the world. Thus, drugs sold with the consent of the patent-holder in a country with low drug prices (because of price controls, for example) could be bought and shipped to markets with higher prices where they might compete directly with the patent-holder's higher priced products.

After the worrisome experience of Brussels in December 1990, the IPC determined to lobby the European and Japanese negotiators directly, making it clear that the IPC would oppose Congressional ratification of a weak TRIPs agreement. Others suggested that stronger messages be sent to the Europeans, including letting it be known that the IPC was considering supporting bilateral negotiations on the model of the earlier negotiation with Korea. As one of the IPC members suggested, "we need to make the Europeans understand that they are not the only game in town."

European governments and European industry were not in perfect accord on the

---

[35]Edmund T. Pratt, Jr., "European Business Must Speak Up for GATT Progress," *Wall Street Journal* (Eur. ed.), January 8, 1991.

terms of an acceptable TRIPS agreement. As one UNICE official explained, "European governments want to get as many LDCs as possible committed to the GATT system. They would rather have a general GATT instrument on intellectual property than a Code among fewer countries. And they are willing to trade off certain property rights in order the achieve this. Originally, industry planned to work first for a Code, and then seek full integration of intellectual property principles into the GATT system. But the governments do not want this." Unlike the amendment of GATT, the adoption of a "Code" did not require the unanimous consent of the GATT contracting parties. However, a "Code" essentially functioned as a separate agreement which bound only those nations that ratified it. Still, the IPC thought a code would allow for meaningful agreement without going for the lowest common denominator.

A UNICE official believed that European Commission officials, in contrast to European national government officials, were strong supporters of European industry's position. In his view, cooperation between United States industry and government had been rather close, though he was not convinced that the United States government had followed industry's recommendations in the end. The Japanese government, he thought, had done what its industry wanted. He nevertheless commented on the high level of American business involvement in public policy making. "American business people and companies are much more active in public affairs at home and abroad than European companies."

Even as the IPC was debating strategies for bringing the Europeans back in line, Clemente was beginning to feel uneasy about the projected course of events. In Clemente's view and that of other IPC members, a bad TRIPS agreement was worse than no TRIPS agreement. "Enshrining a bad TRIPS into a treaty would only make it harder to pursue better terms in bilateral and trilateral negotiations, such as the upcoming free trade discussions with Mexico and Canada." Clemente urged that the IPC use its resources to explore other avenues and identify other pressure points. He also suggested it might be time to increase bilateral pressures such as those created through Special 301. One IPC member suggested the United States should defer forgiveness of loans to Latin American countries until they agreed to adequate intellectual property protection.

Fernandez was more optimistic about the possibility of obtaining an acceptable TRIPS agreement. "At the end of the day," said Fernandez, "the negotiators know that they will have to come to Congress for approval of the agreement. Without a strong TRIPS provision, there will be strong opposition in Congress."

Conclusion

Pfizer and other members of the IPC had managed to exert great influence over the international trade agenda during the 1980s and into the 1990s. Pratt's exceptional level of involvement in public policy making had earned him a very favorable reputation among American trade officials. A UNICE official remarked that the tripartite cooperation among Japanese, European, and United States industry was unique in his memory. "This was the first time that industry from the three areas worked so closely together for a common objective."

But as the negotiations for the Uruguay Round were coming to a close, it was not clear what the outcome would be. The GATT working group on intellectual property had yet to resolve any of the issues being debated. There was no consensus on dispute resolution, subject matter exclusions, minimum patent term, compulsory licensing, transitional periods, or any of the other issues that divided the LDCs and the industrialized countries.

The "Basic Framework" had not addressed a number of issues that had emerged as important to various parties, issues such as "pipeline" protection important to the pharmaceutical industry; protection for "appellations of origin" important to European wine producers; and "international exhaustion" of intellectual property rights sought by the LDCs. Some agencies of the U.S. government, particularly the Department of Defense, NASA, and the Department of Health and Human Services, wanted the TRIPS agreement to include a broad "government use" provision giving the government a right to use patented inventions. Industry, on the other hand, was concerned that broad language would be interpreted inappropriately in developing countries.

It was unclear whether the United States would achieve its objectives in the negotiations. Speaking before Congress in 1991, U.S. Trade Representative (USTR) Carla Hills described the U.S. position on TRIPS.

> Our four basic objectives in these negotiations are to obtain adequate standards of protection that each signatory country must embody in its law in patents, copyrights, trademarks, trade secrets and semiconductor layout design; secondly, effective enforcement provisions that specify how rights holders should be able to enforce their rights internally and at the border; thirdly, a GATT dispute settlement mechanism for intellectual property disputes arising under the agreement; and finally, the right under international law to apply trade sanctions when another country fails to live up to its obligation under the agreement.[36]

Pratt acknowledged the possibility that the best that could be hoped for was a strong "Code" among some GATT members that would gradually come to include all the contracting parties of GATT. He summarized his feelings about the multilateral approach in GATT:

> It was very ambitious of us to imagine that we could achieve an acceptable TRIPS agreement in GATT. When GATT was formed just after World War II, there were only 23 nations involved. Now there are 96, all of whom must agree to any new proposal. Naturally, this is going to make it very difficult to agree on any strong TRIPS provisions. But working through GATT has allowed us to make tremendous progress. We have put intellectual property protection on the world agenda. We have clarified what a good patent agreement must contain.

[36]Testimony of Carla Hills, United States Trade Representative, Hearing of the Intellectual Property and Judicial Administration Subcommittee of the House Judicial Committee, May 15, 1991 ("Hills Testimony").

We have used the momentum of GATT to help forge bilateral intellectual property agreements with the Koreans, the Chinese, the Russians, and with Eastern Europe. Perhaps most important, we have shown how international business can initiate and help shape public policy . . . and that in our interdependent world industry in the United States, Japan and Europe can overcome their differences to mold a unified public policy response.

In the midst of this uncertainty, Pratt, Clemente, and Fernandez were considering what sort of TRIPS agreement Pfizer would be willing to support. The IPC was assessing how to improve the prospects of an acceptable TRIPS agreement as well as alternative approaches to securing intellectual property protection around the world.

EXHIBIT 1 Financial Summary, Pfizer, Inc. and Subsidiary Companies (millions of dollars, except per-share data)

	1990	1989	1988	1987	1986	1985	1984	1983	1982	1981	1980
Net sales	$6,406.0	$5,671.5	$5,385.4	$4,919.8	$4,476.0	$4,024.5	$3,875.9	$3,764.7	$3,496.0	$3,280.9	$3,054.3
Operating costs and expenses:											
Cost of goods sold	2,259.4	2,062.3	2,020.1	1,986.9	1,720.4	1,545.7	1,528.4	1,548.4	1,554.3	1,567.8	1,463.7
Marketing, distribution, and administrative expenses	2,452.7	2,109.8	1,880.9	1,681.1	1,465.3	1,313.2	1,252.6	1,227.0	1,132.7	1,019.6	941.6
Research and development expenses	640.1	531.2	472.5	401.0	335.5	286.7	254.8	229.5	199.4	178.6	161.6
Income from operations	1,053.8	968.2	1,011.9	940.8	954.8	878.9	840.1	760.0	609.6	514.9	487.4
Interest income (expense)—net	61.2	78.8	99.4	60.1	47.1	30.7	2.2	(16.0)	(33.0)	(62.6)	(53.5)
Other income (deductions)—net	(11.7)	(130.5)	(7.5)	9.9	(37.0)	(28.2)	(28.4)	(41.4)	(26.3)	(10.0)	(22.4)
Nonoperating income (deductions)—net	49.5	(51.7)	91.9	70.0	10.1	2.5	(26.2)	(57.4)	(59.3)	(72.6)	(75.9)
Income from continuing operations before provision for taxes on income and minority interest	1,103.3	916.5	1,103.8	1,010.8	964.9	881.4	813.9	702.6	550.3	442.3	411.5
Provision for taxes on income	297.9	231.3	309.4	317.3	300.7	296.4	296.2	248.4	208.6	160.1	149.5
Income from continuing operations before minority interests	805.4	685.2	794.4	693.5	664.2	585.0	517.7	454.2	341.7	282.2	262.0
Minority interests	4.2	4.1	3.1	3.3	4.2	5.3	6.3	5.8	5.4	5.7	7.1
Income from continuing operations	$ 801.2	$ 681.1	$ 791.3	$ 690.2	$ 660.0	$ 579.7	$ 511.4	$ 448.4	$ 336.3	$ 276.5	$ 254.9
Loss from discontinued operations—net of taxes	—	—	—	—	—	—	—	—	—	(52.4)	—
Net income	$ 801.2	$ 681.1	$ 791.3	$ 690.2	$ 660.0	$ 579.7	$ 511.4	$ 448.4	$ 336.3	$ 224.1	$ 254.9
Effective tax rate	27.0%	25.2%	28.0%	31.4%	31.2%	33.6%	36.4%	35.4%	37.9%	36.2%	36.3%
Depreciation	$ 199.9	$ 184.3	$ 176.8	$ 162.0	$ 147.1	$ 129.5	$ 127.3	$ 114.9	$ 110.2	$ 96.9	$ 87.2
Capital additions	547.5	456.5	343.7	258.3	196.1	195.8	182.7	241.8	271.7	290.9	163.9
Cash dividends paid	396.7	364.0	330.1	296.8	269.7	241.2	211.2	183.7	139.8	118.5	105.7

EXHIBIT 1 Financial Summary, Pfizer, Inc. and Subsidiary Companies (millions of dollars, except per-share data) (*Continued*)

	1990	1989	1988	1987	1986	1985	1984	1983	1982	1981	1980
As of December 31:											
Working capital	$1,319.0	$1,593.2	$1,750.5	$2,144.1	$1,728.8	$1,708.7	$1,363.9	$1,217.3	$1,117.8	$1,147.9	$1,089.3
Property, plant, and equipment— net of accumulated depreciation	2,109.8	1,784.1	1,655.1	1,505.9	1,351.5	1,268.5	1,161.7	1,163.3	1,138.5	1,006.7	830.4
Total assets	9,052.0	8,324.8	7,593.2	6,872.3	5,178.5	4,458.7	4,035.7	3,915.8	3,748.0	3,643.1	3,358.6
Long-term debt	193.3	190.6	226.9	248.9	285.4	323.5	341.7	487.4	520.5	691.5	584.9
Long-term capital[a]	5,665.8	5,062.1	4,865.9	4,471.2	3,926.1	3,453.4	2,939.6	2,781.3	2,635.8	2,505.6	2,243.2
Shareholders' equity	5,092.0	4,535.8	4,301.1	3,882.4	3,415.2	2,927.3	2,495.5	2,188.2	1,996.6	1,716.3	1,579.5
Common share data											
Earnings per common share:											
Continuing operations	$ 4.77	$ 4.04	$ 4.70	$ 4.08	$ 3.90	$ 3.44	$ 3.06	$ 2.70	$ 2.11	$ 1.79	$ 1.70
Discontinued operations	—	—	—	—	—	—	—	—	—	(.33)	—
Net	4.77	4.04	4.70	4.08	3.90	3.44	3.06	2.70	2.11	1.46	1.70
Cash dividends paid per common share	2.40	2.20	2.00	1.80	1.64	1.48	1.32	1.16	.92	.80	.72
Shareholders' equity per common share	30.84	27.44	26.00	23.60	20.70	17.87	15.30	13.52	12.70	11.21	10.52
Weighted average number of common and common share equivalents outstanding used to compute earnings per common share (thousands)	168,576	169,696	169,424	170,563	170,796	170,556	169,644	168,555	162,973	157,700	149,223
Number of employees (thousands)	42.5	42.1	40.9	40.7	40.0	39.2	39.2	40.9	40.6	42.0	41.6
Net sales per employee (thousands of dollars)	151	135	132	121	112	103	99	92	86	78	73

[a]Defined as long-term debt, deferred taxes on income, minority interests, and shareholders' equity.

Source: Pfizer Inc. Annual Report, 1990.

EXHIBIT 2   Status of Patent Protection in OECD and Latin American Nations

Nation	OECD Process Patent (year of adoption if relatively recent)	Product Patent (year of adoption if relatively recent)	Nation	Latin America Process Patent	Product Patent
Australia	Yes	Yes	Argentina	Yes	No
Austria	Yes	Yes (1987)	Bolivia	Yes	No
Belgium	Yes	Yes	Brazil	No	No
Canada	Yes	Yes (1983)	Chile	Yes	Yes
Denmark	Yes	Yes (1983)	Colombia	Yes	No
England	Yes	Yes (1949)	Costa Rica	Yes	No
Finland	Yes	(1995)	Cuba	Yes	No
France	Yes	Yes (1960)	Dominican Republic	Yes	Yes
Germany	Yes	Yes (1968)	Ecuador	Yes	No
Greece	Yes	(1992)	El Salvador	Yes	Yes
Holland	Yes	Yes (1978)	Guatemala	Yes	No
Iceland	Yes	No	Honduras	Yes	No
Ireland	Yes	Yes	Jamaica	Yes	Yes
Italy	Yes (1978)	Yes	Mexico	Yes	Yes
Japan	Yes (1965)	Yes (1976)	Nicaragua	Yes	No
Norway	Yes	(1992)	Panama	Yes	Yes
Portugal	Yes	(1992)	Paraguay	Yes	No
Spain	Yes	(1992)	Trinidad and Tobago	Yes	Yes
Sweden	Yes	Yes (1978)	Uruguay	Yes	No
Switzerland	Yes	Yes (1977)	Venezuela	Yes	No
Turkey	No	No			
United States	Yes	Yes			

Source: ALIFAR 1991.

EXHIBIT 3   Members of the Paris Convention

Algeria, Argentina, Australia, Austria, Bahamas, Bangladesh, Barbados, Belgium, Benin, Brazil, Bulgaria, Burkina Faso, Burundi, Cameroon, Canada, Central African Republic, Chad, China, Congo, Côte d'Ivoire, Cuba, Cyprus, Czechoslovakia, Democratic People's Republic of Korea, Denmark, Dominican Republic, Egypt, Finland, France, Gabon, Germany, Ghana, Greece, Guinea, Guinea-Bissau, Haiti, Holy See, Hungary, Iceland, Indonesia, Iran (Islamic Republic of), Iraq, Ireland, Israel, Italy, Japan, Jordan, Kenya, Lebanon, Lesotho, Libya, Liechtenstein, Luxembourg, Madagascar, Malawi, Malaysia, Mali, Malta, Mauritania, Mauritius, Mexico, Monaco, Mongolia, Morocco, Netherlands, New Zealand, Niger, Nigeria, Norway, Philippines, Poland, Portugal, Republic of Korea, Romania, Rwanda, San Marino, Senegal, South Africa, Soviet Union, Spain, Sri Lanka, Sudan, Suriname, Swaziland, Sweden, Switzerland, Syria, Togo, Trinidad and Tobago, Tunisia, Turkey, Uganda, United Kingdom, United Republic of Tanzania, United States of America, Uruguay, Vietnam, Yugoslavia, Zaire, Zambia, Zimbabwe.

Source: WIPO 1990.

EXHIBIT 4 *The New York Times,* Friday, July 9, 1982

In recent days many people have been shocked that Japanese businessmen might have stolen computer secrets from I.B.M. The allegations are the latest twist in the tense worldwide struggle for technological supremacy, but few businessmen, especially those involved in high-technology, research-based industries, can be very surprised.

Their inventions have been "legally" taken in country after country by governments' violation of intellectual-property rights, especially patents. It has been going on for some time, and it is getting worse. Through political and legal dealings, many governments, including Brazil, Canada, Mexico, India, Taiwan, South Korea, Italy, and Spain, to name a few, have provided their domestic companies with ways to make and sell products that under proper enforcement and honorable treatment of patents would be considered the property of the inventors. And now the United Nations, through its World Intellectual Property Organization, is trying to grab high-technology inventions for underdeveloped countries.

As more and more countries yearn for industrialization, it is ironic that less and less respect is given those laws and principles that have attended industrialization in the last hundred years. This is nowhere more true than in the area of patent protection for high technology, where learning how to manufacture a product requires enormous resources but actually manufacturing it turns out to be quite simple. It is in acquiring the knowledge to make new products—computers, pharmaceuticals, telecommunications equipment, chemicals and others—that American companies have been so

good. And it is this knowledge that is being stolen by the denial of patent rights.

For example, India has denied Pfizer the right to exercise its own patent covering doxycycline, an antibiotic used widely around the world. It reserves to Indian companies the right to manufacture and sell that drug, even though the result has been that far less of it is available in India than is needed. Another illustration is Canada's compulsory licensing law, which has obliged Smith, Kline & French to grant patent rights on its antiulcer drug, Tagamet, to a local company that invested nothing in its research and development. The royalty in such a transaction is a meager 4 percent.

Patents are a vital stimulus to technological innovation and a vital part of doing business. In 1883, Western nations met in Paris to write a treaty that firmly conferred international legitimacy on intellectual-property rights—patents and trademarks—and asserted their critical relations to technological innovation. The thought then, which is still valid, was that the enormous human and financial costs attending technological innovation are worth the risks only if the invention is protected from duplication for a period of years in which the inventor can reasonably hope to recoup his costs. Under this arrangement, the inventor is then free to disseminate the technology.

Many developing countries, and some that are clearly developed, do not respect this arrangement. In many cases, however, their laws give the impression that they do, thereby encouraging inventors to place their products on the market. Once a product is on the market, the

information issued with a patent makes it easy to steal the technology unless its protection is enforced.

The irony is that by eroding patent protection, governments are likely to accomplish the opposite of their professed intentions. They may appear to benefit from the inventions they take, but these gains are made at the expense of the system that nourishes industrial creativity.

What's more, the revisions to the Paris treaty being considered by delegates to the United Nations organization would confer international legitimacy on the abrogation of patents. The principle the World Intellectual Property Organization seeks to introduce would enable a nation to deny the inventor the protection of a patent or, worse still, prevent him from exercising his own invention if the product is not made from scratch in that nation.

So far, the United States has opposed such a theft of American technology. Unfortunately, European nations have failed to insist on the respect of these principles of international law and of the international economic system. Canada, Australia and New Zealand have gone even further and argue that for these purposes their nations should be considered developing countries! The competition for world markets and international business is becoming ever more tense, and that is the very reason the United States should insist more than ever that the principle underlying the international economic system be respected and upheld.

Barry MacTaggart is chairman and president of Pfizer International Inc.

EXHIBIT 5   Contracting Parties to the GATT (96)

Antigua and Barbuda	Ghana	Niger
Argentina	Greece	Nigeria
Australia	Guyana	Norway
Austria	Haiti	Pakistan
Bangladesh	Hong Kong	Peru
Barbados	Hungary	Philippines
Belgium	Iceland	Poland
Belize	India	Portugal
Benin	Indonesia	Romania
Botswana	Ireland	Rwanda
Brazil	Israel	Senegal
Burkina Faso	Italy	Sierra Leone
Burundi	Jamaica	Singapore
Cameroon	Japan	South Africa
Canada	Kenya	Spain
Central African Republic	Korea, Republic of	Sri Lanka
Chad	Kuwait	Suriname
Chile	Lesotho	Sweden
Colombia	Luxembourg	Switzerland
Congo	Madagascar	Tanzania
Côte d'Ivoire	Malawi	Thailand
Cuba	Malaysia	Togo
Cyprus	Maldives	Trinidad and Tobago
Czechoslovakia	Malta	Turkey
Denmark	Mauritania	Uganda
Dominican Republic	Mauritius	United Kingdom
Egypt	Mexico	United States of America
Finland	Morocco	Uruguay
France	Mayanmar	Yugoslavia
Gabon	Netherlands	Zaire
Gambia	New Zealand	Zambia
Germany, Federal Republic	Nicaragua	Zimbabwe

Acceded provisionally

Countries to whose territories the GATT has been applied and which now, as independent states, maintain a de facto application of the GATT pending final decisions as to their future commercial policy (28).

Algeria	Guinea-Bissau	St. Vincent and the Grenadines
Angola	Kampuchea	São Tomé and Principe
Bahamas	Kinbati	Seychelles
Bahrain	Mali	Solomon Islands
Brunei Darussalam	Mozambique	Swaziland
Cape Verde	Papua New Guinea	Tonga
Dominica	Qatar	Yuvalu
Equatorial Guinea	St. Christopher and Nevis	United Arab Emirates
Fiji	St. Lucia	Yemen, Democratic
Greneda		

Source: Gatt Director-General.

EXHIBIT 6 The Basic Framework's Fundamental Principles of Patent Protection

Rights Resulting From a Patent

1. A patent shall provide the right to exclude others from the manufacture, use or sale of the patented invention and, in the case of a patented process, the ability to exclude others from the use or sale of the direct product thereof, during the patent term.

Patentability

2. A patent shall be granted for any new, industrially applicable and unobvious devices, products and processes without discrimination as to subject matter, conditions for application, grant or maintenance in force of a patent.

The Patent Term

3. The term of a patent generally shall be 20 years from filing.

Working and Compulsory Licensing

4. A patent shall not be revoked because of nonworking.

5. Compulsory licenses because of nonworking shall be granted only to permit local manufacture. Where justified legal, technical or commercial reasons make it impractical to carry out the invention locally, importation authorized by the patentee which meets local needs shall be deemed to satisfy the requirements for working.

6. Neither exclusive nor sole compulsory licenses shall be granted.

7. Compulsory licensing provisions shall not discriminate against particular classes of subject matter.

8. If a compulsory license is granted, the patentee shall be fully compensated.

9. If a compulsory license is granted, the compulsory licensee is entitled only to immunity from suit under the patent.

Voluntary Licensing

10. Voluntary licensing shall not be discouraged by governments by imposing on the parties to license agreements, terms or conditions which are unreasonable or discriminatory.

Patent Enforcement

11. Nondiscriminatory and equitable civil procedures and remedies shall be available for effective patent enforcement. Remedies shall include preliminary and final injunctions as well as monetary awards adequate to compensate patentees fully and serve as an effective infringement deterrent.

12. Fair, reasonable and effective court procedures shall be available for ascertaining the facts of infringement.

Transition Rules

13. Transition rules shall be developed in connection with these fundamental principles.

Source: "Basic Framework of GATT Provisions on Intellectual Property," Intellectual Property Committee, Keidanren, and UNICE (June 1988), pp. 32–33.

EXHIBIT 7   Should Multinational Pharmaceutical Manufacturers Be Permitted
to Monopolize Production and Sales of Life-Saving Drugs in Poor Countries?

The suggested retail price of a leading brand anti-ulcer drug in the United States is $55.15.[a] The same branded drug in Argentina costs $19.63. A popular anti-arthritis drug sells in the U.S. at a suggested retail price of $169.84.[a] In Argentina, the same branded drug sells for only $35.08. These are only two examples among literally hundreds where the price of pharmaceuticals in the U.S. is dramatically higher than in Argentina.

The reason for the price difference is competition. In Argentina, where the per capita income is only $2,300 (versus $16,497 in the U.S.), this competition has kept prices within reach of average Argentine citizens, and within reach of an overburdened and virtually bankrupt Argentine healthcare system for the aged and poor.

The competition comes from Argentine drug manufacturers who have long produced, under Argentine law, drugs to meet local needs at prices local people can afford. The drugs are identical to those produced by multinational drug manufacturers.

Today, the U.S. Pharmaceutical Manufacturers Association (PMA), representing many major multinational drug producers, is lobbying for swift introduction of restrictive patents. If they succeed at GATT, or succeed by exerting pressure in bi-lateral negotiations, the PMA's multinational companies will have an effective monopoly on pharmaceutical production and sales in Argentina. Drug prices will skyrocket. The strains on the healthcare system will be even more acute—similar action in other countries has bankrupted healthcare systems. People who need the drugs won't be able to afford them, and Argentine unemployment will increase.

Our position is this.

The multinational drug manufacturers are entitled to receive some recognition for the products they invent. However, they should not be permitted to monopolize health markets through the use of restrictive patents. Nor should they be allowed to kill Argentina's infant pharmaceutical industry.

The Government of Argentina has agreed with the U.S. Government that a draft bill will be introduced in Argentina's Congress before September 1991. The bill will address the question of intellectual property rights on pharmaceuticals. This is a significant and positive move towards bringing Argentina into line with the international trading community. But Argentina, like many other countries which have attempted to introduce similar major changes, needs time to make a transition.

The PMA should not be allowed to monopolize pharmaceutical manufacturing and distribution in Argentina. Our country and people cannot afford it.

We are being reasonable. We expect the PMA to do the same.

C.I.L.F.A.

Centro Industrial de Laboratorios Farmaceuticos Argentinos

Esmeralda 130-5° plso, 1035 - Buenos Aires, Republica Argentina

---

[a]Source: *Physician's Desk Reference*

Index

Page numbers in italics indicate illustrations.